FINANCIAL REFORMS and DEVELOPMENTS in CHINA

FINANCIAL REFORMS and DEVELOPMENTS in CHINA

Cheng Siwei

Former Vice Chairman of the 9th and 10th Standing Committee
of the National People's Congress, China

World Scientific

NEW JERSEY • LONDON • SINGAPORE • BEIJING • SHANGHAI • HONG KONG • TAIPEI • CHENNAI

Published by

World Scientific Publishing Co. Pte. Ltd.
5 Toh Tuck Link, Singapore 596224
USA office: 27 Warren Street, Suite 401-402, Hackensack, NJ 07601
UK office: 57 Shelton Street, Covent Garden, London WC2H 9HE

Library of Congress Cataloging-in-Publication Data
Cheng, Siwei.
Financial reforms and developments in China / Cheng Siwei.
pages cm
Includes bibliographical references and index.
ISBN 978-9814317542 (alk. paper) -- ISBN 9814317543 (alk. paper)
1. Finance--China. 2. Economic development--China. 3. China--Economic policy. I. Title.
HG187.C6C3764 2013
332.0951--dc23
2013023790

British Library Cataloguing-in-Publication Data
A catalogue record for this book is available from the British Library.

In-house Editor: Lum Pui Yee

Typeset by Stallion Press
Email: enquiries@stallionpress.com

Printed in Singapore by World Scientific Printers.

Preface

The book now presenting to the readers is some study and thinking about China's financial reform and development from a Chinese scholar (chairman of International Financial Forum, chairman of China Soft Science Association, honorary chairman of Chinese Society for Management Modernization, head of Fictitious Economy and Data Science Research Centre, Chinese Academy of Sciences, Dean of Management School, Graduate School of Chinese Academy of Sciences, head of Division of Management Science, National Natural Science Fund Committee (1996–2004)), a politician (Vice Chairman of Standing Committee of the 9th and 10th National People's Congress), and a leader of democratic parties (Chairman of the 6th, 7th, and 8th Central Committee of China Democratic National Construction Association).

Retrospect my life experience, I can find three turning points: the first one is going back to mainland China from Hong Kong in 1951 and made up my mind to devote myself to my country; the second one is going to United States in 1981 to study business management and expand my study fields; the third one is joining China Democratic National Construction Association in 1995 and engage in political activities. In these decades, I persisted the belief that "to be honest as a man, to be serious to do things, to be diligent in academic study" and hope make my little contribution for the process of reunification of our motherland and revitalization of China.

I think that the goal of academic study and politics is to serve the country, and academic study is the fundamental of political activities.

Thus, I try to use complexity science methodology to analyze the problems in China's reform and development, exploit the characteristics and development patterns of fictitious economy, and study and push the development of venture capital investment in China. I require the applicability, timeliness, and feasibility of every research project. Suggestions should be technically possible, economically reasonable, legally permitted, operationally executive, realizable in practice, and politically acceptable by each social parties, so as to reduce the resistance in execution. I also require to combine quantitative method and qualitative method. The viewpoints should be clear, the arguments should be abundant and solid. China cannot copy the experience of western counties. She can only find the way by combining theory and practice, and realize the great revival of the Chinese nation in the 21th century.

When I get any gain by study or thinking, holding the belief that although any advocating cannot fulfill everybody, I will do my best so as not to ashamed for my heart, I will tell the public by books, papers, lectures, or interview, propose to the leaders, and execute in the work of Standing Committee of National People's Congress. I think that academic research cannot substitute policy decision. However, it can provide support by theoretical exploit, introducing oversea experience, completing the whole framework, and analyzing the problems, and thus promote the scientific and democratic decision making. As a politician, I should use the research results in the practice of National People's Congress, follow the principle of legal governing, maintain the development and stability of our country, protect the benefit of most people. As a leader of democratic parties, I should combine my research with the function of policy participating and discussing, let my party to play an applicable role in the political life of the country.

Political platform provides benefits for my work and study, as well as opportunities for practice. As the chairman of China Democratic National Construction Association, I have several chance in a year to attend the discussion conference with Chief Secretary or Prime Minister, consulting important issues of national development. I can hear the voice from the top, can reflect to them our comments or suggestions. As the vice chairman of Standing Committee of National People's Congress, I also participate the censoring of law drafts, examining the execution of law, hearing the report of governments, investigate in fields. I can access many concrete situation and problems, and propose my comments after study and thinking. Besides, people's letters and comments from the websites also helped me.

I was interested in financial issues when I studied management in UCLA in the period of 1981–1984. However, I really began to study financial reform after the outbreak of Asian financial crisis in 1997, and I focused on the features and development patterns of fictitious economy. I think that fictitious economy is an economic pattern corresponding with real economy, and may play a more and more important role in knowledge society. My research focuses on the development and main features of fictitious economy, the nature and movement patterns of fictitious economy (including credit capital, knowledge capital, and social capital), and the relationship and interaction between fictitious economy and real economy. I also try to use fictitious economy theory to analyze the chaos and self-organization in financial system, financial crisis, inflation and deflation, economic globalization, knowledge economy, and the development of knowledge society.

This book contains the main results of my research on using fictitious economy theory to analyze the financial reform and development of China. It has 12 chapters, and covers almost all aspects of financial reform, including financial globalization, financial system and product innovation, financial crisis, financial safety, financial regulation, mixed operation, capital market, money market, commercial banks, rural finance, futures market, foreign exchange market, derivatives, property market, and insurance industry. The main points were presented in various lectures, especially on International Financial Forum (IFF), which are co-chaired by Prof. Robert A. Mundell and me, and World Economic Forum, as well as my more than 100 published papers. Although my past comments cannot fully represent my viewpoints today, I did not make any modification in this book in order to keep the historical reality and face further tests in practice. Readers can also see the formation and development of my academic viewpoints.

The chapters of this book were written between 2001 and 2009, although some data and descriptions are obsolete, but my basic points of view still remain valid. Here, I summarize my main points on financial reform, so that readers can read and understand easily:

1. The main trend of financial globalization now is the fast expanding of global financial markets, the sharp increase of scale and speed of international capital flow, the increase of virtualization of currencies, exchange rates become policy tools, rapid development of financial innovation, integration of world financial markets. In this process, demands to loosen financial regulation were generated, which was called financial liberalization. However, this kind of liberalization is relative and limited, any country cannot tolerate complete liberalization of financial system in order to maintain national sovereign and safety. Financial globalization has caused significant effects on world economy, politics, and social life, and provides great opportunity for the modernization of China. We should cautiously design the strategy of our financial reform, eliminate the systemic obstacles, strengthen the internal management of financial firms, and speed-up financial innovation.
2. Correctly understand the relation between finance and economy, pay attention to the influence and dependence of finance on economy, and further coordinate their development.
3. Push the market-oriented of financial system, let market play the fundamental role in resource allocation, steadily develop various financial markets, and expand market participants.
4. Financial safety is the kernel of national economic safety. It is a macro concept involving defense of risks from bonds, exchange rates, deposits, and financial markets, finding and solving potential liabilities. Healthy development of real economy is the premise to control financial risk, and strength of financial system is the important guarantee of financial stability.
5. Stock market should be a place for efficient investment and financing, and a place for proper speculation. China's stock market will be hopeful if it can go back to this nature. Now we have three shortcomings for our stock market: one is that financing function

is emphasized, but investment function is ignored; the other is that some stocks are still not fully tradable; the third one is that short sale is still not permitted. We should let stock market to play the fundamental role in resource allocation, set up strict and reasonable exit mechanism, and enhance the quality of listed companies.

6. Improve financial regulation, maintain the market order, and create a fair, impartial, and open environment. According to the theory of scientific development, realize people-orientation, protect the interest of public investors, depositors, and insurers, avoid illegal hurting, and provide necessary right of information. Ask financial institutions to reduce operation costs, improve their service, and get rational profits. Start from information disclosure, introduce market power into regulation according to the process, and improve the regulation along with the development process.
7. Further push the reform of RMB exchange rate regime, from pegging to US dollar to pegging to a basket of currencies. According to the principle "first regulating, then opening", gradually open capital account, and realize the free exchange of RMB finally.
8. Capital is the most scarce resource in rural area. We should greatly develop rural finance, ensure the supply of funds and fulfill the demand of agriculture industry, counties, and farmers. Gradually solve the problems of agriculture industry, counties, and farmers in our modernization process. The target pattern of rural financial system should be: (1) public financial support, and market operation; (2) let policy finance, commercial finance, and cooperation finance play their function; (3) main business should be deposit and borrowing, and with additional business; (4) complete legal system, and let market play the fundamental role.
9. In accordance with the demand of economic development, positively and steadily push the innovation of financial system and financial tools, enhance financial efficiency effectively, solve or transfer financial risks. However, pay attention to over-speculation, and maintain the order of financial markets.
10. Due to the liquidate feature of capital and risk, mixed operation should be the final target of our financial reform. Currently, we should set up powerful coordinate system for financial risk

management, exploit the development of mixed operation and regulation and create conditions for it.

Above points are only personal comments as a scholar. I am pleased that some of them are consistent with the government and other experts, and are realizing gradually. I hope more people concern the issues of our financial reform, provide more suggestions and contributions for enhancing the competitiveness of our financial sector and constructing the a financial system with Chinese characteristics.

The purpose of academic study is to exploit the truth. We must insist on the scientific pragmatic attitude, emphasize academic democracy, be oppose to fame-chasing, power-depending, incompleteness-sticking, incorrectness-covering. I always assert that promotion or honor is determined by the organization, credit or fault is commented by the people. I sincerely hope readers to understand my viewpoints and provide valuable comments.

Lin Zexu once said in a poem: if it can benefit my country, I will never care live or death, and never access or avoid depending on its fortune or misfortune. I want to work together with people with lofty ideals in my rest life, for the prosperity and strength of our country, the development and progress of the society, and the happiness of people.

Cheng Siwei
Director,
Research Center on Fictitious Economy
and Data Science,
Chinese Academy of Sciences

Written on February 10, 2010.

Contents

Chapter 1

Introduction: Finance from the Perspective of Fictitious Economy

Fictitious economy, in contrast with the real economy, is a mode of economic activity with its own structure and evolution process, existing in the economic system. Fictitious economy is a combination of economic activities, related to the circulatory movement of fictitious capital supported mainly by the financial platform, and the relationships resulting from these activities.

Fictitious capital is a kind of resource, established on the basis of a trust relationship, without a real or currency form, without value in itself, but capable of producing profit. The advent of ownership certificates or titles has reflected the dual nature of capital ownership, realized the separation of ownership and the right to use, giving rise to fictitious capital. Fictitious capital consists of three categories: credit capital, knowledge capital and social capital, whose owners, though they do not have any real capital, they do have the ability to obtain the right to use it. As ownership certificate does not have any value in itself and is only the carrier of fictitious capital, it is called secondary fictitious capital.

The development of fictitious economy can be divided into five stages: (1) capitalization of idle capital, (2) socialization of interest-bearing capital, (3) marketization of securities, (4) internationalization of the financial market, and (5) integration of international finance.

Fictitious capital moves according to the following laws: (1) Exchange — re-exchange represents the major movement for fictitious capital; (2) Uncertainty of fictitious capital makes speculation possible; (3) Inflation of fictitious capital could bring about certain risks; (4) Movement of fictitious capital does not create social wealth directly.

Fictitious economic system possesses the following characteristics: (1) complexity, (2) metastability, (3) high risks, (4) parasitism, and (5) periodicity.

The focus of research on fictitious economy includes studying: (1) the relationship between the fictitious economy and the real economy; (2) institutional factors involved in fictitious economic activities; (3) risk generation and prevention in fictitious economy; (4) evaluation system in fictitious economy.

Research methods for fictitious economy include: (1) the method of complexity science; (2) the method of uncertainty decision making; (3) group decision making method; (4) complex data analysis supporting decision making; (5) the method of mathematical finance; and (6) computer simulation method.

Fictitious economy refers to various kinds of activities in which fictitious capital is involved based mainly on the financial platform,[1] while virtual economy refers to economic activities supported by information technology, including the well-known electronic commerce. However, in recent years, it is more commonly defined as the generation and transference of virtual wealth in cyber games especially in foreign countries. For example, Wikipedia's explanation for virtual economy is as follows: "A virtual economy (or sometimes synthetic economy) is an emergent economy existing in a virtual persistent world, usually exchanging virtual goods in the context of an Internet game. People enter these virtual economies for recreation and entertainment rather than necessity. However, some people do interact with virtual economies for "real" economic benefits."[2] On the homepage of Virtual Economy Research Network, it is clearly indicated: "Some online resources, such as domain names, virtual objects in community website and powerful characters, are similar to real goods and real persons that could only be controlled by one person for a certain period of time. Nowadays, virtual goods and properties are being bought and sold by tens of thousands of people with real money in many different markets all around the world."[3] There is also some research regarding this aspect in China.[4]

Studies on virtual economy in China started in 1997. I was then the director of the Management Science Department of the Natural Science Foundation of China and together with the Mathematics Department, we commenced an important research project called "Mathematical Finance, Financial Engineering and Financial Management" at the beginning of 1997. After the breakout of the East Asian Financial Crisis in early July of 1997, the author and some other scholars had tried to analyze it by applying the theory of fictitious economy.[5,6] Studies on fictitious economy flourished especially after the objective of "to deal correctly with the relation between fictitious economy and the real economy"[7] was voiced at the 16th National Congress of Communist Party of China. Up to now, a total of five national seminars about fictitious economy have been conducted and thousands of articles on this topic have been published on domestic newspapers and magazines by Chinese scholars.

Among researchers of fictitious economy in China, three schools of thought or three types of views exist.

The first school believes that fictitious economy is a fictitious value system. Most scholars of this group are traditional economists. As in traditional economics, economy is considered to be a value system itself, which naturally makes fictitious economy a fictitious value system.

The second school holds that fictitious economy is just finance. Most scholars of this group are people in the financial world. To them, fictitious economy is finance and some of them even think that it is not necessary to use the term "fictitious economy".

The third school defines fictitious economy as a mode of economic activities, with its own structure and evolution process, existing in the economic system that is in contrast with the real economy. In their opinion, fictitious economy is the software of the economy. This view was first mooted by the author and it has gained the approval of some scholars of system engineering, natural science & technology.

I believe that research on fictitious economy in China is still at the stage of exploration and no fixed model has yet taken shape. The guideline of "letting a hundred of schools of thought contend" should be pursued and scholars should be encouraged to do research from different perspectives. Coexistence of different thoughts would surely lead to the same destination through different ways. However, as the three schools differ in research philosophies and methodologies, though they may complement one another, only through practice could we discover the correct or most appropriate view or views that suit China's conditions.

I for my part have conducted some exploratory work, trying to apply the principles of complexity science and financial studies — on the various aspects namely the securities market, money market, foreign exchange market, futures and options market, property transactions market, financial crisis, inflation and deflation, commercial bank reform, rural finance, real estate finance, etc. and the associated problems of chaos and self-organizing abilities — under the perspective of fictitious economy. Theories and methods concerning the research of fictitious economy are also involved.[8,9] The aim is to promote the reforms and development of China's financial industry. Each chapter of this book contains to some extent some preliminary research achievement of the author.

1.1. The Emergence and Development of the Theories on Fictitious Capital Theory

1.1.1. *Marxian Fictitious Capital Theory*

In his monumental work *Das Kapital* (Volume 3), Marx put forward the theory of fictitious capital.[10] As Volume 3 of Mark's work was collated based on Marx's manuscript and published by Engels after Marx's death, we could thus say that this is also Engels' contribution to the theory.

According to Marx, the term "fictitious capital" was first used by W. Leatham (a Yorkshire banker) in his *Letters on the Currency* (Second Edition, 1840, London), where it refers principally to 'short drafts' or notes. In the Fifth Section of *Das Kapital* (Volume 3), especially after the illustration of credit in Chapter 25, Marx has conducted an in-depth systematic research on fictitious capital. Marx's theory about fictitious capital could be simply summarized into the following two points:

Firstly, Marx believes that fictitious capital is produced or created on the basis of loan capital or interest-bearing capital and bank's credit system.[11] Under capitalist production, currency could be transformed into capital, through which it changes from one with a fixed value to one with an increasing value. The utility value of currency then is its transformation into capital which produces profit. Therefore, currency, under such circumstance, could be considered as a special commodity, whose owner may lend it to people in need of capital subject to certain laws and conditions and then get back in return both the principal and interest after a certain period of time, according to their agreement or contract. Currency thus becomes a kind of capital that bears interest (interest-bearing capital), while credit is the basis for loans.

However, when currency is lent out as an interest-bearing capital, the owner would not get anything equal in return as they would usually do for ordinary goods. What they get is a certain form of guarantee that promises to pay them back both the principal and interest. This guarantee (usually in written form) is the so-called fictitious capital. After the advent of banks, quite a lot of idle money in the society is gathered together and used as interest-bearing capital. As the use of the credit system gets expanded, banks begin to give out many kinds of credit instead of just loans, thus enlarging the variety of fictitious capital. According to Marx, fictitious capital should include bank credit such as bank notes, value of capitalization such as securities, real estate mortgage bonds, etc.

Secondly, Marx believes that fictitious capital does not have value in itself but has the ability to produce profit through circulatory movement, that is, an ability to produce some kind of surplus value.

According to Marx's theory of labor value, the value of something's utility is the socially necessary labor time that is needed to produce this utility value. Since fictitious capital does not include any labor in it, it has no value at all according to this view.

Marx has also pointed out that surplus value could only be generated through real economic activities: capitalists use currency as capital to exchange for production factors such as employed labor, raw materials, factories, machines, etc., which, through the production process, are used to produce goods that become commodities through a circulation process, after which these commodities are changed back to currency through the exchange process. During this circulatory process in the real economy, surplus value is produced and so is profit. This is a fundamental point of great importance in Marx's work.

In Marx's *Das Kapital* (Volume 3), he has pointed out that fictitious capital could also produce some kind of surplus value through circulatory movement. But strictly speaking, this kind of surplus value is not directly "produced" by fictitious capital but paid in the form of interest to the owner of fictitious capital by functional capitalist (industrial capitalist or commercial capitalist) from their profit (surplus value) according to the contracts between them. This is the reason why Marx has used the words "some kind of" for this concept.

Marx also thinks that capital has two characteristics: (1) It has to have its own value; (2) it has to be able to produce surplus value. As fictitious capital possesses the second characteristic, it is appropriate to call it 'capital'; however, as it does not have the first characteristic, that is, it can not be used to purchase production factors through exchange, it is only a kind of fictitious capital.

We have to agree that Marx has been a far-sighted or a prescient man. It was not that easy to put forward such theory about fictitious capital in the 19th century (He was born on May 5, 1818 and passed away on March 14, 1883.). Of course, after over a hundred years, our understanding of fictitious capital has become much wider and deeper.

1.1.2. *Definition of Fictitious Capital*

I believe that fictitious capital is a kind of resource, established on the basis of a trust relation, without a real or monetary form, without value in itself but capable of producing profit. It could be used to acquire the right to use real capital but it has to promise to pay the owner a certain amount of money in return or to share risk and profit together with the owner. For example, bonds belong to the category of "promising to pay the owner a certain amount of money in return" (or 'promissory note') while stocks belong to the second category, that is "to share risk and profit together with the owner". The most important thing is that the advent of 'ownership certificate' of 'certificate of title' has reflected the dual nature of capital ownership, realizing the separation of ownership and the right to use, which gives rise to fictitious capital.

As we all know, in real economy the exchange process is the exchange of both the ownership and right of use of currency with the commodity bought and these two rights are inseparable. When someone has bought something with a certain amount of currency/money, he/she would no longer enjoy these two rights. But as capital has the duality feature, it could be divided into ownership and right of use, and these could be separable. For example, if someone purchases the bond of a firm with currency, he/she has given the right of use of the currency to the firm. Of course, the firm would give him/her an ownership certificate — the bond — which is the proof for the ownership of part of the currency concerned and would thus give him/her the right to ask for the principal plus interest from the firm. Stocks are proof that the owner enjoys shareholder rights but the shareholder also has to undertake shareholder obligations. As to real estate mortgage bond or bill or certificate, it proves that the ownership of the real property in question has passed to the financial institution or person who has accepted the mortgage arrangement. The mortgagor borrower has reserved the right to use the real property in the agreed period of time, but if he/she fails to return the money on time, he/she would also lose the right to use it. So it's quite obvious that it is exactly the separation of ownership and right of use that has given rise to fictitious capital. This is a very important point, which features prominently in the analysis of many related problems.

1.1.3. *Major Categories of Fictitious Capital*

There are two pivotal points regarding the creation of fictitious capital. First is that real capital has acquired universally accepted evaluation in symbols of value. The second factor is the capitalization of such "soft" factors as science & technology, education and management, which would make it possible to view and evaluate these "soft" factors the way we do for traditional capital — and thus fictitious capital is created. Through such a construction model, the relationships between various kinds of fictitious capital and real capital with valued symbolic evaluation become matched in an economic sense. And with such a relation, we would be able to see the operation and efficiency of the fictitious economic system, which makes this relation the core of many other relations in the fictitious economy.

From the perspective of "soft" factors, fictitious capital could be divided into three categories.

First is credit capital. This type of fictitious capital had already existed in Marx's era and has become the foundation of the financial industry today. For example, banks get deposit through credit, firms issue bonds and stocks with their credit and people who take loans from banks also use their credit to do so. Nowadays, many banks in China would demand for guarantees from loan takers, which is quite similar to old-style Chinese private banks ('money houses') or pawnshops. Banks give out loans to people according to their credit-worthiness; therefore, credit capital refers to the credit financiers use to obtain the rights of use of the capital.

The second category is knowledge capital. Knowledge capital refers to how financiers obtain right of use of capital through their knowledge, technology, trademarks or even standards. The most obvious example would be venture capital investments, where innovators get their capital from venture capitalists with the fruits of their innovation. If the investment fails, they would share the risk and if it succeeds, they would also share the profit. Thus, venture capital investment is a combination of real capital and fictitious capital, which together would create social wealth.[12]

The third category is social capital. The concept of social capital was first put forward by socialists. It is a theory developed on the basis of social network studies in the 70s of the last century and is primarily concerned with the association within the same social network or between different social networks.[13] In the past three decades, the development of both theories and practices of social capital has made quite a lot of progress, with its scope updated constantly, but there are still quite some debates over the definition and function of social capital in socialist circles. Although economists have already noticed the influence of social capital on the economy, this concept has not yet been widely known in the economic circle. The author has included the concept of social capital into the category of fictitious capital and defined it as cooperative relationship and systems or institutions formed through the interaction between members of society. Simply put, social capital is "connection". (or 'guanxi' in Chinese). In China, because of the seriousness and prevalence of corruption, "connection" has become a derogatory term. However, whether at home or abroad, "connection" is actually a very important factor of economic life. During their communication and interaction, members of society increase their mutual understanding and advance the friendship and trust among themselves, thus establishing a cooperative relation between them. And they could also institutionalize such a relation and call it social capital. Social capital plays a positive role in the development of the economy. For example, people have pointed out that Northern Italy is better developed than the south because the North used to be republic system while the south a system of monarchy, and the former system is definitely better for the accumulation of social capital than the latter. In recent years, private equity funds flourish and the capital is raised privately by the general partner of the fund from limited partners. Only if investors could trust the capability and moral character of the general partner will they hand over their money to him and let him help them invest and make profits.

In a word, the owners of credit capital, knowledge capital and social capital basically do not have any real capital of their own. However, they would be able to get the right of use of real capital as long as they issue an 'ownership certificate' to owners of the real capital affirming their ownership and promising to pay them back or share both risks and profits. But the values of these fictitious capitals cannot be determined unless they are combined with real capital to become real money.

When the aforementioned three types of fictitious capital combine with real capital, the rights they endow would be fixed in ownership certificates, stipulating their shareholding proportion or admitting that all profits after interest would be theirs, for instance. As ownership certificate has no value of its own and it is only a carrier of fictitious capital, it is called 'secondary' fictitious capital, while credit capital, knowledge capital and social capital are called original fictitious capital. What we mean by fictitious capital in the remaining of this chapter shall be secondary fictitious capital represented by ownership certificates.

1.2. Definition and Characteristics of the Fictitious Economy

Fictitious economy is a combination of economic activities, related to the circulatory movement of fictitious capital supported mainly by the financial platform, and various types of relationships resulted from within. In real economic activities, capital could only produce profit through a circulatory movement of exchange-production-circulation-exchange-…, but in fictitious economic activities, capital might also produce profit without such a circulatory movement.

1.2.1. *Development of Fictitious Economy*

The development of fictitious economy can be divided into five stages.

The first stage is capitalization of idle currency, which means that the idle currency or money people have in their hands becomes interest bearing capital. The earliest fictitious economy could date back to private commercial lending between individuals. For example, A needs to buy something but he does not have enough money. B happens to have some idle money, so A could then borrow the amount of money he needs and promises to pay B the principal plus interest in return. Thus, A would have the right to use this amount of money to obtain profit through practical operational activities by making use of the function of money as medium of payment, while B still holds the ownership of this amount of money and also has the right to ask A to pay him back both the principal and interest. The certificate of indebtedness held by B could be considered as a kind of rudiments for fictitious capital and its value increases through this circulatory movement of borrowing and paying back. Though B does not undertake any practical economic activity, he has made some money through a kind of fictitious economic activity.

The second stage is socialization of interest-bearing capital, which means that idle money people have is borrowed by banks, which, as an intermediary, would then lend this money out for interest. Besides, firms could also raise money through the issuing of bonds and stocks and promise to pay back the principal plus interest after a certain period of time, or to share risk and profit with investors. Thus, people could use idle money to purchase various types of securities such as stocks and bonds so as to earn interests. We could also see that socialization of interest-bearing capital has given rise to both banks and various kinds of fictitious capital like bonds and stocks. Socialization of interest-bearing capital could also transfer capital from people who do not participate in any real economic activities such as production, circulation, exchange, etc. to people who do. The use of money gathered from different people in large-scale and high-income economic activities would optimize investment directions and increase the efficiency of capital use.

The third stage is marketization of securities. The biggest problem of early fictitious capital was lack of liquidity, which made it very difficult for owners to get currency when in need, thus preventing the transformation of idle currency into interest-bearing capital. Once securities are marketized, they could be freely bought and sold according to their expected value of returns, which would also lead to the emergence of a financial market where fictitious capital is traded (stock market, bond market, money market, etc., for example). Marketization of securities not only makes it much easier for people to get money at any time, increasing the liquidity of fictitious capital, but would also help guide capital to industries and firms with higher expected returns, further increasing the efficiency of the use of capital. However, it has also helped encourage speculation by people taking advantage of price fluctuations in the securities market. In 1898, futures transaction of agricultural products was created and later on industrial raw material such as nonferrous metal and crude oil was also added into this new form of fictitious capital.

The fourth stage is internationalization of financial market, which means that fictitious capital could be transacted among different countries. This process can be traced back to mid-19th century when bonds with fixed interest were issued on the financial markets of Britain, France and Germany by debtor country governments and railway companies. But it was not until the 20s of last century that relatively large-scale cross-country securities investment began, and it was interrupted by the economic depression and Second World War that happened in the 30s of America. Only after 1944 and with the promotion of *Bretton Woods Agreement* and *General Agreement on Trade and Tariff (GATT)* did large scale international financial market gradually come into being. Internationalization of financial market would help guide capital to industries of higher returns, thus increasing the utilization efficiency of capital and at the same time forming a new kind of financial market-foreign exchange market. Futures transaction also gradually becomes fictitious, which means that buying of futures has become a kind of tool for speculation too. After 1960, futures transaction began to show up in various types of financial commodity transactions such as stocks, futures, foreign exchange, etc. In 1973, options transaction appeared for the first time.

The fifth stage is integration of international finance, which means that the relation between domestic financial market of each country and the international financial market is becoming closer and closer, accompanied by increasing mutual influence. Since the 1980s, (1) with the development of economic globalization, the inter-dependence among different countries' economies also grows, resulting in a larger degree of financial liberalization; (2) as the establishment of the floating exchange rate system resulted from the decoupling of US dollar from the gold standard and the increasing financial innovation, the scale of fictitious economy also grows larger; (3) with advances in information technology, the circulation rate of fictitious capital on the financial market also becomes higher together with larger volumes of circulation. All the above mentioned three factors have helped promote the integration of the financial market of each country, resulting in both higher inter-dependence and a larger degree of mutual influence between the economies of different countries. We could say that anything that happens to the financial market of one country could affect the financial markets of all other countries: all the others would feel the impact. This could be clearly seen from the East Asian Financial Crisis that happened in 1997: the liquidity crisis in Thailand had such a big impact on the East Asia, Asia and even the whole world.

1.2.2. *The Laws of Fictitious Capital Movement*

1.2.2.1. *Exchange-re-exchange is a major movement process for fictitious capital*

Whether you are buying bonds or stocks, what you do is to sell the right of use of the real capital in exchange for an ownership certificate and then re-exchange back the right of use of the real capital with the ownership certificate and also profits in return after a certain period of time. This kind of fictitious economic activity makes it possible for capital to increase its value without going through the real economic circulation process.

The movement of fictitious capital includes two interlinked rounds: exchange and re-exchange. The exchange process not only involves the exchange of real capital and ownership certificate (real capital-fictitious capital), but also the exchange of original fictitious capital and ownership certificate (original fictitious capital-secondary fictitious capital). The re-exchange process is a process where the value of fictitious capital is realized through private selling or selling on the financial market.

1.2.2.2. *Uncertainty in fictitious capital price makes it possible for speculation*

Neo-classical economics theory assumes that people conducting economic activities are all "economic persons", who would pursue the maximization of their self-interest and whose behavior is completely rational. According to this theory, the price of a stock is the rational expectation of investors on the future value of real economic variables that might affect stock prices. In other words, the rational price of a stock is the present value of its future returns. However, as winner of Nobel Prize for Economics Herbert Simon has pointed out, for all the people participating in economic activities, their rationality could only be limited. Owing to limited information and knowledge, it is hard for people to understand and predict all kinds of possibilities and they are more likely to make decisions according to their subjective judgment. When they are making decisions, it is not possible for them to consider all the possible solutions[14] and factors. Besides, people's personal values, words and behaviors and actions of other people around would also affect their decision making.

The reason why there are both buying and selling activities on the stock market is that different investors have different expectations for the price of the same stock. Some investors might think that the price of a certain stock has already exceeded their rationally expected price, so they would sell out, while some other investors might think that the price of this stock is below their expected price, so they would buy in. if all the investors are 'completely rational', there would be no transactions on the stock market at all.

Every stock market is a place for both investment and speculation. Generally speaking, "investment" is a kind of long-term investment process where buyers of stocks expect to get relatively high dividends and benefits from their increasing corporate value, while "speculation" is usually a kind of short-term investment where buyers of stocks expect to sell them quickly under favorable conditions so as to make a profit.

In reality, moderate speculation would not only do no harm to the securities market but actually facilitate the operation of the stock market. First, it is good to enliven the stock market, increase market liquidity and speed up capital turnover; second, as speculators are bold enough to undertake the risk associated with newly issued stocks, they would also help promote the issuing of new stocks; third, speculators' buying low and selling high would help 'adjust' the relation between market supply and demand and help stabilize the price of stock. The author believes that a mature stock market should include moderate speculation so that a dynamic equilibrium could be attained between investment and speculation. Although fluctuation would be likely under the influence of external environment, relatively stable operations could still be maintained. Besides its positive effect on economic development, speculation would also help most investors get relatively satisfactory returns.

In fact, many investors in the stock market have both an investing and speculating motivations, but the proportion of each differs for different people and different markets. However, if most investors have very obvious speculating motivations, there would be too much speculation on the market. In that case, the actual operational performance of firms would be ignored by investors. This could lead to disinclination or relative shunning away from blue chips and overheated interest or hot pursuits of stocks with more rooms for speculation, thus diluting the function of the stock market for allocation of resources. Over-speculation would also encourage short-term behaviors on the market as well as illegal market manipulations of 'market makers'. The huge risk that is associated with over-speculation would become a hidden danger that could trigger serious turbulence in the securities market, thus endangering the economy and the society.

1.2.2.3. *Inflation of fictitious capital could bring about corresponding risks*

The basis of fictitious capital is the trust of investors on financiers and the prospective profitability of the investment, and there is no connection between the 'ownership certificates' that financiers give to investors and the real and monetary capital that financiers have in their own possession. When investors and/or financiers are over optimistic about the prospects of the investment project, there would usually be over investment or financing, causing 'inflation' of fictitious capital. When this kind of optimistic estimate goes wrong for subjective or objective reasons, risk would result.

With the development of science and technology and financial innovation, all kinds of financial derivatives show up, which makes people feel dizzy and dazzled. The original aims of these derivatives are to satisfy the different preferences or priorities on security, profitability and liquidity of different investors and also to reduce risk through hedging. At the same time, they also represent a variety of speculation tools in the financial market, which might lead to rapid 'inflation' and expansion of fictitious capital.

Inflation of fictitious capital could be classified into the following categories.

Overestimation/overvaluation: When investors overestimate the value of a certain ownership certificate, fictitious capital gets inflated. For example, when investors are over optimistic about the profitability of a listed company, they would bid high on the stock of this company. Especially in a bull market, many investors would pursue this stock by following others or thinking that someone else would pay a higher price, thus resulting in bubbles, which would bring loss to investors when the bubbles are broken.

Over-indebtedness: When financiers believe that the returns of their assets would be higher than the interest rate of their borrowing, they tend to borrow more so as to gain more profits. But this would make the ratio of their liability to self-owned assets as high as tens or even a hundred. When investors feel that the prospects are not very good and want to retract their loans or refuse to issue new loans, financiers would face the risk of bankruptcy.

Leverage: This refers to a situation where relatively small amounts of capital are used to 'guarantee' or ensure or facilitate transactions involving huge amounts. For example, on futures market for commodities, one can purchase a futures contract with just 5% margin or 'deposit'.

Multiplier Effect: As we all know, because of the multiplier effect of money, the original supply of money provided by central banks become 'multiplied' several times over the original, finally forming the total money supply. Similarly, fictitious capital could also get enlarged through the multiplier effect. For example, a bond holder would be able to get cash from a bank by using his bond as collateral and then use this amount of money as margin to buy futures and other financial derivatives. Thus, the initial capital used to buy bonds could be computed in the book value of the bond and outstanding futures contracts, whose total amount could be as high as 20 times the margin, and outstanding futures contracts of financial derivatives could be enlarged by a factor of several tens. Meanwhile, the risk that the bond holder faces also increases from a low level to a high level. He could get very high returns but could also lose everything or incur huge losses.

Movement of fictitious capital will not create social wealth directly:
As the movement of fictitious capital (fictitious economic activities) stays out of physical production activities, it is not capable of creating social wealth. What fictitious economy can do is redistribute the wealth that is created by the real economy. For example, the stock market only redistributes the wealth inside it while it is the listed companies that create wealth. Trading in stocks and shares could increase the wealth of some people, but what the winners win is the money of people who lose (after deducting stamp duties, commission charged by securities companies and management fees charged by stock exchanges). Therefore, it is only a redistribution of wealth. When the stock market is a 'quick' bull market, stock prices would go up very quickly and there would also be an increasing amount of capital moving in, which makes it seem that no one loses. But when the stock market falls, the last ones to enter would most likely be the ones that lose. Dividend on stocks is a part of profit that stock holders receive as investment returns after listed companies have created wealth. But fictitious economy is able to create wealth indirectly through optimizing the real economy. For example, stock market has the ability to help firms with good performance to get capital at a cost lower than that of bank loans and gradually those firms with bad performance will become 'marginalized', thus realizing optimized allocation of resources.

1.2.3. *Characteristics of the Fictitious Economic System*

The fictitious economic system possesses five characteristic features, namely: complexity, metastability, high risk, parasitism and periodicity.

1.2.3.1. *Complexity*

A complex system is a large-scale, highly integrated, low-transparency, dynamic and open system. Its most fundamental characteristic is the intelligence that is contained in its components, that is, the ability to understand the environment, predict changes and take actions according to preset goals. This is also the intrinsic factor for biological evolution, technological innovation, economic development and social progress.

The stock market is a complex system, composing mainly of natural persons and legal persons (buyer, seller and intermediate agent) who conduct stock trading on the stock market according to a certain set of rules. Though each person has the freedom to make independent decisions based on his own understanding of the environment, his prospective of development of the environment, and preset goals, the decision of each person is also not uninfluenced by other people's decisions and the environment. Although the nonlinear effect among different components of the system could easily lead to a chaos, its self-organizing effect could keep this system in order and stable macroscopically and in the long run.

In stock trading, investors have insufficient knowledge about the present and future market conditions and price changes; investors possess different capacities to invest and to undertake risk, different understanding and estimation of the value of their investment, different investment motivation as well as different expected times for returns. Many investors do not know the methodologies for market trend analysis and do not even have basic knowledge about stock market investment. Owing to the lack of ability to understand and make judgment about market information that keeps coming in, people tend to conduct transactions by blindly following the trends or rumors, or even by just listening to their own instincts. However, it is also because of the interaction between people and the 'guidance effect' that external environment has on people's behavior that makes the stock market take on a certain trend and stay stable for a certain period of time: the so-called bull and bear markets.

1.2.3.2. *Metastability*

A metastable system is a system that is not in equilibrium but could maintain relative stability by exchanging materials and energy with the external environment. It is also called a system with a 'dissipative' structure.[15] Although this type of system could reach equilibrium through self-organization, the stability could be easily destroyed by small external disturbances. However, even after the stability has been destroyed, it could still move between a stable and unstable state within a certain 'range' or 'bounds'. So from a macro perspective, the system is stable within a certain 'region' or 'zone', that is, it has 'regional' stability. But sometimes when the system moves away from its stability, drastic changes could occur that could cause the system to collapse, after which the system could recover its metastability through an in-depth structural adjustment but it could also completely die out. Generally speaking, the bigger its inertia is, the less likely the system will break down.

The stock market is a type of metastable system, which relies on capital exchange with the environment to maintain its relative stability. There are many reasons for its metastability, but the most fundamental reason is the intrinsic instability of fictitious capital.

The intrinsic instability of fictitious capital comes from its fictitiousness. For example, stocks do not have any real value and they only represent a right to get returns. In other words, stocks are just a kind of 'ownership certificates' or 'titles', which enable their owners to demand for a part of the surplus value that is produced by the capital they use to buy securities. When stocks are allowed to be traded on the stock market, as they do not have value in themselves, their prices are not determined in accordance with the objective Law of Value but by people's subjective expectation for their future prices as well as the laws of supply and demand. All of these factors have made it even easier for prices to deviate from the performance of real economic activities. Deviation of stock price from reasonable expectation would result in "bubble", which could be stable as long as capital is injected from outside. However, this is only a fictitious and fragile stability. When there is not enough capital injection from outside, prices would tumble.

Instability of fictitious economic system also comes from the fictitiousness of currency: currency does not have value in itself. Ever since currency was decoupled from gold standard and gold exchange standard, though it could still serve as the medium of payment, it no longer has any value that could be measured by real objects. The value of currency now could only be measured by its purchasing power, which is affected by a host of factors such as currency issuance, interest rate, exchange rate and people's consumption behaviors. The transformation of currency from real to fictitious capital has increased the instability of the fictitious economy.

"Positive feedback effect" existing in fictitious economic system would also increase the instability of fictitious economic system. For example, the more people are buying a certain stock, the more people would follow to buy the stock. This type of mutual influence or reinforcing among people is called "positive feedback effect", which would amplify changes, making stock prices go up and down 'violently'.

1.2.3.3. *High risk*

The so-called risk in economic activities refers to the difference between people's expected returns and real returns, attributable to uncertainties in the objective world, or limited ability to understand the objective world, or mistakes people make on expected return based on their subjective estimation. Stock market features high risk but it could also bring the possibility of high returns.

The high risk that is involved in fictitious economic system comes from the complexity and metastability of the system itself. First, the intrinsic instability of fictitious capital would lead to unpredictable price changes while the increase of financial market transaction and transaction products makes it more complex. Second, people lack the ability to predict changes of the market and environment and could not find a better way of prediction, resulting in mistakes when making decisions. Third, quite a lot of people only have limited 'risk-tolerance' ability and when faced with huge risk, they would feel at loss and even increase their risk if affected by the 'positive feedback effect'. Finally, many people are willing to take high risk so as to pursue high returns and thus many kinds of innovative financial products with high risk and high returns show up, including futures, options, forwards, swaps, etc.

In addition, some activities that violate the laws also result in high risks in the financial market. For example, disclosure of false information could mislead investors; insider trading would do harm to the interests of small and medium investors; hostile market manipulation would allow 'market makers' to get excessive profit.

1.2.3.4. *Parasitism*

There is a close relation between fictitious economic system and real economic system. Fictitious economic system is born out of the real economic system and becomes attached to it.

Because of this close relation between fictitious and real economy, risks born in real economic system, such as risks of accumulated stock of products/inventory, bankruptcy of companies, etc. would be transmitted to the fictitious economic system, resulting in instability; similarly, risks incurred inside the fictitious economy such as drop of stock index and real estate prices, large increase of non-performing loans and large scale depreciation of currency would also exert serious effects on real economy. This is the 'action and reaction' between real economy and fictitious economy. As finance has already become the core of the economy today, real economy could no longer function in isolation of fictitious economic system. If real economic system could be seen as hardware of the economic system, then fictitious economic system would be the software. Both of them are indispensable but software depends on the hardware before it could function.

Stocks are equity certificates that companies limited by shares issue to investors and they are proof of ownership of their holder to the company. As stocks are securities without a stipulated repayment term, investors who have bought stocks on the primary market cannot withdraw their shares but only sell them on the secondary market to other investors. Theoretically speaking, whether on primary market or secondary market, the value of stocks should be determined mainly by the future performance of listed companies, that is, the present value of future returns. Although stock prices fluctuate a lot on stock market, basically speaking, stocks parasitize on listed firms while stock market parasitizes on the real economy. In other words, listed companies may be regarded as the foundation stones of the stock market.

As investors' estimation of stock prices is based on prediction of their future performance, the parasitism of stocks is mainly reflected by the fact that market price is usually affected by information about the issuing company, including information voluntarily disclosed by the company, information about change of external environment and other information circulating in society, etc.

On the other hand, the reaction or 'reverse effect' of the stock market on the real economy cannot be ignored. When stock market goes up, people's confidence towards future economic prospects would also increase. With the help of "wealth effect", consumption would increase, thus promoting economic growth. Similarly, when stock market bubbles burst, people would reduce consumption and sell off their financial assets, leading to economic depression or even economic crisis.

1.2.3.5. *Periodicity*

The evolution of fictitious economic system is also characterized by periodicity, which usually includes the following stages of : increasing growth of real economy, formation of economic bubbles, inflation of currency and credit, increase of asset price, optimism all around, increase of both stock price and real estate price, bursting of economic bubbles caused by external disturbance, drop of financial indices, selling off of real and financial assets by people, reduced or negative growth of real economy. But this is not a simple cycle but a process characterized by wave-like advancing and spiral ascending.

The running of the stock market also features periodicity, with bull and bear markets appearing interchangeably. As stock market is based on optimistic expectation of future returns (fundamentally speaking, on optimistic expectation of economic development) by investors, there would sure be bubbles inside the stock market. Inflation and burst of these bubbles could lead to fluctuation of the stock market, but this fluctuation is a wave-like advancing and a spiral ascending process. For example, on October 19th, 1987 (black Monday) when the US stock market fell drastically, the Dow Jones Index was less than 3000 points but after 13 years, it reached as high as 12000 points or even higher.

1.3. Research Direction of Fictitious Economy

The research direction of fictitious economy includes the following four aspects.

1.3.1. *Relationship Between the Fictitious Economy and the Real Economy*

First, about the relation between the price of fictitious capital and the price of the real capital that it is attached to. Fictitious capital does not have any value in itself and ownership certificate is just a piece of paper, whose price or value depends on people's confidence toward the real capital. For example, generally speaking, the P/E ratio of a stock shouldn't exceed the reciprocal of bank deposit interest rate. If the return of stock is equal to bank deposit interest, it would then be unnecessary for people to buy stocks. Although quite some listed companies have P/E ratios higher than the reciprocal of bank deposit interest rates, some people buy their stocks not because of its present value but their future value, which also means that the estimated future price of the fictitious capital is higher than the present price of the real capital that it is attached to. For another example: in futures market, there is also a difference between the futures price of a commodity and its spot price.

Next is about the relation between the operating circle of fictitious economy and that of the real economy. As we all know, the real economy features periodicity and there are actually three categories of cyclical theories: short-term, medium-term and long-term. The author believes that fictitious economy also features periodicity, but it might not be at the same pace as that of the real economy. There are many factors to consider.

If we analyze the cyclical terms of fictitious and real economy, we would see that they are sometimes at the same 'space' or phase, but sometimes not. People often say that stock market is the barometer of the economy, which is correct to a certain degree but not completely true. Under certain circumstances, the operating cycle of stock market depends on the operating cycle of the real economy. For example, as the stock market is based on listed companies and the real economy, from a macro and long-term perspective, the stock market is capable of reflecting the real economy. The operation of real economy can be represented by Gross Domestic Product (GDP) while the operation of stock market is represented by stock price index, Dow Jones Index for example. Although stock market cycle might go ahead of or lag behind the real economic circle, long-term deviation from the latter is definitely abnormal. It should also be noted that there are quite a number of stocks on the stock market and stock price indices represent a weighted figure calculated by using statistic methods, makes it difficult for these indices to reflect the actual, all round operation of stock market.

In recent years, doubts about the traditional thinking that "stock market is the barometer for the economy" began to show up. It is said that there is no necessary connection between the stock market and the economy, because such things as increasing stock market accompanied by economic depression or falling stock market accompanied by economic progress did happen. The author believe that although the stock market is basically attached to the real economy and should be the leading indicator for the real economy, from the perspective of complex science, the relation between the stock market and the real economy is not a simple linear one-to-one relation but a complex nonlinear relation with multi factors involved. First, GDP is insufficient in reflecting the real economy and neither is stock price index for stock market. Secondly, there are many factors such as international economic environment, social system, government policies, people's confidence, etc., whose effect on GDP and stock price index is not symmetric or 'equally-paced'. Thirdly, under the influence or interplay of many different factors, deviation of the stock market from the real economy in the short or medium term is a common occurrence. The stock market and the development of the real economy are not completely 'in sync'. Finally, as the stock market also reacts to the real economy, the relation between the two becomes more complex and intriguing. What's especially worth mentioning is the fact that when there are such abnormal situations as over speculation, black market maker manipulation and too much policy influence, the development of stock market might go against the directions of the development of the real economy.

Besides, the impact of stock market on the real economy also depends on its scale. The total market value of the stock market of the whole world is about 93% of its GDP, while the figure for developed countries is 130%. As the stock market value of China is less than its GDP most of the time, and part of its stocks are not even allowed to be traded on the market, it would not be appropriate to say that the Chinese stock market is the barometer of its economy. For example, during 2001–2005, the Chinese economy experienced very high growth rate but the stock market stayed a bear market; during 2006–2007 when there was only little increase of economic growth rate, the stock market went crazily high. What's more, the benchmark Shanghai Stock Market index used for China is not fully representative of China's stock markets. For one thing, it does not include stocks trading on Shenzhen Stock Exchange and thus only represents about 70% of the total stock market; on the other hand, it is calculated by using the total market value of stocks trading on Shanghai Stock Exchange as a weight and thus the weight of big-cap stocks is very large, and this could cause 'unreal' price ups and downs that may not reflect the real picture.

The third aspect is about the risk transmission relation between fictitious economy and real economy. Risk in the real economy could be transmitted to fictitious economy, and vice versa. We should study the transmission steps involved in this process, the transmission mechanism, and factors that contribute to this process, etc.

The fourth aspect is about the positive and negative effects of fictitious economy on real economy. Fictitious economy is a double-edged sword: it can do both good and harm to the real economy. We should learn how to make use of the benefits and avoid the harm.

1.3.2. *Institutional Factors Involved in Fictitious Economic Activities*

Although the word "institution" (some would use 'system') has been used very commonly in recent years, the understanding of its essence differs among people. Institution is usually considered by ordinary people to be procedures or rules governing actions that should be abided by all people. However, among the academic circles, it is considered to be a system comprising such aspects as politics, economics, culture, etc. formed under certain 'historical conditions'. The institutional school of economics emerged in America in early 20th century focusing on the study of institutions and also on the analysis of the effect of institutional factors on the development of the society and the economy. According to them, problems of organization and control of economic system are more important than resource allocation, income distribution, the level of income, output and price. They emphasize the impact of factors such as society, history, politics, psychology, culture etc on people's social and economic life and advocate the use of institutional and structural analytical methods to probe these issues. What institutional economics tells us is that in the study of fictitious economy, we must pay close attention and focus on the role and functions of these important institutional elements.

The author once analyzed institutional problems using complexity science methods and concluded that institutions should include two aspects: system and mechanism. System refers to the state and structure at a certain point of time while mechanism means the process and driving force of system evolution. The two aspects are interrelated. System is the starting point and result of evolution while mechanism is the path that evolution follows. Due to the mutually influencing effect among agents inside the system and the interrelation between the system and external environment, a self-organizing effect would emerge inside the system, leading to the formation of the system's hierarchical and functional structure, promoting the development of the system towards a certain direction.

From the developmental process of fictitious economy, we could see that institutions in fictitious economy are the results of evolution and the proposition of "transactions precede regulations" still holds in the area of fictitious economy. For example, before laws and regulation on equity financing came into effect, there was already "South Sea Bubble" in Britain, which was the result of lack of timely regulation on spontaneous emergence of fictitious capital transactions. But this has also proved that without institution, transactions could still proceed. After the Mississippi Bubble, although French politicians were strongly against the stock market and equity financing, the credit bank dealing in moveable property mortgage founded by the Péreire brothers still managed to do business in areas similar to those of today's investment banks by circumventing financial controls. So, it is not easy to find fictitious economic institutions if no transactions involving fictitious economy are found. This is true at least where formal rules are concerned.

On the other hand, we should also pay attention to the reaction of institution to transaction behaviors. After the interaction between institution and transaction, the former would usually become the major factor affecting the further development of the latter or even the transition of its development path. Examples about macro control of institution abound after Keynesian Economics gained its popularity, while financial and monetary policies led by Monetarism and

Supply-side Economics greatly changed the trajectories of both American and European financial system as well as the impact and form of financial system on the real economy. After mid-20th century, the influence of regulation and regulatory rules under different regulation models on the players and components of the fictitious economic system also becomes more apparent.

The author believes that there are three 'layers' or levels for institutional rules in fictitious economy. The first layer consists of formal laws to regulate the behavior of major market participants, fundamental market relations and order of competition in the market. These rules are rooted in different cultures and exert their primary effect on fictitious economic transactions. The second layer comprises relevant regulatory measures, including regulations, guidance, suggestions and advice, that are put forward by administrative supervisory/regulatory institutions guided by legal principles together with their administrative discretions. The third layer refers to the so-called "hidden rules" developed based on daily transaction norms in fictitious economic areas. The three layers are complementary to one another. They might result from obligatory institutional change (hetero-organizing effect) and also from induced institutional changes (self-organizing effect).

According to complexity science, institutional rules could stabilize the expectation of major participants of transactions in fictitious economy. Under a fixed institutional framework, major participants of transactions would know what rules each other would have to follow as they all believe that all people are rational. If this is true, then this system would be appropriate and stable. If under a fixed institutional framework, major participants of transactions cannot play their role to transform business opportunities into reality, then the system should be changed. It is exactly the mutual influence between institutional environment and major market participants that results in the integration of self-organizing effect and hetero-organizing effect, promoting the development and evolution of fictitious economy.

Studies on financial institution should combine normative and positive research methods, adopt various kinds of advanced theories and methods of psychology, sociology, management, mathematical finance, behavioral finance, uncertainty decision-making technology, computer simulation, etc. Both the micro bases and macro effects of institutional evolution should be discussed. The difference in function and aims between policy and theoretical studies must be distinguished. The purpose of theoretical studies is to try to formulate a conceptual system and discover general rules from practice while the objective of policy studies is to develop and test the conclusions of theoretical studies. When it comes to policy studies, simplistic explanation, plagiarism and 'vulgarization' should be avoided; the effectiveness and persuasiveness of research achievement should be strengthened, thus contributing to improving the institutional environment of fictitious economy.

1.3.3. *Risk Generation and Prevention in Fictitious Economy*

Risk may be defined as the difference between expected and real returns. But there are still debates over this definition. Some say that only negative difference should be defined as risk while positive difference is not risk. In other words, when real return is less than expected, then there is risk; when real return is higher than expected, then there is no risk. In fact, it is just a problem concerning the use of unilateral or bilateral measurement of risk. At the moment unilateral measurement dominates but the author thinks that bilateral measurement should be adopted. When real returns exceed expected returns, that means that there is too much 'input' and less of it could also realize the same level of expected returns, resulting in the risk of resource wastage. If risk is considered unilaterally, people would be encouraged to waste resources in order to pursue "insurance"; but if a bilateral method is adopted, people would be encouraged to close the gap between expected and real returns and help realize a reasonable balance between 'safety' and profitability.

Risk comes from the uncertainties existing in the objective world and people's limited capacity to understand it and also from subjective estimation mistakes ('errors of judgment') people make on expected returns. The author thinks that risk could be divided into two categories: objective risk and subjective risk. Objective risk comes from the uncertainties existing in the objective world and people's limited ability to understand it as the objective world is moving and changing all the time and people might not be able to understand it completely. Lenin said: "In order to really understand something, we should be able to master and clearly see every aspect, every connection and every "intermediary" about it'. But we would never be able to do this."[16] When you are studying something at a certain point of time, it would not be possible to get absolute "real-time" result nor really "re-present" the state of the moment because both the environment and it are changing all the time. Besides, as pointed out by the theory of chaos, there are uncertain factors in a certain system. For example, the butterfly effect is the result of accumulation of a series of events of very little probability, which makes it possible that "the flaps of a butterfly could cause a storm". We could see that people are not capable of completely mastering the uncertainties existing in the objective world.

For example, a reasonable price for a stock should be the present value of the future income of the listed company, which depends on the future income and discount rates while the two factors have close relation with the economic fundamentals and should be estimated using data both from the past and the present. But as a matter of fact, both future income and discount rates are not certain because future income depends on the performance of the invested companies which is uncertain and the basis of discount rate is interest rate which would be affected by the market. As both future income for each year and discount rate are not certain, it is not possible to get a reasonable or 'rational' price. Both these two uncertain factors could bring about risk, but this risk belongs to objective risk since it does not change according to people's subjective purpose and we are not able to know changes of the fundamentals of the real and fictitious economy in the future. Although quite a lot of progress has been made as regards to prediction or forecasting techniques or technology in recent years — such as data extraction, database knowledge discovery, symbolic data analysis and group decision making, which could make the prediction of future from past data and expert experience much easier — it is still not possible to predict precisely the future. Therefore, objective risks still exist.

Subjective risk comes from subjective estimation errors people make on expected returns. The development of the stock market relies on people's optimistic expectation. If there is no speculation, bubble or risk, then the stock market would never exist. If all the people are rational investors and could correctly predict the future, then stock prices would be fixed and no transaction would be conducted. What speculators care is not the present value of future income but the difference between buying and selling prices, and that depends on the estimation of future prices. When people are over optimistic, the price of stocks they buy is likely to exceed a reasonable level. Therefore, as long as there is speculation, there would be bubbles and as long as there are bubbles, there would be risks, subjective risks. This type of risk has 'positive feedback' or 'mutually reinforcing' effect, which can be easily enlarged. Generally speaking, people tend to overestimate their ability to undertake risk.

The capacity to withstand or 'tolerate' risks means the ability to ensure safety under a certain probability and certain amount of luck. People tend to overestimate their ability to undertake risk and thus get bankrupted by taking too high risks. For example, A and B play heads and tails. If it is heads, B has to give A one yuan, otherwise, A has to give B his one yuan. The problem is how much money does A have to possess if he does not want to lose all his money with a probability of 90% and under circumstances of 'normal luck'. Ordinary people would think that two yuan would be enough since the probability of heads and tails is 50%. However, the probability of at least one head if throwing twice is only 75%. According to Binomial Theorem, in order to get a probability of 90%, A has to have four yuan as principal under 'normal luck'. As probability follows the law of large numbers in statistics, this means that the 50% probability is only attainable when the coin is thrown a thousand times (or a very large number of times). If it is only for four times, it is not necessarily right. It is quite possible that all the four times are tails, in which case

A would lose all his money. Another example: for several projects each needing an investment of one million yuan with a risk of 80% and returns of five million yuan — as both risks and returns are symmetric, people would usually mistakenly think that as long as they have five million and invest it in five projects, then as long as one project succeeds they would be able to undertake the risk. However, according to "The Laws of Bankruptcy/Insolvency for Risk-takers", if only five million is invested, the probability for at least one of the five projects succeeding is 67%. In order to get a probability of 90%, 14 million would be needed to invest in 14 projects. So it is obvious that five million is far from enough to take the risk. It would therefore be very dangerous if, in a bull market people take loans from banks to 'play' in the stock market by mortgaging their houses. They only see the possibility of 'winning' but do not consider carefully their own abilities to undertake risk.

According to the principles of complexity science, in a complex system with people in it, the subjective estimation of the future differs greatly among people. But the mutual influence and the 'guiding effect' of external environment on people's behavior would result in a self-organizing effect, thus driving the whole system constantly moving towards one direction. Subjective risks in stock market would accumulate under such self-organizing effect and get amplified through 'positive feedback effect', causing stock prices to rise to a much higher level beyond their reasonable prices.

1.3.4. *Evaluation System in Fictitious Economy*

According to system engineering, there are five steps to follow in order to establish a rating or evaluation system. First is to construct an index system consisting of many indices. The second step is to designate methods to measure each index. The third step is to determine the methods for expressing or representing the results of such evaluation — some expressed quantitatively with data while others only qualitatively. The fourth step is to determine methods used to see the quality or veracity of each of the measured results and the final step is to find ways to conduct a comprehensive analysis of the quality of the measured results, combine all the measured results and obtain an integrated rating for the quality of the whole system. Usually, a weighted method is used, that is, to multiply each index with a weight and then add them together. This method has its own limitations though as it ignores the mutual influence among indices, so it needs to be improved through further studies.

1.4. The Methodologies of Research on Fictitious Economy

Research methods for fictitious economy include the following six categories.

1.4.1. *The Methods of Complexity Science*

Complexity science is a science studying complexity and complex systems and is an advanced study for the development of system science. Due to the mutual effect among agents inside the system and the interrelation between the system and external environment, a self-organizing effect would emerge inside the system, leading to the formation of the system's hierarchical and functional structure, promoting the development of the system towards a certain direction. Currently there are about five schools of complexity science,[17] of which the theory of self-organizing, self-study and self-adjustment of systems put forward by Santa Fe Institute in America is more popular or 'mainstream'. For example, in market economies, each company is able to make independent decisions, operate in its own way and also be responsible for its own profit and loss. But the decision making of each of these companies is also affected by that of other companies as well as the external environment. As far as a specific company in the system is concerned, when new competitors arrive, the behavior or actions of this company is likely to change by say, improving its quality or reducing its output or developing new products. As to external environment, when the cost of borrowing changes because banks tighten up or relax their credit policies, the decisions of companies would also change. The reason for some companies' loss or even bankruptcy is their blind expansion and the result of breaks in capital chain when credit gets tightened up. From a macro and long-term perspective, we could see that this self-organizing effect has its own direction, representing the rising and falling stage of the economic circle. It is the same thing when it comes to stock market. Each person has the right to decide what kind of stock to buy, when to buy and to sell, but it is impossible for him not to be affected by the decisions of people around. If all the people around are buying, he is not likely to sell; and also he is not likely to avoid the impact of the environment and public opinions. For example, if all the people are talking about "The Index reaching 10,000 points could be expected" or "ten years' golden bull market", then he would probably feel the need to buy in. With the self-organizing effect, the bull and the bear markets will take shape accordingly.

The first thing we are going to study is how the structure of self-organization is formed. There are two kinds of structure involved. One is hierarchical structure and the other is functional structure. For example, in a company, its organizational structure could consist of work groups, work-sites/work-shops, factories to business units and at last to headquarters, as in a hierarchy. Besides, there could also be cross-hierarchy functional structure, consisting of financial system, personnel system, production system, logistics, etc.

Next on the list for study is how self-organizing effect help promote the evolution of the system, that is, self-organizing, self-study and self-adjustment or self-modification, which means that a system not only could conduct self-organizing but also learn and draw lessons from experience through self-study so as to adapt to changes in the environment. As each member of the system is 'intelligent', for each policy to exert its impact, it has to be able to affect the behavior of members in the system. Otherwise, this policy would exert little effect and be of little use. Some government departments in China always think that policies could do anything and as long as a policy is put into effect, the behavior of market participants would be changed. But it is not necessarily true in reality. As Chairman Mao Zedong pointed out once, "Internal factors are the bases of changes while external factors are just conditions for changes; the external factors could exert their effects because of the internal factors."[18] Policy is an external factor, thus it could only play its role through the change of behavior of members inside the system. For example, during the first half of 2007 when the stock market rose dramatically, the state increased interest rate several times, increased stamp duty and also issued some special bonds, in efforts to prevent the stock market from getting overheated. But people believed that the price wouldn't fall before the 17th Congress of the CPC, not before the Olympic Games. With these thoughts in mind, whatever policies the government put forward, people would still believe that stock prices would not tumble and they continued to buy in at high price. Finally when the index reached over 6100 points, the bubble burst, resulting in a big decline of the stock market and huge loss for investors.

We not only have to study the behavior of individuals but also that of organizations. The behavior of an organization depends on each of its member, including self-organizing effect resulting from the interaction between individual and groups (a group of people in an organization) as well as that between the organization and the environment. However, the organization will also react to its members, so we should learn from institutional economics and take the characteristics of fictitious economy into consideration when studying organizational behaviors.

Four kinds of basic methods used in complexity science are introduced below:[17]

1.4.1.1. *Qualitative judgment plus quantitative calculation*

Among economists in China, some prefer to use qualitative methods while some other like quantitative method more. They actually represent two types of people. One is those who study Marxist economics, including some famous economists. They usually do not receive any quantitative training and almost use no mathematical tools in their published papers, though they possess in-depth knowledge of economics and rich experience and are able to make quick and qualitative judgment. The other group of people comprises those who used to study engineering. They usually have very strong quantitative knowledge and thus like to conduct quantitative calculation, but they also have their own weaknesses, that is, they do not have sufficient economics knowledge. Sometimes the results they obtain from their calculations do not tally with judgments made — based on common economic knowledge. So we should combine these two aspects. On the one hand, we need to learn quantitative calculation techniques and methods while on the other hand we should try to enhance our economic knowledge in making qualitative judgments. Through qualitative judgment we could establish models of concept for both the system as a whole and each sub-system, and then we can transform them into mathematical models. After calculation or simulation we could get quantitative conclusions, for which qualitative methods could be used so as to further advance the knowledge and to find solutions for our problems.

1.4.1.2. *Micro plus macro analysis*

We have to see both the trees and the wood. The goal of micro analysis is to get to know the components and hierarchical structure of the system while the aim of macro analysis is to get to know the functional structure and its formation. For example, when studying the stock market, we have to study individual stocks as well as the market as a whole. The stock market as a whole is not just the simple 'addition' of individual stocks. The emergence of stock market bubble definitely starts with individual stocks. When the value of a certain individual stock is overestimated, bubbles are formed. People holding this stock would try to sell it for profit. In a bull market, these people would not exit from the market and instead use this amount of money to buy other stocks whose prices are likely to increase, including 'trash' stock, 'theme' stock, 'concept' stock, etc., resulting in bubbles in these individual stocks. Finally, the whole stock market would be filled with bubbles. Individual bubbles and bubble in the whole system are different. Some would defend stock market bubbles, saying that "bubbles in China's stock market are structural", which does not make any sense. It is not possible for a stock market to have each listed company in it forming a bubble. There would always be some well-performing companies. Even during the "black Monday" large scale fall of stock market in America in 1987, there were 16 stocks that had gone up in price.

1.4.1.3. *Reductionism plus holism*

Reductionism seeks to find explanation for macro phenomenon from part of the system and its micro structure. For example, using laws of physics and chemistry to explain biological phenomenon is obviously one-sided or biased. The holistic approach emphasizes that the interaction among different parts of a system determines the macro nature of a system. However, without an in-depth understanding of the mechanism of parts of the system and its micro structure, it is also difficult to understand the system as a whole. What complexity science does is to discover the nature and behavior of the system as a whole through the interaction among individuals, which is all based on the understanding of the nature and behavior of individuals in the system. We could say that since the era of Newton, reductionism is used more often as a research method, in which a system is divided into several sub-systems and when all problems in these sub-systems are clearly analyzed, the whole problem would be considered solved. However, people discover in reality that reductionism does not really solve the problem. It needs to combine with holism, which is also one of the 'backgrounds' for the birth of complex science. Holism does not only care about each part of the system but also the interaction among different parts. In other words, it is the principle of 'the whole is larger than the sum of all its parts'. When conducting research on fictitious economy, the study of stock market should be confined to the stock market, likewise for the foreign exchange market and money market. The interaction between them should also be noted. For example, changes in money market, foreign exchange market and real estate market would also affect the stock market as there are also interactions among them.

1.4.1.4. *Scientific deductions plus philosophical arguments*

Scientific theory is a system of concepts which has its own logical structure and has been tested through experiments. When describing scientific theories, scientists would usually try to use symbols and formalize them, making them rigorous axiomatic systems. But the development of science has proved that every theory has its own 'drawbacks' and there would always be some "abnormal" phenomenon and events. We have to use the power of philosophical arguments and speculation to explain them by applying concepts and laws governing the general and the specific, chance and necessity as well as rules such as unity of opposites and the negation of negation.

1.4.2. *The Method of Uncertainty Decision Making*

Fictitious economy features high risk and is faced with both subjective and objective risks, which also means that it has to make 'uncertainty decisions'. There are about four kinds of uncertainty decision making methods.

1.4.2.1. *Quantification of qualitative variables*

Variables could be divided into quantitative, semi-quantitative and qualitative variables. Qualitative variables could be further divided into ordinal and nominal variables. Ordinal variables are variables with no numerical values but they are different from each other and could be sorted by an index, for example, high, medium and low. Ordinal variables could be handled by using certain methods such as multidimensional scaling and generalized quantitative method. Nominal variables do not mean anything by themselves. For example, the number 5 for a basketball player does not make him better than a player with a number of 1. When studying transportation problems, it is convenient to give values for various types of transportation forms, 1 for road transportation, 2 for railway, 3 for waterway, 4 for airway, 5 for pipeline, etc., which makes it easier to establish models and using computers to calculate.

1.4.2.2. *Determination of empirical probability*

This includes data mining/extraction, database knowledge discovery, intelligent data mining, etc. This involves predicting the future by using data from the past. Usually, the longer the time involved is, the bigger will the error be. So the aforementioned methods are more appropriate for short-term or medium short-term predictions instead of medium, medium long-term, or long-term predictions.

1.4.2.3. *Improvement of subjective probability*

Subjective probability is the probability found by experts' analysis and judgment. Subjective probabilities could be improved through group decision making.

1.4.2.4. *Case study and integration of a priori information*

Case study is very important. When doing research, first we have to get statistical data; second we must have the ability to predict and foresee things and finally we have to do case studies. Case study is an individual event. However, a drop of water has the ability to reflect a whole world and we could discover many problems in a specific event — even discover some special examples that do not comply with some general laws. Or course, we shouldn't take the results of case study as general rules. They are just some specific examples after all. Nowadays, the method of induction has been abused by many researchers who take examples given as proofs, which is quite wrong. If examples are proofs, then we could prove that people born in Sichuan Province do not take spices. To find three or four people who do not take spices from the several tens of millions of people there who do is not a difficult job. Lao Zhang is from Sichuan but does not eat spices; Lao Wang is from Sichuan who also does not eat spices; neither does Xiao Li who is also from there. If we conclude from these examples that people from Sichuan do not eat spice, we are obviously wrong. Therefore, examples are not proofs. Besides case study, *a priori* information is also very important. That people from Sichuan like spices is *a priori* information, which we have already known. So we would be suspicious about the conclusion that people from Sichuan do not eat spice. We should not form subjective judgment when doing case studies, but *a priori* information is very important, because it can prevent us from getting confused or puzzled by some superficial phenomenon.

1.4.3. *Group Decision Making Method*

During a decision making process, the judgment of experts is very important while group decision making is an effective method to improve this kind of judgment. I would divide group decision making into two categories: cooperative decision making and harmonized decision making.

In cooperative decision making, each participant has the same goal and what's important is to gather together dispersed opinions and get an optimal decision. In this case, group decision making is better than any individual decision making. Cooperative decision making was first called Delphi (God of Prophecy in Greek mythology) method, which means to gather a group of experts, each of whom is to give their judgment. And then their opinions would be integrated comprehensively and represented in front of these experts who could modify their judgments, if necessary. After several similar processes, opinions would gradually get close and finally reach a conclusion that most people would approve. Today, with the help of various kinds of tools and methods such as computer, decision makers can have sufficient information before hand and then use computer to get an optimal decision.

Harmonized decision is necessitated when there is conflict of interests among participants who nevertheless would like to reach a relatively satisfactory decision. It is a problem of how to reach a compromise (Shapley Value and Nash Protocol Solution, for examples) by using cooperative countermeasure theory. Sub-budget is a very typical example of harmonized decision making. Different departments are discussing sub-budget and each of them wants more for themselves. So each of them would try to compete but meanwhile they all wish to get a result, a decision — for no result means no money. Thus, there are both conflicts of interest as well as compromise in harmonized decision making. I contend that there are many issues here deserving our efforts to study.

In group decision making, difference in knowledge and experience of each participant should be taken into consideration. So should the impact of information asymmetry and their behaviors in the group — to avoid the 'drift' of optimal decision because of the fear and deference for authority or owing to the 'bandwagon effect'. When there is a person with authority in the decision making group, very likely no one dares to say no to him or to challenge him. This then is no longer a group decision making process. Bandwagon effect means people would follow the crowd, which does not have the effect of group decision making. Besides, we should also try to develop and improve democratic centralism by applying modern decision making science and to make it the decision making system with Chinese characteristics.

1.4.4. *Complex Data Analysis Method Supporting Decision Making*

In order to be able to make decisions, we need two kinds of knowledge: knowledge about system quality and knowledge about system evolution — so as to conduct evaluation and prediction. Both these two kinds of knowledge have to be extracted from data, for which we need to use analytic methods of complex data. Currently, popular methods include principal components analysis, factor analysis, cluster analysis, correlation analysis, regression analysis, regression tree and logic data analysis. Partial least squares method, symbolic data analysis and functional data analysis are some other new methods that could be used.

1.4.5. *The Method of Mathematical Finance*

Mathematical finance is a subject that uses mathematical tools and models to study financial problems. When studying fictitious economy, we have to learn to apply the following four methods.

1.4.5.1. *Financial assets pricing*

According to the principle of fictitious economy, pricing of financial assets is actually related to the real economy it is attached to. For example, the pricing of a company's stock is of course related to its assets and performance. But as a matter of fact, there are three types of pricing for assets. First is for tangible assets, which has already had its own set of mature theories and methods in accounting and finance, mainly including depreciation, tangible and intangible wearing off, etc. The second type is for intangible assets. Nowadays, the value of many state-owned enterprises lies in its intangible assets such as trademark, clients (goodwill), technology, skilled workers, etc. If looking just at their tangible assets, we could see that their original values have already 'worn off' completely after several decades. Thus, although there is little tangible assets left for some state-owned enterprises, people are still willing to merge with them, hoping to get their intangible assets. However, pricing of intangible assets has always been a big problem. If the assets are priced too low, these state-owned assets might be lost; if priced too high, no one would be willing to buy them. The third type of pricing is dynamic pricing, in which the value of asset is predicted by taking into account its future value. For many equity investments, especially private equity fund investment, it is very important to look at the future value of the investment. The major function of private equity fund is to merge the enterprises and then manage them to improve their operation, management and administration to increase their values and then to resell them. What private equity fund wants to do is not to set up an 'enterprise group'. Similar to venture capital investment fund, it is to discover the future value of its investment. As to the question of how to discover the future value of enterprises, there hasn't been any good solution internationally and it is still a problem that needs further studying. Without a proper evaluation method, discussing whether there has been loss in the merger would be meaningless since we do not even know the exact value of the enterprise. If the value of the enterprise after the merger increases greatly then there would be no loss, even though the part of benefits investors get might be larger than the enterprise's. However, if the value of the enterprise increases little or not at all, the merger would have incurred loss.

1.4.5.2. *Fractal market analysis*[19,20]

Fractal theory is a branch of nonlinear science that focuses on the description of the structure and form of complex systems with disordered structure. 'Fractal' means that part of a system is similar to the system as a whole in a statistical sense, while fractal dimension, that is, dimension expressed by non-integers, is a quantitative representation and basic parameter for fractals. Fractal market hypothesis is put forward because the traditional effective market hypothesis is not able to explain the trend of capital market price, and fractal market analysis is an attempt to analyze generalized capital market by using a holistic approach and it is able to explain very well the diversity of investors. Fractal market analysis has overcome the limitation of effective market theory and taken into consideration irrational expectation of investors and the nonlinear relation of market's reaction towards information. The most important discovery of fractal market analysis is the dependence of market stability on diversity of investors. When there are many investors with different investment terms on the market, market liquidity is guaranteed and so is market stability.

1.4.5.3. *Autoregressive heteroskedasticity analysis*[21]

Ever since the advent of ARCH (first order autoregressive heteroskedasticity) in 1982, this analysis has been considered a relatively good nonlinear financial time series model by many researchers. In order to get more flexibility, some researchers extended the ARCH model to GARCH (generalized autoregressive heteroskedasticity) model. Many empirical studies have shown that fluctuation of stock returns is time-varying (heteroskedasticity) and nonlinear. GARCH model with a single variable is able to capture the dynamic behavior of this fluctuation by describing this fluctuation as linear function of past prediction of standard deviation. However, the parameters of GARCH model are not stable on the dimension of time and some research has also pointed out that some predicted results based on simple GARCH model are not very good. Thus, various kinds of improvement for ARCH begin to show up, including nonlinear ARCH (NARCH), threshold ARCH (TARCH), asymmetric ARCH (AARCH), quadratic ARCH (QARCH), non-integer order integral ARCH (FIGARCH), ARMA-ARCH, etc. ARCH is a very important method used in mathematical finance and is also widely applied in financial analysis like futures analysis and stock market analysis. But it has its own drawbacks, the most glaring of which is its 'black-box' method or operation. Thus, we need to find a method that is able to combine ARCH analysis and mechanism analysis: we shouldn't have blind faith in conclusions obtained from ARCH analysis.

1.4.5.4. *Financial risk theory*

Financial risk theories include aspects such as the definition, measuring, treatment, control and management of risks. In line with the accumulation of large scale financial data and the development of statistic analytical method, traditional financial risk theories such as options pricing and hedging are faced with challenges.[22]

1.4.6. *Computer Simulation Method*

The last method for complexity science is called computer simulation method, which can be divided into two categories. One is the so-called discrete events simulation, which is a kind of traditional computer simulation method, GPSS, Symscript, for example. The other category is agent-based simulation, which has been widely used in complex scientific research. There are two types of tools for the latter. One is called Swarm Simulation Toolkit, developed by Santa Fe Institute in America and the other is NetLogo, developed by Northwestern University. Other well-known simulation tools include Artificial Life, Cellular Automata, Co-opetition, etc.

References

[1] Cheng, S. W. (1999). Fictitious Economy and Financial Crisis, *Journal of Management Sciences in China*, 2(1), 1–6 (in Chinese).
[2] Virtual economy, Wikipedia. http://en.wikipedia.org/wiki/Virtual_economy.
[3] http://vitual-economy.org/.
[4] Xu, J. (2008). *Fictitious Currency and Fictitious Banking*, Shanghai: Jiao Tong University Press (in Chinese).
[5] Liu, J. M. (1998). *From Fictitious Capital to Fictitious Economy*, Jinan: Shandong People's Publishing House (in Chinese).
[6] Cheng, S. W. (1999). Analysis and Lessons from the East Asian Financial Crisis, in Cheng, S. W. (ed.), Pandect, *Fictitious Economy and the East Asian Financial Crisis*, Beijing: Democracy and Construction Publishing House, pp. 1–50 (in Chinese).
[7] Jiang, Z. M. (2002). To build a moderately prosperous society in all respects, Open up New Vistas for China's Socialism with Chinese Characteristics — Report made on the 16th National Congress of the CPC, November 8 (in Chinese).
[8] Cheng, S. W. (2003). *Collected Essays on Fictitious Economy*, Beijing: Democracy and Construction Publishing House (in Chinese).
[9] Cheng, S. W. (2007). *On Financial Reforms*, Beijing: China Renmin University Press (in Chinese).
[10] Marx, K. (1975). Das Kapital, Vol. 3, translated by Central Compilation & Translation Bureau for Works of Marx, Engels, Lenin and Stalin, 1st Ed., China: People's Publishing House, pp. 525–670 (in Chinese).
[11] Kuruma, S. and Uno, K. (1989). Dictionary of Das Kapital, translated by Xue, J. X., Li, S. G., Wang, J. Y., Tianjin: Nankai University Press, (in Chinese).
[12] Cheng, S. W. (2008). *On Venture Capital Investments*, Beijing: China Renmin University Press (in Chinese).
[13] Portes, A. (1998). Social capital: its origins and applications in modern sociology, *Annual Review of Sociology*, 24, 1–24.
[14] Herbert, S. (1976). *Administrative Behavior*, 3rd Ed., New York: The Free Press.
[15] Prigogine, I. and Nicolis, G. (1977). Self-Organization in Non-Equilibrium Systems, New York: Wiley.

[16] Lenin, V. I. (1986). Lenin's Collected Works, Vol. 10, translated by Central Compilation & Translation Bureau for Works of Marx, Engels, Lenin and Stalin. Lenin, V. I., "Further Thoughts on Labor Union, the Current Situation and the Mistakes of Comrades Trotsky and Bukharin," Beijing: People's Publishing House, pp. 291 (in Chinese).
[17] Cheng, S. W. (1999). Complexity Science and Management, in Cheng, S. W. (ed.), *Complexity Science Exploration*, Beijing: Democracy and Construction Publishing House, pp. 1–15 (in Chinese).
[18] Mao, Z. D. (1991). Selective Works of Mao Zedong, Vol. 1, 2nd Ed. Mao, Z. D., *On Contradictions*, Beijing: People's Publishing House, pp. 302 (in Chinese).
[19] Peters, E. E. (1994). *Fractal Market Analysis*, translated by Chu, H. L. and Yin, Q. (2002), Beijing: Economic Science Press, (in Chinese).
[20] Xiao, Y., Liang, Q. and Wang, L. J. (2008). Theoretical discussions on fractal market analysis in the capital market, Journal of Financial Economics, 16, pp. 85–86 (in Chinese).
[21] Mills, T. C. (1999). *The Econometric Modeling of Financial Time Series*, 2nd Ed., translated by Yu, Z. J. (2002), Beijing: Economic Science Press (in Chinese).
[22] Bouchaud, J. P. and Potters, M. (2000). *Theory of Financial Risks*, translated by Zhou, W. Q. (2002), Beijing: Economic Science Press (in Chinese).

Chapter 2

Financial Globalization and China's Financial Reform

2.1. Introduction

Economic globalization represents "the current world order" and creates a true interdependence between different nations and economies. To date, no consensus has been reached worldwide on the origins and features of globalization. However, it can be argued that the process of globalization had started as early as the emergence of capitalism in western countries. At the outset of the 21st century, the economic relations between different countries are becoming increasingly interrelated, from materials procurement to commodity trading, and from technology transfer to capital export.

The development of economic globalization is characterized by "knowledge as the basis, finance as the heart, information technology as the vanguard, and multinationals as the pillar".[1] Since the 1990s, the progress of science and technology (especially the progress made in information technology), quick flow of capital, globalization of the financial markets of foreign exchange, securities, futures and options in particular, have made financial globalization the heart of economic globalization.

Financial globalization brings about both challenges and opportunities. On one hand, it promotes the free flow of capital, improves efficiency of resource allocation, and speeds up economic growth. On the other hand, it encourages financial speculation, creates economic bubbles, accelerates the transmission of financial risks, undermines the fragile financial system of the developing countries, and increases the gap between the rich and the poor nations. An important task for each nation, therefore, is to develop a sound financial policy, and to reinforce financial macro-control in its economic development. In the meantime, it should also strengthen international financial cooperation, and keep a close eye on the flow of international speculative capital to jointly create a safe, well-balanced, and fair international financial system.

China has achieved tremendous progress through two decades of reform and opening up, and its overall strength and size of economy have been increasing at an astonishing rate. The economic reform in China is a complex system project unprecedented in history. In the face of financial globalization and continuous improvement of the socialist market economy, one of China's priorities is to reform its backward financial industry, and to prevent and eliminate potential financial risks as befitting a big, responsible country. At the Third Plenary Session of the 16th National Congress of the CPC (Communist Party of China) held in October 2003, it was reiterated that "one of the most important tasks facing the country is to deepen the reform of financial businesses, and to improve the financial control and regulatory system".[2] This chapter will focus on the main features of financial globalization and challenges facing China, as well as the progress made so far and the future outlook of China's financial reform.

2.2. Main Trends of Financial Globalization

The development of financial globalization exhibits the following main trends:

2.2.1. *The Virtualization of Money is Intensifying in Each Country*

From a historical perspective, gold had provided an important guarantee for paper money and quickly gained popularity in western countries since 1821 when the United Kingdom first adopted the gold standard system. In 1870, gold became the basis of international currencies, and it was not until the aftermath of World War I that the gold standard system was replaced by the gold exchange standard system. When the United States began to prescribe — after the World War II — the minimum dollar price for gold purchase and sale by foreign central banks, the main European countries decided in 1958 that each of their currencies could be exchanged to gold or the US dollar freely. In 1971, however, the United States decided to put an end to the free exchange between the US dollar and gold at a fixed price (i.e. $35 US dollars per ounce of gold) in international payments, and since then, gold had been replaced by the US dollar and other currencies as the basis of the international monetary regime. When the currency was no longer pegged to gold and could not be exchanged to gold freely at a fixed price, it became the fiat money, and its circulation was conditional on a country's overall credit.

The virtualization of money is intensifying with the separation between the currency and gold, as we can no longer use a "frame of reference" with a fixed value to determine a currency's value — it can now only be measured by its purchasing power. The purchasing power is determined by the relations between the volume of money and the output of real economy[3] when the automatic exit mechanism does not exist in the entire economic system.

2.2.2. *The Exchange Rate has Become a Policy Tool*

With the virtualization of money and fluctuations of purchasing power of each currency, the exchange rate only reflects a currency's international purchasing power, floating with the rise and fall of a country's economic strength. Consequently, each government can use the exchange rate as a policy tool to seek greater benefits in the current and capital accounts. The adjustment of exchange rate is very often a game between the countries involved. Theoretically, if each government coordinates the international exchange rates from a global perspective, the Pareto effect is likely to occur, and each party can have a satisfactory result. In reality, however, the expected coordination effect is hardly achieved, as each country often starts looking after its own interests. This has been obvious from the experience of the developed countries in coordinating international exchange rates in the 1980s.[4,5]

Between 1981 and 1985, Japan's exports witnessed a rapid increase as a result of the depreciation of Japanese yen against US dollar, during which period its exports to the United States increased by 74%, creating a soaring trade surplus against the United States. On September 22, 1985, the finance ministers and central bank governors of G5 countries, including the United States, Japan, Germany, France and the United Kingdom, met at the Plaza in New York to discuss the coordination of exchange policies of G5 to better reflect the economic development of each country and to correct the imbalance of expenses and receipts under the current account. The Plaza Accord reached at the meeting required G5 to take a coordinated action and sanctioned steps to reduce the exchange rate of the US dollar against key currencies progressively.

The Plaza Accord is the first international effort to coordinate exchange rates, and it achieved expected result in the short run. In the first week after the Plaza meeting, the US dollar lost 8% against the Japanese yen and 6% against the Deutsche mark, as the central bank of each country began to sell the US dollar and buy the Japanese yen and Deutsche mark. By December 1986, the US dollar had depreciated about 20% against the Japanese yen and Deutsche mark. If the US dollar were allowed to continue to decline, every country would suffer in the end. On February 21 and 22 of 1987, the finance ministers of G7 comprising the United States, Japan, Germany, France, the United Kingdom, Canada and Italy, met at the Louvre in Paris to discuss measures to stabilize the exchange rates. All parties except Italy accepted the Louvre Accord, agreeing to intervene when the fluctuation of their currencies exceeded a reasonable range. However, the United States did not keep its promise to reduce its deficit, allowing the US dollar to continue to depreciate, especially after the stock market catastrophe of October 19, 1987. In the meantime, an economic bubble began to emerge in Japan as a result of the continuous appreciation of yen, and in 1991, the bubble burst, leading to a long recession of Japanese economy.

The experience of exchange rate game makes some realize that, in a game where there are numerous players and the United States is far stronger than any other player, coordination is always difficult to achieve. A better solution is to reach a regional cooperation first to compete with the United States. This is also the major driving force behind the creation of the Euro. With the development of regional integration, financial integration is expected to speed up, and a good example is the concept of Asian Currency Unit (ACU) developed by the Asian Development Bank (2005).[6]

2.2.3. *The Size of International Financial Markets is Expanding Swiftly*

The size of international financial markets (the developed countries in particular) is expanding swiftly with the growth of the world economy, progress of information technology, and development of financial innovation. In the midst of the incredible economic boom between 1997 and 2000, the world virtual economy — represented by the trade of virtual capital comprising stocks, bonds, and financial derivatives — saw a rapid expansion. By 2000, the aggregate volume of global virtual economy had reached 160 trillion US dollars, the total market cap of stocks had increased to 36 trillion US dollars, the balance of bonds to 29 trillion US dollars, and the over-the-counter trade of financial derivatives to 95 trillion US dollars. In the same year, the total sum of the world's GDP was less than 30 trillion US dollars. The average daily nominal trade of the world's financial markets reached as high as 2 trillion US dollars, 50 times as much as that of the real trade. In other words, only 2% of the daily capital flow goes to international trade.[3]

2.2.4. *The Size and Speed of Cross-Border Capital Flow are Increasing Rapidly*

With the development of the world's financial markets, deregulation of capital flow, and progress of information technology, financial transactions could take place 24 hours a day, and any huge amount of capital can be transferred to a remote place thousands of miles away

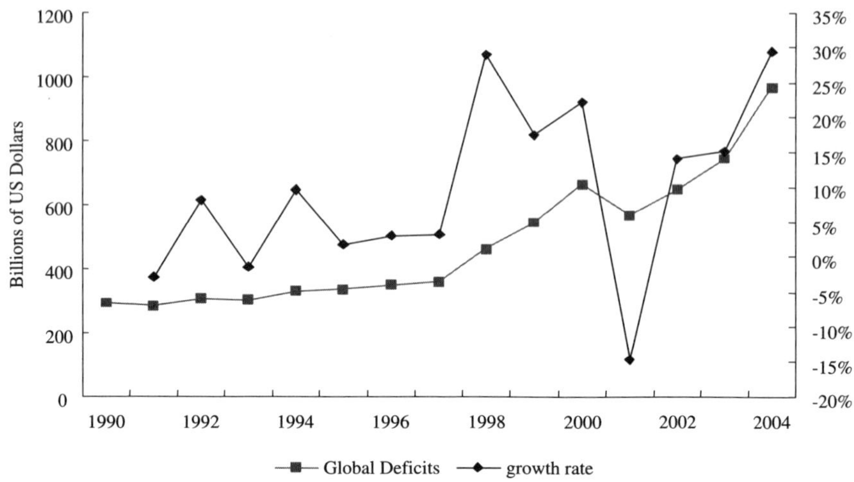

Fig. 2.1. Global Deficits.

within a second. These factors have promoted the cross-border capital flow, and reinforced its short-term tendency. Between 1986 and 2003, the world economy (the real GDP) grew at an average of 3.5% annually, the international trade (including commodity and service trade) grew at an average of 6.1% annually, while the international capital flow grew at a much faster speed.

According to statistics[7] issued by the International Monetary Fund (IMF), the global capital flow, as shown in Fig. 2.1, grew at an average of 8.92%[8] annually between 1990 and 2004; the global deficits were used to represent the net value of the capital flow.

The global capital flow saw a slow growth in the early 1990s, but during 1998–2000, the growth accelerated, reaching as high as 20% annually. Due to the recession of American economy since March 2001, nearly all the regions in the world suffered a concurrent decline which was the most severe one in the past two decades. The "September 11" terrorist attack not only shook the American economy, but also affected the rest of the world, reducing the global capital flow substantially in 2001. Shortly after a recovery in 2002, however, the global capital flow sawrapid growths in 2003 and 2004. The size of the global capital flow in 2004 reached as high as 960 billion US dollars, 29.4% more than the previous year.

As far as the direction of the global capital flow is concerned, the developed countries as a whole saw a capital deficit in the early 1990s, and a capital surplus between 1993 and 1998. But from 1999, they began to see a high current account deficit and the developed countries became a deficit region again. The United States has remained the world's largest deficit nation except in 1991, and its current account deficit in 2004 accounted for 69% of the global deficits. The EU countries have been able to keep a balance between deficit and surplus, and until recently they saw a small surplus. Japan has kept a large current account surplus, accounting for over 20% of the global capital requirements.

The emerging countries had a high current account deficit in the 1990s, but began to have a surplus from 2000. Asia is the major source of capital surplus. Except in 1993, China has been a surplus country since the 1990s, and provided 7.25% of the global capital requirements in 2004. Another important developing country in Asia is India which had remained a deficit country until 2001 when it saw a small surplus.

2.2.5. *Financial Innovation is Speeding Up*

Financial innovation can be defined as creative changes driven by needs and interests in the financial sector. The earliest financial innovation can be dated back to 1957 when the Eurodollar market evolved in London, dealing with dollar-denominated deposits and loans outside of the United States. The Eurodollar market operated free from the regulation of American banking laws, control of American bank interests, and limits imposed by some of the host countries' financial regulations. The emergence of the Eurodollar market provided European banks a channel for dollar funds, and helped American banks avoid the regulation on legal reserves and limits on deposits interest. The commercial notes issued by the controlling parent company were not considered as deposits. The Eurodollar market also provided a refugee for the dollar-denominated exchange reserves of the former Soviet Union and Eastern Europe during the cold war period. Consequently, it had a rapid expansion in the following years. Sterling pound, deutsche mark, and Japanese yen formed an off-shore market successively one after another, which are collectively known as the European monetary market. Currently, the daily trade volume of Eurodollar in Chicago Mercantile Exchange (CME) reaches as high as 2 trillion US dollars.

Beginning from the 1960s, the inflation and interest rates of the United States have been skyrocketing and, coupled with the break-through development of computer technology, integration of international financial markets, and unpredictable fluctuation of exchange and interest rates, financial risks are mounting up in ways that could fundamentally change the demand and supply of financial markets. Many financial institutions realize that their traditional financial products and services are losing sales, and that the old business models are no longer profitable. Similarly, many financial intermediaries find that the traditional financial tools are increasingly difficult to attract capital. Faced with these challenges, financial institutions have to innovate in order to survive, and to develop new products and services to prevent financial risks, ensure transaction safety, avoid financial regulation, and reduce transaction costs. Examples are Negotiable Order of Withdrawal (NOW), Automatic Transfer Saving (ATS), Certificate of Deposit (CD), Monetary Market Mutual Fund (MMMF), and Repo.

With the development of financial innovation, a financial derivative market emerged in the United States and in the United Kingdom after the 1970s. The financial derivative market takes two major forms: the first is the over-the-counter trade of financial products developed by banks and completed through telephone network, and the other is the visible market formed by the organized futures exchanges. The derivatives in the derivative market include futures contract, currency and interest swaps, guaranteed interest contracts, financial futures and options. According to the statistics of the National Futures Association of America, financial futures and options accounted for 92% in global trading of futures and options in 2004. In 2000, the balance of the world's financial derivatives hit 95 trillion US dollars, out of which exchange and option derivatives accounted for 17% respectively, and interest derivatives accounted for 66%.[9]

The emergence of financial derivatives has changed the model of bank operations, allowing multinational banks to develop into universal banks, and off-balance-sheet business to increase exponentially.

2.2.6. *The World's Financial Markets are Increasingly Integrated*

Today, the cross-border financial activities observe the same "rules of game", and adopt the same financial tools, selecting investors and fund-raisers on a global basis. Financial markets in different regions and with different products have been so integrated that capital can not only flow freely through borders in the same type of market, but also be transferred swiftly across different types of markets. The boundary between "long-term capital" and "short-term capital" and between "international finance" and "domestic finance" are becoming increasingly obscure. Alongside this new development, the transfer of risks is speeding up, and even a slight move in one market will affect the whole world.

The 1997 financial crisis in East Asia is still fresh in our memory. The crisis started in Thailand in the latter half of 1997[10] and quickly spread to East Asia and the rest of the world — unprecedented in history in terms of its influence, scope and degree.

Following a heavy sell-off of Thai Baht by some international speculators in mid May of 1997, the exchange rate between Thai Baht and US dollar fell to a historical low in a decade. The Central Bank of Thailand had to use 5 billion US dollars from its reserves to intervene the market. The exchange rate of Thai Baht was stabilized in the short run, but the cost was heavy: the foreign exchange reserves fell sharply, and in the single month of May they declined by 4 billion US dollars; and in the meantime, the foreign exchange rate went up high, creating a heavy burden for businesses, and making prices soar and the stock market go down sharply. On May 20, the finance minister of Thailand announced his resignation, and two months later when the foreign exchange reserves dropped to 8 billion dollars, the Central Bank of Thailand announced it was giving up its effort of intervention, and that it wished to adopt a floating exchange rate system.

The linked foreign exchange rate system (US dollar has 80% of weight) which had been implemented for over 14 years was abolished, and the preferential interest rate in commercial banks was increased to 12.5%, making Thai Baht depreciate by 18% on the same day. As a result, a financial crisis finally broke out in Thailand.

Thailand is an important member of Association of Southeast Asian Nations (ASEAN), having close business and trade relationships with other member countries. After Thai Baht adopted a floating exchange rate system, the foreign exchange markets of other ASEAN members began to fluctuate sharply. Indonesia, Malaysia and Philippines were forced to announce depreciation of their currencies one after another. Even Singapore, with relatively mature financial, monetary and market systems, announced the depreciation of its currency. The financial crisis soon spread to the whole region.

In October 1997, the regional financial crisis began to expand further to East Asia, first to Taiwan, and then quickly to Hong Kong, South Korea and Japan. Beginning from the latter half of 1998, the repercussions of the East Asian financial crisis went beyond Asia, extending to Russia, and countries in South America and Africa. Even the United States and the European Union — the two economic giants — began to feel threatened. The financial crisis slowed down the world's economic growth, down from an average of 3.2% in 1997 to 2.7% in 1998–1999. It was not until the year 2000 that the influence of the financial crisis began to fade away and the world economy recovered as a result of a combined effort in interest reduction by American and European banks, the drastic financial measures taken by the East Asian countries, and China's decision to stabilize its exchange rate.

Financial globalization is not identical to financial liberalization. Financial globalization is a result of the interaction between businesses and markets of different nations, and the evolution of the world's financial system during the economic globalization. There is a demand for deregulation in the process, which some people call financial liberalization. However, the so-called liberalization is only relative; no nation will open its financial system completely to safeguard its sovereignty and safety. As pointed out by Caprio,[11] the weaknesses of financial liberalization policy have been proven in many worldwide financial crises.

2.3. The Challenges of Financial Globalization for China

For the developing countries, financial globalization is a double-edged sword. On one hand, diversification and efficient capital flow improve global resource allocation, and promote international trade growth and economic development of each nation. On the other hand, with the development of financial globalization, international finance often experiences turbulence which produces a magnifying effect with the capital flow, affecting the stability of international financial regime and competitiveness of the developing countries in particular. In general, financial globalization poses the following challenges to China:

2.3.1. *The Opening of the Financial Market Creates an Intensive Competition for Chinese Financial Enterprises*

Under its commitments to the World Trade Organization (WTO) upon ascension in 2002, China would lift geographical restrictions in five years. It would gradually remove restrictions on local currency business, and allow foreign-funded banks to provide RMB services to any categories of Chinese customers and set up business networks in the same city with the same approval procedures as eligible Chinese-funded banks. China would also lift the existing restrictions and non-approval measures on foreign-funded banks in ownership, operation, setup of branches and license, and allow foreign-funded non-banking financial institutions to provide credit service for automobile purchase, enjoying the same treatment with similar Chinese financial institutions. Finally, it would have to allow foreign-funded banks to provide automobile credit business to Chinese residents.

Owing to historical reasons, system deficiency, weak internal control and inadequate financial innovations, China's commercial banks are generally weak in competitiveness. According to my own observation in 2001, the expense of Hang Seng Bank only accounted for 24.4% of its total revenue, while the same figure in our commercial banks was as high as 90%. The pretax margin per capita was HK$1,570,000 at Hang

Seng Bank, which is almost ten times as much as that of our commercial banks. The one-year spread between credit and savings was 1.7–2.2% at Hang Seng, while the same figure reached 3.6% in our commercial banks. In spite of the steady progress of banking reforms, commercial banks in China are not yet as competitive as their foreign counterparts. By international standards, their key indicators, including profitability (pre-tax margin/cost), return on capital, and margin per capita, are relatively low, not to mention the enormous gap in service quality, asset quality, corporate governance and financial innovation. Their advantage of having an extensive business network is often offset by low efficiency and poor service quality. A good example is the foreign exchange business: a significant part of foreign exchange savings in Shanghai is flowing to foreign-funded banks after the business is open to foreign capital. The commercial banks will face great challenges after China fully opens its financial market.

The gap in competitiveness in the securities sector is pretty obvious. In 2002, for example, Morgan Stanley had a total asset equivalent to RMB 6 trillion yuan, net asset equivalent to RMB335.1 billion yuan, and revenues equivalent to RMB245.7 billion yuan, which are 12, 3 and 10-times respectively of the aggregate of Chinese securities companies. The per capita managed assets and margin at Morgan Stanley was 64 and 50 times respectively of the average of Chinese securities companies. The gaps in corporate governance, managerial experience, customer network, incentive system, brand and human resource are enormous.

In futures, insurance and trust industries, China lags far behind the international competition. The Chinese government lacks experience in the regulation of the financial market and financial industry.

2.3.2. *The Flood-in of Foreign Capital will Hit China's Weak Financial System*

The flow of international capital sparked by financial globalization, especially the flow of short-term capital, has stimulated and intensified speculative activities, threatening the stability and safety of international financial markets. As China's market is immature, its legal system not complete and comprehensive (resulting in weak regulation), its financial system will be under greater pressure in the process of financial globalization. The likely significant increase of liabilities in banks will worsen their irrational assets-to-liabilities structure, and increase the systematic financial risks.

In the past two years, China's foreign exchange reserves saw a rapid increase, and in 2004 alone, the new increase amounted to 206.7 billion US dollars, or 77% over the previous year, making up 35% in GDP. In the last quarter, in particular, the average monthly increase reached 30 billion US dollars, much higher than the average level of 12 billion US dollars in the first three quarters. This enormous increase can be largely attributed to the fast growth of China's economy and foreign trade over the years. However, as the total of trade surplus and foreign direct investment in 2004 was less than 92.6 billion US dollars, it is safe to say that a huge amount of speculative capital has flooded into China, and the amount is estimated at 40–80 billion US dollars.

The key driving force behind the phenomenal growth of foreign exchange reserve is the expected appreciation of the Chinese currency. The capital inflow is caused by a number of factors: some foreign-funded banks are stepping up the entry into China's interbank bond market; foreign-invested companies are reducing their foreign exchange savings; the fled capital is flowing back; overseas companies are remitting funds to China through related party transactions or falsified contracts; individual foreign exchange accounts are expanding due to capital transfer from overseas; qualified foreign institutional investors (QFII) are increasing their investments in the Chinese capital market; domestic companies are increasing their foreign exchange accounts by delaying payments and advancing receivables; and the underground money houses are selling US dollars and buying RMB.

According to traditional economic theory, a country's foreign exchange reserves should not fall below 25% of its total export, but should never exceed 30–40%. This is obviously not the case with China: its foreign exchange reserves have exceeded 100%, and to maintain the stability of the exchange rate in the light of the rapid growth of its foreign reserves, China has paid a big price. In 2004, China's foreign exchange reserves reached RMB 5,043.9 billion yuan. Without hedge tools, the Central Bank of China has to increase the money supply to fight the influx of foreign exchange capital and to maintain the stability of the exchange rate. This runs counter to the central bank's conservative monetary policy, and reduces the effect of macro-control. It even ignites the risk of inflation. China uses its foreign exchange to purchase overseas bonds as its reserves, in effect amounting to lending enormous dollar capital to the trade deficit countries. This is not only wasting China's most valuable capital funds, but it is also increasing the strength of its trade competitors. Additionally, there is always a great risk due to the fluctuation of international exchange rates and the economic and social changes of the related countries. The US dollar exchange rate has dropped over 40% since 2002, and its large depreciation shrinks China's foreign exchange assets. The phenomenal growth of foreign exchange reserves intensifies the psychological expectation, and increases the pressure for RMB appreciation.

2.3.3. *The Increasing Integration of Domestic and Overseas Financial Markets exposes China's Financial System to the fluctuations of International Financial Markets*

China received a total of 60.6 billion US dollars in 2004, replacing the United States as the largest recipient of FDI. The inflow of foreign capital and the entry of foreign investment make China increasingly linked to and interrelated with international financial markets. This results, on one hand, in the increasing impact of the developed financial markets on China, as exemplified by the Federal Reserves' adjustment of basic interest rate, and on the other hand, it has brought about the spontaneous involvement of China in international financial markets.

China has experienced a phenomenal growth of its foreign trade over the years, and its foreign trade reliance (ratio between total exports and GDP) is surging. In 2004, China's adjusted GDP reached

US1,931.7 billion yuan, and the total exports was US1,150 billion yuan, increasing the foreign trade reliance to 59.5%. With the increase of its economic activities with the rest of the world, China is increasingly interrelated with international financial markets.

To summarize: financial globalization can on the positive side increase the efficiency of financial resources allocation and promote the financial reform of developing countries; however, the downside is that it could bring about drastic changes in the external environment and make financial reforms a daunting and pressing task for China.

China's path to financial reforms should observe four fundamental principles:

First, we should adhere to the philosophy of socialist market economy as proposed by Deng Xiaoping. The concept of socialist market system is a theoretical innovation with rich contents. It means that the market should be allowed to play a fundamental role in resource allocation to improve economic efficiency and effectiveness. China should draw on the successful experiences of overseas market economies, modifying them with the Chinese context. It is under the guidance of Deng Xiaoping's theory that China has launched the capital market, shareholding companies, venture capital and insurance industries which have promoted the prosperity of the socialist market economy. However, China should maintain and improve its socialist system, ensure social justice and fairness, and protect the legal interests of the weak and underprivileged groups in particular. Efficiency should not be achieved at the expense of social justice. Economic efficiency and social justice are complementary to each other. Economic development should not be achieved at the cost of social justice, because an increasing gap between the rich and the poor will jeopardize social stability. In like vein, social justice cannot be achieved and the people's increasing needs can hardly be met if economic efficiency is sacrificed.

In financial reforms, we should on one hand promote development and improve efficiency, and on the other hand, ensure social justice to protect the legal interests of investors, depositors and insurers. To date, many studies have focused on efficiency improvement, but very few on social fairness and justice.

Second, we should respect the fundamental laws of market economic development. Economic development must observe the basic laws of market, including the laws of value, demand and supply, and competition. Price should not be allowed to divert widely from value, and China's financial competitiveness can only be improved through competition. The development experience of market economy proves repeatedly that any violation of objective laws (e.g. providing subsidy or setting price limit) can only affect the sustainable development of economy in the long run. Resource allocation cannot be optimized when the government tries to protect the backward or limit competition.

Third, we should use the system engineering approach for management. Economic activities fall into two categories: real economy and virtual economy. Real economy generates profits through various transformations of capital. Capital is first transformed to factors of production (i.e. labor, facilities, raw materials and plants) through exchange, then to products through the production process, and finally to commodity through circulation in exchange for capital. This is the operation model of real economy. Virtual economy can be simply defined as "money generating money". Capital is likely to generate profits directly through operations in the capital market. From the perspective of system engineering, virtual economic system is itself a totality in which securities, banks, insurance, futures and foreign exchange markets are interrelated. At the same time, virtual economy is closely related to real economy. If real economy is the hardware, then virtual economy is the software of economy. Software cannot run without hardware, while hardware cannot perform without software. Today, these two forms of economic activities are increasingly interrelated. Overstock in real economy, for example, turns into bad accounts in virtual economy, and problems in virtual economy, such as slump of the stock market, also affect real economy. Therefore, we need to look at economic activities with a system approach, and focus on the interaction between real economy and virtual economy.

Fourth, we should be prudent and meticulous in our planning and advance the reforms as an integrated whole. China is undergoing a transition from the traditional planned economy to socialist market economy, and its reforms and development are path-dependent. We need to be active and prudent at the same time. The first step of the reform is important; it has impact on any of the subsequent steps. When a reform is abrogated and replaced with a new one, losses are almost inevitable. The ups and downs of China's capital market has resulted in great loss of state-owned assets.[12]

Financial reforms should have a clear objective and a well-developed plan. Timing is all-important. When conditions are not appropriate, we cannot have a good result; but if we hesitate when conditions are favorable, we will miss the chance. Every reform measure has two sides, and we must weigh its advantages and disadvantages. A good action can become bad if it is overdone.

2.4. Progress and Achievements of China's Financial Reform

The reform of China's financial system was carried out under the guidance of Deng Xiaoping's theory, and its key objective is to build socialism with Chinese characteristics. When China began its reform and opening up in 1979, the Agricultural Bank of China, the Bank of China, the Construction Bank of China, and the Industrial and Commercial Bank of China were revived one after another. In 1981, Treasury bonds were issued, and in 1984 the interbank loan market was created. In the following years, the note discount market was created in 1985; in 1986 CDs were issued; in 1987 short-term bonds were issued on a trial basis; in 1988 the secondary market of Treasury bonds was set up; and in 1991 the repo market was created. In the early 1990s, Shanghai and Shenzhen Stock Exchanges were launched, and the China Securities Regulatory Commission (CSRC) was established. With the progress of China's reforms and opening up, a market-oriented financial system began to take shape.

The 14th National Congress of the CPC held in 1992 set the reform target of establishing a socialist market economy. In this context, China's financial reforms were further strengthened as banks of different shareholding structures and city commercial banks were established in rapid succession, representing a quick move of China's financial system towards market orientation.

In 2002, China joined the WTO after 15 years of difficult negotiations. To improve the efficiency of its financial system, China has stepped up the reforms of its state-owned commercial banks, and in the meantime, the reforms of securities, futures, foreign exchange and insurance sectors are moving on steadily.

The reforms and development of China's financial sector in the past two decades represent a progressive process of China's financial system moving towards market orientation. The untiring efforts have paid off: China has basically formed a financial system that can meet the development of a market economy.

2.4.1. *The Central Bank System is Continuously Improving*

The People's Bank of China performed a dual role before 1984, serving as the central bank and undertaking credit and savings businesses at the same time. It was not until 1993 that the People's Bank of China began to change its primary function from commercial businesses to the development and implementation of monetary policy to safeguard the stability of currency, and to supervision over financial institutions to maintain financial safety and efficiency. In 1995 the Banking Law of the People's Republic of China was enacted, legalizing the People's Bank of China as the central bank. In the following years, the People's Bank of China promulgated a series of monetary policies and risk regulations, allowing China's central bank system to take on market characteristics. In 1998, it reinforced its functions through the open market operation and use of monetary policy for economic control. On April 28 of 2003, the China Banking Regulatory Commission (CBRC) was set up to take over the regulatory functions of the People's Bank of China. On December 27 of the same year, the "Banking Regulation Law of the People's Republic of China", "Decision of the Standing Committee of the National People's Congress on Revising the Law of People's Bank of China", and "Decision of the Standing Committee of the National People's Congress on Revising the Commercial Banking Law" were adopted at the Sixth Session of the 10th National People's Congress, which prescribed the responsibilities of the CBRC and provided a legal basis for its banking regulations on one hand, and on the other hand, re-established the functions of the People's Bank of China and reinforced its role as the central bank in formulating and implementing monetary policies.

2.4.2. *The Commercial Banking System has been Basically Set-up*

China had started the transformation of specialized banks into commercial banks since the 1980s, and a group of new commercial banks and regional commercial banks were created successively from 1986 to promote the marketization process of China's banking system. During the period, city credit cooperatives were established in major cities, and the reform of financial institutions was carried out to a higher level in rural areas. In 1994, three policy banks were created, and in the following year, the "Commercial Banking Law" was promulgated. In 1999, four asset management companies were established to take care of the non-performing loans of the four state-owned commercial banks. As of 2005, a commercial banking system has taken shape, comprising the four state-owned commercial banks, 13 shareholding commercial banks, 113 city commercial banks, 12 rural commercial banks, and 58 rural cooperative banks. Improvement has also been seen in the external environment and internal management of commercial banks.

2.4.3. *The Securities and Futures Markets Begin to Take Shape*

China's securities market was established after its reform and opening up under the guidance of Deng Xiaoping's theory. After the setup of Shanghai and Shenzhen stock exchanges in December 1990 and June 1991 respectively. Subsequently A-shares, B-shares and H-shares were issued in 1991 and 1993. In October 1992, the Securities Committee under the State Council and CSRC were inaugurated, signifying that a nationwide stock market had been formed. As of December 2005, there had been over 1,381 listing companies, including 109 B-shares companies, with a market cap of RMB 3,243.028 billion yuan. Additionally, there are 122 H-shares companies and 115 securities companies.

On July 1, 1999 the "Securities Law of the People's Republic of China" was put into effect to regulate China's securities market. Between May and June of 2001, the Standing Committee of the National People's Congress organized an expert team to investigate the implementation of the new law. Based on its findings and proposals, the watchdog CSRC strengthened the supervision and pushed forward reforms, while the Standing Committee of the National People's Congress began to revise the "Securities Law".

On April 29 of 2005, the CSRC circulated the "Notice on Pilot Reform of Segmented Shares Structure of Listed Companies" to start the flotation reform. The revised "Securities Law" was adopted at the 18th Session of the 10th National People's Congress on October 27, 2005, and came into force on January 1, 2006.

The futures market in China was set up in 1990, and its development had undergone three phases.[12] The first phase was a booming period, lasting from 1990 to 1995, during which China's futures market saw a rapid growth. By 1995, the total trade volume of the market had exceeded RMB 10 trillion yuan. However, as many regions launched their own futures markets and their regulation lax, grave problems appeared such that the State Council decided to intervene and to rectify. The second phase was an adjustment and rectification period, lasting from 1996 to 2000, during which the futures market saw a recession as a result of rectification and rapid growth of the stock market. By 2000, the trade volume had dropped to RMB 1.6 trillion yuan. The last phase was a restoration and development period, lasting from 2001 till now. Trade volume went up to RMB10.8 trillion yuan in 2003, and 14.7 trillion yuan in 2004, representing a new period of fast development. Presently, there are three commodity futures exchanges located in Shanghai, Dalian and

Zhengzhou, trading 12 futures produces, including copper, aluminum, rubber, fuel oil, bean, soybean, soybean oil, corn, wheat, cotton and sugar.

2.4.4. *The Foreign Exchange Management System is Continuously Improving and being Upgraded*

The reform of China's foreign exchange system can be grouped into three distinct stages: centralized revenue and expenditure system between 1949 and 1978, retaining system between 1979 and 1993, and bank settlement system since 1994. In 1996, China formally adopted Article 8 of the IMF Agreement, removing all exchange limits and realizing full convertibility of RMB under the current account. Based on the market exchange rate, China created a management framework featuring "free convertibility of RMB under the current account, and regulation of foreign exchange under the capital account", and formed a bank settlement system in line with international practice.

To build and improve the socialist market system and to give a full play to market in resource allocation, the People's Bank of China declared on July 21 of 2005 that China would adopt a managed floating exchange rate system with the market demand and supply as the basis and a basket of currencies as a reference for regulation. On July 23, the central bank decided to adjust the range of RMB exchange rate.

After the exchange rate system reform, RMB is no longer pegged to the single currency of US dollar, but to a basket of currencies of countries and regions with which China has important economic and trade ties. Each currency is given a weight in proportion to the country's trade importance to China to form a more elastic RMB exchange rate system. The People's Bank of China will adjust the floating range of RMB exchange rate according to the market maturity and economic and financial situation. In the meantime, it will refer to the global economic and financial situation, the market demand and supply, and the exchange rate fluctuations of the basket of currencies to adjust RMB exchange rate, to maintain its normal floating at a reasonable and balanced level, and to safeguard economic and financial security. The exchange rate reform represents a momentous step forward towards market orientation.

2.4.5. *The Insurance Industry is Developing Steadily*

The insurance industry in China too had experienced a rapid growth since its restoration in 1979. During 1994 to 2005, the premium revenue increased by an average of 19.8% annually, and the total revenue in 2005 hit RMB492.73 billion yuan, out of which property insurance took up 25%, or 122.99 billion yuan; life insurance took up 66%, or 324.43 billion yuan; and health and accident insurance took up 9%, or 45.31 billion yuan. As of 2005, there are 93 insurance companies, with a total assets of RMB1,522.59 billion yuan, among which 6 are insurance groups and holding companies, 35 are property insurance companies, 42 are life insurance companies, 5 are reinsurance companies, and another 5 are insurance asset management companies. Additionally, there are 1,800 insurance intermediaries, and 120,000 insurance agencies, employing over 1.47 million insurance sales persons, and realizing 73% of the total premium revenue.

2.5. Prospects of China's Financial Reforms

Chinese financial reforms represent a progressive process. In the past two decades, the financial sector has followed the principle of conservatism in carrying out the reform and opening up with a measured approach. With China's ascension to the WTO, great changes are taking place in its economic and financial environments. China's finance is increasingly affected by financial globalization, forcing China to step up its financial reforms and to increase the overall quality and competitiveness of the industry.

Maintaining the stability of China's financial system in its integration with international markets does not only arise out of the need to ensure investment quantity and quality, but also represents a response to the need to share the benefits of international capital inflow and to increase its ability to resist the impact of external financial crisis. As a transition economy, it is critical for China to intensify financial reforms, to increase financial efficiency and to ensure financial security for building and improving the socialist market system. In the context of financial globalization, China's financial reforms should be carried out to fulfill the requirements of the Third Plenary Session of the 16th National Congress of the CPC with due attention given to the following aspects:

2.5.1. *Promoting the Reform of the State-owned Commercial Banks and Building a Healthy Banking System*

Finance is the nucleus of modern economy, and banking is the heart of finance. The banking system in China includes the central bank, commercial banks, policy banks and credit cooperatives.

2.5.1.1. *The People's Bank of China should play an enhanced pivotal role in the financial system*

The central bank is the finance regulator of a country, developing and implementing the nation's monetary policies. It should play the central role as the national bank, an issuing bank and banks' bank. After the creation of the CBRC, the People's Bank of China not only continues, as the central bank of China, to issue currency, manage foreign exchange and treasury, settle payments, build financial legal system and analyze statistics, but it also has two additional important functions of anti-laundry and credit investigations. More importantly, it should reinforce its function of formulating and implementing monetary policies. The People's Bank of China should develop monetary policies independently in line with the nation's economic conditions and development objectives, regulate money supply and credit volume, and use monetary policy tools of interest and exchange rates to exercise macro-control. In the meantime, it should promote the interest rate marketization, build an interest rate system and a monetary policy transmission system on the basis of market demand and supply, and guide the monetary market with a combination of rediscounting, open market business and reserve systems. It should give due attention to the prevention of systematic financial risks to safeguard the country's financial security.

2.5.1.2. *Reforms of State-owned commercial banks must be carried out firmly*

Commercial banks are for-profit financial businesses, and their primary roles are: to act as financial intermediary to improve economic efficiency; to help businesses through lending and to promote economic development; to optimize resource allocation to reduce financial risk; and to transmit monetary policy to support macro-control. Commercial banks can be categorized into three levels according to their scope of service: national, regional and community. All commercial banks must follow the requirements set upon by the Third Plenary Session of the 16th National Congress of the CPC, reforming themselves into modern financial enterprises with adequate capital, strict internal control, healthy operation, excellent service, and superior financial performance.

The big four commercial banks in China have spelled out their "roadmap" of reforms on the basis of experiment and practice: to implement the shareholding reform, introduce strategic investors, step up the disposal of non-performing loans, replenish capital base, improve corporate governance, and create conditions for IPO. The roadmap might need necessary adjustments and further specification in practice, but the direction of the reform should be maintained to improve the international competitiveness of Chinese commercial banks and to take a commanding position before China fully opens its banking sector by 2006. Shareholding and city commercial banks should follow a similar approach to improve their corporate governance, to reinforce their internal management, and to create conditions conducive for IPO.

National commercial banks should have adequate capital, good corporate governance and strict internal management. In China, only the "Big Four" and a few shareholding and city commercial banks can meet these requirements. Some urban and rural commercial banks are trying to expand their scope of service, but we need to be prudent and careful. The CBRC should spell out the qualifications for national operation, and encourage commercial banks to become big and strong through mergers and acquisitions. Most of the urban and rural commercial banks should become regional commercial banks, with their scope of service limited to their own regions.

2.5.1.3. *Community banks should be set up on a trial basis*

Community banks are small financial institutions created to meet the demands of community residents and small-sized economic organizations. They operate independently and provide service according to the needs of local economic activities. Community banks usually have a small size, ranging from RMB500 million to 1 billion yuan in assets. Free from the shackles of history, they are more likely to adopt a flexible mechanism. For the time being, they can well control their risks as they are quite familiar with the community they serve. In the United States, there are over 6,000 community banks, with an average of 110 million US dollars in assets, taking up 20% of the savings market share. China should start its experiment with community banks as soon as possible, and push it forward on a larger scale.

Social capital should be encouraged to participate in the restructuring of small- and medium-sized financial institutions, and financial enterprises with different ownership structures should be developed when supervision is strengthened and capital adequacy is maintained. City commercial banks should absorb private capital, while community banks should take private capital as their major source of assets.

2.5.1.4. *Reforms of policy banks to be further strengthened*

The State Development Bank, the Export-Import Bank of China, and the China Agricultural Development Bank should speed up and intensity their reforms to improve their efficiency in supporting macro-control and promoting economic development. On one hand, internal management should be enhanced to prevent all kinds of risks, and on the other hand, research should be conducted on the functions and tools of policy finance to prevent over-commercialization.

2.5.1.5. *Reform of rural credit cooperatives must be continued*

As of 2005, China had 607 urban credit cooperatives and 27,000 rural credit cooperatives, many of which had lost the nature of cooperatives with huge non-performing loans due to absentee owners, inadequate system, poor management and lack of clear policy. The reform of rural credit cooperatives kicked off in 2003, with strong policy support from the government. On a trial basis, rural credit cooperatives can be reformed into regional financial businesses serving the rural community, with shareholding system, shareholding cooperative system and cooperative system as the three major forms of ownership structure. However, as many problems remain unsolved, the reform movement has been a daunting task and the improvement of rural financial service system shall take time.[13]

2.5.2. *To Develop Various Types of and Multi-level Financial Markets in order to Broaden Direct Investment Channels*

The balance of resident deposits has hit RMB12 trillion yuan by January 2005, 13 trillion yuan by May, and 28.72 trillion yuan by December, out of which resident savings have reached 14.1051 trillion yuan. The phenomenal growth of savings can be largely attributed to the narrow channels of direct investment in China. The total cap of the securities market is less than 20% of GDP, and a large proportion of shares are not negotiable. The balance of bonds is less than 30% of GDP, much lower than the international average. The futures market only trades commodity futures with a limited variety of commodities. The monetary, foreign exchange and insurance markets are still underdeveloped. Therefore, we need to develop a multi-type and multi-level financial market, and create an organic and cooperative mechanism that could adapt to different preferences of investors. The same effort should be made to expand the channels of direct investment.

2.5.2.1. *Reforms in division of equities must be promoted and the quality of listed companies improved*

The split share structure reform has been under way, and by January 9 of 2006, 434 listed companies on Shanghai and Shenzhen stock exchanges have completed or kicked off the reform, making up 32% in the total of 1,350 A-share companies, or 37% in terms of market cap. The reform is expected to be completed by the end of 2006.

As a system with a loose structure, the stock market maintains its stability only when it interacts and exchanges with external capital and information.[14] The entry of social securities and insurance capital, QFII and strategic investors will invariably provide a new momentum for the development of China's stock market.

However, what is fundamentally more important is to improve the quality of listed companies. In China's stock market, about 400 listed companies, or 30%, have relatively high investment value and can offer investors with reasonable returns, while the rest have low or no investment value at all. According to the disclosure of 1,353 listed companies in the third quarter of 2005, 36 companies had a negative net asset, 62 companies had a negative net asset after adjustment, and 235 companies had a negative margin, representing 2.66%, 4.58% and 17.37% respectively.[15] Therefore, we need to improve the corporate governance, internal management and profitability of listed companies on one hand, and create a delisting system on the other hand, to allow companies with little investment value to delist through negotiation and acquisitions. Companies with high investment value should be allowed to go for IPO, gradually constituting the "blue chips" in the Chinese stock market. Alongside, a forward sales system should be created. The building of a financial derivatives market can start with the stock index futures.[9]

2.5.2.2. *Bond market should be developed and the issuing of corporate bonds expanded*

The bond market in China is split into interbank bond market and exchange bond market, with the former much larger than the latter in size. In 2004, the interbank bond market issued an aggregate of RMB

2,654.8 billion yuan of bonds, in which 441.39 billion yuan were Treasury bonds, 1,703.73 billion yuan were the central bank's notes, 434.8 billion yuan policy financial bonds, and 74.88 billion yuan subordinated bonds of commercial banks, with a trade volume totaling RMB13.3 trillion yuan (bonds transaction hit 2.5 trillion yuan and repo hit 9.3 trillion yuan). The total value of bonds held in trust in interbank bond market had reached RMB4.6 trillion yuan by 2004, while the figure was only RMB438.84 billion yuan, with the unexpired government bonds repurchase amounting to 108.166 billion yuan.[16]

As one of the major financial tools of businesses, corporate bonds usually have an issuing cost lower than that of stocks. Compared with international markets, corporate bonds are less developed in China, and the quantity issued each year is much lower than the quota approved by the State Development and Reform Commission. In 2004, only RMB32.7 billion yuan worth of bonds were issued. The system for corporate bonds issuance, interest payment and repo should be further regulated, while the quantity issued should be significantly increased. The issuance of corporate bonds should be guaranteed by a company's assets and future earnings, and approved by the CSRC. The interest rate can be determined within a range according to the base rate and the company's credit, and payment must be made annually. A sinking fund should be created to repurchase a certain percentage (usually 3–5%) of bonds at a premium price. The CSRC should perform its regulatory responsibility and take legal actions if necessary. Recently, a few Chinese companies have issued convertible bonds, and their experience should be extended nationwide.

2.5.2.3. *The Issuance of short-term bonds should be rotated*

Most of the Treasury bonds in China are medium- and long-term bonds with a fixed interest rate. Due to low liquidity, they can hardly absorb short-term idle funds. At the 40th Chairman Meeting of the 10th National People's Congress held on December 16 of 2005, a proposal on Treasury bonds balance management submitted by the

Budget Working Committee was adopted, meaning that from 2006, China will follow international practice and use Treasury bonds balance approach to manage issuance of Treasury bonds, and to control its size scientifically to prevent fiscal risk. The change from aggregate management to balance management helps improve the maturity structure of China's Treasury bonds, and creates conditions required for the issuance of rotating Treasury bonds. The author proposed in 1999[10] to issue short-term Treasury bonds with 3-month and 6-month maturity period and to adopt discounted interest. The central bank can sell to large financial institutions through bidding in open market. In practice the new bonds are issued to repay old debts, as the balance management approach can reflect and adjust the demand and supply more dynamically. Acquisitions through bidding can form a weighted average market price, i.e. the interest rate of short-term Treasury bonds. The risk-free interest rate can be taken as the interest base to materialize the regulation of the financial market.

2.5.3. *Duly Adjust the Foreign Exchange Rate and Gradually Realize the Free Convertibility of RMB*

Free convertibility means that a currency holder can freely convert the currency to any of the international reserve currencies. With the increase of economic strength and growth of international trade, China should set free convertibility of RMB as its ultimate objective of reform to adapt to economic and financial globalization. As a first step and a major breakthrough in the reform of foreign exchange rate system, China had followed the requirements of Article 8 of IMF Agreement, and realized the free convertibility of RMB under the current account on December 1, 1996. In the future, when risks can be prevented effectively, limits on cross-border capital transactions should be removed gradually to realize free convertibility of RMB under the capital account.

As its reform of financial and foreign trade systems is not yet completed, it is still too early for China to allow free convertibility of RMB under the capital account. A more pressing task is to improve the foreign exchange system and to maintain the stability of RMB exchange rate at a reasonable and balanced level.

China has long adopted a single dollar pegging system, which is helpful to the stability and development of China's foreign trade, especially when the US has strong economic performance. However, such an exchange rate system reduces the room for macro-control by the central bank, and increases the cost of control, making the performance of RMB over-dependent on the US economic performance. A better choice for China is to use US dollar, Euro and Japanese yen as the base, and to replace the single pegging system with a weighted pegging system, adjusting the weight according to the economic performance of the US, Europe and Japan. The ultimate goal is to realize free convertibility of RMB.[10] This proposal suggests a "three-step strategy" for the adjustment of RMB exchange rate system.

The opening of foreign exchange rate can follow the proposed measured sequence below: (1) China can begin with the deregulation of capital account transactions for commodity and labor trade. (2) The next step is to remove limits on direct investment, first on capital inflow, and then on capital outflow. (3) Limits on short-term capital flow should also be gradually removed. (4) In credit management, China should first consider the deregulation of credit trade between state-owned financial institutions and non-residents, and gradually allow non-financial institutions to enter international financial markets. (5) In the capital market, deregulation of the bond market should precede that of the stock market. A-shares need to be merged with B-shares, but non-residents should register the number of subscription. (6) In the monetary market, exchange transactions between home and foreign currencies should be limited among residents, and non-residents should be encouraged to buy Treasury bonds. (7) In the foreign exchange market, trade should be extended from designated banks to large enterprises, residents and non-residents in succession, but the variety of transactions should be limited.

Through years of efforts, the reform of China's exchange rate system has gained great momentum. Since China adopted a basket of currencies system on July 21 of 2005, RMB has appreciated slightly. To make the weighted pegging system work, China needs to adjust its existing structures of foreign trade, foreign investment and settlement of external debts, and to offset the overweight of US dollar in the basket with a reasonable combination of currencies and weights. In the meantime, China should adopt a managed floating exchange rate system, and duly adjust the target zone of RMB exchange rate. When the market rate is close to the upper or lower limit of the range, the central bank can buy and sell a certain currency through the open market to influence its exchange rate with RMB and consequently the supply of the currency.

China has seen an abnormal growth of its foreign exchange reserves in recent years. Accordingly, it should "strictly control the inflow and loosen the outflow". On one hand, we need to prevent the inflow of huge illegal foreign capital from pushing up RMB and weakening our control over base currency. To this end, China should reinforce its import and export verification system, discouraging the practice of settling the capital items as trade revenues and expenditures and of financing through forward letter of credit. In the meantime, it should also enhance its contract management over joint venture and cooperative projects, prohibiting foreign partners from asking for a fixed return on investment and exchange rate, or cashing in on their ownership before the contracted date. Attention should also be given to the control of various hidden external debts. At the same time, China should loosen its control over the outflow of foreign exchange and gradually remove the foreign exchange quota for enterprises and the compulsory settlement system. Similarly, the quota for foreign exchange banks should be relaxed and the foreign exchange position management removed. The limits over capital outflow should be lifted, encouraging businesses to invest overseas directly. Domestic legal persons and natural persons should be allowed to invest in overseas financial markets.

The capital account in China is increasingly deregulated in recent years. In 60 secondary capital accounts, about half have been open. In principle, the opening of the capital account should be measured and controlled. The timetable should be set in line with the changes of international financial environment and the management capability of the authorities.

2.5.4. *Enhance the Overall Regulation of the Finance Industry and Strengthen International Cooperation*

The regulation of the finance industry rests upon a combination of internal and external controls. First and foremost, the finance industry should strengthen internal control, improve internal control system, and enhance self-discipline. In the meantime, external control should be reinforced, legal system and environment should be improved, and a risk warning and crisis management system created. Additionally, international cooperation should be enhanced. The Chinese finance industry should keep a close eye on the new dynamics of international financial system, and participate actively in the formulation of international financial rules and regional financial cooperation. Counter-measures should be worked out to reduce the impact of external turmoil on domestic economy.

2.5.4.1. *Specify the objectives of financial regulation*

The objective of financial regulation is to ensure the openness, fairness and justice of the financial market by legislation, to encourage and protect fair and orderly competition, to effectively prevent and resolve financial risk, and to protect the legal interests of savers, investors and insurants. China is a transition economy, and presently the government is the regulator of the market and the owner of state-owned enterprises (SOEs) simultaneously. When the two roles conflict, fairness and efficiency of regulation could be compromised. The government should encourage SOEs to improve performance and increase the value of assets through system building, enhanced management, technological innovations and market-orientation. SOEs should not be allowed to speculate on stocks and futures against the regulations, or to acquire bank loans through related party transactions, or even to re-lend the bank loans to other businesses for high interest as such activities could affect adversely the equitableness of the market and increase financial risks.

2.5.4.2. *Start with information disclosure*

The regulation of the finance industry should begin with information disclosure; it should then move on to analysis, publication and disposal of the information so disclosed. The regulator should clearly specify the scope, indicators, depth and frequency of information disclosure and make them known to the public. All information that should be disclosed must be made accessible through media or posted online. Any organization that discloses information should be held liable for the integrity, authenticity and timeliness of information. They must also accept the supervision of the regulator or regulating bodies, disciplinary institution and the public.

After information disclosure, information should be analyzed by professionals. Information analysis not only tells the status and tendency of various financial tools, but could also reveal conflicting or false information and provide clues for the regulator's investigation. The regulator should determine the nature and degree of gravity through analysis and verification when they identify suspicious information, and disclose its measures of disposal (e.g. warning, reprimanding, suspension of business license, etc.) in the first instance to minimize losses. Minor cases can be punished through self-disciplinary institution. A joint litigation system should be created, allowing victims to claim damages under the law.

The regulator should improve the monitoring, warning and disposal system of financial risks, strengthen the process of information disclosure, and create and improve a unified, efficient and safe payment settlement system and a wide, effective and real-time monitoring system. In strengthening financial regulation, the regulator should also support financial innovation, and encourage system and product innovations.

2.5.4.3. *Promote mixed operations steadily*

The finance industry has seen a rapid growth in mixed operation since the 1990s. The United States was the first country to experiment with mixed operation in the 1980s, followed by some European countries and Japan. Mixed operation has two basic models: financial holding company and universal banking. It represents the new development of global financial industry. Mixed operation contributes to capital flow and utilization, helps create a synergy between various financial institutions and the market, and facilitates the systematic control of financial risk. It should become the ultimate goal of China's financial reforms.[17] However, the conditions for mixed operation are still immature in China. What can be done first is to establish a coordination system among the banking, securities and insurance regulators, the central bank and the Ministry of Finance, and to improve the regulatory efficiency. Mixed operation should be pushed forward steadily when the experiments with financial holding company and universal banking show positive progress.

2.5.4.4. *Increase international cooperation*

International cooperation in finance industry should focus on the monitoring of international speculative capital flow. The rampancy of international speculative capital is one of the key factors for financial crisis. The daily trade volume in international financial markets has reached 1.5 trillion US dollars, and the hot money is estimated at 7.2 trillion US dollars. International financial speculators are creating disturbance for abnormal returns. Consequently, even the economists trumpeting financial liberalization begin to favor proper control and regulation. With China's gradual opening of its capital market, we should study how to monitor large foreign exchange and stock trading (especially futures trading) through a declaration system. For huge inflow and outflow of foreign capital, a filing and reporting system should be created, and for huge transactions of financial derivatives, a real-name and deposit system should be introduced. Additionally, the information exchange and financing between the central banks of each country should be strengthened to deal with liquidity crisis and to eliminate any loopholes that can be used by international speculative capital.

The weakening of US economic strength and the ever-increasing gap of inflation rates between leading industrial countries culminated in the collapse of the Bretton Woods system in the early 1970s. Since then, the floating exchange rate and pegging exchange rate had existed side by side, without a stable international monetary system. In five to ten years, the US dollar as a major currency of settlement will be challenged with the maturity of Euro, recovery of Japanese economy, and rapid economic growth of Asian countries. Given the tendency of regional financial integration, China should work with the rest of the world to create a secure, well-balanced and fair international monetary system, which could contribute not only to the prevention of financial crisis, but also to stall the polarization of the world.

Financial globalization is producing profound impact on the world's economic, political and social life, and provides a rare chance for China's modernization. Accordingly, the design of China's financial reform strategy should try to maximize the benefits and to minimize the harms. As long as we can eliminate the structural barrier of finance at the macro level, and strengthen the internal management of financial enterprises and step up innovation at the micro level, the financial reformation of China will invariably succeed.

References

[1] Cheng, S. W. (2001). China's Overseas Investment: Strategy and Management, in Cheng, S. W. (ed.), Pandect, *Devoting Major Efforts to Developing China's Multinationals*, Beijing: Democracy and Construction Press, pp. 1–57 (in Chinese).

[2] The Central Committee of the CPC (2003). "Decision of the Central Committee of the Communist Party of China on Improving Socialist Market Economy" (adopted at the Third Plenary Session of the 16th National Congress of the CPC held on October 14, 2003) (in Chinese).

[3] Cheng, S. W. (2003). *Collections on Virtual Economy*, Beijing: Democracy and Construction Press (in Chinese).

[4] Hashimoto S., (1997). *Japanese Economic Studies: 20th Century System and Japanese Economy*, translated by the Center of Japanese Studies, Fudan University, Shanghai: Shanghai University of Finance and Economics Press (in Chinese).

[5] Song, G. X. and Sheng, Y. F. (2003). Implication of International Exchange Rate Coordination in the 1980s, *Economic Herald*, 10, 54–56 (in Chinese).

[6] Asian Development Bank (2005). *Monetary and Financial Integration in East Asia*, translated by the International Department of the Ministry of Finance, Beijing: Economic Science Press (in Chinese).
[7] IMF (2005). *World Economic Outlook Database*, September 2005.
[8] Yang, H. Z. (2005). *Capital Flight*, Beijing: China Finance Press (in Chinese).
[9] Cheng, S. W. (2005a). Speech on China Financial Derivatives Forum (held on September 26, 2005) (in Chinese).
[10] Cheng, S. W. (1999). Analysis and Lessons from the East Asian Financial Crisis, in Cheng, S. W. (ed.), Pandect, *Fictitious Economy and the East Asian Financial Crisis*, Beijing: Democracy and Construction Publishing House, pp. 1–50 (in Chinese).
[11] Caprio, G., Honohan, P. and Stiglitz, J. E. (2003). *Financial Liberation*, translated by Wang Yonglan, Beijing: China Finance and Economics Press (In Chinese).
[12] Cheng, S. W. (2005b). Exploring a Development Path for China's Futures Market — speech at the 2005 China Futures Market Forum held on January 15, 2005 (to be published) (in Chinese).
[13] Cheng, S. W. (2005c). Reform and Development: Promoting China's Rural Finance, in Cheng, S. W. (ed.), Pandect, *Exploring Effective Path to Develop China's Rural Finance*, Beijing: Democracy and Construction Press, pp. 1–35 (in Chinese).
[14] Cheng, S. W., (2003). Diagnosis and Treatment: Inside the Chinese Stock Market, in Cheng, S. W. (ed.), Pandect, *A Systematic Analysis of China's Stock Market and Regulation Proposals*, Beijing: Economic Science Press, pp. 1–47 (in Chinese).
[15] Li, Z. R. and Cheng, S. W. (2006). On Perfecting the Delisting Mechanism in China's Security Market, *Financial Research Journal*, 11, 17–32 (in Chinese).
[16] China Monetary Society (2005). *2005 China Finance Yearbook*, Beijing: Editorial Board of China Finance Yearbook (in Chinese).
[17] Cheng, S. W. (2004). Mixed Operation is the Ultimate Goal of China's Financial Reform, *Economic World*, 3, 4–8 (in Chinese).

Chapter 3

Causes of Deflation and China's Countermeasures

Deflation is a monetary phenomenon manifested by the decline of the aggregate price level. In studying deflation, we should pay particular attention to the difference between the state of affairs and the process. If a country's overall price decrease lasts for more than 80% of the months in a year, then this country has entered into a deflationary period. Inflation and deflation are two common monetary phenomena. Despite the fact that they both interact with economic activities, we do not have to associate them with good or bad economic performance, or assume that deflation is correlated with economic contraction. Like inflation, deflation has both advantages and disadvantages. Transitory inflation can pose a positive impact on economic development. Only medium and long term deflation can trigger economic recession.

The history of deflation in major Western countries can be divided into three phases. During the 1821–1913 period, currency was based on the Gold Standard. Since money supply was restricted by the Gold Standard, deflation caused by excessive supply of currency was a common occurrence. However, only sustained deflation and an abrupt credit crisis together can ultimately bring about economic recession. In the 1914–1945 period, the Gold Exchange Standard was adopted. Gold reserves during this phase had less dominance over money supply. The influence of interest rate and exchange rate became more pronounced. Governments were also making more interventions in the economies by employing fiscal and monetary policies to control them. However, economic recession can only be avoided or rehabilitated when policies are properly adopted under an effective financial system that boosts people's confidence. The post-1971 deflation occurred when the fictitious or virtual economy was developing rapidly and currencies were completely dissociated or disconnected from gold and turned into unconvertible paper notes and were moving towards becoming fictitious paper currency. This type of deflation is called "modern deflation".

When we are exploring the causes for modern deflation, we shall take into consideration the complexity of the monetary system, the fictitiousness of credit currency as well as the self enforcement of deflation. Deflation is the manifestation of the self organizing effect in the monetary system, and is mainly determined by the future expectations of individuals, enterprises, banks and their corresponding actions. The interaction between the three parties is synergistic. When they have low expectations of the future, they will support and assist each other. Therefore, a credit crisis generated by fictitious money will not only result in deflation, but will also help prolong the deflation until the economy heads into recession.

According to the classification I previously proposed, China's most recent deflation started in June 1997 and ended in September 2000. The causes of this deflation are not only similar to those of other countries, but also feature Chinese characteristics. China's deflation occurred shortly after successfully reversing inflation, accompanied by a system transformation; the Asian Financial Crisis, intensification of the reforms and the continued economic growth. Supply outstripping demand is the primary cause for the deflation in China (that is, income growth lagging far behind economic growth, priorities for savings significantly exceeding priorities for spending, increase of unequal income distribution weakening the overall purchasing power and where a supply structure cannot adapt to changes of the demand structure, etc.). Decline of private investment is also one of the main reasons for China's deflation. In addition, the residual effect of the macro-control and some exogenous elements also fueled the emergence of deflation.

The following policies and measures are suggested: (1) improve the incomes of urban and rural residents, and enhance their purchasing power; (2) improve the expectations of the urban and rural residents for the future economy; (3) adjust the supply structure and expand effective demand; (4) encourage private investment and development of the non-state-owned economy; (5) strengthen financial reforms and improve banking performance and (6) employ fiscal and monetary policies flexibly.

3.1. Introduction

After China curbed the grave inflation during 1992 to 1995 and successfully delivered an economic "soft-landing" in 1997, a prolonged period of price slide was triggered in 1997 exerting an impact on economic development. This situation has drawn wide attention from some economists and practitioners in this field. However, analysis and assertions of this period have differed widely from each other. Although the protracted price decline would normally be described in traditional economics textbooks as a phenomenon of deflation; the definition, criteria for classification, causes, countermeasures for deflation and whether the Chinese economy had really entered deflation are, however, still debated in economist circles.

Deflation represents the opposite of inflation. Over the past 200 years of economic development, there have been fewer deflations than inflations. For this reason, although economists have conducted extensive and in-depth research in the field of inflation, research on deflation has been relatively scarce. The few recent studies on deflation that have been published overseas are mostly based on data and analyses from developed countries — so they cannot describe fully China's situation. As domestic publications are heavily biased towards qualitative analysis and arguments, some of their assertions are not sufficiently supported by reliable and solid data. In this regard, I am going to introduce some preliminary analysis of the classification or criteria, causes and countermeasures for deflation based on the existing research results (employing economic theories, concepts and ideas of project management, complexity science and virtual economy, as well as a combination of qualitative and quantitative methods) and explore the contributing factors for the recent deflations in China, and at the same time endeavor to put forward the major countermeasures that should be adopted based on the findings of the abovementioned theoretical analysis.

3.2. Deflation is a Monetary Phenomenon

Like inflation, deflation in itself is simply a monetary phenomenon. "Currency" is a universally recognized trade medium for circulation, which in our modern society, also includes paper notes and coins.[1] Thus, inflation means the supply of money outstrips the supply of goods, while deflation is defined as a situation where the supply of money is outstripped by the supply for goods. From these definitions, we can regard them as merely monetary phenomena.

Most of the numerous definitions given by various economists tend to relate deflation with the decline of price. For instance, the American economist, Stiglitz J. E., said in his textbook, *Economics*, "deflation means a persistent decline of the price level".[2] Krugman P. L.[3] and Samuelson P. A. *et al.*[4] also defined deflation as "drop of the overall price level".

These definitions have misled many people to the wrong idea that deflation is not simply a monetary phenomenon, but an economic phenomenon. These people tend to associate deflation with economic contraction, or even think that deflation is an economic policy. For example, in the Economics volume of *Encyclopedia of China*, deflation is defined as "a reduction in the volume of currency in circulation or a slowdown of currency issuing rate so as to raise the purchasing power of the currency or to lessen the extent of its devaluation. It is a type of policy adopted to rectify existing fiscal deficit or severe inflation".[5] This definition actually rules out the views of many economists on deflation and attaches to it a political label. But in that book, inflation is defined as a social economic phenomenon: "volume of currency in circulation has exceeded commercial goods demanded, resulting in a rise in prices and depreciation of currency. This is a social economic phenomenon under the condition when currency serves as the circulation medium, manifested by a continued rise in general price level signifying that there is a general decline in price of the goods as represented by currency." This definition has ignored the inherent correlation between deflation and inflation.

From my point of view, the phrase "decline of the price level" is not the definition for deflation, but the manifestation thereof. Ever since Britain first adopted the Gold Standard in 1821, gold acted as a guarantee for the widely circulated paper notes. Consequently, the prevalence of the Gold Standard gradually spread to the whole of Europe and the U.S.A., until in 1870 when it became the basis for world currencies. When World War I erupted, the gold standard was generally suspended due to various reasons, including the prohibition to export gold by some countries.

After World War I, the Gold Standard slowly gave way to the Gold Exchange Standard. By the 1970s, the role of gold in the international monetary system had officially come to an end. With the "de-linking" of money and gold, currency had become more 'fictitious' or become 'virtual' because people could no longer use a stable "reference unit" to measure money. People had to use the purchasing power of money to measure its value. In addition, in the absence of the automatic exit mechanism as originally put in place by the Gold Standard in the overall economic system, the purchasing power of currency was then determined by the relation between the volume or quantity of currency and the actual economy. For this reason, the increase of the purchasing power generated by "decline of price" is considered the equivalent of "decrease of currency quantity". That would mean the "decline of overall price level" can be used as the classification criterion for deflation.

I consider *deflation as a monetary phenomenon, manifested by the decline in aggregate price level.*

The aggregate price level is normally measured by the price index (price index of mainly consumer products and services). In 2001, the National Bureau of Statistics of China set out and promulgated the new fixed consumer price indices that live up to the international standard based on new classification and methods. These indices can be used to measure the aggregate price level.

Chain price index will generally be employed to facilitate the observation of the aggregate price level. If this index is greater than 100%, the currency is considered inflated, while if less than 100, the currency is considered deflated. Some Western scholars believe, as governments tend to amplify inflation, when the price index is below 101% and index growth is less than 1%, we can assume that the economy is facing deflation. However, this view needs to be further justified and we shall take "deflation occurs when the price index is less than 100%" to be the classification criterion in this paper.

In my opinion, when we are studying deflation, we need to distinguish 'state of affairs, or situation' from 'process'. When the aggregate price level at one stage is lower than that of the preceding stage, we can call it deflation (or precursor of deflation). This phenomenon refers to a state of affairs or a situation. But if the aggregate price level maintains a downward trend, we can call it deflationary period (stage), and this is a process. It is relatively easy to tell a deflationary phenomenon since its standard or criterion is universally recognized. However, when we are trying to judge if a country is in the deflationary period, there is no consensus on the classification criteria. There is a "unitary element" theory, a "dual elements" theory as well as "triple elements" theory. The proponents of "unitary element" theory advocate the definition of deflation as the opposite of inflation. Deflation is a general prolonged decline of the price of goods and services; they propose that "prolonged decline" does not necessarily mean the price level must be "low". "General" decline means an overall and extensive price drop of goods and services, rather than for a specific product or sector. The proponents for "dual elements" theory believe that the emergence of deflation, accompanied by economic contraction, requires two conditions. One is the persistent price drop of goods and services, and the other is the sustained decrease of money supply. The underlying difference between "triple elements" theory and "dual elements" theory is that "triple elements" theory takes economic recession as the classification criterion and not a concomitant of deflation. That means they consider deflation firstly as a monetary phenomenon, related to decline of money in circulation. Secondly, deflation will lead to a fall of price; and thirdly, it is generally concurrent to economic contraction.

Since deflation is a monetary phenomenon, we do not need other classification criteria other than the aggregate price level. Therefore, I technically agree with the "unitary element theory", though I think the classification criteria need to be further scrutinized and quantified. My proposition is, when a country has experienced an overall price drop for 80% of the time during the year, we can conclude that this country has entered a deflationary period, or as we would say, deflation has emerged.

Some people propose that we should take a sustained decline of the overall price level within 12 months as the classification standard, which I personally consider inappropriate. If we look at a specific point in time (say, end of each month), there are three possibilities for the movement of the aggregate price level compared with the previous month; increase (inflated), decrease (deflated) and even, with the probability for the former two scenarios more likely. Thus, the aggregate price level is in constant flux, and may fluctuate due to various internal or external factors. For instance, there might be a transitory rise during a persistent, sustained declining period. However, if we look at the period (say a year), although the overall price might fluctuate, if it is on the upward trend for most of the time, there is inflation; whereas, if it is on a downward fall for most of the time, a deflation appears. In this regard I suggest for a certain period, if the price index is greater than 100 for more than 80% of the time, we can regard it as inflation; or if it is less than 100 for over 80% of the time, we call it deflation.

Attention should also be paid to the point that, from the time signs of deflation start to show until it starts to pose a destructive impact on economic operations, there is a time lag. Statistics from other countries indicate that the impact on the price level from money supply will be manifested only about one or two years later. If we take a relatively shorter period, deflation would have been alleviated before it has any marked impacts. Earlier statistics from certain countries recognized deflationary periods as lasting at least one year. For this reason, I would advise studying statistics of more than a year to investigate the occurrence of deflation. It is also suggested we call deflation that lasts for less than 24 months as transitory deflation, and a deflation lasting for over five years as long term deflation, and deflation in between, as medium term deflation.

Some economists believe when the price index is greater than 100, inflation will only occur when the inflation rate continues to grow. On the contrary, if the inflation rate starts to decline, it should be called *disinflation*. I do not totally agree with this view, though.

As deflation and inflation are common monetary phenomena, despite their being linked with economic phenomenon, we do not have to necessarily associate them with economic performance or assume that there is an inevitable correlation between deflation and economic recession. If we attach a political tag to deflation, assuming that to admit deflation is to acknowledge economic recession, it will prevent us from giving an in-depth analysis of the rules of deflation or objectively judge the occurrence of deflation and its impact on economic development when appropriate measures should be taken.

My view is that: like inflation, deflation has both its advantages and disadvantages. Transitory deflation can sometimes have a positive impact on economic development. Only medium term and long term deflation will result in economic recession. To this end, as long as we stay clear- and level-headed and take timely and appropriate countermeasures, we can take advantage of its positive impacts on economic development while at the same time minimizing its destructive or negative influences.

3.3. A Review of the History of Deflation

Since deflation is a monetary phenomenon, when we are reviewing the history of deflation we shall have to take into consideration the history of money, paying particular attention to its interaction with economic phenomenon.

Based on my preliminary research, the history of deflation in the West can be divided into three phases.

3.3.1. *1821–1913*

Money is the only 'circulating' asset, and is also a type of asset which can be traded for other commodities at any time. Metal (gold or silver) had been used as currency for at least 4,000 years, and the coinage system has existed for approximately 2,600 years. In 1821, Britain first adopted the Gold Standard. It was a monetary system where the price of gold was fixed or maintained against the currency. Currency could be freely converted to gold against the fixed weight of gold. Later, Germany, France, the U.S.A. and many other countries also followed in the footsteps of Britain. Since the major Western countries all adopted the Gold Standard, deflation at this stage was closely correlated with the Gold Standard based monetary system.

The advantage of the Gold Standard is that it limits the power of governments or banks to issue paper currency — excessive issue of paper currency — thus avoiding the subsequent currency depreciation while stabilizing exchange rates. Since the ratio of currency to gold for each country is fixed, the volume of currency issued is linked to the gold reserves of the country based on this ratio. The disadvantage is that since the growth rate of the gold reserves is very slow, this restricts the volume of currency issued or issuable. Such restriction meant that the needs of the increasing aggregate supply for currency increase could not be met for each country for its economic development. There was no flexible adjustment of money supply, and as a result this could easily lead to deflation, obstructing the interactions between the economies in different countries and even limiting the capacity for combating deflation for countries with deficit spending. As the paper money issued by the governments at this stage was guaranteed by equivalent amounts of gold, even frequently occurring transitory deflations did not usually generate economic contraction.

In the period 1839–1843, deflation occurred in the U.S. During this deflationary period, price dropped by 42%, investment decreased by 23%, the stock market went down by 34% and the number of banks came down by 23%, whereas spending increased by 21% and actual GNP grew by 15%. These data indicate that this deflation did not cause an economic contraction.[6]

Ever since the end of the American Civil War in 1865, the U.S. had seen stable economic growths which were mainly attributable to the export of agricultural products, extensive railway construction and large-scale industrialization. The agriculture industry in the U.S. had enjoyed rapid growth owing to the influx of immigrants, land exploitation and operational expansion. As a result, the volume of agricultural products exceeded 70% of American exports and total railway tracks increased from 30,600 km in 1860 to 150,200 km in 1880 (up to 8,000 miles of railway lines were laid in 1870 alone). By 1900, this figure had reached 193,000 km. At the same time, industrial development, favored by growing investment, enhanced management and horizontal acquisition, had far surpassed agricultural development. Meanwhile, the industrialization process was also accelerating. During the period 1869–1878, the ratio of industrial GDP to agricultural GDP was 1.66 and, during 1897–1901, it had jumped to 3.26.

Despite the U.S. economy enjoying aggressive developmental momentum, because the growth of gold reserves could not catch up with the growth of the demand for currency, price of goods clearly took a downward trend. From 1865 to 1897, GDP kept increasing for 23 years out of the 32 year period, of which only nine years saw a decline of GDP, whereas M2 money supply decreased for 12 years and increased for 20 years. However, the wholesale price index for the U.S.A. had dropped for 22 years, increased for eight years and was even for two years; the price index for farm products slid for 22 years, picked up for nine years and was even for one year. The consumer price index declined for 22 years, rose for three years and was even for seven years. As we can see here, when the economy was on the Gold Standard, falling prices definitely did not trigger economic recession.

However, during the period 1865–1914, the U.S. economy did encounter two recessions, one during the 1873–1878 period and the other in the 1893–1896 period. These two economic recessions were caused by the joint impact of a prolonged price decline and a credit crisis.

In the history of money development, ever since people's idle money were turned into interest generating capital, and accompanied by the emergence of credit currency, money began to become 'fictionalized'. Banks, as intermediary institutions, can accept deposits of idle money from citizens and loan out to generate interest. People can also choose to purchase all kinds of marketable securities with their idle capital to generate interest. At this time, the depositing documents and the marketable securities actually represent fictitious capital. Socialization of interest generating capital can direct the capital from those depositors who do not use them for real economic activities, so that the idle funds can be used for relatively sizable and more profitable economic activities, thus improving the utility of capital.

In this regard, activities that are used for directly generating money through utilizing fictitious capital are called the fictitious economy.[7]

Further development of the fictitious economy is manifested in the marketization of marketable securities. This means marketable securities can be freely traded based on their expected returns. That was how the financial market for the exchange of fictitious capital came into existence (namely, stock market, bond market and monetary market, etc.). The marketization of marketable securities not only makes it possible for people to liquidate their marketable securities at any time, but also greatly improves the liquidity of the fictitious capital; it can also direct capital to more profitable industries and thus further increase capital utility. In 1898, futures exchange for farm products also came on board, and this later spread to industrial raw materials such as non-ferrous metal, heavy oil, etc., as new forms of fictitious capital.

The existence of banks leads to the expansion of credit currencies, which are used as trade medium and means of payment such as checks, remittances and promissory notes. However, as a large part of the credit currency was not secured by corresponding amounts of gold, their value is fictitious. Once a credit crisis is triggered, people will rush to convert their credit currency to gold, which in turn causes banks with insufficient gold reserves to close, as a result of a run on the banks. A credit crisis is thereby generated, making the deflation even worse.

Despite price declining for six consecutive years during the 1865–1871, period the U.S. managed to maintain relative financial stability and its GDP continued to grow. However, the negative effect of the protracted price decline manifested gradually, which slowly lowered the profits of the financing enterprises. As a result, the reduced profits not only pushed up the volume of total debts, but also made it more unlikely for these enterprises to clear their debts or even to put them into insolvency. During this period, the number of annual insolvent enterprises jumped from 500 to 2,900, and the total annual volume of debts also climbed from $17,600,000 to $85,300,000.

The consequence of the prolonged excessive supply of currency is the shrinking credit market and the rise of the discount rate. In 1871, the discount rate for private capital in New York increased from 4.7% in July to 9.8% in December, and by October 1872, this figure had gone above 12%. In September 1873, numerous banks that were previously supplying capital for railway constructions went insolvent, and people started to withdraw their deposits from the banks. The collapse of the credit system caused prices to further slide and interest rates climbed dramatically (discount rate for private capital reached 17% in October of the same year), which accelerated the insolvencies of banks, industrial and commercial enterprises and precipitated the fall of the stock market. Even the Stock Exchange of New York was shut down for ten days. With the government's initiatives to acquire treasury bonds to alleviate the tension of the financial market, the situation began to improve by the end of 1873. This was accompanied by the recovery of the credit market. However, as money supply was restricted by gold reserves, money was still in short supply, and the sluggish industry and commerce sector still could not fully recover.

The wholesale price index, price index of farm products and consumer price index maintained a downward trend until 1879, with their decline reaching 33.8%, 33.3% and 20% respectively within a six year period. From 1872 till 1878, the number of insolvent enterprises increased by up to 14.4%. In 1878, this figure jumped to 10,500, hitting a historical high. From 1873 till 1878, the total volume of debts hovered at a relatively high level, having accumulated to $1,201 million during the 6 year period. During this period, increase of new railway lines had slowed down, the stock market became stagnant, prices kept sinking, the unemployment rate went up, and the economy entered into a recession.

Under such circumstances, the U.S. government began to increase reserves through importing gold and buying silver for minting coins etc, helping to increase money supply somewhat. Simultaneously, the government encouraged both domestic and foreign investors to invest in railway and other industries. From 1878, railway stocks and industrial stocks registered an obvious rebound, and newly constructed railway lines had grown markedly, which stimulated the development of other sectors and accelerated the recovery of the general economy. In 1879, the price index of farm products, the wholesale price index and the consumer price index all began to improve, while M2 money supply also saw a substantial growth. In 1879 and 1880, the GDP growth rate reached 12.55% and 11.87%, respectively. As a result of the price increases, industry and commerce started to flourish and the number of insolvencies and total volume of debts both dropped dramatically. The U.S. economy had quickened its recovery pace. In 1879 and 1880, the poor harvest of the farming industry abroad caused the price of farm products to pick up, bringing new opportunities for the U.S., whose agriculture industry accounted for 90% of the export volume. In 1880, the trade deficit of the U.S. was $169 million, whereas in 1881, this figure became a positive $163 million in the black. Favored by the joint effects of all the above elements, the five year long (1873–1878) deflation in the U.S. finally came to an end.

From the late 1870s to the early 1890s, the U.S. economy had as a whole, maintained an upward development trend owing to continued railway constructions, increased exports of agricultural products and the considerable amount of capital inflow from Europe. However, restrictions of the Gold Standard on money supply still existed. During 1888–1892, the decline of the wholesale price index, the price index of agricultural products and the consumer price index were 11.6%, 8% and 0.87% respectively. By contrast, the GDP growth kept going up. The total volume of debt for the same period increased from $124 million to $190 million. Besides, since 1888, construction of new railway lines had slowed down remarkably. As a whole, the U.S. economy had manifested a downward trend since 1892.

In March 1893, the gold reserves in the U.S. Treasury went below $100 million. Stock prices in the New York Stock Exchange were also sinking dramatically. Foreign investors all started to sell stocks of U.S. enterprises and to purchase gold. $72 million worth of gold flew out of the U.S in 1893. As depositors lost their confidence in the stability of dollars, they queued up to withdraw their deposits. To defuse the effect of the withdrawals and to prevent further risks, banks had to reduce or suspend the granting of loans to industry and commerce. In the same year, 15,200 enterprises in industry and commerce went insolvent with debts totaling $347 million. 450 banks had to close down and the U.S. GDP declined by 8% against the same period in 1892.

After 1893, prices continued to fall: during 1893–1897, the wholesale price index decreased from 78 to 68, the price index of agricultural products dropped from 72 to 60 and the consumer price index fell from 90.7 to 83.5. In spite of the transitory economic upturn in 1895, negative economic growth came back again in 1896. During 1893–1897, the growth range of exports for agricultural products and the lengths of railway lines laid continued to decline for years.

At the beginning of 1897, the U.S. economy was slowly reviving. The discovery of gold mines in South Africa and Alaska had contributed partly to its economic recovery. Gold could now be refined from low grade ores through applying cyanogens reaction technology, as a result of which a sharp increase of gold supply was generated. Money supply increased accordingly, causing the price of farm products and other commodities to rise. A second reason was US's accelerating industrialization process. At the end of the 19th century, industry had become the main economic sector for the U.S. economy. The third reason is the increase in the volume of exports, attributed to the sustained growth of exports of agricultural products. All the above factors worked together to bring the U.S. economy out of the deflation that lasted from 1893 till 1896.

The economic recession that occurred during 1873–1879 in Britain has to a greater degree reflected the influence of a credit crisis. In the 1870s, Britain injected tremendous amount of investments into the U.S. and central Europe, accompanied by the export of a great amount of various industrial products to these countries. In 1873, a general financial panic was triggered as a result of shrinking railway constructions, and this affected the interest rate of Britain through the financial market, causing financial enterprises to adopt stricter credit terms. Consequently, money supply declined. In September 1873, in the light of the slump of the U.S. stock market, the Bank of England discount rate started to rise, reaching 9% on November 7. At the same time, the crisis in the U.S. and central

Europe dealt a heavy blow to the exports of Britain. Export volume of iron, in particular, dropped from 3,958,000 tonnes in 1872 to 2,594,000 tonnes in 1876. In addition, the number of British enterprises that had gone insolvent and the total debts of insolvents increased dramatically. The British wholesale index had been falling from 120 in 1873 to 99 in 1879 (1913 = 100); while GNP decreased by 10.7% against the same period. By 1880, the price index started to recover and the retail product index went up to 103. By then, Britain had finally come out of the economic recession period.

It can be observed from this period of history that as money supply is restricted by the Gold Standard, deflation generated by oversupply of money would be a common phenomenon. It is only under the joint effects of a chronic deflation and abrupt credit crisis that an economic recession occurs.

3.3.2. *1914–1945*

After the outbreak of World War I in 1914, almost every country started to use unconvertible paper notes or to restrict gold exports. From the end of World War I till 1928, many countries switched to the Gold Exchange Standard. That means these countries could fill up the gold reserves of their central banks by converting their currencies (dollars and pounds) to gold. However, due to the impact of the Great Depression in the 1930s, Britain and the U.S. officially suspended the Gold Exchange Standard in 1931 and 1933, respectively. By 1937, the Gold Exchange Standard was almost defunct.

The international transactions of fictitious capital can be traced back to the mid 19th century, when governments of debtor countries including the U.S. and some railway companies issued bonds at fixed interest rate in the financial markets of Britain, France and Germany. However, only until the 1920s did relatively sizable securities investment start to emerge, whereby the economic relations between countries were further strengthened. At that time, exchange rates were exerting a bigger impact on economies.

After the end of World War I, during the period 1918–1920, the GDP of the U.S. showed a sustainable growth and prices kept rising.

To discourage speculations in the stock market, ever since December 30, 1919, the Federal Reserve Bank of New York had raised the discount rate several times. In less than one year, the discount rate had almost doubled. At the same time, money supply fell substantially, resulting in a credit crisis. The increase of interest rates also discouraged investment, and figures for commerce and industries had also been falling since the summer of 1920. The number of insolvencies had increased, prices continued to fall and the unemployment rate was rising. Despite the circumstances, the Federal Government did not increase their governmental expenditure, but instead converted the budget in 1920 from a deficit to a surplus, and this ushered the U.S. economy into recession. After 1922, lowered interest rates stimulated investments. Business and industry began to recover and prices started to go up again. In 1923, the U.S. finally stepped out of the deflationary period, which had lasted for more than two years.

From 1923 to 1928, the U.S. economy thrived. At the beginning of 1928, to curb the speculation activities of the stock market, the Federal Reserve System began to restrict money supply with a view to increasing loan interest rates. During the first half of 1929, the Federal Reserve Committee mandated all Federal Reserve banks to grant only "loans for production" and to suspend loans used for securities speculations. However, this produced the opposite effect as tremendous amounts of banking capital were flushed into the stock market, keeping the stock market strong. By contrast, enterprises were faced with deteriorating problems of capital shortages, which caused manufacturing and construction industries to drastically cut down production. Then came October 24, 1929 — the famous "black Thursday" in history. It was on this very day that the stock market started its significant downward plunge, losing $25 billion of capitalization in less than three months, which exceeded the total net income of the whole U.S. economy. The collapse of the stock market caused the insolvency of numerous banks and triggered a general financial panic. With the runs made by the public on the banks, the Great Depression which lasted four years in U.S. history, thus began.

During 1929–1933, prices in the U.S. dropped by 32%, investment decreased by 91%, the stock market went down by 27%, the number of banks shrunk by 42%, actual consumption fell by 19% and actual GNP declined by 30%.[6] The unemployment rate had been rising dramatically since 1930, reaching up to 18.3% on average. The incomes of employed workers fell even faster than prices. From 1930 till 1933, M2 money supply registered negative growths for four consecutive years, averaging at –8.7% annually. In 1933, the ratio of currency held by the public to total deposits was 2.1 times the figure in 1930.

When President Roosevelt took office on June 3, 1933, he made a series of policies to stimulate economic recovery. The Agriculture Adjustment Administration, the National Industrial Recovery Act, the Federal Securities Act, the Glass-Stegall Act of 1933, the Securities and Exchange Commission, and the National Labor Relations Act, etc. were promulgated or enacted, as the case may be. The U.S. Government also set up a series of federal funded institutions to increase various loans, such as reconstruction financial companies and housing loan companies, etc. In addition, it also increased the exchange rate of gold to the dollar from $20.67 to $35 per oz, which substantially raised money supply and enabled M2 money supply to grow from 1934, and an average growth rate of 9.1% was achieved during the 1934–1937 period. The producer price index and consumer price index started to rebound; so did the GDP. From 1934 till 1936, the annual growth rate averaged 13%, thus bringing the U.S. out of the most severe economic recession in history.

The prolonged deflation that occurred in Britain from 1920 till 1933 was caused by the British government's attempts to resume the Gold Standard. During 1918–1920, Britain's economy maintained a sustainable growth. However, the British government switched to restrictive monetary policies in an effort to regain the price/value of the pound. As a result, money supply, price levels and GDP saw a protracted decline from 1921, resulting in a three year long economic contraction. When Britain resumed the Gold Standard in 1925, the overvalued pound had a serious impact on exports, leading to a huge trade deficit. At the same time, to prevent capital outflow, the British government resorted to a high interest rate policy, giving another devastating blow to economic development, and again pushing the

British economy into recession. In 1931, Britain was forced to abandon the Gold Standard, an act which brought about significant depreciation of the pound, and together with the British government's protectionist trade policies, this finally brought Britain out of the chronic economic recession.

The two deflations experienced by France at the beginning of the 20th century (1921–1922 and 1931–1936) are to a great extent caused by external factors. In 1920, under pressure from Britain and the U.S., the French government adopted tight monetary policies to hold back the depreciation of the Franc, leading to the decline of money supply. Prices had dropped in both 1921 and 1922, resulting in a transitory or short–term economic contraction. Fortunately, the French government took timely steps to stop the depreciation of the Franc and to lower interest rates, allowing its economy to gradually rebound. During 1923–1930, although the French government had adopted a package of policies including stabilizing exchange rates, balancing the budget and raising interest rates, prices sustained an upward trend as a consequence of the increase of net capital inflow and national income. In 1931, the depreciation of the English pound and the U.S. dollar, as well as the decline of prices in the international market — all these assisted in lifting up the value of the Franc and cutting down exports. Furthermore, the French people rushed to buy bank drafts from the Central Bank of France, resulting in the decline of the money supply. Consequently deflation occurred and prices went down continuously. France then faced a six-year economic recession. To increase money supply and stimulate demand, the French government adopted various measures including depreciating the Franc, prohibiting individuals from purchasing gold and purchasing bulk amount of T-Bills so as to push up prices. From 1937, the French economy started to revive.

One could discern from this period of history that the limits on money supply from gold reserves had gradually ebbed away. By contrast, interest rates and exchange rates had become more influential, and governments began to take greater interventionist measures to manage the economy. However, economic recession could only be avoided or its severity reduced if governments adopt sound fiscal and monetary policies, a healthy and solid financial system is in place and people have confidence in the economy.

After the outbreak of World War II, economies of various countries were turned into 'war economies' and accordingly, deflation was totally absent. Because of this, some economists considered that the war had favored Roosevelt's New Deal, rehabilitating the U.S. economy and triggering rapid economic growth.

3.3.3. *Post-1945*

The Great Depression of the 1930s and the outbreak of World War II jeopardized the globalization process of the financial market. At the end of World War II, mainland Europe was totally devastated by the war, and the economy had to be revived by injecting tremendous amounts of capital. At this juncture, the U.S. introduced the "Marshall Plan" ("the Plan") to help Europe get back on its feet. However, the attendant conditions for freedom of international trade and international payment that came along with the Plan paved the way for U.S. capital to directly enter the European Market. Propelled by the subsequent Bretton Woods Agreement and the General Agreement on Tariffs and Trade, the international financial market slowly came into being. Globalization of the financial market at the time steered capital to better performing industries within the international arena, thus substantially increasing capital utilization. Simultaneously a new financial market took shape in the form of the foreign exchange market. Futures exchange activities were becoming more fictitious. That meant the purchase of futures became a means for speculation. Since the 1960s, futures exchange activities covered transactions in stock, bonds, foreign exchange as well as other financial products.

After World War II, the minimum dollar price for foreign central banks to purchase or sell gold was set by the U.S. government. In 1958, it was stipulated in major European countries that for international payment, each country could convert its own currency to gold or dollars. However in 1971, the U.S. suspended the free conversion of dollars at a fixed price (35 dollars for each ounce of gold). Since then, the international monetary system was merely based on dollars and other paper notes, and the obligatory role of gold in the world currency conversion came to an end. Currency has been totally "de-linked" from gold since it could no longer be converted into gold at a fixed price. Henceforth, currency can only be issued based on the total credits of that country, signaling that currency has developed into fiat money. This change has significantly increased the fictitiousness of currency.

In the international monetary system, despite the obligatory function of gold having come to an end in the 1970s, it is still the most reliable reserve asset. Therefore, 45% of the world's gold reserves are held by various governments and central banks, and used as an internationally recognized medium of payment.

With the emergence of the floating exchange rate, advances in financial innovation, rapid development of information technology, increase of financial freedom and the development of economic globalization as a result of the suspension of the Gold Standard, the world financial industries have become more integrated. The financial markets in individual countries are now more closely associated with the international financial market and they are influencing each other to a greater extent. The advance of fictitious capital has been rising substantially in the financial market with increasing capital flows, creating a constant increase of the scale of the fictitious economy.

Under the "multiplier effect", currently the total scale of the global fictitious economy has far exceeded that of the entity or real economy. According to some preliminary statistics that I have collected, the gross global fictitious economic volume by the end of 2000 had reached $160,000 billion, of which stock capitalization and bonds outstanding amounted to $65,000 billion, while financial derivative instruments OTC transactions amounted to around $95,000 billion. However, the sum of the GNPs of all the countries for that year only totalled approximately $30,000 billion. That is to say, at the end of 2000 the scale of the fictitious economy was five times that of the entity economy. The daily flow volume of global fictitious capital has reached beyond $1,500 billion or 50 times that of the actual global daily trade volume. In other words, only 2% of the world's working capital is used for international trade, while the rest is used for income generating activities in the financial markets. It is foreseeable that, with the development of e-commerce and e-currency, the scale of the fictitious economy will further expand.[8]

From the end of World War II till the beginning of the 1970s, all countries were busy rejuvenating their economies. The U.S. was also enjoying sustainable economic growth. During 1949–1974, the wholesale price index in the U.S. increased by 1.4%. The occurrence of deflation was unlikely.

After 1971, as money supply totally freed itself from the restrictions of gold reserves, governments could ensure money supply by increasing the printing of paper notes. In addition, as the world was relatively at peace, many nations were taking all kinds of measures to propel their economic development. So the aggregate price level manifested an upward trend for most of the time. However, the defeat in the Vietnam War and the failings of the grandiose "Great Society Plan" caused severe inflation in the U.S., which further led to the economic recession in 1973–1975.

Since the 1980s, the world has as a whole maintained economic growth. During this period, chronic deflation has been very rare. The only event worth our attention is the deflation that occurred in Japan in the 1990s. After 1991, with the collapse of the bubble economy, the economic growth rate of Japan kept falling until it entered into a prolonged economic recession. Since 1992, the wholesale price index of Japan had maintained a downward trend, and this trend became even clearer after 1998. In 1997 and 1998, Japan suffered from negative economic growth. The average annual growth rate of M2 money supply dropped from 11.8% at the end of the 1980s to below 4% by the end of the 1990s. Unemployment rate had been rising continuously, reaching 4.7% in 1999, and hitting a historical high since the two world wars. Since 1998, the Japanese government had taken various measures in attempts to stimulate the economy and improve the economic structure. However, little result had been achieved in this regard.

After the 1990s, there was a prolonged decrease of the inflation rate (disinflation) in a number of countries. Starting from the third quarter of 1997, China, Singapore, Sweden, Switzerland and many other countries were struck by deflation one after another. At the same time, the disparity between the actual world output and potential output has reached a historical high since the 1930s. The deflation of post-1971 took place when the fictitious economy was developing dramatically and currency was becoming increasingly fictitious. Its causes are different from that of the previous two stages. In this paper, this type of deflation is defined as modern deflation and I am going to further explore its causes and consequences.

3.4. Causes and Consequences of Modern Deflation

The causes for deflation are complicated — requiring more extensive and in-depth research work — but there has been no general academic consensus so far.

The earliest person to systematically study deflation is the U.S. economist, Irving Fisher. When he was studying the Great Depression in 1929–1933, he advocated that the initial excessive debt and the subsequent deflation were the two major variables. When the equilibrium in economic system was destroyed by excessive debts, the liquidity of debt will trigger the following nine chain reactions assuming there were no other contributors factors affecting price: (1) cheap sale of assets; (2) shrinking saving deposits and slowing circulation; (3) falling prices; (4) accelerating corporate insolvencies; (5) lowered profits; (6) contraction of industry and commerce; (7) spread of pessimism and loss of confidence; (8) further drop of currency circulation and; (9) rise of real interest rate concomitant with drop in nominal interest rate.

These nine steps of chain reactions do not necessarily follow the chronological order they have been listed: there will exist some other reactions of which certain individual steps might be repeated. Except for the first and the last reaction or step in the logical sequence (debt and its interest rate), all other changes stem from falling of prices. It is also note-worthy that the decline in cash supply, savings and the speed of circulation of money also has a direct impact on the decline of the transaction volume.

Excessive debt will lead to deflation, and deflation will in turn raise the actual scale of outstanding debt. When excessive debts exceed the threshold scale, the more the debtors pay back, the more debts they owe, thus creating a vicious cycle. For example in the case of U.S., the Great Depression begun in 1929, by September 1933, as the aggregate price level dropped by an accumulated 75%, the real debts had actually increased by 40% [(100% – 20%) × (100% + 75%) – 100% = 40%] even though the liquidation of debt has lessened 20% of the nominal debt volume. Under such circumstances, output and real income would drop sharply and continuously, adding more instability to the economy.

From Fisher's point of view, (1) if deflation is not generated by excessive debt, it will be less destructive; (2) if the decline of price levels triggered by excessive debt is averted by inflation, the fluctuations of the economic variables will be leveled off; and (3) if excessive debts do not reach the threshold scale, economic equilibrium will be attained through fluctuations.

Amid the initial conditions for producing excessive debt, the most common one seems to be the availability of extraordinary or unusual investment opportunities that could make substantial profits. Low interest rates, however, are the biggest contributor for excessive debt. Compared with non-production debt bubbles, debt bubbles resulting from dabbling in new profitable investment opportunities will grow bigger and faster. The psychological elements that have trapped the public into the vicious debt circle include: (1) high returns in the long term; (2) big profits in the short term; (3) imprudent investment decisions; and (4) people becoming credulous of fraudsters.

The school of monetarists headed by Friedman M. claims that currency supply is the main determinant of economic activities, and that currency volume exerts a profound impact on economic activities and price levels. Therefore, the best method to achieve the objective of monetary policy is to set up the objectives for the growth rate of money supply. According to the following formula, [Currency stock × Speed of money circulation = Price × Gross production Output]. In the long run the fluctuation of money stock is normally greater than the speed of money circulation (total expenditure/money stock), and it determines the future speed of money circulation. Nevertheless, the gross production output is mainly determined by non-monetary elements. Therefore, the fluctuation of money stock is correlated with the price level. Since inflation is caused by the expansion of money supply, it can be reversed by moderate control of the money supply. Friedman has reiterated that "inflation is a monetary phenomenon no matter where it occurs and when it occurs." As the counterpart for inflation, deflation's main cause is undersupply of money. Friedman believes the volume of money supply is controlled mainly by monetary authorities extraneous to the economic system. In this sense, money supply is exogenous. For instance, the excessive and prolonged tight monetary policy of the central bank will generate a decline of money supply and represents a failure to meet the needs of development of the entity economy. As spending declines causing supply to outstrip demand, the aggregate price level will also go down.[9–10,5]

Friedman's theory was supported by relevant monetary statistics in the U.S. prior to the 1970s. However, with the abolishment of the Gold Standard, development of financial innovation and the continuous globalization of the financial market, this theory has met with more and more challenges. For example, Tobin J.[11] believes that currency is endogenous. The volume of currency is jointly determined by the monetary authority, commercial banks and non-banking financial institutions within the economic system rather than being directly controlled by the monetary authority itself. Deflation caused by short supply of currency due to increase of the currency value created by the endogenous elements of an entity economy is called endogenous deflation. For example, if the supply of commodities and services expand due to technological development and institutional innovation until it exceeds demand, a surplus will be created and the aggregate price level will go down.

In recent years, the mainstream views from international economic circles have emphasized and analyzed the causes for deflation mainly from the supply side. They assert that accelerating globalization, technological progress and high investment rate, etc., have generated a global production surplus, thus creating deflation.

Shilling A. G.[12] cites 14 forces that lead to deflation — basing mainly on the U.S. situations:

1. End of the cold war led to global cuts in defense spending.
2. Major-country government spending and deficits are shrinking.
3. Central banks continue to fight the last war — inflation.
4. G-7 retirements lead to reduced benefits and slower growth in incomes and spending.
5. Restructuring continues in English-speaking lands and will spread.
6. Technology cuts costs and promotes productivity.
7. The internet increases competition and slashes prices.
8. Mass distribution to consumers reduces costs and prices.
9. Ongoing deregulation cuts prices.
10. Global sourcing of goods and services curtails costs.
11. The spreading of market economies increases supply.
12. The dollar will continue to strengthen.
13. The Asian Contagion will intensify global glut and reduce worldwide prices.
14. U.S. Consumers will switch from borrowing and spending to saving.

A year later, Shilling again preached his major points of view and clearly pointed out that deflation is unavoidable. A global deflation has begun and the above deflationary forces will be enough to put the world into long term deflation.[6]

Although depression has not arrived, Krugman[13] already sees the return to the stage of depression economics, which studies world economic depressions. He highlighted the deflation in Japan in the 1990s, believing that apart from contributing factors from the supply side, elements from the demand side should also be taken into consideration. Reasons for insufficient demand vary with the national system, stage of economic development and social conventions, etc. For the Japanese economy, its slow population growth and the sharply reduced labor force resulting from emigration have devastated expected corporate returns and, in consequence, enterprises were unwilling to expand their domestic investments. In the early 1990s, the collapse of the Japanese bubble economy discouraged corporate investments and led to a lower expected income of the public, which further accelerated the falling of aggregate demand and ultimately bringing about deflation. Krugman believes that in a slightly inflationary environment, price decline is not a result of high price, but a consequence of the low expected price or high nominal interest rate. He points out, the Japanese economy was pushed into a "liquidity trap", allowing for a negative actual real interest rate where savings and investment are sufficient to keep employment rate high. That means the public will have higher expectations for the future than for the present. So, even if the nominal interest rate is lowered to zero, saving would still be more desirable than investment. In such a case, there is nothing monetary policies can do to curb deflation; deflation should be allowed to take its course — though it led to a protracted Japanese economic recession.

With insufficient information from the capital market, people who are expected to receive increased incomes are restricted by capital liquidity. The consumer loans they obtain cannot offset the increased savings from people with lowered incomes, leading to a rise in savings and causing a real interest rate lower than that obtained under complete market oriented conditions. This will create conditions for a "liquidity trap".

In Krugman's opinion, even if the capital can be completely liquidated, as the degree and extent of integration level of the commodities and the labor markets is limited, the opportunities for the public to convert their savings into better investments abroad under the low interest rate regime are restricted. Besides, since many labor intensive industries have fairly low tradability, savings will not be significantly reduced through investing abroad. Thus, capital export cannot totally rectify the "liquidity trap" problem.

I would like to stress the following three points in discussing the causes of modern deflation:

The first point is the complexity of the monetary system. The monetary system is a subsystem of the financial system. According to complexity science,[14] the monetary system is a complex system comprised of various relevant agents, including individuals, enterprises and banks, etc. Each agent is not only the payee of currency, but also the payer. Although each agent independently controls its actions based on certain rules and its expectation for the future, its actions are certainly influenced by the decisions of other agents and the environment. The interaction, influence and effect between agents will generate a self-organizing effect and create a systematic level structure and functional structure, allowing the system to evolve towards a certain direction. Deflation is an indication of the self organizing effect. Monetary system is an open system and it is closely associated with the external environment. When the external environment changes, it will bring about changes in the behaviors of various agents and also changes to the organization through their interactions, pushing the system structure to adapt to the changed environment. The monetary system also manifests the dissipative structure in the metastable state, which has to be stabilized by the continuous money throughput with the environment.

The second point is the fictitious nature of credit currency. With the suspension of the Gold Standard and development of the credit system, currency has turned into unconvertible credit currency with a greater variety and increasingly expanding size and volume. Apparently, it has become increasingly more fictitious in character. As credit currency is guaranteed by the government, banks or corporate credit, if people start to lose confidence in them, a credit crisis will result. As a consequence, depositors will draw their deposit and cash out the commercial notes to increase cash holdings or purchase government bonds, which will in turn lead to a decline of money supply or even deflation. Even for the paper notes that are guaranteed by the national governments, they too are to some extent fictitious and their real value will decrease if the government decides to issue more paper notes or announce the depreciation of the country's currency. Credit crisis generated by the fictitious nature of currency will not only generate deflation, but also can result in a protracted deflation leading to economic recession.

The third point is the self-strengthening or self-increasing nature of deflation. Although deflation is a monetary phenomenon it falls into the fictitious economic category. It is also closely associated with entity economy. Since fictitious economy both originates from and relies on the entity economic system, risks engendered in the entity economy, such as overstock and enterprise insolvency, etc., will be passed on to the fictitious economic system, spurring dramatic changes of the fictitious economy. Risks occurring in the fictitious economic system, such as the dramatic fall of stock index, collapse of real property prices, considerable amounts of non-performing loans, and substantial depreciation of currency, etc., will also seriously affect the entity economy.[7] My view is that the cause and effect of deflation are not only bi-directional; they interact in ways that one responds or reacts positively to the other, thus making deflation self-strengthening.

In a monetary system, people earn money through labor and investment returns and pay out money through consumption, depositing and investment. The proportion of the income that goes to consumption is the real spending power. Depositing is to save money for future consumption, which is also a low risk, indirect investment. In contrast, direct investment is a means to seek profit with comparatively bigger risks. People's income distribution structure is influenced by historical customs and conventions, social systems, income level and personal preferences, etc. The most important factor, however, is the people's expectation for future income. When people do not have good expectations of their future income (for instance, there is economic recession and the stock market is going down, etc.), they tend to increase saving and reduce spending and investment, leading to the decrease of the demand and supply. Due to the buffering effect of inventory, demand will decrease more or faster than supply, thus bringing down the aggregate price level and generating deflation. If people expect that the future price level will go down, they will try to defer or delay current spending, thus contributing to deflation. If people's desire for immediate spending becomes extremely low, a "liquidity trap" might emerge. Under such a scenario, even when the nominal interest rate drops to zero, it is still difficult to motivate spending and deposits in banks will keep increasing.

Business enterprises are mainly engaged in production, circulation, trade and other entity economic activities. They not only receive money through selling their products and financing activities, but also give money away through purchasing raw and production materials, paying workers, repaying loans, distributing dividends, depositing and paying taxes. When an enterprise cuts its operating cost through technological progress and efficient management, it could reduce the price of its products because of lower cost or competition. This phenomenon contributes to deflation. When enterprises have negative expectations of the future (for example, excessive products supply and increase of interest rate, etc.), they tend to reduce production volume and retrench employees and, in the end, cut price in order to reduce inventory stock. This will normally push down the aggregate price level and bring in deflation.

Banks are mainly engaged in depositing, credit and other fictitious economic activities. They obtain money through taking in deposits and repayment of loans, and then they utilize the money so obtained in extending loans and paying interest. When banks have low expectations of the economic prospects (such as economic recession and credit crunch, etc.), they will increase interest rate and impose stricter loan terms, which will eventually cause a situation of tight money supply and deflation.

The interactions between the abovementioned agents are often synergistic. The actions they take when they do not have good expectations of the future reinforce each other. For instance, when people's purchasing power weakens and the interest rate is increased, business enterprises will cut down price to reduce inventory in order to minimize working capital. However, lower prices will make people delay their purchase and wait for even lower price, which in turn forces enterprises to further reduce their prices. Another reason is that the increase of unemployment rate will reduce people's income in general, forcing people to save more. This will further weaken consumers' purchasing power. When enterprises receive lower profits because of price cuts, they will experience operational difficulties or could even go insolvent. At the same time, banks' performance will deteriorate due to the decrease of loan applications and increase of non-performing loans. As a result, people's confidence in banks will suffer and they might rush to the banks to withdraw their deposits, creating a shortage of money supply. When things get worse, this could even spark off runs on banks and lead to more insolvencies.

The influence of the capital market on deflation manifests itself in two aspects. First, when the price starts to decrease while the stock market is still booming, part of the money supply will be diverted to weaken the stimulating effect on demand, thus fueling deflation. The other aspect is that when the stock market is at a continuous downturn, people will cut down spending due to the contraction of wealth and shift from investment to saving, which will also generate deflation. History has proven that, when there is long term or medium term deflation, the stock markets are likely to fall.

Under the market economy, the Central Bank and the Chinese Government are supposed to stay out of the monetary system and adopt various policies to influence the agents of the monetary system to enable its self organizing effect to adapt to the changes of the environment. For instance, the Central Bank could utilize the three monetary policy instruments viz. re-discounts, open market operations and reserves system to apply macro-control on the monetary market. It can also influence the self organizing function of the monetary system by issuing more paper notes in line with the government's money issuing system. The Government can exact an influence on the operations of the entity economy and further affect the self organizing function of the monetary system by changing taxation rates, and by increasing or reducing government expenditure.

3.5. Emergence and Features of Deflations in China

Although academic opinions differ on definition and classification criteria of deflation, the protracted decline of China's aggregate price level is an obvious fact. Please see Fig. 3.1 for the fluctuations of China's Consumer Price Indices from 1997 to 2001.

In accordance with the classification standard/criteria proposed in this paper, the most recent deflation in China began in June 1997 and ended in September 2000. During this period, which lasted for

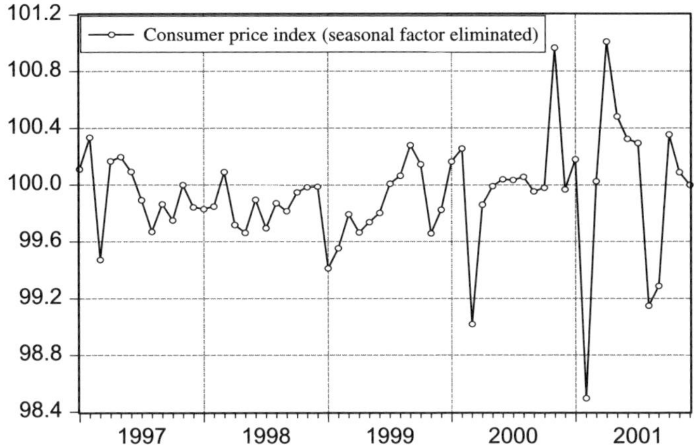

Fig. 3.1 Chain Consumer Price Indices (excluding seasonal factors).

40 months, the aggregate price level for 32 months was lower than 100%. From the statistics, it would appear that China had averted deflation, but some underlying factors of deflation still existed. Deflation could make a come-back. In this regard, it will be of great significance to scrutinize the causes and the special circumstance and background of this deflation, and to summarize the experience and lessons learned in combating inflation for both theoretical and practical purposes.

Generally, the factors contributing to this deflation could be summarized as follows:

(1) Insufficient effective social demand:[15,16] on this view China's deflation falls into the category of endogenous deflation caused by decrease of currency volume as a result of insufficient effective social demand. The reason for this decrease is that the entity economic phenomenon including decline of industrial production growth, lower business profitability and increasing unemployment rate, etc., have rapidly eroded the expectation of domestic manufacturers and consumers for the future. As a result, business enterprises were less willing to invest, production investment shrunk, people were more inclined to save and the retail volume

for social consumptions dropped remarkably. Investment products and the consumables market entered into a period of stagnation, and the aggregate price level was further brought down, creating an inertial operation with the interaction between deflation and an accelerating economic slowdown. Presently, the underlying reason for the decline in aggregate demand is the hold-up or 'stand-off' of various economic indicators in the economic processes including income, savings, investment and consumption, etc., in adapting to the financing system, the organic structure of industrial capital, the dual economic structure in urban and country, patterns of consumption and so on.

(2) Inadequate private investment[17–18]: some people think the major determinant of the deflation in China is the institutional "credit crunch" and the subsequent falling social (private) investment demand. The key element that generates "credit crunch" in the aggregate economy is not the tight monetary policy, but a series of economic micro-structural factors. For example, the performance of SOEs is deteriorating and banks could not afford giving out more non-performing loans. In addition, credit policy discrimination on private investment of state–owned banks blocked the borrowing channels for SMEs. The government's strategy of stimulating the economy by expanding governmental investments is proving to bring little effect. Lagging private investments became the underlying factor which underscored the efforts to reverse the economic downturn. The fundamental reason for the lack of private investment is the impact of institutional contraction. This means to say, when the government is adopting expansionist fiscal policy to reverse the economic downturn, it has also made some centralizing and administrative arrangement and measures to minimize risks, resulting in the co-existence of the instrumental expansion of macro policy and institutional contraction. This has, to a great extent, offset the effect of the expansionist policies and created certain new distortions of the real situation.

(3) External impact: proponents of this school reckon that the deflation in China originated from the impact of external factors.

Reckless investments and repetitive or redundant constructions during 1992–1993 had exacerbated relative production capacity surplus, thus creating conditions for the emergence of deflation in China's economy — objectively speaking. Due to China's high dependence on the world economy, the worldwide economic crisis and deflation exerted a serious impact on China's economy. This impact first generated an immediate fall in export volume. With the decline of external demand, enterprises have to dump their products onto the domestic market. This further dampened the domestic market, which was already suffering from serious market surplus. The external impact also led to the decline of foreign direct investments, weakening the adjustment capacity of China's economic structure. The export decline also led to a reduction of the base currency for purchase of foreign exchange, resulting in an endogenous tightening of currency supply in circulation. In conclusion, the present deflation can be classified as "imported" deflation.

(4) Production capacity surplus:[19] some people believe that production capacity surplus is the primary cause for the deflation in China. Presently, China's real economic growth rate has gone much lower than its growth increase trend, and the expansion of the production gap has led to the idleness of tremendous amount of social production capacity. Reckless investment and repetitive constructions are the underlying reasons for the production capacity surplus.

(5) Insufficient money supply:[20] the underlying idea behind this concept is, since 1993, the time lag effect of the five-year long restrictive monetary and fiscal policies, as well as the restrictive policy in 1998, especially from the banking sector, caused the over-exercise or implementation of restrictive policies and decline of money supply, which, as a consequence, caused the emergence and growth of the deflation of 1998.

(6) Excessive debts:[21] On this view, the deflation in China is caused by excessive debts accumulated from the long-term low performance of the SOEs. With the enhanced regulation on financial institutions and restrictions on banks' credit give-out, low performing SOEs can no longer receive loans, and this put them into

> even worse operational difficulties. Increased risks for bank loans, increase of non-performing assets and decline of interest rates combine to force banks to become more prudent in paying out capital. At the same time, product capacity surplus generated by low performing repetitive investments, brought the aggregate price level further down and reduced the profit of SOEs. The pressure for repaying principal and interest had grown and SOEs were faced with an operational predicament. As the aggregate price level dropped, the real interest rate increased, and so did the enterprises' debt ratio. In addition, the financial liquidity pressure for enterprises further added up to their operational difficulties. Consequently an endogenous and self-intensifying deflation was created.

Some of the views expressed above do make sense in some aspects. China's deflation not only shares common features with other countries, but also features China's own characteristics. In my opinion, China's deflation occurs in the context of its special situation or background as expressed in the following five aspects:

(1) The deflation in China took place during its transition period. In 1992, Deng Xiaoping proposed the grand concept of constructing a socialist market economy, urging China to transform from the traditional planned economy to a market economy. In 1997, this transformation was still at its inception, characterized by the sustained influence of the old system, unchanged government functions, relatively weak market strength, poor performing SOEs, low growth of fiscal income, slow financial reforms and a newly established capital market. All these institutional elements contribute to the deflation in China.

(2) Deflation arrived in China shortly after China curbed inflation. In response to the expanding inflation between 1992 and 1995, the government adopted restrictive fiscal and monetary policies, and achieved some good results by successfully delivering an economic "soft-landing". However, due to the policy inertia and time lag (policies take time to implement), negative influences emerged, catalysing deflation.

(3) Deflation in China began during the outbreak of the Asian Financial Crisis. Since July 1997, the financial crisis that began in Thailand quickly spread to other countries and regions in East Asia, bringing devastating impacts. After weighing the pros and cons the Chinese government adopted a package of policies in a timely manner — for instance, announcing that the Yuan would not depreciate. Despite China not being directly affected by the crisis, the international environment and domestic countermeasures taken at the time favored the emergence of deflation.

(4) China's deflation occurred during the intensification of its reforms. After more than ten years of reform, China has seen significant development of the economy and continuous improvement of people's living standard. In 1997, China's reforms entered the breakthrough stage and most reform measures that are beneficial to the general public have been basically implemented. As the reform goes further, some adjustments have to be made regarding vested interests and people are required to sacrifice their short-term interests for the long–term interests. All these add up to the uncertainties of the expectation for future income. This, together with the undeveloped social security system, helps to encourage people to cut down on spending, ultimately ushering in deflation.

(5) Deflation emerged when the economy was still growing. Ever since its reform and opening up, China economy has enjoyed a concerted and continuous economic growth. Between 1978 and 1997, China's annual GDP grew by 9.8%, about three times the world average for the same period. During the deflationary period, the years 1998, 1999 and 2000 still saw growth rates of 7.8%, 7.2% and 8.3% respectively. For this reason, some people claim that deflation did not happen in China at all. However, it is this very characteristic of China that we should pay our due attention to while studying the deflation in China.

We shall now use a combination of qualitative and quantitative methods to further discuss the causes for deflation in China.

3.5.1. *Lagging Demand is the Main Cause of China's Deflation*

Since the reform and opening up, China has seen concerted economic growth and continuous improvement of people's income level. However, society's growth of aggregate demand has fallen behind that of the aggregate supply, which I believe, is the main reason for China's deflation. My analysis covers the following four aspects:

3.5.1.1. *Income growth is way lower than economic growth*

According to my calculations from the statistics, the average growth rate for China's GDP from 1988 till 1997 is 8.6%, whereas the growth rate for the annual disposal income for urban and rural residents averages at 5.5% and 3.0% respectively. This shows the aggregate demand growth is lagging far behind the aggregate supply growth. China has switched from an economy of shortages to a buyer's market, where supply of goods is growing significantly. This could lead to deflation.

3.5.1.2. *Priority for saving rather than for spending*

In China, saving is a traditionally ingrained behavior and people count on saving to achieve financial security for their family and descendants. With the increase of income, the proportion of income that goes to consumption in the income structure has gradually come down. According to a sample survey,[22] in 1990, per capita surplus for urban and rural residents (difference between income and spending) was 243.9 Yuan and 199.54 Yuan respectively. By 2000, this figure had climbed to 1,318.81 Yuan and 732.79 Yuan respectively. Most of this surplus was put into savings. From 1990 till 1997, the total balance amount held on deposit for China at the end of the year for urban and rural residents increased from 711,980,000 Yuan to 4,627,980,000 Yuan, with an annual growth rate of 26.4%. With the intensifying of reforms in SOEs, housing, medical service and education, etc., people are faced with more economic pressures. What is more, their expected incomes do not look very promising. Therefore, people tend to cut down on immediate or current spending to increase savings. In rural areas in particular, Chinese peasants have always been small producers with unstable expected income and they are more vulnerable to risks and are highly security-minded. Therefore, they tend to save rather than spend. This is especially the case when the price is decreasing, as people expect the price to go even lower and delay immediate spending or consumption.

3.5.1.3. *Unequal distribution of income has weakened the aggregate purchasing power*

With the rapid development of China's economy and the transformation of the economic system, income gaps between residents of different regions have widened. Ratio of the consumption level between the urban and rural residents has grown from 3.0 in 1990 to 3.5 in 1999, and the Gini coefficient, which is used to measure the difference in income distribution, has increased from 0.30 in 1988 to 0.47 in 1997. (In my proposition, the Gini coefficient is calculated separately for urban and rural areas to better accord with the dual economic structure of China). In 1997, the percentages of residents in rural areas whose per capita falls into the range of less than 3,000 Yuan, 3,000–5,000 Yuan and above 5,000 Yuan, against the total number of rural residents are 79.88%, 15.18% and 4.94% respectively.[23] Some empirical studies have proved that low income residents have a relatively higher tendency for spending than saving. In contrast, high income residents tend to save more and spend less. As the purchasing power of the low income residents in urban and rural areas is fairly weak, and the small number of high income residents has a relatively lower consumption tendency, taken as a whole the overall purchasing power of the urban and rural areas will be weakened by the increasing gap in income distribution.

3.5.1.4. *Supply structure has not adapted to the changing demand structure*

With the income growth of the urban and rural residents, the Engel's coefficient (proportion of income that goes into food) dropped from 54.2 and 58.8 in 1990 to 39.2 and 49.1 in 2000. Ownership of consumer durables was also rapidly improving. In 2000, the number of color TV sets in 100 households was 116.56, refrigerator 80.13, and washing machine 90.52; in rural areas, number of TV sets in 100 households was 101.71, (half being color televisions, with the other half being black and white televisions), refrigerator 12.31, and washing machine 28.58.[22] Earmarked by the planning economy, a great number of Chinese enterprises did not recognize the importance of market research and marketing. They are not very sensitive to the prominent changing demand structure of urban and rural consumers, and they have been slow in product change and updating business information. According to the statistics from relevant departments, the absolute surplus of industrial products has reached 70–80% presently in China. On the other hand, there is still a big shortage of hi-tech products, which we have to rely largely on imports. An example to illustrate the point: with huge oversupply in the textile industry and the protracted price decline of textile products, we are still importing an excess of 6 billon dollars worth of high-end textiles each year. With a high rate of production idleness (in 1998, the idle production capacity was 17.9%), a lot of stock is stuck in warehouses, and goods have to be sold at very low prices. As the supply structure cannot adapt to the demand structure, price has to be slashed down, which will further dampen the spending desires of urban and rural residents and ultimately generate deflation.

3.5.2. *Decline in Private Investment is an Important Precursor for China's Deflation*

As previously discussed, decline of consumption demand will lead to decline of investment demand. However, decrease of investment demand will make it even more difficult to tailor supply structure to consumption needs, and this in turn leads to the decline of consumption demand and deflation.

After the reforms and opening up, in line with the progress of the economic reform, private investment has manifested a concerted growth. Due to its profound impact on optimizing allocation of market resources, adaptation to the consumption needs, improving capital utilization and raising economic vitality, etc., the influence of investment on economic development has become more visible.

Share of private investment in China's GDP has grown from 4.2% at the beginning of the 1980s to 11–12% at the first half of the 1990s.

However, after 1996, while actual investment by the government was increasing continuously, private investments declined dramatically, showing a zero growth or even negative growth. This is in part caused by the fact that the investors' desire for investment is largely determined by their anticipation of the future economy and market performance, or in other words, expectation of the investm ent returns. This expectation is based on consumption demand as well as forecast of the future price levels and interest rates. A stagnant market, price decline, oversupply and income decrease combine to lower the expectation of future economic prospects. As a result, investors became more prudent to risks. The other point is that banks were already burdened with huge amounts of non-performing loans and they anticipated more uncertainties from business enterprises. They are more reluctant to lend, thus creating the "credit crunch". As China's credit policy has always favored SOEs rather than private investments, the impact of credit crunch hit private investment hard, which as a consequence, jeopardized people's investment in private firms. Besides, since Chinese residents invest mainly through the banking system, the stock market is in fact a speculative market for most people rather than an investment channel. That means limited investment channels have also impeded the development of private investments.

Since 1995, governmental investments have seen an upward trend. After 1997 in particular, it enjoyed even bigger growth. The growth rate in 1998 had more than doubled as against the previous year. However, since governmental investments focused on infrastructure constructions under the orders and direction of various levels of government, these investments fueled the demand for production materials, and the payments for labor have mostly been converted into savings with no major effect on increasing spending power at all. Therefore, the declining private investment, being a critical component in the consumption of Chinese residents has become an important contributor to China's deflation.

3.5.3. *The Inertial Effect of Macro-Economic Control Contributed to the Emergence of Deflation*

In my opinion, since the government lacks experience in macro-control in the market economy, it suffers from the inertia effect while setting and implementing macro-control policies. Newton's First Law of Motion (which introduces the concept of inertia) states that "if an object is at rest, it stays at rest; if it is moving, it keeps moving — unless otherwise disturbed by external forces". New economic policies tend to encounter a lot of obstacles when being promulgated and implemented, and normally economic development will progress very slowly during periods of adjustment. During 1992–1995, to combat the deteriorating deflation and prevent an overheated economy, China adopted a tight monetary policy. By 1996, money supply, economic growth rate and price increase had all dropped to a reasonable level. Despite money supply having started to go down from 1995, there was still a great concern that inflation might make a come-back. The monetary policy of 1997, set in force by the Government, still focused on anti-inflation measures and the restrictive monetary policy was carried forward, until it led to a shortage of money supply.

The influence of insufficient money supply on deflation can become aggravated because of the following two factors. One is that the banking sector tried to retain loans to substantially increase the reserve or savings rate. The discrepancy between saving and lending for financial institutions headed by the four commercials banks kept growing, which respectively amounted to 1,028.8 billion Yuan in December 1998, 1,272.6 billion Yuan in December 1999 and 1,369.3 billion Yuan in September 2000. At the end of September 2000, reserves in the Central Bank totalled 1,438.8 billion Yuan, with 737 billion Yuan of excess reserve savings.[24] This has the effect of seriously blocking the channels for transferring savings to spending. The other is that a substantial part of the money supply drifted into the stock market for speculations rather than being channeled into spending and investments.

Another manifestation of policy inertia is the hold-up of the adjustment in nominal interest rate. Nominal interest rate is the sum of real interest rate and inflation rate. Given that nominal interest rate is relatively stable, fast changing inflation rate will definitely lead to greater fluctuations of real interest rate. If inflation rate keeps dropping and the nominal interest rate is not lowered accordingly, consumers will tend to increase savings to enjoy the relatively higher real interest rate, while enterprises will suffer from heavier debt and higher financing cost. All these elements can attribute to deflation. In June 1997, China entered a deflationary period. However, the nominal interest rates for one year deposit and loan at the time still reached 7.47% and 10.08% respectively — which discouraged spending in general, and forced enterprises to get rid of their stocks to repay loans. The result of this was a stagnant aggregate demand. From October 23, 1997 till June 10, 1999, China had lowered its nominal interest rate 5 times. However, owing to the presence of other factors, China's countermeasures taken to reverse deflation have achieved little effects.[25–26]

A third manifestation of policy inertia is that with the slow transformation to the market economic system, some government officials are still intoxicated with pursuing political power, which they still widely use to allocate resources. This has prevented the market from genuinely exerting its fundamental function of resource allocation. The adjustment of China's economic structure has made rather slow headway and the reforms in industries such as telecommunications, electricity and finance, etc., are still struggling. In addition, China is in the economic transition period, and the 'lag or inertial effect' from previous old policies are still affecting investment, consumption and other economic imperatives. Considering that China's financial market is still not very developed, the interest rate is not yet fully driven by the market, and existing financial institutions are still to a great extent under policy oriented and planning oriented management, some policies are adopted for raising money supply and some for stimulating consumption demand, etc., many positive effects or outcomes of economic reforms will be offset by such factors as lagging supply structure and low expectation of the future, etc. In the meantime, the impact of monetary policies on investment will also be diminished by effects of the substitution of labor.[27–29]

3.5.4. *External elements also Partly Attribute to the Emergence of Deflation*

Economic globalization signifies mutual dependence in the true sense of the term. It has strengthened the economic ties between countries to an extent that a slight move by a single party may affect the whole situation. However, while our country is enjoying the benefits of resource exchanges between countries, we must bear corresponding economic risks. From 1995 to 1996, as a result of international trade protectionism rearing its ugly head, the impact of foreign trade on China's economic growth weakened. Although this did not bring about major fluctuations of the macro-economy, it did lead to a downwards trend in the performance of Chinese export-based enterprises. In 1997, as a consequence of the Asian Financial Crisis, net export volume dropped substantially. Between 1995 and 1996, foreign investment stopped growing and even declined slightly in 1997. Decline in foreign trade and foreign investment brought some direct and indirect effects to the domestic economy. In addition, decrease of net export volume, through channels of issue for foreign exchange, will reduce money supply. Nevertheless, based on the results of quantitative analysis, external elements are not the main factors for triggering a prolonged deflationary period.

3.6. Major Countermeasures for Deflation

As a result of the new package of policies from the Chinese government such as expanding fiscal deficit, increasing money supply and lowering interest rate, etc., China has successfully reversed the deflation which lasted from June 1997 till September 2000. However, after September 2000, the threat for deflation had still not completely disappeared. Monthly deflation still emerged from time to time (from October 2000 till March 2002, there were 7 monthly deflations, 1 break-even and 10 monthly inflations, of which 9 were with price index lower than 101%). Based on the analysis of the causes for China's deflation, the following policies and measures are suggested:

3.6.1. *Increase the Incomes of Urban and Rural Residents and Intensify their Spending Power*

As China is currently at the 'reasonably well-off' development stage and transition period, cultivating the spending power of urban and rural residents is not only a critical prerequisite for achieving social stability and sustainable development, but it is also a fundamental measure geared to prevent deflation. The key to cultivating people's spending power is to increase the income of the medium and low income groups.

At present, the low income group in China comprises mainly of laid off workers from SOEs, peasants in the farming industry or regions of poverty as well as poverty stricken urban residents. Appropriate measures need to be taken to increase their income level. A 'minimum standard of living' system for urban residents should be implemented, in which they will be given food coupons and clothing coupons instead of cash allowances. As for laid off employees from SOEs, the government should make a commitment for systemically transforming costs by establishing individual accounts for each laid-off worker with amounts of compensation based on the term of service and rank of the laid off worker concerned. Each month, a certain amount of money can be withdrawn from the account. Those who are not re-employed will also be able to claim unemployment benefits and subsistence allowance. With regards to low income peasants, in addition to reducing taxes to alleviate their burdens, the government also needs to re-adjust the economic structure in order to create more income generating channels.

At present, the middle income groups in China include mainly governmental officials and employees from various state departments and organizations. We need to improve their salaries, allowances from their work units and implement performance-related evaluation system to eliminate illicit income and ultimately achieve an income increase through regulated process. At the same time we should further cut down the number of civil servants and employees of public organizations, and encourage them to independently look out for other jobs in society.

Expanding the scale and scope for granting of loans is also one of the effective measures to increase spending power. Production loans in rural areas should be steadily promoted to cater to the capital demands of rotational agricultural productions. Another proposal is to establish individual credit records in big or medium sized cities to encourage people to take up consumption loans.[30]

3.6.2. *Improve Expectation for the Economic Prospects of Urban and Rural Residents*

Improving the expectations for the economic prospects of urban and rural residents is an essential measure that could stimulate spending and investments. The following support measures should be taken:

Firstly, the government should disclose the long term objectives of economic development and regularly release information on its policies, including monetary objectives and implementation plans[31] in order to improve the transparency, openness and creditability of the Central Bank's monetary policy — to ease out suspicion and stop spreading of rumors from the public. One very good example was that after the outbreak of the Asian financial crisis, our government expeditiously announced that the Yuan would not depreciate, and this effectively prevented a general panic among members of society. In times of deflation, relevant information should be released to allow for rational deflationary expectation from the public to mitigate over-saving and to avoid a 'liquidity trap'.

Secondly, the government should take steps to improve the social security system, which subsumes four levels or strata (social aids, social service, social security and commercial insurance), four component forces (government, society, organizations and individuals) and four aspects (unemployment, pension, medical services and accident insurance). It should formulate and form a rational structure for China's social security system based on the principle of "clearly demarcated scopes, division of responsibilities, mutually complementing each other, reasonable support and share of bearing burdens, different regional treatments and overall balance and equilibrium" in constructing a comparatively stable but dynamic social security system with Chinese characteristics to replace the tendency of urban and rural residents to seek ways to self-security and protection and thereby stimulating current or immediate consumption.

The third step the government could do is to strengthen the protection of consumers' rights, revamp and regulate the market, crack down on fake and inferior or shoddily produced goods and commodities, and safeguard the 'nine consumers' rights' including the Right to Know, Right to transactions at Arm's Length and Right to Recourse when aggrieved, etc., to reduce consumers' worries when purchasing goods — thus promoting the positive development of the consumer market.

3.6.3. *Modify the Supply Structure and Increase Effective Demand*

Adjusting supply structure in line with the changes in the demand structure is an effective way to increase real demand and stimulate spending. New economic growth spots and new economic cyclical periods cannot be created without the supply structure becoming able to adapt to all immediate and current needs of the consumers in terms of product variety, quantity and price, etc., and without possessing the capacity to foresee the future needs of the consumers in advance. That is why we should emphasize technological and system innovations and overcome all obstacles with full conviction and determination to adjust the supply structure.

Adjustment of supply structure should focus on two aspects. On one hand, the government should act out fully its function as the "visible hand" in drawing up structure adjustment plan to resolutely eliminate obsolete and unmarketable products, cut down surplus production capacity, shut down badly managed and poor performing enterprises and restructure inefficient corporations, using various legislative, administrative, economic and disciplinary means.

On the other hand, in order to bring into play the market's "invisible hand", it is imperative to direct enterprises to look for business opportunities during the deflationary situation. Production costs could be lowered by adopting new technology and improving management. Businesses whose market forecasts are unpromising or which are lacking competitiveness should be down-sized or even wound up. New market opportunities are to be sought through market segmentation and demands forecast. Technology oriented products, patent products and feature products should be made and at the same time, core abilities and strengths of the enterprises should continue to be cultivated and closer partnership or strategic alliance established with other enterprises, etc.

3.6.4. *Encourage Private Investment and Development of the Non-State Economy*

Non-state economy, mainly constituted by private investment, is one of the critical components of China's market economy. It has been proven that private investment and governmental investment are inter-dependent and complementary to each other. With the strengthening of investment system reform, private investment will make up the major part of investment. The growth of private investment not only helps to encourage the mushrooming of numerous vitalized private SMEs, but it also promotes the establishment of multiple-shareholding enterprises, thereby accelerating economic development, improving employment rate and alleviating deflationary pressures in China. It is suggested that encouraging private investment should begin from the aspect of market entry, to be followed by presence of fair competition, reducing liabilities or burdens and facilitating financing and protecting the property rights of the investors through legislation. Currently, savings are concentrated in the four state–owned commercial banks, resulting in relatively abundant capital but inadequate loan give-outs. The banks would therefore wish to hold national bonds rather than selling them to the Central Bank. By contrast, small and medium–sized financial institutions have more loan demands, but less funds and capital to pay out. In this regard, I suggest granting more re-loans to the four commercial banks and relaxing the existing restrictive regulations on re-loans for SMEs. Support for re-loans should only be provided to SMEs that enjoy better reputation and performance so that they will become more capable of lending support to the development of private investment and that of the non-state economy.

3.6.5. *Intensity Financial Reform and Improve Banks' Performance*

Credit crunch does not only cause deflation, but is also an important factor leading to economic recession. Under the dominant planning economic system of the past, the four state–owned commercial banks, Industrial and Commercial Bank of China, Agricultural Bank of China, Bank of China and China Construction Bank formed a 'monopoly' — being the "the government cashier" with certain privileges granted by the government. However, with the development of the socialist market economy, institutional and structural contradictions, such as overlap or mix-up of party and government functions, government and corporate functions, lack of incentive system and undeveloped system of legal and corporate personalities — all begin to emerge to affect their operational performance and competitiveness as financial enterprises. In addition, these banks are also overstaffed, with low level of management capability, high ratio of non-performing loans and a constant drain on various kinds of assets, resulting from ineffective macro-supervision, etc., The per capita assets and performance indices are far lower than that of their overseas peers. For instance, according to the annual report of Hang Seng Bank in 2000, its costs only accounted for 24.4% of its income, whereas for China's state–owned banks, this figure ran as high as 90%. The per capita EBITA of Hang Seng was 1,570,000 HKD, several tens of times higher than that of state owned banks; its one–year interest rate was 1.7–2.2%, whereas interest rate from state–owned banks was 3.6%. In accordance with China's pledge after joining the WTO, by December 2006, China's banking sector standards would have to be more in line with international practices, giving the same treatment for both domestic banks and foreign banks. By then, state–owned commercial banks would be confronted with severe challenges. For this reason, we shall have to carry out fundamental reforms to the wholly state–owned commercial banks in line with the spirit put forth in the national conference on financial work with a view to turning state–owned commercial banks into modern financial enterprises with developed governance structure, adequate operational system, clear operational objectives, satisfactory financial performance and relatively strong international competitiveness by continuously improving their operational performance and competitiveness.

To prevent deflation from coming back, it is necessary to improve the performance of commercial banks by carrying forward financial reforms. Therefore, the following measures should be taken:

Firstly, the issue of the banks' non-performing loans must be addressed. One of the factors that attributes to deflation is that non-performing loans ('defunct' currency) have considerably weakened China's money supply. In this regard, we should recall or 'digest' these loans through auction, internal transfer or debt for equity swap, etc., after investigating carefully each case and obtaining verification thereof.

Secondly, steadily and progressively promote the marketization of interest rates. Presently, with the relatively low interest rate in China, commercial banks have become more self-restrained, SOEs' demands for investment in SOEs have declined and the expansionist mechanism for interest rates has been curbed. All these combine to help create a favorable opportunity for the marketization of interest rates. Thus, we should gradually relax restrictions on loan interest and allow commercial banks to fix loan interest by themselves based on the credit-worthiness of the borrowers and credit risks, and at the same time widen the floating range for the interest rate of bank loans. Risk premium should also be decided by the commercial banks themselves. This will not only motivate banks to grant loans, but also favor the implementation of the policy of expanding internal demands.

Thirdly, we must be wary and vigilant against the possible but clandestine flow of bank funds into the stock market. When the aggregate price level and interest rate are both low and the stock market is enjoying good returns, improper bank funds are more likely to flow into the stock market, which will further lead to investment shrinkage and consumption decline for economic entities, resulting in the emergence or deterioration of deflation. The Central bank and China Securities Regulatory Committee should jointly enhance supervision and impose regulations, and should mete out punishment expeditiously and judiciously on violators.

3.6.6. *To Employ and Manage Fiscal and Monetary Policies Flexibly*

Adopting fiscal and monetary policies to address deflation can and does to a certain extent bring some positive effects on the adjustment of the short-term economic situation. However, in the long run, it could worsen the macro-economic balance. For this reason, correct estimation of the impact on macro policies is required, with particular emphasis placed on the appropriate quantitative limitation. In addition, flexible adjustment and control should be the key in preventing deflation and inflation from inter-converting into each other.

As an illustration, despite the fact that expansionary fiscal policies can be effective in the short term, their effects will gradually fade away. If we fail to achieve an overall balance on the basis of economic structural adjustments, disadvantages will outweigh advantages in the long run. Without developing new capital resources, sustainable economic growth cannot be achieved solely by relying on expanding fiscal deficit.

Lowering interest rate may, to some extent, curb deflation. However, when public desire for consumption and investment is too low, a "liquidity trap" will easily emerge and it will be difficult for monetary policy to play an effective role.[32–33] For example, from May 1, 1996 till June 10, 1999, interest rate was lowered seven times but the sum of various saving deposits in the financial institutions, however, still jumped to 15,487.61 billion Yuan at the end of 2001, from 7,603.37 billion Yuan at the end of 1996 (of which savings deposits for urban and rural residents increased from 3,852.08 billion Yuan to 7,376.24 billion Yuan).[34]

As previously discussed, according to complexity science, environmental factors such as policies can only come into play through the self organizing effect of the monetary system itself, and this requires patience on the part of policy makers to wait for the self adjustment of the internal monetary system. On the other hand, we should try to avoid amplifying policy strength and striving for immediate results, as such untoward actions could destroy the self organizing mechanism of the system and bring about opposite effects.

During the establishment and development of China's socialist market economy, we will inevitably encounter various problems that foreign market economies have experienced throughout their development.[35–36] However, as long as we adhere to the theoretical foundations, draw on the experiences of other countries, improve our policy structure and analyze the difficulties in a down-to-earth manner in keeping with modern times, we would be able to gain and accumulate experiences obtained through actual policy implementation and reap good theoretical results that befit the actual conditions prevalent in our nation.[37–40]

References

[1] Encyclopedia Britannica (1998). International Chinese Edition, Encyclopaedia Britannica, Inc.

[2] Stiglitz, J. E. (2000). *Economics*, 2nd Ed., New York: W. W. Norton & Company Inc.

[3] Krugman, P. R. and Obstfeld, M. (1999). *International Economics Theory and Policy*, 4th Ed., Translated by by Hai W., Cai, R., Guo, H. Q., Beijing: Renmin University Press (in Chinese).

[4] Samuelson, P. A. and Nordhaus, W. (1998). *Economics,* 16th ed., New York: McGraw Hill Companies, Inc.

[5] The Encyclopedia of China (Volume of Economics) (1988). Beijing: Encyclopedia Sinica Press.

[6] Shilling, A. G. (1999). *Deflation*, New York: McGraw Hill Companies, Inc.

[7] Cheng, S. W. (1999). Fictitious Economics and Financial Crisis, *Economic Affairs*, 3, 4–9 (in Chinese).

[8] Cheng, S. W. (2001). *China's Economic Reform and Development,* Vol. 1, Beijing: China Renmin University Press (in Chinese).

[9] The New Palgrave Dictionary of Economics (1996). Beijing: Economics Press.

[10] The Encyclopedia of China (public financing, taxation, finance, price) (1993). Beijing: Encyclopedia Sinica Press.

[11] Tobin, J. (1971). *Essays in Economics, Vol. 1: Macroeconomics*, Amsterdam: North-Holland Publishing Co.

[12] Shilling, A. G. (1998). *Deflation*, Short Hills: Lakeview Publishing Co.

[13] Krugman, P. L. (1999). *The Return of Depression Economics*, New York: W. W. Norton & Company, Inc.

[14] Cheng, S. W. (1999). Complexity Science and Management, *Bulletin of the Chinese Academy of Sciences*, 14(3), 175–183 (in Chinese).

[15] Fan, J. P. (1998). New Phenomenon of the Current National Economy: Deflation, *Urban Finance Forum*, 11, 9–12 (in Chinese).

[16] Zhuo, T. Y. (1999). In-depth Obstacles of the Aggregate Demand and its Expansionary Path, *Economic Research Journal*, 1, 9–17 (in Chinese).

[17] Fan, G. (1999). Overcoming Credit Crunch and Reforming Banking System, *Economic Research Journal*, 1, 3–8 (in Chinese).

[18] Macro team of Institute of Economics Chinese Academy of Social Science, Zhang, S. G. (1999). Investment, Cyclical Fluctuation and Institutional Deflationary Effects, *Economic Research Journal*, 3, 16–25 (in Chinese).

[19] Hu, A. G., Wu, Q. G., Shen, B. X. and Cheng, J. S. (2001). *China Challenging Deflation*, Beijing: China Planning Press (in Chinese).

[20] Zeng, L. H. (1999). Monetary Supply Analysis in 1998 and Monetary Growth Interval in 1999, *Economics Information*, 4, 18–21 (in Chinese).

[21] Macro-group of China Economic Research Center of Beijing University (2000). *Studies of Deflation in China: 1988–2000*, Beijing: Peking University Press (in Chinese).

[22] National Bureau of Statistics of China (2001). *China Statistics Yearbook*, Beijing: China Statistics Press (in Chinese).

[23] Cheng, S. W. (2001). Analysis and Exploitation of China's Rural Market. in Cheng S. W. (ed.), *An Analysis of China's Rural Consumer Markets.* Beijing: Democracy and Constructions Press, pp, 1–40 (in Chinese).

[24] Wang, H. C. (2002). Bad Structure of Fund Circulation, *Capital Markets Magazine*, 3, 44–48 (in Chinese).

[25] Xie, P. and Sheng, B. X. (1999). Deflation and Monetary Policies, *Economic Review*, 8, 14–22 (in Chinese).

[26] Yu, X. J. (1999). Analysis of Effectiveness of Monetary Policies in 1998, *Economic Review*, 3, 34–40 (in Chinese).

[27] Topic Team of The Research Bureau of PBOC (1999). Analysis of China's Monetary Policies, *Economic Review*, 3, 26–33 (in Chinese).

[28] Liu, G. D. (1997). *Studies of Monetary Polices During the Transitory Period In China*, Beijing: China Financial Press (in Chinese).

[29] Liu, X. L. (1998). *Studies of Monetary Policies During the Transitory Period In China*, Chengdu: Southwestern University of Finance and Economics Press.

[30] Topic Team of The Research Bureau of PBOC (1999). Major Problems Faced by Chinese Credit Monetary Policies in 1999 and Relevant Suggestions, *Financial Review*, 5, 27–34 (in Chinese).

[31] Chen, P. S. (1997). Asymmetrical Information and Policy Information Disclosure: Analysis of the Influence of China's Monetary Policies, *Economic Research Journal*, 12, 3–32 (in Chinese).

[32] Liu, L. (1999). If China's Economy is Experiencing "Liquidity Trap", *International Finance Review*, 10, 50–55 (in Chinese).

[33] Liu, X. F. (1999). "Japanese trap" and China's Current Macro-Economic Realities, *Economic Review*, 8, 40–47 (in Chinese).

[34] Liu, J. Q. and Guo, Z. F. (2002). Studies of the Relationship Between Savings Rate and Economic Growth of Chinese Residents, *China Soft Science*, 2, 24–27 (in Chinese).

[35] Keynes, J. M. (1936). *The General Theory of Employment, Interest, and Money*, London: Macmillan and Co.

[36] Skene, C. L. (1992). *Cycles of Inflation and Deflation*, Westport, Connecticut, USA: Praeger Publishers.

[37] Liu, S. C. (1999). Deflation: Neither Overlook Nor Overestimate, *Economic Review*, 10, 23–30 (in Chinese).

[38] Zhang, Y. J. (2000). *Theories and Realities of Deflation*, Beijing: China Economic Press (in Chinese).

[39] Luo, Z. Y. (1999). *On Deflation*, Beijing: Economics Press (in Chinese).

[40] Qian, Xiao-an (2000). *On Deflation*, Beijing: The Commercial Press (in Chinese).

Chapter 4

Systematic Analysis and Proposals for Improvement and Modification of China's Stock Market

4.1. Introduction

According to traditional financial theories, the financial market can be classified into capital market and money market by the relevant credit period of either more or less than one year (with the former also being called the medium and long–term capital market and the latter the short–term capital market). Equity financing and debt financing are the two financing methods in the capital market, while debt financing plays a dominant role in the money market. However, with the popularization of mixed operations by financial institutions, improvements in the degree of integration in the international financial market, and the rapid development of financial innovations, the boundaries between the traditional capital market and the money market are becoming blurred.

With the development of capitalistic production and increasing expansion in the size of enterprises, the capital needed for their development and expansion can hardly be furnished by individual capitalists or even several capitalists in partnership. Joint stock companies operated by pooling dispersed money capital through stock offerings started to emerge from the 17th century, and had prevailed in Europe and America by the 19th century. Personal, private capitals were incorporated into social capital through joint stock companies, and this boosted the establishment and development of large capitalist enterprises. Joint stock companies have become the main organizational form for contemporary large enterprises.

Given the necessity of stock purchase and sales, stock exchanges started to emerge in the United Kingdom and the U.S. over the second half of the 18th century, and stock markets were subsequently established in many other countries one after another. With the advent of the 20th century, especially after the Second World War, stock markets witnessed rapid growth across the world. In the last ten years of the 20th century, rapid growth in the world's stock markets hit an unprecedented record. The World Bank statistics[1] indicate that the value of the global stock market totalled US$9.4 trillion in 1990, accounting for 50.7% of the combined GDP of all countries, and this figure surged to US$36 trillion by 2000, accounting for 119% of the combined GDP of all countries. The number of listed companies went up sharply from 25,424 in 1990 to 49,612 in 2000. In developed countries, the stock market is not only a barometer reflecting economic climates, but has become a major driving force for economic development as well as an important factor causing fluctuations in economic ups and downs.

The earliest stocks (shares) of China were issued by the Shipping Merchants Bureau established in 1873, while the Chinese Stock Exchange dates back to the early 20th century. In 1914, The 'Northern Government' of the Qing Dynasty enacted the Stock Exchange Law and established the Beijing Stock Exchange in 1917. The stock market of New China was established under the guidance and theory of the late Deng Xiaoping following the launch of reforms and the 'opening up'. The inauguration of the Shanghai Stock Exchange in December 1990, marked the modern beginning of the stock market of New China. Thereafter in June 1991, the Shenzhen Stock Exchange was founded, and the Securities Commission of the State Council and the China Securities Regulatory Committee were set up in October 1992, which resulted in the nationwide coverage of stock issuance and symbolized the official formation of China's nationwide securities market.[2]

In order to establish a securities market in China (as the largest developing country which had adopted a planned economic system for a long time), what was needed was not only far-sighted leaders at the top like Deng Xiaoping, but also practical efforts to overcome various difficulties and exploring ways for development in line with Chinese national conditions. With the support of the State Natural Science Fund Committee, the author had organized a group of experts and scholars in 2001–2002 to conduct a systematic analysis of the development of the Chinese stock market in the first ten years (from December 1990 to December 2000), and led the law enforcement inspection team of the NPC Standing Committee in 2001 to monitor the implementation of the Securities Law of the PRC (hereinafter referred to as the Securities Law). My overall impression is that the Chinese stock market is still in a fledgling stage, with remarkable achievements made on the macro level, but many problems still exist at the micro level.

This chapter proposes to use the ideas of fictitious economy and the methodologies of complexity science (the higher stage in system science development) to carry out systematic analysis of the development of the Chinese stock market in the first ten years of its development. It is proposed that progress made be recognized and problems identified herein. Some major recommendations are then presented for the stock market in China which is now undergoing a period of adjustment and modification.

4.2. Fictitious Economy and Stock Market

The author had proposed a theory of Fictitious Economy[3] in 1998 for the purpose of studying the Asian Financial Crisis. It is the author's intention to attempt to make use of the theory to probe into issues connected with the stock market.

4.2.1. *Overview of the Fictitious Economy*

Fictitious Economy is a new term which has emerged in recent years, the definitions of which are varied but are primarily of three types. One refers to transactions of fictitious capital including securities, futures and options (Fictitious Economy); another refers to economic activities conducted on the basis of information technology (Virtual Economy) — some would call it digital economy or information economy. The third refers to visual economic activities done by computer simulation (Visual Economy). Some inter-connections exist among these three definitions, with the first definition to be elaborated herein.

The idea of Fictitious Capital was initially raised by Marx, who made a detailed analysis of Fictitious Capital in Section 5, Volume 3 of *Das Kapital*, especially in Chapter 25 and thereafter in respect of credit and Fictitious Capital. He held that Fictitious Capital was created on the basis of loan capital (interest bearing capital) and bank credit systems, including stocks, bonds and real estate mortgage bonds. Fictitious capital itself carries no value, which is different from real capital. However, it can generate profits through circulatory or cyclical movements (creating a certain form of surplus value), which is a common feature of real capital. Despite numerous new items (e.g. futures, options and various derivative financial products) and new circumstances (e.g. currency departing from the gold standard and economic globalization) which emerged with the global economic development after more than a century, Marx's analysis of Fictitious Capital still plays an important guiding role in the current study of Fictitious Economy.

According to the author's understanding, the so called Fictitious Economy refers to economic activities relating to circulatory movements that occur primarily in the financial system, or simply activities that directly 'use money to generate money'. People engaged in fictitious economic activities do not personally participate in substantive economic activities such as the production, circulation and exchange of commodities; they only conduct deals involving fictitious capital. However, given that fictitious capital does not have any value itself or its value is fictitious, transactions in fictitious economy are dependent upon the subjective forecasts of the parties to the deal of future incomes and fictitious economic activities (just as the real economy) and are likely to be either profitable or making losses.

According to the concepts of system science, Fictitious Economy can be treated as a system, the features of which may be researched from the perspective of the internal structure of the system and the relationship between the system and the environment — so as to discover the laws of system evolution.

The fictitious economic system is a kind of complicated system, composing mainly of natural persons and legal persons (investors, investment receivers and financial intermediaries) who carry out fictitious economic activities in the financial market according to certain rules. Complexity science concepts hold that though every individual has the freedom to make decisions independently according to his personal strengths and surrounding environment, his understanding of the development prospect and preset targets, it is inevitable that his decision making is affected by other people's decision making. Although some chaos and confusion may ensue because of the nonlinear effect among system components, the self organizing function of the system may yet give rise to some orderliness and stability.[4,5]

When people have readily available idle money, other than increasing consumption and savings, they would like to use the idle money for investing for profit. From the perspective of Fictitious Economy, all financial market instruments are fictitious capital. When investors purchase financial market instruments with their idle money, they are actually exchanging the right to use the money for certificates of equity, thereby obtaining the right to benefits from future incomes and assets of the issuers of the financial instruments. In making decisions for investment, therefore, people have to consider three issues including: how much the expected or forecast incomes will be, whether these incomes can be realized and whether the investment money can be returned promptly when necessary. That is to say, investors have to weigh the profitability, security and liquidity of the financial instruments to be purchased prior to investment. Theoretically, the profitability of financial instruments is negatively correlated with security or liquidity, and its security is positively correlated with liquidity. To cater for the demands of different investors, various financial instruments or vehicles have emerged in the financial market.

Financial vehicles can normally be divided into two types according to whether their credit period is more than or less than one year.

The first type comprises capital market instruments, including stocks, mortgaged loans, corporate bonds, treasury bonds of more than one year, consumer loans and commercial bank loans. The second type comprises money market instruments, including treasury bonds of less than one year, large-amount negotiable CDs, commercial bills, bank acceptance bills, repurchase agreements and inter-bank borrowing agreements. Financial market instruments can also be classified into equity and debt instruments according to the nature of investment. Investors could only receive dividends from issuers of equity instruments rather than directly recovering the principal, though they could recover principal and interest from the issuers of debt instruments.

The existence of the secondary financial market enables investors to sell their financial instruments at hand and obtain cash at any time, which greatly improves the liquidity of financial instruments. However, given the uncertainties in the prices of financial instruments in the secondary market, investors are likely to attain high profits or suffer huge losses in encashing their financial instruments. Therefore, financial market instruments are sometimes called paper money.

It can therefore be concluded on the basis of the above theory that the money market is a liquidity oriented debt instrument market, the debt market is a security oriented debt instrument market, and the stock market is a profit oriented equity instrument market.

The earliest origins of fictitious economy began with interpersonal commercial loaning. For example, if A is in urgent need of purchasing certain raw materials or goods but has insufficient capital, while B has a sum of idle money, A offers to borrow some money from B and pledges to repay the principal with interest within a period of time. In so doing, A obtains the right to use the sum of money and gains profits through substantive economic activities with the money borrowed. On the other hand, B retains the title to this money on the strength of an IOU as well as the right to claim for the repayment of the principal with interest when the period of the loan matures. In this case, the IOU in B's hand is the prototype of fictitious capital which realizes appreciation or gains value through the circulatory actions of loaning and repayment. B is not engaged in actual economic activities, but only makes money through a fictitious economic activity.

It can be seen therefrom that the first phase of fictitious economic development is the capitalization of idle money, or the transformation of idle money in people's hands into interest bearing capital. The second phase is the socialization of interest bearing capital, in which banks act as intermediaries that take idle money from their owners and lend the money out for interest. People can also use their idle money to purchase various interest–bearing negotiable securities: the certificates and negotiable securities are also fictitious capital. The socialization of interest–bearing capital can divert capital from people who are unable to use it (for real economic activities including production and circulation) to those who are able to do so, while centralizing or collecting scattered capital for large scale and highly profitable economic activities, thus improving the capital utilization efficiency.

The third phase of fictitious economic development is the marketization of negotiable securities or negotiable securities which can be freely traded for forecast profits. This has given rise to a financial market engaged in fictitious capital transactions (e.g. stock market, bond market, money market, etc.). The marketization of negotiable securities not only enables people to encash their negotiable instruments in hand, but also greatly improves the liquidity of fictitious capital. Additionally, this marketization can also direct capital to industries with sound forecast profits which further improves the utilization efficiency of capital. There also emerged in 1898 the futures trading method of farm products, a new form of fictitious capital, which subsequently involved industrial raw materials including nonferrous metal and oil.

The fourth phase of fictitious economic development is the internationalization of the financial market — whereby fictitious capital can be traded across borders. Though this process dates back to the 19th century when debtor countries including the U.S. and railway companies issued fixed rate bonds on the financial markets of the UK, France and Germany, it was not until the 1920s when large scale cross border securities investment emerged. The global economic recession and the eruption of the Second World War in the 1930s brought the financial market internationalization process to a standstill. Only after the Second World War, boosted by the Bretton Woods Agreement and the General Agreement of Tariffs and Trade, did a huge international financial market come into being. The internationalization of the financial market helped divert capital to profitable industries in the international arena so that capital utilization efficiency greatly improved, and at the same time a new financial market was born — the foreign exchange market. Futures trading is also becoming increasingly 'virtual' in that futures purchase has become a means for speculation. Since the 1960s, futures trading emerged in transactions of financial commodities including stocks, debts and foreign exchanges. Options trading too began in 1973.

The fifth stage of the development of fictitious economy is international financial integration, or closer relationships between the home financial market of various countries and the international financial market, bringing about intensifying mutual impact. With the formation of floating exchange rates after the severance of the U.S. dollar from the gold standard, the strengthening of financial innovations, rapid progress of information technology, expansion of financial freedom, and the promotion of economic globalization, fictitious capital moved increasingly faster and grew larger in volume in the financial market, enlarging the scale and size of the fictitious economy.

Under the multiplier effect, overall scale of the current global Fictitious Economy has significantly exceeded the real economy. The global economic aggregate had hit US$160 trillion by the end of 2000, including around US$36 trillion in stock market value, US$29 trillion in bond balances, and US$95 trillion in the over-the-counter trading balance of financial derivative instruments, while the combined GDP of all countries totaled only approximately US$30 trillion for that year, indicating that the scale of Fictitious Economy was five times as much as that of real economy. The average daily flow of global fictitious capital amounted to more than US$1.5 trillion, approximately 50 times the average daily real trade volume across the world. This means also that only 2% of the daily capital flow in the world has been used for international trade, with the remaining involved in money-for-money activities in the financial market. It can be expected that with the development of electronic commerce and electronic currency, the scale of Fictitious Economy will further swell.

A close relationship exists between the fictitious economic system and the real economic system, with the fictitious economic system deriving from and 'attaching' to the real economic system. The real economic system involves the production of material resources and economic activities including distribution, exchange and consumption in respect thereof — considered circulation of capital. For example, capitalists in the sphere of production would, after obtaining capital from the financial market, spend it on the purchase of equipment, raw materials and on manpower to be inputted into the production process. They subsequently sell their products with proceeds which become their capital again, thus the circulation of capital. Capitalists utilize the said proceeds and the surplus value obtained therefrom to repay the principals with interest as contracted — thus a round of fictitious capital circulation is completed.

Given the close relationship between the fictitious and real economic systems, risks derived from the real economic system (such as excessive inventory stock and corporate bankruptcy) tend to be passed on to and destabilize the fictitious economic system. On the other hand, the risks in the fictitious economic system, such as stock index plummets, housing price dives, bank NPL surge and significant currency depreciation, also have serious impacts on the real economy. Nowadays when finance has become the economic core, the fictitious economic system is indispensable for the operation of the real economy. If the real economic system is considered as a hardware of the economic system, the fictitious economic system could be considered a software of the economic system.

4.2.2. *The Virtual or Fictitious Nature of the Stock Market*

Given that the stock market belongs to the fictitious economic system, its features can be probed into from the perspective of the system's internal structure and the mutual impact between the system and the environment in accordance with the views of system science.

The author presented five features of the fictitious economic system in an article published in 1998 for the first time. An in-depth analysis is hereby made on the five features as to the stock market.

4.2.2.1. *Complexity*

The features of a complex system normally include: large scale, high degree of coupling, low transparency, dynamic state and openness. But its most essential feature is that its components possess some 'intelligence' -the ability to understand the environment they are in, to forecast its changes and take actions according to preset targets. This is also the intrinsic characteristic for biological evolution, technical innovation, economic development and social progress.

The stock market is a complex system, with its major components being primarily natural and legal persons (buyers, sellers and intermediaries) who conduct stock trading in the stock market according to certain rules and regulations. Every one of them has the freedom to make independent decision in accordance with his understanding of the environment, development prospect as well as the prescribed target. The decision of each of them cannot be unaffected by the decision making of others. Although chaos and confusion manifest themselves because of the non-linear impact among components, the system's self organizing function can enable the system to show some macro orderliness and stability over the long term.

The theories of neoclassical economics presume that those engaged in economic activities are all "economic people" who seek the maximization of their own benefits and whose behaviors are completely rational. In accordance with this theory, stock prices are the rational forecast of investors as to the future value of the stock, taking into consideration real economic variables that may affect the stock price. The value of a stock should be equal to the present value of its future profit. However, as pointed by Herbert Simon, a Nobel Prize Laureate, people engaged in economic activities may only be rational in a limited way, and as they are also limited in terms of information and knowledge, they can hardly understand and forecast various possible results, and can only make decisions according to subjective judgments, without considering all possibilities. Moreover, people's values and the words and deeds of the people around tend to affect the correctness of their decisions.

In securities trading, investors do not have sufficient information on current and future market conditions and price changes. Since investors have different capacities for withstanding and absorbing risks and also varied investment capabilities, their understanding and judgment of investment differ vastly and their investment objectives and expected returns vary too. Many investors do not understand the technical analysis of market movements, nor do they possess any basic knowledge about stock market investment or capabilities for understanding and making judgment in the face of large amount of market information. Many of them rush into trading for profit taking in transactions. They listen to rumors, believe in them, and often act on personal or emotional impulses, which inevitably lead to chaos in the stock market. However, the mutual effect of the actions between investors and the external environment which plays a guiding role in people's behaviors have made the stock market show a particular trend seen from the macro and long–term perspective. That is why the stock market can and does maintain relative stability over a certain period of time — hence the so called bull and bear markets in stock exchange.

4.2.2.2. *Metastability*

The so called metastable state is a system which is distant from an equilibrium state, but can maintain relative stability through exchanges of substances and energy with the external environment. In system sciences it is called a system with dissipation structure. Though this system can attain stability through its self organizing function, its stability is prone to destruction by even minor external disturbances. The system could still function within a certain range or confined area and it could alternate between a stable and 'wandering' state. From a macro view it can be said that the system is stable within a certain confine, or is stable regionally. However the result of the loss of stability could also bring about dramatic changes and could cause a system crash or collapse. When a system crashes or collapses, its intrinsic structure could re-organize to revert to its former metastable state, or it could go into extinction. Generally, the greater the inertia of the system, the smaller will be the possibility of crash or collapse.

The Stock market is a metastable system requiring exchange of capital with the external world to maintain relative stability. There are many reasons why the Stock market is metastable, but the fundamental reason is the inherent or intrinsic instability of virtual/fictitious capital.

The intrinsic or inherent instability of the virtual capital stems from its own fictitiousness. The shares or the stocks are by themselves without any real value. They represent the rights to proceeds or incomes and are a form of title of ownership. They allow the holder the legal right to the residual value in the purchase of the stock or securities after paying the capital sum required. When stocks are being traded in the Stock market, their prices are not determined by objective rules of valuation but rather by the people's expectation of their future value — bearing in mind that the stocks themselves are valueless. What is more, the prices of stocks are also subject to the laws of demand and supply, making them having little to do with real economic activities. When the price of stocks steers very far above their reasonably forecast value, an economic 'bubble' is born and external capital injection is required to maintain the price stability. In other words, this is a fictitious or virtual stability and when there is insufficient capital injection, prices of stocks will tumble.

The instability of a fictitious economic system can also be attributable to the fictitious character of currencies. The fact is, currencies do not possess real value. When currencies became un-pegged from the Gold Standard and the Gold Exchange Standard, though they do represent a means for exchange (to pay and be paid) they do not genuinely possess values based on a certain real physical entity. This means the value of a currency could only be gauged by its purchasing power and this in turn is affected by the volume of currency issued, interest rates, exchange rates, people's consuming patterns and other economic variables. The fictitiousness of currencies therefore contributes to the increased instability of fictitious economy.

The presence in the virtual/fictitious economy of the effect of 'positive' feedback also helps to exacerbate the instability of the fictitious economy. When more people purchase a particular stock, this will result in yet more people purchasing that stock. This is what is meant by the effects of 'positive feedback' — the mutual influence exerted by people. The result is that all effects become amplified and 'multiplied', causing the price of stocks to rise or fall sharply.

4.2.2.3. *High risks*

Risks in economic activities refer to the difference between the expectant profit and the practical profit. Such a difference comes not only from the vicissitudes and uncertainties of the objective world and the limitations of people's capability of understanding the world, but also from a subjective and false estimation of the expectant profit. In the stock market, high risks and the possibility of high profits co-exist.

The high risks of the stock market stem from its complexity and metastability. Firstly, the internal instability of stocks leads to a frequent and irregular change of its prices. The expansion of the stock market exchanges and the increase in the variety of exchanges add to their complexity. Secondly, people are not 'up to the mark' in making a good estimation of the possible changes in the market and its environment. Till now, there is still no effective way of estimating the expectant profits. As a result, many wrong and mistaken decisions have been made. What's more, many people have a very limited capacity for assuming or withstanding risks. When confronted with high risks, they will be simply at a loss and might even increase the risks as a result of the positive feedback effect. Finally, a number of people will be willing to take risks for the sake of high profits. This has stimulated the continuous emergence of high risk and high profit financial products, such as the stock index futures and options.

Furthermore, some on-going illegal activities also lead to high risks in the stock market. Such activities may include: (1) the publication of untrue information, which will mislead investors; (2) occurrence of internal dealings (or insider trading) which could jeopardize the interests of the small and medium investors; and (3) hostile manipulation of the market, making huge profits for the manipulators.

Research findings show that people are inclined to overestimating their capacity for assuming risks and will likely go bankrupt as a result of assuming overly high risks. For example, for a project with an investment of one million Yuan, risk possibility of 80% and a return of five million Yuan if successful, people will always make a false conclusion that if they invest five million Yuan on five projects, they can take the risks so long as one of the five succeeds because the risks and returns are believed to be 'symmetrical'. However, on calculations based on the rules of "Rules of Bankruptcy for risk-takers', there is only a 67% probability of success in one of the five projects if only five million Yuan is invested on them. If one wants to make sure that the probability of success in at least one project is 95%, then one will have to invest 14 million Yuan on 14 projects. It can be seen that an investment of only five million Yuan is far from being sufficient to assume the risks.

4.2.2.4. *The parasitic nature*

Stocks represent the evidence of stockholding issued by limited liability companies to their investors. They imply that ownership of the company 'belongs' to the stockholders. As stocks are a kind of portfolio securities without a given date of realization, investors cannot withdraw once they have taken up the stocks in the primary market, but can only sell them to other investors in the secondary market. Theoretically speaking, whether it is traded in the primary or secondary market, the worth of the stocks is mainly determined by the future performance of the company, equal to the value of the future profits. Notwithstanding the unpredictable fluctuations of the stock prices in the stock market, in the final analysis stocks are parasitic on the company and the stock market is parasitic on the entity economy.

As investors' judgment about stock price is based mainly on the prediction of the future performance of the company, the parasitic nature of the stocks is mostly demonstrated by the ways that their market prices are influenced by information about the company that has issued the stocks. Such information may come from the said company on its own disclosure, or by changes in the external environment, or information circulating in society.

The parasitic nature of the stock market is mostly expressed in the ways its working cycle is dependent upon that of the entity economy. The working or functional index measuring the entity economy is Gross Domestic Product (GDP) while the corresponding index measuring the performance of the stock market is the share price index (like the Dow Jones index). Although the stock market index may go below or lag behind the economic index, a protracted deviation from it would be clearly abnormal. We should also notice that as there are lots and lots of varieties of stocks in the stock market, the share price index is computed by selecting a few from them in a statistical method and cannot give an accurate and comprehensive reflection of the stock market's performance.

On the other hand, the counter-actions of the stock market upon the entities economy cannot be overlooked. The rise of the stock market will strengthen people's confidence in the prospects of the economy and increase their consumption as a result of the "wealth effect", which will promote the development of the economy. Similarly, when the stock market bubble bursts, people will not only reduce their consumption but also strive to sell cheaply all kinds of financial assets in panic, leading to economic recession and even an economic crisis.

In recent years, some people have raised their doubts about the traditional idea that, "the stock market is the barometer of the economy". They believe that the happenings in the stock market are not necessarily connected to the performance of the economy. Indeed, there have occasions when a rise in the stock market is accompanied by a fall in the economy, or a fall in the stock market is accompanied by a rise in the economy. Personally, I think in the long run and from a macro point of view, the situation of the stock market should on the whole reflect the performance of the entity economy, for the reason that the stock market is based upon and relies on the entity economy. From the viewpoint of complexity science, the stock market and the economy are not simply connected in a one–to–one linear relationship, but by a non-linear, very complex one. Firstly, the GDP cannot fully demonstrate the situation of the entity economy; neither can the share price index comprehensively reflect the conditions of the stock market. Secondly, stock markets are subjected to the influences of many factors, such as the international economic situation, social systems, policies of governments, people's confidence and so on. In addition, the influences of these factors upon the GDP and the share price index are not symmetrical or synchronous. Thirdly, due to the impact of many factors, it is often the case that the situation of the stock market deviates from that of the entity economy in the short or medium–term. For example, in economic recessions when investment returns are meager in the entity economy, people tend to invest in the stock market to promote its rise. Lastly, as a result of the counter-action of the stock market upon the entity economy aforementioned, the relationship between the two has become so bewildering and confusing that it is hard to tell the effects of their mutual influence. It should be specially pointed out that when there are abnormal situations like excessive speculation, underhand manipulations and exceedingly strong impacts of policies in the stock market, the performance of the stock market will deviate from the entities economy — but this is not sufficient to negate the parasitic nature of the fictitious economy.

4.2.2.5. *Periodicity*

In general, the evolution of the fictitious economy takes on the characteristic of periodicity. Usually, the process is as follows: faster growth of the entity economy, formation of economic bubbles, gradual expansion of money and credit, universal rise in the prices of various assets, prevalence of optimism everywhere, continuous rises in stock and real estate prices, bursting of the bubble economy as a result of external turbulence, dramatic fall of all financial indices, underselling the real assets and financial assets in succession, and slowdown or even negative growth of the entity economy. However, the periodicity is not simply a cycle or mere repetition; it is a kind of wave motion — like an upward spiral.

The functioning of the stock market is also periodic with the bear and the bull market appearing alternately. Since the stock market is mainly based on investors' optimistic expectation of future profits (optimistic expectation of economic development in the final analysis), there is no doubt that bubbles do exist in the stock market. The expansion and bursting of the bubbles cause fluctuations in the stock market. But such fluctuations represent a kind of wave-like motion moving in an upward spiral. For example, on October 19, 1987 (Black Monday) when the US stock market nosedived, the Dow Jones index was less than 3,000 points. However, 13 years later, the Dow Jones index hit over 12,000 points.

4.2.3. *Connection and Interactivity Between the Money Market and the Capital Market*

The money market and the capital market are interrelated components of the financial market. A standard and optimized money market can direct the surplus capital holders to change their savings into investments in the capital market. The fluidity and the short–term nature of the tools in the money market can make the investment necessary complements to the capital market and an important way of reducing risks. In a developed financial market, the money market and the capital market possess different characteristics and tools. But the combined use of the capital circulation and other financial tools make the two constitute an integrated financial market system.

The connection between the money market and the capital market is mostly manifested in that the main bodies of the two markets do overlap. Some financial and non-financial organizations have entered the money market and the capital market as well. All the financial and non-financial organizations are likely to invest in the money market, and such activities facilitate the balancing of their own assets structure by utilizing their liabilities in the money market. In addition, the diversity of the tools in the money market has provided many opportunities for investments and profit taking. In those countries that allow financial organizations to get involved in other industries, in particular, financial organizations should make dynamic adjustment to their capital structure so as to make the largest possible profits under a certain amount of security. Profits from investment in money market in many financial organizations have accounted for an increasingly larger portion of their gross earnings. Along with the application of modern technology in the finance industry and changes in financial supervision concepts, the main body of investment in the money market is also becoming diversified. In a developed financial market, the money market and the capital market are inter-dependent and the distinction between the two has become more and more blurred.

In a developed financial market, except for the central banks, the participants of the market can operate in the money market and the capital market simultaneously. For example, a securities company can hold a large number of stocks and long–term bonds and at the same time holding short–term bonds and participating in short–term loans at a daily interest and making repurchase within the industry. In this way the company can adjust the fluidity and security of its capital accordingly and also earn some interests. Moreover, the high risks of the tools/instruments in the capital market force investors to favor and make use of tools in the money market so as to establish good investment structures in an effort to disperse risks. The participants of the market also need to operate in the two markets at the same time to ensure the fluidity of capital. Although the two markets are different in the light of their tools, yield rate and risks, their main market structures are fundamentally the same. So by comparing the prices of their tools, yield, fluidity and risks, people are able to make dynamic or appropriate adjustments to the structure of their assets and liabilities.

The interaction between the money market and the capital market is mainly observed in the two way flow of capital. In theory, there is some kind of equilibrium between the money market and the securities business according to the Gordon growth model. When they are in equilibrium, the share price is inversely proportional to the interest rate in the money market. If any one of them rises or falls, the other one will certainly fall or rise respectively to reach a new equilibrium between the two. When the interest rate falls, investors often tend to make a short term loan at a daily interest from people in the same industry or sell short–term securities in the money market to get the necessary capital for the long–term securities in the capital market. As capital flows from the money market to the capital market, prices of the long–term securities will go up. When the interest rate rises, investors tend to sell their long–term securities to invest in short–term securities. As capital flows from the capital market to the money market, prices of the long–term securities will go down. Thus, when prices of the securities go up, their demand will decline and capital will flow from the capital market to the money market; conversely, when prices of the securities go down, capital will flow from the money market to the capital market.

The fact is: the actual situation is much more complicated than that in theory. For example, when the money market is not optimized and devoid of effective market tools, more capital will flow to the capital market; another example is when the requirements for financing in the capital market are too lax, a large amount of credit capital will flow to the capital market.

Some scholars attempt to analyze the financial market according to the traditional law of value, believing that when the price of some tool in the financial market exceeds its value, its price will go down; otherwise it will go up. However, I believe that the tools in the financial market are some kind of fictitious capital and do not possess value in themselves. So the law of value is not applicable, but the law of supply and demand is still applicable here. When demand for a certain tool in the financial market exceeds its supply, its price will go up, or otherwise it will go down. The reason for the change in the relationship between demand and supply is not the deviation of the price from the value but the self organizing effect of the investors' activities.

The financial market falls under the fictitious economy system and has its own internal complexity. Although every main entity in the market is independent in decision making according to its own expectation of the future and in a micro point of view there is quite a lot of random fluctuation and chaos, the decision of every one of them in the market is inevitably subjected to the influences of the decisions of others and the environment. This will leads to a self organizing effect. So, from a macro point of view, the development of the financial market does exhibit some degree of certainty and also follow some undefined and fuzzy rules. I think in our analysis of the financial market we should give full consideration to the decision making of the main entities or bodies in the market, especially those decisions which appear irrational.

For example, when selecting a tool in the financial market, investors who lay particular emphasis on profits probably favor the tools concerning equities, whereas those who emphasize security probably favor the tools related to debts and liability. When the stock market is in a bull market, investors will have greater confidence in the rise of the stock market. At this time, not only those investors who lay particular stress on profits will increase their investment but also those who lay particular stress on security will turn to the stock market, as they believe that the risk of losses is smaller. In this case, the impact of increasing the interest rate in the money market so as to reduce the amount of capital flowing into the stock market will be much smaller than is the case if a bear market is in place. According to the law of supply and demand, an increasing amount of capital flowing into the stock market will inevitably lead to a rise in the stock market, and thus further strengthening investors' confidence and attracting more capital into the market.

When the stock market rises sharply, those investors who place particular attention on profits will even give up the logical principle of equilibrium between risks and profits and invest at high prices, believing that some other investors may offer even higher prices. For example, since 1995, greatly encouraged by the successful listing of companies like Netscape, Amazon and America Online, people were convinced of the fable that "investing in the internet industry for one year is equivalent to investing in traditional industries for 100 years". What followed was a sharp and dramatic rise in the share prices of the internet-related or web-based stocks on the NASDAQ. In May, 1995, the online bookstore "Amazon.com" was listed. By November 30, 1998, its share price had risen by 2,300%. Although its turnover was US$293 million with a loss of US$61 million, people still expected it to have good prospects. So they continued buying into its stocks, hoping that they would profit substantially in the future. Three months later, it rose by a further 400%, with a total market worth of US$40 billion. Before Christmas in 1999, the NASDAQ index breached the 4,000 points level and continued to go higher. On March 10, 2000, it reached 5,048 points, the highest point in its history up till then.

However, in reality the facts show that if a company gets listed before it reaches the stage of maturity it is actually shifting the risks that its investors should otherwise assume to the public. In 1999, 486 companies issued their stocks in the U.S. Of these 242 were newly started internet companies. Their average annual turnover was US$18,500,000 while their average annual loss was US$17,800,000. Of these 242 companies, 224 of them have no record of making profits. There was such a sharp disparity between the share price and company performance that investors gradually lost confidence in these companies, leading to the final slump in internet stocks in 2000. The NASDAQ index slid down from its highest point all the way and could not recover. In 2000, it registered the largest drop in 30 years — 39.3% in one year, losing about US$300 million in market value. At the beginning of 2001, the NASDAQ index continued falling rapidly. On March 12, it fell below the 2,000 points level and at the lowest even dropped to about 1,400 points. According to the statistics of Webmergers.com, from January 2000 to May 2001 at least 493 Internet companies had gone bankrupt, of which 55% of them had declared insolvency in the first five months of 2001.

Conversely, if investors lack confidence in the stock market, even if there are frequent cuts of interest rate it will be difficult to stimulate capital to flow into the stock market. For instance in Japan, due to the economic downturn in recent years, the stock market could not be vitalized although the interest rates of banks have reached the lowest point.

We could see that the interactive relationship between the capital market and the money market is quite complex. However, we should not just look at the antagonistic effect of the two — "as one falls, the other rises" — we should also discern their mutually complementary effects.

4.3. China's Stock Market: Still at a Preliminary, Infant Stage

After the Shanghai stock exchange and the Shenzhen stock exchange were successively established and had started to issue "A-shares" in December 1990 and June 1991 respectively, the special shares denominated in the Yuan ("B-shares") and the overseas investment shares listed abroad (such as the "H-share") were later issued in 1991 and in 1993 respectively. However, since it is still at an early stage of development, the stock market in China is far from being 'perfect' or fully developed. Investors, listed companies, securities companies and China's Securities Regulatory Commission are in all respects lacking in experience, and have undergone many ups and downs in the course of their development. Amidst the sudden and sharp rises or slumps in the stock market, there are a series of problems behind the scenes such as insider dealings, dissemination of false information, sham investment projects out to cheat investors, market manipulation, over-speculation, etc.

On July 1, 1999, the "Securities Laws of PRC" took effect ("Securities Laws" for short hereinafter), aiming to regulate China's stock market. The promulgation and implementation of the Securities Laws has accelerated the progress of the legalization and standardization of China's securities market. The regulatory and supervisory departments in the securities market thus have a clearer idea about their roles and functions. The standard performance and operation of the listed companies and the securities companies — the main bodies of the market — can be continuously improved and investors have become more aware of the laws and have more confidence in the market.

Early in 2001, the Standing Committee of the National People's Congress, in accordance with the law, decided to carry out an inspection on the enforcement and implementation of the Securities Laws.

The Standing Committee of the National People's Congress formed an inspection team for the enforcement of the Laws and I had the honor of being the head of the team. We carried out the inspection from the middle of May to early June 2001. The inspection team first listened to the (oral) reports about the enforcement of the Securities Laws made by China's Securities Regulatory Commission, State Economic and Trade Commission, People's Bank of China, Supreme People's Court and the Supreme People's Procuratorate. Then four sub-committees (headed by Zhou Zhengqing, Li Yining, Zhou Daojiong, and Zhang Xiao) were dispatched to Shanghai, Shenzhen, Chengdu, and Wuhan to carry out inspections on the spot. Additionally we arranged for five cities — Beijing, Guangzhou, Lanzhou, Harbin, and Xiamen — to carry out some self-inspection of the enforcement of the Securities Laws in these cities.

The four inspection sub-committees listened to the reports about the enforcement of the Laws made by local governments, Securities Regulatory Office accredited by China's Securities Regulatory Commission, the Shanghai Stock Exchange and the Shenzhen Stock Exchange. They also hosted several conferences inviting some listed companies, securities companies, related intermediary services organizations, agencies, investors, experts and scholars. They also did site inspections of the Shanghai Stock Exchange, the Shenzhen Stock Exchange, some listed companies and securities companies. After returning to Beijing, the teams then hosted several related conferences and listened to the views, comments and suggestions from all circles. The Standing Committees of the Municipal Congress of the above five cities also, as required, reported the results of the inspection to the Standing Committee of the National People's Congress. When the inspection was all over, I had the honor of making a report to the 22nd session of the 9th National People's Congress on behalf of the inspection teams.

I have been paying attention to the development of China's stock market for many years. Through this inspection, I was able to obtain a more profound understanding of the situation and problems of the market. I had a general impression that the stock market is still at a preliminary, early stage though great achievements have been made from a macro point of view, though there are still quite a few problems — viewed from a micro perspective.

In the past ten years, China's stock market has made notable achievements, becoming stronger after starting from scratch. The market size and performance have improved greatly. By the end of 2000, the gross stock market value of our country had reached 4,809.09 billion Yuan (of which the "tradable" market value was 1,608.8 billion Yuan); domestic listed companies number over 1,088; and more than 56 million accounts have been opened by investors on the Shanghai and Shenzhen Stock Exchanges. Besides, there are around 34 securities investment funds with over 55 billion Yuan in total funds.

China's stock market has played an important role in amassing the capital dispersed in society and translating them into large amounts of long term capital. By the end of November 2000, our stock market has raised an accumulative total capital of 944.32 billion Yuan. Out of this figure, domestic listed companies have raised 484.61 billion Yuan, overseas listed companies 143.91 billion Yuan (US$17.38 billion) and red chip shares 315.8 billion Yuan (US$38.14 billion).[6]

A great number of state owned enterprises have gone public. IPOs create a direct financing channel in upgrading traditional industries, reducing their liabilities, speeding up the pace of technical reform and application of new technologies, and helping to promote the restructuring of properties and commodities. More importantly, listings have notably promoted the transformation of the operating mechanism of state owned companies — energizing these companies. Listed companies have to learn to practice corporate governance by establishing a system of legal persons required by the modern enterprise system. Through listing of companies the stock market helps to accelerate the implementation of scientific decision making, facilitate market based operations, socialized monitoring and promotes awareness of legal responsibility in companies, play a model and pioneering role in the establishment of the modern enterprise system by state–owned enterprises thus paving the way for the improvement of the overall quality of the national economy.

The ten years' development of China's stock market has shown that the security market plays an important role in the nation's economic development. As Comrade Jiang Zemin pointed out, "The security market is essential for the socialist market economy; a healthy, orderly and secure security market plays an important role in optimizing resource allocation, transforming economic structure, raising greater social capital and driving the development of the national economy."

While affirming the achievements of the securities market, it should be made clear that compared with the mature security market in developed countries or regions, China's securities market is still at the preliminary, early stage and there are still some issues to be solved. Based on our analysis, there are eight aspects of the problems facing the securities market.

4.3.1. *Small Scale and Insufficient Depth*

Although our country's stock market has developed relatively quickly, its scale or size is still on the small side. According to the data of the World Bank, China's stock market value accounted for only 1.6% of the total value of the world's stock markets, while the U.S. accounted for 46.2% and Japan 12.6% respectively. The proportion of China's stock market value to GDP is 33.4% while the U.S. is 181.8%, Japan 104.6% and the Hong Kong Special Administration Region 383.2%. Moreover, there is a large number of non-tradable shares (state–owned shares and legal person or corporate shares), with tradable shares accounting for only about 1/3 of the total capital stock. As a result of the small scale and the prevalence of excessive speculation, China's stock market cannot be regarded as a barometer for the economy, and this is one distinct characteristic of the Chinese stock market — being still in the early stage of its development.

The key problem of a small scale stock market is its weak stability. In systems engineering, stability refers to the capability of a system to restore to its original state after deviating from the original state following some disturbance. As the stock market is a fictitious economic system featuring a dissipative structure, its main disturbance comes from the change in the net inflow amount of capital (reflecting the demand of buyers) and the amount of tradable capital stocks (reflecting the supply of sellers). On the whole (from a macro point of view), when the net capital inflow increases while the amount of tradable capital stocks remains the same, the stock market value will rise; and when the amount of tradable capital stocks increases (including newly listed companies and new stocks issued by listed companies) while net capital inflow remains the same, the stock market value will fall. Similarly with individual stocks (micro), when net capital inflow increases (more purchases than sales), share prices will rise; and when the net capital inflow decreases (more sales than purchases), the share prices will fall. Theoretically the larger the scale of the stock market, the better will its stability be, and similarly for individual stocks.

The sudden and sharp rise and slump of China's stock market in the past ten years were to a large extent caused by the serious imbalance in the relationship between capital and tradable capital stock (outstanding capital stock). In such a case the price of a stock was determined mainly by the amount of capital chasing after the stock, so it cannot properly reflect the internal value of the stock.

For example, before May 1992, there were only eight listed companies on the Shanghai stock exchange, including the Yanzhong Company. They were called the "Eight Ancient Stocks", and their total tradable stock capital was less than 80 million Yuan, which was far from meeting the demands of investors. So in the market there were only purchases but no sales of the stocks or in other words, there was 'only price but no market.' On May 21, 1992 when new stocks came on to the market and trading was 'unleashed', the Shanghai stock index rose from 616 points the day before to over 1,265 points. On May 25, it reached another new high of 1,420 points. It did not fall below 1,000 points until two months later when a large number of new stocks were also listed.

Some listed companies entrust large amounts of capital raised to securities companies for financing, which is actually a circuitous route for the raised capital to go back to the stock market and will thereupon further lift up the prices of stocks and weaken the stability of the market. Furthermore, it will weaken the capacity of the stock market in raising capital and optimizing resource allocation, and would increase tremendously the possibility of speculation in the market.

In addition, stocks listed and issued in the past ten years, especially before 1996, were from small companies with not only small capital but also small scale of operation and small total capital stock and tradable capital stock. By the end of 2000, of the 1,076 listed companies, 307 companies had less than 50 million shares of tradable capital stock, accounting for 28.53%; 409 had 50 to 100 million shares, accounting for 38.01%; and 360 had over 100 million shares, accounting for 33.46%. Because of the small scale or size of listed companies, the manipulators (commonly called "the Market Maker" or the 'banker') do not need a large amount of capital to 'meddle' in the market and raise the prices of stocks. What's more, these companies can further expand their capital stock by donating or transferring the stocks, thereby further increasing the stock capital and pushing up stock prices for the 'Market Maker'.

4.3.2. *Over Half of the Stocks are Non-Tradable*

In China, shares of listed companies can be divided into state–owned shares, legal person shares and public shares. In order to prevent the erosion and dissipation of state assets, as well as to ensure that the state takes the control over key industries and companies, and taking the capacity of the market into consideration, the state–owned shares and the legal person shares are still not allowed to enter the market and be traded at present. Only the public shares are allowed to be traded on the stock market. Owing to the fact that the tradable stocks' market value accounts for only 1/3 of the total market value, most of the listed companies' stocks in our country are in fact non-tradable.

The fact that more than half of the stocks are non-tradable has led to many consequences: it artificially magnifies the scale or size of our stock market, greatly reduces its stability and makes for easy manipulation by the Market Maker. What's more, it will lead to an imbalance in the interests between the holders of public shares and that of the holders of state-owned and legal person shares. As the interests of shareholders of the latter two are not directly reflected in the stock price, they usually adopt a speculative attitude toward the rise and fall. For example, to make sure that the rights issue by their listed holding company can reach a high price, they often release some good news (including false news) to stimulate the rise of their stock prices, and sometimes they even manipulate the market directly to uplift it by adopting all kinds of unscrupulous measures. When the stock price goes down, they will still provide rights issue to increase the supply of stocks in order to gain more capital from society, making the stock price fall even lower. Under the present condition, getting listed is still some kind of highly valued and precious 'resource' — with government support and the concerted actions of dominant shareholders, these listed companies can easily undergo asset re-organization at a low cost even if they are suffering severe losses. The enormous amounts of non-tradable stocks also lead to the problem of "same stock with different prices". That's to say, the value of non-tradable stocks is far lower than that of tradable stocks, which makes it hard to maintain fairness within the stock market. Although we treat non-tradable stocks like tradable stocks, when calculating the total market value it is still somewhat difficult for investors to buy the non-tradable stocks at its market value when they go on sale.

From May 19, 1999 to August 30, 2001, the total market value of China's stock market rose by 90%. The total value of the A-shares in the Shenzhen and Shanghai stock exchanges amounted to 4,610.2 billion Yuan with tradable market value of 1,459.2 billion Yuan. In such a situation, some relevant governmental organizations decided to reduce holdings of state-owned shares at market value, an action which intensified "the same stock with different market values" dilemma. With the net inflow of capital gradually decreasing, a large number of state-owned shares entered the stock market, which inevitably led to the fall of the market. What's more, investors were not satisfied with the set price of the state-owned shares and dumped their shares one after another, causing the bubbles in the market to burst and the stock market to slump further.

The fact that more than half of the stocks are non-tradable also prevents the optimization of the system of legal person management in listed companies. Furthermore, as the state-owned shares make up the majority of stocks in many listed companies, the management of these companies are free from the supervision of investors and the general meetings of shareholders become perfunctory. Illegal activities such as release of false information, insider dealings, fraud and manipulation of the market — despite repeated prohibitions — become the order of the day.

4.3.3. *More Transactions to be Made but No Transactions Involving Buying and Selling Short*

'Short trading' or 'fictitious transaction' is a kind of credit transaction, including fictitious purchase and sale, or 'selling and buying short'. Investors borrow capital to buy in or borrow securities to sell out. Investors only need to pay a certain amount of 'caution money' to the securities dealers, and they can do business without any capital or holding any securities. In a mature stock market, the trading mechanism allows not only large amount of transactions, but also fictitious ones — as described above. Both individual stocks and stock indices can be traded in fictitious transactions. But as China's Securities Laws clearly stipulate that only transactions with real stocks can be transacted, and such fictitious transactions are forbidden. So at present the exchange mechanism in our country's stock market is still a 'one-sided' mechanism that encourages more transactions but forbids fictitious transaction, thus making it a 'one-sided' market.

A one-sided market will encourage investors to speculate excessively and to deal short term, throwing the market into a speculative atmosphere of "more transactions". That is to say, only by pushing up the stock price can investors make profit by purchasing at low prices and selling at high prices. Once there is good news, there is a stampede of investors. In order to avoid risks, transactions are for very short-term, thus causing large fluctuations in the stock market. As the exchange mechanism is one-sided, investors, securities companies, listed companies, regulatory departments and the government all hope that the stock market will rise more often than fall. In such situation, both individual stocks or the stock price index tend to maintain an upward trend for a long time. However, once the stock market falls continuously, most investors will be 'stuck' or will suffer losses when they dump their shares in a hurry, giving rise to a series of problems. As most investors can do nothing but simply observe when the stock market persistently falls, the vitality or 'genki' (energy and spirit) of the stock market will also be diminished.

The biggest problem of a "one-sided market" is that it cannot eliminate investors' systematic risks. According to empirical research findings,[7] our stock market fluctuates within a wide range with high risks overall. What's more, systematic risks account for a rather high proportion of risks overall. In the U.S., the U.K. and France, the proportions of systematic risks to risks on the whole are respectively 26.8%, 34.5% and 32.7%. However, in China, the proportion is high at 65.7%. Without a mechanism allowing fictitious transactions or necessary hedge tools to offset risks, it will be very difficult to avoid systematic risks unless investors withdraw completely from the stock market.

Withdrawing capital from the stock market can be seen as a passive fictitious transaction ('trading short') for investors.[8] That is to say, they foresee that the general developing trend of most stocks or individual stock will go down so they sell the stocks for cash. They will keep themselves away from the market and just look on to avoid being 'stuck' and to evade or reduce potential losses. The purpose of passive fictitious transaction is to avoid risks, and in such a case, capital appreciation cannot be realized for the moment because investors' capitals are indisposed. So it is uncommon for investors to do fictitious transaction and sell the shares. Some investors will purchase individual stocks at low prices, expecting to make profits after the prices soon touch the bottom line and begin to rally.

Of course, it will also be propitious to speculators to introduce the mechanism of allowing fictitious transactions. According to the Securities Laws, fictitious transactions are forbidden mainly for preventing and keeping away all possible risks and their proliferation. But weighing on the whole, the introduction of the mechanism will be more conducive to guarantee the stable functioning of the spot market. In the light of the actual functioning of the stock market, 'unorthodox' or 'irregular' credit transactions exist all the time, with their ups and downs. It is advisable to introduce the credit transactions of shares and share index futures when conditions are ripe and mature. Doing so will result in the gradual attainment of a balance amid the scramble among multi-'short trading' and to curb excessive speculation and the tendency toward short term transactions, thereby directing investors toward value oriented investments.

4.3.4. *Significant Influences of the Policies*

A great deal of evidence has shown that government policies as well as official remarks and comments are indeed among the key reasons that brought about the abnormal changes in the stock prices of China's stock market. For example, from 1991 to 2001, 25 of the highest or lowest points of the Shanghai Stock Exchange index corresponded with the release of related policies and information on those days. That is why the academia and the public describe vividly China's stock market as "a policy oriented market".

As already stated, the stock market on the whole reflects the changes in the situation of the entities or real economy. But it may go beyond or lag behind the changes thereof. We should also be cognizant of the fact that the stock market, no matter in which country or region, is under the influences of not only changes in the situation of the entities economy but also that of governmental policies, official remarks and comments. This is because firstly, the stock market (no matter in which country or region) will respond to the related governmental policies and important information. Secondly, when there are violent or unusual fluctuations in the stock prices, any government would come up with policies hoping to influence the direction of the stock market.

The prices, profits and fluctuations of a highly efficient and healthy stock market should be subjected to the influences of the entities economy on the macro level and in the long run. Its response to policies should also be moderate and appropriate. If the government interferes too much in it, or if it overreacts to policies, or the stock prices, profits and fluctuation are constantly driven by policies, that means the market has severe limitations and can't play its basic role of optimizing the resource allocation effectively and thus becomes "a policy-oriented market".

According to our research, the inter-relationship among our country's economic cycle, stock market and policy cycle is as illustrated by Fig. 4.1.

According to Fig. 4.1, from 1991 to 2000, both the policy cycle and the stock cycle have gone through one and a half cycles, almost in synchronization. It provides justification for the hypothesis that our stock market is closely linked with policies. From 1991 to the first half of 1996, the functioning direction and pace of the three cycles are

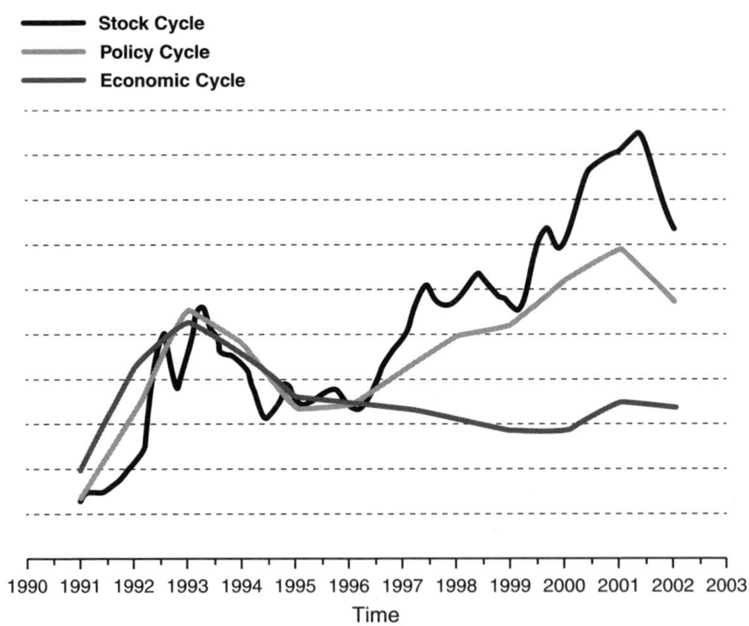

Fig. 4.1. The Relationship between China's Economic Cycle, the Stock Market Cycle and the Policy Cycle during 1990–2003.

almost the same, presenting obvious synchronization. However, after the latter half of 1996, the notable deviation of the stock cycle from the economic cycle originated mostly from the functioning of the policy cycle. That is to say, the great bull market since the latter half of 1996 was supported by the policy cycle instead of being promoted by the rise in the economic cycle.

By adopting the CGARCH (components generalized autoregressive conditionally heteroscedastic) model to describe the characteristic of China's stock market fluctuations with time, we have made an analysis of the impacts of policies upon the fluctuations. It shows that in our stock market there is short–term and obviously also long–term volatility with time. Short–term material fluctuation is often caused by the interference of government policies and it will interrupt the regression process (process of declining fluctuation) of long–term fluctuation to revert to an average value. What's more, it will shift to become an even greater fluctuation. It can therefore be seen that, policy interferences are the direct cause of tremendous changes in the fluctuation of our stock market and contribute to its volatility.

We also researched on the issue of whether our stock market overreacts to policies. By "overreact" we mean the phenomena that an event (such as a policy announcement) leads to change in stock prices beyond the anticipated and rational range. Its reflection in the market is that after the event, the share prices will go through dramatic changes beyond the anticipated range, then the opposite situation will occur and the prices will restore to the anticipated and appropriate level. The main reason for the overreaction is that investors usually overestimate the effects of the current information while underestimating that of the past information. They will react irrationally to the present information and then prices will fall or rise beyond the anticipated range. After a period of time when investors do make rational estimations and begin to re-consider the effects, share prices will go through reverse amendments. In such a process, the over-risen or over-fallen stocks will over-fall or over-rise respectively. By adopting the method of "event study" in an analysis of four representative events of new policies (the promulgation and implementation of the Securities Laws on 1 July 1999; the release of the news that "insurance capital has come into the market" and "rights issue for investors in the secondary market" on 14 February 2000; "notice on rights issue for listed companies in 1996" on 27 January 1996; and an editorial by the People's Daily entitled "understanding the present stock market in a correct way" on 16 December 1996), we find that China's stock market do overreact to policies.

Policy cycles have much more impact than economic cycles on the functioning of the stock cycles in our country: market prices, profits and its fluctuation are all policy driven over the long–term and always respond too much to policies. We may conclude that our stock market comes under the influence of policies to an excessive extent, bearing the characteristic of "policy oriented market."

The consequence of a ten year long "policy oriented stock market" in China is that many investors (especially small and medium investors) developed the tendency of being excessively dependent on information about policies. Also as a "one-sided stock market", profits can only be made in a bull market. So many investors are convinced that rises are the general trend while falls are only temporary. They believed that the government also does not want to see falls and will always take measures to support or 'save' the market in the end. "A policy oriented market" will also help encourage more excessive speculation. Once a favorable policy is revealed, investors will scramble for stocks and rush to purchase one after another, soon lifting the stock index to high points and bringing about the rapid expansion of bubbles in the stock market. Furthermore, "a policy oriented market" lends advantages to 'Market Makers' or 'bankers' to manipulate the market. They always manage to raise the prices of individual stocks by making up and spreading false "insider information" together with various speculation techniques; they then cash out and rake in huge profits.

4.3.5. *A Serious Tendency Towards Excessive Speculation*

Every stock market is a place for both investment and speculation. Generally speaking, "investment" refers to the long–term investments of purchasing shares in the hope of enjoying high dividends while "speculation" refers to short–term investments of purchasing stocks in the hope of quickly making profits by selling them at higher prices.

Generally, moderate speculation activities will do no harm to the securities market. On the contrary, they are helpful to its proper functioning. There are three reasons for this. Firstly, these moderate speculations can help vitalize stock transactions, increase the liquidity of the market and accelerate the active turnover of capitals. Secondly, speculators dare to assume the risks of newly issued shares, an action that promotes the issue of new stocks. Thirdly, investors' speculative activities of "sell at high while buy at low" help to adjust or develop the relationship between supply and demand in the market, thus facilitating the stability of share prices. In my opinion, a mature stock market is one with moderate speculation and a dynamic balance between investment activities and speculation activities. It may fluctuate as a result of influences from the outside environment, but generally it could usually maintain stable and smooth functioning. Furthermore, in helping to promote the development of the economy, it can also bring about relatively satisfactory returns to most investors.

As a matter of fact, many investors in the stock market have motives of both investment and speculation, but the proportion of the two varies with the people and the specific conditions of the stock market. If the speculation activities of most investors are very significant, this will lead to a market with excessive speculation. At such times investors usually tend to brush aside the business performance of the companies. Blue chips will be snubbed while those shares worthy of speculation will be chased after, which will greatly weaken the stock market's objective of resource allocation. Excessive speculation will also encourage short–term activities and lay the basis for 'Market Makers' to manipulate the market. The tremendous risks accompanied by excessive speculation will be a serious potential cause of turbulence in the securities market and this could hinder further the development of the economy and society.

The key criterion for judging whether a stock market is excessively speculative is to see whether investors value the short–term prices or long–term value of investment objects (listed companies), and whether the market deviates from the rule of symmetry between risks and profits.

From the point of investment, the share prices should be equal to the spot value of their expected revenues (called rational prices) so the fluctuation of share prices should not exceed that of the rational prices determined by dividends. But due to the influences of speculation, the fluctuation of share prices may exceed that of the rational prices. To test the excessive speculation and effectiveness or 'validity' of the stock market, *Shiller* in 1981 put forward the famous testing method of "variance limit."[9] He defined the "future discounted present value of actual dividends" as the post-event rational stock prices. The proportion of the fluctuation of share prices (variance) to that of the post-event rational stock prices (variance) can indicate whether the fluctuation is excessive or not. In my view, it can on the whole represent the extent of speculation in the market. According to Shiller's calculation, fluctuation of the Dow Jones index of the U.S. from 1928 to 1978 was 13 times that of the post-event rational stock prices. Fluctuation of the S&P Index from 1878 to 1978 is 5.6 times of the post-event rational stock prices. We selected a sample data from the Shanghai Stock Exchange from January 1993 to December 2000 to test the variance limit, and found that fluctuation of the Shanghai Stock Exchange Composite Index was 69 times that of the post-event rational stock prices.

The notable deviation of share prices from the rational prices in China's stock market is also reflected in that dividends have a very limited illustration or explanatory capability of stock prices. According to our research, in China, the illustration capability is 10% (1 year) and 20% (2 years); however, in the U.S., it is 48% (1 year) and 53% (2 years).

From the two reasons aforementioned, we can see that the extent of speculation is much higher in our stock market than that of the U.S.

It should also be pointed out that the activities of listed companies have also encouraged speculation in the market. China's listed companies seldom pay out dividends. Even if they do, it is usually in the form of giving bonus shares rather than cash. By the end of 1999, only eight listed companies on the Shanghai and Shenzhen Stock Exchanges have shared profits of over one billion Yuan every year. In 2000, stamp duty collected from the stock market and commissions from the investors to securities traders amounted to more than 90 billion Yuan. The total amount of listed companies' profits was about 50 billion Yuan and total dividends for allocation about 14 billion Yuan. As investors can hardly make profits from dividends, they have to 'go all out' to strive for profits from price differences between sales and purchases, which increases speculation in the market.

The P/E Ratio is the proportion of stock prices to earnings after tax. The higher the P/E ratio is, the better the investors' anticipation for the future of the stock. So investors are willing to hold the shares at higher prices to gain future profits. In the stock market, only those shares that are widely regarded as worth investing by investors will have their P/E ratio reaching relatively high levels. However, after carrying out a statistical analysis of the stock market we find that there is a strong negative correlation between the companies' business performance and their P/E ratio. The stock prices of those companies with poor performance are always relatively high while the prices of those listed companies with sound financial status are relatively low. On the whole, the P/E ratio of blue chip type listed companies are much lower than that of those with very poor financial status. This goes to show the excessively speculative direction of China's stock market.

To judge whether our stock market deviates from the rule of symmetry between risks and profits, we have made an analysis of the data classified according to the CITIC Style index system. It is composed of three scale-styled indices and six sub-indices of scale, value and growth. The scale indices include overall market index (Zhongxin overall market), medium stock index (Zhongxin medium stocks) and the small stock index (Zhongxin small stocks). The six sub-indices consist of: overall market value index, overall market growing index, medium stocks value index, medium stocks growing index, small stocks value index and small stocks growing index. The value indices have a high ratio of liquidation value to total market value (B/P value for short). The growing indices have a low ratio. According to the data, the liquidation value per share of the overall market and medium value stocks is slightly higher than the growing stocks in our stock market, but the gap is not so remarkable (about 10%). However, the gap of the liquidation value per share between small value stocks and small growing stocks is extremely large (two times). There is a notable distinction between growing stock prices and value stock prices: the average prices of the growing stocks are obviously higher than the value stocks.

According to the data, the profits per share and the profit margin of liquidation value per share in the overall market stocks are higher than that in the medium stocks. The financial status of the small stocks is the worst. In the large stocks and medium stocks, the financial status of "growing stock" companies is universally better than the "value stock" companies. Among them, the growing stocks in the overall market is the best, with the profits per share and the profit margin of liquidation value per share about 50% higher than the value stocks. Companies with the growing stocks in the overall market generally boast abundant assets, promising industry prospects and support from government policies. But what is worth mentioning is that the small value stocks have remarkably better financial revenues than the small growing stocks. This is because most of the companies running in the red have concentrated on the small growing stocks. Their profits per share and profit margin of liquidation value per share are negative, evidencing that these stocks on the whole are running in the red.

In a normal stock market (with moderate speculation), risks (fluctuation of share prices) and returns (profits gained in the fluctuation of share prices) are on the whole symmetric. That is to say, the higher the profits of a stock, the greater the corresponding risks will be. Thus, no risks (no fluctuation of share prices) means no returns (profits from speculation). But in a market with excessive speculations, it may differ from the rule of symmetry regarding risks and returns. The relationship between risks and returns of various shares in China's stock market from January 1998 to December 2000 is shown in Fig. 4.2.

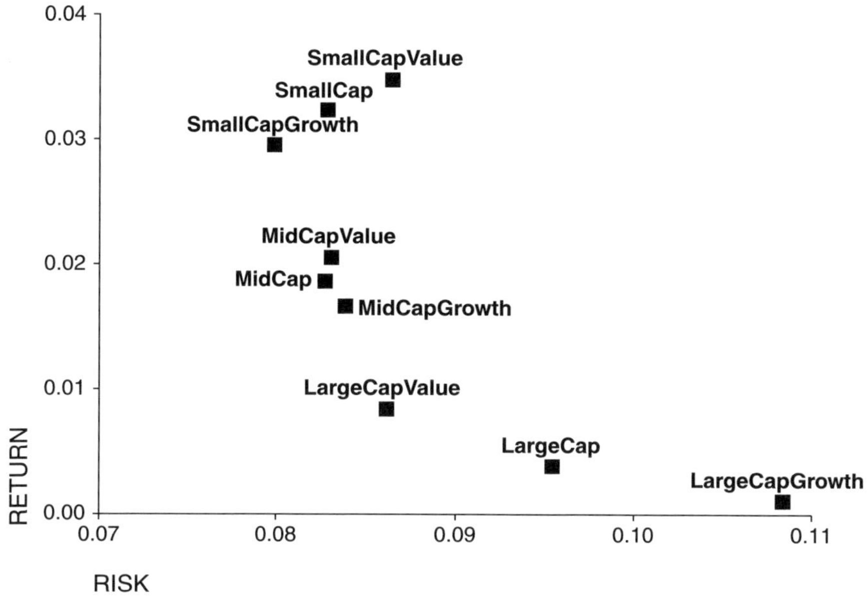

Fig. 4.2. The Risk-Return Relationship of the Various Styles of Shares in China's Stock Market from January 1998 to December 2000.

The vertical axis in the figure represents the market rate of returns, using the price differential between end of the month and that of end of the previous month — to estimate the average yearly share price at the end of the month concerned. The horizontal axis represents the market risks, measured using yield variance. In the chart, LargeCap, LargeCapValue, LargeCapGrowth represent the broader/overall stock market, large-value and large-growth respectively; MidCap, MidCapValue, MidCapGrowth refer to medium stocks, medium value stocks and medium growth stocks respectively, while SmallCap, SmallCapValue, SmallCapGrowth refer to small stocks, small value stocks and small growth stocks respectively.

From Fig. 4.2, we can see that in our stock market, small stocks with poor financial status and poor business achievements bore the highest market yield while those overall market stocks with the best business performances bore the lowest market yield. Within tradable stocks of the same scale, yield of the value stocks are universally higher than the growing stocks, while the growing stocks with the best business performances bore the lowest yield and the highest risks as well. This is because these companies boast a fairly large stock scale/size and a limited "content", which makes it hard to bring sudden and huge profits to investors in a short period of time. So investors usually have no interest in their stocks. Such a situation has led to a serious underestimation of their internal/inherent value and these stocks have thus become the "blue rubbish chips of the market". On the contrary, some shares with poor performance, such as PT and ST shares are being greatly sought after over the long–term.

The above situation speaks volumes to the fact that China's stock market has deviated from the rule of symmetry between risks and profits. But such a distortion, to a great extent, comes from the 'Market Makers' arbitrage by using asymmetric information. Most investors can hardly resist the tempting profits of low risks and high returns. It is reported that in 1999,[10] of the 44 million stock investors, 29.66% of them made profits and 4.56% of them broke even. That is to say, 65% of them suffered losses and 50% of them suffered heavy losses of over 35%. In addition, an online survey revealed that in the bull market of the year 2000, only 39.68% of stock investors made profits in the secondary market from January to October; 43.22% of them suffered losses and 17.09% of them broke even.

4.3.6. *Lots of Bubbles in the Stock Market*

Financial asset bubbles refer to the deviation of prices from their base value. It is a sudden rise in price of one or a series of assets in the continuous process of financial operations. Following the initial price rises, there will be anticipation for further rises in the future. New speculators will be lured to invest, which will bring about the phenomenon of asset prices rising much higher than their rational prices. What interest the speculators are the profits to be gained through purchase and then sale of the assets instead for their own use or for their capacity to earn profits. Expansion of the bubbles will lead to temporary prosperity and even 'fanaticism', but the bubbles will eventually burst after assets are amassed to a certain degree, after a financial assets price slump, followed by recession of the economy and even an economic crisis.

Our considered view is that speculation, bubbles and risks co-exist. Where there are speculations there will be bubbles, and where there are bubbles, there will be risks. The stock market is a speculative one, so there is no doubt that bubbles do exist. Expansion and bursting of the bubbles lead to the fluctuations of the stock market, bringing risks to investors.

A moderate amount of bubbles, just like speculations, would be advantageous to the workings of the stock market. A moderate amount of bubbles will help strengthen people's confidence in making profits by speculating in the market, and so attract more capital into the stock market. But a continuous expansion of such bubbles will induce people to speculate excessively and finally lead to their panic when the bubbles break down. At this time, people's dumping of their stocks might lead to an "excessive rectification or overcorrection" of the stock market. In such a scenario, share prices become lower than their rational prices, constituting "macula" or 'sunspots' (negative bubbles).

Some scholars have proposed classifying the bubbles in the stock market into two types: 'rational' bubbles and 'irrational' bubbles. By the former is meant those bubbles formed when share prices deviate from their rational prices for a short period of time; by the latter we mean those formed when investors' activities are irrational because of an often ineffective market, incomplete information and difference in investors' anticipation. In the latter case, investors may continue to purchase shares when share prices are already fairly high, believing that they can sell the shares at even higher prices. This is the so called "stupid gambling".

There are also some scholars who proposed to classify them into certain bubbles and random bubbles; once the former is formed, it will sustain a stable growth along with time with no connection with anticipation; whereas the scale and change of the latter are all uncertain, depending on anticipation and other random factors — and they may break down any time. Random bubbles are closer to the actual situation of the stock market and are thus more typical.

I would propose classifying bubbles into 'objective' bubbles and 'subjective' bubbles in accordance with the scientific principles of decision making and uncertainties. Objective bubble results from the existing uncertainties in the economy; while the subjective bubble stems from people's false and subjective estimation of the stock market's prospects. As stated above, the rational prices of shares is equal to the spot value of their future profits, and are dependent on their future profits and interest rate. Both of the two are closely associated with the fundamental aspects of the economy and should be forecasted based on their past and present data. It is true that in recent years with the rapid development of information technology, the forecast techniques have been greatly improved. Many new techniques have appeared, such as data extraction, discovery of knowledge in the database, symbolic data extraction, intelligent extraction and so on. These have greatly improved the veracity of the forecast. To some extent, they enable us to grasp the changes in the business performance of companies, the developing trend or direction of the interest rate variation and to help investors to adjust their investment strategies accordingly. However due to the uncertainties in the objective world and people's limitations to comprehend, there will inevitably be some difference between the anticipated and actual results. Bubbles formed under such conditions exist objectively or independently, so we may call them objective bubbles.

The principles of complexity science dictate that in a complex system with people's participation, their subjective estimations of the future differ in a myriad of ways. However, the mutual influences among people and the inductions of the outside world on people's activities will develop a kind of self organizing effect and stimulate the system to persistently and eventually move toward one direction. The subjective bubbles in the stock market result from this self organizing effect. What's more, it may result in reinforcing 'positive feedback' (stupid gambling), rendering share prices to rise far higher than their rational prices.

In the stock market, price/earning ratio (P/E value) is the ratio of a listed company's share price to the net earnings per share. It is an important indicator reflecting the probability of formation of bubbles. The higher the P/E ratio is, the more likely bubbles may form. In essence, the P/E ratio is the relative price of the share. It can directly reflect the severance between share price and its market value, serving as a very significant index for judging the rationality of share prices and the formation of financial bubbles. A number of factors may affect the general P/E ratio, and the most important factors are potential for economic development and the interest rate in the market. In normal cases, maximum acceptable P/E ratio should not exceed the reciprocal of yield (discount rate) acceptable to investors. For example, in 2000, taking the interest rate of five year fixed deposits (2.304% after deducting the interest tax) as the discount rate, the maximum acceptable P/E ratio is 43.4.

From 1996 to 2000, the growth rate of Shenzhen's aggregate index number is 461.40% while in Shanghai it is 273.41%. In 2000, the average P/E ratios of A-shares at the Shenzhen and Shanghai stock exchanges were respectively 58.22 times and 56.03 times, both of which are much higher than the maximum acceptable ratio in the corresponding period. As the profits used in the calculation of P/E ratio are accounting profits, it is estimated that on average, about 10% of the publicized profits are from investments in the stock market. In addition, the calculation of the average P/E ratio does not include those companies running in the red. So the actual P/E ratio could be even higher.

Dividend rate is the ratio of dividends to share prices. An excessively low dividend rate indicates that share prices are too high and that too many 'bubbles' exist. According to statistics, from 1996 to 1999, on average only 26 listed companies in a year gave out cash bonus, accounting for only 3.3% of the listed companies for each year. In 2000, the percentage returns in cash of the 61 companies that have publicized their annual returns was only 0.83% on average. But in the corresponding period, the interest rate of bank deposits was 2.25% (1.8% after deducting the interest tax). Furthermore, in 1995, the dividend rates in the Shenzhen and Shanghai stock exchanges were only 20% to 50% of the public debt yield, which showed that share prices were on the high side.

The bubbles of our stock market can be divided into three levels or strata: first level bubbles are from the securities amortization on issuing and listing in the primary market; second level bubbles are from the profits of price differences in the securities exchanges in the secondary market; and third level bubbles come from the profits of price differences resulting from the rise of share prices after listed companies' takeover, purchase and re-capitalization.

By applying the dynamic first order autoregressive model, we can find that there are still relatively too many bubbles in the present stock market, compared to the mature stock markets abroad. From 1991 to 2000, cumulative bubbles in the aggregate indices of the Shenzhen and Shanghai stock exchanges were respectively 63.4% and 58% per year. However, the Dow Jones index only registered 19.5% in the corresponding period. After comparing the developing trend of the bubbles with that of the aggregate indices, we could discern that notable rises in the stock indices were always accompanied by more bubbles at the same time. This accounted for the fact that rises in the overall market were to a large extent, prompted by the bubbles. Although the bubbles are declining year on year, there are still too many of them compared with the situations in mature markets. Since August 2001, with the fall in our stock market, the number of bubbles has been declining. But due to various reasons, some bubbles (such as the first level bubbles) are still hard to eliminate.

4.3.7. *Prevalence of Short–Term Acts*

By short–term acts, we mean that a round of share trading is completed within six months to make short–term profits, something which is a prevalent phenomenon in today's stock market of China. When investors are engaged in such acts, they usually "chase the rising share while abandoning the falling share", which is the characteristic of speculation. They will not pay much attention to the achievements of the companies and will make decisions for investment mainly according to information about market exchange (technical analysis) or some other information. This has created a Chinese stock market with the following marked features: high P/E ratio, no favor to blue chips, high turnover rate and high fluctuations.

Turnover rate is the ratio of "total amount of transactions" to "tradable shares", or "total contract value" to "total negotiable market capitalization". Turnover rates at the Shanghai and Shenzhen stock exchanges are much higher than that of mature stock markets in Western countries. The turnover rates at the Tokyo and London stock exchanges are smaller than 50%. In recent years, turnover rates in the stock markets of New York, Hong Kong SAR, Thailand and Singapore are all less than 70%. But in our stock market, average turnover rate from 1992 to 2000 in the A-share market was 400% annually, which meant that investors in the secondary market usually held a share for only about three months on average. Every year the turnover rate of a few individual shares reached 1,000% or even as high as 2,000%.

Blue chips in China's stock market are not favored and objects of investors' pursuit. A more important cause for the rise and fall in the stock market is the size of the stock. The direction of the stock market is mainly determined by various factors of anticipation, Market Makers, policies and rumors. The share prices, to a great degree, are 'divorced' from the business performance of the companies concerned.

Our research also shows that 76.3% of investors complete a round of stock trading within half a year and only 7.3% of them take longer than a year. That is to say, at present most investors are engaged in short term transactions and long–term investors account for the least. Moreover, a fair number of the investors are doing very short–term transactions, that is, 27% of them complete their 'round' of transactions in less than a month. From this we can see that short term acts of investment are universal in China's stock market.

Investors in China's stock market attach the greatest significance to the official policies and the domestic and international environment; second in importance are the Market Makers, followed by the company's fundamentals. According to a random sample survey, 40.6% of investors know little or even nothing about the workings of the relevant company — which all go on to show that generally investors in China's stock market commonly carry out short–term investments.

At present, investors in China's stock market can on the whole be divided into three major types: institutional investor, private investor and private equity fund. The acts of all the three types of investors exhibit clearly the characteristic of being short–term investors.

Institutional investors are mostly securities investment funds and securities companies. They possess the advantages of being large scale or size, having abundant capital and professional staff. It is natural that they are tempted by the motive to manipulate the market for quick gains. Driven by prospects of sudden huge profits, their acts will inevitably be short–term. The securities companies are devoid of their own capital, so they will adopt either legal (such as using shares as security for loans) or illegal means (embezzlement of clients' cash deposits, covert interbank lending and clandestine taking of deposits) to obtain capital to gain sudden and huge profits by speculating in the stock market. Such short–term capital with high costs will inevitably lead to short–term transactions.

Private investors in our stock market are mainly composed of small and medium investors. They have few channels to gain information and the authenticity of the information cannot be ascertained. So they cannot make rational judgments for making long–term investments. They possess a limited amount of capital and their investment in the stock market accounts for a large proportion of their family's total assets, so they cannot withstand or assume the risks of losses caused by long–term investment in the stock market. As a result of excessive speculation and bubbles in our stock market, investors are less aware or less 'sensitive' to the possible risks and they are willing to bear higher risks than compared to the anticipated corresponding risks of their actual profits. They have actually become speculators who are partial to risks.

A privately offered or 'equity' fund means a fund established to collect capital via non-public means from a few specially designated investors. Owing to their lack of appropriate legal foundation, there is at present still no public and legitimate privately offered fund in our country. They exist in other disguised forms such as a 'works studio', handling the financial affairs of their clients and as company or contractual privately offered fund. It is estimated that as of 30th June 2001, the amount of privately offered funds reach about 700 to 900 billion Yuan, mostly in the form of 'handling the financial affairs of clients'. As these amounts represent short–term capital, the handlers or fund-mangers will be forced to make short–term investments under the pressure of repaying the principal and interest.

4.3.8. *Market Makers: Punishment must be Meted out for their Manipulation of the Market*

Market manipulation is defined as activities by individuals or institutions carried out for making profits for themselves through manipulating stock prices by means of cheating, misleading and creating untrue prices to lure other people to enter the stock market. On the surface, market manipulation activities are camouflaged as securities investment activities. However, in actual fact, they constitute illegal use and abuse of investors' rights to buy and sell shares.

Market manipulation activities are listed as forbidden by the "Provisional Regulations on the Administration of Share Issuance and Trading" promulgated by the State Council in 1993 and the "Provisional Administrative Rules Forbidding Fraudulent Securities transactions" by the State Council Securities Supervision Commission in 1993. In 1999, the "Stock Act or Securities Laws of the PRC" came into force, and it made further provisions prohibiting market manipulation activities. It forbids in explicit terms anyone to obtain malfeasant or irregular profits or to transfer risks by the following behaviors: (1) individually or in collusion with others, purchase or sell shares with a view to manipulating the trading prices of shares by using the advantage of accumulated capital or that of being in possession of shares, or that of information leverage; (2) to collude with other people and trade at pre-arranged time, price and means or to sell and purchase securities that they do not possess or hold, such as to affect share prices and trade volume; (3) to take one's stock as the trading object and purchase and sell to oneself without transferring the ownership, so as to affect the share price and trade volume; (4) to manipulate share prices by other means — for example, to manipulate the share prices by timing their transactions at the beginning or closing time of the market or by misrepresentation.

China's securities market is an emerging market. Owing to many factors including the market itself, the legal structure and framework, supervision and law enforcement and so on, market manipulation also exists in China's stock market (as has happened in many mature stock markets at their early stage) and is very serious in some markets.

As a rule, the way of judging whether there is market manipulation of a share price is to identify the abnormal fluctuations. Guojun[11] and others adopted the "excess share price amplitude" (to subtract share price index amplitude at the corresponding period from the share price amplitude) as the indicator for measuring manipulation by Market Makers. The ratio of dominant shareholders (the proportion of "the total shares of individual shareholder owning over 100,000 shares" to "total tradable capital stock") is used to weigh the Market Makers factor. After an analysis of the data from the Shenzhen stock exchange, the results showed that Market Makers had notable influences on excess swings or 'amplitude' of share prices. We therefore come to the conclusion that there are Market Makers manipulating the Shenzhen stock exchange.

From June 1996 to May 2001, the China Securities Regulatory Commission has all together investigated and punished 16 cases of market manipulation. Comparing the fluctuation ranges of the 16 shares' integrated index with that of the weighted composite index in Shenzhen and Shanghai stock exchange, the growth rate of the former is 50% larger than that of the latter. The standard deviation of the former is two times that of the latter. If fluctuation of the weighted composite index is to be representative of the market, we may conclude that fluctuation of the share price caused by manipulation is about two times that of market fluctuation.

The most important ploy of market manipulation in our stock market is the commonly called "taking the Market Maker's seat or becoming a Market Maker". Its fundamental *modus operandi* generally includes the five stages of: accumulation of shares over time, raising the share price, causing share price turbulence, pushing up the share price to a high level and then finally selling the shares.

Market Makers manipulating the market are mostly institutional investors, including securities companies, funds companies, listed companies and (or) their major shareholders, other institutional investors and substantial capital holders. Of the 16 cases of market manipulation investigated and punished by China Securities Regulatory Commission, seven of the manipulators were securities companies. What's more, although one of the manipulators was not a securities company, a securities company has provided the necessary funds for the manipulator.

By manipulating the trading price and trade volume of the stock market to produce false illusions and change the relationship between supply and demand, the Market Makers manage to mislead other investors to follow blindly, chasing after the rising shares and abandoning the falling shares. The Market Makers will either sell out the shares after manipulating them to higher prices to gain huge profits or collect more shares after manipulating them to lower prices so as to subsequently gain profits by raising their prices. Other investors who do not know the facts will either carry on with absorbing shares abandoned by the Market Makers at a high price and thereby locked in or 'stuck', or dumping them at low price to suffer immediate losses. This will seriously infringe the legitimate rights and interests of the investors, and erode the justice and fairness of the stock market. Furthermore, it will destroy the sound running of the stock market and interfere with the healthy development of the economy. Besides, market manipulation also creates an ill effect upon the credit fluctuation and collateral loans of the banks.

As stock transactions have the characteristic of being centralized and quick, so risks could be spread out rapidly. If not properly controlled, the risks of certain stock transactions may evolve into a systematic risk to the whole stock market and lead to its collapse. A very important reason for the collapse of the U.S. stock market in the 1930s was market manipulation. Many other countries and regions also legislate to forbid and punish market manipulation, thus reducing the room for Market Makers to manipulate.

Although the Stock Act/Securities Law has forbidden market manipulation acts in explicit terms, Market Makers are not under close surveillance or restrictive supervision for the reason that our stock market is a one-sided market where everyone expects more rises and less falls. Some people even think that Market Makers are indispensable to the stock market and that they are the "discoverer of stock market potential" or "voluntary/unpaid analyst of changes in share price". They advocated that people should approach and follow the Market Makers. These appeasing and conniving remarks have led to the prevalence of market manipulation.[12] The 16 cases already investigated and prosecuted represented only a very small fraction of the actual extent of manipulation. It should be pointed out that objectively, the dominant or shareholders of sizeable shares in the market are not the same as Market Makers who manipulate the market. These shareholders should play the role of making more rational investments instead of obstructing the fairness of the market.

4.4. Effective Measures to Standardize, Manage and Develop Our Stock Market

In my opinion, the abovementioned eight aspects of the problems are the major ones of our stock market that we must address. They have not only 'destroyed' the fairness and justice of the stock market, but have also made people speculate fanatically to earn sudden and huge profits, thereby seriously infringing the rights and interests of most investors and greatly undermining the stock market's roles in optimizing resource allocation and promoting the development of the national economy. We must find out the reasons that cause these problems and take effective measures to standardize, control, manage and develop our stock market.

"Recommendations by the CPC Central Committee on formulating the 10th five year plan for national economic and social development" stresses that it is necessary to "standardize, control, supervise and develop the stock market", and proposed that the stock market should "support the commercialization of new high technologies", to "encourage large and medium sized state owned enterprises to implement and enforce stockholding system by getting listed through proper channels", to "breed and develop institutional investors", to "strengthen supervision over the market and publication of information about listed companies", to "adapt to the trends of cross-border investment, actively explore various ways of utilizing long and medium term foreign investment channels such as acquisitions, mergers, investment funds and securities investment". These guidelines have further demonstrated the direction for the development of our stock market.

Since the bull market which occurred from May 1999 to July 2001, the market value of our stock market has been declining. The market value at the end of 2002 had dropped by 20.3% compared with that of 2000 (tradable market value dropped by 22.5%). We may therefore conclude that China's stock market has entered a period of adjustment and consolidation. We should grasp the opportunities open to us to expeditiously and seriously 'sum up' the experiences and learn the relevant lessons, and regulate or manage the stock market conscientiously and in a down-to-earth manner, laying emphasis on the following eight aspects:

4.4.1. *Define and Clarify the Guiding Theory*

It is known to all that China's stock market developed under the guidance of Deng Xiaoping's Theory. After thoroughly summarizing the experiences and lessons learned in economic development since the founding of the PRC and using the achievements of contemporary human civilization as reference and encouraged by the progressive principles of Marxist theory, Deng Xiaoping put forward the innovative viewpoint that market economy is also applicable to the socialist system. As early as 1979, he pointed out that "it is absolutely wrong to say that market economy only exists in capitalist society or that the only market economy is a capitalist economy." Why should market economy be disallowed in a socialist society? We should not simply equate market economy with capitalism." He later reiterated his viewpoint time after time, relieving people's misgivings about the development of the stock market in a socialist system and stimulating the establishment of the Shanghai and Shenzhen stock exchanges. In his speech delivered during his visit to Southern China in early 1992, he pointed explicitly that "planned economy is not equal to socialism, because it also exists in capitalist society; market economy is not equal to socialism, because it also exists in the socialist society. Both planning and the market are economic measures." He further added: "whether stocks and the stock market are good or dangerous, whether they are exclusive to capitalist society and cannot be applied in socialist society-we should resolutely have a try at it, let us allow it and see what happens. If we find that they are good and after a one to two year trial, then we open up; if not, we just redress or rectify them or shut them down. We may shut them down rapidly, slowly or leave some parts."

In line with the spirit and contents of a series of speeches made by Deng Xiaoping, in 1992, the 14th National Congress defined the grand objective of establishing a socialist market economy. Our achievements in the past ten years also proved that it is thoroughly possible and quite necessary to use for reference, those advanced operation modes and management methods (including shareholding system and stock market) that reflect the regulation and running of modern socialized production.

Of course, we should be fully aware that we still have a long way to go: we have to make long and arduous efforts in order to develop the stock market in the World's largest developing country that practices the socialist system. We should not only research into and absorb and learn the experiences and lessons of foreign stock markets accumulated through their several hundred years of existence. More importantly, we should ponder and explore the paths of their development that accord with China's national conditions.

In my opinion, the development of China's stock market should be compatible with the socialist market economy system. The essence of the socialist market economy lies in that on the one hand it will play the fundamental role of resource allocation to improve the efficiency of economic development and on the other hand, it should adhere to the principle of socialism to guarantee justice and fairness in society. We should take steps to boost the healthy development of China's stock market, and give full play to its function in optimizing resource allocation to promote the development of the economy. Meanwhile, we should pay close attention to the standardization, proper management, control and supervision over the stock market. We must investigate and punish all illegal activities to provide equal and fair opportunities for all investors in the market to make profits.

We can conclude from the developmental course of virtual or fictitious economy, that value securities are the products of socialization of interest-added capital, while the stock market is the outcome of marketization of securities. The fundamental role of the stock market is to provide opportunities for investors to make direct investments and for companies to directly seek financing. Risks in the stock market are rather high to investors, so only those companies whose expected share yield is higher than the bonds are worth investing. On the other hand, companies need the investors to share the risks, and in this regard they have to provide fair profits for sharing with the investors in order to attract the capital of investors. The guiding principle of adjusting or managing China's stock market is to allow it to return to its fundamental function. On the one hand, we should enable investors to invest their capital in deserving companies, to make independent decisions on whether to hold the shares or to sell them for cash, and to let speculators assume corresponding risks. On the other hand, we should enable companies with profit making potential to raise the needed capital and to drive those companies deserving no investment out of the market through investors' choice. Only in this way can the stock market play the role in optimizing resource allocation. We should prevent firmly excessive speculative acts in the stock market. We should never allow the stock market to become a place for a few people to speculate madly or to make huge profits quickly, nor allow it to become a place for a few companies to absorb capital without restraint or to obtain finance at rather low costs.

4.4.2. *Strengthen and Improve Market Supervision*

In October 1992, the State Council decided to establish the State Council Securities Supervision Commission and China's Securities Regulatory Commission to centralize supervision and regulation over China's stock market and to extend the experimental locations of stock issuing from Shanghai and Shenzhen to the whole country. According to the "reform program on the system of securities supervisory and regulatory organizations" by the State Council, China's Securities Regulatory Commission has completed the system reform of implementing vertical leadership over local securities supervisory and regulatory organizations. It has also established nine securities regulatory offices, two offices under direct control and 25 specially appointed offices. Pursuant to the requirements of the Stock Act/Securities Laws, securities supervisory departments have cleared up and closed down several stock exchange markets that were opened before the implementation of the Act. They have also changed the stock issuing system from "examination and approval system" to "authorization system". They help to intensify the obligations of listed companies and institutions concerned to disclose relevant information. They have supervised and urged the listed companies to optimize corporate governance, implemented the "three separations" of assets, personnel and financial affairs between listed companies and shareholders. They have also strengthened the routine supervision and regulation over listed companies, re-classified the securities companies for better management, improved regulation and guidance over intermediary service business such as investment consultancies and reformed the registration and settlement system. All these measures have been effective in ensuring the normal functioning of the stock market and preventing illegal activities. China's Securities Regulatory Commission has investigated and punished many illegal activities of listed companies and securities companies, such as illegal financing, covert or behind-the-scene transactions, market manipulation and fraud. Procuratorial organs have investigated into some illegal cases and the people's courts at all levels have prosecuted and tried several such cases.

As a legal securities supervisory and regulatory organization, China's Securities Regulatory Commission, despite its supervisory and regulatory powers, is still quite far from fully fulfilling the requirements of the Act/Securities Laws and the expectations of the people. I propose to improve its working from the following four aspects:

First of all, the responsibilities of the securities supervisory and regulatory organizations must be clearly spelt out. The main responsibility of the securities supervisory and regulatory organizations is to safeguard the justness and fairness of the securities market to let the stock market return to its fundamental role as an organ for direct investment and direct financing. On the one hand, the stock market should try to provide an equal investment environment for all to enable the investors to strive for reasonable profits under the prerequisite of bearing the risks by themselves. As small and medium investors have poor and limited avenues to information and weak capacity to bear risks, they are the relatively vulnerable groups in the stock market. That is why the relevant authorities must investigate and punish firmly and timely all kinds of illegal activities that rob the wealth of the small and medium investors. At the same time, the system must prevent a situation whereby the actions of some majority shareholders in listed companies jeopardize or side-line the interests and rights of the small shareholders. On the other hand, a just, fair and open authorization system should be established to offer equal market access to companies of different types of ownerships. Good companies that provide higher returns for investors should be given more opportunities to obtain financing. The requirement for no-risk arbitrage in the primary market should also be abrogated to prevent the market from becoming a place for "misappropriation" for some companies. Securities supervisory and regulatory organizations should not be made responsible for the rise or fall of the stock market, nor be seen as a support or savior of the market at the behest or assuming the role of owners of state assets. In some unusual and extremely necessary cases, securities supervisory and regulatory organizations may request the government, through legal means and processes, to intervene temporarily and moderately in the market.

Secondly, it is essential to grasp the key points of market supervision and regulation. Publication of false information is a universal problem among listed companies in their raising of capital by floating shares, during listing, share allotment, and publication of their annual reports. First of all, some companies, in order to get listed, will overvalue their capital, falsify reports of their profits and fabricate their strengths. Secondly, some listed companies will, against the will of the investors, change the purpose and object of the raised capital at will, and thus indirectly causing false information about the company. According to what I have known in Shanghai, 40% of listed companies changed the use of the raised capital within two years; 10% of them changed the use of the raised capital within a year. A fairly high portion of the raised capital returns to the stock market through many channels and join in the speculation. Thirdly, a few listed companies deliberately publicize false information. Some companies, in order to cater to the Market Makers' speculation of their own shares, will announce some misleading information at different times. For example, in January 2001, a majority shareholder of Daqing Liandong announced that the company would give out a large number of bonus shares, and this caused the stock price to go up. But later on, two shareholders released remarks to deny those made by the majority shareholder, causing the stock price to slump. Many investors suffered heavy losses as a consequence. According to the Xiamen municipal government, among the 16 listed companies in the city, 20% of them have publicized false information. In light of the results of the inspection on law enforcement, the situation in some places could be even worse.

It can therefore be seen that the emphasis of supervision and regulation should be placed on the publication of information. We must take effective measures to prevent false fabrication and avoid changing the use of the raised capitals at will, which will jeopardize the interests of investors. We should further improve the criteria on information publication, accelerate the process of internationalization of accounting standards, ensure the authenticity, veracity, comprehensiveness and completeness, standardization, timeliness of listed companies and related intermediary organizations in their publication of information. Publication of correct and accurate information not only alters the asymmetry of information among investors so as to prevent a handful of people from making profits by using insider information and from cheating by using false information — but also facilitates discovery of the actual problems. After the publication of information, professionals like CFA (certificated financial analyst) and the investors can make an analysis of the problems themselves and submit them to the securities supervisory and regulatory organizations. The securities supervisory and regulatory organizations may publicize them once the problems are confirmed and verified and will deal with them according to the seriousness and importance of the problems. Attention should also be paid to strengthen supervision over securities companies, listed companies, intermediary organizations, appointed mass media and some stock commentators in order to prevent their mutual collusion and publication of false information to mislead public opinion and investors.

We must not forget also to bring the market in to play its role. Although securities supervisory and regulatory organizations are indispensable to the healthy development of the stock market, the self organizing effect of the market should also be brought into play. As to those related proceedings of stock issuing, listing and transactions, we should try to avoid administrative examination and approval as far as possible. The related processes can be openly applied for and authorized according to procedures; or the companies concerned can apply to be put on the records of the securities supervisory and regulatory organizations after making independent decisions in the light of market conditions. The self-regulatory and self-disciplining organizations such as the stock exchanges and the securities industry association should effectively play the role of bridging and bonding between the government and the stock market. For example, they can inspect and assess their associates or members annually in areas of financial status, business achievements and service quality; they could guide their associates' business activities, investigate any illegal activities and punish them according to the association's regulations. They could settle the conflicts among them, safeguard their legitimate rights and interests, provide them with legal and business education, organize visits and facilitate exchange of ideas, and offer accreditation of qualifications etc.

Lastly, we should constantly strengthen our supervisory and regulatory measures. By utilizing advanced information technology, we should establish a real time transaction monitoring system and an inspection and pre-warning system connecting the whole country by internet. We should identify timely any abnormal events like unusual fluctuations of share prices and analyze the causes in order to take quick counter measures. We should grant the China's Securities Regulatory Commission the necessary power to investigate and punish illegal activities through legal proceedings to prevent surreptitiously withdrawing of funds and the absconding of suspected criminals to avoid punishment. We should further improve the working staff of the securities supervisory and regulatory organizations to elevate their political, ideological, professional quality and specialty skills. Securities supervisory and regulatory organizations, banks, courts and procuratorial organs should strengthen their co-operation, establish a centralized law enforcement co-ordination system and intensify the efforts in the fight against serious illegal securities activities.

4.4.3. *Improve the Quality of Listed Companies*

At present, many of our listed companies are unworthy of people's investment because of their poor quality. The assets yield of our stock market in 1999, 2000, and the first half of 2001 was 4.01%, 3.58% and 1.83% respectively. According to a joint research finding recently made by Shanghai University of Finance and Economy and Brunel University in the U.K.[13], 70% of the listed companies in our country are in a state of depreciating value. Although there are fair profits on the book, these profits are "bought" with the raised money, so these companies are 'rich' on paper only. These 'profits' cannot be translated into cash profits to create value for investors. Additionally, as it does not cost much to create falsified accounts, about 20% of the listed companies do just that. After eliminating the factor of possible falsification of accounts, we find that listed companies display increase in capital and profits, but a notable decline in creating more value.

According to our investigation, a very important reason for the low achievements and lack of development sustainability is that the listed companies have no rational or effective corporate governance structure. By the end of 2002, 1,233 companies have been listed domestically. Most of them are from formerly state–owned enterprises. This has led to our stock market having 40% of state–owned shares that are not tradable, with some listed companies reaching as high as 80%.

Corporate Governance is sometimes called 'corporate artificial person governance' structure. It is a system that determines the allocation of the company's fundamental powers (including senior management, control over corporate resources, power to distribute net profits, etc.), that is to say, the system decides who have these powers and under what circumstances. It is set up to settle the disputes over objectives, as between owners and governors, after the separation of ownership and governance. There are also people who argue that corporate governance means a system that aims at supervising and controlling all the companies' management and performance.

Some of China's listed companies are strictly under the control of their majority shareholders, and some of them have one set of organization but two names or entities so to speak. Some listed companies mix together their personnel, financial affairs and assets with those of the shareholders, thus allowing listed companies to become the "ATM or automatic teller machine" of majority shareholders and the group company. For example, in the past few years, the Monkey King company successively lent out 900 million Yuan to its holding group without being repaid; an account payable of 260 billion Yuan was improperly dealt with, which hollowed out the company's capital and threw it into a state of insolvency. Some companies are active in raising capital but passive in allocating the profits — against the interests of investors. For example, in 1999, 69.1% of the listed companies in Sichuan province did not share profits (give out dividends) and in 2000, 49.1%. Even some companies with outstanding achievements do not give dividends with the excuse of being in dire needs of capital, to the dissatisfaction of investors.

Intervention by local governments with respect to market entry, the process thereof, and the withdrawal mechanism for listed companies have seriously eroded the function of the stock market in optimizing resource allocation. For example, according to the Stock Act/Securities Laws, once the listed companies have lost legal capacity, their listing should be suspended or terminated (delisted). But owing to the intervention by the relevant local governments, some companies that had lost their legal capacity for some time could not withdraw from the market for a long period of time, an occurrence which has severely affected the working efficiency of the securities market.

The main direction for listed companies in adjusting their proprietary rights structure is toward plurality in shareholding. "Decisions by the CPC Central Committee on some important issues concerning the reform and development of state-owned enterprises"[14] pointed out that plurality in shareholding is conducive to the shaping of standard corporate governance. Except for a very small number of companies that should be state monopolies, we should actively develop companies investable by numerous parties. Plurality in shareholding is not only opportune to realizing the objective of public ownership in companies, diversifying forms of ownership, but it also enables the government to solve the problem of the over — dependence of companies on the government and the government having to be indefinitely responsible for the companies. This is done by letting investors take their proper positions or posts.

The problems of unclear proprietary rights and confusion between ownership and managerial authority existing in collectively-owned and privately-owned companies should also be addressed by means of plurality in shareholding.

Theoretically speaking, the general meeting of shareholders is the supreme authority in plural shareholding companies. But owing to the high fluidity and large number of shareholders (transactions of shareholding or 'equities' is quite frequent in the stock market), in practice the board of directors will exert the authority and act on behalf of all the shareholders. As a result of the concentration of shareholding and decentralization of public shareholders, majority or dominant shareholders or insiders might manipulate the board, making it hard to form an independent board to guarantee a wholesome managerial and decision making mechanism. According to a questionnaire survey, only 3.4% of people agreed that the board supervisory commission should be the major controlling body within the listed companies. Due to unreasonable or inequitable shareholding structure, many business managers' interests cannot be safeguarded through a transparent mechanism. In such a situation they will always decide in the interests of the dominant or majority shareholders or themselves when making decisions, at the expense and to the detriment of small and medium shareholders. In such cases, the achievements and performance of the companies are more dependent upon the quality and "conscience" of the managers or upon the open mindedness of the dominant shareholders.

We should treat the problem of "one dominant shareholder" by looking into its root cause and symptoms. On the one hand, effective measures should be taken to solve the problem of dominant shareholders controlling the capital of listed companies. We should supervise stringently the implementation of mutual-assurance between the dominant shareholders and listed companies according to the Act/Securities Laws, forbidding listed companies to provide guarantees for dominant shareholders. Transactions between the dominant shareholders and listed companies should be carried out in accordance with the Act and be publicized in pursuance of the regulations.

It should be made clear by providing guidelines in documents the qualification, requirements, payment, rights and responsibilities of an independent director to allow him to take on the role of supervising. On the other hand, the shareholding structure of listed companies should be adjusted or modified. Since presently it is somewhat impossible to increase the proportion of tradable shares in the stock market, shares could be exchanged among state–owned enterprises. We should make sure that each listed company has at least three dominant shareholders and we should also ensure a healthy, proper and legal system of meetings of shareholders, board of directors and board supervisory commission.

4.4.4. *Lead Investors to Change their Modes of Thinking*

The numerous small and medium investors are not only active participants but also vulnerable groups in China's stock markets. In the process of adjusting and improving the securities market, multiple measures, political as well as legal, should be taken to protect their rights and interests.[15] It is also necessary to educate them to lead them to change their modes of thinking.

First of all, investors should take a correct attitude toward the stock market. They should be told that there are risks to investing in the stock market, and the more speculations there are, the greater the risks will be. If they have deficient capability to assume the risks, most of the time their long–term investments will suffer great loss even though they might have had made profits by speculation. This is especially true of small and medium investors. They should therefore avoid excessive speculation and had better choose listed companies with high investment value.

Secondly, investor's analytical ability should be improved. With better publication of information available, investors should be able to make independent analysis of the value and developing trend of individual stocks and adopt appropriate investment strategies. They could avoid losses by not believing hearsay or by not blindly following the actions of the Market Maker.

Lastly, investors should improve their awareness of the law and regulations. According to my investigation in Shanghai, Shenzhen, Wuhan and other places, many small and medium investors have never read the Stock Act/Securities Laws and do not even know what legitimate rights and interests they enjoy. Investors should learn how to enforce their rights, including rights to own shares and rights to dispose of them at liberty. They should also be told they have the right to information, right to knowledge of material events and the right to vote, right to share in the distribution of the profits allocation of residual properties and so on.

4.4.5. *Actively and Vigorously Foster Institutional Investors*

At present, the tradable shares in our stock markets are rather dispersed, and institutional investors account for too low a proportion. According to statistics, of all the share accounts with the Shanghai stock exchange in 2000, individual investors made up 99.6% while institutional investors a mere 0.44%. The situation in Shenzhen stock exchange is similar. Tradable public shares are highly dispersed among individual shareholders, with the result that public shareholders do not have effective and direct control over listed companies with a strong tendency toward "hitching a ride".

Fostering institutional investors is critical to improving the investment structure of our stock market. The first step is to further develop the securities investment fund, especially "open" funds, trying our best to make "open" funds become the mainstream of the fund industry within five years. The system of fund registration and issuing should be gradually established to create an environment conducive to mechanism innovation in the market. Additionally we should be innovative in creating new varieties of funds to suit insurance and social security capitals, and market the bond market fund and money market fund at opportune times. We should do research on expanding the business scope of fund management companies, allowing them to deal with business like privately offered funds and consigned assets management etc. We should relax the qualification requirements on fund management companies and fund proposers or initiators. We should gradually permit various institutions and natural persons to engage in establishing fund management companies, explore new shareholding structure in these management companies and choose qualified fund management companies to get listed on a trial basis.

Secondly, we should accelerate the pace of fostering institutional investors. We should explore various flexible ways for insurance capital to enter into the market, and encourage fund management companies to make bold innovations in designing a particular variety of fund to suit specifically insurance capital so as to better serve the insurance companies. We could allow on a trial basis insurance companies, either exclusively funded or in joint ventures, to manage the insurance capital. When the conditions are ripe and mature, we may allow insurance companies to participate in establishing fund management companies to further participate in the development of the fund industry and the securities market of our country.

Lastly, we should vigorously explore a market-wise and specialized management system of social security fund. When the social security fund has achieved a certain scale, we may relax the restrictions on investment and gradually open the securities market to the social security fund. We will introduce the competitive mechanism in which to explore and establish a marketwise and specialized management and supervision system of social security fund, with the consigned or entrusted special organizations as the leading management house. We would vigorously and actively explore a variety of management modes for our social security funds, including consigned fund management companies or other insurances like annuity insurance, investment-linked and profit-sharing schemes launched by the life insurance companies, in order to realize the positive interaction between the social security fund market and the securities market.

4.4.6. *To Facilitate the Transformation of Securities Companies into Modern Investment Banks*

Securities companies grow with the development of the stock market. By the end of 2002, there were altogether 126 securities companies and more than 3,700 securities sales departments in various institutions. On the whole, most of the securities companies are doing fine. But there are also some institutions that are involved in illegal and regulation-violating activities. Market manipulations were still rife and some securities companies themselves played the role of Market Makers, or participated in manipulating share prices, gravely undermining the orderly transactions of stocks. Some provided overdrafts to their clients and even appropriated clients' deposits. Some of them even participated in malicious speculation, financed for their clients, sold or purchased shares for their clients, and opened private accounts to trade shares. It is therefore necessary and expedient to take effective measures to rectify and punish the illegal and criminal activities of the securities trading and serving organizations — including their market manipulation, malicious speculation, provision of overdrafts to clients, and the misappropriation of clients' deposits.

At present, China's securities companies are generally very small. There is still a rather large gap in terms of capital strength, business scope, volume and management experiences, compared with the investment banks overseas. The total registered capital of all the securities companies in our country is less than that of a famous foreign investment bank, not to mention the financing capacity. Right now the business scope of securities companies in our country mainly covers securities underwriting and securities brokerage. Other businesses including merger & acquisitions, leveraged buyout, project financing, assets management, and risk investments are yet to be opened up. Our securities companies are not well prepared to underwrite shares in the international market, and far from being able to meet the requirements for further development of the multinational corporations in our country. It is therefore recommended that we lend our strong support to two to three securities companies with good fundamentals and to urge, encourage and groom them to develop towards becoming the modern investment bank.

Great efforts should be made to improve the moral integrity and professional skills of people in the securities industries. It is necessary to establish an incentive mechanism and punish severely illegal acts like fraudulent trading. At the same time, we should enforce strictly qualification and certification tests and accreditation for people in the securities business. Establishing a qualification board for Certified Financial Analyst (CFA) whose standard requirements meet our needs and are up to international standard is strongly recommended.

4.4.7. *Standardize and Develop other Intermediary Organizations and Agencies*

According to the Stock Act/Securities Laws, the intermediary service organizations including accounting firms, law firms and assets valuation offices should provide related services for share issuing and listing. But some organizations, for their self interests, breach professional ethics, fabricate false accounts and provide false certificates. Some even answer to the illegal or unreasonable demands of listed companies, providing whatever accounts or reports asked for, thus throwing open the doors for the false 'packaging' of listed companies. For example, in the first half of 2000 in Sichuan province, four listed companies were investigated for suspected illegal activities involving three certified accountant firms and an assets valuation office.

It is necessary to intensify the self discipline of intermediary organizations, improve the work ethics and moral integrity of the working staff, and strengthen the supervision over and monitoring on intermediary organizations. Accounting firm should play its role professionally and ethically (as certified public accountants) in auditing, providing independent, objective and true audit reports and giving out correct related data, and be answerable and responsible to investors, share issuing companies and society at large. They should adhere to professional rules and conduct as well as follow relevant technical criteria, improve their professional skills and maintain their good and trusted image among the public. Those who are negligent, in breach of contracts or who cheat or lie — resulting in losses suffered by the relevant auditing units or other interested parties — should be investigated into in accordance with the law and could be prosecuted in administrative, civil and criminal proceedings.

Law firms engaged in securities business should guarantee the authenticity, veracity and integrity of their written legal opinions and other legal documents, and be forbidden from providing false certification. In addition, we should raise the qualifications of lawyers engaged in securities business and gradually train and produce lawyers who specialize in securities business and the relevant laws.

Valuation reports on assets or properties from valuation offices represent an important basis upon which state–owned enterprises transform into a shareholding system and for listed companies' recapitalization. The authenticity, veracity, objectivity and integrity of the valuation should be respected, safeguarded and guaranteed. Any attempts to change at will the valuation reports to cater to the wishes of the evaluated entity must be forbidden. We should refer to international benchmarks to set down the valuation method and procedures to suit our national conditions. In particular, the valuation of intangible assets should be standardized strictly. Attention should also be paid to train and foster a group of qualified assets evaluators or valuers.

Another unhealthy phenomenon in China is that some investment companies, investment consultant firms and finance companies start to engage in financing business and control a large amount of capital to speculate in stocks after they have registered in the relevant commercial business management departments. This has led to bad influences on the stock market and should be regulated through legal measures immediately.

4.4.8. *To Further Improve the Legal System/Framework for Securities*

After the promulgation and implementation of the Stock Act/Security Laws, it has become expedient for securities supervisory and regulatory departments to set down necessary codes and relevant implementation regulations because the contents of the Act are just guidelines. It is also necessary to 'tidy up' the relevant, past regulations to accord with the new laws, and to promptly formulate new regulations to implement provisions and policies according to the law and the development of the market. Up till July 2001, with the State Council approval, China's Securities Regulatory Commission has issued five administrative 'codes' or 'directives' including, "Rules and regulations of the Review Committee on Share Issue", "Approval Procedures for Stock Issuance", and formulated and issued more than 130 departmental regulations including "Regulations for the management of new shares issue for Listed Companies', "Securities Companies Inspection Regulations". At the same time, pursuant to the requirements of the law, more than 250 codes, regulations and regulatory documents have been cleared up and 114 have been abrogated. The Shenzhen and Shanghai Stock Exchanges have also cleared up and formulated a number of regulations in accordance with the provisions of the Stock Act/Securities Laws and other supervisory regulations.

However, the existing implementation regulations still cannot meet the needs of the development of the stock market. Some regulations are not in harmony with the Stock Act/Securities Laws and there is a lack of co-ordination and some conflict between laws. Firstly, according to the Stock Act, if investors suffer losses in the stock exchange because the issuer has released false information, the issuer, directors, supervisors and managers should assume related responsibility of compensating the victims. But owing to the lack of specific provisions, it is difficult for an individual investor to lodge a complaint. Moreover, in many cases it is very difficult for the complainant to furnish proof and the courts will be of the view that the existing regulations are not specific enough and do not apply to the cases at hand. For example, an investor in Sichuan province sued the Honguang Corporation but the court considered that there was no or insufficient proof hence 'no case' to put on file for investigation and prosecution. On January 9, 2002, the People's Supreme Court issued the "Notice on accepting and hearing civil cases involving false statement in the stock market". Thereafter on 9 January 2003, the court further issued "Provisions on hearing civil Damage/compensation cases resulting from false statements in the stock market". These provisions have provided powerful legal redress and protection for the rights and interests of investors. Secondly, law enforcement departments have not yet maintained uniform guidelines and criteria in investigating illegal activities and criminal cases in the stock market, thus has impeding the investigation and of some cases. Thirdly, the relationship between the Stock Act and some contents of the Code of Civil Law is unclear or undefined. For instance, law enforcement organizations could carry out execution proceedings against the deposit of caution moneys of clients in securities companies and even arrest people. This has adversely affected the orderliness and smooth running of the stock market.

As the Stock Act came about during the Asian financial crisis, some of the relevant measure were not well-prescribed, whereas some were rather rigidly prescribed in order to effectively avoid the risks. In addition, developments in the stock market have led to some new problems, affecting the enforcement of Stock Act. It is recommended that we do a thorough research into the problems and propose legal redress in accordance with the needs of its development, in areas such as cross industry business, share index futures, entry of social security capital into the market, development of the stock market after ascension into the WTO, and the limits of law enforcement on securities supervisory and regulatory organizations. As to the guideline provisions in the Stock Act, they should be implemented by making detailed rules to effectively carry out the spirit and letter of the Stock Act. For example, securities market supervisory and regulatory rules/regulations, listed companies supervisory and regulatory regulations, securities company management regulations and so on. We should carry out research into the relationship between the Stock Act and company law, trust law, civil law, law of civil suits, criminal law, and code of criminal procedure, and make revisions or give interpretations about related laws when necessary. By doing so, we can co-ordinate their relations and provide effective support and assurance for law enforcement. Securities supervisory and regulatory organizations should try to constantly consider and explore new situations and problems through practices and innovations and further develop and improve China's stock market.

The Stock Act is a fundamental law relating to China's stock market. Only if all the supervisors, working staff and investors know and understand the Stock Act and act in accordance with it can we guarantee its effective implementation. Efforts should be made to further study, publicize and implement the Stock Act. The mass media and securities regulatory and supervisory organizations should be encouraged to publicly promote knowledge of the Stock Act and the related regulations by all means possible. The Shanghai stock regulatory office has requested the securities companies to give a free copy of the Stock Act to every new investor and this action is to be welcome and should be popularized. Leaders at all levels, supervisory staff and principals of securities transaction institutions should take the initiative to study and implement the law. They should be forbidden from illegally intervening with the market and should try to be the role-models in administering, supervising and regulating in accordance with the law. Listed companies, securities management institutions, securities investment consultant institutions, securities staff and the media should further study, publicize and understand the Stock Act in accordance with the requirements of their work. Investors should study thoroughly the Act and strengthen their awareness of risks and self protection, and learn to safeguard their legitimate rights and interests.

At present, China's stock market is at a low ebb and the situation provides an excellent opportunity for adjustment and consolidation. I am convinced that under the efficient leadership of the Central Party Committee and the State Council, the stock market can be rejuvenated and get back onto the broad and correct path for healthy development through the next two to three years of arduous efforts and hard work.

References

[1] World Bank (2001). World Development Indicators, The World Bank.

[2] Zhou, Z.Q. (ed.) (1998). Knowledge of the Securities, Beijing: China Finance Press (in Chinese).

[3] Cheng, S. W. (1999). Fictitious Economy and Financial Crisis, *Journal of Management Science*, 1, 1–6 (in Chinese).

[4] Cheng, S. W. (1999). Explorations of Complexity Science, in Cheng S.W. (ed.), *Complexity and Management*, Beijing: Democracy & Construction Press (in Chinese).

[5] Cheng, S. W. (2001). *Studies on Economic Reforms and Development in China*, Vol. I, Beijing: China Remin University Press (in Chinese).

[6] Zhou, X. C. (2000). Speech on Ten Years' Forum of Securities Market, Hexun, December 16 (in Chinese).

[7] Liu, S. C. and Shen, P. (ed.) (2000). *Chinese Capital Market Theoretical Research Collection*, Beijing: Social Science Literature Press (in Chinese).

[8] He, X. N. (2002). A Study of China Stock Market Making Empty Mechanism. (Somoney.com.cn, accessed on April 11.) (in Chinese).

[9] Shiller (1981). Do Stock prices Move too much to be Justified by Subsequent Changes in Dividends? *American Economic Review*, 76, 421–436.

[10] Wei, Y. H. (2001). Is the Chinese Stock Market "Zero Sum Game" of One Gained, Two Balanced and Seven Lost? Guangdong & Hong Kong Information Daily, December 5 (in Chinese).

[11] Guo, J., Zhang, S. and Chen, J. G. (2002). The Empirical Study of the Characteristics of the Bankers' Manipulation in Shenzhen Stock Market, *China Soft Science*, 9, 27–33, 53 (in Chinese).

[12] Chen, Z. R. and Huang, Y. Z. (2001). What is the Way of the Foamed Chinese Stock Market? *China's Economic Information*, Issue 20 (in Chinese).

[13] Wang, K. G. (2002). *Studies of the Development and Innovation of China's Security Market*, Shanghai: Shanghai People's Press (in Chinese).

[14] The Fourth session of the 15th Central Committee of the Communist Party of China (1999). Decision on Several Important Issues of Reform and Development of State Owned Enterprise of the Communist Party of China, Beijing: People's Press (in Chinese).

[15] Xia, Z. Q. (2002). Eight Major Factors Restricting Savings from Entering into the Stock Market, *Jinghua Times*, April 17 (in Chinese).

Chapter 5

Strategic Thinking about the Development of China's Money Market

Money market is a market for short–term debt securities with high liquidity. Its key functions include but are not limited to: promoting the supply-demand equilibrium of capital and supporting the economic development; pooling together idle funds and increasing the efficiency of capital utilization; driving the capital movement and optimizing capital allocation; implementing monetary policy and enhancing macro control. Despite the prevailing belief in the academic world that the history of the money market can be traced back to the discount market in early 19th century U.K., the transition from the early money market to the modern money market was not completed until after World War II, when the money market saw significant development characterized by rapid growth, rapid market change and ever increasing innovations.

If the money market related questions are studied with the fictitious economy and complexity science theories, all financial market instruments may be considered as fictitious capital. By buying these instruments with the idle funds at hand, investors actually exchange their right of using the money for written evidence of equity and thereby obtain the right to claim the instrument issuers' income and assets generated in the future. In doing so, the investors have to make a trade-off between returns on the one hand, and security and liquidity on the other. As the instruments traded in the money market are mainly those with high liquidity and the ability to rapidly realize the liquidation of the fictitious capital, the design of these instruments embraces such features as short–term credit, credit reputation or credit-worthiness, risk linked interest rate, bulk trading, liquidity through collateralization and compliance with legal regulations. The interrelationship between the money market and the capital market is manifested mainly by the overlapping of market players and the two way movement of capital. As part of the fictitious economy system, financial market, with its inherent complexity, is a combination of micro randomness or uncertainties and macro certainty. Hence, the decision making behaviors of people have to be examined in studying financial markets, especially those concerning irrational behaviors.

China's money market emerged in the early 1980s and experienced ups and downs until after 1998 when its development got back on the right track. However, there is still a huge gap between the conditions of the existing money market and that of the target model. The main lessons to be learned are: (1) the money market can never serve as a market for long–term borrowings; (2) no bank shall be allowed to establish its own intermediaries; (3) the money market should be unified, not fragmented; (4) the Central bank should regulate, rather than simply restrict or prohibit; (5) the Central bank should not neglect the policy function of the money market; and (6) the development of China's money market should never be divorced from China's specifics. China's target model of money market development is composed of the following elements: diversified market players, diversified market instruments, market based interest rates, standardized operations, networked transactions and efficient regulation.

Currently, the market players in China's money market are facing such problems as the "monistic" structure of the market participants, lack of self discipline in their behavior, low competitiveness and outdated financing concepts. It is suggested that intermediaries be developed, entry barriers be lowered, direct financing by companies be encouraged and money market funds be established.

The problems with the 'tools' or 'objects' (the instruments) on the current money market in China are, *inter alia*, sub-scale market, uneven development among sub-markets, lack of connection between sub-markets and unbalanced development between the primary and secondary markets. It is suggested that short–term bonds be developed in a standardized way, interbank borrowing market be expanded and financial innovation be steadily promoted.

Market based interest rate is a prerequisite for the effective operation of the money market. In China, however, the interest rates for most instruments on the money market are determined by reference to the bank deposit and loan interest rates, rather than based on their own particularities and the market supply and demand. To realize market based interest rate, a base rate should be imposed throughout the market to be followed by the establishment of a reasonable interest rate structure (including risk structure and term structure). It is suggested that the interest rate of T-bills (short-term government bonds) formed through bidding prices be adopted as the base rate for the money market. With that base rate as the benchmark, people who have a surplus of capital and those in need of money could work out interest rates of various money market instruments under the rules of the market.

Commercial banks are the most important participants in China's money market. It is believed that radical reforms should be made to transform all the wholly state-owned commercial banks into financially healthy and internationally competitive modern financial companies with well established governance structure, good operational mechanism and clear operation target so as to continuously improve their performance and competitiveness. The People's Bank of China (PBOC) as the Central Bank of China is not only responsible for the regulating of the money market, but is also obliged to construct and improve the monetary policy implementation mechanism and to realize macro control of the market through re-discount, open market operation and reserves policies.

Online transactions will be the trend of trading on the money market. The construction and operation of information network and settlement network must be speeded up. Online trading and networking have taken shape in China but the scale and scope of services should be enlarged, quotation system improved, market analysis increased, and settlement and payment system refined.

Under the socialist market economic system, regulation of the money market should be done by providing guidance with policies, making timely adjustments, preventing risks and maintaining the principle of fairness and equality. Meanwhile, "top-down" administrative regulation and "bottom-up" public supervision should go hand in hand to continuously increase the effectiveness and efficiency of regulation. The Central bank should also play its part in information disclosure in efforts to develop the system and abolish monopolistic privilege.

5.1. Introduction

Money originated as a universal equivalent in the commodity exchange to overcome the limitation of barter in the process of human and social development. When people had surplus money, private lending occurred and idle funds became interest generating capital. With the socialization of the interest generating capital, the financial market emerged whereby lenders and borrowers realized lending and borrowing purposes using various market instruments.[1] According to classical definition, the money market is a financial market that issues and transfers credit tools with a maturity of up to one year. The money market can be defined in a broad as well as a narrow sense. In its broad sense, the bank credit market should be included in the money market. Peter S. Ross, a U.S. economist, thinks that the money market provides a marketplace and a mechanism where people with short term surplus cash can lend money to those with short–term cash deficit.[2] In its narrow sense, only the exchange of short–term debt instruments is included in the category of money market. For example, the U.S. financial scholar, Marcia Stigum thinks that the money market is a wholesale market for low risk, high liquidity, short–term debt instruments.[3] In this article, the author shall elaborate on the money market in its narrow sense and defines the money market as an exchange market for short–term debt instruments with high liquidity.

The key characteristics of the money market are:

1. Trading is conducted between the people with cash surplus and those with cash deficits as reflected in the current accounts, instead

of the capital accounts, of the financial institutions (companies).

2. Short–term trading is the norm, with a maturity of up to one year, or three months for most transactions.
3. Products traded are various short–term credit instruments with high liquidity, including mainly short–term bonds and notes, e.g. treasury bill (TB, T-bill), bank acceptance bill, commercial notes, negotiable certificate of deposit (NCD), repurchase agreement (Repo), federal fund, Eurodollar, interest rate and currency swap, note issuance facilities, money market deposit (MMD), money market deposit account (MMDA), negotiable order of withdrawal account (NOW account), etc. A variety of instruments in the money market meet the different needs of both money borrowers and lenders.
4. Each instrument forms a market and each such market is closely related to the others. The combination of these markets as a whole form the money market.
5. There are numerous and various types of market participants. For example, the borrowers in the U.S. money market include domestic and foreign banks, the Treasury Department, companies of all types, the Federal Home Loan Banks and other federal agencies, dealers in money market instruments, and many states and municipalities. The lenders include most of the above plus insurance companies, pension funds (public and private), and other financial institutions.
6. Wholesale is the major form of trading and each transaction involves a vast amount of money. Normally, transactions are entrusted to dealers who have professional experience and are familiar with a particular market.
7. Lenders' transaction in the money market is a high liquidity and low risk investment with a certain rate of return.
8. Credit and trust is very important in the transactions on the money market. Deals are normally conducted over the phone and often involve a huge amount of money. Once the deal is closed, no party shall renege even if he finds it less profitable than expected. In case unintended mistakes occur, both sides shall try to solve the problems amicably.

The role of money markets in economic development is expressed mainly in the following four aspects:

1. Promoting equilibrium between capital supply and demand, and supporting the development of the economy. Funds can be raised in the money market to rapidly make up the short–term deficit when a company is short of money or a company could invest its short–term surplus. A company's capital flow has its ups and downs. For example, before payment is received for a batch of products sold, the company might not have enough money to pay for the raw materials for the on-going production and it needs to borrow money from the money market. Once the company receives the payment for the goods sold, it might have some extra money for the time being after making repayments, and the extra money can be invested in the money market. In countries with developed market economy, the treasury departments and local governments also take money markets as important means to adjust the short–term capital surplus or deficit.
2. Pooling together idle funds and increasing utilization efficiency. When companies and individuals deposit their idle money into their bank accounts, the bank is responsible for turning the money into interest generating capital. Apart from investment loans and consumer loans, the money market is another important interest generating channel. Thanks to the ability of the money market to gather the funds from all banks into a strong pool of lendable money, an integrated banking system is formed which does not only satisfy speedily the big demands for short–term capital, but also increase the liquidity and utilization efficiency of capital. In addition, the money market is a major place for the management of liquidity of financial institutions and money supply of commercial banks.
3. Promoting capital circulation and optimizing capital allocation. The money market can, through the market mechanism, shift rapidly the short–term capital to the lenders to obtain the biggest return, and thus enable the borrowers to get access to the capital needed at the lowest cost. In so doing, the money market manages

to leverage the market mechanism to encourage and cultivate the good and 'superior' while discouraging or discarding the bad or inferior, thus increasing macro economy efficiency.

4. Propagating and implementing monetary policy and tightening macro control. The money market plays an important role in the conductive mechanism of monetary policies by providing the government with effective means of macro control of the economy. The conduction and propagation of the Central bank's market oriented monetary policies, whether through credit loans (quantity) or interest rates (price), can never steer away from the money market. For instance, the open market operations, re-discount windows and interest rate adjustment of the Central bank have to go through the money market to have their impacts and effects felt on the economy as a whole. Only the mandatory planning-oriented credit monetary policy does not need the money market conduction mechanism.

Although a notion prevails in the academic world that the history of the money market can be traced back to the re-discount market emerging in the U.K. in the early 1900s, it was only after World War II that the world money market gained substantial development, characterized by rapid growth, rapid market change and ever increasing innovations. For example, in the U.S., a country with the most developed market, current daily transactions reach hundreds of billions of dollars, dozens of times larger than in the 1960s. The sizes of various markets change all the time, such as the rise of the U.S. interest rate swap market in the 1980s, the emergence of options and related products, and the rapid expansion of the commercial notes market which dwarves even the short term T-bills market etc.

The most remarkable feature of the U.S. money market is their ever increasing innovations. Compared with other financial markets, the U.S. money market' innovations are the least regulated. Whenever one wants to launch a new money market instrument or use a new method to operate the existing instruments, the odds are that it will not prohibited. Moreover, if the results are clearly remarkable, it will be widely copied and popularized.

The development of China's money market lags far behind that of those developed countries such as the U.S. It is increasingly difficult and untenable for the existing money market to satisfy the growth of China's socialist market economy. The author attempts here to make a preliminary study on the strategic issues in the development and regulation of China's money market by applying complexity science, fictitious economy and system engineering theories and methodologies based on world money market practices and China's specifics.

5.2. History of World Money Market

As an important part of financial market, the money market was born during the development of the modern market economy. Money markets in different countries and regions grow with the development of the economy, matures over time with their practices and explorations, and are closely related with the special historical and cultural backgrounds and the developmental paths of the countries or regions concerned. There has never been a universal model for all the countries, whether it is the transitional form from the early money market to a modern one or the improved modern money market itself. However, by looking back at the history of the world money market, one can find some common features and laws in the development of the money market.

Currently there are four types of money markets in the world: the first type concerns the money markets such as those in the U.S. and the U.K. which are developed, highly market oriented and facing minimum government intervention. The second type subsumes the money markets such as in Japan, Germany and France which are also very developed and highly market oriented, but with much government interventions. The money markets of Singapore, Hong Kong, Taiwan, South Korea, Philippines and other emerging market economies fall into the third type, which possesses certain special characteristics in some aspects, but there are still rooms for improvements. The fourth type includes money markets in China, India, Indonesia and other developing countries, which are still 'under construction'. Of the above four types, the first type represents the mainstream of the world money market and is also the focus of this section.

The rise of capitalist society in Europe drives the growth of the market economy and creates conditions for the birth of the money market. The development of the world money market can be roughly divided into two stages, the traditional money market (commercial note and T-bills market) from the early 19th century to the 1950s, and then the modern money market which is still under development. Countries and regions do not enter into the modern money market stage from the traditional all at the same time, and neither do they follow the same paths.

It is commonly believed that the earliest money market was the discount market that occurred in early 19th century in the U.K. At that time, bank credit was leveraged to discount notes based on commercial credit, and commercial notes were used not only in most of the domestic transactions but also as a common settlement instrument in foreign trade. Some banks subsequently began to discount the commercial notes in Germany, France, Italy and other European countries, but the scale was small. Based on the numbers published at the beginning of 1873 in London, Paris, New York and Germany, the deposit balance in English banks accounted for 66.3% while the other three accounted for 7.2%, 22.1% and 4.4% respectively. The most concentrated area for banks in the U.K., Lombard Street of London became one of the biggest financial centers in the world, capable of providing vast sums of short term capital with good security and reasonable profitability.[4] However, for quite a long time afterwards (the period from early 19th century to the mid 1950s), there was only note discount market in the money market of the U.K. It was not until the end of the 19th century, that the English discount market began to expand from the discount of commercial notes to the operation of T-bills and short–term bonds issued by the treasury department. After the 1930s Depression, the discount of commercial notes came second to the discount of T-bills. It was not until after 1959 when the idea was mooted in the Radcliffe Report that discount companies should discount commercial notes, that commercial notes replaced T-bills as the most important discount instrument in the discount market.

The U.S. money market developed later than that of the U.K. but the commercial note market was the earliest money market in the U.S. In the War for Independence the American Civil War, the secondary market of issuing financing bills to raise war funds was very active. The abnormal or 'distorted' economic prosperity resulting from the growth of the military industry during World War II again stimulated the development of the money market, especially the state bond and T-bill market. After the war, the money market with T-bill and state bond as dominant instruments was further developed with state support and the Wall Street of New York replaced London's Lombard Street as the world's biggest financial center.

After World War II, the devastated and ruined European mainland was badly in need of material sand capital. The U.S. offered to help Europe to get back on its feet through the "Marshall Plan" which also benefited the U.S. itself by paving the way for entry into European market with international trade and payment liberalization bundled with the aid plan. The conference at Bretton Woods in 1944 made the U.S. dollar the world currency and the only international currency linked to gold, which facilitated the acquisition and merger of European companies by the U.S. Multinational Corporations ("MNCs"). The General Agreement on Tariffs and Trade (GATT) entered into in 1948 reduced trade barriers and increased trade opportunities for US overseas subsidiaries. In addition, the U.S. government encouraged domestic enterprises to invest overseas by providing diplomatic, legal and taxation support, while promoting investment freedom and security, enabling the U.S. MNCs to grow rapidly. With the development of MNCs spearheading globalization of the economy, cross border capital flow, as well as international technology transfer and international trade proliferated. However this also brought about many financial problems. At the same time, with the progress of science and technology, many new industrial sectors, such as computer, semiconductor and petrochemical industries emerged, and their rapid growth required a huge amount of capital. The internationalization and diversification of capital supply and demand accelerated the development of the money market into a new phase.

In the late 1950s, a variety of new money markets appeared in parallel with the discount market in the U.K. The most important one is the Eurodollar market that arose around 1957 in London,[5] where U.S. dollar deposit and loan business was operated outside the U.S., and its object was the US capital in U.S. dollars circulating outside the country. In this market, one can be free of restrictions from U.S. banking regulations, control of U.S. bank interest rates and some financial regulations of the host country. The Eurodollar market developed rapidly for several reasons. First of all, a large amount of capital in U.S. dollars that was badly needed by the banks of the U.K. and other countries, was raised in the market. Secondly, the market enabled the U.S. banks to evade regulations on reserves and restrictions on the deposit interest rate, with the benefit that commercial notes issued by the parent companies of the banks would not be considered as deposits. Thirdly, the market provided a place for the former Soviet Union and Eastern European countries during the cold war to deposit U.S. dollars with relatively little political risks. Soon the off-shore markets of English pounds, German marks, Japanese yen and other freely convertible currencies followed and were called universally the Eurocurrency market. There emerged also the interbank borrowing market, CD market, local institutional bond market and so on in the U.K. By the 1980s, the aforementioned new markets in the U.K. had grown larger than its discount market.

Beginning from the 1960s, the supply-demand position in the financial market was largely changed with the increased financial risks resulting from the soaring inflation rate and interest rate in the U.S., as well as other factors like the rapid development of computer technology, integration of international financial markets, and the unpredictable and uncontrollable fluctuations of interest rate and foreign exchange rates. A great number of financial institutions found that the traditional financial services and products were faced with the decline of sales, and the old operation model was not profitable any more. Many financial intermediaries also found that it had become increasingly difficult for traditional financial instruments to attract the capital required for their survival. To survive and develop, financial institutions had to work hard on financial innovations, develop new products and services so as to prevent financial risks, ensure the security of transactions, get around or circumvent the financial regulations and reduce the transaction cost.

For instance, to evade the regulation prohibiting interest payment for check deposits, a mutual savings bank in Massachusetts found in 1970 that as long as a check was named as NOW (notice of withdrawal), an account issuing NOW can be regarded as not a checks account defined in law. In this case, the interest becomes payable, and savings and loans associations and mutual savings bank can attract more loan funds. In addition, in order to evade the regulation, ATS (automatic transfer service) was created, i.e. the surplus in a checking account can be transferred automatically into an interest paying savings account once the balance in the checking account exceeds a certain amount; only when the savings account holder issues checks will the amount of the checks to be honored be transferred automatically from the savings account into the checking account. At the end of the business day, deposits above a certain amount on the checking account of a company shall be automatically transferred to a one day repo investment and the bank may pay interest to the company.

For another illustration: Citibank launched negotiable CD in 1961 to avoid the regulation on the upper limit of term deposit interest rates which attracts capital with high rates of return and increases its liquidity in a transferable manner. However, it can hardly attract medium and small investors as the minimum amount required for CD is 100,000 dollars. Therefore, MMMF (money market mutual fund) came into being in the U.S. in 1972 which can be purchased at a fixed price (normally one dollar). The fund could accumulate the scattered money to invest in short–term money market securities (for example T-bills, commercial notes, CD, etc.). Investors can also issue checks on the capital held by means of shareholding. As the shares of MMMF are not deposits in law and are free of regulations on legal reserve and prohibition on interest payment, a higher rate of interest than that for bank deposits can be paid.

The third example is the occurrence of repo in the U.S. in 1969 aiming to evade regulations on deposit reserve and premium. Under the repo (repurchase options) system, banks borrow money from holders of large amounts of short–term capital with T-bills as the collateral and execute a written agreement which guarantees the 'buy back' or re-purchase within a certain period of time (normally one day to two weeks) at a certain price (equal to principal + interest), and which provides that the collateral shall belong to the money lender in case of default. Currently, repo has become an effective financing tool for U.S. banks, and big corporations are its most important lenders.

In the 1970s, financial derivative markets emerged in the U.K., the U.S. and other countries with the growth of financial innovations. These kinds of markets can be classified into two types: one is OTC (over the counter) trading, a market composed of financial products issued by banks but where most transactions are completed through telephone network; another is the 'tangible' market formed by financial futures trading. Currency derivatives traded on the derivative market include forward contract, money and interest rate swap, FRA (forward rate agreement) and financial futures and options, etc.

Although interbank borrowing market occurred in Japan as early as 1903, the actual development of its money market was only seen after World War II. Before 1969, the interbank borrowing market consisted mainly of unsecured interbank lending businesses. At the same time, the money market with the "repo market" feature emerged. From 1970, the Japanese money market began to liberalize with numerous innovations on money market instruments. The Euroyen market emerged in 1972 when discount activities, public sales of notes and repos by the Bank of Japan (the Central Bank) began to appear in the discount market in big cities. In 1975–1976, certain measures were taken by the Ministry of Finance of Japan to drive the standardization of repo market.

The liberalization of money market which began in 1978 quickened the development of the Japanese money market. In October of the same year, the Japanese money market introduced short–term credit instruments with a maturity of only seven days, and this was followed by another initiative to allow three year coupon bonds to circulate in the market. After April 2, 1979, the "standard interest rate system" was abolished for the interbank borrowing market and note market in Tokyo, under which system, the interest rates for the interbank borrowing market and paper market were determined by both lenders and borrowers through the short–term capital operating companies, and these rates can hardly be changed once set. On May 10, 1979, negotiable CD was introduced in the market and in the same year, the Japanese Ministry of Finance allowed non-Japanese residents to take part in the repo market. In October 1979, freely floating interest rates were implemented in all the discount note market. In the following year, the Japanese government announced the abolishment of the regulation on the highest price for bonds sales. The market was then fully liberated while the Bank of Japan representing the government can only exert its influence through the market. At the end of 1980, the Japanese government adopted another liberalization initiative by removing foreign exchange regulations on many currencies, and only those covered in the Law of Foreign Exchange and Foreign Exchange Control were excluded in the liberalization. In 1984, restrictions on Yen exchange were lifted and the minimum amount for CD was lowered. The terms for note transaction were reformed and further shortened in 1988. Finally in the 90s, the modes of interbank borrowings and lendings were reformed.

The Canadian money market emerged as early as the 1930s but was confined to short–term T-bills. In the 1950s to the 1960s, the country's financial system changed considerably with the rapid development of the economy. Since 1953, incorporated banks and large securities investment companies had begun the co-operation led by the Bank of Canada to build a modern money market. After the mid 1950s, many short–term financial instruments (except T-bills) emerged and expanded rapidly the businesses in the money market, such as corporate notes, bonds and short–term bonds issued by local governments. Most non-bank financial institutions took part in the money market transactions towards the end of the 1950s. From the 1970s, a large number of affiliates of foreign banks began to join the banking industry of Canada, issuing short–term financial instruments to raise money in the Canadian money market, providing credit loans to commercial and industrial companies, and became important participants in the Canadian money market at the beginning of the 1980s. At the end of 1980, the short–term commercial notes issued by these affiliates accounted for 18% of the total amount of instruments in the Canadian money market.

In the 1990s, with the wide application of information technology in financial areas and the integrated development of the international financial market, a number of innovations in financial instruments, modes of transactions and forms of financial organization emerged in the U.S. and other countries in their increasingly active and structurally complex money markets. Currently, the U.S. money market has developed into a sound market system consisting of numerous sub-markets and has become the most advanced money market in the world. However, attention should be paid to the increased risks, as well as the liquidity of the global money market with the development of the liquidation-based currency forward contract, currency futures contract, currency options, currency index futures and currency swap market.

In spite of the different development paths of the money markets in different countries and regions, economic globalization and increased consolidation of the international financial market has gradually narrowed the gap between various money markets and chances are that they will all become like and uniform money markets although they have taken different paths to arrive.

5.3. Fictitious Economy and the Money Market

According to traditional financial theory, the financial market can be divided into the capital market and the money market based on whether the credit term is longer than one year or less (otherwise called the mid-long term capital market and the short–term capital market respectively). There are equity financing and debt financing in the capital market while there is mainly debt financing in the money market. However, with the popularity of mixed operations practiced by financial institutes, and the integration of the international financial market, as well as the rapid development of financial innovations, the boundary between the traditional capital market and the money market has become increasingly blurred. In the present article, the fictitious economy theory,[6] put forward by the author in 1998 to study the East Asian financial crisis, is applied to explore related issues in the money market.

5.3.1. *An Overview of Fictitious Economy*

Fictitious Economy is a new term which has emerged in recent years, the definitions of which are mixed but are primarily of three types. One refers to transactions of fictitious capital including securities, futures and options (Fictitious Economy) — also known as 'digital' economy or information economy by some people. Another refers to economic activities conducted on the basis of information technology (Virtual Economy). The third one refers to visual economic activities simulated by computers (Visual Economy). Some associations do exist among these three definitions, with the first definition to be elaborated herein.

The idea of Fictitious Capital was initially raised by Marx, who made a detailed analysis of Fictitious Capital in Section 5, Volume 3 of *Das Kapital*, especially in Chapter 25 in respect of credit and Fictitious Capital and thereafter. He held that Fictitious Capital was created on the basis of loan capital (interest bearing capital) and bank credit systems, including stocks, bonds and real estate mortgage bonds. Fictitious Capital itself carries no value, which is different from real capital. However, it can generate profits through circulatory movement (a certain form of surplus value), which is in common with real capital. Despite numerous new items (e.g. futures, options and various derivative financial products) and new circumstances (e.g. money departing from the Gold Standard and economic globalization) which emerged with the global economic development — after more than a century — the analysis of Marx on Fictitious Capital still plays an important guiding role in the current study of Fictitious Economy.

According to the personal understanding of the author, the so called Fictitious Economy refers to economic activities relating to circulatory movements primarily in the financial system, or simply activities directly 'generating money from money'. People engaged in fictitious economic activities do not personally participate in substantive economic activities such as the production, circulation and exchange of commodities, but only conduct deals of fictitious capital. However, given that fictitious capital does not have any value itself or its value is fictitious, it is primarily reliant upon the subjective forecast of the parties to the dealing of future income and fictitious economic activities (just as the real economy) and could be either profitable or loss making.

It can be concluded from the above that the first stage of fictitious economy's development is the capitalization of idle money, i.e., the idle money held becomes the capital capable of generating interests. The second stage is the socialization of interest generating capital, i.e., with banks as the intermediaries, borrowing idle money from people and lending to others to generate interest. At the same time, people can use their idle money to buy marketable securities to generate interest themselves. The CDs and marketable securities that people hold are called the fictitious capital. The socialization of interest generating capital can improve the utilization of capital by directing the flow of money from the people who cannot use it in productions, circulations or other physical economic activities to those who can, and pooling together the scattered capital for large scale and highly profitable economic activities.

The third stage is the "marketization" of marketable securities, i.e., marketable securities can be traded freely based on the expected returns with the result that a financial market for fictitious capital transactions (such as stock market, bond market and money market, etc.), is created. This "marketization" can improve not only the liquidity of fictitious capital with its capability to readily cash out the marketable securities, but also the efficiency in capital utilization by making the capital flow into the industries with good returns. In 1898, futures transaction occurred involving agricultural products, followed by non-ferrous metals, petroleum and other industrial materials–falling into a new type of fictitious capital.

The fourth stage in the development of fictitious economy is the internationalization of the financial market in which fictitious capital can be traded across the board. This process dated back to the mid-1800s when the U.S. and other debtor countries and railway companies issued bonds with fixed interest rate in the financial market of the U.K., France and Germany. However, it was not until the 1920s that cross country securities investments grew to a certain scale. The depressed world economy in the 1930s and the breakout of World War II stalled the whole process. It was not until after World War II and the signing of the Bretton Woods Agreement and GATT that a sizable international financial market came into being. Internationalization of financial market facilitates the flow of capital to the most profitable industries within the international community, and improves significantly the utilization of capital. Meanwhile, a new type of financial market — the foreign exchange market — was created. Futures trading becomes more and more virtualized, involving purchase and sales of futures as a type of speculation. Since the 1960s, stocks, securities, foreign exchanges and other financial products began to be involved in futures transaction. Options transactions occurred later in 1973.

The fifth stage of the development of fictitious economy is the integration of the international financial market, i.e., local financial markets become more and more closely related with the international financial market with increasing impact on each other. With the establishment of floating interest rate system as a result of the separation or 'un-pegging' of the dollar to gold, increasing financial innovations, the advancement of information technology, the increased financial liberalization and the globalization of the economy, increasing amounts of fictitious capital are flowing more and more quickly in the financial market and the scale of the fictitious economy has been increasing continuously.

Under the multiplier effect, overall scale of the current global Fictitious Economy has significantly exceeded the real economy. The global economic aggregate had hit US$160 trillion by the end of 2000, including around US$36 trillion in stock market value, US$29 trillion in bond balances, and US$95 trillion in the over-the-counter trading balance of financial derivative instruments, while the combined GDP of various countries totaled only approximately US$30 trillion for that year, which indicated the scale of Fictitious Economy was five times as much as that of real economy. The average daily flow of global fictitious capital amounted to more than US$1.5 trillion, approximately 50 times the average daily real trade volume across the world, indicating that only 2% of the daily capital flow in the world has been used for international trade, with the remainder involved in money-for-money activities in the financial market. It can be expected that with the development of e-commerce and electronic currency, the size of Fictitious Economy will further swell.

5.3.2. *Role of Money Market in the Fictitious Economy*

In accordance with the viewpoints of system science, Fictitious Economy can be treated as a system, the features of which can be researched from the perspective of the internal structure of the system, and from that of the relationship between the system and the environment, so as to reveal the law of system evolution.

The fictitious economic system is a kind of complex system, composing primarily of natural persons and legal persons (investors, investees or investment receivers and financial intermediaries) who carry out fictitious economic activities in the financial market according to certain rules. Complexity science holds that although every individual has the freedom to make decisions independently according to his personal strengths and surrounding environment as well as his understanding of the development prospect and preset targets, his decision making cannot avoid being affected by other people's decision making. Despite the chaos and confusion that could easily be caused by the non-linear effect among the components of the system, the self organizing function of the system may give rise to some orderliness and stability.[6,7]

When people have readily available idle money, they aspire to invest the money for profit, besides increasing consumption and increasing savings. From the perspective of Fictitious Economy, all financial market instruments represent fictitious capital. When investors purchase financial market instruments with their idle money, they are actually exchanging the right to use the money for certificates of equity, thereby obtaining the right to benefits from future incomes and the assets of the issuers of the financial instruments. In making decisions for investment, therefore, people have to consider three issues including: how much the predicted incomes are, whether the predicted incomes can be attained and whether the investment can be cashed promptly when in need. In other words, investors have to weigh the profitability, security and liquidity of the financial instruments to be purchased prior to investment. Theoretically, the profitability of financial instruments is in a negative correlation with security or liquidity, and its security is in a positive correlation with liquidity. For the purpose of meeting various investors' demands, various financial instruments have emerged.

Financial vehicles or tools can normally be divided into two types according to whether their credit period is more than or less than one year. One type is capital market instruments, including stocks, mortgaged loans, corporate bonds, treasury bonds of more than one year, consumer loans and commercial bank loans. The other is money market instruments, including treasury bonds of less than one year, large amount negotiable CD, commercial bills, bank acceptance bills, repurchase agreement and interbank borrowing agreements. Financial market instruments can also be classified into equity and debt instruments according to the nature of investment. Investors can only receive dividends from issuers of equity instruments rather than directly recovering the principal, but they can recover principal and interest from the issuers of debt instruments.

The existence of the secondary financial market enables investors to sell their financial instruments in hand and obtain cash at any time, which greatly improves the liquidity of financial instruments. However, given the uncertainty in the secondary market prices of financial instruments, investors are likely to attain high profits or suffer huge losses in encashing the financial instruments. Therefore, financial market instruments are sometimes called paper money.

On the basis of the above concepts it can be said that the money market is a liquidity-oriented debt instrument market, while the debt (bonds) market is a security-oriented debt instrument market, and the stock market is a profit-oriented equity instrument market.

The money market can be considered as a debt instrument market which focuses on liquidity, the stock market as an equity instrument market focusing on returns and the bonds market as a debt instrument market focusing on security. Given the fundamental differences between the three markets, and considering the increasingly quickened flow of capital, the author proposes to define the money market as an **exchange market for short–term debt instruments with high liquidity.**

As the instruments traded on the money market are highly liquid and capable of liquidating the fictitious capital quickly, the design and construct of money market instruments has the following characteristics:

(1) Short credit term: normally one day (overnight lending) to three months. Owing to the short maturity period, the price fluctuation of debt instruments is small and the investment risk is quite low. The risks for investors include market risk or interest rate risk, re-investment risk (i.e., the risk that arises when investors re-invest the earnings gained from their financial assets in some other assets with lower profit at some time in the future), default risk, liquidity risk, inflation risk and policy risk, etc. Generally speaking, the risk avoiding capability of the money market instruments is stronger than that of capital market instruments. For instance, the price of short–term securities in the money market is more stable than that of bonds and stocks and they can be sold at discount, so the default risk is smaller.

(2) Credit reputation and trust based: according to traditional 'real bills theory', notes shall not be accepted unless the issuance of the notes is based on the real, physical transaction. For example, a company that sells a batch of products and has not received the payment can, with the purchase/sales contract and delivery order, issue commercial notes of an equal amount. This kind of notes are acceptable during the process of acceptance, discount or transfer. The notes market referred to here is based on the real economy and has a higher degree of security. However, in the modern money market of today, it is hard to verify the physical or real transactions of the money market instruments, and decisions can only be made based on the credit of the money market

instrument issuers. For example, as long as the note issuers always fulfill their obligations for payment and establish a good credit standing, the notes issued will be widely accepted. In recent years, with the improvement of the credit rating system and the advancement of information technology, purchasers can get accurate and timely information about note issuers more easily, thus promoting the development of the commercial note market.

(3) Interest rate increases with the riskiness: by the rule of 'higher risk higher returns', the interest rate of debt instruments should increase with the degree of risks. For example, the T-bill market is the least risky, so its interest rate is the lowest; the interest rates for the repurchase market and negotiable CD market are lower than that of commercial notes.

(4) Bulk trade. With the low rate of returns in the money market, only large scale transactions can reduce the cost. For example, in the U.S., money market, brokers can earn only one dollar for a million dollar transaction, so only those deals of more than 100 million dollars are worth doing. Owing to the huge amounts involved in transactions, individual investors can hardly enter into the market but they can do it indirectly through MMMF (money market mutual fund).

(5) Pledge can be used to transfer liquidity. Each economic participating 'body' (such as companies, governments and families) may adjust its asset structure based on the realities and dynamics of the economy and themselves, to realize the best combination of liquidity, security and returns. In fact, the asset structure depends largely on the current interest rate structure, rate of return, price level and expectation factors for each asset. The money market is an integrated place or 'portfolio' for liquid financial assets. Its existence can increase the liquidity of the assets, link up the short term capital lenders and borrowers, and hence improve the efficiency and effectiveness of capital utilization. For example, commercial banks could acquire short–term capital through the repo market with long–term bonds as collaterals and thus the liquidity of its asset portfolio is improved.

(6) Efforts made to evade regulations and control. As the liquidity of the money market tools or instruments is high and its rate of return low, creators of these instruments attempt to get round or circumvent financial regulations legally thereby trying to increase the returns. Financial innovations of many varieties emerge consequently. Apart from giving new opportunities to the investors, these innovations also present new challenges to the monetary administration authorities. For example, Eurodollar was created to evade the regulations on deposit reserves and overseas loans of U.S. banks and MNCs in U.S. financial law. Eurodollar is free of both restrictions of bank interest rates in the U.S. and certain regulations in the host country. NOW (notice of withdrawal) came into being to evade the regulations prohibiting interest payment for check deposits. CD was launched to avoid the regulation on the upper limit of term deposit interest rates; repo was created to evade regulations on deposit reserves and premium. Economists have put forward different theories to explain the above phenomena. Silber W. L., for example, thinks that financial innovations are the "self defense" behaviors of financial organizations to maximize the profit and reduce external restraints (various regulations and rules). Kane E. J. believes that financial innovations are created when the external market forces and market mechanism match the internal need of the financial organization, thereby side-stepping the financial controls and regulations. Institutionalists such as Davies S., Sylla R. and North D. think that as part of the economic system, financial innovations represent reforms of the system, and the economic system and these innovations are related in the way that each takes the other as cause or effect and each constrains the other.

5.3.3. *Relationship and Interaction between Money Market and Capital Market*

The money market and the capital market are interrelated components of the financial market. A standard and optimized money market can direct the surplus capital holders to change their deposits into investments in the capital market. The fluidity and the short–term of the tools in the money market can make it complementary to the capital market and these tools are an important way to reduce risks. In a developed financial market, the money market and the capital market boast different characteristics and tools. But a combined use of the capital circulation and other financial tools make the two constitute an integrated financial market system.

The connection between the money market and the capital market is mostly manifested in that the main bodies of the two markets overlap somewhat. Some financial and non-financial organizations have entered into the money market and the capital market as well. All the financial and non-financial organizations are likely to invest in the money market, which facilitates the equilibrium of their own assets structure by utilizing their liabilities in the money market. In addition, the diversity of the tools in the money market has provided many opportunities for investments and profit-making. Particularly in countries that allow financial organizations to get involved in other industries, these financial organizations should make dynamic adjustments to their capital structure so as to make the largest possible profits under a certain amount of security. Profits made from investment in money market in many financial organizations have accounted for an increasingly larger portion of their gross earnings. Along with the application of modern technology in the finance industry and changes in financial supervision, the main body of investment in the money market is also becoming diversified. In a developed financial market, the money market and the capital market are inter-dependent and the distinction between the two has become more and more blurred.

In a developed financial market, except for the central banks, the participants of the market can operate in the money market and the capital market at the same time. For example, a securities company can hold a large number of stocks and long–term bonds and at the same time can hold short–term bonds and participate in short–term loans at a daily interest rate and make repurchases within the industry. In this way the company can adjust the fluidity and security of its capital accordingly and also earn some interests at the same time.

Moreover, the high risks of the tools in the capital market force investors to favor and make use of tools in the money market so as to establish good investment structures in attempts to spread out risks. The participants of the market also need to operate in the two markets at the same time to ensure the fluidity of capital. Although the two markets are different in that their 'tools' are different, their yield rate and risks, their main structures are almost the same. So by comparing the prices of their tools, yield, fluidity and risks, people can make dynamic and informed adjustments of the structure of their assets and liabilities.

The interaction between the money market and the capital market is mainly displayed in the two way flow of capital. Theoretically speaking, there is some kind of equilibrium between the money market and the securities business according to the Gordon growth model. When they are in equilibrium, the share price is inversely proportional to the interest rate in the money market. If any one of them rises or falls, the other one will certainly fall or rise correspondingly to reach a new equilibrium. When the interest rate falls, investors often tend to make a short–term loan at a daily interest rate from people in the same industry or sell short–term securities in the money market to get the necessary capital for the long–term securities in the capital market. As capital flows from the money market to the capital market, prices of the long–term securities will go up. When the interest rate rises, investors are inclined to sell the long–term securities to invest in short–term securities. As capital flows from the capital market to the money market, prices in the long–term will go down. Thus, when prices of the securities go up, their demand will decline and capital will flow from the capital market to the money market; when prices of the securities go down, capital will flow from the money market to the capital market.

But of course the actual situation is much more complicated than that in theory. For instance, when the money market is not optimized or is 'imperfect' and devoid of effective market tools, more capital will flow to the capital market. For another example: when the requirements for financing in the capital market are too lax, a large amount of credit capital will flow to the capital market.

Some scholars attempt to analyze the financial market according to the traditional 'law of values', believing that when the price of some tool in the financial market exceeds its value, its price will go down, otherwise it will go up. As far as I am concerned, I believe that the tools in the financial market are a kind of fictitious capital and do not possess value themselves. So the law of values is not applicable, but the law of supply and demand is still applicable here. When demand for a certain tool in the financial market exceeds its supply, its price will go up, otherwise it will go down. The reason for the change in the relationship between demand and supply is not the deviation of the price from the value but the self organizing effect of the investors' activities.

The financial market is a component of the fictitious economy system and possesses an internal complexity. Although all main bodies in the market are independent in decision making according to their own expectation of the future and in a micro point of view there is quite a lot of random fluctuation and chaos, the decision of every main body of the market is inevitably subjected to the influences of the decisions of others and the environment. This will lead to a self organizing effect. So, from a macro point of view, the development of the financial market also features some period of certainty and fuzzy rules. I think we should give full consideration to the decision making of the main bodies in the market, especially those decisions which appear irrational.

For example, when selecting a tool in the financial market, investors who lay particular emphasis on profits probably favor the tools concerning rights and interests, while those who place particular emphasis on security probably favor the tools related to liability. When the stock market is in a bull market, investors have greater confidence in the rise of the stock market. At this time, not only those investors who emphasize profits will increase their investment but also those who emphasize security will turn to the stock market — since they believe that the risk of losses is smaller. In this case, the impact of increasing the interest rate in the money market so as to reduce the amount of capital flowing into the stock market will be much smaller than in the case of a bear market. According to the law of supply and demand, an increasing amount of capital flowing into the stock market will inevitably lead to a rise in the stock market, thus further strengthening investor confidence and attracting more capital into the market.

When the stock market rises sharply, investors who emphasize particularly on profits will even give up or 'forgo and forget' the logical principle of equilibrium between risks and profits and invest at high prices, believing that some other people may offer even higher prices. For example, since 1995, greatly encouraged by the successful listing of companies like Netscape, Amazon and America Online, people were convinced of the myth that "investing in the internet industry for one year equates to investing in traditional industries for 100 years". What followed was a sharp and dramatic rise in the share prices of the Internet 'concept' stocks on the NASDAQ market. In May, 1995, the online bookstore "Amazon.com" was listed. By November 30, 1998, its share price had risen by 2,300%. Although its turnover was US$293 million with a loss of US$61 million, people still anticipated that it would have good prospects. They therefore incessantly bought into its stocks, hoping that they would profit substantially in the future. Three months later, it rose by a further 400%, with a total market worth of US$40 billion. Before Christmas in 1999, the NASDAQ index breached the 4,000 points level and continued to go higher. On March 10, 2000, it reached 5,048 points, the highest point in its history up till then.

But in reality, a company that's got itself listed before it reaches 'maturity' would lead to disastrous consequence, because it actually shifts the risks to the public, which should be otherwise be assumed by its risk-taking investors. In 1999, 486 companies issued their stocks in the U.S.; of which 242 were newly started internet companies (new Internet start-ups). Their average annual turnover was US$18,500,000 while their average annual loss was US$17,800,000. Of these 242 companies, 224 of them have no record of making profits. There was such a sharp contrast between the share price and company performance that investors gradually lost confidence, leading to the final slump in internet stocks in 2000. The NASDAQ index slid from its highest point and went down all the way and could not recover. In 2000, it registered the largest drop in 30 years - 39.3% in one year, losing about US$300 million in market value. At the beginning of 2001, the NASDAQ index continued falling rapidly. On March 12, it fell below the 2,000 points level and at the lowest even dropped to about 1,400 points. According to the statistics of Webmergers.com, from January 2000 to May 2001 at least 493 network companies had declared insolvency or applied for bankruptcy, of which 55% of them did so in the first five months of 2001.

Of course, if investors have no confidence in the market, even if there are frequent reductions of interest rates it will be difficult to stimulate capital to flow into the stock market. For example, in Japan, due to the economic downturn in recent years, the stock market could not be vitalized although the interest rates of banks have reached their lowest point in history.

We can therefore conclude that the interactive relationship between the capital market and the money market is quite complex. One should not just look at their mutually antagonistic effect of "as one falls, the other rises and vice versa"; one should also study their collaborative and complementary effects.

5.4. Experience Gained and Lessons Learned in the Development of China's Money Market

In spite of the existence of some rudiments of money market before the liberation of China, it was not until the implementation of reforms and the opening up policy that the real efforts to explore the country's money market began. The prevailing view is that China's money market originated in the early 1980s and experienced numerous ups and downs in the subsequent 20 years before getting on track in 1998. However there is still a large gap compared with the developed money markets of advanced countries. An objective review of the history and a careful summary of the experience and lessons of the development of China's money market[8] are expedient in formulating the future development strategies of the market.

China's money market developed earlier than its capital market: T-bills were launched in 1981, interbank borrowing market established in 1984, note discount market in 1985, CD in 1986, pilot project involving short–term financing bills issued by companies in 1987, secondary T-bill market in 1988 and T-bond repurchase market in 1991. However, owing to the ineffective system and mechanism, underdevelopment of market, out-dated investment concepts of investors, incomplete design and lack of experience etc., almost all sub-markets experienced the process of "once deregulated, things go out of control — once out of control, things are closed down."

Take the interbank lending market as an example. It is a tough process involving 'three rises and three falls'. In October 1984, the People's Bank of China replaced the highly centralized credit capital management system of "centralized deposits and loans" with the system of "actual loans and deposits" allowing interbank borrowings, which changed fundamentally the top-down credit capital allocation. The Interim Regulations of the People's Republic of China on the Administration of Banks promulgated by the State Council published in January 1986 provides clearly that professional ('commercial') banks can lend and borrow from each other. With the publication of the Regulations, the interbank borrowing market was established in Guangzhou and four other cities. In March 1988, branches of state–owned commercial banks set up joint ventures through membership, and established financing companies specializing in interbank borrowings. However, the People's Bank of China issued directives in October of the same year to ask for improvement and rectification, and even ordered the closing of the related financing companies in 1989.

In March 1990, the People's Bank of China issued the 'Interim Measures for the Management of Interbank Lending', which puts forward for the first time the standards for the interbank borrowing business and percentage requirement. However, the market became chaotic in 1992 and there were over 1,170 provincial, regional and county level intermediaries in June 1993. At the end of May 1993, state–owned banks borrowed 105.5 billion Yuan from outside the system and rectifications started again in June 1993. In September 1995, the People's Bank of China started to build a unified interbank lending market to monitor all the interbank lending/borrowing activities. In November of the same year, the People's Bank of China issued directives to close down 50 financing centers, capital markets and various kinds of intermediaries built by commercial banks, sparing only the 43 financial centers established under the leadership of the People's Bank of China.

On January 3, 1996, a unified interbank lending/borrowing market began to operate. In that year, the cumulated turnover was 587.1 billion Yuan, down by 41% against the previous year. In July 1997, the financing centers of the People's Bank of China began to clean up the overdue capital and the interbank borrowing volume went down to 414.9 billion Yuan in that year. In October of the same year, the financial centers of the People's Bank of China stopped operating interbank borrowing business. In March 1998, the People's Bank of China cancelled all the financing centers. At the end of 1998, the financing center of the People's Bank of China collected over 16 billion Yuan of overdue capital and cleaned up more than 40 billion Yuan of 'chain' or 'linkage' debts. At that time, work was completed in 7 of 43 financing centers in Shanghai, Wuhan and Chengdu which were then eliminated and 1/3 of the branches had completed 50%–80% of the clean-up task. During this period, the credit funds borrowed in the interbank borrowing market kept decreasing (down from 820.5 billion Yuan in 1995 to 98.9 billion Yuan in 1998) until the recovery in 1999.

The National Interbank Lending/Borrowing Center was established in Shanghai in 1996. At the end of 2001, there were 553 members in the interbank borrowing market, with a turnover of 4,905.491 billion Yuan in 2001, of which 81.8% came from bond repurchase, 16.5% from credit interbank borrowing and 1.7% from cash transactions.

The development of the note discount market has also been an arduous journey. Through years of experiment, the People's Bank of China and the Industrial and Commercial Bank of China issued in 1985 the Interim Measures for the Acceptance and Discount of Commercial Draft, and the Accounting Procedures in the Acceptance and Discount of Commercial Draft to promote the usage of notes in commercial credit activities between industrial and commercial enterprises. In April 1986, pilot trials on using acceptance and discount of commercial notes to work out overdue loans were conducted in Beijing, Shanghai, Guangzhou, Chongqing, Wuhan, Shenyang, Harbin, Nanjing and other cities. The pilot schemes allowed banks to make note discount to industrial and commercial businesses, but the notes discounted were limited to commercial acceptance bills and bank acceptance bills arising from commodity exchanges. Re-discount business between professional banks was also allowed. In 1986, the People's Bank of China issued the Interim Measures of the People's Bank of China for re-discount when some branches of the bank began to handle its re-discount businesses. However, serious issues occurred in the market, such as irregular cash flow, uncontrollable behavior, notes related cases, forged notes, etc. Bank note acceptance and discount business was stopped in 1988.

In November 1994, to promote commercial note acceptance and discount business, the People's Bank of China arranged special funds for the re-discount of discounted notes in five industries (including coal industry) and four products (including cotton). In 1995, the People's Bank of China extended the re-discount to livestock products in some regions and added a certain re-discount amount. The re-discount balance in the People's Bank of China at the end of the year was 32.2 billion Yuan, with cumulative amount of 84.4 billion Yuan. In 1995, the National People's Congress passed the Law on Negotiable Instruments. It promoted the growth of the notes market by driving the development of commercial notes issued by companies, commercial banks' discount amount and the Central Bank's re-discount amount, as well as the formation of the regional note market. In 2000, the amount of the cumulative commercial notes issued across the country was 744.5 billion Yuan with a balance of 367.6 billion Yuan. Cumulative discount amounted to 644.7 billion Yuan with a balance of 153.6 billion Yuan while cumulative re-discount was 266.7 billion Yuan with a balance of 125.8 billion Yuan.[9]

The pilot scheme of short–term financing bills issued by companies initiated by the People's Bank of China in 1987 was not successful. Some high performing companies were allowed to issue short–term financing bills of 3, 6, 9 and 12 months to other companies and individuals at a monthly interest rate of up to 6% (equal to the interest rate for working capital loans). Provincial branches of the People's Bank of China reviewed and approved the applications for the issuance within the outstanding balance limit set by the People's Bank of China. The outstanding balance at the end of 1988 was only 1.2 billion Yuan. In February 1989, the People's Bank of China issued the 'Notification on Problems in the Issuance of Short term Financing Bills', which clearly set forth that the short–term financing bill market was going to be formally opened after the pilot and provided that this kind of short–term facilities could be transferred between companies, traded in the capital market and issued on an agency basis or underwritten by financial institutions. As a result, the issue volume increased with the cumulative volume reaching 99.3 billion Yuan from 1987 to 1995. However, transfers only happened in a few cities and no secondary market was actually formed. A considerable number of companies failed to pay back when their financing bills became due and they had been issuing new debts to pay the old debts. After 1996, bond repayment crises arose one after another in some provinces and cities.

The development of negotiable CD market ended up as a failure too. In the latter half of 1986, the Bank of China and the Bank of Communication began to issue CDs before the People's Bank of China granted its permission to all the other state–owned commercial banks to do so. In May and November of 1989, the People's Bank of China issued successively the 'Measures for the Administration of Negotiable Certificates of Deposit and the Notification on Problems in the Transfer of Negotiable Certificates of Deposit'. From 1990–1993, around 50 billion Yuan worth of negotiable CDs were issued by commercial banks, all under quota/indicator management by the People's Bank of China and at an interest rate 5%–10% higher than that of term deposit with the same maturity. It was effective in attracting more deposits. However, as the minimum amount bought by individuals was only 500 Yuan and most of the buyers were individuals, the liquidity was poor and no secondary market developed. In 1998, the People's Bank of China issued directives to stop the issuance of CDs.

Starting from 1981, the year of the first issuance of T-bills in China, T-bills were issued once a year with terms ranging from three to five years, but there was only an issuing market and no circulating market. In 1988, pilot circulation and transferring of T-bills scheme was conducted in 61 cities in two batches. The scale of T-bill issuance was significantly increased as the "underwriting" was organized by the Ministry of Finance to introduce the market mechanism into the primary market. In 1993, the T-bill market saw another great development, i.e. the establishment of the primary dealer system. A large amount of national debt was issued through "underwriting" or "open tender or bidding system" to deal with the primary dealers only — and then from the primary dealers to the brokers and from the brokers to the investors. The system was established in 1994 when a large amount of national debt was issued to institutions and distributed by these institutions to individual investors. With the system, the 3 year T-bill deposit acceptable in advance (although not on the market) was launched and national debt terms and types further diversified. State–owned commercial banks were allowed to hold national debts. Spot, repurchase and futures transactions of T-bills were launched in transaction networks such as the Shanghai Stock Exchange, Shenzhen Stock Exchange and Wuhan Stock Exchange. Taking the Wuhan Stock Exchange as an illustration, its total volume of T-bills traded reached 456.6 billion Yuan in 1994, of which 211 billion Yuan was from spot and 245.6 billion Yuan from futures. Since the suspension of T-bond futures transaction in 1995, spot and repurchase transactions became the dominant transactions in the secondary national debt market. In 1997, the People's Bank of China asked all commercial banks to exit from T-bond repurchase and cash transactions at the Shanghai Stock Exchange, Shenzhen Stock Exchange and local stock exchange centers. In the following year, local stock exchange centers were closed and interbank T-bond repurchase transactions were centralized at the National Interbank Lending/Borrowing Center.

In 1996, the Ministry of Finance and the People's Bank of China, after mutual discussions and with the approval of the State Council, decided to restructure the China Securities Exchange System Company Limited to 'China Government Securities Depository

Trust & Clearing Co. Ltd'. (hereinafter referred to as the Clearing Corporation) to handle the registration, trust service and settlements of state bonds throughout the country. Participants in the interbank bond market are required to open bond trust accounts with the Clearing Corporation and the accounts are managed according to their category. Type A members can both act as dealers and can also handle agency businesses; Type B members and 'indirect' settlement members can only act as dealers. Bond settlement is processed through the central bond bookkeeping system of the Clearing Corporation, while the capital settlement for bond transactions is by means of transfer. By the end of 2001, there are over 670 members in the market (mainly the headquarters of state–owned commercial banks and their authorized branches, insurance companies, other commercial banks, foreign banks, Rural Credit Co-operatives Associations, some securities companies and fund management companies), of which only 358 members participated in the transactions. Interbank repurchase (one way and unilateral) transaction settlement was 4,009.796 billion Yuan in 2001 and the volume was 1,534.298 billion Yuan in the stock exchanges in Shanghai and Shenzhen.

The development of China's money market during the past two decades could be described as going through many ups and downs. Even today there is still no sizable market and the market itself is still underdeveloped. The author thinks that the following lessons can be learned:

Firstly, the money market cannot serve as a market for long term borrowings. The role of the money market in the financial system was originally to 'cover positions'–to provide money supply — through the management of short–term liquidity. However it failed to play its part in the 12 years before 1997. Commercial banks did not take the money market as the place for liquidity management and cash management, but tried to make money at the cost of liquidity and turn the money market into a long–term debt market. Many financial institutions, without considering the operational risks and repayment abilities, expanded loans and investment with "over-borrowed money" to support local governments financing for repeat constructions. Branches of state–owned banks lent the money to their trust investment companies or used the money to grant loans, invest in the stock market and real estate to avoid regulations, with terms as long as 3–5 years. Some agencies and local governments, in violation of the regulations that prohibit non-financial institutions from participating in interbank borrowing activities, misappropriated or diverted credit capital and expanded fixed assets investment in the name of inter-lending. Some 'grassroots' banks got round the credit limits and grant loans to companies by means of inter-lending. Some financial institutions involved in inter-lending activities violated the regulations on interbank borrowing interest rate and the extension of terms, and increased the interest rates and extended the terms without authorization. Some other financial institutions involved in inter-lending activities violated against discipline and fee standards by accepting cash, rebate and other "commissions". According to some preliminary statistics, at the end of May 1993, money raised around the country reached 100 billion Yuan, with the net amount lent outside the system by state–owned banks reaching 105.5 billion Yuan. The interbank borrowing interest rate rose above 18%. The malpractices aforementioned destroyed the order of the financial market and resulted in large amounts of overdue loans and huge financial risks. It was reported that there was still an outstanding and overdue amount of more than 16 billion Yuan at the end of 1998.

Secondly, no bank shall be allowed to establish its own intermediaries. Banks are the key players in the money market — they can be both the lenders and the borrowers. However, they are definitely not intermediaries. In the course of development of China's interbank borrowing market, banks have established their own intermediaries for the reason of "not allowing fertile waters to flow onto the fields of others". Such a practice can neither optimize capital allocation nor disperse risks. Banks had established lending markets at provincial, regional and county level in 1992, with up to 1,170 lending institutions, leading to serious problems such as too many 'points of contact', multiplicity of lending/borrowing as well as incurring huge losses. After 1993, the People's Bank of China decided to operate inter-lending businesses itself and cancelled gradually the financing centers, capital markets and various intermediaries established by commercial banks, sparing only the 43 financing centers established under the leadership of the People's Bank of China. Most of these intermediary financing centers in the money market were section-level organizations within provincial branches of the People's Bank of China. In some representative offices at the region or city level, the people working in the financing centers were also those staffed in the capital planning sections. The practice of the Central bank in establishing intermediaries in the money market specializing in the profit making businesses confuses its roles as the market organizer and the market regulator and such practice facilitates corruption and bureaucracy, distorts the information regarding market interest rates and risk mechanism and weakens the regulatory powers of the Central bank on the money market. The Central bank finally decided to close all the financing centers in March 1998.

Thirdly, the money market should be unified, not fragmented. Most inter-lending transactions before 1996 were conducted within provinces, cities and autonomous regions, and financing centers were doing businesses in their own ways. With the largely different interest rates of different inter-lending markets and the presence of regional protectionism restricting cross-province capital flow, it was difficult to create a united market. Additionally, the T-bond repurchase markets in different places differed in many aspects: T-bond trust confirmation, real bond pledge percentage, fees and trading and liquidating rules were different, as well as different and incompatible trading rules in the marketplaces. In fact, the same institution was even required to pay a membership fee when they joined a different local market. The People's Bank of China had delegated most functions of the money market to branches in provinces, cities and autonomous regions. Before June 1993, the behaviors of branches and sub-branches of state–owned commercial banks had become quasi legal person/entity-based. Under such circumstances, a centralized risk and liquidity control system was yet to be completed and branches lent out large amounts of capital to gain from a high rate of interest, part of which was lent to the trust investment companies and non-financial companies controlled by the bank itself. As a result, economic bubbles increased and large amount of bad debts were cumulated. Sometimes, even branches and sub-branches within one commercial bank lent money to each other. In fact, the so called inter-lending was covering up the non-book loans and the incomes became concealed accounts like a private coffer. These behaviors resulted from the laggard commercial bank reforms in China, the localized behaviors of branches and sub-branches, the substandard credit granting system and risk control system of the banks, and led to huge restructuring and standardization cost thereafter.

Fourthly, the Central bank should regulate, rather than simply restrict or prohibit. Due to the short history of China's money market and the lack of experience, plus the incomplete system construct, there were inevitably some problems in the establishment of a sub-market at the very beginning. Instead of simply closing the market, the Central bank should carefully study the root causes and find the solution. There were also many serious problems at the initial stage of the establishment of China's security market. With both system reforms and effective guidance, the market has gradually improved. However, reforms much depend on the 'reformation paths'; each step backward incurs certain reform costs and it is likely to provide excuses for wrong-doers to escape responsibility and opportunities for them to abscond because of the defects of the system.

Fifthly, the Central bank should not neglect the policy function of the money market. Before 1997, the People's Bank of China was not successful in leveraging the important role of the money market in the implementation of monetary policies; neither had it launched any open market operations. The loan limit management under the planned economy (i.e. credit plan) became the key tool for monetary policies. This remained unchanged until the issuance of the 'Interim/ Provisional Regulations on the Management of Open Market Operation and Primary Dealers' by the People's Bank of China in 1997, which, *inter alia,* clarified the relationship between the People's Bank of China and primary dealers, the qualification, rights and obligations of primary dealers, the scope of instruments and transaction modes for open market operations. In 1988 changes came when the

Central Bank conducted open market operations in the bond market. The volume of transactions was 176.1 billion Yuan that year and increased to 707.6 billion Yuan in 1999. The base currency placed through the open market operations by the Central bank was 190.7 billion Yuan, accounting for around 50% of the newly increased base currency in the same year. In 2001, the Central bank conducted open market operations 54 times through repurchase and cash buy in (sell out) and the annual volume was 1,678.142 billion Yuan.

Sixthly, the development of China's money market should never steer away from China's specifics. The development of the money market in Western countries is a bottom-up process, i.e., laws to regulate the market came after the invention of instruments. When the market economy develops to a certain stage and new financing demands and competitive environment emerge, new financial instruments or financing methods are created spontaneously to meet these new demands. This creation is followed by the promulgation of financial laws and regulations by the government to regulate and standardize these newly created instruments. In China, under the traditional planned economy, the money market as well as the financial market as a whole develops through a top-down process, the other way around compared with Western countries. At a certain phase of economic development, the government puts forward a theoretically ideal market framework (which often suffers from lacking actual practicing and test) whenever it feels that 'the time is ripe or opportune for launching reform initiatives'. Then, new things will be added to the old framework based on actual operations from time to time. That is why the money market of China, either its birth or its growth, is greatly affected by the government's decision making. In building and improving the socialist market economy, the cultivation of the money market should neither follow the traditional top-down model nor taking everything from the Western bottom-up model. It should rather combine both models, reduce government intervention gradually, encourage banks' innovation, work hard to review and roll out new innovations through experience, and strengthen continuously the effectiveness of regulation.

As China's money market has long been underdeveloped, with relatively low capital turnover efficiency, it has so far failed to fully play its role of driving the development of the national economy. Private finance has grown illegally and rapidly as enterprises and individuals are not able to borrow money through a well established money market and have to turn to private individuals with idle capital. It is well known that "underground banks" are very active along the coastal areas and regions with quite developed 'private economy', and some have even become the mainstream providers of short–term capital in a few cities. They are able to rapidly allocate millions of capital within one day and some can even handle notes discount businesses. Some of these "underground banks" collude with triads and are engaged in illegal economic activities. These problems can hardly be solved effectively simply by "blocking" and "prohibiting". The best way is to regulate and guide the market by actively developing the money market, so as to prevent the possible financial and political risks.

It is the considered view of the author that the target model of China's money market should have the basic features of a mature money market, including mainly diversified market players, diversified market instruments, market based interest rates, standardized operations, networked transactions and efficient regulation. What follows is a preliminary discussion on how to groom and develop China's money market from these aspects.

5.5. Diversified Market Players

Diversification of market participants (subjects or participants in the market) is an important condition for the soundness and maturity of the money market. A developed money market is often a market with diversified transaction subjects, and is normally open and all-inclusive.

In the very beginning, transactions in the money market were confined between banks and big corporations. The function of the money market then was mainly to raise short–term capital for enterprises or to satisfy the needs of commercial banks in liquidity management. After that, as required by the government driven economic development and with the emergence of T-bills and other new financial instruments, the government and the Central bank gradually entered into the money market which began to serve as an important place to implement the monetary policy of the Central bank. With the development of financial innovations and financial deregulations, both variety and scale saw continuous increase in the money market along with the growing number of money market instruments. We now have improved financing efficiency, reduced transaction cost and increased attractiveness of the market to lenders and borrowers. In addition, with the lowered entry barriers in many countries, deregulations on the participation of many institutes, there have been more and more market participants. In addition, with the occurrence of intermediaries specializing in money market transactions and the reduction of transaction cost, many under-qualified dealers have managed to take part in the money market directly or indirectly. This has rendered the money market in some countries becoming a market composing of the Central bank, commercial banks, non-bank financial institutions, investment institutions, intermediaries, companies, governments and affiliates, Central banks and commercial banks of other countries, citizens, foreign residents and many other participants.

However, it should be remembered that due to the differences in the development and government management regulations on the money market in different countries, the participants of their sub-markets are different. For example, the main participants in the U.S. commercial note market are large (domestic and foreign) companies, commercial banks, insurance companies, annuity organizations and foreign investors. The main players at the federal fund market are limited to some financial institutions, e.g. commercial banks, deposit and loan associations, some federal agencies and government securities dealers, with commercial banks taking a dominant position. In the T-bills market, the main players are (federal, state, local) governments, the Federal Reserve Bank, commercial banks, non-financial companies and foreigners. The European money market in London allows all financial institutions around the world to trade in the market. In Japan, by contrast, the money market is strictly divided into interbank market and short–term open market. The interbank market, as the market for banks and other financial institutions, includes mainly city banks, local banks, mutual banks, trust banks, long–term credit banks, foreign banks, insurance companies, security companies and short–term fund companies (intermediaries). The open market is the short–term capital market for domestic financial institutions, companies, individuals, foreign banks and foreign currency authorities, with the exception that individuals are not allowed to participate in the bond repurchase market.

It should also be pointed out intermediaries, as the participants of the money market, have special meaning and significance. They can be roughly classified into two categories.

The first category includes those brokers who are pure intermediaries not involved in transactions. In countries with a developed money market, brokers are common. They normally contact lenders and borrowers through telephone. If the deal is closed, they shall ask for a certain percentage as commission of the turnover from both sides. Intermediary brokers between lenders and borrowers appeared with the increase of the amount lent and borrowed, concomitant with the continuous development of lending market and its increased complexity. In addition, there are the U.S. Federal Fund brokers and British bank brokers who play an important role in improving transaction efficiency and reducing the transaction cost.

The second category includes financial companies that act both as intermediaries as well as taking part in transactions. They normally take borrowed money from the domestic banking system and other financial institutes, and then apply the capital in the trading of short–term negotiable securities, cash discounts, repurchase and other transactions. They can also raise money through re-discount by the Central bank and act as the 'conduit' of monetary policy to a certain extent. Typical examples of financial companies in the short–term securities market are British discount banks, Japanese short–term capital operating companies, etc. Take Japanese short–term capital companies for instance. Their role is mainly as currency intermediary in both the interbank borrowing market and the notes market. At the same time, they independently operate some other businesses such as short–term capital, short–term government securities, CDs and bank acceptances, etc. They also act as foreign exchange brokers. They play an important role in capital flow in the money market of Japan by serving not only as the conduits for the one remaining local capital to flow to the metropolitan financial institutions but also as the important channel for banks (mainly the city banks) to keep deposit reserves. They are the conductors and propagators for Japanese banks to execute the monetary policies in Japan. As the ultimate lender, The Bank of Japan conducts open market operations and grants loans through short–term capital companies.

To promote the development of the money market in China, the restrictions placed on the type of participants should be reduced and diversification of market players should be promoted. Since all market participants need to increase the liquidity and to borrow or lend capital, the diversification of market participants can better leverage the role of supply and demand mechanism in the money market to satisfy most of the demands of both lenders and borrowers, thus further improving the financial efficiency and promoting the development of the economy. Currently, there are four major issues regarding the participants in the money market of China.

5.5.1. *The "Monistic" Structure of the Market*

Among the existing participants in the money market of China, state–owned commercial banks occupy the dominant position, but the level of their activeness is not very satisfactory. Business enterprises have relied heavily on bank loans for a long time and they seldom raise money through the money market. The government finance departments have not become a big and important provider of regulated short–term financial instruments. The Central bank does not hold a large number of short–term securities that can be utilized for active adjustment and this makes it hard to exert macro financial control through the money market. This kind of structure limits the growth of the money market as it has resulted in the tendency towards similarity of demands in the money market and the lack of liquidity.

5.5.2. *Lack of Self Discipline*

Currently, China's state–owned commercial banks and enterprises lack initiatives and self discipline. Under such circumstances, the behaviors of transacting participants are not restrained by their repayment abilities and operating risks. Profit driven misconducts such as uncontrolled borrowing, unauthorized fund raising and forged repurchase occur endlessly. Moreover, since the participants' main purpose is to make money and speculate, their creditability will definitely be compromised. Some operators in certain state–owned enterprises regard financing channels as the place to make money, thinking that they only need to borrow money but are not responsible for repayment. It is therefore difficult for the notes market or the company bond market to develop healthily. Some state–owned banks use short–term capital raised in the money market for long–term investments by means of 'chain' debts. Some financial institutions make high risk investment in real estate, securities, foreign exchange, etc., with the money borrowed from the money market, which not only affects adversely their credibility but also leads to serious financial risks.

5.5.3. *Low Competitiveness and Weak Strengths*

The level of capital sufficiency of most state–owned commercial banks have not met the requirements of the Basel Agreement and this will definitely impact on their transactions in the money market. In 1998, the Ministry of Finance issued 270 billion Yuan special T-bonds to make up the state–owned commercial banks' own capital, and this improved the capital restructuring of state–owned commercial banks. The capital of most state–owned enterprises, especially short–term capital, is in deficiency, making them lose many business opportunities, and sometimes even affecting their normal, routine operations.

5.5.4. *Backward Financing Concepts and Ideas*

Indirect financing has long been the main approach to capital allocation in China. Both companies and individuals are used to saving money with and getting loans from banks; they know little about various other direct financing methods, especially the various instruments in the money market. As illustrations, consider this: the total deposits of the financial institutions in 2000 was 12.38 trillion Yuan, of which 6.43 trillion Yuan was from residents' deposits, 4.41 trillion Yuan from company deposits, with only 1.61 trillion Yuan from stocks (market value) and only 86.2 billion Yuan from company bonds. The over dependence on indirect financing leaves the money market as a much neglected direct financing channel thereby reducing the needs for money market and hindering its development.

Based on the specifics of the country, it is proposed that diversification of participants in the money market should be promoted through the following four initiatives.

5.5.4.1. *Proactively develop the intermediaries*

Intermediaries (brokers and financial companies) play an important role in the money market. Most transactions in the money market are completed through brokerage intermediaries as (1) the transaction cost can be reduced with the service of professional brokers, which includes but not limited to matching the volume and the term for the borrowers and the lenders; (2) they could carry out searching and providing information on best prices; (3) they act as witnesses for both sides of the transaction; and (4) they can provide service for some anonymous dealers. In addition to the fact that they can help both sides close the deal rapidly and satisfactorily, and thereby reducing the transaction cost, these intermediaries can leverage the economies of scale to promote the healthy and rapid development of the secondary market. In addition, some intermediaries can help to conduct and implement monetary policies in the open market operations. Currently, the money market is short of intermediaries. It is suggested that some qualified investment trust companies be allowed to take part in intermediary businesses and play a role similar to that of financial companies. When the money market reaches a certain scale, brokers can be allowed to enter into the market.

5.5.4.2. *Relax the entry barriers*

Market entry regulation should be developed based on the actual situation and market requirement, and should reflect the principle of fairness, justice and openness. Upon this principle, qualified players can enter the market while unqualified ones must exit the market. For example, as long as a bank has a legal person status and meets the Basel requirements and other conditions for entry into the market, it should be allowed to enter into the interbank market. The development of the notes market entry system should focus on the qualification of primary market debt issuers, their creditability, capital sufficiency and debt service capability. Any other participant is allowed to join the secondary market as long as the source of capital are legal.

5.5.4.3. *Encourage direct financing by companies*

Due to the financing structure, property rights and other factors involving enterprises, over the years it has been difficult to put their liquidity management in a proper, correct and appropriate status. In addition, long–term over-dependency on bank loans, existence of market fraud and weak sense of awareness of contractual terms in the notes market, these enterprises and companies lose the motivation and initiative to seek finance through the money market. The extensive utilization of notes has been undermined.

5.5.4.4. *Establish money market fund*

The money market mutual fund ("MMMF") in the U.S. is an 'open-ended' fund issued to the public. One can buy shares in the funds at a fixed price (normally at one dollar) and MMMF managers can invest the money on profitable short–term money market instruments (e.g. T-bills and commercial notes, etc.). In addition, fund buyers can issue checks on the capital held through shareholding in the fund. As an open-ended fund, MMMF collects the money of many institutions and individuals, and invests in the money market for profit, hence attracting many institutions and individuals to participate in the money market.

5.6. Diversified Instruments

The diversification of objects for transaction (money market instruments) is another important condition for the development and improvement of the money market. A developed money market is normally a market with diversified objects for transaction and is able to provide rich choices and flexible transferability for the market participants, not only for the varieties of high quality market instruments, but also for the continuity and interaction between these instruments. Along with the development of the money market, the instruments have been continuously undergoing innovation, enrichment and improvements.

As aforementioned, commercial notes and bank acceptances were the only two instruments that could be traded at the beginning of the development of money market. Later, interbank borrowing business developed gradually with the establishment of the central banking system in countries, aided by the strengthened banking regulations and increased demand of banks for daily liquidity. Due to the involvement of the government and monetary authorities, there emerged T-bills, short–term T-bonds, the Central Bank's financing bills and other new credit instruments. After World War II, Eurodollars, CDs, NOWs and many other new money market instruments were created amidst varied demands and the development of financial innovations.

The characteristics of the development of the money market instruments can be summarized as follows: firstly, there is a great variety of credit instruments and objects for transactions; secondly, the frequent innovations of credit instruments help promote a prosperous and active market; thirdly, there are many credit instruments to be traded in each sub-market. e.g. in the U.S., CD market is composed of markets for different CDs, the domestic negotiable CD market, Eurodollar CD market, Yankee CDs issued by foreign banks in the U.S. to investment institutes (non U.S. citizens), etc.; and fourthly, there are many credit instruments with national or regional features, e.g. the exchange fund bills in Hong Kong, Korean monetary stabilization bonds and commercial invoices, etc.

Listed below are the current problems of China's money market instruments.

5.6.1. *Small Scale/Size of Market*

The money markets in developed countries have grown to a considerable scale. In the U.S. for example, the yearly balance of the main money market instruments in 1995 was 2,080 billion dollars.[10] Based on the data collected by the author, the yearly balance of the main instruments in 2000 in the U.S. was 5,400 billion dollars. Compared with these developed markets, the money market in China is much smaller. Based on the data quoted in the articles of Li Yang and other scholars,[11] the turnover in the money market in 2000 was 5,864.028 billion Yuan (around 700 billion dollars), accounting for 65% of the gross domestic product. The author thinks that if the comparison was based on a balance calculation according to the international practice, the gap of the money market scale in China with that of the U.S. could even be bigger. For example, the data from the Clearing Corporation says that the interbank bond market transaction settlement amount was 4,094.03 billion Yuan in 2000 while the face value of the bonds entrusted by the corporation on December 31 was only 2,004.655 billion Yuan. The balance of commercial notes, discount and re-discount accounted for only 49.4%, 23.8% and 47.2% of the turnover respectively on December 31, 2000.

(1) *Unbalanced development*

The money market in a developed country is a system composed of numerous sub-markets. In each sub-market, there is one type of money market instrument and professional service is provided for market participants. All sub-markets develop basically in a balanced and harmonious manner. For example, in the U.S. money market, the harmonious development of sub-markets enables the market to act as an integrated whole and they play an important role in raising short–term capital and the conduction of monetary policies. Major sub-markets include the T-bill market, federal fund market, commercial note market, CD market, and the rest are supporting markets.[12,13] By contrast, most of the sub-markets except the interbank borrowing market and repurchase market in China, such as commercial note market and short–term bond market, still lag far behind.

(2) *No Connection between sub-markets*

In a mature money market, sub-markets are closely connected and capital can flow freely between one another. Market participants can make rapid selection and replacements based on the profitability, risk exposure and liquidity to form a complete money market system. While in China, most sub-markets are independent and basically closed markets which are formed around their primary markets, and a unified money market system cannot be formed easily or conveniently. In addition, the isolation between sub–money markets in China prevents their development. For example, transactions in the notes market are conducted mainly among the Central bank, commercial banks and companies, while the bond market is artificially divided into Shanghai stock exchange market, Shenzhen stock exchange market and interbank bond market. The interbank borrowing market is confined to commercial banks. Apart from the above problems, some sub-markets (such as CD market) are even forced to close due to too much risk exposure.

(3) *Unbalanced development between primary market and secondary market*

In the money market of China, the primary market and the secondary market are not developed in a balanced way. Great importance is attached to the primary market by the participants while the secondary market is often neglected. The liquidity of the instruments on the money market is reflected mainly in the secondary market. Some money market instruments, such as CDs, short–term bonds and commercial notes, lose their liquidity due the underdevelopment of the secondary market and consequently their development is impaired.

Based on the actual situation in China, the following four initiatives are proposed to diversify the instruments:

(1) *Regulate the development of short–term bonds*

Short–term bonds include short–term T-bonds and short–term company bonds with a maturity of 3, 6 or 12 months. The short–term T-bond is the short–term debt instrument issued by the government and is an important tool for the government to manage the capital balance. Because of its short maturity term, they are easily marketable, and their prices could be adjusted according to changing market conditions. Another advantage is that the government can guarantee payment of the bond debts through taxation and money issuance. That is why the short–term bond is the money market's instrument with the best liquidity and highest security. For this reason too, it can also act as a tool for the Central bank to conduct open market operations and adjust money supply in the market.

Let me take an example. The fiscal year for the U.S. federal government is from October 1 of the previous year to September 30 of the current year. Because the personal income tax, an important source of tax, cannot be fully collected by April, short–term T-bonds can help the Treasury Department manage the seasonal deficit. This kind of T-bonds is sold at a discount and held mainly by the banks. The government pays in cash when bonds are due, based on the face value.

Currently, T-bonds in China include common T-bonds that are issued regularly and special T-bonds that are issued irregularly. Common T-bonds include mainly certificated T-bonds, book entry T-bonds and bearer T-bonds, with a maturity of 3 months, 6 months, to 1, 2, 3, 5, 7 and 10 years. Special T-bonds include mainly specific bonds, special purpose bonds (bonds to raise money from pension fund, unemployment insurance fund and other social insurances), specialty bonds, bonds with special holders (issued to the top four state–owned commercial banks (the "Big Four") to make up the capital of wholly state–owned commercial banks) and dedicated bonds, bonds for specific investments (10 year coupon bearing bonds for infrastructure investment urgently required for the development of the national economy and social development issued by the Ministry of Finance to the Big Four). Since 1981, common T-bonds in China have been dominated by the medium term (3–5 years) T-bills and there are only 3 month, 6 month and 1 year products issued on a small scale. Company bonds, otherwise known as enterprise bonds, include financial bonds, industrial bonds and utility bonds, etc., with financial bonds as the main financial bonds. There are very few short–term bonds.

According to the statistics of the Clearing Corporation, the debt issued in the national interbank bond market was 474.853 billion Yuan in 2001, increasing by 21.6% over that of 2000, of which the debt issued by the Ministry of Finance accounted for 44.7%, the National Development Bank 44.2%, the Import and Export Bank 10.3% and China International Trust and Investment Corporation 0.8%. In the total amount of the issued debt, debts with a maturity of 10 years or above account for 39.9%, 5–10 years 29.1%, 1–5 years 23% and only 8% for those below one year. It can be seen that the scale of the short–term bond market in China is small and hence the short–term bonds cannot act as a monetary policy tool.

(2) *Enlarge interbank borrowing market*

Interbank borrowing is a kind of credit based borrowing between banks at an interest rate agreed between lenders and borrowers. The key function is to satisfy the temporary (usually overnight) capital demand. As the purpose of the interbank borrowing in the U.S. is to meet the legal reserve requirement, the target object of borrowing is its deposit in the Federal Reserve System so it is called the federal fund.

Currently, the interbank borrowing market in China includes 1 day, 7 day, 20 day, 30 day, 60 day, 90 day and 120 day products with 7 day products as the major one with few overnight transactions. For example, the percentage of the turnover within one day in 1996, 1997 and 1998 was only 2.16%, 6.49% and 5.9% of the total respectively. It can be seen that the interbank borrowing market in China is used mainly for short–term financing, rather than adjusting deposit reserve positions which is supposed to be the key role of the market.

Another drawback is that the volume of interbank borrowing transactions in China is small. Based on the statistics of the National Interbank Borrowing Center, the amount borrowed in the interbank borrowing market was 808.2 billion Yuan in 2001 which was only 16.5% of the turnover of the center.

To promote its development, the interbank borrowing market should be gradually linked up with the deposit reserve system of the Central bank to leverage its role in deposit position adjustment.

(3) *Promote flow/circulation of company capital*

The company is the cell of the market economy and an important participant in the money market. Fund raising and investments are the two basic tasks of financial management of a company. Owing to the limitations of the system and mechanism on the company over the years, financial management, especially liquidity management has remained at a low level and has been inefficient, as the main channel of short–term capital movement is to apply for bank loans or deposit money with banks.

To encourage companies to raise money from the money market to make up their short–term capital deficiency, commercial notes and bank acceptance notes should be developed actively. Commercial notes are a kind of short–term debt instruments that are issued by big banks or companies, and sold mainly to international intermediaries and other enterprises. Bank acceptance notes are issued by a company and accepted by a bank which promises the payment by a fixed date. The bank then puts the "accepted" seal on the note it guarantees and asks the company to deposit a certain amount of money into its bank account at a certain cost to the company. The company uses the above two types of notes to pay the money borrowed for purchasing goods or labor, and notes holders can sell these notes at a discount and get back cash in the secondary market.

There are no commercial notes for the purpose of raising fund for companies in China. Most commercial notes are transferred to bank acceptance drafts with which the payee company shall get cash in another commercial bank, which may re-discount the drafts to yet another bank or with the Central bank. However, as commercial banks acquire a dominant position, they become also the main risk undertakers and this is not beneficial to the development of the notes market. It is suggested that commercial banks' special sections dealing with notes and notes operation companies should compete for the note acceptance and discount business so as to act as the custodian of note trading (instead of discounting) on behalf the clients.

To attract companies to invest their short–term capital surplus in the money market, CDs and other money market instruments (with higher rates of return than the current bank account interest rate) and those instruments with high liquidity such as repos should be developed. It is suggested that commercial banks issue CDs of more than 100,000 Yuan — mainly to companies and enterprises — requiring that payment of principal with interests be made when due and these CDs can then be traded in the secondary market.

Repos are mainly used by commercial banks to borrow money from big companies to adjust their 'position' of money supply. They are in fact short–term loans with T-bills as the collateral (with a term of no longer than two weeks), and their main function is to use mid and long–term debt instruments for short–term financing. Borrowers sell their T-bills to lenders at an agreed price and promise to repurchase these T-bills at a slightly higher price within the term agreed in the agreement. If the borrowers cannot repurchase the bonds when due, these T-bills will be possessed by the lenders. Currently, the T-bond repurchase market is mainly operating between banks in China. In 2001, the total turnover in the interbank T-bonds repurchase transactions took up 72.3% of the total. Going forward, initiatives should be taken to encourage big companies to enter into the T-bonds repurchase market.

(4) *Steadily promote financial innovations*

The financial innovation of the 1960s generated various types of derivatives that played an important role in driving the development of the money market and increasing financial operation efficiency. The negative influence of financial innovations should be prevented while realizing its positive impact. Active but cautiously steady explorations in the derivatives market within the money market are proposed to leverage its role in risk management, for appropriate control of speculations and to improve the regulatory rules. Once the architecture for the government bond and quasi government bond market is established, the above bond derivatives should be introduced at the right time. In addition to the free convertibility of the Yuan, off-shore Yuan based bonds (normally called Euro Bonds) should also be developed.

5.7. Market Based or Market-Oriented Interest Rate

The money market is a highly liquid market. Both capital surplus holders and borrowers interact with each other in this ever changing and highly competitive market to find the most profitable market instrument and transaction conditions. Interest rate, as the cost of using capital, is the barometer and regulator of market supply and demand. It proves that the pre-requisite for the effective operation of the money market is a market-based interest rate, i.e. a floating interest rate that adapts to different degrees of risks, liquidity and terms through the market driven mechanism.

In the free trading money market, each market participant makes a comprehensive prediction and analysis based on its performance, capital supply, change in the macro environment and other factors to decide the interest rate through consultations. Transactions made by the money market participants in sub-markets are based on their understanding of risk exposure, liquidity and profitability. As the secondary market brings liquidity to the money market instruments, capital can flexibly transfer between highly substitutable instruments. Market participants select different money market instruments in different situations and this behavior makes these instruments interrelate with each other more closely and hence increases the effectiveness of the money market.

When the level or degree of transparency is high and the level of asymmetry of information is relatively low, the market interest rate of a particular instrument will evolve in transactions of this money market instrument within a certain period of time. In spite of the different liquidities and risks of various money market instruments, the gap between different money market instruments is not that big as each market participant can replace or substitute the instruments and adjust their own capital structure according to their own needs. In China, the interest rates of most money market instruments are determined by referring to the bank deposit interest rate, rather than being based on the market supply and demand and the characteristics of the instruments themselves. This has the effect of making the difference of interest rates between different money market instruments bigger, rendering these instruments irreplaceable or un-substitutable as among them.

The pre-condition to realizing market based interest rate is to determine base interest through the market before setting up a reasonable interest rate structure. The interest rate structure of the money market includes risk structure and term structure.[13] In risk structure, interest rates are determined based on the difference in risk and the liquidity of money market instruments, whereby the interest rate of the money market instrument with the lowest risk and highest liquidity shall be selected to be the base interest rate. The interest rates of other money market instruments should be the base interest rate plus risk premium according to the principle that return is positively related to risk. The term structure of the interest rate means for those instruments with the same risk and liquidity, the interest rate of the instruments with the longer term is computed by adding the expected short–term average interest rate and the liquidity premium according to the investor's preferred short-term instruments. In addition, the taxation and exemption regulations on the earnings of money market instruments may affect the structure of the interest rate. For example, although U.S. municipal bonds are more risky than short–term T-bonds, the interest rate of the former may be lower than the latter as the federal income tax is exempted for its interest income.

With government backing which almost guarantees no risk of default, plus the advantage that the cashing out can be completed rapidly and at a low cost, short–term T-bond is the instrument with the lowest risk and highest liquidity. Therefore the interest rate of short–term T-bond should be taken as the base interest rate for the money market. However, owing to the small scale of the short–term T-bond market in China, the issue interest rate is determined by referring to the bank deposit interest rate for the same period of time; the market mechanism is yet to be formed and short–term T-bonds have not played its part in fostering the market based interest rate mechanism as expected. As early as 1999, the author had proposed issuing 3 month and 6 month short–term T-bonds and adopt discount calculations. Under the proposal, the Central bank can conduct "wholesale like" auctions over the open market business counter to large financial institutions on a fixed-term rolling basis regularly. As the actual operation is to replace new debts with old debts periodically, the market supply and demand situations can be reflected dynamically and adjusted timely. Acquisition through bidding can help create a market based, weighted average closing price, i.e. arriving at the interest rate of short–term T-bond. Widely recognized as free-of-risk, this interest rate can be taken as the base interest rate for the money market which is helpful to the rationalization of the money market interest rate structure.[14]

As the interbank borrowing market is a market with large scale transactions and short credit terms, and both lenders and borrowers hold a lot of market information, the interest rate for interbank borrowing can reflect the supply and demand situation of the money market capital. In this sense, this rate is the most sensitive money market interest rate and a key factor affecting the returns of other money market instruments. That said, this sub-market within the money market is most closely related with other sub-markets and any minor change in it could disperse rapidly, spreading to the whole market and resulting in change in the returns structure and transaction scale of other sub-market instruments in the money market. For the same reason, all participants would watch closely the interbank borrowing market in order to grasp the dynamics of the interest rate for the money market. LIBOR (London Inter-Bank Offered Rate), for example, is the interest rate agreed by five British banks at 11:00 am each day for the 3 month and 6 month transactions, and interbank borrowings are conducted based on this interest rate with 10 million dollars as the unit of transactions.

In developed countries, the interest rate for interbank borrowings is normally taken as the indicator interest rate of the Central bank's monetary policy. The Central bank judges the money supply in the market before deciding what actions to take. For example: relaxed monetary policy will lower the target interest rate of the interbank borrowing market while tightened monetary policy will increase the interest rate. It can be seen that the interest rate for interbank borrowings has a certain impact on the formation of the interest rates of all other instruments in the money market.

In 1996 CHIBOR (China Inter-bank Offered Rate) was introduced when the National Interbank Borrowing Center was established in Shanghai, establishing a market-based interest rate. Some people suggest that CHBOR be adopted as the base interest rate in China's money market because it has a huge influence and strong referential role. The author disagrees. Firstly, the interest rate for interbank borrowings is not the one with the lowest risk, and secondly the scale of the interbank market is quite small in China, with a small percentage of overnight borrowings. Therefore, CHIBOR can hardly reflect the supply and demand situation as precisely as LIBOR; neither can it function as the base interest rate. In addition, since the interest rate on deposits and borrowing in the banks' assets and debts are still strictly regulated as planned, adopting the interest rate for interbank borrowings would not be appropriate. Moreover, the market participants' behavior is not standardized and often quite speculative. The interest rate for interbank borrowings fluctuates greatly and can hardly serve as a market stabilizer.

Under the guidance of the base interest rate, capital surplus holders and borrowers can, under the rules of the market, devise different interest rates for money market instruments. Each market participant can also adjust their own investment portfolio based on their own specifics and prediction of the future interest rates.

5.8. Standardized/Regulated Operation

In a mature money market, the key players are various financial institutes, including deposit institutions (banks, credit co-operatives, etc.), contract-based savings institutions (life insurance companies, pension funds, government retirement funds, etc.), and intermediaries and dealers (e.g. financial companies, etc.). Their capital source, capital operation, business proceedings and operations follow certain rules and are closely linked with the Central bank of the country. Some even act as the propagator of monetary policy to an extent.[8]

Deposit institutions (of which banks dominate) acquire the capital mainly from saving deposits of individuals and other organizations to be applied in individual loans (mainly consumer loans), institutional loans (mainly industrial and commercial loans), mortgage loans and T-bonds, etc. Banks, as the biggest financial institutions between the capital surplus holders and the borrowers, can reduce the transaction cost through economies of scale and the 'reverse selection factor' arising from information asymmetry (lending money to people who are most untrustworthy) and moral risks (borrowers apply the loan into the high risk speculative business rather than the pre-assigned areas). In the money market, banks acquire money by selling some financial instruments, and then use the money to purchase other financial instruments (assets) to make profit. This process is called "asset transfer." Banks should attract those surplus capital holders to deposit and pursue the maximum benefit for them through financial innovations without violating the relevant regulations.

The source of capital of the contract-based savings institutions is the insurance premium paid to keep the insurance policy valid and in force, or the forced savings by the employers and employees. The capital is mainly utilized in company bonds, mortgage loans, T-bonds, stocks, etc.

The capital source for financial companies is commercial notes, stocks, bonds, etc., and the areas of application include mainly individual loans and institutional loans.

Commercial banks are the key participants in the money market of China. During the past long periods of planned economy, the four wholly state-owned commercial banks — the Industrial and Commercial Bank, the Agriculture Bank, the Bank of China and China Construction Bank - act as the "cashier" of the government and thereby acquired a certain monopoly position and some privileges.

With the development of the socialist market economy, the inner contradictions in the system and mechanism (such as lack of distinction between the party and the organ of state power; no clear line between government regulation and company governance, lack of initiative and regulation mechanism and obsolete legal person governance system) have affected the performance and competitiveness of these financial companies. Moreover, they often face problems as being overstaffed with poorly qualified personnel, poor management, extremely high rate of non-performing loans, huge loss in various assets and ineffective macro regulations making their per capita asset and benefit indicators much lower than their counterparties overseas. For example, according to the annual report of Hong Kong's Hang Seng Bank in 2000,[15] its operating cost only accounted for 24.4% of the revenue, while the percentage is normally around 90% for state–owned commercial banks. The per capita EBIT (per capita pre-tax profits) was 1.57 million HKD, over a dozen times higher than state–owned commercial banks; its one year deposit/loan interest rate difference was 1.7–2.2%, while it was 3.6% for state–owned commercial banks. Even though the shareholding banks restructured based on the modern company model of governance, their HR management and other management areas still follow in the 'old patterns and ways' created under the planned economy, and it appears that their operational modes keep reverting to what is typical for state–owned banks.

With China's ascension into the WTO, foreign banks in China should be able enjoy equal treatment as the domestic banks by December 2006, and those wholly state-owned banks shall have to face real challenges. This requires radical reforms to the wholly state-owned commercial banks in accordance with the spirit of the national financial work conference held recently by China's Central Government[16,17] to restructure them into internationally competitive modern financial institutions with a sound corporate governance structure and operation mechanism, clear operational goals, healthy financial status as well as ever increasing performance and competitiveness.

The People's Bank of China of China, being the Central bank of China, is responsible for the regulation and supervision of the market, and the establishment and improvement of mechanism for the smooth conduct of the money market.[18] The Central Bank is further tasked with realizing macro control of the money market through three monetary policy instruments, namely re-discount, open market operation and the reserve system.

The effective operation of the re-discount system depends on the development of the notes market. Without a developed notes market, commercial banks will not be able to rely on the specific channel of average discount for its capital operation. Without it, neither can the Central bank guide the market interest rate or adjust the market capital supply by adjusting the re-discount rate.

The Central bank puts or re-collects the base currency (base amount of money) in the market through money market instruments in the process of open market operations and influences the overall economy through the monetary derivative mechanism of commercial banks. Through this channel, the monetary policy will immediately exert its impact on the money market and transmit that impact to the other areas of the national economy.

The implementation details of the legal reserve system are closely related to the development of the interbank borrowing market (a submarket of the money market) and the operation of the interbank borrowing market provides the market information for the Central bank to adjust the reserve rate and formulation of macro regulations.

5.9. Networked/Online Transactions

With the rapid developments of information technology, there emerges in the money market the trend towards trading network characterized by exchange media center, internet technology and remote online transaction. For example, the open market and the so called the "Fourth Market" (bilateral tele-transaction market) are on the way to being integrated to become the unified electronic transaction network. Internet or online trading has its advantages of high efficiency, high speed, convenience and transparency. The Net (or Web) is helpful to increasing the consistency and efficiency of the market and could help better realize the market's statistical function as well as facilitating regulation by the Central bank.

Information and settlements are the two essential requirements for the operation of the money market. Therefore to enable online, Internet trading, it is essential to construct (and to ensure their proper running) and operate information network and settlement network. The information on the money market (such as interest rate, transaction volume, etc.) are an indispensable part of the economic information having a great impact on the economy. This information must be transmitted to market participants through networked information system (web-based) and must minimize the efficiency loss arising from information asymmetry. The role of the computer-based, networked (web-based) settlement system is to rapidly and accurately complete the settlement to ensure safe and smooth transactions.

The main function of the information system is to publish government announcements, debt issuing announcements by the debt issuers, market information and related information and data. The current money market information system includes "China Money Net" established by the National Interbank Borrowing Center, "China Debt Information Net" set by the Clearing Corporation and "Financial News."

China Money Net, at www.chinamoney.com.cn, opened on June 12, 2000, provides public information and market participant oriented information. Currently, three quotation systems have been opened, namely debt repurchase, spot bond trading and credit lending.

China Debt Information, at www.chinabond.com.cn, opened in late September 1998, provides information on various bond markets, including bond type, scale, issue status, market dynamics, statistics, business training, members' forum, regulations and laws, research update, etc.

Financial News is a nationwide and comprehensive economic paper founded by the People's Bank of China and seven other financial institutes. In addition to the reports on market dynamics that appear from time to time, special columns are launched on daily financial market analysis and money market, carrying articles analyzing money market related laws and regulations, money market construction and operations, as well as information on the interbank bond market and national interbank borrowing market. Its website is www.financialnews.com.cn.

Although the money market network in China has reached a certain level and plays an important role in the development of the money market of the country, there are still many shortcomings and improvements should be made in the following areas:

(1) *Enlarge scope of service*

Currently, the transaction network in China's money market exists mainly to serve the interbank bond repurchase, credit lending and spot bond trading. With the development of financial innovations and banks' information system, steps should be taken to transform promissory notes, big-amount negotiable certificates in the form of paper rights and endorsements. Transaction networks are to be constructed for notes, CDs and other financial derivatives to realize paperless transaction. Efforts should also be made to build a unified financial network by linking up the networks of financial institutions, the money market and the capital market.

(2) *Improve quotation system*

Reform is required in the existing quotation system of the interbank bond market in order to facilitate the smooth conduct of the inter-bank spot bond trading. To do this, first we implement "real prices + virtual names", i.e. the quotation system discloses the identities of the two parties only after the deal is closed, but "real names + potential prices" is allowed when quoting the intentional price. The second step is to quote the real price, i.e. the price should not be changed once quoted and accepted by both sides of the transaction. Third, both price and volume should be quoted at the same time and the deal must be closed once one party's quotation is the same as the other party's, or the other party's volume quoted is smaller than that of the quoting party. Disagreement is only allowed when the price or volume exceeds what is quoted. Fourthly, defaults should be stopped. The Interbank Borrowing Center regulates the behaviors of quotation makers through the market information system. In the event of any violations or non-compliance with quotations, compensation (damages) or penalties shall be imposed based on the seriousness of the breach. Fifthly, information on transactions in the money market should be further opened. Public market transaction information should be open to the public and the range of information provided for the medium and small sized investors should be extended. Sixthly, the information service should be improved. The quotation system should contain a large amount of political, economical, financial and market information for the investors.

(3) *Increase market analysis*

Analysis of the money market dynamics is the scientific basis for investment and financing activities. The transaction network can transmit all the information timely to all the related parties and this facilitates market analysis. Market analysis should be intensified while promoting the networked transaction to improve the development of the money market. Financial market analysis is a professional and knowledge based business for which the CFA (Chartered Financial Analyst) system is set up in the U.S. So far, only about several tens of thousands of people have been certified as CFA. Currently, the country is short of both talents and experience in financial analysis. It is proposed that China introduce the CFA qualification system and step up talent development based on China's specifics.

Money market analysis involves evaluating the profitability, risk and liquidity of money market instruments and identifying better opportunities or possible loop-holes by applying theories like risk-return relation, loanable funds, term selection and liquidity premium. One basic task is to construct the earnings curve reflecting the term related interest rate change to provide reference indicators for investors. With the improvement of bilateral quotation system, T-bond earning curves can be drawn, which can act both as an important basis for new debt pricing and create the necessary conditions for the birth of futures and other derivatives. The T-bond earnings ratio created by the liquidity in the secondary market is an important reference for all investors and of great help in promoting the market based interest rate by disclosing the overall level of market interest rate and providing a scientific basis for the Central bank to develop its monetary policies.

(4) *Improve settlement method*

Currently, the Clearing Corporation is only allowed to conduct settlements for interbank cash transactions and closed repurchase, and not multiple-type settlement service for open repurchase and collaterals, nor other businesses. The settlement business is handled with the order matching the requirements sent by both sides of the transaction. Bond transaction settlement is real time and transactions include gross settlement, i.e. FOP (free of payment), delivery upon payment or payment upon delivery. Currently, DVP (delivery versus payment) is not available.

DVP not only facilitates simultaneous cut-over of capital and bonds but also builds a flexible, efficient and secure liquidity adjustment mechanism. This requires the support from the administration agency on the one hand and the seamless connection between the bond bookkeeping system of the central settlement organization and the national payment system supported by the Central bank on the other hand.

(5) *Improve payment system*

Currently, the key products traded in the money market of China include bond repurchase and interbank borrowing, of which short–term transactions within seven days take up about 70% of all the transactions and the daily turnover surpasses 100 million Yuan. It requires the capital transferring system to transfer on the same day of settlement the payment from the payer's account to the receiver's account and all operations are finally confirmed. Transactions in the debt instrument market require also the seamless connection between the settlement system and the payment system to realize the simultaneous transfer and payment, so as to maximize the efficiency and minimize the risk. Currently, the capital settlement in the money market is supported by the electronic interbank system of the People's Bank of China. Although the transferred and received payment is finally confirmed, the system cannot satisfy fully the requirements of the money market as there are too many steps in the transfer from the payer's account to the receiver's account. Problems of delays, too many steps in the processing and the inability to connect with debt settlement system exist.

According to international experience, the modern payment system led and managed by the Central bank should adopt real time gross settlement (RTGS), targeted at the institutional players of the money market. When completed, the transfer of large amounts of capital possesses finality. Besides, the system should also be closely connected with the bond settlement system to realize simultaneous bond and capital settlement, and automatic repurchase financing. The latter is to have a commercial bank or the Central bank sign the automatic repurchase agreement beforehand which provides that when the commercial bank's situation does not allow a large sum transfer, the Central bank will automatically arrange with the bank short-term repurchase financing and pledge the commercial bank's qualified bond entrusted in the bond settlement system. Once the commercial bank has received the transferred payment, it will immediately purchase back all bonds pledged and repay the capital. This flexible, efficient and secure liquidity adjustment mechanism can ensure the efficiency of the real time gross settlement and the security of the Central bank's capital, as well as increase the interest of commercial banks in buying bonds and taking part in bond transactions.

5.10. Efficient Regulation

Ten years ago, Mr. Deng Xiaoping raised the great idea of the socialist market economy in his visit to the south. The author thinks that this theory clarifies the way to solve the contradiction between efficiency and fairness in the development of the country, i.e. to leverage the role of the market in resource allocation and pursue the high efficiency in economic development on one hand, and continue to adhere to the socialist system and protect the fairness and openness of the society on the other hand. This theory should also be the basic principle in guiding the formulation of China's financial regulation, i.e. to fully make use of the financial market — a creation of the highly developed market economy in Western countries — to speed up the economic development of China without compromising the protection of investors, especially the legal interests and rights of medium and small investors.

The author is of the view that under the socialist economic system, the government should regulate the money market through providing guidance with appropriate policies, timely adjustment and control, in regards to risk prevention and safeguarding of justice, and constantly increase efficiency and effectiveness by combining top-down administrative regulation and bottom-up public supervision. In the course of development of the money market in China, regulation should be focused on the following areas:

5.10.1. *Use the Position of the Central Bank as Leverage*

As the regulator and the player in the money market, the Central Bank can and does participate directly and indirectly in it. The indirect participation of the Central Bank lies in influencing the level of reserves of commercial banks through monetary policies, 'forcing' them to adjust their positions in the money market and hence to influence the supply of money in the money market. Through direct participation, the Central Bank influences the capital supply in the money market through open market operations. As a result, the short–term interest rates fluctuate; capital supply, long–term interest rates in the capital market, followed by the capital supply-demand and the overall interest rate of commercial banks are affected. Thus, through direct participation, monetary policies are thrust upon the participants in the economy and the Central bank obtains an effective control of the economy. Generally speaking, indirect participation happens in the interbank borrowing market, while direct participation occurs in the short–term security market (including notes market and T-bond market).

The Central bank can also create certain money market credit instruments necessitated by the monetary policy. This not only promotes the development of money market, but also enables the Central bank to effectively participate in the money market to ensure the implementation of the monetary policy.

The People's Bank of China is the Central Bank of China. Currently, its control of the macro economy is realized through direct adjustments — mainly by influencing the operational behavior of financial institutions dominated by commercial banks through the size of loan, credit and cash plans. With the development of the money market in China, the monetary policy imperatives of the Central Bank shall change from direct control to indirect control, i.e. to adjust and control the economy through reserve system, re-discount policy and open market operations.

5.10.2. *Increase Information Disclosure*

Information disclosure is a manifestation of the open and fair principle of the money market. The purpose of information disclosure is to increase transparency, making the information accessible to all participants and reducing the loss caused by information asymmetry. It aims to provide accurate and complete market information to the public in a timely manner, which facilitates the analysis and monitoring of the market and helps people to avoid risks of various types. The supervision by a developed country on the financial market normally begins with information disclosure. This is followed by analysis, announcement and disposal.

The regulatory authority should make clear rules on the scope, indicator, depth and frequency of information disclosure and make these rules publicly known. Under the principle of equal rights to knowledge, all market related information required to be disclosed should be able to be searched or accessed freely at relevant media or networks. The company disclosing the information should be responsible for the timeliness, completeness and accuracy of the information, and accept the supervision of regulators, disciplinary organizations in the relevant industry, and the public.

With information disclosure, professionals can analyze the information. The analysis helps determine the status and dynamics of the instruments on the money market for the reference of market participants, and helps identify contradictory or false information that could form the basis of investigation.

Upon discovery of suspicious elements or circumstances in a case, the supervisory or regulatory departments should, through analysis and investigation, identify timely the nature and seriousness of any wrong-doing, if any, and determine the type of punitive measures (such as warning, reprimand, suspending operation, disqualification, etc.) to be taken. The result of the investigation should be published expeditiously to reduce the damage caused. In less serious cases, punishment can be meted out by industrial associations and other self disciplinary organizations. In addition, group litigation system should be set up to allow the victim to claim compensation or damages from the people found liable.

5.10.3. *Strengthen System Constructs*

To ensure the orderly operation, and the sustainable, healthy development of the money market, the Central Bank is obligated to regulate and manage the participants, transaction behavior, financing scale, financing term, financing interest rate, etc. The Central Bank in China adopts mainly administrative measures in its approach to regulations. Under this approach, government has to be responsible for solving problems as and when they arise. This is an ad–hoc approach (the Chinese saying is 'treat the head when there is headache and treat the foot when there is foot-ache') that could hinder the future reforms because of inertial factors involving policy implementation. A comprehensive set of money market regulations should be established to clarify the regulators and the regulatory authority, provide in detail what to regulate with effective regulation measures, and to cut down as much as possible direct interventions by the Central Bank. At the same time, industrial self discipline and public supervision should be further reinforced, concurrent with the development of the society and economy, and participants should exercise self disciplinary management in addition to following market rules and moral principles.

5.10.4. *Abolish Monopolistic Privileges*

Under the planned economy system, the "Big Four" established their monopoly position in the money market and acquired some privileges with government support. There is little ground for criticizing the former arrangement given the situation at that time. However, under the socialist market economy, monopolistic privilege is one of the important reasons for market inefficiency and corruption. As the financial reform goes under way, monopoly and privilege must be abolished and banks should compete equally as financial institutions to realize the healthy development of the financial system and maximize the social benefit. The equal position or status of each participant, in addition to the diversification of participants, should also be realized to increase the operational efficiency of the money market.

References

[1] Bagehot, W. (1999). *Lombard Street*, New York: John Wiley & Sons.

[2] Cheng, S. W. (1999). Fictitious Economy and Financial Crisis, *Journal of Management Science in China*, 1, 1–6 (in Chinese).

[3] Cheng, S. W. (1999). Analysis and Lessons from the East Asian Financial Crisis, in Cheng, S. W., (ed.), Pandect, *Fictitious Economy and the East Asian Financial Crisis*, Beijing: Democracy and Construction Publishing House, pp. 1–50 (in Chinese).

[4] Cheng, S. W. (2001). *China's Economic Reform and Development*, Vol. 1, Beijing: Renmin University Press (in Chinese).

[5] Dai, G. Y. (2001). *Studies of China's Monetary Policy Conduction Mechanism*, Beijing: Economic Science Press (in Chinese).

[6] Li, Y. (2001). Chinese Money Market: Theory and Practice, *Chinese Money*, 1, 18–21; 2, 26–30 (in Chinese).

[7] Lin, M. Z. (2001). Treat the Development of Note Market Correctly, *Financial News*, September 7 and September 14 (in Chinese).

[8] Mishkin, F. S. (1998). Monetary Finance, Beijing: Renmin University Press (in Chinese).

[9] Peters, E. E. (1999). *Complexity, Risk, and Financial Markets*, New York: John Wiley & Sons.

[10] Questa, G. S. (1999). *Fixed-Income Analysis for the Global Financial Market*, New York: John Wiley & Sons.
[11] Rose, P. S. (1997). *Money and Capital Markets: Financial Institutions and Instruments in a Global Marketplace*, 6th Ed., New York: McGraw-Hill.
[12] Shan, Y. Q. (2002). Commercial Bank 'Trader' Taste will be Dense, *China Economic Times*, February 8 (in Chinese).
[13] Stigum, M. (1990). *The Money Market*, 3rd Ed., New York: McGraw-Hill.
[14] Wang J. Z. (Ed.) (1994). *International Financial Market*, Tianjin: Nankai University Press (in Chinese).
[15] Xie, P. (2001). Lessons and Arguments in the Development of Money Market in China, *Chinese Money*, 1, 6–9; 2, 17–20 (in Chinese).
[16] Yang, Q., Chen, D. R., Chi, D. X., Son, X. X. (2001). *Money Market and Investment*, Jinan: Shandong People's Publishing House (in Chinese).
[17] Hang Seng Bank, *Annual Report 2000* (in Chinese).
[18] Xinhua News Agency (2002). The National Financial Conference in Beijing, *People's Daily*, February 8 (in Chinese).

Chapter 6

The Reform of China's State-Owned Commercial Banks: Objectives and Measures

6.1. Introduction

Commercial banks are for-profit financial service enterprises with savings and lending as their key products. Other businesses include trust, lease, deposit, exchange, consultancy and financing services. In some countries, commercial banks are also involved in securities and insurance business.

Finance is the nucleus of modern economy, while banking is the heart of finance. In any given country, commercial banks constitute the most important component of its financial system, and play a leading role in the national economy and financial operation under a market economy system.

The leading role of commercial banks in the development of national economies and the running of financial services can be seen from the following:

1. As a financial intermediary, commercial banks help uplift and improve economic efficiency. Commercial banks bridge the gap between the demand and supply of capital. When individuals and organizations put their idle money into banks, the latter has the duty to turn it into interest-bearing capital to be used as investment loans and consumer credit. By pooling the idle money,

commercial banks reduce the transaction cost between the demand and supply sides and satisfy their diversified needs, thus improving the efficiency of capital use. They allow capital to flow, through the market mechanism, to those who can provide maximum returns. Such a competitive mechanism improves the efficiency of macro-economic operations. Additionally, the banking system pools the funds of each bank through the monetary market and creates a powerful credit treasury to meet the enormous demand for short-term capital, thus improving the capital liquidity and efficiency of use.

2. Lending support to business operation and promoting economic development. Commercial banks play a pivotal role in helping businesses finance for short-term capital needs or invest with short-term surplus. In most businesses, capital liquidity fluctuates with operations. When a business, for example, sells its products but does not receive the payment in due course, it may not have adequate funds to purchase raw materials for production and has to borrow money from a bank; but when it receives the payment, it can put the surplus into a bank for interest revenue after paying back its debts. Therefore, commercial banks can lend support to business operation and promote business development.
3. Optimizing capital allocation and reducing financial risk. Commercial banks are often better informed and placed than individual investors through their professional analysis and investigation of a borrower's credit and capital use, which helps, in turn, optimize capital allocation and reduce the savers' (indirect investors') risk. Banks invest in different projects to diversify risks. Additionally, commercial banks allow depositors to draw their deposits at any time as contracted, and protect the interests of petty depositors through a deposit insurance system such that no bank squeeze (run on the bank) will happen to affect social stability.
4. Transmitting or propagating monetary policy and supporting macro control. The central bank's monetary policy transmission mechanism, regardless of its credit (quantity or volume) transmission or interest (price) transmission channel, is dependent on commercial banks. The open market business, rediscount

windows and interest adjustment of the central bank must work on the economy through commercial banks. As an important transmitter of monetary policy, commercial banks can be used by the government as an effective means to exercise macro control.

Enormous and fundamental changes have taken place since the 1980s in the banking sector of the developed countries like the United States. With the rapid progress in economic globalization, information technology and financial innovation, the financial markets of each country are becoming increasingly interrelated such that the external environment and the internal management of commercial banks are undergoing continuous changes.

In the first three decades after the founding of the People's Republic of China between 1949 and 1978, China had implemented a "unified" financial system with centralized planning and management. The banking sector was under the strict control of the central government, with all businesses centering on the implementation of the government's plans. The People's Bank of China had a dual function: as a government institution and a commercial bank. All its business decisions were subservient to the government. During the "Cultural Revolution", China's financial system was almost ruined under the influence of the "leftist" ideology, and banks had basically become the "treasury house" and "cashier" of the government.

It was not until 1979 that China entered a new era of "reforms and opening up". With the widening and intensification of the financial reforms, the People's Bank of China began to function as a central bank, and the banking sector witnessed a rapid and steady growth. By 2003, a commercial banking system had been formed, comprising the big four commercial banks ("Big Four"), 11 shareholding commercial banks, 112 city commercial banks, and three rural commercial banks. In the meantime, the external environment and internal management of commercial banks were being greatly improved.[1] It is recognized that, however, the present conditions of the commercial banks do not match or are not commensurate with the need of developing a socialist market system, not to mention meeting the challenge of global financial integration. The reform of commercial banks and the reform of the state-owned commercial banks in particular, have become the keys to China's financial structural reforms.

With the progress of the reform, commercial banks have attracted wide attention, including from the academic community. The literature shows that, in 2004 alone, there were over 2,776 papers published in domestic journals on the topic of commercial banks. The writer has been keeping a close eye on virtual/fictitious economy since 1999, and studying the reform of commercial banks from different perspectives. Some of the research findings have appeared in books.[2–4] This chapter attempts to review the development of China's commercial banks, and analyze their status quo with concepts from complexity science, virtual economy, management science and monetary banking, exploring the objective model and implementation steps, and it is hoped, providing policy support for the reform of the state-owned commercial banks.

6.2. Development of China's Commercial Banks

The earliest form of banks can be traced back to 2000 B.C. when the Babylon Temple first began money exchange. However, it is generally accepted that modern banks first appeared in 1580 in Venice of Italy. In China, organizations closest to banks were 'money houses' and exchange shops which first appeared in the Ming Dynasty. Some foreign-funded banks began to develop business in China after the Opium War, and grabbed huge profits with their privileges. The Oriental Bank was the first bank in China founded in 1845 by a Briton, and the first Chinese bank was China Merchants Bank founded in 1897.[5]

In the 1930s, the ruling Kuomintang government developed a financial system comprising primarily the Central Bank, Bank of China, Bank of Communications, China Peasants Bank, Central Trust Administration, Post Office Savings Administration, and Central Cooperative Treasury. In addition to these banks, some national capitalists created a few private banks and money houses, with about one third of them located in Shanghai. Given the size and nature of these banks, they had played a limited role in economic operations then.

With the irreversible victory of the people's liberation war, the Communist Party established the People's Bank of China in Shijiazhuang on December 1, 1948 to issue Renminbi-denominated paper notes and coins. In February of the following year, the People's Bank of China was relocated to Beiping/Peking (former name of Beijing). During the period before and after the founding of new China, the 'bureaucrat' banks were taken over, suspended or reformed into specialized banks according to the "Common Program" adopted at the first plenary session of the Chinese People's Political Consultative Conference. The four banks jointly owned by the government and merchants were changed into state and privately-owned-banks. Private banks were restructured and reformed, and all the privileges of foreign banks were abolished, and foreign currencies were prohibited from circulating in China.

After the founding of new China, a "unified" banking system was created under the planned economy system. Banks were not categorized into specialist banks with specialized departments, with every bank being an internal part of the People's Bank of China. Consequently, the People's Bank of China had become both a commercial bank to handle savings, credit and exchange businesses and a central bank to exercise the country's macroeconomic control. During the "Cultural Revolution", banks began to lose their independence under the influence of the "leftist" ideology. In September 1969, the People's Bank of China was merged to the Ministry of Finance to become one of its subsidiaries. In the eyes of some top leaders, banks were no more than a "treasury house" and "cashier" of the government. They had equated budgetary capital to credit capital, and used administrative means to replace the market functions of banks.[6]

The banking system was not restored and reestablished until October 1976 when the "Cultural Revolution" was put to an end. At the Third Plenary Session of the 11th National Congress of the Communist Party of China v(CPC) in 1978, the "leftist" ideology was 'rectified', ushering a new era of reform and opening up. The banking sector was brought back to track under the guidance of Deng Xiaoping's theory. Since 1977, the development of China's commercial banks has gone through the following periods:

6.2.1. *Reconstruction Period (1977–1986)*

The headquarters of the People's Bank of China resumed its ministerial level status in March 1978, but its dual role as a commercial bank and the central bank was left unchanged. Beginning from early 1979, the Agricultural Bank of China was restored to deal with rural financial business. The Bank of China split from the People's Bank of China to specialize in foreign trade credit and exchange business. The Construction Bank of China split from the Ministry of Finance to handle long-term investment and loans, and the Investment Bank of China was set up in 1981 to deal with loans from international financial institutions and other sources of capital for re-loaning to domestic businesses. On September 17, 1983 the State Council decided that the People's Bank of China would only perform the role of the central bank and that the Industrial and Commercial Bank of China would be set up to undertake the credit and savings business. By then, the banking system was firmly established, comprising the central bank and the four specialized commercial banks.

In October 1984, the "Decision on Restructuring the Economic System" was adopted at the Third Plenary Session of the 12th National Congress of the CPC. The banking system quickly expanded to develop the "planned commodity economy". In 1985, the People's Bank of China promulgated the policy that "specialized banks are allowed to undertake overlapping businesses", and that "banks and businesses can choose each other to their best interest", encouraging the "Big Four" to improve through moderate/measured competition. The new policy had broken the "system of centralized supply and use of capital". In the meantime, the "Big Four" began to expand their businesses to the vast rural areas, providing loans for the booming township and village enterprises.

6.2.2. *Period of Expansion (1987–1996)*

The country's reform and opening up provided great impetus for the reform and development of the banking sector. In December 1986, Deng Xiaoping called for "a great leap forward in financial reform to turn the banks into real banks".[7] In the following year, the People's Bank of China proposed to set up a socialist financial system, with the banks as the principal and various financial institutions as complementary players under the leadership of the central bank. Guided by the spirit of the 13th National Congress of the CPC in 1987 and the 14th National Congress of the CPC in 1992, the banking sector had seen a rapid growth.

As early as the beginning of the reform and opening up, it was made clear that the state-owned specialized banks should operate as real commercial banks. However, it was simply impossible (for them to so act) as they had to undertake policy credit and commercial credit businesses at the same time. At the Third Plenary Session of the 14th National Congress of the CPC held in November 1993, the Central Committee proposed "the establishment of policy banks to separate policy business from commercial business". As a result, the State Development Bank, Export-Import Bank of China, and the China Agricultural Development Bank were created successively in 1994, making possible the move of specialized banks towards commercial banking. On May 10, 1995 at the 13th Session of the National People's Congress, the "Commercial Banking Law of the People's Republic of China" was adopted, stipulating the nature and status of commercial banks as well as their relations with other financial institutions in the market. The new law had provided legal guarantee for commercial banks to operate autonomously and to improve assets quality. By 1996, the "Big Four" had 153,069 subsidiaries and branches, employing over 1,686,800 employees.

Similar growth was seen in other types of banks. The Bank of Communications was restructured as a shareholding public bank in July 1986. Since then, another 12 shareholding banks were founded, including the CITIC Industrial Bank, China Merchants Bank, Shenzhen Development Bank, Yantai Housing Savings Bank, Bangbu

Housing Savings Bank, Fujian Industrial Bank, Guangdong Development Bank, Everbright Bank of China, Huaxia Bank, Shanghai Pudong Development Bank, Hainan Development Bank, and China Minsheng Banking Corporation Limited. These banks have 3, 748 branches in total, employing over 85,500 employees.

In January 1986, the Ministry of Postal and Telecommunication and the People's Bank of China jointly promulgated the "Agreement on Opening Postal Savings Business" in the name of investment owners and business regulators respectively, deciding that post office savings business would be launched on a trial basis in 12 cities including Beijing and Tianjing. The "Postal Law of the People's Republic of China" adopted in 1986 stipulated post office savings as a part of legal business of postal companies. With postal savings business spread nationally, a "quasi-banking system" was created. In 1995, the People's Bank of China began to experiment with the setup of urban cooperative banks on the basis of urban credit cooperatives. In February of the same year, the first urban commercial bank in China — Shenzhen Commercial Bank — was created, and by 1996, a total of 18 urban cooperative banks had been in business.

6.2.3. *Period of Intensified Reforms (1997–2002)*

After two decades of reforms and development, a vast banking system had been established by 1996, in which the "Big Four" were the pillars, playing an important role in supporting and promoting the nation's economic and social development. However, the old ideology and historical burden from the planned economy were not easy to shrug off, while system building was slow in progress during the initial period. All these had added to the difficulty of the reform movement. The financial crisis in Southeast Asia in 1997 warned China that due attention should be given to risk prevention and management in commercial banks. At that time, the main problems of the "Big Four" included the following four aspects:

First, the financing of credit capital retained the strong 'flavor' of a planned economy. With the change from appropriation to loans, fiscal subsidies to state-owned enterprises (SOEs) were gradually replaced by bank loans. In 1985, financing from financial channels only accounted for 24.2% in the total subsidies for SOEs, but in 1994, the ratio had increased to 43.6%. As many SOEs had a low profitability and a high liability ratio, they relied heavily on banks for financing when government subsidy was cut off, and most of these loans became non-performing loans (NPLs) of banks.

Second, there was too much government interference/interventions in bank operation. Governments at all levels had directly interfered with the operation and management of banks, forcing banks to make loans to enterprises in financial difficulties to arrange for the laid-offs of staff and to pay the due taxes, or even to bridge the fiscal deficit. In some provinces, banks were even directed by the local governments at the end of year to lend to enterprises to pay taxes so as to realize the objective of fiscal revenue.

Third, in their fervor to maximize profits and making their interests to be the top priority, the banks seemed to have preference for expanding scales and increasing expenditure. On one hand, they were fond of expanding the scale and size, and on the other hand, they increased expenses substantially by building luxurious offices and training centers, leading to significant decline in margins and profits. During 1989–1998, the balance of credit assets in the "Big Four" had increased by 11 times, the overhead by 8.9 times,[8] while the total profit only by 26%.

Fourth, the banks' internal control was weak, lacking effective means of risk prevention. The practice of making new loans to recover the old, extending arbitrarily and 'rotating drafts' was widespread in the country. In the non-credit assets, there were problems of discrepancies between book entries and goods in-kind, misuse of book items, etc. In 'off-sheet' business, illegal making and acceptance of bills, and excess loans and credit were not uncommon. Weak management, ineffective auditing and lenience with cases of shirking responsibility had further increased the risk of bank assets.[1]

The Chinese government had attempted to hasten and enhance the reforms of and supervision over commercial banks since 1998.

However, the reforms before 2002 were merely implemented superficially, centering around changing the operational mechanism, improving management system, changing business scope, and adjusting business networks. The supervision over state-owned commercial banks was also weak.

6.2.4. *Crucial Period of Consolidation (Since 2003)*

China had joined the World Trade Organization (WTO) after 15 years of difficult talks and negotiations. As part of its WTO ascension agreement, China promised to lift geographical restrictions in five years; to eliminate gradually restrictions on local currency business, and allow foreign-funded banks to provide RMB service to all kinds of Chinese customers; to allow foreign-funded banks to set up business networks in the same city, with the same approval procedure as applicable to Chinese-funded banks; to lift the existing restrictions and non-approval measures on foreign-funded banks in respect of ownership, operation, setup of branches and license; to allow foreign-funded non-banking financial institutions to provide credit service for automobiles 'consumption' (enjoying the same treatment as similar Chinese financial institutions); to allow foreign-funded banks to provide automobile credit business to Chinese residents.

In the light of progressive opening and entry of foreign capital in the financial sector, our commercial banks, and especially the state-owned commercial banks, are facing important challenges as described below:

6.2.4.1. *Low competitiveness*

Haunted by historical burdens, system deficiency, weak internal control and inadequate financial innovations, China's commercial banks are generally poor in competitiveness. According to my own observation in 2001, the expense of Hang Seng Bank in Hong Kong only accounted for 24.4% of its total revenues, while the same figure is as high as 90% in our commercial banks. The pretax margin per capita is HK$1,570,000 at Hang Seng Bank, which is more than ten-fold that of our commercial banks. The one-year spread between credit and savings is 1.7–2.2% at Hang Seng, while the same figure is as high as 3.6% in our commercial banks.

6.2.4.2. *High proportion of non-performing assets (NPAs)*

By 2002, the NPLs in financial institutions had amounted to RMB2,598 billion yuan, excluding the NPLs of RMB1,400 billion yuan transferred to the four asset management companies. By 2003, the NPLs remained as high as RMB2,440.6 billion yuan, accounting for 15.19% in the total of loans. The average proportion of NPLs is as high as 19.74% in the "Big Four", while the same figure is only 5% in the top 100 international banks.[1] According to the statistics of the 'five-classification system', the NPLs in key commercial banks had reached RMB1,827.45 billion yuan by the first quarter of 2005, taking up 12.4% of the total volume of loans.[8]

Table 6.1 NPLs of Key Commercial Banks as of Q1, 2005.

	Amount million (100 yuan)	As a percentage of total loans (%)
Total NPLs	18,274.5	12.4
Among which: second-tier loans	3,410.1	2.3
doubtful loans	935.3	6.3
Loss-incurring loans	5,511.4	3.7
		As a percentage of total loans in commercial banks (%)
Key commercial banks	17,128.4	12.7
State-owned commercial banks	15,670.5	15.0
Shareholding commercial banks	1,457.9	4.9
Urban commercial banks	1,073.8	11.5
Rural commercial banks	36.2	6.1
Foreign-funded banks	36.0	1.2

Table 6.1 shows that the NPLs in the commercial banks account for 86% of the total of financial institutions, and 15% in the total of their loans.

6.2.4.3. *Low capital adequacy ratio (CAR)*

Beginning from the early 1980s, the state as the owner suspended its capital injection to the commercial banks. It was not until 1998 after the outbreak of the financial crisis in Southeast Asia did the government issue RMB270 billion yuan in bonds as supplemental capital of the "Big Four". However, a regular channel of supplementary capital was yet to be established. For a long period, the CAR of the "Big Four" had been well below the statutory requirement of 8%. Additionally, there was a huge gap in the reserves for dead accounts. In 2003, the commercial banks were allowed to issue subordinated bonds to increase their subordinate/subsidiary capital. By year end, the State Council decided to restructure the Bank of China and the Construction Bank of China as shareholding banks, and injected USD45 billion through the Central Huijin ('Remittance')Investment Company to supplement their capital. It is reported that by 2004, the overall CAR of 113 urban commercial banks was only 1.36%.[9]

To meet the aforementioned daunting challenges, the Chinese government decided to strengthen its supervision and speed up the reforms of commercial banks. Beginning from 2003, the reform of commercial banks has been carried out to higher levels, representing a new period of 'fortification' and consolidation. The focus of the reform has been shifted to structural reform (including systems and mechanisms) and establishment of modern financial enterprises.

According to the "Decision on the Plan for Restructuring the State Council" adopted at the First Session of the 10th National People's Congress held on March 10, 2003, the China Banking Regulatory Commission (CBRC) was founded on April 28, 2003, to replace the People's Bank of China in the exercise of its regulatory powers. At the Third Plenary Session of the 16th National Congress of the CPC held in October of 2003, it was decided to "deepen the structural reform of financial enterprises, enhance the financial control mechanism, and improve financial regulatory system".[10] At the Sixth Session of the 10th National People's Congress held on December 27, 2003, the "Law on Banking Regulatory Management of the People's Republic of

China", the "Decision of the National People's Congress on Amendments of Banking Law of the People's Republic of China", and the "Decision of the National People's Congress on Amendments of Commercial Banking Law" were adopted, providing legal legitimacy for the CBRC to exercise its regulatory function on one hand, and repositioning the People's Bank of China on the other hand to reinforce its function of formulating and implementing monetary policies.

The reform of the commercial banks is being accelerated. The Bank of China, the Construction Bank of China and the Industrial and Commercial Bank of China are making preparations for an overall IPO through shareholding reform. Some shareholding banks and urban commercial banks are seeking to improve corporate governance and internal control through the introduction of strategic investors and the CBRC is strengthening its supervision over commercial banks. However, we must be aware that the reform of commercial banks is a daunting task — it requires clear objectives, careful and meticulous planning, recognition of regional and local differences in approach, and steady and step-wise implementation.

6.3. Reforming Commercial Banks into Modern Financial Enterprises

At the Third Plenary Session of the 16th National Congress of the CPC held on October 14, 2003, the "Decisions of the Central Committee on Improving Socialist Market Economy" was adopted to strengthen the reform of financial enterprises, commercial banks, securities companies, insurance companies and trust investment companies to transform towards modern financial enterprises with adequate capital, strict internal control, efficient and healthy operations, excellent service, and superior financial performance.[11]

Shareholding is the main organizational form of modern enterprises, adopted by commercial banks worldwide. It is conducive not only to the development and growth of commercial banks, but also to the improvement of corporate governance and internal management. Among the 2002 Top 1,000 Banks published by *The Banker*, all the banks in the list were shareholding banks except the "Big Four" of China, and more interestingly, most of them were listed companies. The main feature of shareholding commercial banks is that shareholders undertake extent or scope of responsibility in proportion to their shares and banks undertake liabilities against their total assets. Shareholders as investors of banks enjoy owner's equity rights commensurate with their investments and participate in important decisions of banks, while the 'legal personality' of banks enjoys the legal personal assets formed through shareholders' investment, and possesses civil rights and assumes liabilities according to the law.

At the Third Plenary Session of the 16th National Congress of the CPC, it was decided that "selected state-owned commercial banks can take the lead in shareholding reform to speed up the disposal of NPAs, replenish capital base and create conditions for IPO". The shareholding reform is the foundation of all other reforms of commercial banks, as well as an important chain of the structural reform of the financial sector. According to the state regulations, SOEs must change their operational mechanism in line with the law and regulations when they are reformed into companies. They have to progressively check fund sources, clarify ownership, liquidate credits and meet liabilities, evaluate assets, and establish a standardized internal management system.

The shareholding reforms of the Bank of China and the Construction Bank of China kicked off at the end of 2003, and the main features included: to establish a standardized corporate governance and a strict internal system of rights and liabilities; to form a sound financial control and risk prevention mechanism; to expedite the disposal of NPAs through debt restructuring; and to develop solid financial fundamentals and to incorporate strict financing criteria.

It is recognized that the shareholding reform of state-owned commercial banks is an arduous and complex task, demanding careful and meticulous planning and step-wise or gradual implementation as suggested below:

6.3.1. *Clear Definition of Ownership and Property Rights*

The first priority of shareholding reform is to define ownership and clarify ownership structure. Ownership involves the property rights of corporate legal person and its related powers, and the property rights represent a company's economic benefits, including rights to physical entities, quasi-property rights, claims and intellectual property rights, etc. The corporate legal person enjoys ownership, and rights of use, transfer and disposal. Ownership rights structure refers to the distribution of property and related powers. In general, the property rights of corporate legal person are jointly owned by various owners according to their relative shares, and so is the distribution of power.

Like many other SOEs, the commercial banks in China are fully owned by the state. However, the problem of "owner's absence or absentee owners" does exist. Theoretically the state is the owner of the commercial banks, but in practice it is difficult for the state to exercise its powers as an owner. Firstly this makes the management of SOEs misconstrue themselves as the owner's agent, giving rise to such perennial problems as failure to supervise, abuse of power and "insider control". Secondly it makes the local officials and management of SOEs think that the debts of SOEs to banks are only an internal problem since both are owned by the state. As a consequence, "the government undertakes unlimited liability, while the banks are controlled by insiders".

The key of the ownership reform is to turn the state-owned commercial banks into shareholding companies or limited liability companies, allowing the state capital to enter banks in equity form. The state or its proxy organization can send representatives to attend the shareholder's general meeting, and enter the board of directors through elections so that ownership is separated from operation. In some countries like the United States, the government directly holds the shares of commercial banks, but in China, it is more appropriate for government-related investment companies or funds to hold shares. To this end, the State Council decided to form the Central Huijin (Remittance) Investment Company on December 16, 2003. This company is wholly owned by the state, with the Ministry of Finance, the People's Bank of China and the State Administration of Foreign Exchange as its major shareholders. Huijin is responsible for injecting capital to the Bank of China and the Construction Bank of China which are experimenting with the shareholding reform. It acts as an investor, supervises them to implement the reform measures and helping to improve corporate governance for competitive investment returns. The creation of Huijin signifies that the Chinese government has begun to establish the investor model of financial capital in the form of investment companies. However, the system and mechanism need further improvement in many facets of its running.

The Central Huijin Investment Company is created with the following objective in mind: representing the state in exercising the rights and obligations of an investor in large state-owned financial enterprises, safeguarding financial stability, preventing and eliminating financial risk; utilizing foreign exchange reserves effectively to add value.

As of September 2005, the company had recorded the following investments:

Injecting USD22.5 billion to the Bank of China in December 2003;
Injecting USD20 billion to the Construction Bank of China in December 2003;
Injecting USD2.5 billion to the Investment Company of the Construction Bank of China in December 2003;
Injecting RMB3 billion yuan to the Bank of Communications in June 2004;
Injecting USD15 billion to the Industrial and Commercial Bank of China in April 2005;
Injecting RMB10 billion yuan to Yinhe Securities Company in June 2005;
Injecting USD5 billion to the Import and Export Bank of China in July 2005;
Injecting RMB2.5 billion yuan to Shenyin Wanguo Securities, plus a RMB1.5 billion loan in August 2005;
Injecting RMB1 billion yuan to Guotai Junan, plus a RMB1.5 billion loan in August 2005;
Injecting RMB5.5 billion yuan to Yinhe Holdings in August 2005;
Injecting RMB10 billion yuan to China Everbright Bank in September 2005.

Obviously, the business scope of Huijin has extended from injecting capital to the Industrial and Commercial Bank of China and the Construction Bank of China to injecting capital to other commercial banks and securities companies. Some scholars have questioned the legal status of Huijin and the legitimacy of its injecting capital to commercial banks with the state foreign exchange reserves,[12] while others have voiced different views over the positioning of Huijin.[13] They argue that the macro objective of maintaining financial stability and the micro objective of making profit cannot be achieved at the same time; Huijin should function as a purely government-related holding company, and like Temasek Holdings* of Singapore, it should not be involved in any commercial business. Some even maintain that Huijin should be a non-profit organization.

In my view, the legal status of Huijin is in question, when it overemphasizes the maintaining of financial stability like the State-Owned Assets Management Commission, because the latter was approved by the First Session of the 10th National People's Congress. As a limited liability company, Huijin' board of directors and top management are government officials and public servants, which obviously conflicts with the regulation in the "Company Law" that "public servants are not permitted to hold concurrent positions in companies as members of board of directors, members of supervisory board, or members of management team". The argument that Huijin is a non-profit organization is even more unconvincing, because Article 5 in the "Company Law" has made it clear that "companies operate independently with all their legal person assets, and are responsible for their own profits and losses". To conclude, overemphasis on Huijin's macro function to turn it into the "State-Owned Assets Management Commission" in the financial sector (making it look like a financial fire brigade) is contrary to the direction of the structural reform of China's finance.

---

*Temasek Holdings is an investment company formed in June 1974 according to the "Company Law of Singapore". It holds shares in 20 large "government-linked companies (GLC), taking up 12% in GDP of Singapore. Temasek manages over USD55 billion of capitalized assets, but its annual operation expenses are less than USD30 million.

We would advise that Huijin be organized as a holding company according to the "Company Law", wholly owned by the state and with investment in financial enterprises as its key business. It should possess the property rights over all its assets, and perform the responsibility of an investor in financial enterprises it invests; and the return on equity (ROE) and return on investment (ROI) should be used as the key measures of performance — which can in fact support, at the micro level, the macro function of the People's Bank of China to maintain the financial stability.

6.3.2. *Introducing Strategic Investors*

At the Fourth Plenary Session of the 15th National Congress of the CPC, it was decided that "except for a few enterprises that must be monopolized by the state, companies with diversified investments should be encouraged".[14] Equity diversification is not only conducive to the realization of the policy that public ownership is the key component commensurate with the co-development of multi-ownership economy, but also helps solve the problem of enterprises' over-reliance on the government to undertake unlimited liability.

Equity diversification helps eliminate problems arising from the "overwhelming majority of the state-owned shares", especially problems arising from "insider control" in state-owned commercial banks. It can improve their corporate governance and internal management. In this context, the shareholding reform is not simply to change a bank's name to a "limited liability company" or a "shareholding company"; more importantly, it should move towards the realization of equity diversification.

In recent years, many commercial banks have been active in introducing overseas strategic investors to elevate their reputation, increase capital and improve management. Overseas (offshore) financial institutions are seeking active involvement in China's commercial banks through equity investment as they see great opportunities in this market and they do realize the close relations between the banking sector and the Chinese government.

The first case of introducing strategic investors occurred in 1997 when the Asian Development Bank (ADB) invested in China Everbright Bank. In September 1998, International Finance Corporation (IFC) acquired 5% of shares in the Bank of Shanghai. In 2001, the Hong Kong and Shanghai Banking Corporation (HSBC) and Shanghai Commercial Bank (Hong Kong) acquired a total of 18% of shares in the Bank of Shanghai. In October 2001, IFC acquired 15% of shares in Nanjing City Commercial Bank; in January 2003, Citibank acquired 5% of shares in Shanghai Pudong Development Bank; and on December 17, 2003 Fujian Industrial Bank reached an agreement with Hang Seng Bank, IFC and Singapore Direct Investment Company in Fuzhou, allowing Hang Seng to acquire 15.98% of its shares. By 2004, overseas financial institutions had invested in 10 Chinese banks, totaling USD2.663 billion. The realized investment amounted to USD2.408 billion, and to add the working capital of foreign-funded companies, the actual use of foreign capital had reached US3.786 billion in the banking sector.

Entering 2005, the pace of introducing strategic investors has been stepped up. As of September 2005, seven shareholding commercial banks and another seven urban commercial banks have introduced strategic investment with foreign investors successively. Following Everbright Bank, Pudong Development Bank and Fujian Industrial Bank, Xinqiao Capital acquired a controlling number of shares (17.89%) in Shenzhen Development Bank, while General Electric (GE) will invest USD100 million to acquire 7% of its share. HSBC acquired 19.9% of shares in the Bank of Communications — the first bank that went public on overseas market; China Minsheng Banking Corporation sold 1.1% of its shares to IFC, and 4.6% to Temasek. In early September, Pangaea Capital Management Singapore LTD acquired 6.9% of shares (289 million legal person shares) of Huaxia Bank through bidding, with a total investment of RMB1.0115 billion yuan (RMB3.5 yuan per share). The Deutsche Bank of Germany is reported to have reached a preliminary agreement with Huaxia Bank to purchase 14% of its shares (in its bid to be a strategic partner,) totaling USD330 million. Citibank has expressed its wish to increase its shareholding of Pudong

Development Bank to 19.9%. On September 6, Standard Chartered will invest in Bohai Bank as the sole overseas strategic investor through its wholly-invested/wholly owned company in Hong Kong — Standard Chartered Bank (Hong Kong) — to acquire 19.99% of its shares, investing a total of US123 million.

Following the Bank of Shanghai and Nanjing City Commercial Bank, a number of urban commercial banks, such as Xi'an City Commercial Bank, Bank of Beijing, Hangzhou City Commercial Bank, Ji'nan City Commercial Bank and Nanchong City Commercial Bank, have completed restructuring and introduced overseas strategic investors. Xi'an City Commercial Bank sold 5% of its shares to IFC and Scotiabank (2.5% of shares each) at a price of RMB53.76 million yuan; Bank of Beijing sold 19.9% of its shares to ING at a price of RMB1.78 million yuan (IFC purchased 5% of shares); Hangzhou City Commercial Bank sold 19.9% of its shares to the Commonwealth Bank of Australia; Ji'nan City Commercial Bank sold 11% of its shares to the Commonwealth Bank of Australia at a price of USD75 million; Nanchong City Commercial Bank has reached a strategic partnership agreement with Deutsche Entwicklungs Gesellschaft (DEG), Sparkassen International Development Trust (SIDT) and Sparkassenstiftung fuer Internationale Koopepation (SBFIC): DEG and SIDT will subscribe €3 million and €1 million shares respectively, taking up 10% and 3.3% after rights issue, with SBFIC providing technical support.

In the meantime, the three state commercial banks of China are stepping up the introduction of strategic investors too. On June 17, 2005 the Bank of America invested USD2.5 billion to acquire shares in the Construction Bank of China, and promised to subscribe another USD500 million at its IPO, amounting to 9% in total; Temasek invested US1.466 billion to acquire 5.1% of its shares, and promised to subscribe another USD1 billion at its IPO. It is reported that Credit Suisse First Boston will subscribe USD500 million at its IPO. Temasek also invested USD3.1 billion to acquire 10% of shares in the Bank of China, and promised to subscribe another USD500 million at its IPO. Royal Scotland Bank will invest USD1.6 billion and join hands with Merrill Lynch (investing USD750 million) and a private fund (investing USD750 million) of Li Ka-shing to acquire a total of 10% of shares in the Bank of China. UBS and ADB are also negotiating with the Bank of China, and will invest USD500 million and USD100 million to acquire 1.6% and 0.3% of shares respectively. Goldman Sachs, Allianz and American Express will invest a total of USD3 billion (Goldman Sachs USD1.8 billion, Allianz USD1 billion, and American Express USD200 million) to acquire 10% of shares of China's largest bank — the Industrial and Commercial Bank of China. The purpose of this arrangement is to help the bank to go public in overseas markets in 2007. The programs involving the Bank of China and the Industrial and Commercial Bank of China will be finalized very soon, although they need to be approved or adjusted by the authorities. The Agricultural Bank of China is also accelerating its shareholding reform and introduction of strategic investors.

As of September 2005, 19 overseas financial institutions have invested in 16 Chinese banks, with a total investment of USD16.5 billion, excluding the Bohai Bank which will soon begin business, and Fushan Commercial Bank acquired by Fujian Industrial Bank (24.98% of shares of the bank controlled by foreign capital) with RMB500 million yuan.

There are four important issues involved in the introduction of strategic investors: the share price of Chinese banks, definition of "strategic investors", further relaxation of the equity restrictions, and the effects of strategic investors on China's financial safety.

(1) *Is the banking industry selling cheap?*

A recent argument is that the banking industry of China is selling cheap as the state-owned commercial banks under-price their shares to introduce strategic investors. The price for acquiring 10% of shares in the three commercial banks is set at USD3 billion, which is obviously very low, given the profitability, business network, brand and credit reputation of the banks. Take the Industrial and Commercial Bank of China (ICBC) for example. It has over 22,000 business networks, controlling about 20% of assets of China's banking sector. In 2004, it realized a profit of RMB74.7 billion yuan. At the price of USD3 billion, the foreign investors didn't pay any premium to acquire 10% of equity, and can get a return of 100% in less than four years, not taking into account the premium of the bank after its IPO.[14]

To me, the above argument is not well-grounded. First, the choice of strategic investors and pricing of shares are conditional on the two-way choice making and negotiation between the vendor and the purchaser. The state-owned commercial banks in China are often haunted by such problems as 'historical burdens', overstaffing, irrational structure, excessive interference from the government, occasional scandals, strict restriction on the shareholding percentage by foreign capital, and different taxation, accounting and labor systems from international markets. These are potential risks for foreign capital. Among the numerous overseas banks, only a few have ventured to invest in China; so there is no "flooding in" of foreign investors as reported in the media. Foreign investors often ask for "systemic discount" to these factors during the negotiation, making it difficult for the Chinese side to raise the price.[15] Additionally, reserves for bad accounts and NPAs are inadequate in the state-owned commercial banks and that the equity rights and profitability are overvalued. In 1999, for example, when IFC invested in Bank of Shanghai, the net asset per share was RMB2.1–2.2 yuan according to the Chinese accounting principles. However, according to the auditing made by the PricewaterhouseCoopers, it was only 1.07 yuan after drawing USD2 billion from the owner's equity as reserves for bad accounts. The final price was set at RMB1.41 yuan[16] as a compromise. Even at the compromised price, some foreign investors are worried about the potential risks and are demanding "risk guarantee". For example, Huijin promised that the net asset per share of the Bank of China and the Construction Bank of China wouldn't be below the acquiring price of the foreign investors, and that if IPO does not show success in three years, Huijin would have to buy back the equities from the foreign investors.

Second, we must be aware that the commercial banks in China are not as competitive as their foreign counterparts, with their creditability relying mainly on the country's reputation. In a monopolized market, almost everything in the banks is controlled by the state: the interest rate is determined by the state, the foreign exchange of businesses is required to deposit at banks in RMB, the top management of banks is appointed by the state, all capital is provided by the state, and the NPAs are disposed by the state. When compared with international standards, the key indicators of performance at the commercial banks in China, including profitability (before-tax margin/cost), returns on capital and margin per capita, are relatively low. It is also obvious that there are gaps in service quality, asset quality, corporate governance and financial innovation. The advantage of an extensive business network is often offset by low efficiency and poor service quality. A good example is the foreign exchange business: a significant part of foreign exchange savings in Shanghai is flowing to foreign-funded banks when the business is open to foreign capital. My view is that the exchange of equity for advanced technology and management is a win-win transaction for both sides.

Third, most of the foreign investors had focused more on the future value when they decided to invest in the Chinese banks. Given the uncertainties, the valuation of the same bank can be widely different. For example, the market value of the Construction Bank of China was estimated at RMB403-475 billion yuan by Morgan Stanley, but the estimate of Goldman Sachs was much lower, at about RMB281.7-368 billion yuan.

According to the terms of the strenuously negotiated agreement, the net assets of the three commercial banks are valued at a premium of 10–17%, with the selling price well above the net assets. Additionally, the shareholding percentage of foreign capital is set at below 25%. The IPO experience of the Bank of Communications and the Construction Bank of China on Hong Kong market shows that the entry of foreign capital can help improve the reputation of Chinese banks and contribute to a premium listing. Moreover, as the Chinese side owns the largest shares, it has obtained most of the benefits.

The above analysis demonstrates that there are no cheap sales of our commercial banks. Of course, these banks will be able to sell a better price if they simply wait until the reform makes significant progress. However, this is not possible as China would be opening its market to foreign capital by 2006.

(2) *Definition and scope of strategic investors*

Strategic investors are traditionally defined as investors who hold shares for long term and are helpful in upstream and downstream products, market, management or social relationship. The CBRC has proposed four guidelines for the introduction of strategic investors: long-term shareholding, corporate governance optimization, business cooperation, and avoidance of competition. In most cases, these four guidelines have been observed, and some strategic investors have even agreed to provide technical support. in these aspects. For example, the Bank of America not only agreed to send 50 experts to the Construction Bank of China, but also promised not to open any new branches in China and it closed its retailing business. Another example is the Bank of China which will be cooperating with the Royal Scotland Bank in credit card services and corporate banking, and BC is developing close collaborative relationship with RSC in corporate governance and risk management.

In addition, the scope of strategic investors is fast extending to investment companies, funds and enterprises. Presently most of the strategic investors in our commercial banks are from overseas. Cross-holding between banks and involvement of domestic investment companies and enterprises should also be encouraged in the future to better realize equity diversification.

(3) *Relaxing the equity rights requirement of foreign capital*

On December 8, 2003 the CBRC promulgated the "Measures for the Administration of Equity Investment in Chinese-Funded Financial Institutions by Foreign-Funded Financial Institutions", prescribing the conditions and procedures for equity investment by foreign-funded financial institutions. According to the

"Measures", the shareholding by a single overseas financial institution was increased from 15% to 20%, but the total of foreign capital could not exceed the ceiling of 25%. The "Measures" were put into effect on December 31, 2003. As most of the commercial banks with overseas investment have approached the ceiling, some suggest a further loosening of the percentage equity rights control on foreign capital.

A further relaxation of the percentage control can bring more benefits than potential disadvantages. It not only helps attract more foreign capital and increase the capital strength of China's banks, but also encourages them to improve their corporate governance and internal management. Additionally, the implementation of this relaxation can increase the confidence of overseas investors. As a start, the amount of equity rights held can be increased to 33% and finally to 49%. Nevertheless, this does not mean that all banks should allow up to 49% of shareholding by foreign capital. In the "Big Four", the shareholding by foreign capital should not exceed 33% in order to maintain the state's control.

(4) *Jeopardizing China's financial safety?*

During the past two decades of reform and opening up, the question was raised repeatedly whether the introduction of foreign capital would jeopardize the country's security. Now some people are worried about the financial security because of the introduction of overseas strategic investors — so this issue deserves scrutiny and analysis.

A nation's financial security is a macro concept, concerned primarily with the prevention of risks in public bonds, exchange rate, savings and financial market.[17] Due to the parasitic and meta-stable nature of the virtual/fictitious economy, the healthy development of real economy is the prerequisite to preventing financial risks. The improvement of micro foundations of financial system provides important assurance for financial stability. It must be realized that, under the old, traditional system, huge NPLs, 'moral hazards' and low efficiency of state-owned banks constitute the largest threat to our financial stability.

The purpose of introducing foreign strategic investors is not solely for 'importing' capital, but more importantly for the improvement of our system through external force. It's true that foreign investors come in for profit, and their practices and mindset could be widely different from us, but our fundamental objectives are the same: to make banks become successful. The entry of foreign capital is conducive not only to the rectification of the abnormal "government-banks-businesses" relations existing under the planned economy, but also to the improvement of the micro foundations of our financial system.

According to one report,[16] the dividends of the Bank of Shanghai before 1999 accounted for 20% of its profit, but when the foreign shareholders entered the board of directors, they proposed to balance the short-term and long-term interests of shareholders to realize the combination of "maximization of shareholder returns" and "the bank's long-term development". Since then, the dividends had been decreasing from 20% to 10%. This is to improve the bank's ability of 'self-accumulation and self-development'. By concerted efforts involving all parties, the bank has seen an enormous growth over the past five years. By 2004, the total assets of the bank had reached RMB220 billion yuan, with an ROA of 18.42%, CAR of 10.4%, NPLs of 4.99%, and pre-tax profit of RMB1.815 billion yuan. The equity investment of foreign capital has also helped increase business cooperation between Chinese-funded and foreign-funded banks. For example, the HSBC was helping the Bank of Shanghai to launch a Visa card for overseas customers.

According to one report, Ji'nan City Commercial Bank had increased its CAR to 8.88% after one year of introducing the strategic investment of Commonwealth Bank of Australia, and completed six projects in IT, credit management, risk management, marketing, financial management and capital management. With the upgrading of credit classification system, the bank's ability to control credit risk has been greatly improved.

According to its commitment to the WTO, China will gradually lift its restrictions over foreign-funded banks, which means that the competition in this market will be intensifying. In 10–15 years, foreign capital is estimated to occupy 30% of China's market share. Given the low competitiveness of China' commercial banks, it is not wise for them to compete 'head-on' with foreign-funded banks. A more sensible approach is for them to develop a collaborative relation with foreign-funded banks, and make themselves better, stronger and bigger so as to take up the biggest share of the cake.

However, issues of principle should not be compromised. For example, during the negotiation between Citibank and Pudong Development Bank, the two sides had disagreed on the choice of applicable law and jurisdiction. Finally, the American side made great concessions and agreed to use Chinese law as the applicable law for registration and Singapore law as the applicable law in case of disputes. In introducing strategic investors, the top management of banks should maintain state secrecy (keeping state secrets) in accordance with the relevant laws and regulations of the state.

6.3.3. *Stepping up the Disposal of NPAs*

There are four factors contributing to the high proportions of NPAs within the banking sector. The first factor is that many loans had been approved because of government directives. Under the planned economy, the banking sector had long been taking the role of "bank cashier", giving out loans according to government instructions and planning. The situation has improved since 1994 when the three 'policy banks' were created and since 1995 when the "Commercial Banking Law" was promulgated. But government officials were still reluctant to give up their control over the banks' credit, instructing banks to make loans to designated industries and businesses and "image-keeping projects" or asking banks to 'inject blood' to save SOEs in great financial difficulties or on the verge of bankruptcy. Banks were asked to foot the bill for losses incurred resulting from wrong decisions and corruption. The second factor is the poor performance of SOEs. With decreasing subsidies from the government, they turn to banks for capital needed for their blindly ambitious expansion. When these businesses fail, their losses become the NPAs of banks. The third factor is the loss arising from the 'moral hazards' of employees within the banking sector, and the last factor is the loss arising from bad decisions and poor management.

The classification of NPAs in the banking sector has shifted since 2002 from the 'four- to the five-category system', leading to a great difference in the final result. By 2002, for example, the NPLs on the four-category system were RMB1,702.362 billion yuan, or 21.41%; but using the five-category system, they reached RMB2,077.036 billion yuan, or 26.12%, an increase of 4.71%.[16]

The replacement of the four- by the five-category system represents China's integration with international practices, and a change in loan quality evaluation from the parameters of 'post mortem' (overdue, stagnating, non-performing etc.) to that for the proper steps to be taken before any serious events occur (normal, cause for concern, suspicious, losses etc.) to identify and solve problems in the first place. The CBRC decided on July 13 of 2003 that the wholly state-owned banks and shareholding commercial banks should replace the four- with the five-category classification from 2004.

To help banks dispose the NPAs, China created Xinda, Huarong, Great Wall and Orient asset management companies respectively for the Construction Bank of China, the Industrial and Commercial Bank of China, the Agricultural Bank of China and the Bank of China in 1999. In 2004, a total of RMB140 million of NPAs were removed.

The creation of "one-to-one" asset management companies to remove the NPAs of commercial banks has given rise to a number of problems. First, as the asset management companies were derived from the state-owned banks, they had inherited the banks' old governance and management approach, and lacked system innovation. The same problems would arise when they dispose of the NPAs. Second, the "internal transfer" of NPAs does not contribute to the solution of the problem as the cause of and question of who were responsible for NPAs were not seriously analyzed. Third, these asset management companies were created in a great rush, with many loopholes and without proper planning and regulations in regard to asset pricing and methods of NPA disposal. Fourth, the duration of the management companies was set at ten years when they were created, which induced the short-term self-profiting behavior and 'moral hazards' of the management and staff. Without appropriate supervision, problems are almost inevitable.

The auditor-general Li Jinhua disclosed in his 2004 auditing report the auditing results of the balance sheets of Xinda, Huarong, Great Wall and Orient and their subsidiaries.[18] A total of RMB554.4 billion of NPAs were audited, accounting for 39% of their acquisitions. In general, these management companies had played an active role in saving the banks' NPAs and preventing and eliminating financial risk. However, illegal practices and improper management were also found in the four companies. As of 2004, they had disposed of a total of RMB675 billion of NPAs, taking up 53.9% in the total. The accumulated collected cash reached RMB137 billion yuan, with a cash collection rate of 20.2%. Flouting with regulations and non-standard management disclosed in the auditing involve a total of RMB71.549 billion yuan, or 13% of the audited capital.

The main problems found in the auditing report comprise three aspects. The first involves the illegal spin-off and acquisition of NPAs. Some commercial banks and asset management companies were too lenient in evaluation of NPAs, allowing bad loans which should not be 'removed' to be transferred to the asset management companies. The result was that a substantial part of financial claims were difficult to honor, while the cause and persons responsible for NPLs were not investigated thus covering up the illegal practices and financial crimes in the loan process. The second involves the disposal of NPAs at an undercut price. Some management companies had flouted the procedure, while others were found guilty of false valuation, collusion, and under-price repurchase, resulting in a great loss of the state-owned assets. The last involves disorder in financial management. Embezzlement of recovered funds for personal gains, and off-account savings were rampant in some asset management companies.

The disclosures of the auditing shocked the nation. The Budget Working Committee of the National People's Congress proposed an all-out and thorough audit of the four asset management companies, while the banking regulatory body has promulgated the "Guidelines for Disposal of Non-Performing Assets", requiring financial institutions to establish a standard system of NPA disposal, improve the decision mechanism and operational procedure, adhere to the principle of "openness, fairness and justice", and improve the transparency of disposal through public disclosure to realize maximum recovery. Mr. Zhou Xiaochuan, Governor of the People's Bank of China, has made eight proposals, including legislating on NPA disposal, attracting private and foreign capital, reforming the four asset management companies, pricing through market simulation to avoid light restrictions, establishing an internal incentive system, reforming the disposal procedure and work procedure, promoting the growth of intermediaries, and taking measures to handle the interests between the management companies and the acquired companies of NPAs.

Some commercial banks have taken action to cooperate with foreign capital in NPA disposal. On July 9, 2002 the Construction Bank of China and the Asset Management Company of Korea signed a memorandum of understanding and training service agreement in Beijing. On June 5, 2003 the Industrial and Commercial Bank of China signed a MOU in Beijing with an American company on strategic cooperation in NPA disposal, including establishing a joint venture to dispose a total of RMB1 billion of NPAs, creating a joint venture service entity, and developing assets management training programs. On July 8, 2003 the Construction Bank of China signed an agreement in Beijing with Morgan Stanley on pilot/trial transactions of NPA disposal. This is the largest project of its kind in China, as well as the first project of Morgan Stanley to acquire NPAs of Chinese state-owned commercial banks through a "one-to-one" agreement.[1]

It is worth our vigilance to note that, as the banking reform is not yet properly in place, the absolute value of NPLs is increasing though their relative value is decreasing. In 2000, the NPLs of the "Big Four" reached RMB2,743.9 billion yuan, with a balance of RMB1,350 billion yuan after a removal of RMB1,393.9 billion yuan. But as of 2004, the NPLs had amounted to RMB1,696.7 billion yuan according to the 4-category system, a net increase of RMB346.7 billion yuan and as high as RMB1988 billion yuan according to the 5-category system, a net increase of RMB638 billion yuan.

The disposal of NPLs in commercial banks needs to be more market-oriented, attracting domestic and overseas investors to the NPL market. The NPL market had originated from the US savings and loan crisis in the 1980s. The international interest in China's NPL market has been mounting up in recent years. Next to Japan, China's NPL market is the second largest in Asia, with a tota size of about USD500 billion. According to an estimate by PricewaterhouseCoopers, the accumulated international investment in China's NPL market was merely USD10-15 billion, which means that the market potentials are huge.[19] After the East Asian financial crisis, the international banks and funds had seen high returns in the NPL markets of Korea, Thailand, Japan and Malaysia during 1998–2002, with an average of 20–30% of ROI. China is an emerging market, and it is estimated that more overseas investors will enter this market in the coming years. In April 2004, ADB formed a joint venture fund with IFC, which is the first fund investing in China's NPL market.

In the meantime, the NPL market should also be open to domestic private capital. There is a huge amount of idle capital in China, part of which can be directed to the NPL market, given the gloomy stock market and a tight control on the investment in real estate. As a start, private equity funds can be launched on a trial basis, and encouraged to enter the NPL market where the risk is under strict control.

The NPLs of commercial banks should be disposed with different approaches and assimilated step by step. The NPLs before 2003 are "old accounts": some were created by the government and therefore need to be covered by the government through capital injection or 'getting rid of — removal', and the rest, together with the "new accounts" after 2003, need to be absorbed by the banks themselves.

Some suggest the disposal of NPLs through asset securitization. However, as most of the NPLs of the "Big Four" are claims difficult to realize, and the generation of steady future cash flow is still in question, securitization of NPLs is actually to transfer the risk to investors of the stock market. This is obviously inappropriate for the time being.

6.3.4. *Replenishing Capital Base*

Constrained by ownership structure, the "Big Four" have a single source of capital, funded primarily by the state through injection of fiscal capital or issuance of financial bonds. This approach is easy, but the fiscal capital is not unlimited. With the expansion of banks, the state is not likely to inject capital unendingly, while issuing bonds will only increase the state's debt burden. Capital injection by the state can only lead to banks' over-reliance on the state and the state's over-control on banks, both of which are detrimental to the market-oriented banking reform.

According to the Basel Agreement,[20] the minimum requirement of CAR for commercial banks is 8%, and supplemental capital must be confined in the 100% of core capital (i.e. core capital should not be below 4%). CAR is calculated as regulated assets divided by risk-weighted assets, where risk-weighted assets equal to credit-weighted assets plus 12.5 times (capital requirements for market risk and operation risk). Wang Xiaofeng.[21] compared the CAR between banks in China and banks in the US, Japan and India based on the materials published by the Banker in 2003. The average of CAR is 7.63% in China (12 banks), 13% in the US (72 banks), 10.83% in Japan (27 banks), and 12.23% in India (20 banks).

China's commercial banks must replenish their capital base and increase their CAR to qualify for IPO. In December 2003, the state injected USD45 billion through Huijin to launch a shareholding reform in the Bank of China and the Construction Bank of China on a trial basis. When interviewed by the Xinhua News Agency, the spokesman for the State Administration of Foreign Exchange pointed out that the use of foreign exchange reserves should not be considered as fiscal allocation but rather as capital injection.[22] On April 21, 2005 the shareholding reform program of the Industrial and Commercial Bank of China was officially approved by the State Council, in which a total of USD15 billion of capital was injected.

It should be noted that capital injection by the state is merely an expedient or temporary measure to help the commercial banks qualify for IPO. To increase the CAR of Chinese-funded banks up to international standards, steps must be taken to increase the numerator and reduce the denominator of the capital adequacy ratio simultaneously.

The numerator of CAR is the regulatory capital of commercial banks, including core capital and supplemental capital. The core capital in China's commercial banks includes paid-up capital, capital reserve, surplus reserve and retained profit, and the supplemental capital includes reserve for loan risk, reserve for investment risk and long-term bonds with a five-year maturity or above. The regulatory capital can be increased through the following measures:

(1) Introducing strategic investors; this can increase the paid-up capital directly.
(2) Balancing the proportion between retained earnings and dividends. Some commercial banks are often motivated by short-term interests, resorting to all means to 'whitewash' the accounts and giving generous dividends to please shareholders. This is like 'killing the goose that lays the egg'. It is advised that the banking regulatory committee or authority set a reasonable proportion between retained earnings and dividends, allowing adequate capital and surplus reserves. Commercial banks with CAR below the requirements should keep their dividends at the minimum.
(3) Improving the reserve system for NPLs. The reserve for bad accounts had been kept at 0.5% in the "Big Four", far below the international level. On the basis of the five-category classification system, we can draw on the international experience to establish reserves for NPLs, and set 1%, 10%, 20%, 50% and 100% respectively for loans of "normal", "cause for attention",

"subordinated", "doubtful/suspicious "and "loss" — the 5 category classification.

(4) Issuing subordinated bonds. Issuing long-term subordinated bonds is an important source of capital replenishment in international banks. The analysis by Merrill Lynch Securities shows that, in international banks, common shares account for 60% in their capital structure, subordinated bonds 25%, and preferred shares, minority equity and other forms of capital 15%. According to the Basel Agreement, (commercial banks are allowed to book the subordinated term bonds less than 50% of the core capital as supplemental capital.) On December 9, 2003 the CBRC issued the "Circular on the Inclusion of Subordinated Term Bonds in Supplementary Capital", allowing banks to issue subordinated term bonds to designated creditors with not less than five-year maturity.

(5) Issuing convertible bonds. Convertible bonds and convertible preferred shares are the two key forms of convertible securities. In China, enterprises are allowed to issue convertible bonds only. The holders of convertible bonds shall have the right, in addition to those of common bonds, to convert the bonds to common/normal bonds. According to China's regulations, convertible bonds can be included in tier-two capital, or tier-one capital when converted to common bonds.

(6) Appropriate tax reduction. The tax burden of commercial banks is in general too heavy in China, and tax reduction is necessary to promote banking reforms. However, the proceeds generated from tax reduction should be used to increase CAR, rather than as profit for distribution.

The denominator of CAR is the risk-weighted assets. Measures should be taken to reduce the amount of risk assets. Loans to individuals and enterprises are the key business of the commercial banks in China, but these assets have a relatively high risks. According to the existing regulations of the CBRC, their risk weighting is 100%. Loans account for 60% of the total assets of China's commercial banks, and the same figure is about 40% in some of the overseas banks. One way is to reduce the high-risk loan business, and increase the low-risk loan business, such as housing mortgage, intermediary business and 'off-the-statement' business.

It should also be noted that, according to the Basel Agreement, when the expected loss exceeds the approved reserves, the balance should be deducted from the core capital and supplementary capital, with 50% from each. The reduction of NPLs contributes to the increase of CAR.

6.3.5. *Setting up Good Corporate Governance and Continue to Improve it*

Due to the problem of 'owner's absence/absentee owners', governors of state-owned commercial banks not only act as the management, but also as the owner's representatives. Some of them arrogate all powers, and put their own interests before the interests of the state. A few of them even violate the laws and regulations. The introduction of strategic investors is an important step in the shareholding reform to improve the corporate governance of the commercial banks and to check such blatantly wrong behavior.

Corporate governance is a system arrangement that defines and determines the basic power of a company, including the appointment of the top management, control of corporate resources, and distribution of earnings. It is set up to address the issue of difference in objectives between the owner and the management after the separation of ownership and operation. Corporate governance is also considered as a set of system arrangements helping the owner to monitor and control the management and performance.

According to the modern management theory, factors contributing to a company's performance are two-fold: one is the market structure, and the other is the corporate behavior. Corporate behavior includes the leadership quality, internal management and business strategy. These are all related to corporate governance. Besides such factors as the history, culture, legislation and economy of each country, corporate governance is also affected by ownership structure, decision model and strategic objectives.[23]

In a diverse-shareholding company, the shareholders' general meeting is the ultimate governing body in theory; but in practice, it is often the board of directors that exercises the owner's power, as the number and turn-over of shareholders is overwhelmingly large through frequent equity trading on the stock market. Therefore, the core of corporate governance is the power, structure, and work mechanism of the board of directors.

The legal regulations about the power of the board of directors are more or less the same round the world, including those concerning the appointment and removal of the top management, and the overall supervision over the corporate strategy, management and financial affairs. However, the structure of the board of directors differs from country to country. China will implement its new "Company Law" from January 1, 2006, which prescribes that the board of directors shall comprise 3–13 members for limited liability companies, and 5–19 members for shareholding companies. All the members of the board are elected through shareholder's general meetings. At present, apparently overseas strategic investors are concerned with the role of the board of directors, performance of the management, internal auditing, risk control, and nomination of independent directors. They demand for seats in the board of directors and key positions in the special/ad–hoc committees, such as chairperson of the risk management committee, compensation committee and auditing committee. Their other concerns include the functions of each ad–hoc committee, charters of the board of directors, and the deliberative system.

The board of directors appoints the general manager and is held responsible/liable for the consequence of its choice. In China, candidates are screened and assessed for "reliability" and "obedience". This is one of the key factors contributing to the low performance of the state-owned commercial banks. The general manger of a commercial bank should be a professional banker with practical business experience and ethics, expertise in banking, strong leadership qualities and a good sense of risk prevention. Some people are worried about the reliability of professional bankers. Such a worry is unwarranted, because with strong incentives and good supervisory system, a capable individual can always be reliable, while a poor system will make a usually, reliable individual unreliable.

Independent directors are also known as external directors. They have no stakes in the company in question and their primary responsibility is to protect the interests of small shareholders. The new "Company Law" requires all listed companies to introduce independent directors, but such specifics as the qualifications, procedures of appointment, compensation, power and obligations are yet to be approved by the State Council. In the writer's view, at least one third of the board members of a multiple-ownership bank should comprise of independent directors, and the position of chairperson of the risk management committee, compensation committee and auditing committee should be assumed by independent directors.

6.3.6. *Encouraging Shareholding Banks to Obtain Finance through IPO*

The development of commercial banks often relies on financing through the capital market. In 2002, there were about 900 banks listed on the New York Stock Exchange, taking up 30% in the total. Another 900 banks were listed on NASDAQ, accounting for 19% in the total. Citibank, Chase Manhattan etc are just a few examples. On the Tokyo Stock Exchange, there are 160 banks, and on Hong Kong Stock Exchange, there are over 40 banks, including the blue chips of HSBC and Hang Seng Bank.

Since 1991, five shareholding banks, including Shenzhen Development bank, Shanghai Pudong Development Bank, China Minsheng Banking Corporation, China Merchants Bank and Huaxia Bank, have gone public in domestic market, while the Bank of Communications and the Construction Bank of China went IPO in Hong Kong. From a strategic view point, China's commercial banks should actively create conditions for IPO, and replenish capital base through the capital market. They should expand their size, open overseas branches, and improve their corporate governance and internal management in accordance with the rules of the capital market. But tactically, the IPO model ('spin-off' or by overall listing), location (domestic or overseas), timing, 'rhythm', choice of underwriters, and pricing still need our further study and scrutiny.

'Spin-off' listing is a popular model adopted by most of the large-sized SOEs. For the state-owned commercial banks, the first important step is to form group holding companies, and restructure the assets under the overall framework of group holding reform. Premium assets qualifying for IPO should be restructured as subsidiaries for public offering. The listed subsidiaries should reverse-takeover or acquire the group assets through capital operation, and ultimately realize the overall listing of the commercial banks.

The Bank of China had a spin-off listing experience. On July15, 2002 the Bank of China (Hong Kong) Limited announced its initial offering of 2.298 billion shares to investors in Hong Kong, taking up 25% of the total equity, among which 2.174 billion shares were sold globally at a price range of HK$6.93-9.5 per share. The objective was to finance HK$14.3-19.5 billion, equivalent to USD2-3 billion. The company offered its shares globally, and 50% were subscribed by the finance groups and real estate developers in Hong Kong. Before its IPO, the company had a total of HK$7.4 billion of NPLs transferred to an asset management company registered at Cayman Islands to meet the listing requirement of the Hong Kong market.

A spin-off listing enables a subsidiary to meet the listing requirement immediately and improves its competitiveness in the stock market, but at the same time it increases the burden and difficulties of the parent company. As the listing company is closely related to its parent company, related transactions between them seem inevitable. In China, embezzlement of capital by the parent company is not rare. This not only harms the interests of public investors, but also jeopardizes the healthy development of the stock market. If all factors are taken into account, an 'overall' listing seems to be a better choice.

In the case of the "Big Four", the problem with an overall listing is their enormous size and 'heavy historical burdens', making them difficult to meet the listing requirements. Given the gloomy domestic market, the government decided to list them on overseas markets and turn them into real companies. There is not much flexibility in timing as the commercial banks are hungry for IPO. Due attention should also be given to the listing sequence and interval between each listing of the banks. As the domestic underwriters are less known in international markets, and are less experienced, overseas securities companies are preferred.

On June 23, 2005, the Bank of Communications went public on the H-share market of Hong Kong, thus becoming the first bank from the mainland to realize an overall listing in overseas market. The bank issued a total of 4.684 billion H-shares, with an over-subscription of 205 times for individual investors and 27 times in the case of institutional investors, which is the fourth largest over-subscription in the IPO history of Hong Kong. The listing price was set at HK$2.5, but the share opened at HK$2.8 on the first day, and closed at HK$2.825, 13% higher than the listing price.

On October 27 of the same year, the Construction Bank of China had a successful IPO on Hong Kong market, offering 26.486 billion of H-shares, out of which 1.986 billion shares were sold in Hong Kong, and the rest were international 'allocated' shares. The nominal value of each share was RMB1yuan, and the listing price was HK$2.35. The total capitalization amounted to HK62.2 billion, recording a historical high in Hong Kong. The share opened at HK$2.375, and closed at HK$2.35 on the first day. The Bank of China and the Industrial and Commercial Bank of China are scheduled to launch IPO in one or two years' time in off-shore market.

The determination of listing price is a major decision in the listing process. If it is priced too low, the interests of original shareholders will be harmed; but if it is priced too high, the fluctuation will be big. The pricing process is often designed by the primary underwriter, with the final approval of the top management of the bank in question. The pricing models include the P/E, P/B, DDM and comparative valuation against peers.

The Bank of Communications used the P/E and P/B indices, and priced its shares together with such factors as asset quality, profit model, expected revenue growth and improvement of management techniques. There were five principles involved. The first was the market principle — to benchmark against the P/E and P/B of peers. The second principle was to protect the interests of old shareholders — not to price the share too low. The third principle was to take into account the interests of new shareholders — not to price the share too high because the investors can be very disappointed if the share price goes down below the listing price after IPO. The fourth principle was to safeguard the national interests and the fruits of the banking reform — to avoid the devaluation or loss of state-owned assets. The last principle was to maintain the stability of share price after IPO. After a series of negotiations with the primary underwriter, the Bank of Communications finally decided to choose the upper limit of the price range, pricing its shares at HK$2.5 per share, with a P/B of 1.6 times.[24]

The important principle observed by the Construction Bank of China during its IPO process was to curb short sell and increase long-term stability. In its initial road-show, the bank set the price range between HK$1.8-2.25 per share in Hong Kong, and then increased to HK$1.9-2.40 in London, and finally fixed at HK$2.35 in New York on the basis of the market reaction.[25]

The commercial banks can replenish capital, increase awareness and improve corporate governance through IPO. However, the challenge is also huge, as the shareholding reform, capital replenishment and disposal of NPLs were completed in a great rush through strong government support, and many of the in-depth problems remain unsolved, such as the internal 'moral hazards' and external administrative interference. These problems are likely to prop up after IPO, exposing the listing companies to the legal actions of investors and the severe punishment of the regulatory authorities. Therefore, IPO is only the first step for the state-owned commercial banks in their long journey to join the ranks of global leading banks. They must strengthen their reforms, improve management, make business grow, and continuously improve their international competitiveness through innovations.

6.3.7. *Improving Internal Management*

Commercial banks are financial enterprises, with both the general features of businesses and the peculiarity of finance. Chinese commercial banks, especially state-owned banks, still have a number of problems in system, mechanism, mentality, tradition, organization, staffing, skills and business, among which the most serious are overstaffing, overlapping of duties, bureaucracy, and low efficiency. Therefore, increased efforts must be made to improve the internal management in the following aspects:

6.3.7.1. *Organizational management*

The state-owned commercial banks in China are structured in line with the division of administrative regions. Despite a centralized legal person system, they have retained a five-level hierarchical structure from the headquarters down to sub-offices. Internally, they are organized into different departments in line with business or product categories. For example, some banks have international business department, real estate credit department, settlement department, and capital business department, and supporting departments as labor department, personnel department, education department, and administration department. The weakness of the structure is that the vertical 'delegation chain' is too long, and there are too many horizontal staffing departments, resulting in slow response, low efficiency, poor service quality, and insider control. One suggestion is to draw on international experiences and establish a market-oriented, customer-centered and product-pillared structure through process restructuring. Vertically the structure has three levels from the headquarters to strategic business units (SBUs) and to branches, and horizontally, it entails three lines of market, strategy and supporting functions. The first line includes customer relations management departments grouped according to the categories of customers, and financial products management departments grouped according to the products. The second line includes strategic planning, risk management, finance and administration departments. The third line includes human resource management, operation center and technical support, responsible for processing customer data and business operation.

6.3.7.2. *Customer relations management*

The clients of commercial banks include businesses in the finance industry, domestic business enterprises and multinationals. To attract and retain these customers, commercial banks often implement the account managers system to provide premium and effective services. Account managers are responsible for developing new customers, providing savings, lending and exchange services for customers, and act as their investment consultants. As the bridge between banks and customers, account managers coordinate the relations between them, externally representing banks to contact and provide service for customers, and internally representing customers to require banks to provide services they need.[26]

6.3.7.3. *Financial products management*

Commercial banks usually have a number of financial products, including cash, securities, trade financing, loans, etc. With the diversification of needs for financial products and customization, the design, valuation and management of financial products are increasingly complex. The management of each product line requires special skills and expertise, which are often beyond the capability of account managers. Therefore, banks need to create a product managers system to develop financial products that can meet the specific needs of customers or the market.[27]

6.3.7.4. *Risk management*

There are all kinds of risks involved in bank operation, including credit risk, country and transfer risk, market risk, interest risk, liquidity risk, operational risk, legal risk, and reputation risk. The business of a bank is essentially to realize returns through risk-taking activities, and a bank's core competence is its ability to manage risks. To this end, a bank needs to create the position of risk manager who evaluates business risks. The risk manager can form a CRM team (team of Risk Managers) with the account manager and product manager. The account manager centralizes the contacts with customers and brings back the customer's needs to the product manager who designs and delivers the most appropriate product and service. The responsibility of risk control and management rests with the risk manager. The accounting of businesses is centralized in the finance department while the processing of businesses is centralized at the operation center.

6.3.7.5. *Strategic management*

Strategic management is the highest level and the first priority of modern management. Management involves strategy formulation and strategy implementation. The strategic goal is the soul of a business, formulated on the basis of an objective analysis of the future. The strategic goal includes performance objective, proprietor's equity objective, customer interest objective and social benefits objective at four levels. The strategic management department of a bank should study various factors, including the society, industry (competition) and market (customer), as well the bank's internal resources and core competence before it formulates an appropriate strategic goal and proposes the key measures and steps to realize the goal. Sometimes adjustment and fine-tuning is necessary during the implementation to adapt to the new changes.

6.3.7.6. *Human resource management*

As a financial service company, a bank's operational effectiveness is largely dependent on the quality of its employees. In recent years, however, many young talents have left the state-owned commercial banks, because in a pyramid structure, they have little chance of getting promoted to higher positions. Therefore, commercial banks should learn from businesses about human resource management, and establish a business manager line parallel to administrative positions, providing the same compensation and welfare as the latter. To complement this, a systematic training and appraisal system should be developed. Banks should work with reputable universities to set up Masters program in finance (FMBA) for business managers above the middle level in order to nurture a team of highly professional and high quality bank employees.

6.3.8. *Promoting Financial Innovation*

Beginning from the 1960s, the supply and demand of the financial market has been greatly changed by sky-rocketing inflation and interest rate in the US, rapid development of computer technology, integration of international financial markets, and the financial risks arising from the fluctuation of exchange and interest rates. Many financial institutions find that traditional products and services have lost their popularity and that the old business model is no longer profitable. Also, the traditional financial tools are not attracting capital — capital that determines a bank's survival. Financial institutions will have to innovate in order to survive and grow, they need to research and develop new products and services to prevent financial risks, ensure transaction security, and reduce transaction costs.[4]

Most of China's commercial banks are confined to traditional savings and lending business. Business innovations only account for less than 10% in the total revenues of the shareholding banks, while in some western countries, the percentage is as high as 40%.

Financial tools innovation includes monetary capital mutual funds, junk bonds, commercial bills market and asset securitization. Monetary capital mutual funds were less than USD4 billion in 1977 in assets, but in 1999, the size had reached USD1500 billion. Junk Bonds were first issued by an investment bank in 1977, and by the late 1980s, the total business volume in junk bonds had exceeded USD200 billion. Commercial bills are short-term securities issued by commercial banks and enterprises, and in 1999, its size reached USD1200 billion, becoming the fastest growing financial tool. Commercial bill market became part of the money for the transaction of mutual funds, and attracted enormous capital from pension funds and insurance funds.

The most important financial innovation in the past two decades is asset securitization which originated in 1970. Asset securitization is the process of turning non-liquid assets into liquid assets to be exchanged in the capital market. For example, commercial banks pool real estate mortgages as assets and issue small cap securities to be sold to third parties and investors. During the process, they charge service fees, recover interest and principal, and dispose NPAs. In 1999 alone, the size of asset securitization reached USD1000 billion. Today, asset securitization has been extended to auto loans and credit card receivables.

6.4. Conclusions

If the reform of commercial banks is the key of China's financial structural reform, then the reform of the "Big Four" is the key to the reform of commercial banks. To meet the financial challenges after its ascension to the WTO, China has developed the "road map" for the reform of the "Big Four" — restructuring through shareholding reform, introducing strategic investors, stepping up NPL disposal, replenishing capital base, improving corporate governance, and creating conditions for IPO. The road map is in implementation, and although it needs necessary adjustment, fine-tuning and further specification in practice, the direction of the reform should be upheld to improve the international competitiveness of the commercial banks before China fully opens its market by 2006. It should also be realized that IPO is merely a continuation rather than the end of the reform. Further efforts need to be made to improve the banks' corporate governance and internal management, and to develop them into modern financial enterprises with adequate capital, strict internal control, secure operation, premium service and superior financial performance.

References

[1] The Chinese Finance Society (2004). *China Finance Yearbook 2004*; Beijing: Editorial Board of China Finance Yearbook (in Chinese).

[2] Cheng, S. W. (2003). *Collection of Essays on Virtual Economy*, Beijing: Democracy and Construction Press (in Chinese).
[3] Cheng, S. W. (2002). Causes and Countermeasures: Analyzing China's Deflation, in Cheng S. W., (ed.), Pandect, *Theoretical Analysis of Deflation and the Real Problems Lies Ahead of China*, Beijing: Economic Science Press, pp. 1–37 (in Chinese).
[4] Cheng, S. W. (2002). Nurturing and Supervision: Design of China's Monetary Market, in Cheng S. W., (ed.), Pandect, *Strategic Consideration on Developing Money Market in China*, Beijing: Economic Science Press, pp. 1–46 (in Chinese).
[5] Editor-in-Chief Committee of China Encyclopedia (1993). *China Encyclopedia: Finance, Taxation, and Price Volume*, Beijing: *China Encyclopedia Press* (in Chinese).
[6] Editorial (1979). The whole Party should place great importance on the roles of banks, *People's Daily*, March 18 (in Chinese).
[7] Deng, X. P. (1993). Works of Deng Xiaoping, in Literature Editorial Committee of the CPC Central Committee (ed.), Vol. 3, *Enterprise Reform and Financial Reform*, Beijing: People's Press, pp. 192–193 (in Chinese).
[8] Wang, Q. and Hu, C. (2004). The Paths of the Reforms of Wholly State-owned Commercial Banks, *Economy and Finance*, 1, 31–33 (in Chinese).
[9] Xu, G. (2005). RMB Will Not Necessarily Keep Appreciating, *New Fortune*, 52, 42–44 (in Chinese).
[10] Xinhua News Agency (2003). Improving Financial Supervision, *People's Daily*, June 20, pp. A6 (in Chinese).
[11] The Central Committee of the CPC (2003). Decision of the Central Committee of the Communist Party of China on Improving Socialist Market Economy, The Third Plenary Session of the 16th National Congress of the CPC (in Chinese).
[12] Chang, J. (2004). A Legal Analysis of Capital Injection to State–owned Commercial Banks through Foreign Exchange Reserves, *Legal Science*, 4, 95–99 (in Chinese).
[13] Chen, G. (2005). China's Banking Sector Is on Big Sale, People's Web, http://finance.people.com.cn/GB/1045/3701900.html (in Chinese).
[14] The Central Committee of the CPC (1999). Decision of the Central Committee of the Communist Party of China on State-owned Enterprise Reform and Development, The Fourth Plenary Session of the 15th National Congress of the CPC (in Chinese).

[15] Zhao, J. and Wu, Y. S. (2005). Five-tier Discounts for Foreign invested Shares, and Huijin Claims No Cheap Sell of China's Banking Sector, *21st Century Business Herald* (in Chinese).
[16] Han, G. B. (2005). Foreign Shareholders Investing in the Bank of Shanghai, *People's Daily,* January 24 (in Chinese).
[17] Cheng, S. W. (2004). Financial Security Is the Key to the National Economic Security, *Economic Circle*, 6, 4–9 (in Chinese).
[18] Li, J. H. (2005). Working Report on the Auditing of 2004 Budget Implementation and Other Fiscal Revenues and Expenses, The 16th Session of the 10th National People's Congress held (in Chinese).
[19] Li, S. Y. (2004). PwC: China NPL Investor Survey 2004, *International Financing*, 1, 62–66 (in Chinese).
[20] Basel Committee of Banking Supervision (2004). International Convergence of Capital Measurement and Capital Standards, A Revised Framework, Bank for International Settlements.
[21] Wang, X. F. (2004). Basel Agreement and Capital Adequacy Ratio of China's Commercial Banks, *Dalian Maritime University Journal*, 4, 60–64 (in Chinese).
[22] China News (2004). Huijin Injects Foreign Exchange Reserves to Banks, China News Web, January 6 (in Chinese).
[23] Cheng, S. W. (2000). Chinese Enterprises' Management: Problems and Countermeasures, Beijing: Democracy and Construction Press (in Chinese).
[24] Wu, Y. S. and Zhang, Y. Z. (2005). IPO of the Construction Bank, People's Web, September 19 (in Chinese).
[25] Tian, J. R. (2005). The Interview of Guo, S. Q. by the People's Daily: to speak about the IPO of the Construction Bank, People's Web, October 28.
[26] Liu, H. Y. (2004). The Role of the Account Manager System in the Strategic Development of State-owned Commercial Banks, *Business Research*, 18, 128–129 (in Chinese).
[27] Meng, L. (2004). A Tentative Study of the Product Manager System at Commercial Banks, *Xi'an Finance*, 11, 42–43 (in Chinese).

Chapter 7

Seeking Effective Ways to Develop Chinese Rural Finance

China is a densely populated and underdeveloped country, featuring uneven development with the rural population being the biggest population segment. To fully realize the strategic goal of constructing an all round and better off ('medium income for reasonable comfortable life') society by 2020, it is imperative for us to step up agricultural developments, maintain the stability of the rural society and seek to improve rural incomes. In the current stage of development, we should aggressively develop rural finance to ensure sufficient capital supply with a view to meeting the financial needs of the agricultural industry, the rural areas and farmers in order to steadily resolve the 'three agricultural issues', which are of strategic importance to China's modernization drive.

Since the founding of New China, the evolution of China's rural financial system can be categorized into the following five phases:

(1) burgeoning phase (1949–1957); (2) stagnant phase (1958–1976); (3) recovery phase (1977–1984); (4) development phase (1985–1995); and (5) reform phase (from 1996 till now).

Though the past few years had witnessed the 'deepening' and intensifying of the rural reforms in various aspects and some headway having been achieved in this regard, the rural financial sector is still faced with serious challenges, which can be summarized as follows:

(1) many peasant households still face the problem of insufficient credit loans and serious outflow of rural capital; (2) farmers' lack of

access to loans offered by financial institutions, giving rise to 'people's finance' — improper and sometimes illegal financing or lending provided by non-financial organizations; (3) small scale loans that do not fully fulfill the needs of rural households; and (4) services provided by financial institutions are too restricted or not diverse, and agricultural insurance is seriously lagging behind.

To eradicate the existing rural financial problems, we need to first look at the social and economic factors, etc., in rural China before we attempt to further enhance the institutional constructions of rural finance.

At present, small scale peasant economy still forms the dominant part of China's rural economy, characterized by peasant households, individual ownership, small scale production, primitive production conditions, co-existence of self sufficiency and trading business commodities, strong attachment of farmers to land and the bond with friends and relatives. The saving and borrowing behaviors of the rural population show comparatively strong cautionary, self-protecting saving tendency; though there is increasing acceptance for credits from institutions, a big percentage of credit is through interpersonal lending (from friends and relatives).

The fictitious economy of rural China has just progressed from the capitalization of the idle money to the initial stage of the socialization of interest generating capital. Owing to the dual nature of our economic structure, the socialization level for interest generating capital in the rural area is still relatively low. Most farmers choose to deposit their idle money in banks for precautionary purpose, and only a small number of farmers lend their idle money to township and village enterprises (TVEs) or subscribe shares from them. For this reason, there are few farmers that own stocks or bonds. Moreover, due to non-access to formal financial channels, some informal financing activities still and do exist to some extent. It is foreseeable that, in the coming 10 to 20 years, the fictitious economy in rural China will stay at the socialization stage of interest generating capital, where indirect financing activities will be extensively carried out through financial institutions.

Risks in the fictitious economy in China's rural areas are mainly credit risks. Owing to the immature credit system in China's rural financial sector, commercials banks are reluctant to extend credit loans to peasant households; instead they focus on granting collateralized loans, including guaranteed loans, mortgage loans or pledged loans. Currently they primarily offer small scale loans and mutually guaranteed loans to rural households.

As entity economic activities based on small scale peasant economy have slow pace, and progress is minimal, peasant households engaged in organized, larger-scale farming, TVEs and the agricultural industrialization in which farmers work with companies have appeared in the entity economic activities in the rural areas, triggering dramatic changes in the rural financial demands. However, this situation contrasts with that of relative shortage of capital supply and increasing commercialization, forcing many peasant households to go for 'informal financing', to satisfy their financial needs.

The target models for the construction of China's rural financial system should be the following:

(1) financial support and market operation; (2) adopting A-3-tier system in which each plays its respective role; (3) focusing on deposit and loans, with supporting service package; and (4) existence of good legal framework.

To realize these objectives, I hereby put forward the following suggestions:

(1) extend policy driven financing functions of the Agricultural Development Bank of China (ADBC) with the focus gradually shifting to "green-box" projects of the WTO; (2) adopt effective measures to lower transaction cost and defuse risks — offering discounts, tax reduction or subsidies to agriculture support undertakings so as to motivate commercial financial institutions to support agriculture; (3) continue and improve small scale credit loan system tailored for rural households; improve and expand mutually guaranteed loans system; (4) ensure that the proportion that goes to agriculture support from the loans extended by the Agricultural Bank of China shall

not be less than 12% and that from the loans extended by rural commercial banks shall not be less than 60%; (5) establish loan guarantee firms and develop agricultural production insurance; (6) vigorously and steadily restructure rural co-operative financial institutions based on the principle of "voluntary participation, democratic management, sharing risks and dividends based on shares". The Government will formulate preferential policies such as business tax exemptions and income tax exemptions, reduce reserve against deposit and offer moderate amount of re-loans when credit amount exceeds deposit amount, etc.; and (7) combine the "lead" and "block" approach to encourage private capital to buy stocks from commercial financial institutions and transform various kinds of "savings foundations" and "co-operative foundations" to co-operative financial institutions with a view to harnessing and regulating 'popular' finance as a common but informal and improper way to obtain credit.

7.1. Introduction: The Significance of Developing Rural Finance

China is a densely populated country that features relatively low levels of development as well as uneven development, with the rural population making the biggest population segment. Agriculture, rural areas and farmers (also referred as the three 'agriculture' issues) are an important problem whose solution we have to prioritize in the process of modernization.

First of all, the solution to problem will determine food security. China has a population of 1.3 billion. This means if there is a short supply of food, relying on import from international market will not be the solution. In recent years, China's grain production has slightly fallen, accompanied by a persistent shrinkage of farming areas. Grain output has also been declining, reaching a historical low in 2003, with only 430 billion kilograms.

Secondly, China's modernization cannot be realized without resolving the aforementioned three agriculture issues. From the point of view of Modernization Theory in the West, the so called modernization entails industrialization and democratization. Agriculture industry is the foundation for industrialization. At the inception of industrialization, capital was accumulated from the difference between the prices of agricultural products and industrial products. In addition, the labor force such industrialization demanded largely relied on farmers becoming workers. Industrial development is also partly determined by the rural consumption market. As 60% of the Chinese population are located in rural areas, without the improvement of the purchasing power of the rural population, the industrialization process would not have been possible in China.[1,2]

One of the important indications of industrialization is urbanization, which is to drive rural labor force to migrate to the urban areas. It took Britain over 200 years to reduce the percentage of rural population from 70% to 30% in about 1850, and it took the U.S. about 100 years to approximate this figure in 1930. Presently, the ratio of urban population to rural population in China is 40% to 60%. It is axiomatic that the task to migrate out the rural labor populace is extremely urgent.

One of the main criteria for realizing democratization is the intellectual and educational level of the rural population. Proper understanding and exercise of democracy is based on certain literacy and education level, combined with the level of economic development of that country. Some undeveloped countries, which are still impoverished with a large percentage of illiterate population, have blindly copied Western democratic systems. Some countries have even allowed the existence of over 100 political parties, with the resulting scuffling for power seriously worsening the living conditions of their people. This is a sobering lesson to be kept in mind in the development of China.

Thirdly, socialist modernization will not be attained without resolving the ‘three agriculture’ issues. The modernization of China differs from the modernization in Western countries. The modernization we want is socialist modernization, which not only consists of industrialization and democratization, but also includes all out efforts to narrow down the income distribution gap and to work towards realization of common prosperity. Currently in China, the dual economic structure still exists: there are still distinct disparities in the economic development level, economic modes of economic activities and operations, etc., between the rural and the urban areas. This dual economic structure exists as a result of various historical reasons. After the outbreak of the Opium War in 1840, the feudalistic society, which had existed for over 2,000 years in China, gradually broke up and rural China was transformed into a semi-feudal society, whereas urban China was gradually relegated to a semi-colonial society. Since then, the urban and rural economies have been developing on two different tracks, giving rise to the dual economic structure. After the founding of New China, the dual economic structure remained throughout the development of the new democratic society and the initial stages of socialism. According to statistics, in 2003, the urban per capita income was about three times that of the rural per capita income, and the urban purchasing power was about four times that of the rural purchasing power. Social services for urban residents, including social security and education, were far better than that of the rural residents. If this dual economic structure is not eliminated, the gap between the rich and the poor will never be narrowed, nor will common prosperity, social equality and justice be achieved, which in the end will impede the socialist modernization of China.

In conclusion, to realize the grand objective of constructing a better off and all round society by 2020, we have to conscientiously resolve the ‘three agriculture issues’ to accelerate the development of the agriculture industry, maintain the stability of the rural society as well as increasing the income of peasants.

According to development economics, economic growth can be divided into three categories: growth generated by capital infusion, growth created by the labor force and growth engendered by ‘integrated’ factors (including management, technology and education, etc.). At present as rural China contains significant labor surplus, the steps to transfer the labor surplus to industry and the service sector should be quickened. General factors, however, require a relatively lengthy process from ‘input to output’; they take a long time before their effects are felt. Besides, institutional innovation, improved management, technological development, application of research, and developing compulsory education and vocational education, etc., all entail capital support. This indicates that the most urgent task now is to channel more funds to the three agriculture issues with a view to stepping up the rural economic development. Only through developing the rural economy with agriculture as the core, can social stability of the rural society and farmers' income be improved. So my proposition is that, in the present stage, we should develop vigorously rural finance to ensure sufficient capital supply in order to satisfy as far as possible the financial needs of agriculture, rural areas and farmers, and fundamentally solve the strategically significant three agriculture issues that have plagued China's agriculture sector in the process of modernization.

With the construction of socialism with Chinese characteristics and the development of the socialist market economy, the government is placing increasing importance to rural financial issues. In addition, rural finance has drawn the attention of some scholars. Based on some sources, up to 100 papers on rural finance have been published in various academic publications and some books on the subject have also been published. I started to study rural financial issues from 1999, and since then I have conducted some investigation and given my thinking on this issue. Upon this premise, I attempt to explore various issues relating to the building of the rural financial system by employing relevant theories including institutional economics, complexity science, fictitious economy, etc.

7.2. Development of China's Rural Finance and the Challenges it Faces

The origin of modern rural finance in China can be traced back to the early days of the 1920s, when the first rural credit co-operative was established in Xianghe county of Hebei Province. In the early 1930s, the areas ruled by the Kuomintang, were experiencing a situation of great rural economic crisis and bankruptcies of rural households. Following the 'finance rescuing' activities carried out by related public benevolent associations, some commercials banks participated in the "Return Capital to peasants" movement to channel funds to the rural areas. The Kuomintang's central and local governments also set up special functional departments and other financial units to carry out rescue activities and provide funds to the rural areas. These measures had to some extent achieved certain effects in helping farmers to repay debts, reclaiming land use and purchasing necessary production materials and subsistence etc.[3] In the Central Soviet Area of China and various revolutionary bases under the control of the Chinese communist party, numerous rural credit co-operatives were established which, to a great extent, fulfilled the financial requirements of rural China, and contributed to the consolidation and development of the revolution bases.

After the founding of New China, development of China's rural finance can generally be classified into the following five phases.

7.2.1. *The First Phase: Burgeoning Period of the Rural Finance (1949–1957) (consists mainly of the activities of rural credit co-operatives (RCCs))*

At the end of 1949, there were over 800 rural credit co-operatives throughout China. During 1949-1953, under the backing and guidance from the government, rural credit co-operatives (hereafter referred as RCCs) were extensively experimented in rural areas. By the end of 1953, the number of RCCs in China had increased to 9,841. Upon the establishment of relatively comprehensive and democratic management system to run them, RCCs were the major credit bodies for counties or 'administrative villages. Farmers pay to buy shares upon joining the RCCs and are distributed with dividends based on their share of contributions at the end of the year. Another avenue is represented by credit departments and credit teams, set up as subsidiaries of the Supply and Marketing Co-operatives (SMCs). Since 1955, production, sales & supply and credit co-operatives movements in rural China have spread widely and RCCs have made dramatic progress. At the end of 1957, RCCs were established in 80% of the county capitals, with a total number of 88,368 RCCs, raking in capital of 1,060 million Yuan and membership stock capital of 310 million Yuan. Despite RCCs suffering from being small scale and ineffective management, their co-operative nature has been manifested in the observed results and they have enjoyed relatively healthy overall development.

Shortly after the founding of New China, the rural financial business came under the administration of various departments of the People's Bank of China (PBOC). To adapt to the new dynamics of the rural economic development after the Land Reforms and to enhance the administration on rural credit co-operative association, the Agriculture Co-operative Bank was officially set up on August 10, 1951, with the approval of the Government Administration Council of the Central People's Government. The Bank was charged with the responsibilities of rendering investment appropriation service for agriculture, forestry and irrigation, etc., and to take up the job of leading the operations of RCCs. However, the Agriculture Co-operative Bank was dissolved in 1952 and the rural financial sector was moved under the administration of the Rural Financial Administration Bureau under PBOC. Later, with the approval of the State Council, the Agricultural Bank of China was officially incorporated. Its main missions are to direct rural credit associations, extensively mobilize rural surplus capital, utilize rationally national agriculture loans, assist with agricultural production development and step up the socialist transformation of small scale peasant economy. However, because the division of responsibilities between grassroots Agriculture Bank of China under county level and the PBOC was ambiguous and that both banks suffered from lack of staff and insufficient funds, in April 1957, the State Council decided to dissolve the Agricultural Bank of China and have it taken over by the PBOC.

7.2.2. *Second Phase: Stagnant Period for Rural Financial Development (1958–1976)*

In 1958, RCCs were placed under the administration of people's communes and in 1959 were again transferred to the administration of the 'production brigades'. Under the regime of the extreme left, the co-operative system was seriously undermined and 'distorted'. The production brigades were not only controlling the financial administration and business operations of the co-operatives, but also took charge of accounts and this ultimately deprived them of their autonomous status. With the damage done to the normal credit relationship, enormous amount of capital was embezzled and savings were decreasing dramatically, from two billion Yuan at the end of 1958 to 0.97 billion Yuan at the end of 1962. Despite the autonomy of RCCs being restored in 1962, their business and operations were still subject to the leadership of PBOC. In 1993, Agricultural Bank of China was re-established, with the objective of centrally managing agriculture funds and agriculture loans as well as taking charge of the operations of RCCs. However, this ended shortly when the Agricultural Bank of China was dissolved for the third time in December 1965. Consequently, RCCs again fell into the hands of people's communes and production brigade/teams. During the Cultural Revolution, RCCs were nominally administered by peasants. This practice crippled the cadres' teams, endangered funds security and ruined business activities of RCCs. In many places, RCCs were almost pushed to the brink of bankruptcies.

7.2.3. *Third Phase: Recovery Period for Rural Finance (1977–1984)*

In 1997, the State Council issued the circular of "Several Provisions on Rectifying and Enhancing Banking Administration", which stated *inter alia,* "Rural credit co-operatives are not only collective financial associations, but also grassroots units of the state banks". It was also stipulated that RCCs should be subject to the administration of PBOC. In February 23, 1979, in the Circular on Restoring Agricultural Bank of China [1979] No. 56 issued by the State Council, it was formulated that the major tasks for Agricultural Bank of China is to manage centrally agriculture funds and engage in granting agricultural loans, lead RCCs and develop rural financial sector. It was also stipulated that RCCs are not only collective financial associations, but also the grassroots units of Agricultural Bank of China. By then Agricultural Bank of China had integrated the functions of policy-based appropriation administration, commercial loan business and administration of collective financial associations, indicating that the "official" nature and monopolist status of ABC was established. Since all the saving and loaning business of Agricultural Bank of China were carried out in line with the government's planning, its administration of the RCCs fell into the same, set patterns of old. Despite RCCs having 'recovered' somewhat during this period, they were slowly losing their autonomy and gradually relegated to the subordinate position to tow the official line.

7.2.4. *Fourth Period: Development Period (1985–1995)*

There are five 'phases' in the development during this period, namely:

(1) *Commercials banks started to make inroads into the rural areas*
In October 1984, the Third Plenary Session of the 12th Central Committee promulgated the "Decision on Carrying out Economic Reform by the Central Committee of the CPC". With a view to developing "Planned Commodity Economy", China's commercial financial system expanded enormously, consequently breaking the monopoly of the Agricultural Bank of China in the rural areas. In 1985, it was made clear in the "Ten Policies to Further Invigorate the Rural Economy" by the Central Committee of the CPC, the Agricultural Bank of China shall put in place corporate management in order to improve capital utilization. PBOC also issued corresponding circulars on policies, which stipulate that the four big banks can engage in 'moderate' competition with each other in their business scope and "banks can choose enterprises and enterprises can also choose banks". This, as a result, ended the "supply system" dominated by "unified collection and allocation of funds by the state". It was also clarified in these policies that Agricultural Bank of China should be geared towards the business of procurement of agricultural by-products. Subsequent to the implementation of these policies, some commercial banks began to tread into the territory of rural China to channel funds to the burgeoning TVEs.

(2) *RCCs continue to reform*
In 1984, the State Council forwarded the "Provisions on the Administration of Rural Credit Co-operatives" as circular No. 105, which put forward the transformation of RCCs into civilian based

co-operative financial associations responsible for their own management decisions, profits and losses. Later, the Agricultural Bank of China launched a series of reform measures in respect of democratic management, business management and organizational structuring, etc., which significantly stimulated the development of RCCs. At the end of 1995, there were a total of 50,219 RCCs throughout China that had independent accounting operations and 2,409 county unions of RCCs, with a total equity of 63.2 billion Yuan, with paid-up capital valued at 37.8 billion Yuan and total assets of 985.7 billion Yuan. The balance held on various deposits amounted to 717.3 billion Yuan, of which saving deposits totaled 616.9 billion Yuan, accounting for more than 60% of the rural savings. The total sum of various loans was 517.6 billion Yuan, accounting for over 60% of agriculture production loans, over 80% of the loans for rural households and over 70% of the loans for TVEs.

(3) *The rural policy based finance began*
In accordance with the decision of the State Council, Agriculture Development Bank of China (ADBC), an exclusive 'policy' bank tasked with managing loans for procurement of agricultural by-products, was established in June 1994. It was charged with the following responsibilities: pooling agricultural policy funds, providing agricultural policy-led finance services in compliance with national regulations, appropriating policy agriculture funds based on national credits to serve the development of the agricultural industry and rural economy. Its primary credit service includes: providing discount loans from the national special reserve funds for main agricultural products including grain, cotton, edible oil, meat, sugar, etc.; offering loans for agricultural procurement, transportation and wholesale; extending loans for enterprises involved in the process for grain, cotton and edible oil; granting 'poverty alleviating loans and economic development loans to poverty stricken areas; offering industrial loans for impoverished counties; granting loans for integrated agricultural development and other agriculture–based fiscally allocated

discount loans, loans for infrastructure and technological progress loans for small–scale agriculture, forestry, husbandry and irrigation works.

(4) *The Rise of Post Office savings*
In January 1986, with the co-ordination of the State Council, the Ministry of Postal & Telecommunications as investor and PBOC as business supervisor, jointly released the "Agreement on Establishing Postal Savings Service", and began to run pilot post office savings outlets in 12 cities including Beijing and Tianjin, etc. In the *Postal Laws of The People's Republic of China* enacted at the end of 1986, postal savings were defined as one of the business functions of postal business enterprise, allowing postal savings service to quickly spread to the whole of China, and post office savings became one of the important forces in the savings services of rural China.

(5) *The 'quiet' emergence of Informal finance*
In the earlier days of the 1980s, with the prevalence of the household contract system, rural co-operative foundations (RCFs) appeared in 1984 during the process of sorting out the properties of the grassroots in rural areas. These foundations were set up as community mutual assistance associations on the basis of voluntary participation, mutual benefit and availability of compensation. Funds of these foundations came mainly from collective capital and in part from the capital of farmers through purchase of shares. The deposits with these foundations were characterized by relatively longer deposit term and lower interest rates. RCFs primarily extended small–scale loans to peasant households within the counties or villages. By the end of 1992, RCFs had been established in 17,400 counties and 112,500 villages throughout China, respectively accounting for 36.7% and 15.4% of the total number of counties and villages, with total pooled funds of 16.49 billion Yuan. After 1992, individual contributions of stock capital in the RCFs rose dramatically. In addition, dividends distributed against individual shares were higher

than collective stocks. From 1994, RCFs started to take short–term deposit in the name of agent fee and offered large–scale loans to TVEs, with the interest rate for both deposit and loans higher than that of RCCs.[4] This practice not only changed the nature of RCFs, but also increased the potential risks faced by RCFs.

7.2.5. *Fifth Phase: Reform Period for Rural Finance (1996–present) (primarily dedicated to aggressively pressing forward the reforms of RCCs)*

In August 1996, the State Council promulgated the "Decisions on Reform of the Rural Financial System", putting forward initiatives for carrying out profound reforms on rural financial systems. This "decision" requested the separation of RCCs from Agricultural Bank of China, and on this basis its objective was to transform RCCs into a true financial institution that featured purchase of stocks by farmers, democratized management and dedication to serving the members. At the end of 1996, there were a total of 49,532 RCCs at grassroots level throughout China and 2,409 credit co-operative unions. The sum of various deposits totaled 879.4 billion Yuan, of which savings deposits amounted to 767.1 billion Yuan. Assets amounted to 1,445 billion Yuan and the sum of various loans stood at 629 billion Yuan, of which agricultural loans reached 148.7 billion Yuan, out of which increased agricultural loans accounted for up to 40% of the total loans. At the end of the same year, the "separation" was largely completed. This practice, however, gradually gave rise to the discovery of various potential risks such as low performing assets, severe loss making and insolvency, etc., that were accumulated over time.

To strengthen supervision and administration on RCCs and effectively avoid and defuse risks, in June 1997, the State Council took the initiative to set up the Administration Bureau of Rural Co-operative Finance with a view to carrying forward the reforms of RCCs and intensifying administration and supervisions of RCCs. In the same year, PBOC issued the "Rules on Administration of Rural Credit

Co-operatives" so as to transform RCCs into a co-operative mechanism, in which farmers can voluntarily buy shares, implement democratic management and receive financial service. In 1998, the State Council forwarded "Provisions on Further Rectifying and Standardizing Administration of Rural Credit Co-operatives" stipulated by PBOC, and reiterated its determination to transform RCCs into co-operative institutions that feature the voluntary purchase of shares by farmers and implementation democratic management with the primary function of serving the members.

In 1998, Premier Zhu Rongji, put forward his request for 'deepening' the financial reform in rural areas: turning RCCs into an important tie connecting the vast number of farmers and a major force in rural financial sector streamlining farmers' access to loans. The main content of this reform is to transform the ownership system of RCCs, and clarify the risks and accountabilities.

In January 1999, the State Council issued a document announcing a unified elimination of rural co-operative fund associations. In the same year, PBOC launched a pilot scheme to reform RCCs in Jiangsu Province, including (1) combining legally registered RCCs and county credit unions into one legal entity based on asset and capital verification; (2) transforming the operational mechanism to improve the financial service standard & operational management of RCCs; (3) clarifying ownership rights and optimizing corporate governance structure to realize self regulation and self development of RCCs; (4) removing 'historical burdens' through internal system transformation, increasing profit and lowering cost, and gradually absorbing non-performing loans with the assistance of policy support; (5) establishing Rural Credit Co-operative Association of Jiangsu Province. To quicken the pace of the experimental reform, the Government launched a package of fiscal financial support policies with the following policy terms: (1) spin off or remove the bad debts and 'wholly non-performing loans' from the non-performing loans for RCCs, and to offer discount re-loans (interest-free) from the special funds against 50% of the loans removed with a total amount of five billion Yuan with a five year expiry period; (2) from 2000 onwards, PBOC will provide equal amount of loans from Central Bank of China to RCCs in Jiangsu Province to match the annual savings deposited into postal savings outlets in counties or units under county levels within Jiangsu Province; (3) with respect to seasonal idle capital, PBOC will establish special depositing service based on the basis of capital guarantee; (4) allow RCCs to adopt flexible interest rate floating regimes; (5) in principle, the withdrawal ratio of bad debt reserve is increased from the previous 1% to 2%, which can be even higher in individual cases; (6) transfer taxes and administrative charges for RCCs based on collateralized assets to be levied in line with policies for straightening out RCFs; and (7) withdraw a certain percentage of special fund as risks compensation from the retained tax from RCCs in Jiangsu Province, as part of the budget to help RCCs to mitigate their serious losses.

In May 2003, with the approval from the State Council, the reform of RCCs which started in Jiangsu Province, was extended to eight provinces and municipalities (Jilin Province, Shandong Province, Jiangxi Province, Zhejiang Province, Shanxi Province, Chongqing City, Guizhou Province and Jiangsu Province). According to the overall requirements of "clarifying ownership rights, strengthening discipline mechanism, intensifying service functions, moderate governmental support and the overseeing of local government", the reform of the management system and ownership rights of RCCs shall be stepped up to gradually transform RCCs into a community based regional financial institution, dedicated to providing service for farmers, the agriculture industry and the economic development of the rural areas. Farmers, rural merchants and various economic units can voluntarily buy stocks of this regional financial institution. These efforts will ultimately allow RCCs to effectively fulfill their roles as the major force of rural finance, acting as a tie between the farmers. It is hoped that it will play a pivotal role in the financial sector to better support the rural economic adjustment, increase rural income and engender a harmonious development of the urban and rural economy. The main contents of the pilot scheme are: (1) clearly defined ownership rights and the property relationship, optimize corporate governance structure, and classify various property relationship based on different circumstances of various corporate units; and (2) reform RCCs' management system and move RCCs under the administration of local governments.

To carry forward the reform of RCCs, the Government has formulated the following four supportive measures:

Firstly, provide subsidies for poor-performing RCCs that are offering too much capital guarantee discount interest rate for their capital guarantee depositing services as mandated by the Government. The Ministry of Finance will verify the amount for capital guarantee discount interest granted by RCCs during 1994-1997 and subsidize them with state appropriation in installments.

Secondly, from January 1, 2003 till end of 2005, corporate income tax for RCCs in the experiment regions of West China will be exempted. With respect to RCCs in other experiment regions, their corporate income tax will be reduced to 50% and from January 1, 2003, all RCCs in the experiment areas will be levied only 3% of normal business tax.

Thirdly, to provide appropriate amounts of capital support to RCCs in the pilot areas, there are two measures. One is to continuously issue low interest re-loans from the special funds to RCCs by the PBOC. The other is to use the bill of the central bank through the PBOC. The interest rate for the re-loans shall be half the interest rate for that for reserves deposits in financial institutions, with the terms ranging from three years, five years to eight years depending on the conditions of the specific region. Special re-loans shall be centrally borrowed and repaid by the provincial governments. The Central Bank bills issued by the PBOC shall not be purchased by RCCs with cash, but rather, they should be used in exchange for non-performing loans of the RCCs with two year expiry period. Interest shall be paid by appropriate interest rate. The bill shall not be circulated, transferred or collateralized, but it can be cashed in advance. These two measures are to be chosen by the region under the experimental reforms and RCCs according to their respective conditions.

Fourthly, flexible interest rate regime shall be adopted where 'popular' financing is relatively active. A flexible floating interest rate regime shall be permitted for RCCs. The loan interest shall float within the range of one to two times the benchmark interest rate. Small scale loans extended to rural households shall not float upwards, whereas individual loans that bear relatively bigger risk can float slightly to the upper end (but not exceeding 1.2 times the benchmark interest rate). With respect to loans for disaster affected households, it can even float downwards moderately.

In August 2004, a working conference on strengthening the experimental reform of RCCs was held by the State Council. After reviewing the implementation of the experiment reform in the previous stage, it was decided to extend the pilot scheme to 21 provinces and municipalities including Beijing. The State Council also requested that these eight provinces and municipalities where the pilot scheme had been first carried out should seek to push the reforms of RCCs 'deeper and wider'. The newly included provinces and municipalities for this experimental reform shall focus on the key aspects and they are to carry out all policies based on the spirit and guidance of the State Council. Extensive support and guidance shall also be given by the local authorities to encourage and lead rural households and people from all walks of life for their active participation and support.

In recent years, reform of rural finance has been strengthened in various aspects and remarkable progress has been achieved in this regard. However, farmers' access to loans remains a problem. The financial service rendered by the financial institutions so far cannot keep pace with farmers' financial needs, and many problems and difficulties remain. The development of rural financial sector is still faced with grave challenges, which can be summarized as follows:

(1) *Insufficient supply of credit funds and serious outflow of rural capital*

Since 1998, loans extended to agriculture and TVEs by various financial institutions accounted approximately to a mere 11% of the total amount of loans granted by all financial institutions. Yet this figure was still going downwards. From 1999 to 2002, the figure was 11.7%, 11%, 10.8% and 10.5% respectively. In 2003, the added value in agriculture took up 14.8% of GDP. However, the outstanding loans extended to agriculture by financial institutions occupied less than 6% of the total loan amount. On the other hand, the amount deposited by rural households outstripped the amount of loans they obtained, and the disparity between deposit and loan was growing year by year. This disparity increased from 735.79 billion Yuan in 1997 to 940.37 billion Yuan in 2001. What is more note-worthy here is the outflow of tremendous amounts of rural capital. Postal savings outlets and commercial banks, as the principal outflow channels, are siphoning off a huge chunk of rural savings away from the countryside. Postal savings outlets currently are only handling saving deposits, and all the funds they receive are re-deposited with PBOC for interest. The rural postal savings held on balance increased from 171.06 billion Yuan at the end of 1997 to 442.14 billion Yuan at the end of 2002. In addition, a considerable amount of rural funds have flowed from the countryside through state–owned commercial banks. According to a survey conducted in 61 counties in Anhui Province, the deposit held on balance by the four state–owned commercial banks increased by 23.7 billion Yuan in 2003, which contrasted with a decrease of 3.51 billion Yuan for the loans they gave out. Other outflows occurred through RCCs purchasing bonds, removing capital and extending loans to urban clients. Presently, the bonds purchased by RCCs throughout China are valued at 200 billion Yuan approximately.

(2) *Loans from formal financial institutions are not easily accessible to rural households, thus giving rise to the prosperity of 'popular finance'*

One of the important business functions of RCCs is to extend small–scale loans and mutually guaranteed loans to rural households. Based on relevant statistics, at the end of March 2004, there were an accumulated 58 million rural households that have received small–scale credit loans, and roughly 11 million rural households have received mutually guaranteed loans. However, according to a sample survey conducted by the National Bureau of Statistics of China, most farmers have little access to loans from formal financial institutions (banks and RCCs), and they rely primarily on 'popular finance' (obtaining finance from private individuals or certain 'private' business entities) as their source of credit. From 2000 to 2003, 65 Yuan were borrowed from financial institutions per person per year and 190 Yuan through popular finance, accounting respectively for 25% and 75% of the total credit amount. In economically developed regions such as Jiangsu and Zhejiang Province, popular finance enjoys even greater vitality. Of the total credit amount channeled to farmers in these two provinces, funds that were provided by banks and RCCs only took up 22.9% and 16.8% thereof, and rural households that had obtained loans from banks or RCCs occupied merely 2.9% and 2.5% respectively.

(3) *Small–scale Rural credit loans cannot fully satisfy the demands of the rural households*

Small–scale credit loan 'ceilings' or quotas accessible to rural households are too limited, generally below 5,000 Yuan. Moreover, the small–scale loans service targeted at rural households features short repayment periods, ranging from 6 months to 1 year. In some cases, the repayment periods are reduced to 2 or 3 months, which, as a result, fail to correspond with the production cycle of the forestry and aquaculture industry, causing the farmers to fail to repay loans on time. In the end, it adds up to more difficulties for rural households to obtain more loans. In addition, as industrialized operations such as large-scale planting, aquaculture and farm products processing, etc., require comparatively large amounts of capital and longer production cycle, they normally involve high investment and high risks at its start-up. For this reason, small–scale loans have failed to meet this type of financial demand.

(4) *Services offered by financial institutions are relatively 'simple' and limited. This includes, among others, the seriously under-developed agricultural insurance service*

In most rural areas, only conventional depositing and credit services are available, whereas other services including settlement, insurance, consultancy and foreign exchange services are rare. In recent years, agricultural insurance service has been shrinking constantly. In 2003, premium income from agricultural insurance in China stood at only

460 million Yuan, accounting for merely 0.44% of the premium income of property insurance. In 1992, premium income from agricultural insurance in Jiangxi Province constituted 3.5% of the total premium income of all insurances, which decreased to 0.15% in 2002. In 2003, the premium income of agricultural insurance in Liaoning Province amounted to only 2.24 million Yuan, less than one tenth of the figure in 1993.

Faced with such severe challenges, we should be clearly aware that it is impossible to push forward the development of Chinese rural finance simply by taking stop-gap measures (the Chinese say 'treat the head for headache, treat the foot for foot-ache'); rather, we shall have to conduct in-depth theoretical analysis and thinking based on the actual circumstances of the three agriculture issues in order to strengthen the institutional system of the rural financial sector.

7.3. Fictitious Economy and Constructions of the Rural Financial System

Although the word "system" or 'institution' had been widely used in recent years, people's understanding of its nature differs. People tend to take it as a regulation or code of conduct that everybody shall follow and abide by. The academia, however, consider institution a system established under certain historical circumstances including political, economic and cultural factors, etc. Institution economics (which emerged at the inception of the 20th century) has been dedicated to institution studies and analyzing the impact of institutional elements on social economic development. According to their propositions, the organizing and control aspects in the economic system is more important than resource allocation, income distribution, income, output and price level, etc. The proponents of institution economics highlight the enormous impact of social, historical, political, psychological and cultural factors on the social economic life, and they suggest using the institutional analysis and structural analysis approaches. Institution economics tells us to eradicate the long standing rural financial problems such as the absence of loan access for farmers. It is imperative to analyze first the social and economic factors in China's rural area prior to talking about enhancing the construction of the rural financial system.

Complexity science is the science that studies complexity and complex systems, and it is an advanced level in the development of system science. Complexity science emerged in the early 1980s of the 20th century, and currently it is still at its research and development stage. Although five schools of complexity science have emerged so far, including kinetics, chaos, adaptive system, structure and postmodernism, a mature paradigm has not been established.[5] I once employed complexity science to analyze institutional issues, concluding that an institution shall include both system and mechanism. System refers to the status and structure of the institution at a specific time, whereas mechanism refers to the evolving process and contributing factors of the system. System and mechanism are sometimes interdependent. System is the starting point and consequence of the evolution of institutions whereas mechanism is the path of the evolution. Owing to the interactions between various agents, and between the system and the external environment, a self organizing effect will be generated within the system, generating a hierarchy and functional structure of the system, propelling the system to evolve towards a certain direction. As system is dynamic and stays in a constantly evolving process, merely employing static structural analysis such as power analysis, interest group analysis and regulation analysis to study system will not be enough. As pointed out succinctly by the prominent institutional economist, Noth D. C.: "we live in a dynamic economic world; our theories, however, are static".[6]

Fictitious economy is the counterpart model of the entity economy. To put it simply, in entity economic activities, capital generates profits through inter-conversion with entity activities through the cycle of trade-production-circulation-trade (trade = exchange). With respect to fictitious economic activities, however, capital can still generate profits without this cycle. Fictitious economy has developed through the following stages: capitalization of idle currency, socialization of interest generating capital, marketization of marketable bonds and globalization of the financial market, etc. Presently, it has entered into stage of the integration of global finance. Fictitious economic system is characterized by complexity, metastability, high risk, parasitism and periodicity, etc. As entity production activities do not fall into the category of fictitious economy, fictitious economy itself does not create any physical wealth, but can relocate the wealth created by the entity economy, by which it can directly generate money without going through the entity economic cycle.[7] I once used the fictitious economic approach to study China's capital market, venture capital, deflation and financial crisis, etc and have obtained some initial results.[8] By the same token, this approach can be applied to the studies of the rural finance.

7.3.1. *The Rural Economic System in China*

Throughout the lengthy feudalist society in China's history, peasant economy, which was mainly constituted by peasant proprietors and serfs, had been the dominant economic system in China's rural areas for a very long time. After the founding of the People's Republic of China, despite the rural areas having successively undergone the Co-operative Movement, People's Commune and Cultural Revolution, etc., inflicting serious damage to the peasant economy, and that peasants' social status has been changing constantly, peasant economy, however, has remained prominent in China's rural areas with the following characteristics.

(1) The peasant household is known as the basic unit. At present, the individual household is the basic production and living unit for China's rural folks. With the assistance of other family members, peasants can complete the production process of farm products independently: they normally do not need external co-operation. Family members live together and they collectively own their properties.

(2) Peasant economy is based on individual ownership. Individual peasants can obtain long-term rights of use for small pieces of land by signing 'farm use' (tenancy farming or leases) contracts. They are also, to different extents, equipped with agricultural tools; they possess farm animals and other production materials.

Under relatively favorable policy environments, peasants tend to have higher operational independence and work enthusiasm and this in turn adds to the stability of the rural society.

(3) Small production scale and unsophisticated production conditions. Each peasant household owns a small piece of land and their tools are limited to manual farm tools. They rely mainly on physical labor and animal power to carry out their production. As the production scale of peasants is limited, they are less capable of coping with natural catastrophes and market risks. These could bring about poverty or even bankruptcy, thereby posing potential threat to social stability.

(4) Self sufficiency co-exists with trading of farm commodities. Part of the farm products that peasants produce is used for their own subsistence, while the remainder is sold in exchange for cash to purchase daily necessities from the market.

(5) Farmers are strongly attached to the land. The longstanding and deep-rooted peasant economy has resulted in peasants' strong attachment to the land. Although the source of income of rural households has been diversified and many peasants are migrating to the cities for employment, their customs, beliefs, culture, integrity and emotions are 'imbedded in the soil', which cannot be eliminated or substituted[9] easily.

(6) Farmers are intimately 'bonded' with friends and relatives. Although the peasant economy is a self-sufficient economy with the peasant household as the basic unit, households who live in the same village maintain a close relationship with each other. They help each other and stay close to each other. This type of closeness will create various kinds of informal rules that could have effects on rural economic operations.

In studying China's rural economy we should on one hand learn the characteristics of the peasant economy, which is still dominating the rural economy, analyzing its status quo. On the other hand, we should pay attention to the changes that have occurred in rural China since the reform and understand its development trend.

7.3.2. *Saving and Borrowing Behaviors of Rural Households*

According to institutional economics, people's habits, social conventions and behavioral models play a vital role in a society. From the narrow view of the definition of rural finance, peasant households are the main depositors and borrowers in rural areas. For this reason, to study problems of rural finance, we shall first of all have to explore the saving and borrowing behaviors of the rural households.

Owing to the development and income disparities between different regions, the saving and borrowing behaviors of rural households differ from each other. However, the following characteristics are common to most of them:

7.3.1.1. *Farmers have relatively strong propensity towards 'self-protecting' or 'precautionary' savings.*

As farmers in China have always been small producers in China's history, they suffer from unstable income, and are very vulnerable to risks. For these reasons, they have a strong tendency for self-protection and self-security and are more inclined to choose saving over spending. We can assert that the motive for the saving behavior of the Chinese farmers is mainly precautionary. These behaviors can be labeled as purposeful, long-term and compulsory for the sake of future consumptions that could be beyond their affordability at that time. The consumption behaviors of peasant households are not only determined by their income, but also influenced by social conventions, local customs and consciousness for self security. In general, they can be considered as relatively conservative. Most households are only spending a bit more than usual when they are building houses or getting married, and at other times they are very frugal. In addition, the absence of rural social security and a production insurance system has to a great extent, tied up the consumption behaviors of the rural population, especially the current consumption behaviors of relatively wealthy households.[2] According to statistics from the National Bureau of Statistics of China (NBSC), from 1986 to 2003, the average net income of Chinese peasant households rose from 423.8 Yuan to 2,622.2 Yuan, with annual growth rate of 7.3% leaving out the inflation factor. Moreover, the savings growth for rural residents has far exceeded their income growth.* Although in recent years the Government has attempted to tone down the saving tendency of the residents through lowering interest rate and levying interest tax, etc., savings in rural areas have maintained a sustainable growth, which goes to prove that the motive for savings in the rural areas is not to obtain interest, but represents a kind of self protection behavior.

7.3.1.2. *Borrowing has become more socially acceptable*

Owing to the deep seated self protection and security tradition of the small–scale peasant economy, most peasants see debts as a bad thing, something shameful. For this reason, when they have financial difficulties, they will first switch to other sidelines of production or other jobs to increase income. If they still do not get out of the crisis, they will turn to their friends or relatives. They will only go to financial institutions when they are left with no choice. In recent years, however, with the development of the market economy, debt has become more acceptable and the number of rural borrowers has been growing continuously.**

7.3.1.3. *Borrowing from friends and relatives still makes up a big percentage*

According to a sample survey conducted by the agricultural investigation team from the NBSC, from 2000 to 2003, on average each peasant borrows 65 Yuan from banks and RCCs per day and 190 Yuan through private financing, which respectively accounted for 25% and 75% of the total credit amount. On investigation, personal lending

*According to the statistics from a survey conducted on over 20,000 households by the Office of Fixed Observation Points under the Ministry of Agriculture, from 1986 to 2002, the average per capita income increased from 510.22 Yuan to 2,775.62 Yuan; and the year-end per capita savings (including cash in hand) grew from 224.16 Yuan to 2,209.01 Yuan. Based on my calculation, if we take out the inflation factor, the annual growth rate of per capita income averaged 3.2%, whereas per capita savings achieved an average annual growth rate of 7.1%.

currently occupies the biggest share in popular finance. Most peasants will lend money to their relatives or friends upon requests. When I was doing some surveys in Hunan Province, I found that one peasant with good creditability had obtained loans from a RCC four times, of which three times were for his friends or relatives. This phenomenon appeared mainly because of the deep-seated bond with friends and relatives in rural China. This phenomenon could also be partly caused by the weakening financial service, strict requirements and tedious procedures for loan applications, etc. Since small–scale lending between friends and relatives in the rural areas does not requires IOUs and most of the times it is interest–free, and the borrowers will still do their utmost to return the money, even when they have to work as a free helper or use other "humanized or courtesy" means to pay back the money. However, with the development of market economy in rural China and the growth of credit, more and more lenders are requesting for IOUs and interest charges. Some peasants, who are in dire need of capital, have to go to loan sharks when they fail to borrow money from their friends or relatives.

7.3.3. *Status Quo of the Rural Fictitious Economy*

From the perspective of the five development stages for the fictitious economy in rural China, the Chinese rural fictitious economy has just entered the second stage, that is, from the capitalization of the idle money to the early stages of the socialization of interest generating capital.

The first developmental stage of fictitious economy is the capitalization of the idle money, which becomes interest generating capital. Fictitious economy can be first traced back to the commercialized personal lending activities. For an illustration: A needs to buy seeds, fertilizer or pesticide urgently, but he himself does not have enough capital. B happens to have some idle money, so A can borrow some money from B and promises to return the principal and interest within a certain period of time. Through this activity, A obtains the use of the capital and can create profits through entity economic activities with this capital functioning as a means of payment. On the other hand, B maintains the ownership of this amount of money holding the IOU and the rights to receive the principal and interest from A when the loan is due. The IOU that B possesses in his hand is the rudiment of fictitious capital which can attain capital increase through the lending and repaying cycle. In the process, B is not involved in actual economic activities, but obtains profits through a type of fictitious economic activity. In this way, the idle money of B becomes interest generating capital.

As previously discussed, the personal lending relationship in rural China is mainly built upon the relationship with friends and relatives. Since small–scale lending is normally interest–free and does not require IOUs, it does not fall into the category of fictitious economy. However, with the development of the market economy in rural China and the increasing credit amount for each borrowing, more and more lenders are asking for IOUs and interest charges.

When some people hold idle money and lent out money to generate interest, others want to borrow money to meet various needs. However, the transaction may be realized due to the absence of connection (they are not friends or are not related) and guarantee between the two parties. At this juncture, credit intermediaries step in to satisfy this special need. When a credit intermediary successfully helped the borrower and lender to reach an agreement, it will charge a certain amount of handling fee or 'guarantee fee' from the borrowing party.

The second development stage for fictitious economy is the socialization of interest generating capital. As fictitious economic activities are usually limited by small scales, inability to optimize investment and vulnerability to risks, a need for the socialization of interest generating capital is created and banks come into the picture. As intermediary organizations, banks pool the idle capital from the public and then lend out to people who need capital and can generate profits. If enterprises conduct indirect financing through banks, they have to bear relatively higher cost, but the cost for direct financing such as issuing bonds to the public is lower than paying the interest of the bank loans. Investor can at the same time enjoy returns that are higher than bank interest. Moreover, business enterprises can pool capital through issuing stocks to share its risks and profits with the investors. This means people can purchase various marketable bonds such as stocks, bonds, etc., to earn interest. In the end, the socialization of interest generating capital produces banks and other forms of fictitious capital such as bonds and stocks, etc. The socialization of the interest generating capital allows social capital to move from the hands of people who are not engaged in entity economic activities such as production, circulation and trade, etc., to the hands of people who can apply it to entity economic activities by pooling the dispersed capital from various owners for large-scale and highly profitable economic activities in order to ultimately optimize the investments direction as well as improve capital utilization.

Owing to the existence of the dual economic structure, the socialization level for interest generating capital in the rural area is still relatively low. Most farmers choose to deposit their idle money in banks for self security purpose, and only a few farmers will lend their idle money to TVEs or buy stocks. For this reason, farmers that own stocks or bonds are very few. Moreover, due to the insufficient supply of funds from formal financing channels, some informal financing activities still exist. It is foreseeable that, in the upcoming 10 to 20 years, the fictitious economy in rural China will sustain at the socialization stage of interest generating capital, in which indirect financing activities will be conducted out through financial institutions.

The fictitious economic mechanism is intimately associated with the entity economic mechanism. Fictitious economy is endogenously created by the entity economic system, and is dependent on the entity economic system. Risks that are generated in the entity economic system will be passed on to the fictitious economic system, triggering a certain amount of instability. In return, risks generated in the fictitious economic system will have a profound impact on entity economy. In an era where finance has become the economic centerpiece, entity economy cannot survive without the company of the fictitious economy. That means, if we call the entity economic mechanism the "hardware" for the economic system, then the fictitious economic mechanism would be the "software" for the economy.

There are two types of risks for the rural entity economy. One is natural hazards. This type of risks refers to losses caused by various disasters that human force cannot cope with. The other type is market risks, referring to losses created by changes of the market demand and price. Both types of risks can deprive farmers of their ability to repay the loans. In consequence, risks could be further passed to the fictitious economic system, becoming non-performing assets of financial institutions.

Risks from the rural fictitious economy consist mainly of credit risk. Credit risks refer to risks posed by the possibility that borrowers do not repay loans at the due time as stated in the contract. This in part is linked to the risks of the entity economy, but is also partially caused by the bad creditability of the farmers and local authorities who are not keen on repaying their loans. Due to the immature credit system of China's commercial finance, commercials banks are not motivated to extend credit loans to farmers. Instead, they are mainly engaged in granting collateralized loans, including guaranteed loan, mortgage loans and pledged loans, etc.

At present, credit loans in the rural financial sector are mostly small–scale credit loans set up for the purpose of alleviating the difficulties for farmers to obtain loans. The RCCs will issue loan certificates based on farmers' credit assessments and each loan transaction ranges from 2,000 to 10,000 Yuan, for which guarantee (in the form of guarantors etc.) is not needed. In 2002, small scale credit loans were provided by RCCs. By the end of March 2004, the total amount of outstanding loans reached 136.5 billion Yuan. To minimize risks, some RCCs request guarantee even for applicants with loan certificates. In addition, each application needs to go through a tedious verification and review process. This actually converts credit loans into small–scale guarantee loans.

Of the above three types of collateralized loans, mortgage loans occupy only a minute share. This is because farmers' personal properties are limited in quantity and cannot be easily valued and liquidized or realized for cash. Moreover, it is not appropriate to use the houses or contracted lands of the farmers as collaterals either. Pledged loans account for a slightly bigger share, which include bankbooks and treasury bonds, etc. Guaranteed loans take up the bulk of collateralized loans, in which the guarantor shall undertake the joint responsibilities and obligations for all the debts stated in the loan agreement.

To solve the problem of absence of guarantee for loans to peasant households, in 2002, PBOC promulgated the "Directives and Opinions on Administration of joint-household guaranteed loans by Rural Credit Co-operatives", mandating RCCs to provide guaranteed loans business to members of the mutual, joint-household guarantee team, which is voluntarily made up five to ten non-related households with capital needs. The underlying principle for loan provision is "joint guarantee, regular savings and repayment by installments". Members of the joint guarantee team undertake the joint responsibilities or liability of the borrower. If the borrower cannot repay his/her loan in due time, the joint guarantee team shall repay it on the borrower's behalf. Because of the mutual supervision between member households, this practice has somehow reduced instances of breach of loans agreement thus reducing credit risks. For this reason, mutually-guaranteed loans developed considerably. By the end of 2004, the outstanding mutually guaranteed loans totaled 65.2 billion Yuan. In fact, the actual amount of outstanding loans has far surpassed this figure if we include small–scale credit loans which have also adopted this practice. However, because of the pressure exerted by mutual supervision, borrowers are too cautious and prudent when selecting projects and conducting operational activities, and the banks' costs for pre-loan approval investigation, loan reviews and post-loan overseeing are also high.

It can be seen from the above discussion that when we are studying relevant issues on rural financial constructions in China, we should start from the status quo ante of the rural entity economy and analyze the conditions from both capital demand and capital supply in order to design the target models for the institutional constructions of China's rural financial sector.

7.3.4. *Chinese Rural Entity Economy and Its Derived Financial Needs*

China's peasant economy, which has existed throughout China's long history, has progressed from the 'set out to work in at the break of dawn to coming home at dusk; digging well for drinking and working on the fields for food' form of self-sufficient status to today's situation of both self sufficiency and commodity trading. As a matter of fact, economic activities involve purchasing fertilizers, pesticides, farm tools, seeds and other production materials by paying money. After farm products made through the production process, a small part is kept for the subsistence of the farmers themselves, the rest is sold in the market in exchange for money to purchase other necessities. The farmlands that most peasants work on are quite small and they primarily rely on primitive production conditions. Their income is mainly used for maintaining their primitive production process, purchasing living necessities, building houses, celebrating marriages, holding funerals as well as paying for education, medical services, etc. When their income cannot satisfy their consumption needs, or they encounter natural disasters or other crises, their needs for financing service will arise.

Since China's opening up and reform, the income levels of Chinese farmers have improved substantially. However, due to the low productivity of the small scale peasant economy, the over-supply of agricultural produce and the heavy burdens of rural taxes and administrative charges for farmers, etc., a great number of peasant households cannot maintain their production and subsistence. Consequently, they have to turn to side or peripheral business or relocate to survive. Based on statistics from the NBSC,[10] per capita income of the rural households stood at 2,622.24 Yuan, in 2003, of which 1,165.58 Yuan came from farming, forestry, husbandry and fishery, accounting for merely 44.4% of the total income. This figure was much lower than the 66.6% in 1990. Per capita living expenditure for rural households was 1,943.30 Yuan, of which cash spending amounted to 1,576.64 Yuan. Both figures were higher than the incomes of farming, forestry, husbandry and fishery.

With the slow progress of the entity economic activities based on small–scale peasant economy, the following three entity economic forms have appeared on the center stage of the rural entity economy, changing dramatically the financial needs of rural China.

(1) Emergence of households with sizable production. Some peasant households that are engaged in the farming and aquaculture sectors are seeking expanded production in order to get out of poverty. As many peasant households suffer capital shortage, they often need to borrow money from their friends, relatives or financial institutes in the initial stage of the expansion. However, due to the lack of adequate credit records, financial institutions would not take the risks to extend loans to these rural households. With the expansion of the production, the amount of capital that peasant households need have also increased accordingly. As a result, they are more inclined to borrow from financial institutions. Obviously financial institutions are more willing to provide loans to large farming and aquaculture producers with good creditability and development prospects.

(2) Development of township and village enterprises (TVEs). In the mid 1980s, TVEs, derived from the rural collective economy, sprang up in relatively developed areas in Jiangsu Province and quickly spread to other places of China. Benefiting from the comparatively flexible operational model, TVEs can better adapt to the changing market demands. Spurred by full support from the government, TVEs' output registered an average annual growth rate of over 20%. At the same time, its employment increased at an annual growth rate of more than 10%, becoming a critical contributor to the increase of rural incomes. However, starting from the 1990s, development of township and village enterprises has gradually slowed down, and many county and village collective enterprises have been transformed into individual, private or stockholding enterprises. With the increasing commercialization of the financial institutions, loans offered by financial institutions could no longer meet the financial needs of the vast TVEs. Some

informal financial institutions therefore stepped in, intending to provide high interest loans to TVEs.

(3) Rise of agriculture based industrialization model of "company + household". In the late 1980s, agriculture based industrialized operations characterized by company-led households prevailed in the east of Shandong Province and then gradually spread to the whole of China. The principal intention is to engage in processing agricultural products or trading enterprises and create a 'flagship' to lead peasant households to engage in specialized production through orders made in contracts, thus bringing closely together production and processing and sales of farm products. As this mechanism moves forward the market economy of rural China without changing fundamentally the operational mode of the individual household and their land tenancy rights, it is more in accord with the current circumstances of our nation's agriculture, its rural areas and the Chinese peasants. Remarkable progress has been achieved in this regard in recent years. Based on some news sources,[11] at present there are 372 national key flagship enterprises, 1,839 provincial key flagship enterprises and over 20,000 other flagship enterprises in China. In 2002, the "production order" model for the farming sector was extended to 327 million *mu* (a Chinese unit for area), taking up roughly 24% of the total agricultural acreage sown, of which about half were completed by flagship enterprises. Since agriculture based production is seasonable, requiring tremendous amounts of capital infusion at the initial stage of the production cycle, peasant households or flagship enterprises have to borrow funds from financial institutions.

7.3.5. *Organizational Behaviors of the Supply Channels and Financial Institutions of China's Rural Finance*

The supply channels or conduits for rural finance sector can be divided into four areas: policy based finance, commercial finance, co-operative finance and 'popular' finance (informal finance), which are respectively incorporated by policy based banks, commercial banks, RCCs and private money houses. As previously discussed, short capital supply is the fundamental problem for China's rural finance. I propose that, to investigating the causes for this problem and to come up with effective solutions, we shall first have to analyze the organizational behavior of related financial institutions.

Organizational behavior is a study of human behaviors and experiences as well as the organization itself in an organization setting.[12] From the perspective of complexity science, the behavior of an organization is determined by its self organizing effect created by the interactions between the components of the organization (individuals and groups), and between the organization and the external environment. The organization, in return, will also affect the behaviors of its components. Therefore, while analyzing the behaviors of a financial institution, we shall not only study the behaviors of its internal members, but also shall pay attention to the setting or circumstances in which they are placed.

7.3.5.1. *The Agricultural Development Bank of China (ADBC)*

The ADBC is currently the major policy based financing channel in China apart from state fiscal allocation. ADBC was founded in June 1994 and it completed its establishments of provincial level branches at the same year. Its county level transactions were temporarily entrusted to Agricultural Bank of China (ABC). In 2002, the establishment of county level branches was completed. At the end of 2003, it had established approximately 2,000 branches of various kinds, of which there were 35 primary branches, 294 secondary branches, 1,602 subsidiary banks, 3 branch offices and 34 credit groups employing a total of 59,000 people.

As the credit business for agricultural development and poverty alleviation that ADBC was initially established for were officially handed over to ABC in March 1993, currently its business functions are limited to providing policy based loans for agricultural procurement (of food crops, cotton, oil etc), serving as a capital management agent.

This is by no means close to the government's requirement to provide policy based financing to support agricultural development. As a result of the orientation of this function, ADBC has concentrated too much on completing the assigned tasks of agricultural procurement and stockpiling, rather than carrying out other banking functions. Since it had failed to develop other financing channels, the sources of its funds were limited to re-loans from the Central Bank. At the end of April 2004, various outstanding loans held by ADBC totaled 684.7 billion Yuan and deposits of 24.8 billion Yuan, of which funds borrowed from the Central Bank were valued at 630 billion Yuan, accounting for 92% of its outstanding loans.

7.3.5.2. *Agricultural Bank of China (ABC)*

ABC, established in 1950, has been dissolved and re-established four times and consolidated three times. According to the regulations in the fourth restructuring of ABC by the State Council in 1979, its main functions include centrally managing agriculture support/subsidy funds, handling rural credit business and directing the operations of RCCs with a view to developing the rural financial sector. As such, ABC can be categorized as a specialized bank that is dedicated to rural financial operations. From 1985, despite some commercials banks starting to flock to the rural financial market to provide loans to the burgeoning township and village enterprises (TVEs), ABC remained the biggest agriculture based commercial bank. However, with the rapid development of the urban economy and the slight slowdown of the growth of TVEs, the four state-owned commercial banks including ABC all started to withdraw from the rural financial market or merge their financial units from the late 1990s to focus on more profitable operations. According to some news report,[13] from 1999 to 2002, the four commercial banks merged a total of 31,000 outlets below township level. At the end of 2003, their outstanding loans totaled 13,717.36 billion Yuan, of which only 282.86 billion Yuan went to agriculture and TVEs, accounting for merely 2.06%.[10]

When ABC was withdrawing from the rural market, it shifted its business focus to support agricultural industrialization. In this regard, it formulated relevant credit policies and provided services to support contract farming and flagship enterprises that implement the "company + base + peasant households" model. By the end of 2003, loans outstanding for agricultural industrialization amounted to 65.4 billion Yuan, of which up to 39.9 billion Yuan was extended in the same year. Amid the 371 key flagship enterprises published by related national ministries and commissions, 238 of them have received support from ABC, obtaining outstanding loans totaling 15 billion Yuan. At present, ABC is still engaged in some policy based financial activities, including the granting of poverty alleviation loans and loans for agricultural infrastructure constructions focusing on electricity network reconstruction and rural urbanization loan, etc.

7.3.5.3. *Rural Credit Co-operatives (RCCs)*

After the founding of New China, RCCs have enjoyed continuous development, overcoming various types of difficulties from time to time. By the end of 2003, there were a total of 35,544 legally registered RCCs throughout China, the number of which decreased by 2,547. Of the 35,544 RCCs, 31,448 were village level RCCs, 153 were town level RCCs, 2,460 were county unions of credit co-operatives, three were rural commercial banks, one was rural co-operative bank, 65 were co-operative fund associations at county level and seven were provincial co-operative fund associations.

Theoretically, RCCs are collectively owned co-operative financial units, are made up of shares subscribed by farmers. They handle deposits and short–term loans in different localities. Their assets and equities are collectively owned, and internal democratic management style is implemented within RCCs. Their profit, except the part for collective reserve, is normally distributed through dividends. However, in the actual development of RCCs, most of them are operating more like a subordinate unit or grassroots institution of the state banks, and developing towards commercial finance.

The reasons that contribute to this phenomenon may be described on the following two aspects:

The first is the hazy definition of ownership rights. Based on the Constitution of RCC, its ownership belongs to its members. But in fact the percentage of equity held by internal staff and external investors has been increasing. Together with the mandatory interventions of the authorities, RCCs are in reality under the control of inside forces. As a result, Member's Representative Assembly, Board of Directors and the Supervisory Board are as good as non-existent because they could not perform their functions. This has resulted in RCCs deviating from their business objective: they function mainly to pursue profits, even for the 'insiders'. Presently, although some RCCs are running in the red, their staff members still enjoy relatively high pay.

The second aspect is the lack of policy support. RCCs are engaged in providing service to the vast number of dispersed rural households. This not only necessitates a network of numerous outlets, but also requires RCCS to send their staff to the remotely located households to handle business. Besides, loans granted to the farmers are normally of small amount, which consequently raises the transaction cost. As these RCCs also lack effective remedial measures to cope with various risks, such situations inevitably lead to a decline in their profits. Owing to many factors, including the 'ownerless' structure, inadequate mechanism, ineffective management and outmoded policies, tremendous amount of non-performing loans and suspended accounts have been accumulated over time. RCCs are heavily burdened, with some deprived of their capacity to support the agricultural industry. By the end of 2002, 53.46% of the RCCs are running in the red, with debts reaching 177.9 billion Yuan. Under such circumstances, many RCCs have to maintain their operations by relying on the refinancing of the PBOC. In the absence of governmental policy support, many RCCs are no longer keen on lending out small–scale loans for supporting agricultural productions and operations. Based on a questionnaire survey conducted by a township branch of PBOC in 2002 targeted at all credit administrators in the county unions of RCCs, 70% of the credit administrators were biased against small–scale loans. Because of the prejudice credit administrators hold against small–scale financial service, it is more difficult for the impoverished and low income peasants to obtain loans.

7.3.5.4. *Private 'money house'*

As the financial supply from formal financial institutions cannot meet by far the rural credit demands and the strict and tedious loan application procedures are keeping rural households away, various forms of private finance (informal finance) other than the existing personal lending come in. Amid these informal financial forms, private 'money house' becomes the main player.

After the reform and opening up, private money houses started to appear in some developed regions. Private money houses stem from credit intermediaries, and they are mainly engaged in saving and borrowing business to earn the difference between savings rates and borrowing rates. In the second half of 1984, in Wenzhou of Zhejiang Province, the local government approved the setting up of four private money houses. Some of the private money houses were doing quite well.[13] In January 1986, the State Council promulgated the "Provisional Measures on the Administration of Banks", stipulating that private individuals are not allowed to open banks or other financial institutions, or run any type of financial operations. From then on, although private money houses in Wenzhou had been suspended, the activities and practice of rural private lending did not cease entirely. After the mid 1990s, the rising capital demand of the rural economic development and the declining capital supply resulting from the withdrawal of commercials banks as well as the elimination of rural co-operative fund associations, had created rooms for the development of informal finance led by private money houses. Their client base not only included peasant households and TVEs that needed to develop production and sustain their business, it also included some local authorities at village level and villagers committees that urgently needed capital to carry out their assigned tasks. The appealing higher saving rates that private money houses offered helped them to attract idle capital of the farmers. Despite their slightly higher borrowing rates, the much faster loan application procedures seemed worth-while. Therefore, both borrowers and depositors have relied on the existence of private money house and have supported its development. However, since private money houses are banned as illegal financing activities, their activities have to be kept underground and sometimes they show up as credit intermediaries. Based on a survey conducted by Agricultural Bank of China, Wenzhou Branch, approximately 83.3% of the farmers were once involved in private financing activities. The private credit scale of Wenzhou city accounted for one third of the whole rural capital market. Shockingly, part of some bank's capital even became the "principal" for loan sharks.[14]

7.4. Target Models for the Institutional Constructions of China's Rural Finance and Related Policy Recommendations

From the above analysis, we are made aware that the reform of the rural financial system is an arduous task and we need to identify a development path that best suits China's realities and specifics. From my point of view, to explore this issue further, we need first of all set up the target models for constructing China's rural financial system and then, based on the analysis of current situation of China, put forth specific measures and steps to achieve these target models and put up relevant suggestions on formulating policies towards achieving them.

7.4.1. *Target Models for the Institutional Construction of China's Rural Finance*

Based on the current conditions of China's rural areas and the experiences from other countries, the target models for China's rural financial system prior to 2020 ought to possess the following four characteristics:

7.4.1.1. *Fiscal support, market-based operations*

Before 2020, Chinese agriculture will still remain a weak and disadvantaged 'industry' and farmers will stay as the disadvantaged groups of the population. To develop agricultural financing, we need to bring into full play the "visible hand" of the government to provide appropriate fiscal support. However, fiscal support should not be implemented by means of extending direct loans to the rural areas or providing government subsidies to rural households. Rather, it should be carried out by various types of financial institutions through prudent policy formulation and institutional operations led by the "invisible hand" of the market to optimize capital utilization. The government ought to provide funds to policy driven financial institutions for their start-up and capital needs, support their bonds issuing as well as offer necessary policy support to agriculture based commercial financing institutions and RCCs through policy financial institutions. The Government will also need to provide preferential policies (such as cutting down on reserves requirements, tax deduction, etc.), and necessary fiscal supports (namely, credit guarantee, loss compensation, etc.), to RCCs and some agriculture supporting commercial institutions. Besides, relevant government departments will have to provide financial assistance to and invest in the rural social welfare services to promote the development of the said social welfare services by means of various subsidies.

7.4.1.2. *A3 tier system in which each plays its respective role*

China's rural financial system should consist of policy driven finance, commercial finance and co-operative finance, with a clear cut division of duties and responsibilities with each participant focusing on its assigned roles.

The underlying function of policy driven finance is to employ all kinds of financial instruments to drive the economic and social development of rural China through fiscal support provided by state financial units. The main scope of business for policy finance includes granting medium or long–term loans to farmers for their agricultural production and development — on favorable terms. Policy finance should also offer transaction cost compensation and risk interest rates to commercial banks in their loan give-outs to farmers, as well as giving reinsurance subsidies for relatively bigger natural disasters/hazards borne by insurance companies. They can also extend low interest loans for low returns projects such as improving agricultural production conditions and expanding production in addition to direct investment.

The main function of commercial finance is to provide various financial services to peasant households, TVEs and flagship enterprises through various forms of financial institutions and market oriented operations. Its main business scope includes absorbing savings locally, providing short–term or long–term production-based loans to farmers, and supplying working capital and loans for technological upgrading to TVEs and flagship enterprises as well as notes discounts.

The main initiative for co-operative finance is to provide basic, simple financing services to its members and local farmers, through co-operative financial associations which are voluntarily set up by farmers. Its main business covers providing small scale, short–term and low interest rate production and consumption loans, and assisting farmers to receive loans from policy driven financial institutions or commercial institutions.

7.4.1.3. *Focus on deposits and credit services; integrated support services*

In the 10 to 15 years to come, the major business functions of the rural financial institutions will continue to focus on deposits and loans business dealing with rural households. With the development of the rural market economy, it is imperative to develop gradually other financial services such as settlement, arbitrage, financial consultancy, leasing, trusts, insurance, credit card, safe deposit box, marketable bonds issuing and trade intermediary service, etc., to foster a more mature and comprehensive rural financial service system.

7.4.1.4. *Good and comprehensive legal system and developed market*

Developing rural finance entails the effective existence of a good and comprehensive legal system to regulate the behaviors of the major market participants and to define the fundamental relations between them as well as the competitive environment. The legal system for the

Chinese rural financial system shall be established in line with the fundamental codes of the *Constitution*, with the *Agriculture Law* and *Finance Law* as the parent laws. Upon reviewing various rural financial laws of other countries, it is proposed that laws including *Law* of *Agriculture Loans*, *Agriculture Credit Law*, *Agriculture Insurance Law* and *Co-operative Finance Law* etc., should be promulgated in China, to be supplemented with appropriate codes and regulations.

With the development of the market economy in China's rural areas, fund raising will become more dependent on the financial market, which includes, among others, issuing bonds. As such, we need to cultivate aggressively China's bonds markets. Apart from treasury bonds, policy related financial bonds and corporate bonds, there is a need to extend the variety of agricultural bonds, and establish a bonds issuing and regulatory system. The rural insurance market can be initiated from production insurance to guard against natural hazards and market risks, and later extend to property insurance, life insurance as well as other insurances.

7.4.2. *Intensify and Strengthen the Functions of Policy Financial Institutions*

ADBC is by far the sole policy related financial institution for rural areas. Its functions need to be significantly intensified so that it can develop towards a professional bank for granting agriculture loans.

Currently the main business of ADBC is limited to policy related financing business for agricultural procurement. However, ABC, classified as one of the commercial banks, also engages in certain policy based financing business such as granting discount loans for poverty alleviation. This practice, however, is underscored by the fact that profit driven commercial banks overlook the low returns policy related finance business in pursuit of their own interests, or even flagrantly ask for government subsidies under this pretext. Some commercial banks had extended the discount poverty alleviation loans to some wealthy farmers who did not really need funds. Some of them even went as far as embezzling the procurement funds set aside for agriculture produce, or transferring the losses in their commercial operations or risks onto other policy based operations that they are entrusted to. In my view, it is inappropriate for governmental departments to be directly involved in policy based financial activities by means of direct appropriation or subsidies. If they do so, this will result in the government exerting excessive interventions on financial activities, bringing about problems of preferential treatments for some parties. In this regard, we should bestow all policy related financial functions to ADBC only. To realize this objective, it is advisable to take the following steps to 'adjust' and restructure ADBC.

The policy based financing business of ABC such as granting discount government loans for poverty alleviation should be handed back to ADBC, and the functions and roles of ADBC need to be more clearly defined.

The policy finance business involving poverty alleviation subsidized interest loans handled by ABC should be handed over to ADBC as soon as possible, and the mission and functions of ABDC should be more clearly defined.

The principal capital of ADBC should be replenished and increased, its ownership rights established and its corporate governance system improved. It is suggested to ratify a capital amount worth 50 billion Yuan, which shall be paid out jointly between the central government and the local government in the ratio of 7:3. The directors shall be appointed based on the proportion of shares and three more rural financial experts shall be hired as independent directors to form the Board of Directors. The State Council will appoint the Chairman of the Board, and the General Manager shall be nominated and appointed by the Board of Directors with the approval of the State Council.

In the upcoming five years, the policy based financing functions of ADBC shall be steadily extended. Firstly, long–term low interest or interest free loans shall be offered for rural infrastructure constructions (such as roads, telecom and electricity network constructions) and social development projects (namely, heath clinics and cultural centers, etc.). Secondly, low interest loans shall be extended to low returns projects tailored for improving agricultural production conditions and expanding productions in addition to direct investment. Thirdly low interest loans are to be provided to RCCs. Fourthly, offer appropriate amount of compensation for transaction cost and subsidies for interest rate risks under the entrustment of the Ministry of Finance, and provide reinsurance subsidies to insurance companies for relatively more severe natural disasters, etc. A major part of the funds for the above mentioned items shall come from fiscal appropriation; another part is to be paid by relevant funds set up by the governmental departments.

According to the rules of WTO, China's agriculture support policies that might lead to 'trade distortions' and compromised commitments are called "yellow" policies.[15] Apparently, rooms for discount rural financial service and subsidies will become more restricted. As such, we should try our best efforts to create conditions to guarantee the smooth operations of agriculture support finance and rural co-operative finance. At the same time, ADBC shall be allowed to offer credit guarantee to credit plans of government-driven projects, shifting its attention to scientific research, technological transformation, reserves for food safety, rescue and assistance work during natural disasters, environmental protection as well as adjustment of the agricultural industrial structure that fall into the "green box" category of WTO.

7.4.3. *Encourage Commercial Banks to Support Agriculture*

Of the four big commercial banks in China, Agricultural Bank of China (ABC) was meant to be the bank for exclusively delivering rural financial service. However, as the transaction costs for agriculture support loans are relatively high and the business entails high risk, not only has ABC slowly withdrawn from the rural areas and reduced its functions for providing agriculture support, even the rural-rooted RCCs have slowly drifted away from their originally intended roles and re-oriented towards commercialization. For these reasons, to motivate commercial banks to support agriculture, it is imperative to take some effective measures to cut down the high transaction costs and high risks.

The principal contributors for the high transaction cost for agriculture support projects can be summarized as follows: (1) small scale of the loans. It is axiomatic that the cost for processing one loan of two million is far lower than the cost for handling 40 loans of 5,000 Yuan each; (2) rural loan applicants are normally widely dispersed in different locations and credit administrators have to spend a lot of time investigating the local circumstances and process the applications; (3) owing to the low education level of rural loan applicants, credit administrators have to help them fill out the loan application forms and go through relevant procedures; and (4) as the transaction volume of the banks at the grass-roots level is too low, the banks or other financial institutions can hardly cover the expenses for their operations.

Since there is not much room to reduce the transaction cost for agriculture support loans, some people have suggested increasing borrowing interest rates. However, this will aggravate the existing burdens of the rural lenders and impede the development of the agriculture industry. Therefore, I am advocating for the loan discount or subsidy approach, which will not only prevent farmers from being victimized by heavier burdens, but can also encourage commercial banks to participate enthusiastically in agriculture support financing. The funds set aside for discount service and subsidies shall be shared between the central government and the local governments from their budgets and granted through ADBC.

Risks for agro support projects lie in the following three aspects:

First is the risk of natural disasters. When big natural catastrophes occur, farmers will be unable to repay their loans. This type of risk can only be defused through insurance. Since this kind of insurance features low insurance premium and high amounts of payment in cases of occurrence of natural catastrophes, commercial insurance firms are not very keen on offering this low profit insurance to farmers. For this reason, government subsided reinsurance service should be offered to insurance companies by the ADBC.

Second is market risk. When demand for farm products decline or its price starts to go downward, rural incomes will go much lower than expected — which will consequently badly affect farmers' repaying capability. To mitigate this kind of risks, agricultural industrialization shall be aggressively promoted and the implementation of the 'production order model' (procuring more orders to boost production) speeded up. At the same time, we shall develop the futures market for agricultural products to use 'hedging' to minimize losses caused by market risks.

The third is credit risk, which refers to the risks that the borrower does not repay the loan because of reasons other than the above mentioned factors. This type of risks could be defused by a combination of steps.

Considering the current circumstances of the rural areas, it is suggested that agriculture support institutions be divided into two tiers. Agricultural Bank of China (ABC) shall serve mainly flagship enterprises and large TVEs, the major players of the agricultural industrialization; whereas RCCs shall cater to rural households, and small and medium sized TVEs. Rural commercial banks, however, can serve both tiers.

During the implementation of the pilot scheme for RCCs in Jiangsu Province, rural commercial banks were established in Changshu, Zhangjiagang and Jiangyin. I have visited Jiangsu twice (2002 and 2004) to investigate the newly born rural commercial banks, which came into existence during the development of the rural financial sector. In general, it has achieved some good results. The features that are common to this type of county level commercial banks can be summarized as follows: (1) they operate in the form of a stockholding system or joint stock system, so they have clear-cut ownership rights; (2) they serve mainly local customers. They have the benefit of symmetrical information, but suffer high cost in cases of breach of agreement from their customers; (3) they have a widespread business network. Since they are closer to the farmers, they can better perform their agriculture support functions; and (4) they comprise good internal system and management. We shall gradually and conditionally expand this program to pilot counties and take effective steps to support its development, continuously perfect its governance system and protect its independent legal status to shelter their operations from the abuse of power by local government and provincial associations.

To encourage the support for agriculture development from commercial financial institutions, the following measures are proposed:

Firstly, continue and improve the small scale credit system for rural households and give priority to relatively more impoverished households, for the purpose of maintaining the basic/simple re-production needs (such as purchasing seeds, fertilizers, pesticides and normal farm tools, etc.), and other contingencies. Each loan amount shall be limited to within 5,000 Yuan and the credit term shall correspond to the agricultural production cycle, with the borrowing rate equal to or slightly lower than the market driven rate. Technically, these types of loans do not require any guarantee, but the credit administrators should co-ordinate with the villager representative committees for credit verification of the borrowing farmers.

Secondly, improve and expand 'mutually guaranteed' loan system, where the funds will be primarily used for supporting farmers for moderate production expansion, house building and university education expanses for their children, etc. The loan ceiling is 50,000 Yuan and the term is normally less than a year.

Thirdly, to offset the transaction cost and risks for the above two types of loans, sales tax for RCCs and rural commercial banks should be repealed. If there are still losses, the ADBC can consider disbursing appropriate amounts of discount loans. Otherwise, ADBC can entrust some policy related financial business to the RCCs and rural commercial banks by paying them some administrative fees.

Fourthly, regulate the development of the rural postal savings service. It is suggested that postal savings outlets pool the rural savings and re-deposit them into ABC under the same conditions as for the other commercial financing institutions. These funds can be re-loaned to RCCs and rural commercial banks to alleviate the funds shortage.

Fifthly, continue to remove the 'historical burdens' (remnant practices and thinking of the past) of RCCs. Fiscal subsidies, tax reductions and exemptions, including interest compensation for capital guarantee depositing service by government, temporary exemption of income tax for RCCs under the reform in West China, appropriate capital support provided to RCCs by PBOC through re-loans and special bill and extended interest rate floating range for RCCs under the experiment reform, shall be implemented in a concerted and serious manner.

Sixthly, establish credit guarantee companies. These types of companies can be jointly incorporated by local departments and private investors to provide credit guarantee for loans extended to large agricultural and aquaculture producers. According to my investigation in Jiangyin City at Jiangsu Province in June 2004, Fumin Guarantor Company, Ltd., played an important role in supporting farmers to expand production moderately and to make profit. At present, the 'guarantee rate' of this company stays within 1:5-8 and the due collection rate is 100%, earnings after tax is roughly 5%, and 5% of the registered capital is kept as the risk reserve.

Seventhly, it is stated that the proportion that goes to agriculture from the outstanding loan of ABC shall not be less than 12% and the proportion from rural commercial banks shall not be less than 60%. For projects that are in line with the country's industrialization policies and are also critical to the agricultural development, ADBC can consider offering appropriate interest discount to offset the relatively high transaction cost incurred by ABC.

Eighthly, develop agricultural production insurance. Agriculture producers can buy insurance for their future income and apply for mortgaged loans from banks to cover production cost. For instance, when pig farmers purchase piglets, they can buy insurance from insurance companies, and apply for mortgaged loans with insurance policies to purchase fodder.

7.4.4. *Support Development of Co-operative Financial Associations*

In some countries with market economy such as the U.S, France and Japan, etc., rural co-operative financial associations are very developed, and have become the main component of the rural financial sector. The Chinese Government has reiterated several times that

RCCs are co-operative financial associations. In addition, it was stated in the recent rural financial reform that RCC shall play its role as the main force of the rural financial industry. However, various factors, including excessive interventions from the local governments, ambiguous property right, high level of internal control and lack of effective policy supports, are not only causing economic losses for RCCs, but also are transforming them into commercial financial institutions.

Ever since the reform movement of RCCs was launched in 1999, overall China has curbed the deteriorating losses of RCCs. This can be exemplified by the fact that RCCs managed to reduce losses and increase profit for three consecutive years. In 2002, 23,643 RCCs throughout China were making profits, accounting for 66.52% of the total number. Based on this figure, the number of profit making RCCs increased by 3,047, with the total profit reaching 5,923 million Yuan. In 2002, 11,901 RCCs were making economic losses, the number shrunk by 5,664 against 2001, with the losses totaling 11,707 million Yuan. After the breaking even, losses in 2001, 2002 and 2003 were respectively 3,050, 7,203 and 5,322 million Yuan. By the end of March 2004, the balance held on deposits totaled 2,578.3 billion Yuan and total loan outstanding amounted to 1,888.5 billion Yuan, of which agriculture support loans accounted for 43.3%, and loans for TVEs occupied 32.6%. For the total outstanding agriculture support loans, the proportion granted to rural households and agricultural economic organizations was approximately 4 to 1.

In accordance with the internationally affirmed "the Seven Principles of Co-operatives", which are respectively — voluntary and open membership, democratized member control, members economic participation, autonomy and independence, education, training and information, co-operation among co-operatives and concern for community — the rural co-operative financial associations are organizations made up of the voluntary subscriptions of the farmers and are organized in a democratic manner based on the "one member, one vote" principle. These associations are self-help and self-benefiting non-profit organizations, which serve primarily their rural members. However, owing to some remaining institutional problems, currently the majority of RCCs have not genuinely become co-operatives and they are still far away from fulfilling the role of leading the rural financial sector.

During the experiment reforms launched to RCCs, there are three options for RCC's ownership structure, which are respectively, shareholding system, joint venture and co-operative system. Provinces that are involved in the experiment reform can choose their own co-operative system depending on their regional conditions. They can also select their operational form between shareholding commercial bank, joint venture banks or co-operatives. For this reform, RCCs are moved under the administration of the provincial governments by setting up a supervision and administrative mechanism under which "the co-operatives will be self-restraining and responsible for their own losses and profits, but regulated by the provincial governments to enforce their compliance with laws and regulations, and their responsibilities are subject to the macro control and overseeing of the central government". It is foreseeable that, without effective support and directions to the rural co-operative financial associations, most RCCs will gradually become commercial financial institutions. When these financial institutions 'got carried away' in their effort to reduce cost and avoid risk, they will deviate more and more from satisfying the capital needs for low or medium income farmers. This will further stimulate the growth of private 'informal' or personal finance in rural areas.

In the construction of the rural financial system, it is imperative to recognize the weak position of RCCs and the fact that the rural 'informal finance' is growing, and to draw on the forces from all sides under the support and directions of the government to restructure the RCCs steadily and actively. I hereby put forward the following suggestions:

Firstly, encourage some of the RCCs which insist on continuing to go the co-operative path to transform into real co-operative financial organizations. The constitution of the RCCs should be modified based on the co-operative spirit with a view to attracting farmers with capital needs. Members/representatives assembly should be held regularly in line with the principle of "one member, one vote". Co-operative Council and Board of Supervision shall be selected in conformity with the regulations of the constitution. RCCs' directors shall be appointed by each co-operative Council. To avoid too much control by the internal staff, members' share shall account for more than 70% (including the original collective share) and staff share shall be limited to below 20%. Preferentially favorable policies such as business tax and income tax exemption for RCCs, provision of small deposit withdrawal reserve and moderate re-loan services for borrowing over the amount deposited etc., should be provided by the central and local authorities.

Secondly, encourage RCCs to serve the local farmers. Apart from conventional financial business such as settlement, remittance and savings, etc., co-operative financial organization should also be allowed to provide consultancy or intermediary services such as bonds exchange, insurance purchase and leasing. At places where co-operative financial associations have been established, RCCs can be entrusted by ADBC to handle some policy based business and paid certain business handling fee. Otherwise they can also be entrusted by the commercial banks to perform credit assessments on the farmers.

Thirdly, help RCCs to set up a mechanism to share risks and profits. As a county associated union, RCC is a primary legal personal entity. It operates independently, is responsible for its own losses and profits. Interest is not payable on the subscriptions of the members, but dividends will be distributed to the members at the end of the year.

7.4.5. *Regulate 'Popular Finance'*

The supply-demand equilibrium for the rural financial sector has not been maintained; it is very difficult and costly for farmers to obtain loans from normal financial institutions, and the interest rate for depositing at formal financial institutions is low. As rural economy developed, it is an indisputable fact that popular finance has gained popularity in the rural areas of China. Apart from the rise of various traditional financing forms such as 'rotating credit associations' and private money houses, other forms of fund raising such as 'savings foundations' and 'funds foundations' are also operating in a "half open, half underground" state. Based on the survey targeted at over 20,000 farmers throughout 31 provinces and municipalities by the Policy Research Office of the CPC, Central Committee and the Observation Office from Ministry of Agriculture, popular financing is still the primary financial channel for counties and rural areas. In 2002, the amount lent to each farmer averaged 1,414 Yuan, increased by 394 Yuan than 2000, of which 71.8% came from popular finance (up by 24.1%) and the amount lent to each rural household averaged 1,015 Yuan approximately. Moreover, interest bearing popular finance (most of which charge high interest rates) made up 53.3% of this amount. If we round the number of the rural population to 200 million, in 2002, capital paid out to farmers from the rural private financial market ('curb market') reached over 200 billion Yuan, of which interest bearing loans exceeded 100 billion Yuan.

The 'curb market' (activities involved in popular/informal finance) in the rural areas has, to some extent, accelerated the development of the agriculture industry as well as the side productions and operations, and has helped solve some problems for the livelihood of the farmer. Various government and regulatory departments at all levels have always attempted to ban and discourage private financial activities, and the 'curb market' has never been integrated into the regulatory scope of the state. The vitality of popular finance and its unregulated activities will seriously affect the financial order of the rural areas and make it more difficult for farmers to pay back their loans. As such, I propose a combination of 'guiding' and 'blocking' approaches to put the unregistered forms of popular finance under control.

Firstly, protect the legitimate rights of the borrowers and lenders engaged in the informal financing activities, and restrict interest rates. In the "Opinions on Hearing of Loan Cases by the People's Court" promulgated on August 13, 1991, it is stated that "the People's Court shall protect the legal rights and interests of the borrowers and lenders based on the principles of voluntary participation, mutual benefit, equality and legitimacy, and high interest rate restriction in hearing loan cases." It is also stipulated in Article 6 thereof that "interest rate for private loans can be moderately higher than banks and the local People's Court should try cases based on the actual circumstances, but the interest rate for loans shall not go above four times the interest rate of banks (including the base rate); the portion (of interest) that exceeds this ceiling will not be protected by law." This regulation should be maintained but it is suggested that "four times" be changed to "three times".

Secondly, encourage infusion of private capital into commercial financial institutions. We should allow rural commercial banks to absorb subscriptions from natural persons in the rural areas by stipulating that each natural person shall at least purchase 50,000 Yuan shares and that dividends will be distributed against the shares they hold. People who are running underground money houses would automatically suspend their previous financial operations and try to clear all the remaining problems. As for those runners who are politically reliable, professionally competent and also keen on public welfares, they shall be given the opportunities to work in the commercials banks.

Thirdly, guide the various savings foundations and rural fund foundations to convert to co-operative financial associations. The proportions that are privately owned by households can be transferred to shareholding or savings on a voluntary basis, whereby the contributors will benefit from dividends or interest in line with the constitution of the associations. The transformed structure and procedures shall be carried out under the regulations formulated by the China Banking Regulatory Commission. Again, for people who used to manage these associations — those who are politically reliable, professionally competent and also keen on public welfares — they can enter the Council or Board of Supervision through democratic elections or be hired by the Council of the Association.

Fourthly, crack down hard and unflaggingly on 'rotating credit associations', pyramid investment associations and other illicit financing activities. Better educate the vast rural population to understand the risks and undesirable and bad outcomes of these illicit fund pooling activities. As for those who run these illegal associations, they shall be tracked down and brought to justice. Other illegal forms of financing activities shall be checked and counseled in a timely fashion and dealt with accordingly. Underworld elements and loan sharks in the rural areas shall be cracked down mercilessly and brought to justice.

In the process of building a 'better-off society' — in which people enjoy reasonably comfortable life in all aspects — in China, the rural financial sector imparts a profound impact on the development of the agriculture industry, increase of rural incomes and the stability of the rural society. To develop the rural financial system, we should pay special attention to the unity between periodicity and continuity. On one hand, we should not go beyond the realities of current circumstances and pursue unrealistic development; on the other hand, we should not be too tied up by the realities and ignore conflicts and other contradictions. We shall step up the development of agriculture and social undertakings through developing the rural finance in order to lay a solid foundation for realizing the modernization of China.

References

[1] Cheng, S. W. (2001). *China's Economic Reform and Development*, Vol. 1, Beijing: China Renmin University Press (in Chinese).

[2] Cheng, S. W. (2001). *Analysis and Exploration of China's Rural Consumption Market,* Beijing: Democracy and Constructions Press (in Chinese).

[3] Yu, Y. (2002). *Investigation of the Rescue of China's Rural Finance*, Hohehot: Inner Mongolian People's Press, (in Chinese).

[4] Zhang, X. S. and He, A. (eds.) (2002). *Transformation and Innovation of Rural Finance*, Taiyuan: Shanxi Economic Press (in Chinese).

[5] Cheng, S. W. (1999). Exploration of Complex Science, in Cheng, S. W. (ed.), Chapter 1 *Complexity Science and Management*, Beijing: Democracy and Constructions Press (in Chinese).

[6] Noth, D. C. (2003). Institution, Contract and Organization, in Claude, S. (ed.), *Understanding of the System*; Beijing: Economics Press, pp. 15–18.

[7] Cheng, S. W. (1999). Fictitious Economy and Financial Crisis, *Journal of Management*, 1, 1–6, Beijing: Democracy and Constructions Press (in Chinese).

[8] Cheng, S. W. (2003). *Discussions on Fictitious Economy*, Beijing: Democracy and Constructions Press (in Chinese).

[9] Zhang, J. (ed.) (2003). *China's Rural Financial System: structure, transformation and policies*, Beijing: China Renmin University Press (in Chinese).

[10] National Bureau of Statistics of China (2004). *China Statistics Yearbook*, Beijing: China Statistics Press (in Chinese).

[11] Lin, D. G. (2004). Understanding the Situation, Focusing on the Key Areas and Comprehensively Improve the Industrialization of Agriculture, *Management and Administration on Rural Co-operative*, 6, 9–11 (in Chinese).

[12] Nicholson, N. (2003). Blackwell Encyclopedic Dictionary of Organizational Behavior, in Nicholson, N. (ed.), Translated by Lin, Z. Y. and Yan, L. H., Beijing: International Business University Press.

[13] Zheng, Z. Y. (1993). *Perspective on Financial Phenomena in Wenzhou*, Hangzhou: Zhejiang University Press (in Chinese).

[14] Jia, J. H. and Wang, Y. (2003). Unbalance and Rectifications of Rural Financial Market, *China's Township and Village Enterprises*, 8, 31–32 (in Chinese).

[15] Cheng, G. Q. (2000). WTO's Rules on Agriculture and China's Agricultural Development, Beijing: China Economics Press (in Chinese).

Chapter 8

Status Quo and Prospects of China's Venture Capital Industry

8.1. Features of Venture Capital and International Developments

Venture capital refers to risk investment in new technology projects that involve high risks but offer the prospect for high returns. It is, in essence, a speculative investment in a portfolio of high risks and high returns projects, realizing divestment of owner's equity though sale or initial public offering (IPO) of successful projects. This allows investors not only to offset losses in unsuccessful projects but also to realize high returns.

Venture capital has five main features[1]:

1. It is a (very) risky investment. As venture capital supports chiefly innovative technology and products with high risks in terms of technology, economics and market, its average success rate is merely 30%. According to some veteran American venture capitalists, only one third of their invested projects achieved great success, one third broke even, and one third incurred huge losses. However, as the returns on investment (ROI) of successful projects is usually very high, these risk projects can still attract some investors for speculation.
2. It is a portfolio investment. To diversify risks, venture capital is often invested in a project portfolio with multiple projects,

offsetting losses of unsuccessful projects and realizing returns through divestment of successful projects after sale or IPO.

3. It is a long-term investment. Venture capital realizes returns through divestment typically after three to seven years during which incremental capital is needed for projects with prospects of success.
4. It is an equity investment. Venture capital is an equity capital, not a debt capital, focusing more on the prospects of growth and added value of assets than the short-term profit or loss of invested projects. It expects high returns through divestment. Venture capital supports businesses (often called venture companies) that typically have a negative cash flow and operating losses during the growth period. General investors are reluctant to invest, but venture capitalists start more from the perspective of owner's equity, willing to invest as long as a venture company's value could grow and increase.
5. It is a kind of professional investment. Venture capital is not limited to the funding for entrepreneurs, but also offers expertise, experiences and networks to help them succeed through involvement in improving organization structure, business direction, financial management and management staffing.

The United States (US) is the first as well as the country with the largest amounts of venture capital. A rigorous study of American experience is of great value to the development of China's venture capital industry.[2]

As a special form of investment, venture capital can be traced back as early as to the 1920s and 1930s when some wealthy American families and individual investors provided 'seeding fund' for such projects as Eastern Airlines and Xerox that later achieved huge success. But the world's first venture capital firm is credited to American Research and Development Corporation founded in 1946. The American venture capital industry did not show its strength and become an important force of the economy until the mid 1990s after several ups and downs, going through formation in the 1950s, growth in the 1960s, recession in the 1970s, recovery in the 1980s, to setbacks in the early 1990s.

There are two types of statistics on the size of venture capital: one is the commitments to venture capital funds, and the other is the actual input, or the amount raised by venture capital backed companies.

Beginning from 1992, venture capital has seen a rapid growth in the US, and the returns on investment (ROI) have been on the increase. During the two decades between 1975 and 1994, the average ROI was merely 13.1%, but in 1995, 1996 and 1997, the number jumped to 48%, 40% and 36% respectively.

The most rapid growth was seen during 1996–2000, with the actual investment input, number of backed projects and average input intensity in 2000 being 7.6, 2.5 and 3.1 times that of 1996 respectively. In 1998, 1999 and 2000, in particular, the actual input doubled each year. In early 2000, there were around 7,000 venture companies in the Silicon Valley, with about 30 people becoming millionaires each day, 500 new ventures start-ups, and the same number going bust.

The statistics of American venture capital between 1998 and 2005 are shown in Table 8.1.

Based on the data, we can describe the changes of American venture capital as in Fig 8.1.

As shown in Fig 8.1, American venture capital began to fall in 2001 after it reached the peak of 100 billion US dollars in 2000. However, a quarterly analysis shows that American venture capital began to decline from the second quarter of 2000. It was 5.081 billion in Q1, 8.323 billion in Q2, 8.969 billion in Q3, and 15.813 billion in Q4 of 1999. The peak came in Q1 of 2000, reaching 19.354 billion, but it began to fall from Q2, from 18.927 billion in Q2, to 16.764 billion in Q3, 13.71 billion in Q4 of 2000, and 10.11 billion in Q1 of 2001. This tendency coincides with the development of American economy. In 2002, 2003 and 2004, the American venture capital remained at 18–20 billion US dollars.

Table 8.2 shows that American venture capital would rise slowly.

It also shows that most of the funds raised in 2000 and 2001 were used for investment. The percentage of investment was 79.94% and 67.43% in 2000 and 2001 respectively. But the ratio went down sharply from 2002 onwards, to 58.66% in 2002 and 17.92% in 2004.

Table 8.1 Statistics of American Venture Capital during 1998–2005

	1998	1999	2000	2001	2002	2003	2004	2005
Commitments to VC Funds	/	202	249					
Total Amount Raised (100 million US dollars)	/	345.4	690.8					
Actual Input (100 million US dollars)	163.4	452.2	852.8	345.7	209.6	185.8	210.4	2139
Number. of Venture-Backed Projects	2200	3874	5447	2934	2190	2007	2120	216.2
Average Input Intensity (10K/project)	500	700	1100					

Source: The data in the above table is adapted from The PricewaterhouseCoopers MoneyTree Survey in Partnership with VentureOne.

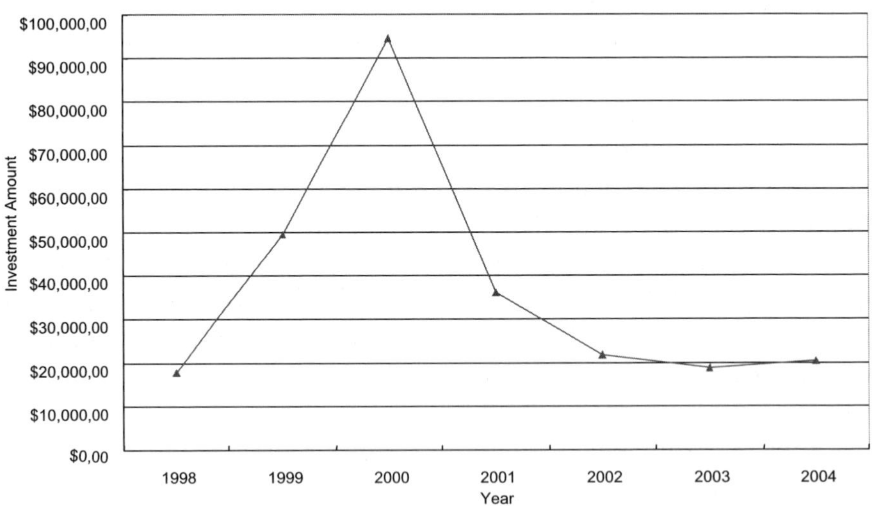

Fig. 8.1 Total Amount Raised by Venture Backed Companies in US (million US dollars).

Table 8.2 Total Commitments to Venture Capital Funds in US (million US dollars)

	Total Commitments	% of Investment	% of Non-investment	Balance
1999	$44,540.26	94.54%	5.46%	$2,432.78
2000	$64,029.30	79.94%	20.06%	$12,841.52
2001	$38,839.38	67.43%	32.57%	$12,651.27
2002	$11,380.00	58.66%	41.34%	$4,704.90
2003	$7,853.20	35.93%	64.07%	$5,031.25
2004	$15,765.60	17.92%	82.08%	$12,940.30
2005	$	%	%	$

Source: The data in the above table is taken from The PricewaterhouseCoopers MoneyTree Survey in Partnership with VentureOne.

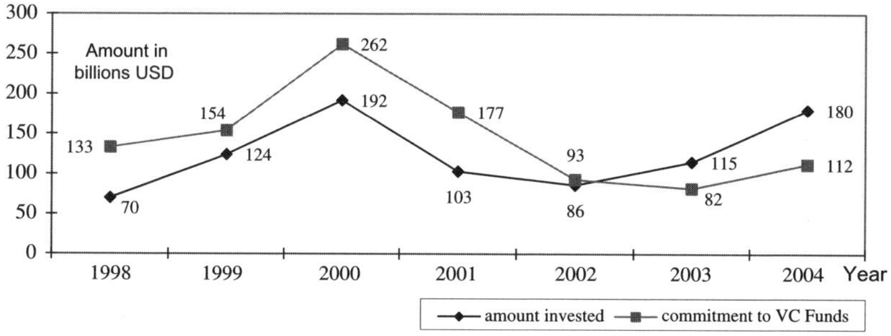

Fig. 8.2 Total Commitments to Global Venture Capital Funds and Actual Amount Raised by Venture Backed Companies during 1998–2004.

Source: The data are taken from The PricewaterhouseCoopers/Venture Economy/ NVCA/CVCA Annual Report/EVCA Annual Report/AVCJ Report/Latin American Private Equity Investment Analysis/SAVCA Private Equity Survey.

There are abundant venture capital funds in the US, but the venture capitalists are increasingly cautious after the collapse of the dot.com bubble. The total amount raised has reached 53.6 billion US dollars, and with the development of American economy, the venture capital industry can be expected to continue to grow.

The global venture capital has experienced a similar development to that of the US. The total commitments to global venture capital funds and the actual amount raised by venture backed companies during 1998–2004 are shown in Fig 8.2.

Table 8.3 Top 10 Venture Capital Countries

Ranking	Country	Amount (Billion US Dollars)	As of the World %	As of GDP (%)
1	US	113.7	64	1.0
2	UK	23.7	13	1.1
3	Japan	6.6	4	0.1
4	France	6.5	4	0.3
5	Germany	4.7	3	0.2
6	Spain	2.4	1	0.2
7	Netherlands	2.1	1	0.4
8	Sweden	2.0	1	0.6
9	Italy	1.8	1	0.1
10	China	1.4	1	0.06
	Other	12.0	7	0.0
	Total	176.9	100	0.3

Global venture capital is concentrated in Central North America and Europe. In 2004, North America accounted for 66% of global venture capital investment, an increase of eight percentage points over 1998; Europe accounted for 26%, an increase of two percentage points over 1998. The Asia-Pacific accounted for 6% in 2004, a decrease of one percentage point over 1998. The rest of the world went down from 11% in 1998 to 2% in 2004.

Table 8.3 lists the top ten countries in terms of investment amount, percentage of the world, and percentage of GDP.

A close look at the global venture capital reveals a few common features in its development.

8.1.1. *Venture Capital is Playing an Increasing Important Role in Promoting Economic Development*

The experiences from the US and other developed countries show that venture capital can promote economic development in the following aspects:

8.1.1.1. *Promote economic growth and increase employment*

In the 1980s, for example, the US improved its economic efficiency through adjustment of economic structure, streamlining and deregulation, but it lost 44 million jobs in the meantime. It was venture capital that created a new market and a large number of businesses that offered 73 million new jobs, and which sustained American economic growth in the 1990s by supporting the development of science and technology.

According to the survey of the Organization of Economic Cooperation and Development (OECD), the number of new businesses created in the US during 1984–1991 was four times that of France, and eight times that of Denmark. Between 1992 and 1996, 85% of new jobs were created by small businesses. The statistics by American National Venture Capital Association show that over ten million Americans were employed by venture backed companies in 2003, with a total sale of 1.8 trillion US dollars.

The United Kingdom (UK) lost its competitiveness in the world market in the early 1980s due to economic difficulty, policy mistake in science and technology, slow-down of emerging industries, and recession of traditional industries. Given the worsening economy, the UK government resorted to venture capital to promote economic growth. In the following decade, it formulated a series of measures to support the development of venture capital, resulting in an average increase of 30% annually. In 1984, the total investment by British venture capital funds was 190 million pounds, and by 1996, the number had reached 18.528 billion pounds, 97.52 times that of 1984. In 1997, the UK became the world's second largest country of venture capital, accounting for 20% of venture capital investment in Europe. In the UK today, 90% of funds needed by science and technology are provided by venture capital, and 85% of venture capital is used to develop new industries. With the help of venture capital, the investment in biological engineering and information technology (IT) has increased by nine times over 1984, allowing the UK to take a leading position in the world. Each year, about 15% of new jobs are created in association with venture capital, and in the recent decade, a total of one million new jobs were created by small- and medium-sized high-tech firms.

8.1.1.2. *Promote technological innovation and entrepreneurship*

Venture backed companies are generally more focused on R&D, and biotechnological and medical companies, in particular, invest a significant part of venture capital in R&D, which not only promotes technological innovation but also improves a nation's overall quality and prestige.

A developed venture capital market offers thousands of young Americans not only more job opportunities, but also opportunities of entrepreneurship. In the US, venture capital allows many entrepreneurs to realize their start-up dreams. In sustaining social and economic development and realizing high returns for investors, these entrepreneurs create huge wealth for themselves.

In recent years, a number of high-tech firms have stepped onto the world stage from the Silicon Valley. These venture incubated 'babies' have grown to become the pillars of American economy. During the years before and after 2000, about 1,000 venture companies were created each year in the Silicon Valley, among which about one third succeeded, one third merely survived, and one third failed few years later.

8.1.1.3. *Improve business performance*

Statistics show that, during 2000–2003, venture backed companies had better performance than any other companies in creating job opportunities and sales volume. The new jobs created by venture companies are increasing by 6.5% annually, while employees employed by other private businesses are decreasing by 2.3% annually. Similarly, the sales of venture companies are increasing by 12% annually, while the same number for other American domestic companies is merely 6.5%.

8.1.1.4. *Improve investing efficiency and returns*

In general, the ROI of venture capital is higher than that of other investment tools. During 1965–1985, for example, the average ROI of venture capital was 19%, two times that for stocks, and five times that of long-term bonds. In the UK in 1996, the net ROI of venture capital funds was 14.2%, higher than any other financial products in the same year (11.7% for stocks, 7.6% for bonds, and 6.1% for cash assets). Even though the global venture capital was experiencing a hard time in recent years, the ROI had maintained at a high level.

8.1.2. *Venture Capital is Directed towards High-tech Industry*

Most of the venture capital funds have flowed to such high-tech industries as IT and life science In the US, for example, there are over 4,000 venture capital firms, with a total investment of 100 billion US dollars, helping to establish the US as a global leader in information industry, and allowing the Internet, biological engineering, healthcare and semiconductor industries to become the fastest growing industries. Each year, thousands of high-tech projects are supported by venture capital. The investment structure of American venture capital is shown in Fig. 8.3.

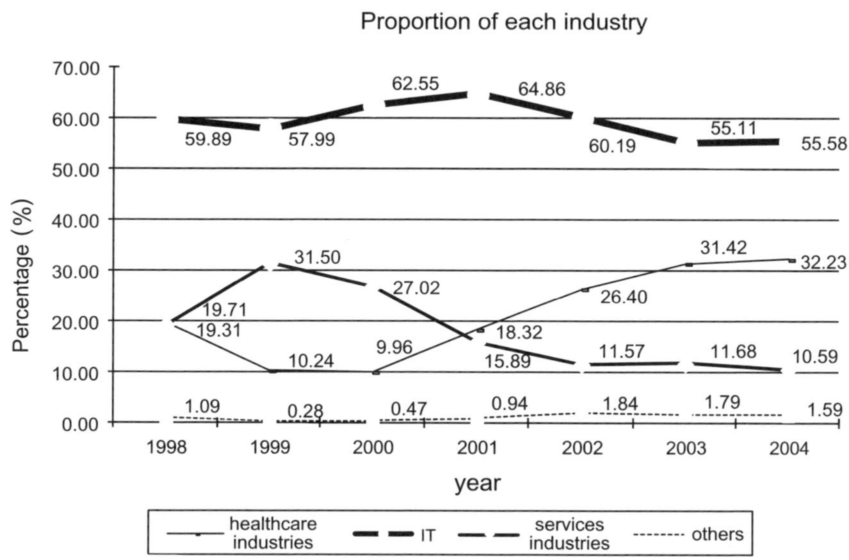

Fig. 8.3 Investment Structure of American Venture Capital.

As shown in Fig. 8.3, the IT industry accounted for 60% in the total of venture capital investment. The biotechnology industry kept increasing to over 30%. The service industry was decreasing, taking up about 10%, and the rest of the industries accounted for 2–3%. The same is true of Europe.- where venture capital goes primarily to IT and biotechnology.

8.1.3. *Equity Sale is the Main Exit Route of Venture Capital*

When a venture backed company succeeds, the venture capital firm wants to cash its owner's equity through divestment. The most common method is IPO or equity sale (i.e. to sell the venture to a big company through mergers and acquisitions or to sell to employees or other start-up entrepreneurs).

As venture companies usually are of smaller size despite their rapid growth, and they require constant injection of capital for their growth, their business performance indicators do not meet the requirements of traditional securities market. It is therefore necessary to create a new security market for small and medium-sized enterprises (SMEs), and for high-tech firms in particular. The small capital market of NASDAQ, for example, is created to meet the financing needs of high-tech SMEs and to provide a divestment exit for venture capital. Such a market is often called the second board. When a listed company has grown more 'mature', it can be upgraded to the national market of NASDAQ (i.e. the primary market). The dual structure of the stock market makes relisting after LBO possible.

IPO was the primary exit channel of global venture capital before the 1980s. The 1990s saw the most intensive exits of venture capital, but the percentage of IPO was decreasing. From 2000, the exit of venture capital has become increasingly difficult with the recession of the world's economy. Both the number and value of exited projects went down sharply, especially through IPO. In 2000, about 1,883 venture companies exited through IPO, and funds raised through IPO were 210 billion US dollars. In 2003, the numbers were further reduced to 864 and 50 billion US dollars respectively. It was not until in 2004

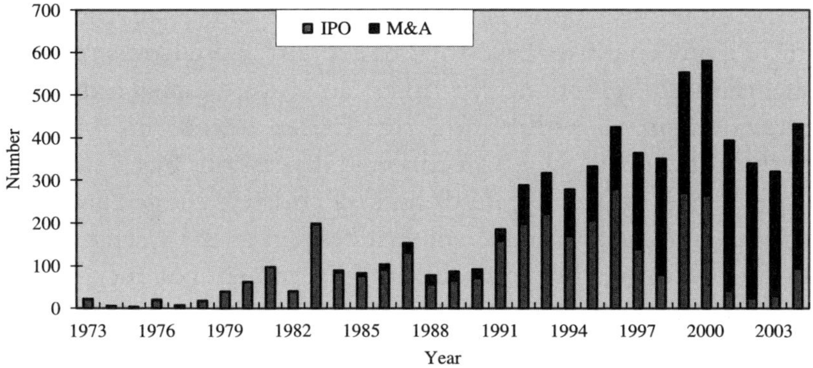

Fig. 8.4. The number of venture projects that withdraw by IPO and M&A in the U.S. during 1973–2004.

Source: PricewaterhouseCoopers/Thomson Economic Committee/NVCA 2004 Annual Report.

that exit through IPO had a slow recovery — the number and value of exited venture companies jumped to 1,516 and 124 billion US dollars. However, equity transfer has replaced IPO as the main exit channel.

Fig. 8.4 compares the number of projects exited through IPO and the number of projects exited through mergers and acquisitions (M&As) for the period 1973–2004 in the US.

In 2000, 264 venture companies exited through IPO in the US, and 316 through M&As. In 2003, the number of venture companies exited through IPO dropped sharply to 29; in 2004, the number climbed to 93, with a total of 11.014 billion US dollars in raised funds. In the same year, the total amount exited through M&As reached 15.21 billion US dollars, involving 333 projects.

In recent years, the percentage of exit through IPO went down to 10% in Europe.

8.1.4. *Venture Capital has Strong Support and Encouragement from the Government*

Although venture capital plays an important role in economic development, its inherent risk is so high that investors are reluctant to invest without the support of the government. Therefore, the government of many countries have tried to support and encourage venture capital through legislation. The American venture capital industry, for example, began to wither after the 1970s, despite its remarkable growth in the 1960s, due to economic depression, bleak stock market, regulation of pension funds and oil crisis etc. Urged by venture capitalists and entrepreneurs, some statesmen in the Carter administration worked together to create an environment conducive to venture capital. During 1978–1981, five laws were passed to encourage the development of venture capital. The 1978 legislation, for example, reduced the capital value added tax from 49.5% to 28%, providing a direct incentive for long-term equity investment, and consequently, the commitments to VC funds increased by ten-fold in 1979. The 1981 Economic Recovery Tax Law further reduced the capital value added tax from 28% to 20%, allowing the commitments to VC funds to double in the same year.

The supportive measures include tax reduction, government guarantees, and risk subsidization.

8.2. Venture Capital in China: Background[1,3,4] and Development

The development of venture capital industry in China falls into three periods:

The first is the inception period lasting from 1985 to 1996. After the reform and opening up, China sent a large number of scholars to the US for further studies, some of whom, including the author, began to notice the important role of American venture capital in promoting industrialization of high technology, and attempted to introduce the concept to China. In the "Decisions on the Structural Reform of Science and Technology" adopted in March 1985, the Central Committee of the Communist Party of China proposed that "venture capital can be set up to support the R&D of fast changing and high-risk technology", representing the emergence of China's venture capital industry.

In September 1985, the State Council approved the establishment of "China New Technology Venture Capital Company", the first of its kind in mainland China. In 1986, the State Commission of Science and Technology for the first time mapped out the strategy for the development of China's venture capital industry. In the following years, some provinces and departments set up a number of small businesses involved in financing for high-tech projects. However, owing to obstacles brought borne of old mindset and system, the gap between technological and economic reforms, lack of financing channels, immaturity of capital market, irrationality of allocation system, and ambiguity of intellectual property rights, China's venture capital industry had a very difficulty time in its development. A few venture capital firms even went astray, using funds to speculate on stocks, futures and real estate. In the end, they were forced to close because of violations of laws and huge losses.

Since 1990, foreign (off-shore) investors began to set up venture capital funds in China, such as IDG, Walden China, etc. The management of these funds had extensive experience in venture capital, but most of them agreed that the market environment for venture capital in China was still immature and under-developed. Consequently, the majority of funds were invested to support the re-production and expansion of existing enterprises, rather than to support the growth of high-tech companies.

The second phase is the emerging period lasting from 1997 to 2001. With the intensification and progress of the reform and opening up, the conditions for China's venture capital industry are becoming increasingly 'mature', and what's more, the development of China's socialist market economy gives rise to the need for venture capital. First of all, the socialist market economy provides a solid foundation for the development of venture capital industry. Second, China has many valuable scientific innovations and discoveries 'waiting' to be commercialized and industrialized. Third, high-quality management teams are being formed in China. Fourth, Chinese residents have huge bank savings that can be used in direct investment. Fifth, the consultancy service industries in technology, finance and law are growing fast. Last, the Chinese securities market is getting increasingly developed. All these have helped to provide a favorable environment for the development of venture capital in China.

In the "Decisions on the Structural Reform of Science and Technology" during the 9th Five-Year Plan promulgated in 1996, the State Council reiterated the importance of capital venture for China. Against this backdrop, some departments and regions began to experiment with venture capital actively.

In March 1998, the Central Committee of China National Democratic Construction Association submitted a proposal to the First Plenary Session of the Ninth Congress of the People's Political Consultative Conference on the development of venture capital in China. The proposal was listed as No. 1 proposal, winning great attention and support from the government and society, and a new round of development for China's venture capital was ushered in.

At first, the relevant departments under the State Council came into the picture by directing implementation, and the State Development Planning Commission gave a positive response to the above proposal. Second, some local governments took immediate action, and those of Beijing, Shanghai and Shenzhen, in particular, announced supporting measures and policies successively. Third, venture capitalists at home and abroad were optimistic about the future of China. The Ministry of Science and Technology and IDG, for example, were working together for possible cooperation. Fourth, many domestic high-tech firms turned to venture capital for support and growth. Fifth, there were extensive research and discussions on venture capital. Workshops and seminars were held on a regular basis, and the National Commission of Natural Science Fund and the Ministry of Science and Technology completed several research projects on venture capital, putting forward a few policy recommendations on legislation, management and financial support for venture capital. Sixth, the mass media did a wide coverage on the topic, and played an important role in disseminating the idea. Despite old mindsets, inadequacies of system and law, problems and mistakes, China's venture capital industry witnessed a rapid growth during this period.

The efforts and initiatives made between 1997 and 2001 laid a solid foundation for the development of China's venture capital.

According to some (incomplete) statistics, there had been only 38 venture capital institutions by 1996, but this figure had increased to 246 by 2001. The total funds managed by venture capital institutions had only been 3.608 billion Yuan, but had increased to 40.526 billion Yuan by 2001. The five-year growth was remarkable. Today, Beijing, Shanghai and Shenzhen have become the centers of China's venture capital. By 2001, the three cities had a combined 150 venture capital institutions, accounting for 60% nationally. The total funds involved had reached 28.783 billion Yuan, taking up 70% nationally. Each of the three cities has its own special feature. Beijing has Zhongguancun Park where innovative enterprises are concentrated, Shanghai has Zhangjiang High-tech Park supported by high-tech industries, and Shenzhen has a high-tech industry belt formed by the activities of an annual high-tech trade fair.

The third is the period of adjustment. Starting from 2002, under the influence of the global economic slowdown and recession of international venture capital, China's venture capital met with great difficulties and entered a period of adjustment or some might call 'consolidation'.

The development of China's venture capital industry after 2002 has displayed the following characteristics:

8.2.1. *The Total Volume of Venture Capital and Investment has been Growing Steadily, but the Percentage of Local Venture Capital has been Diminishing*

Since official statistics on venture capital are unavailable, questionnaires have been used to collect related information. The profile of China's venture capital during 2001–2005 is shown in Table 8.4.

As China lacked relevant laws and policies to encourage venture capital, no 'exit channel' was available, and the capital market was consistently gloomy. The majority of local venture capital institutions were 'buried' or stuck in the invested companies, with little chance of profit-making or exit, which greatly reduced their ability to reinvest. Consequently, the capital increment and number of venture capital institutions experienced a significant decrease. However, since

Table 8.4 Profile of China's Venture Capital During 2001–2005

Year	No. of Samples	Total Volume of Venture Capital (100 million yuan)	Percentage of Foreign Capital (%)	Number. of Investment Projects	Total Volume of Investment (100 million yuan)
2001		405.3	21.9	210	50.0
2002					55.9
2003	180	325.3	5.0	315	37.1
2004	141	438.7	15.0	325	37.8
2005	150	464.5	33.9	307	54.7

the overseas venture capital institutions were optimistic about China's economic outlook, they had increased their businesses in China steadily and this had somewhat offset the reduction of China's venture capital institutions in number and investment. Some of the local venture capital institutions had turned to financial and intermediary service markets, withdrawing their capital from venture capital fields.

Meanwhile, more and more international venture capital firms began to set up their China investment funds, or increased their investment in China. In June 2005, for example, Intel announced the setup of a 200 million US dollars fund focusing on Chinese high-tech firms. In July, Accel Partners announced the setup of joint venture capital fund in China, involving a total of 250 million US dollars. In August, Softbank Asia successfully raised a total of 643 million US dollars, 70% of which were planned for investing in Greater China.

According to some (incomplete) statistics, 40.7% of China's venture capital is controlled by foreign-owned or foreign-related institutions. In fact, an increasing number of overseas venture capital firms are coming into China. 3i and Blue Run, for example, set up their representative offices in China in 2005. In a total of 19.571 billion yuan (equivalent to 2.416 billion US dollars) raised in 2005, 85.95% was associated with foreign-related venture capital institutions, while the local firms accounted for merely 14.05%. In the first half of 2006, about 40 international venture capital institutions will come to Beijing for partnership with Chinese firms, bringing along a total of five billion yuan.

8.2.2. *There are still Gaps between Local and Overseas Venture Capital Institutions in Mindset and Practice*

In 2005, the most active international venture capital institutions were IDG, Softbank Asia, TDFVC, DFJ, Intel Investment, 3i, Warburg Pincus, and Acer Technology Ventures, and the top local performers included NewMargin Ventures, Shenzhen Capital Group, Legend Capital, Merchants Technology, Shandong High-tech Investment, and Tsinghua-LH. In the 150 venture capital institutions involved in the questionnaire, 114 were local firms, and 36 were foreign-related firms. A comparison between the two reveals that they are significantly different in several significant aspects:

Investment strength. International venture capital institutions are generally superior to local counterparts in investment strength. The 36 foreign-invested firms control a total of 67.545 billion yuan of capital, among which 18.907 billion yuan can be invested in China, with each firm having an average of 526 million yuan of capital. To contrast, the 114 local firms controls a total of 29.414 billion yuan of capital, among which 27.543 billion yuan can be invested in China, with each firm having an average of 248 million yuan of capital.

Investment intensity. International venture capital institutions are also superior to local firms in investment intensity. In 2005, they invested in 143 projects, involving a total of 3.11 billion yuan, with an average of 21.75 million yuan for each project. The local firms invested in 215 projects, involving a total of 2.358 billion yuan, with an average of 10.97 million yuan for each project, almost half of their foreign counterparts.

Investment stage. International venture capital institutions tend to invest in the early stages of new ventures, but in the recent years, local venture capital firms began to increase their investment in projects in the start-up and growth stages. In 2005, the percentages of investment by foreign-invested firms in the start-up, growth, expansion, and maturity stages were 14.7%, 43.1%, 26.5% and 15.7% respectively, and the same numbers were 22.5%, 42.8%, 20.3% and 14.4% for local firms. No significant difference can be observed between the two.

Number of talents. International venture capital institutions have more professional managers than local firms. 32% of them have 10–20 managers, 43% have 5–10 managers, and 18% have less than 5 managers, while in local firms, the percentages are 19%, 36% and 38% respectively.

Investment focus. The focus of China's venture capital is quite close to the tendency of global venture capital, i.e. IT, biotechnology and new materials. However, the investment focus of foreign-invested institutions is quite different from that of local firms. The top five industries invested by foreign-invested firms are semiconductor (48.0%), IC (11.9%), telecommunications (10.8%), new energy (9.3%) and Internet (3.4%); for local firms, they are medical service (11.2%), new materials (8.0%), biotechnology (7.2%), new energy (5.3%), and software (5.0%). Obviously, the foreign-invested firms are more interested in semiconductor and IT, while local firms focus more on medicine and biotechnology.

8.2.3. *Beijing, Shanghai and Shenzhen are Three Preferred Locations for Venture Capital*

The questionnaire shows that each major area had some venture capital in 2005, but 83% of foreign venture capital was concentrated in Beijing, Shanghai and Shenzhen, and the remaining 17% was spread in the east part of China. In recent years, the three cities are taking up increasingly more shares in the total of China's venture capital. In 2003, the percentage was 51.0%, and in 2004 and 2005, it was further increased to 55.0% and 59.9%. Among the three cities, Beijing, Shanghai and Shenzhen accounted for 31.2%, 11.2% and 17.5% respectively in 1995, with foreign venture capital taking up 71.2%, 63.6% and 25.4% respectively. From an annual perspective, the three cities are also the most preferred locations for venture capital, taking up 50% in the total of China's venture capital.

8.2.4. *Overseas IPO has Become an Important Exit for Projects Backed by Foreign Venture Capital*

In a total of 1,597 projects invested by 118 venture capital firms in 2005, 56.6% are still in operation, 19.3% have exited through equity transfer, 11.5% have exited through IPO, 8.8% are preparing for IPO, and 3.8% are in liquidation.

In a total of 553 exited projects, 55.9% exited through equity transfer, 33.1% exited through IPO, and 11% exited through liquidation. Among the projects invested by local firms, the percentages of the three channels were 69%, 17% and 14% respectively; and for projects invested by overseas firms, the percentages were 35%, 58% and 7% respectively.

Most of the venture capital institutions choose to exit through IPO on overseas markets due to the gloomy local capital market and regulation of foreign exchange under the capital account item. In a total of 183 projects exited through IPO, 139 had IPO on overseas markets, taking up 76%, and 40 had IPO on the local markets, taking up 24%. This is particularly true of foreign venture capital institutions. As they are prohibited from setting up venture capital funds in China, they have both fundraising and divestment on overseas markets. In a total of 126 projects with IPO, 112 (88.9%) have IPO on overseas markets, and 14 (11.1%) have IPO on the local markets.

The most favorite market for overseas IPO is NASDAQ. To date, there are 25 Chinese companies listed on NASDAQ, creating a "Chinese board". As overseas investors are optimistic about China's economy, most of the Chinese companies on NASDAQ have an impressive performance, such as Sina.com, NetEase, Sohu.com, SNDA, Focus Media and Baidu. Suntech Power had a similar performance when it went IPO on New York Stock Exchange in 2005. The same is true of companies listed on the primary and growth boards of Hong Kong and Singapore.

8.3. Prospect of China's Venture Capital

Entering the 21st century, the world's economy is exhibiting three new tendencies: knowledge economy is becoming the new form of society, virtual economy is becoming the new model of economic activities, and web economy is becoming the new means of economic operation. All of them constitute a great challenge to China.

To meet the challenge, we first of all need to increase the efficiency of knowledge transformation, allowing knowledge to be quickly transformed into factors promoting productivity; second, we need to increase the efficiency of capital operation for high returns; and third, we need to improve the efficiency of economic operation for a balanced, harmonious, and rapid growth of economy. China is facing the task of increasing the three efficiencies simultaneously, and venture capital is one of the most important means to realize the three improvements by supporting innovation.

At the 16th National Congress of the Communist Party of China, Mr. Jiang Zemin proposed the objective to build a well-being society, pointing out that "venture capital should be allowed to play a role in the national economy, and a viable system should be created to support technological innovation and entrepreneurship in capital operation and talent pooling". The knowledge economy is featured by the dominance of knowledge-based industries in the economic structure, and the leading role of knowledge-related factors in the economic growth. In the meantime, knowledge factors will be the most critical factors to productivity, and knowledge cost will take up the largest share of products. Whoever possesses knowledge, he captures the commanding height of technology. Technological innovation and industralialization of high technology supported by venture capital will allow China to become a "brain country" in an era of knowledge economy that creates knowledge, and possesses core technology with proprietary intellectual property rights, rather than a "skeleton country" that merely applies knowledge and introduces technology.

In a peaceful environment, the competition between countries is primarily the competition of economic strength, which essentially involves the competition of strength in science and technology. In the competition of strength in science and technology, strength of talents is the most critical factor, especially their innovative ability. China's international competitiveness can not be improved without an abundance of talents with innovative competence. In this sense, venture capital provides a stage for innovative talents to convert their innovations to commercialized products and technology, and to realize their own value while creating wealth for the society and investors.

The building of a well-being society requires China to develop its venture capital industry unswervingly. However, as China is a developing country transiting from a planned economy to a market economy, the development of its venture capital must be a long process — its progress is much dependent on the deepening of the reform and development of science and technology.

In 2001, the writer put forward a development objective for China's venture capital industry: to create a sound venture capital system in 10 years, with the actual amount of investment reaching 10 billion yuan annually. To realize the objective, a three-step strategy should be followed:

8.3.1. *Promote China's Venture Capital Industry under the Existing Legal Framework*

Venture capital consulting and management companies can be created, for example, to evaluate, recommend and manage venture projects for investors. There are two major sources of projects. First, China has a total of 30,000 scientific achievements annually, among which 27,000 projects are not able to be converted to commercialized products. In such a huge amount, it is not difficult to find viable projects with great potentials. The second source is the inventions or patents by overseas Chinese scholars. Before the legislation of a venture capital law, projects can be recommended to individual investors, allowing innovators and investors to create joint venture firms to realize the transformation of scientific achievements. The evaluation of venture capital projects should be combined with management to ensure its objectivity and accuracy.

When individual investors have abundant capital and are willing to unite, they should also be allowed to set up venture capital firms according to the Company Law, directly involved in venture capital businesses. These types of companies are usually controlled by the government, and funded by investment companies affiliated to the government, with an objective to promote the development of local venture capital and high-tech industry. Venture capital firms of small size often seek common or strategic investors.

8.3.2. *Create Venture Capital Funds and Develop Related Regulations and Administrative Methods to Absorb Domestic and Overseas Capital*

Venture capital is often invested in a cluster of projects, among which projects with chances of success need huge supplemental capital. Therefore, venture capital funds must absorb adequate social capital to meet the increasing need for fundraising. Overseas venture capital funds have three basic types: independent funds, funds associated with large companies, and funds associated with financial institutions. As a special form of private placements, venture capital funds should be managed with specific regulations and administrative methods, especially on fundraising, management, monitoring, and liquidation of funds, as well on qualifications, rights and obligations of fund champions. When such regulations are in place, venture capital funds can raise funds from domestic and international investors, and turn consulting or investment funds into fund managers, operating as a limited partnership company.

8.3.3. *Establish a Sound Venture Capital Investment System and Provide Necessary Support and an Exit for Venture Capital*

The government should encourage venture capital through legislation, including preferential policies in capital contribution, subsidy, warranty, interest discount and tax reduction, and regulations on

M&As of venture companies. The government should also formulate laws and regulations to regulate venture capital intermediaries.

Despite difficulties and setbacks, China's venture capital industry has basically completed the first stage after seven years of painstaking efforts. Currently, private placements and limited partnership are still prohibited in law, and domestic venture capital institutions are primarily established in the form of limited liability corporations, operating as investment companies or investment management companies. In organization structure, 104 venture capital institutions out of a total of 132 firms in the 2005 survey adopted the limited liability corporation form, taking up 79%; 12 firms adopted the shareholding company form, taking up 9%; and only seven firms adopted the limited partnership form, taking up 5%. In operation model, in a total of 110 venture capital institutions covered in the 2005 survey, 47% were operating as investment companies; 16% were operating as investment management companies; and 37% were operating as investment + investment management companies. Presently, China's venture capital is operating in line with the corporation system, and major decisions must be approved by the board of directors. Such a corporate governance arrangement is meant to solve the inconsistency of interests between the owner and the management. To realize the shift to a limited partnership system, project managers should be given more empowerment and autonomy under the existing framework of corporate governance prescribed by the Company Law, facilitating the creation of venture capitalists for China, and the creation of a group of qualified general partners when venture capital firms operate as limited partnership companies in future. Many venture capital firms are blind in investment, often making hasty decisions without serious investigation and evaluation. Therefore, some of them have tried to set up an advisory committee to help with their decision-making. It is well advised that China's venture capital firms should not create a pyramid structure with too many layers like general companies. A flat and semi-autonomous learning organization is more appropriate, with only two levels consisting of a general manager and several project managers, each of whom is supported by 1–3 assistants.

China's venture capital firms can use the soft commitment approach in fundraising. First, the registered capital is contributed by shareholders, ranging from 30 to 100 million yuan. Second, 10–20% of the registered capital is allocated as seed funds to support projects at the start-up stage. Third, venture capitalists make a soft commitment to invested ventures. The right of capital contribution is allocated according to percentage of equity ownership, but can be transferred among shareholders. Shareholders involved in venture capital should be committed to capital contribution according to percentage of equity ownership when projects recommended by managers are approved by the board of directors. Capital can be injected through the venture capital firm, or directly to the venture company. One benefit of such a soft commitment is that capital is contributed only when viable projects are identified, avoiding the embarrassment of having a huge amount of capital in hand but without viable projects to invest. There is a high risk that venture capital is not invested in venture companies, but in the speculation of real estate, futures and stocks. The second benefit is to prevent moral hazard which is likely to occur when several millions of funds fall into the hand of the management of companies with poor corporate governance. The third benefit is to give priority to exiting shareholders in capital contribution, with the gap covered by external investors.

To promote the development of China's venture capital industry, continued efforts need to be made in the following six aspects:

8.3.3.1. *Establish venture capital funds and operate under a limited partnership system*

China's venture capital industry is still in the experiment and exploration period. There is no effective system to regulate the organization form, fundraising means and operation mechanism of venture capital firms. The most acute problem is lack of commercial credit, giving rise to dishonor of contracts, delay in payment and even financial frauds. On one hand, some technology holders are accustomed to "iron bowel", with a weak sense of responsibility for investors, and even refuse to accept the monitoring of investors. On the other hand, some venture capital firms are reluctant to take risks in business development, and prefer to speculate in securities and real estate for short-term gains, which weakens the role of venture capital in supporting innovations. China should draw on the American experience, and create venture capital funds operating under a limited partnership system.

In the US, venture capital institutions have basically four types: venture capital firms affiliated to banks, venture capital firms affiliated to large companies, government-supported small and medium-sized venture capital firms, and independent venture capital firms. As independent venture capital firms usually have an impressive operating performance, venture capital firms affiliated to banks and large companies are turning into independent venture capital institutions. Most American venture capital institutions are created in the form of limited partnership, because according to the American Taxation Law, only income tax is levied on investment revenues of partnership. Venture capital funds consist mostly of general partners and limited partners. The general partner is the venture capitalist, contributing 1–2% of registered capital, but taking responsibility for the operation with unlimited liability for the funds. The limited partner is not involved in operation, with limited liability for the funds. The partnership of each fund usually lasts for 7–10 years, and a limited partnership company has 3–9 general partners, managing several mutually-independent funds. The benefit of such an organizational form is to allow a balance of rights and obligations and a high degree of flexibility and efficiency for venture capitalists.

8.3.3.2. *Formulate and implement laws and regulations conducive to the development of venture capital*

With the development of China's venture capital, the National People's Congress is stepping up the legislation on venture capital. On December 25 of 1999, the Congress adopted the decision to amend the Company Law of the People's Republic of China, making it clear that "Qualified high-tech shareholding companies should be encouraged to raise funds directly in the securities market to promote the development of high-tech industry. The national industry policy and requirement for high technology should be observed when high-tech shareholding companies go IPO in the capital market. An independent trading system should be created for high-tech shareholding companies in line with their features, with their stocks being traded independently on the existing stock exchange. Given the lack of experience and high risk, the work should be pushed forward in measured steps". "The State Council will provide separate regulations for high-tech shareholding companies on the percentage of non-cash contribution by the founder in the form of industrial property right and non-patent technology, as well as on qualifications for IPO". The original Company Law had requirements on a company's size (i.e. no less than 50 million yuan for registered capital) and operating performance (i.e. profit for three consecutive years) for IPO, which are two major barriers for high-tech firms to go public. High-tech firms exhibit two features during the growth stage: they are small in size, and need continuous capital injection for growth, resulting in negative cash flow in early periods. Therefore, the amendment of the Company Law creates conditions for IPO of high-tech firms and provides an exit for divestment of venture capital.

In the meantime, the National People's Congress has started the legislation on venture investment funds, including on securities investment funds, industry investment funds and venture capital funds. However, as it was generally thought that the conditions for the establishment of industry investment funds and venture capital funds were still immature, the Investment Fund Law was finally reduced to the Securities Investment Fund Law, which was adopted on October 23, 2003. In April 2002, the Standing Committee of the National People's Congress adopted the Trust Law, representing that China's trust industry was put on a fast track.

On October 27 of 2005, the Company Law and the Securities Law of the People's Republic of China were adopted at the 18th Session of the 10th National People's Congress after important revisions, and came into effect on January 1st of 2006. The revision of the above two laws has drawn on international experiences and taken into account China's realities, which is of great significance to the development of China's businesses and capital market, as well as to the development of China's venture capital industry.

The amendment of the Company Law is a comprehensive revision. Only 20 articles of the existing Company Law remains intact, and all the other articles are revised with important additions or deletions. The revised Company Law contains 12 chapters with 219 articles. Although the number of articles has been greatly reduced, its philosophy of legislation is more scientific, structure is more rational, and contents are more substantial. Compared with the original one, the revised Company Law has the following benefits for venture capital:

First, it creates a "threshold" for the setup of companies. The setup of shareholding companies is no longer approved by the departments authorized by the State Council or the provincial government; and any investor can establish a shareholding company as long as the related requirements prescribed by the Company Law are met. The new law also allows the setup of "one person company" with only one shareholder. The minimum for registered capital is reduced from 100,000–500,000 to 30,000 yuan for limited companies, and from 10 million to 5 million yuan for shareholding companies. These revisions are conducive to the establishment of innovative small- and medium-sized enterprises (SMEs).

Second, the registered capital is contributed in installments. General companies are allowed to contribute in two-year installments, and investment companies are allowed to contribute in five-year installments. Therefore, investors can inject capital according to the actual needs of operation, and improves the efficiency of capital utilization by avoiding excessive capital surplus in the initial periods. This will help realize the "soft commitment" in fundraising.

Third, it loosens the requirement that accumulated external investments should not exceed 50% of a company's net assets. The original requirement is a fatal barrier to venture capital firm. If only 50% of capital can be used for external investment, the remaining 50% will be of no investment value. The new Company Law allows investment in other businesses, and lifts the restriction on the percentage between investment amount and net assets.

Fourth, it loosens the means of contribution by shareholders. The new Company Law prescribes that "shareholders can contribute in cash, or in non-cash assets, such as physical assets, intellectual property rights, and rights of land use that can be transferred according to the law; however, assets not allowed by the law and administrative regulations are excluded". Therefore, claims, rights offering, mineral rights, and exploration rights can all be used as assets of contribution. Also, the percentage of non-cash assets is increased from a maximum of 20% to 70% to facilitate the development of venture capital. If the percentage of intellectual property rights is set too low, technology holders are reluctant to seek cooperation with domestic venture capital firms.

Fifth, in the chapter of limited company, it prescribes that dividends, priority of capital contribution and right to vote can be exercised not in proportion to the percentage of contribution. In the meantime, protection for shareholder's equities is increased, making it clear that shareholders can request to audit the accounts of the company concerned. Before the establishment of a limited partnership, these prescriptions help venture capitalists reinforce control on invested companies.

The new Securities Law also has several important revisions. First, it expands the means and scope of securities trade, and empowers the State Council to develop separate regulations and rules on divided operation, divided regulation, actual transaction, stock financing, involvement of SOEs in stock trade, and entry of bank capital in the stock market, which were all strictly controlled in the original law. The method to manage securities companies is changed, and in the meantime, the risk control mechanism for securities companies is improved. Second, the power for the regulatory authority is increased, while the control for the exercise of power is enhanced, with strict prescriptions on related legal responsibilities. Third, the legal responsibility is reinforced, with the number of articles on punishment is increased by one third to 47. Fourth, the protection for investors' interests is expanded and enhanced. The new law requires the creation of a protection fund for stock investors, prescribing that the transaction funds of investors are trusted to the third party, and no embezzlement of stocks or funds of clients is allowed. Fifth, the transparency for information disclosure is increased. The new law clearly spells out the legal responsibilities respectively for the issuers, listing companies, management of listing companies and intermediaries.

On November 14 of 2005, approved by the State Council, the State Development and Reform Commission promulgated the "Interim Measures for the Administration of Entrepreneurial Investment Companies" together with another ten ministries and commissions. Coming into effect on March 1, 2006, the Interim Measures formally recognizes the status of venture capital industry, and eliminates the prejudices and problems in its development. In the meantime, the Interim Measures provide specific regulations, on the basis of the Company Law and Securities Law, on investment, financing, and exit of venture capital, as well as on legal protection and regulation of the industry. Despite inadequacies and deficiencies, the Interim Measures have promoted the development of venture capital industry.

Along with the above developments in legislation, the Promotion Law of Venture Capital should be drafted to promote the development of China's venture capital, including protection for investors' equities and innovators' intellectual property rights, setup of venture capital funds by private placements and a second board, and policies and measures encouraging venture capital, such as tax reduction, subsidy and interest discount, and loan warranty by the government.

Other related laws and regulations also need to be revised. The existing partnership enterprise law, for example, should add contents on limited partnership to facilitate the adoption of a limited partnership system by venture capital funds, while the existing tax law should prescribe that only individual income tax instead of corporate tax is levied on partnership enterprise.

8.3.3.3. *Provide an exit channel for venture capital*

During 1997–2000 when venture capital was heat across the world, not a few people called for the setup of a second board to provide an exit for venture capital. However, to allow growth companies to finance in the capital market at that time was actually to transfer the risk of venture capital institutions to public investors. Given the need to promote the development of venture capital and to prevent risks at the same time, the Standing Committee of the National People's Congress revised the Company Law in 1999, allowing high-tech firms to go IPO in the high-tech board of the Shanghai and Shenzhen Stock Exchanges.

Despite the decision, some people were still trumpeting the setup of a second board, asserting that "where there is no second board, there is no venture capital". Consequently, the decision was not implemented promptly. When the heat of global venture capital receded, the setup of the high-tech board was delayed, not to say the second board.

The writer proposed a "three-step" strategy for the setup of a second board in 2002. The first step is to select 30–50 small cap stocks with high-tech content approved by the China Securities Regulatory Commission, and create a separate board. As the listing qualifications are not lowered, and the number of these companies is limited, the shock wave on the market will not be significant. The second step is to lower some requirements, and to gradually expand the board. The last step is to separate the board from the primary board to create a complete and an independent second board.

After much research and preparation, the SME board was launched in the Shenzhen Stock Exchange on May 28, 2005. On June 2nd, the first SME went IPO. As some people were worried about the definition of high-tech firms, the name of SME board was adopted. The SME board is an integral part of the existing primary board, observing the same laws and regulations as the primary board. Although with the same requirements as the primary board on IPO and information disclosure, the SME board operates independently, with independent regulation, code and index.

Some question that many SMEs with good operating performance but not up to the listing requirements might be excluded since the threshold for the SME board is based on the existing primary board. After weighing the strengths and weaknesses, the existing requirements for IPO were maintained so that the SME board could be launched without delay.

The launch of the SME board represents the building of a multi-layer capital market in China. It provides a means of financing for SMEs and a channel of exit for venture capital through the capital market, as well as a new investment opportunity for the vast investors. However, it must be recognized that the launch of the SME board is merely the first step of a long march, and painstaking efforts must be made to develop the Shenzhen Stock Exchange into a multi-layer capital market like NASDAQ.

After the launch of the SME board, the Shenzhen Stock Exchange has been focusing on the system building to create a board of creditability. Up to date, the regulations that have been promulgated include "Specific Regulations on Listing Companies on the SME Board of the Shenzhen Stock Exchange", "Specific Regulations on Transactions on the SME Board of the Shenzhen Stock Exchange", "Guidelines for Good Faith of Listing Companies on the SME Board of the Shenzhen Stock Exchange", "Guidelines for Recommendation for the SME Board of the Shenzhen Stock Exchange", and "Guidelines for Behaviors of Board Members of Listing Companies on the SME Board of the Stock Exchange". These regulations are of great significance to the internal system building and regulation of operation of listing companies on the SME board.

The SME board achieved substantial growth over the past year. By 2005, 50 firms went public on the SME board, among which 38 were private enterprises, and 12 were state and collective-controlled enterprises. The total amount of funds raised reached 12 billion yuan, with an average of 119–473 million yuan per stock; the total of shares issued reached 1.38 billion, with an average of 13.4–15 million shares per stock. The average total capital was 91.16 million shares after issuance.

Today, the SME board has become an important element of China's capital market, with its trade volume taking up 12% of the primary board of the Shenzhen Stock Exchange. Additionally, its overall quality is much higher than that of the primary board — the percentage of shares held by institutional investors reaches as high as 30%. In a total of 50 listing companies, 33 are high-tech firms, taking up 66%.

By November 21, 2005, the split-share reform program has been passed in all the 50 companies, making the SME board the first board to realize "full negotiability".

In terms of overseas listing, with the abolishing of the "Circular on Certain Issues Relating to Improvement of Foreign Exchange Administration for Acquisitions with Foreign Capital" and "Circular on Certain Issues Relating to Registration of Offshore Investments by Domestic Individuals and Registration of Acquisitions with Foreign Capital" issued by the State Administration of Foreign Exchange, and the promulgation and implementation of "Circular on Certain Issues Relating to Financing of Domestic Individuals through Offshore Special-Purpose Company and Foreign Exchange Administration for Return Investment", the channel for offshore IPO has been opened, and the government's regulation has been more standardized.

8.3.3.4. *Train Venture Capital Talents*[5]

Where is the greatest difficulty in the development of venture capital? Some may think it is the inadequacy of capital, or lack of a second board in China. As a matter of fact, the greatest difficulty lies in the lack of talents, especially the lack of qualified venture capitalists.

Managers of venture capital funds (i.e. general partners) are often known as venture capitalists. Although they only account for 1–2% of the total investments in the funds, they take full responsibility for the management of the funds. They are generally versed in one specific area, and are experts of management and finance, playing a critical role in the success of venture capital. Their primary role is to use their expertise and experience to raise funds and make investment decisions. They need not only to identify projects with chance of success from hundreds and thousands of project proposals, but also to sit on the board of directors of invested companies to guide their growth and development. In addition to regular pay from the management fees (usually 2.5% of the total amount of the fund), the most significant part of general partners' revenues come from investment returns (i.e. 20% of ROI), which motivates them to find good projects, improve their performance and win trust of investors.

The primary role of venture capitalists is to support innovators in their entrepreneurial efforts, and to help investors speculate. To this end, venture capital must be operated by professionals. This is a pressing issue in China. First, China has a large number of scientific achievements to be transformed to commercial products, but the evaluation of the commercial prospect is much dependent on experienced talents versed in technology, management and finance. At present, most of the venture capital has not been invested just because of a lack of ability to evaluate venture capital projects. Second, innovators have an enthusiasm for entrepreneurship, but lack the expertise and experience of financing and management. They have to be matched by venture capitalists if they wish to realize the commercialization of their innovations. Third, both foreign capital and private sector have a willingness to invest, but can not find trustful agents, facing a dilemma that the reliable is not competent, and the competent is not reliable". Before they can find reliable and competent agents, they will not feel safe to make substantial investments.

Venture capitalists should sit on the board of directors of venture firms, with the primary responsibility to exercise financial control (i.e. regulating financial management and making decisions on incremental capital, closing, IPO and sale) and help establish a powerful management team, including CEO, CPO, CFO, and vice presidents of sales and business development. It should be made clear in the agreement that venture capitalists have the final say on major financial and HR issues. There is a fallacy among Chinese innovators that anyone with strong technical background can be a good CEO. But according to the statistics in the US, only 50% of founders are suitable for the position of CEO, and another 50% are not. In the eye of the American venture capitalist Randy Komisar,[6] a web company needs different qualities for the CEO at different stages of growth. In the start-up stage, the CEO should have the spirit of innovation and perseverance; in the growth stage, the CEO should have a strong organization capability and a strong sense of market; and in the mature stage, the CEO should have the capability of strategic management, sticking to the strategic direction while adapting to the environment. It is difficult for an entrepreneur to possess all these qualities simultaneously, and therefore, a company needs to choose the most proper CEO at different growth stages. Chinese innovators should have a self-knowledge, not attempting to ruin their companies by assuming the position of CEO if they are not qualified.

Venture capitalists have five major tasks to support innovators in their entrepreneurship. The first task is to judge the commercial prospect of an innovator's achievements. Such a judgment is based on their experience and business intuition. The second task is to help the innovator develop a business plan. The third task is to organize the innovator to introduce his product and business plan and convince investors for investment. The fourth task is to help reach an agreement between the innovator and investors and create a venture firm. The last task is to represent investors to sit on the board of directors, to make decisions on major financial and HR issues, and to take responsibility for restructuring and divestment.

Venture capitalists support investors' speculation in four ways. First, they help investors identify from thousands of proposals viable projects with the prospect of commercialization. Second, they judge the qualities, personality and ability of the innovator from initiative contacts and cooperation. It is indeed the most critical ability for a venture capitalist to judge the qualities of the entrepreneur. If the entrepreneur has personality problem, even the project with the largest chance of success does not deserve investment. Third, they represent investors on the board of directors, monitoring and guiding the management for success. Fourth, they help select the best timing for divestment through IPO or sale, and realize high returns for investors.

Venture capitalists should possess five qualities. The first quality is entrepreneurship, sense of responsibility, and acute business intuition. Venture capitalists should be able to distinguish between good and bad projects. The second quality is interpersonal skill. Venture capitalists should be able to judge the qualities, ability and credibility of the innovator. The third quality is knowledge of business management, financial operations and related laws and regulations. Most innovators are strong in technology, but often lack knowledge in management, finance and law. Venture capitalists should be able to cover the gap. The fourth quality is expertise and practical experience. If a venture capitalist is an expert himself, his communication with the innovator will be easy and smooth. In the US, many venture capitalists have a strong technical background, and before going in for venture capital, they usually study for another degree in finance or management. The last quality is good relations with the finance, technology, legal and government sectors, which is particularly important in China. Some local venture capital firms employ expatriates with a PhD or MBA degree as the general manager. However, despite their profound knowledge of technology and management, they can hardly succeed in the Chinese environment if they know so little about China.

There are various ways to develop Chinese venture capitalists. The first is to identify and train talents with potentials in practice. The second is to send managers with venture capital management experience abroad for special training. The third is to employ overseas Chinese with overseas experience in venture capital investment. The last is to create an incentive system for venture capitalists.

8.3.3.5. *Create a culture that encourages the development of venture capital*[7]

During the transition from a centrally planned economy to a socialist market economy, it is not strange that many problems still exist in the legal system, habits of government management, procedures of administration and people's mindset. These problems have been formed due to historical and cultural factors, and are not going to disappear overnight. Therefore, we must first of all create a culture that encourages the development of venture capital, and gradually change the old ideas and concepts deeply rooted in the people's mind.

Broadly speaking, the culture entails all the abilities and habits acquired as a social member, and influences an individual's values and behaviors. Values are objective properties that can meet an individual's certain need, such as economic value, cultural value, scientific value and historic value. Values reflect an individual's preferences in objective and action. A culture conducive to the development of venture capital should include the following aspects:

The first is to develop entrepreneurship. Entrepreneurship is closely related to venture capital. The word "entrepreneur" should not include all the managers and executives. Obviously, managers and executives without entrepreneurship or innovative spirit are not entrepreneurs. It is important in China to develop entrepreneurship, encourage creativity, innovation and risk-taking, and tolerate failure at the same time.

The second is to develop integrity and business ethics. In venture capital industry, integrity and business ethics are very important; venture capital can only succeed when venture capitalists and innovators build trust and learn to cooperate. Many of the problems in China are related to integrity and business ethics. For example, some investors try every means to delay the promised capital or to withdraw after investment, while some innovators commit one technology to several investors simultaneously and cooperate with the one promising the highest returns. Venture capital is a combination between knowledge capital and real capital; it uses real capital to support knowledge capital and social capital. However, the biggest problem with virtual capital is the uncertainty of its value, which often cannot be determined until it is cashed. On the other hand, without virtual capital, venture capital has no object to support.

The third is to create an environment for free dialogue and discussion. Any new things can not be perfect from the very beginning, and won't be accepted until a consensus is reached through free discussion and free exchange of views.

8.3.3.6. *Establish a supporting system for venture capital*

Over the years, China has established a supporting system for venture capital, which includes:

The first is to hold venture capital forums. According to an incomplete statistic, there are about ten forums held each year on venture capital, among which the China Venture Capital Forum, jointly organized by the Central Committee of China National Democratic Construction Association and the Ministry of Science and Technology, is the most famous. Held annually in April, the Forum has been successfully launched for eight consecutive years.

The second is to set up research institutions. In 2003, the China Venture Capital Research Institute (Hong Kong), co-funded by China Venture Capital Company and The Polytechnic University of Hong Kong, was launched in Shenzhen. After three years of operation, the institute has been running smoothly.

The third is to publish the quarterly *Journal of China Venture Capital.*

The fourth is to publish the *China Venture Capital Yearbook*, which began to have an English version since 2004.

The fifth is to launch the venture capital website. The objective is to make it the most important website as VentureOne in the US that can provide the most updated information on the venture capital industry.

The sixth is to publish a series of books on venture capital. Up to date, five books have been published, covering the role of government in venture capital, and project evaluation, etc.

The last is to train talents for China's venture capital. Approved by the Ministry of Education, the People's University of China has offered a PhD program on venture capital.

It has been proved by facts that a spiral development is the general law of development for virtual economy, including for venture capital. In early 2006, the Chinese government proposed the objective of building an innovation-oriented country, which provides a rare chance for the growth of China's venture capital. Along with the rapid and coordinated development of Chinese economy, the venture capital industry will continue to grow as long as we work hard and develop the right policies.

References

[1] Bygrave, W. D. and Timmons, J. A. (1992). *Venture Capital at the Crossroads*, Boston: Harvard Business School Press.

[2] Cheng, S. W. (2001). *Studies on Economic Reforms and Development in China*, New York: Oxford University Press.

[3] Cheng, S. W. (2004–2006). *China Venture Capital Yearbook*, Beijing: Democracy and Construction Press.

[4] Cheng, S. W. (1998–2006). Proceedings of China Venture Capital Forum, Beijing: Democracy and Construction Press.

[5] Komisar, R. and Lineback, K. L. (2000). *The Monk and the Riddle*, Boston: Harvard Business School Press.

[6] Quindlen, R. (2000). *Confessions of a Venture Capitalist*, New York: Warner Books.

[7] Saxenian, A. (1996). *Regional Advantage*, Boston: Harvard University Press.

Chapter 9

Analysis and Suggestions on Chinese Housing Reform

The system of housing and administration should include laws, regulations and policies that are related to construction, distribution, exchange, management of housing whose objectives are the regulation of the relationship between the parties concerned in housing. The establishment and improvement of the housing system have a lot to do with human existence and development, as well as social stability and economic progress. Housing has gone through 30 years of difficult process since China began to make housing reforms from 1979. Although it has made remarkable achievements, the overall progress is less than ideal. The basic philosophy and concept of reform is correct, but when policies are implemented in practice, lots of obstacles and difficulties need to be overcome — as manifested in the slow progress of low-cost housing construction, the lack of regulations on affordable housing, and a chaotic commercial housing market.

In allusion to this situation, I have put forward the following eight basic ideas representing my understanding about the housing problem:

- houses are a special 'commodity' with the characteristics of necessity, durability, immobility and high-value;
- real estate is a 'pillar' industry of the national economy;
- real estate industry has the dual functions of residence and investment;

- purchasing or renting a house are the two ways to achieve "home ownership";
- we need to distinguish between two different types of housing — 'protective' or 'safeguarded' housing (affordable housing for the less wealthy) and commercial housing;
- both government and the market should cooperate closely to solve the housing problem;
- protective housing is only meant to cover low-income families who have no housing or have housing difficulties;
- focusing on developing the regulatory role of the commercial housing markets.

In order to improve our country's low-rent housing system, it is recommended:

- low-rent housing system should be incorporated into social security, and the obligation to provide low-rent housing needs to be effectively implemented by governments at all levels;
- there must be clear definition in the classification of people with low income and those who have experienced difficulties;
- determining basic standards of housing security that fits the condition of China;
- increasing rental availability of houses for low-income families;
- increasing low-rent housing guarantee/safeguarding fund;
- strengthening the implementation and management of the low-rent housing-related policies, establishing and improving the management of the low-rent housing organization.

Affordable housing problems in China are mainly:

- short supply;
- high prices;
- many economically affordable housing fall into high-income people because of careless omission on the qualification requirement;
- due to remote location and incomplete support facilities, living costs are high.
- In order to regulate country's affordable housing system, I propose

- moderate standard;
- apportion/partition the property;
- impose heavy penalties on fraud;
- mete out severe punishment for corruption.

After analyzing the major issues of Chinese commercial housing market, I believe that

- protective housing and the commercial housing should not be mixed-up or 'confused';
- actual demand of Chinese commercial housing is large;
- there exists structural imbalance between supply and demand of Chinese commercial housing;
- Chinese commercial housing prices consist of land costs, construction cost, taxes and net profit, each counting for a quarter;
- Chinese commercial housing market bubble do exist.

In order to promote the healthy development of Chinese commercial housing market, I suggest:

- develop and perfect laws and regulations of the commercial housing market;
- strengthen and improve macro-control of the commercial housing market;
- adhere to the correct views/orientation of public opinion;
- nurture and develop the second-hand housing market;
- promote real estate financial innovation, e.g establish pilot projects for real-estate investment trusts (REITs) and mortgage-backed securities.

9.1. Introduction

Since ancient times, clothing, food, houses and transportation were classified as the four basic needs of human livelihood as well as the basic elements of the existence and development of human society. Of the four, housing provides inhabitants a safe, comfortable, nice-looking and convenient place to live. With technological development and social progress, people's demands for housing have become 'higher'. Therefore, the housing problem is becoming an increasing concern and a major issue in national, social and economic development. Housing policy is a common problem faced by governments around the world.[1]

As early as in 1933, cities were given three functions by the Athens Charter, including habitation, work and visit, and habitation was regarded as the main function of cities. With the rapid growth of populations after World War II, housing problems have become more and more urgent and acute. In October 1978, the U.N. set up the center for human habitation. As the leading organization in charge of coordinating the development and activities of human habitation in the UN, the center supports and works with all the national governments, local governments, non-governmental organizations and private sectors to promote the cause of global human habitation.

The UN General Assembly in 1982 passed a resolution assigning the year 1987 as "International Housing Year" in the hope that before 2000 all the homeless people of the world would be provided a house equipped with tap water and sewage pipes. The U.N. would try to provide public transport and improve the urban infrastructure to stop the rapid expansion of cities. The year 1987 was defined as the International Year for providing shelter abbreviated to International Housing Year. More than 130 countries including China registered in the U.N. and took part in the activities of the International Housing Year. In the second U.N. assembly for human habitation held in Istanbul in June, 1996, the proposals of "all humans enjoying adequate housing" and "sustainable development of human habitat in the process of urbanization" were made the 'globally important' themes. It was emphasized in the Istanbul Declaration that the challenge of human habitation is a global issue. In order to solve the global housing problem and improve the living conditions of people, international, national and local governments should build good work together with each other. The international society should strengthen monetary support by funding and help speed up transfer of technology.

In 1997, the United Nations Human Habitat Committee adopted a resolution at the 16th conference, calling for quick actions to be taken by all governments to formulate or implement housing strategies and policies, and to help coordinate to the greatest extent efforts to motivate, secure and increase reasonably contributions to housing supply by public, private and non-government industries, through cooperation among governments in the housing supply process. The development of human habitat in the city and that in the countryside should synchronize with each other. Once the housing development in the countryside is neglected, large population will migrate from the countryside to the city, making the housing problem in the city more serious. It is reported that in the developing countries, there are at least 0.6 billion city residents living in dilapidated houses where the conditions of drinking water, sanitation, drains and garbage collection are far from adequate, causing sustained threats to their life and health. Every year, millions of city residents are evicted from their houses violently, bringing about daily increases in the number of homeless people. It is estimated that so far, the number of homeless people has reached 0.1billion. Till 2008, it is expected that over half of the world's population (3.3 billion) will be living in the city area, and over 1 billion of the population will be living in the slums. In December, 2001, the U.N. General Assembly adopted Resolution 56/206, upgrading the United Nations Human Habitat Center to the United Nations Human Settlements Program, UN-Habitat for short. UN-Habitat is dedicated to promoting the achievement of two major objectives, namely "all humans should enjoy adequate housing" and "sustainable development of human habitat in the process of urbanization". The mission of UN-Habitat is to implement the *Human Habitat Agenda*, passed in June, 1996 on 2nd Human Habitat Conference held in Istanbul, Turkey, so as to make contributions to the U.N.'s systematic efforts in achieving the aim of eradicating poverty and promoting sustainable development. One of the major tasks of UN-Habitat is to help speed up the formulation of policies, strategies, building of a supply system, establishing housing and social service, and to encourage governments to realize progressively and comprehensively the peoples' rights to housing.[2]

Housing problem is a very serious and acute issue in our country. Because of the planned economy of the past, in which high savings and low consumption, high employment rate and low salaries featured, the construction of houses was conducted under the national plan for investment of infrastructure and basic housing. During the twenty years from 1958 to 1977, with the dominance of the "leftist" ideology of "production first, living second" and "rebuilding first, erecting new house second", the investment for basic housing construction was cut. By 1978, the per capita living space in urban areas had decreased from 4.5 square meters in the early years of the construction of new China to 3.6 square meters. As a result, many people have fallen into the disadvantaged group with housing difficulties and the shortage of houses has become a serious social problem.

Early in September 1978, the late Comrade Deng Xiaoping had posed the question of whether we could solve the housing problem through more ways — like allowing private construction, or letting the government provide citizens with building materials to build their own houses, the repayment of which materials could be done by installments — which are potentially promising. On April 5, 1980, in a conversation with the leading members of the Central Committee of the CPC, Comrade Deng also mentioned, "On the problem of housing, a series of polices on house building in urban areas and house distribution should be considered. On one hand, urban residents can either buy houses or build their own ones. On the other hand, both new houses and old ones can be sold, and people can choose to pay by lump-sum or by installments in 10 to 15 years. In accordance with the house price, we should gradually adjust the rent to a higher price so that people will consider buying houses economical; otherwise people won't buy houses if the rent is low. Moreover, we should make a difference on house rentals for different places. For instance, houses in the busy business center of the city and in the remote areas, houses in a place where transportation is convenient and where that is inconvenient, as well as houses in the urban area and in the rural area. And in future when the rent is raised, subsidies should be given to the workers with low pay. All the policies mentioned above should be linked in our consideration. Besides, we can encourage the private sector to build houses jointly with the government, or to manage all by themselves. There should be new designs for housing in the rural villages. In addition to houses with quadrangles, there should be multi-storey buildings, in order to save on cultivated land. Those buildings should also meet the different requirements for different areas and different people." This farsighted speech by Deng Xiaoping not only established the framework for the reform of the housing system but also started a series of the exploration on the theory and practice of the housing reform system.

The reform of China's housing system started from 1979. After 30 years of difficult process, it has made remarkable achievements. By the end of 2008, the area of living space per capita has reached 27 square meters in urban housing construction area (according to household registration demographics/census).[3] Chinese achievements in the housing system reform also received international recognition. Up to November 2005, China has obtained 12 United Nations Habitat Awards. However, the overall progress is still less than ideal. The fundamental idea of reform is largely correct, but when actually implemented, lots of obstacles and difficulties need to be overcome. Construction of low-cost housing is still slow; economically suitable houses lack regulation and there is a chaotic commercial housing market.

At the Fifth Session of the Tenth National People's Congress, Premier Wen Jiabao pointed out that: 'The real estate industry plays a major role in economic development and in improving the living conditions of the people. As such, we need to promote the continued progress and healthy development of the real estate industry. First, realizing that China is a nation of vast population and limited land and in view of the level of economic development at the present stage, we should carry out rational planning, scientific construction, moderate consumption, and the development of energy-saving and environmental buildings. We are attempting to build and design houses with Chinese characteristics. Second, the real estate industry should focus on the development of ordinary commercial housing for the masses. The Government should pay particular attention to and help solve the housing problems of low-income families, increase taxation and make supportive policies towards the end, establish and improve low-rent, low cost housing system, improve and standardize the system of economically affordable housing. Third, we should make a 2-prong approach — through proper government co-ordination and adjustment and market mechanism — to maintain and regulate a reasonable extent and scale of real estate investment, optimize the supply structure of commercial housing, strengthen supervision and regulation of housing prices, control real estate prices so as to avoid skyrocketing prices, and maintain a reasonable level of house prices. Fourth, we need to regulate the real estate market so as to maintain order, strengthen market supervision, punish those involved in illegal activities in real estate development, trading, intermediary and other sectors. Local governments at all levels must be responsible for the real estate market regulation and supervision.

I have been concerned about Chinese housing system reform for years, and conducted some researches on housing issues together with some experts and scholars. In the light of our research findings, and upon my personal reflection and analysis, I hereby present in this chapter on how to further promote Chinese housing system reform and towards a healthy development of Chinese housing market, to explore and put forward some views and suggestions.

9.2. Understanding the Fundamental Issues of Chinese Housing

Owing to some lingering problems of history, plus the fact that in today's China there are many diverse interests, the housing problem in our country appears to be very complicated. Since the housing reforms began, home prices has become the focus of concern by people from all walks of life and the controversies about home prices and the real estate industry are becoming more and more heated. I think this is a representation or manifestation of a democratic and open society, which should be encouraged and supported. Unfortunately, some remarks posted online distort the facts, while others are too extreme. Yet some others even try to politicize the discussions about the housing controversies. What's worse, a few individual experts and scholars have made some unrealistic, impractical suggestions meant to inflame readers, trying to become 'heroes' and to appeal to the sentiments of the masses. In addition, some media reports have added fuel to fire by writing sensational news, resulting in some irrational interference to the reforms of Chinese housing system. In order to carry out further the reforms of Chinese housing system, the study of Chinese housing problems should be comprehensive, systematic, and in-depth. I put forward the following eight fundamental issues of our housing problem in the hope of righting the wrong and false ideas and to reveal the truth and promote better understanding of the issues.

9.2.1. *Housing is a Special Commodity with Four Characteristics*

The first one is necessity. Housing is a necessity for human existence. With the increase in population and people's incomes, the demand for housing will grow. If the needs of human beings other than housing are not taken into consideration, the price elasticity of demand for housing could be considered to have a large rigidity — so the effect of a change in house prices on demands is relatively small. The second is durability. At present the life span of normal houses generally reaches 50 years or so, with an annual natural renewal rate of 2%. Therefore, the main motivation for consumers updating their houses is not because the houses they live in have exceeded their useful lives, but rather it is because of the change in income, family size, nature of work, environment, and aesthetics. This will create new demands for housing, and improve the development of second-hand or secondary housing market. The third is the high-value nature of housing. Housing is a high-value commodity whose value usually reaches more than four times of the annual household income. In developed countries, whether it is a loaned purchase or rent/tenancy, living expenses, plus electricity, water, property management fees account for 20% to 35% of household income. Therefore, the state should pay special attention to and enhance housing support to those low-income families with housing difficulties. The last one is immobility. As housing is not removable (immovable property), people have to change housing as a result of changes in the workplace. Since the value of the property depends on their location and the surrounding environment, such as quality and availability of nearby schools and shops, cleanliness of the environment, maintenance of law and order and so on, house prices in big cities are higher than those in medium and small cities; prices of those in urban centers are higher than those in the countryside. Thus, in the formulation of relevant policies, we should distinguish between cities and regions instead of having a unified national standard.

9.2.2. *The Real Estate Industry is a 'Pillar' of National Economy — A Very Important Component of it*

Experience both at home and abroad has shown that there is a huge potential in the demand for housing construction. The construction industry boasts high degree of industrial linkage — linking it to other industries — and no technological barriers. It can stimulate the development of construction, building materials, light industries, electronics and dozens of others. The housing construction industry absorbs a huge number of people, and play an obviously important role in economic growth. It is estimated that under the current situation in our country, each 100 yuan invested in housing construction funds can create 170–220 yuan worth of demands for related industries. A 10% increase in housing construction brings about a one percentage point increase in GDP growth. The construction of every 10,000 square meters of housing space creates 100 job opportunities, while 100 job opportunities in housing sector will create 200 vacancies in related industries. The housing sector can stimulate the need not only for steel, cement and other materials required for construction, but also helps stimulate the appliances, furniture, as well as service industries like house moving and property management. Therefore, many countries regard the real estate industry as a pillar industry of national economy, and attach great importance to its development.

9.2.3. *Real Estate Possesses the Dual Functions of Residence and Investment*

Its residential function is to provide residents a safe, comfortable, pleasant and convenient place to live, and the price depends on buyers' rational judgments. On the other hand, the main function of investment is to maintain and increase the value of the house for its owners in which case the price depends on the buyer's expectation of the price increase. Among a variety of investment vehicles, the principal means of preservation and price increase of people's properties is through commercial housing investments.

9.2.4. *Purchasing or Renting Houses are the Two Ways to Achieving "Home Ownership"*

At present, the urban homeownership rate in our country has reached about 72%, among the highest in the world. However, objectively speaking, there still exist the problems of demand and supply for renting. Maintaining a certain number of houses for rent is conducive to housing turnover, which can promote the development of the housing market. The key to maintaining a balance between renting and purchasing is to determine or decide reasonably on the price of housing rentals and this means keeping a general balance between the actual rent charged and the virtual private housing rent. The so-called virtual rent includes deposits interest of down payment, interest and amortization charges of mortgage loan, as well as property management expenses. The virtual rent is not only an important yardstick to judge whether there is a balance between renting and purchasing, but also a crucial means for market regulation. The Government should strengthen the macro-management of the housing rental/lease market, mainly through taxes, subsidies, and other means to adjust the rent-purchase balance and to protect the legitimate rights and interests of tenants and homeowners.

9.2.5. *We Need to Distinguish Two Different Types of Housing — 'Protective' Housing and Commercial Housing*

In the primary stage of socialism, China is implementing the socialist market economic system. To solve housing problems, on the one hand, the government needs to act in accordance with the concepts of socialism in providing adequate housing security for low-income groups with housing difficulties. On the other hand, it should abide by the principles of market economy to satisfy the reasonable demands for housing of the majority. The main responsibility of government is to spearhead the building of 'protective' housing, try hard to meet the housing needs of all the low-income groups and those with housing difficulties, and prevent unqualified people from getting the protective housing by "seeking a vacant seat" or "hitching a ride". Commercial houses are a commodity and not a 'public' goods, whose prices are determined by a number of market factors; therefore the prices change as these factors change. Like fluctuations in stock market, the housing market is also constantly fluctuating. The government's macro-control affects the price of commercial housing and prevents, to a certain extent, the situation of 'rising too fast up or going too far down' for the price of houses. However, it is not appropriate and also impossible for the government to set prices of commercial houses. It is the house-buyers themselves who decide on the time, location, as well as the size, level of decor, financing and so on of their houses.

9.2.6. *The Government ('the Visible Hand') and the Market ('the Invisible Hand') Should Cooperate Closely to Solve the Housing Problem*

Looking at the evolution of housing policies around the world, most countries eventually adopt the mode of "formulating market regulations is primary and providing government support is supplementary". Learning from the common mode, we should make use of the market's fundamental function of resource allocation to produce different houses — to adapt to different needs and to achieve the dynamic equilibrium between supply and demand. At the same time, the government needs to establish a housing market system and classify markets in accordance with the order of entry into the market, type of houses, geographical locations, forms of transactions, purpose of the purchase etc. At the same time, the government must assume the responsibility of protecting the interests of low-income groups.

The market and government should co-ordinate with each other in that government should give more consideration to ensure social justice and fairness while the market should adhere more to the laws of value, supply and demand, and rules of competition. There have been individuals who think that houses are 'public goods' and they have appealed to the government to adopt the policy of "Secure housing for all". To me, this is actually a call for return to the "welfare housing" of the planned economic system, which not only goes against the general direction of the socialist market economic reforms, but also creates a huge burden to the state's financial capacity.

9.2.7. *'Protective' Housing can only Cover Low-Income Families who have no Housing or who Face Housing Difficulties*

On account of the facts that China will still be at the primary stage of socialism for a long period of time, and its per capita GDP and financial revenue are still at a low level, protective housing will only be available to a portion of the urban population, accounting for about 30% of low-income groups without housing (including the migrant workers who have worked in urban cities for more than two years) and those with housing difficulties (housing area per capita is less than 40% of the local level), estimated around 20 million or so. Besides, the average area of protective housing per-capita should not exceed 60% of the local per-capita housing area, which restrictions should apply to the standards of low-cost housing and economically affordable housing. If proper and meticulous planning is carried out, and appropriate policies gradually implemented, it is quite possible to meet the protective housing needs of all the low-income groups within 3-5 years.

9.2.8. *We should Emphasize the Regulatory Role of the Commercial Housing Markets*

Since most of the housing needs of urban residents must be met by the commercial housing market, we should endeavor, on the basis of a careful analysis of actual demands for urban residential housing, to work hard to develop and perfect a commercial housing market system, in line with our situations. We should strive to increase effective supply, improve the intermediary system and provide financial support. Furthermore, the government should carry out a modest and effective macro-control on commercial housing market and focus on those middle-income groups without housing. In response to the demands of improving housing condition, people's intention of buying a second housing and that of making investment purchase, the government should pay more attention to the market's inherent regulatory role and should not interfere too much with it. The government does not need to devise special preferential policies favorable to commercial housing industries, but should just let housing developers make their own decisions, take responsibility for their own profits and losses, and bear their own risks.

9.3. Efforts to Improve China's Low-Rent/Low-Cost Housing System

Low-rent housing is a kind of public commodities or 'goods' provided by the government for the low-income groups with housing difficulties to realize their home ownership. The distribution of low-rent housing is implemented primarily by providing rent subsidies, supplemented by the policy of directly providing rented housing to qualified families or by reducing the housing rent. The property rights of low-rent housing belong to the state, and such housing is for rent but not for sale. Although China's housing reform policies had proposed establishing low-rent housing system in 1998, the construction of low-rent housing has been slow in progress. In 2006, the Ministry of Construction released information about the construction and implementation of low-rent housing system in Chinese urban areas, showing that the total housing funds for the lowest-income families reached 4.74 billion, and 329,000 of the lowest-income families have already been emplaced to the low-rent houses under the low-rent housing system. However, nationwide, there are still more than 70 cities above the prefectural level that have not established low-rent housing system. Besides, less than 50% of the cities in Fujian, Henan, Yunnan, Jilin, Gansu, Inner Mongolia provinces (autonomous regions) have implemented the low-rent housing system.

During the "Two Congresses" in 2005, I proposed to the leaders of the Ministry of Construction that we should speed up the construction of low-rent housing. Thereafter, I was working on the supervision of PhD students in relevant research and at about the same time, I was involved in a field trip organized by Organization of the Central Committee of China Democratic National Construction Association to investigate the low-rent housing system in the United States and Europe. After discussing with the leaders of the Ministry of Construction, I have put forward six recommendations as follows:[4]

First, low-rent housing system should be put under the purview of social security, and governments at all levels should take responsibility in implementing relevant policies and giving full support. According to a survey, until the first half of 2006, China has invested only six billion-odd yuan in low-rent housing, the actual 'security' coverage of which was probably less than 15% — so that needs to be greatly improved. To integrate the existing 'secured housing' policies, we must speed up legislative process concerning housing security, develop medium to long-term programs and annual implementation plans for secured housing and make it an important indicator in the assessment of local government performance.

Second, we need to make it clear that the scope of the secured housing policy should cover low-income families with no housing or people with housing difficulties. The state should give support to low-income families who have no housing, or the families who have housing but the per capita living area/space is far below the 'level of protection'. According to the survey conducted by the Ministry of Construction, altogether 8.2 million families are eligible for such protection, about half of which are the 'minimally living/surviving' families. Low-rent housing system should also cover the families of migrant workers who have been working more than two years in urban areas. Since they create wealth for the urban and live in the cities, the government should provide them with secured housing.

Third, the basic housing security standards/requirements should be determined to fit the conditions of our nation. Under the premise of ensuring the basic functions of housing, per capita living space of each household cannot be more than 60% of the average local residential living area. We should provide full or part subsidies as per the family incomes. Those minimally living households should be provided with full subsidies, while other low-income families with housing difficulties are to be given part subsidies to cover the shortfall in their rental payments.

Fourth, more rental housing should be made available for low-income families, to be realized by two means. On the one hand, the government should take the lead in constructing low-rent houses for small households, taking into full consideration some social factors. For instance, it is not advisable to build a large number of low-rent housing blocks concentrated in one particular place as it might lead to demarcation between rich and poor communities. On the other hand, rental of second-hand houses should be encouraged. When people move to a better house, but they are not allowed to sell their old house or they do not want to sell it, their old house then can be used for low-rent housing. The government shall subsidize the rent according to market prices.

Fifth, we should increase funds for low-rent secured housing. This requires establishing national and provincial housing funds, and in more impoverished areas of Western China, funds should be transferred to support housing programs. According to one survey, families with housing difficulties in the western regions number about twice that in eastern regions, but the housing funds (house provident funds) for the western region is much less than that for the east. We must try to ensure that 5% of net income from land transfer will be used for the construction of low-rent housing and we should try to steadily increase the proportion to 15% in some areas that warrant this proportion.

Sixth, we must not only strengthen the inspection and management on low-cost housing-related policies but also establish and improve the management of low-rent housing organizations. At present, there are 179 million urban households in total, of which 8.2 million families are in need of housing (accounting for less than 5%.) From our current economic development and revenue situation, it is possible to support all the families in need of housing by 2010.

After the above six recommendations have been approved by the leadership of the State Council, I had discussed further with the Ministry of Construction on how to implement them. It has been clearly stipulated by the Ministry of Construction that all cities and counties in China have to establish the "low-rent housing" system before the end of 2008. On November 12th, 2008, leaders of Housing and Urban-Rural Construction stated that in the next three years we need to add two million units of low-rent housing, four million units of economically affordable housing, and complete reconstruction/renovation projects involving more than a million squatter settlements in forestry, agriculture and mining regions. The total investment will reach 900 trillion, averaging 300 trillion annually. I believe that by 2011, China is expected to have established a relatively sound low-rent housing system, but I also recommend the establishment of specialized agencies responsible for the examination of qualification for requirements, determination of subsidies, rent collection, housing allocation and searching for sources of housing.

9.4. Regulate Rigorously the 'Economically Affordable/Suitable' Housing System in China

Economically affordable housing is a commercial housing program in the nature of social security in which houses are built by real estate enterprises or through fund collection under the auspices of local governments in accordance with national planning. Its predecessor was the "comfortable housing project" in the 1990s, and was renamed as 'economically affordable housing' in 1998. Over the next few years, the economically affordable housing has developed rapidly, with yearly increase in investment, new construction areas, sales volume and sales areas, but the proportion of new construction area and sales area began to decline from 2000. With the exposure of problems of an unreasonable system, a stream of questioning about such housing sprang up, including the following:

The first is short supply. Since 2000, the annual newly-started construction area is approximately 50 million square meters, and the sales area is around 40 million square meters, which can only meet the needs of about 400 thousand purchasers. This is mainly because of lack of initiatives on the part of the local governments to build economically affordable housing. The land required of economically affordable housing is allocated by the executive, the relevant taxations levied are halved and the price is approved by the pricing department. In comparison with the construction of commercial buildings, revenue collected by local governments is greatly reduced and there is a lot of additional work and trouble for the local government in construction, distribution and management. As a result of very low profit margins (3%) stipulated by the government, some developers are not enthusiastic about building economically affordable housing: some of them even do shoddy work or use inferior materials for construction, resulting in poor quality houses. Some developers collude with government officials to use their power for personal gain by selling some 'lucky' house number at a high price of tens of thousands or even hundreds of thousands, thus making it very difficult for people who are really in need to purchase these economically affordable housing.

The second problem is about the high price of 'economically affordable' housing: it is plainly impossible for the low- and middle-income families with housing difficulties to afford them.

The reason for the high prices is mainly due to the government's desire of increasing revenue, the overwhelming varieties of various kinds of "rent-seeking" activities, and no limitation on irregular exploitation and selling of economically affordable housing by developers — like the arbitrary reducing of green areas, unpermitted expansion of construction areas and even the appearance of large number of units with more than 100 square meters. Besides, the rise in building and construction standards also increases the cost of building the houses. In addition, it is not uncommon for developers to give false reports on their costs by quoting higher figures than they actually are.

The third is the oversight in reviewing the qualification of those wishing to purchase economically affordable housing, leading to a number of economically affordable houses being bought by some high-income families. One reason is because of the difficulties in collecting accurate information from the applicants. Furthermore, some applicants become 'qualified' to purchase these houses by giving false information or bribing government officials. A large number of rich families who have Benz, BMW or other high-class cars live in the community of economically affordable housing — there is a unit with seven air-conditioners in the house! Some people even rent or resell their affordable housing for profit. A survey of one Beijing real estate agency shows that the rentals of economically affordable housing in two communities named Huilongguan and Tiantongyuan at the Changping District accounted for 78.8% of the total rent/lease transactionss in the district, while the second-hand housing transaction volumes in the two communities are increasing day by day too.[5] Some individuals even buy several units of economically affordable housing and combine them into a mansion.

The last problem of economically affordable housing is the oversight of many planning authorities of such housing. The houses are placed in remote areas with little regulation and planning; the units do not fulfill the correct requirements of economically affordable houses and the types of houses built are not suitable. Although these economically affordable housing in many cities are priced lower, the living costs are relatively higher. In addition, the prices of economically affordable housing in some cities are not much lower than that of commercial housing. Coupled with other unfavorable factors like complicated application procedures, cumbersome process of transfer and exchange, many qualified applicants are discouraged from purchasing these 'economically affordable' houses.

In short, one can say that the economically affordable housing is neither "economical" nor "suitable". It has even been proposed by some academics that the economically affordable housing program should be abolished.[6]

In order to regulate, standardize and improve the economically affordable housing system, governments at all levels have introduced certain management measures. On November 30, 2007, the Ministry of Construction as well as other six departments issued the "The Management of Economically Affordable Housing", clearly indicating that economically affordable housing buyers have merely the limited property rights.[7] The Shanghai municipal government and other local governments also introduced their own appropriate measures to manage the local economically affordable housing.[8]

Despite having many problems over the past decade, the economically affordable housing system has indeed helped solve the housing difficulties for some medium- and low-income families, playing an important role in providing housing support. As long as the system is further improved and strictly enforced, the economically affordable housing will remain an indispensable part of our nation's housing supply system.

According to the theory of complex science, a system consists of two aspects: body and mechanism. The body refers to the system's states and structure at a given point of time, while mechanism means the system's evolution process and driving forces. They are interdependent with system being the starting point and the result of the evolution while mechanism the path of evolution. The interaction between the different system agents and between the system and the external environment help produce a self-organizing function in the internal system, forming the system hierarchy and functional structure, and promoting the evolution of the system towards a certain direction.

As the exogenous or external factor, Government policies will not really be effective unless they change people's standard of behavior.[9] Therefore, in considering the approaches to manage the economically affordable housing, the following provisions should be adopted to minimize the possibilities of people's attempts to "hitch a free ride", or "to get a bargain" or even to engage in profiteering.

9.4.1. *Maintain Moderate Standard*

The economically affordable housing should set the 'standard' equal to that for low-rent housing's as its nature is to provide housing protection or security and it aims mainly to meet the needs of low and middle income families. In this way, it can on one hand greatly simplify municipal governments' management procedures in building and taking back the buildings; on the other hand, this makes some people with good incomes unwilling to live in them and it deters people with higher incomes from trying to make profits by disposing of it, as well as eliminating some middle-income buyers' complaint about their not meeting the conditions of purchase (these people think that the buyer's income plus the state subsidies is higher than their actual income). When the low-income families' incomes grow, they could be allowed to purchase low-cost rented housing.

9.4.2. *Part Property to be Vested in Government*

Affordable housing is commercial housing with housing protection nature, the price difference between which and the same commercial housing is compensated by publicly financed subsidies, and this represents part of the property that shall be vested in the Government. The affordable rental housing is not allowed to be rented, directly traded in the market or privately transferred. If the low-income families want to improve their housing conditions because of their income growth, governments could purchase the part property rights at the price in the second-hand housing market.

9.4.3. *Heavy Penalties for Fraud*

All kinds of fraud such as concealment of properties, under-declaration of income and overstating the number in the households in purchasing affordable housing shall result in cancelation or withdrawing house owners' eligibility for affordable housing, and severe punishment will be meted out to those found guilty of such frauds.

9.4.4. *Corruption Must be Severely Dealt with*

It is the key to the management of affordable housing system to improve the transparency of administration of land allocation and to punish collusion between officials and businessmen. The recent incident of "six consecutive house numbers" of the third phase affordable housing in Wuhan Yujia Tou District is a case in point: it is suspected that intermediaries had colluded with the staff of the relevant departments to fraudulently 'draw' house numbers of affordable housing.[10]

9.5. Analysis of Commercial Housing Market in China

Since China suspended the welfare housing allocation system and implemented the commercialization of houses in 1998, the housing market in China has achieved rapid development. From 1997 to 2008, the newly started construction area/sites, the completed construction area and sales area of Chinese housing have all shown upward trend, with an increase of 2.4, 1.4 and 8.6 times respectively. Furthermore, housing conditions of most of the urban residents have improved, and over 80% of China's registered urban households have their own commercial residential properties.

Over the past decade in the development of China's commercial housing market, difficulties come up in areas such as construction, sales, management and control of the commercial housing market. These difficulties have to some extent led to some misguided decision-makings made by the government as well as the behavior of buyers because of continuous debates, controversies and divergent opinions.[11] As a result, China's commercial housing market is still in a chaotic state. In order to promote the healthy development of China's commercial housing market, the following should be carefully analyzed:

9.5.1. *'Protective' Housing and Commercial Housing should be Differentiated*

Protective housing and commercial housing are two very different things in nature, the former being public commodities provided by the government, with prices determined by the government based on an appropriate level of protection, while the latter is freely on sale in the open market where price depends on supply and demand. However quite a few people mix them up intentionally or unintentionally when expressing their views. For example, some say 70% of the people in China cannot afford housing, and in order to ensure social equity, the government should try to bring down prices. But the fact is — for urban low-income families (which account for 30% of the total number of households) — even if house prices are reduced by 50%, they still cannot afford. So such views actually represent the interests of the middle and high income families, many of whom want to improve housing conditions and who want to buy a second suite at a lower price. If house prices are reduced by 50%, it will not only cause enormous harm to the commercial housing market, but will also cause great damage to the country's economic development; it could even lead to more than 70% of China's urban households owning real properties to have their properties devalue considerably.

The lessons of American "sub-prime crisis" show that, it is difficult to solve the housing problem of low-income groups.[12] During the Clinton and Bush administration periods, in order to garner for the support of low-income groups (mainly blacks and Hispanics) and to promote economic development, they regard the increase in the percentage of home ownership as one of their main ruling objectives. Thus the U.S. governments have often attached great importance to the mortgage industries (including Fannie Mae and Freddie Mac, two government-sponsored lending giants) to relax their lending standards or requirements. Some councilors in the United States also advocated: "Let all blue-collar families own their own homes." In order to achieve that, the United States Department of Housing and Urban Development tailored the mortgage lending policies to encourage the development of sub-prime mortgage loans, required "Fannie Mae and Freddie Mac" to buy more "affordable" mortgage loans for low-income families and ethnic minority families, and asked them to view the multi-billion dollar investment in the sub-prime mortgage loans as public commodities for the development of low-income housing. In 1996, HUD indicated that the "Fannie Mae and Freddie Mac" should issue 42% of the mortgage loans to the families whose incomes are below that of the average of the borrowers, and the percentage should be up to 50% in 2000 and 52% in 2005.

As the U.S. housing market was booming during that time, driven by the "Fannie Mae and Freddie Mac" loans, more and more banks began to offer loans to high-risk borrowers, including illegal immigrants, trying to get higher returns by high-risk loans. At the same time, the average difference between the normal mortgage interest rates and the sub-prime's fell to 280 base points in 2001, then further reduced to 130 base points in 2007. In addition, mortgage loan audits (mortgage underwriting) were also becoming more liberal: 40% of all the sub-prime mortgages in 2007 were automatically issued without appropriate assessment and records. This stimulated the entire sub-prime mortgage market, which prompted the issue rate of the sub-prime mortgages to increase by nearly ten-fold from 1994 to 2003 with an annual growth rate of 25%. In 1994, the sub-prime loans' value accounted for only 5% of the total loans' value, but increased to 13% in 1999 and even to 20% in 2006.

Normally, demands for housing will come down when the price rises, which helps to control the rise of the prices. However, the U.S. government used policy instruments to support the development of the sub-prime mortgage industry. This, coupled with the Fed's low interest rate policy, led to prosperity in the U.S. housing market starting from 2002. At the same time, many low-income families got loans to buy their own housing when in fact they could not afford and they fell into the trap. These and other policies encouraged housing investment and speculation. In the 2005, 28% of buyers purchased housing for the sole purpose of investment, while 12% buyers purchased homes for vacation. Speculators purchased existing housing and 'forward delivery housing' by making use of high leverage rate, which greatly increased the risk of the market.

After the first sub-prime crisis in 2007, it was difficult for many low-income families to escape paying high monthly interests through refinancing after the initial concession period. They therefore couldn't pay off the loans and lost their right of redemption. In September 2008, U.S. house prices dropped by an average of 20% or more from the peak in mid-2006. By March 2008, it was estimated that there were 8.8 million borrowers (accounting for 10.8% of all owners) whose housing became negative assets, and this figure would rise to 12 million in November 2008. As a result, many borrowers intentionally breached contracts, and mortgage fraud cases became common occurrences. What's worse, the sales volume of American new housing fell by 26.4% in 2007, which is the greatest figure (23.1%) since 1980. At the end of 2007, there were nearly four million homes for sale, of which nearly 2.9 million units were unoccupied.

The rise in mortgage defaults reduced the values of securities such as MBS, CDO, etc., which weakened the bank's net assets and financial position. "Fannie Mae and Freddie Mac" were also taken over by the U.S. government due to insolvency (until June 30, 2008, the net asset value was only 114 billion U.S. dollars, but the mortgage loans totaled 5.1 trillion U.S. dollars, nearly half of which were outstanding accounts.)

9.5.2. *There is a High 'Effective Demand' in Chinese Commercial Housing Market*

Since housing is a necessity and people always have the desire to improve their living conditions (from the mere pursuit of space to the pursuit of the functional qualities, environmental quality, service quality and taste), the demand for commercial housing in China will continue to grow with population, income and socio-economic development — but only if the buyers have the ability to make a purchase, can this need be effective.

Many people in China view the price earnings ratio as the criteria for evaluating effective demand, and conclude that since China's price earnings ratio is more than 3–6 times that of the international standard, the majority of our people do not have the ability to buy commercial housing. Only when the prices are reduced greatly, can the demand effectively increase, promoting China's commercial housing market. However, in fact, in spite of the fluctuations of commercial housing prices in the past decade, the overall trend is that house prices are rising faster than falling. In addition, the newly begun areas, completed areas and sales areas of commercial housing all show positive growing trends, showing that the above argument does not reflect China's actual situation at all.

The price earnings ratio (for housing) should not be calculated by comparing the national average commodity prices with the average per capita annual income of people, for the reason that the housing needs of low-income families in China (who account for 30% of the total urban households), cannot possibly be met by the commercial housing market. We should calculate it by what was defined as the "Urban Indicators Guide" from UNCHS (United Nations Centre for Human Settlements) — "the ratio between the free market price of dwelling units and the annual income of medium households." The UNCHS says that it is not an "international practice" that the price-income ratio should be 4 to 6, and points out that when comparing the price-income ratios in different countries, special care must be taken. Some scholars in China had made a 'benchmark' by using the average income per capita in Beijing to purchase 100 square meters housing in downtown Beijing priced at 30 thousand per square meter to conclude that the price-income ratio in Beijing is 20 to 30. That conclusion is really sensational!

My students and I established a house purchasing power model from the consumption structure of urban residents and the mode of financing for housing purchase. Taking the relevant data for Beijing in 2004 as an example, we made an empirical analysis on the purchasing power of higher-, high-, medium-, low- and lower-income families, and calculated the affordable housing prices of all these families and the price-income ratio when the house price can be paid through the housing consumption mode. The results show that the acceptable price-income ratio of medium-income families was 7.6.[13]

When analyzing the effective demand, the following factors should also be taken into consideration:

First, as the housing needs of middle-income families without housing are more rigid — some of them may pay the mortgage down payment with the support of parents and close relatives — their purchasing ability is thereby greatly increased. Others may choose to rent first; with the later income and savings increase, their purchasing power will gradually grow stronger to bring about an effective demand in the future.

Second, there are buyers who want to improve their existing housing conditions or wish to purchase a second set of house. These people could sell or rent their original houses, and in this way their purchasing capacity will greatly exceed the price-income ratio calculated from their incomes.

Third, price-income ratio is just a static figure; as long as people's income growth rate is greater than the growth rate of the price of houses, the effective demand for commercial housing will grow continuously.

Fourth, our mortgage-backed loans have not been securitized. So when the stock market is at the downturn, the investments for commercial housing will increase, resulting in a lot of money flowing into commercial housing market. Besides, in the expectation of the appreciation of RMB and inflation, both investment demand and speculative demand will increase greatly. As domestic and foreign funds pour into the commercial housing market of Beijing, Shanghai, Shenzhen, Hangzhou and other cities, the housing prices there go up sharply.

9.5.3. *The Structural Imbalance Between Supply and Demand in China's Real Estate Market*

Based on the fact that the number of vacant, unoccupied commercial houses in China is large, some scholars assert that the supply of commercial housing in China is so excessive that the prices will fall, and the land area for newly commenced commercial housing will decrease as well. However, the truth is that both the prices and the new land areas for commercial housing are surging forward and spiraling upwards. We need to explore further to find out why that is the case.

The supply in commercial housing market necessarily includes stock and the new increase. The stock means the total number of commercial houses available for people to move in, while the new increase refers to the newly completed houses during a certain period (usually for one year). The current new increase is bound to become part of the stock in the next period, while the stock will become less due to depreciation, urban re-development and other reasons, so that the stock and new increase of commercial houses should maintain a relatively reasonable ratio. Vacant commercial housing refers to the housing areas that haven't been sold or leased at the end of each construction period, including those commercial houses completed in the current period or from previous ones that are available for sale or lease but haven't been sold or leased out yet. It takes a certain period (usually one year) for the new increase to become stock; however, the existing stock keeps decreasing, so the number of vacant houses (vacancy volume) in commercial housing should be larger than the total sum of both the sold and the leased commercial houses in the coming year. Thus, maintaining a certain vacancy volume in the commercial housing market is not only necessary but also reasonable.

The large vacancy volume of commercial housing in China is due to the structural imbalance of supply and demand, resulting in the over-supply of high-class commercial housing and over-demand of those in the middle and low–end market. Since a single unit of high-class commercial housing is much larger than that of middle and low–end market, the vacancy volume appears larger than what it really is.

The equilibrium of Commercial housing supply and demand is dynamic and constantly shifting, affected by a variety of factors. The development of commercial housing market is closely related to the financial system. Home buyers rely on banks for mortgage, while developers rely on banks for loans. Thus house prices and loan interest rates have become the main factors affecting the housing market. In accordance with the principles of economics, housing developers will increase their housing supply when price of housing goes up; meanwhile demand for housing will decrease and vice versa. The decline in interest rates will increase the supply and demand; when interest rates rises, both supply and demand will fall.

At a certain level of price and loan interest rates, market supply and demand reach an equilibrium, which shows us how the market (the "invisible hand") plays a fundamental role in allocating resources in housing market.

The equilibrium of supply and demand also depends on the future price expectations of both sides. If the future price is expected to fall, the developers will hurry up trying to sell off their houses, while buyers prefer to wait before they finally buy, which results in oversupply; if the house price is expected to rise, developers will increase prices of housing and may even try to keep them in the stock, while the buyers are eager to buy, which often result in short supply.

According to the principles of dialectics, everything is in a state of constant change or development, which means balance is relative, while imbalance is absolute. Newly emerging sciences of complexity argue that although each individual spontaneously decides when and where to buy which house, their decision-making is inevitably affected by others' and the external environment. Buyers, developers, banks and government mutually influence each other, generating a self-organizing force in promoting the market to a certain direction. The market seems to be unordered from the micro and short–term perspective, but from macro and long-term perspective, it is developing towards a certain direction. The market is 'going forward in a wave-like motion': the housing market is periodically going up on a spiral.

9.5.4. *China's Commercial Housing Price Consists of Four Major 'Components'*

As mentioned earlier, China's effective demand for commercial housing in the market is still relatively strong. The main reason of rising house price is insufficient effective supply. The imbalance between effective demand and effective supply implies that the price of China's commercial housing won't significantly decrease.

Overall, housing price can be divided into four major components. The first is the land cost; the second part is miscellaneous costs (referred to construction and installation costs), including the pre-construction cost, infrastructure cost, construction and installation cost, public facilities cost, indirect development expenses, unpredictable expense, financial expense, management expense, marketing expense and etc. The third component consists of payable tax, including mainly business tax, additional city construction tax, education surcharge, value-added tax of land, income tax and etc. The fourth component is the net profit of the project.

Disclosing publicly the costs of commercial housing has provoked a lot of controversies and heated debates. Many developers are against the disclosure; they emphasize that the cost of commercial housing is a business secret, and it may involve some 'gray' areas. We therefore come up with a new concept known as "reference or benchmark cost" to estimate the housing cost in view of the fact that in China, the objective situations are uncertain and there is insufficient or incomplete information available.[14]

In 2005, we studied three cases based on the reference/benchmark cost. The first case is a housing project in Beijing with a price of 8211 yuan per square meter, in which the land cost is 1411.0 yuan (17.2%), construction cost 2583.9 yuan (31.5%), tax 1693.9 yuan (accounting for 20.6%), and net profit 2522.2 yuan (30.7%). The second case is another housing project in Shanghai, with a price of 17,059 yuan per square meter, in which the land cost is 4900.0 yuan (28.7%), construction and installation cost 3683.4 yuan (21.6%), tax 3425.56 yuan (accounting for 20.1%), and net profit 5050.0 yuan (29.6%). The third case is a project in Fuzhou, the selling price per square meter is 3900 yuan, in which the land cost is 742.9 yuan (19.0%), construction and installation cost 1713.6 yuan (33.8%), tax 750.7 yuan (accounting for 19.2%), and net profit 1088.7 yuan (27.9%). From these three cases, we find that the total project cost (land cost plus construction and installation cost) accounts for almost half of the end price. The other half is gross profit (net income and tax). Although China's commercial housing market has changed a lot since 2005, the price composition analysis above is still worth our reference and deeper thinking.

First, land cost accounts for approximately 40–60% of the total project cost, or 20–30% of housing price. This proportion is credible. For example, according to an investigation conducted by Federation of Real Estate Industry Chamber of Commerce from July to October 2008, land cost accounts for 58.2% of the direct housing development cost;[15] Just like what Lu Xinshe, vice minister of Ministry of Land and Resources had said in a press conference conducted by State Council Information Office on June 23, 2009 — that the system of Land and Resources survey results showed that land price in China currently accounts for 15%–30% of the housing price, averaging 23.2%.[16] As land is a scarce resource, its price will definitely continue to rise in the future.

Second, construction and installation cost only account for a quarter of the housing price. This component consists of the cost of materials and labor. However this "concrete" cost ratio is comparatively low by international standards. Of course China's housing price shouldn't directly follow the international ones. It is predictable that the cost of this component will rise as the construction materials and labor cost rise.

Third, tax accounts for about 20% of housing price. Since the newly revised corporate income tax law took effect on January 1, 2007, income tax rate has decreased from 33% to 25%, tax should weigh less in housing price composition. However, value-added tax in 2005 was not considered in the aforementioned three cases because of lax collection. The State Administration of Taxation started a comprehensive liquidation program of the value added tax on real estate companies from February 1, 2007. If the value-added tax on land were recollected based on the provisions, the tax in the three cases above will account for 26–33% of the housing price. After offsetting the decrease of income rate, tax accounts for about 25% of housing price.

The fourth component is the net profit of developers, which accounts for about 30% in housing price, and about 25% after adding value-added tax, including certain "gray" cost — the expense incurred for "rent-seeking". As commercial housing developments requires a number of governmental approvals, this component is quite considerable but difficult to quantify and ascertain.

To sum up, the land cost component in the housing price will be going up instead of down. So it looks like the only way to lower the housing price is to reduce the profit margin, which is determined by tax levied by the governmental and the net profit of developers. Without a compromise between government and developers, the housing price won't go down. Tax involves governmental revenue, so is unlikely to decrease. One must not forget that investing in commercial housing is a kind of relatively high-risk investment. Because of the market risk and financial risk and the requirement of a large amount of capital, the profit margin of commercial housing project in general should not fall below 15%. It is therefore quite obvious that under normal circumstances, China's commercial housing prices won't fall significantly: instead it will go up in the long run.

9.5.5. *The Bubble of China's Commercial Housing Market does Exist*

Since 2003, commercial housing sales price in Shanghai, Hangzhou and other places has been rapidly and continually rising. Domestic and international academia have had heated debates about "whether the real estate bubbles exist in certain areas of China". Historically the real estate bubble burst is an event with a small probability, but once the bubble bursts, it will cause a lasting and devastating effect to the economy and social development of a country or region.

Not long ago, in the United States the "sub-prime" crisis was caused by the commercial housing market bubble burst. After a series of enlargements, the US sub-prime crisis eventually led to the global financial crisis, which dragged United States and many other countries into recession. China has not fully developed its financial system: with less financial innovations (like financial derivatives etc) and relatively stringent regulations on housing loans, it does not have problems of subprime crisis. However, the possibility and problem of China's commercial housing market bubble should be our concern and focus of our attention.

Asset price bubble refers to the trading in high volumes at prices that are considerably at variance with the assets' intrinsic, base values.

During a continuous process of business operations, the price of one type or a series of assets suddenly rise, followed by people's long-term expectations that prices would continue to rise. Such a situation attracts new speculators into the market, making the price of assets much higher than rational.[17] These speculators are interested in selling the assets for profits and quick gains rather than using the assets themselves or utilizing their profitability. The inflated bubble will cause a temporary boom or prosperity, but it's doomed to burst when it amassed itself to a certain size. When the bubble bursts, this will result in the asset prices collapse, economic recession, and even a financial crisis.

We therefore believe that speculation, bubble and risk coexist. Where there is speculation, there will be bubble and risk. Currently China has ample liquidity, limited options for direct investment, undeveloped securitization of mortgages — so people tend to purchase commercial houses to mitigate the effects of inflation and to increase revenue. In this way, commercial housing could be regarded as either an investment or even items for speculation, making commercial housing market speculative too. Bubbles definitely exist there. The inflation and burst of bubble caused fluctuations in the housing market, putting investors at risk.

Just like any speculation, if the size of the bubble is appropriate, it's good for the housing market. Because an appropriately sized bubble will help enhance people's confidence in making money, attracting more capital into the housing market and make it more active. However, it may lead to over-speculation, and finally the burst of the bubble. The atmosphere of panic will spread. People would rush to sell their houses in the market, resulting in an "over-correction" — the price of commercial housing falls lower than its rational price, producing what is known as "sunspots" (i.e, negative bubble).

According to the principles of scientific uncertainty in decision-making, housing bubbles can be divided into two categories: 'objective' bubble and 'subjective' bubble. Objective bubble is formed because of the objective reality of economic uncertainties while subjective bubble exists due to the wrong expectation of the future. Commercial housing price is affected by supply and demand, land cost, construction and installation cost, tax rate, interest rate and etc., which are all related to economic fundamentals. We need past and current data to predict the changes. It is true that developments in Information Technology and forecasting techniques have improved tremendously; more new techniques showed up, such as: data extraction, discovery of knowledge from database, symbolic data analysis, intelligent extraction and many other new technologies. There is now greater accuracy of prediction, enabling investors to adjust their investment strategies based on the predicted interest rate and trend of housing market. However, due to the uncertainties of the objective world and our limited knowledge of the uncertainties, it's inevitable the predicted results and real results will not be identical. That is why the objectively existing bubble is called objective bubble.

According to the principle of complexity science, even if in the same complex system, people's subjective estimations of the future vary widely. But the interaction among people, as well as the external environment are exerting an influence on people, forming a kind of self-organizing force, to guide people's behavior and propel the whole system to move towards a certain direction. Subjective bubble in the housing market is formed by this self-organizing force. What's more, the production of positive feedback — also known as 'extensive foolishness' — will push the housing price much higher than its rational price.

The rational price of commercial housing is an abstract concept, which is hard to determine. We could only use an approximate, reasonable price to substitute it. Based on the above benchmark cost analysis result and the practical conditions of China's Real Estate Market, we recommend that the reasonable price should be 3.5 times the construction and installation cost (net profit of the developers is around 12.5% of the housing price). When the price rises above 3.5 times of the construction and installation cost, we can say that a housing bubble has been created.

Land cost is a major factor affecting housing price, so real estate bubbles will lead to housing bubbles. Since 2003, the "Public bidding, Auctions and Listed land grants" approach has been widely promoted across the country, land cost is escalating in certain cities and the frequency of "prime sites" increasing. According to reports, on June 30, 2009 afternoon, after nearly a hundred rounds of bidding,

Franshion Properties China Limited of Sinochem won the bid for the land located in Road No.15, Fangxing Guangqu (known as No. 15 place) at the cost of 4.06 billion yuan. Its floor price is up to 15,321 yuan per square meter.[18]

We[19] have studied rational expectations equilibrium in the short-sighted (myopic REE) theoretical framework. The introduction of "negative dividends" proved that land price is a 'discounted martingale' under the real discount rate. From 1986 to 1990, eight Japanese Governor Prefectural offices created a real estate bubble warning/alert model in which the inflation rate was subtracted from the land price. Based on this model, we have conducted an empirical analysis on housing market bubbles of 16 key cities in China. Our results showed that in 2004, Hangzhou, Shanghai and Shenyang had serious real estate bubble problems. Signs of overheating also appeared in housing markets of Chengdu, Chongqing and others.

When the housing price is more than 3.5 times of its construction and installation cost, the extra income (bubbles) is gross profit, allocated between the developer and the Government. As added value land tax is collected based on Grade 4 progressive tax schedule, the more the bubbles there are, the more the government will collect in taxes.

Because the housing and real estate industries are of mammoth size and scale, when the house values are very high and bubbles burst, it may cause a huge impact on the whole national economy through credit, investment, consumption, and other means. We should therefore establish rules and formulate policies to guard against excessive speculation in the commercial housing market.

9.6. Suggestions on Promoting the Healthy Development of China's Real Estate Market

Because housing is a necessity, involving the interests of millions of households, the Government has the responsibility of not only to ensure that needs of the low-income families for housing are taken care of, but also has the responsibility to let the market play its fundamental role of resource allocation — through legislation, macro-control and public opinion guidance etc. The government should try to eliminate gradually the state of disorder or chaos in the market, and to contain the over speculation in the market to promote the healthy development of commercial housing.

9.6.1. *Enacting and Improving Laws and Regulations on Commodity Housing*

Real Estate Law is the legal avenue for enacting and implementing real estate policies and regulations. The Law also helps to settle real estate disputes, recognizing and protecting real estate ownership, and it provides a legal basis for securing the works of real estate administrative departments.

Since the adoption of reform and opening-up policies, China has enacted a set of laws and regulations on real estate. With the Law of Land Administration and the Law of Urban Property Administration as the core legislation, relevant and related laws included and consolidated and various regulations complemented, the legal framework for real estate has taken shape.[20] But the quality of legislation is yet to be improved, and I think enhancing systematic legislation is most important.

Laws on real estate encompass civil laws, economic laws and administrative regulations and involve six big sections: capital operation, design and planning, land requisition and demolition, construction, sales and leasing, and property management services. Therefore regulating land transfer, leasing and managing the inter-relations between real estate development, evaluation, transferring, leasing, registration, mortgage, intermediate agencies as well as property management service entities should all be based via legal means and go through the relevant legal, authorities. Any laws and regulations on real estate should be formulated for the following three purposes: (1) to regulate the behavior of market players, including purchasers, tenants, developers, banks, government, intermediary agencies etc. (2) to regulate basic market relationships, such as contract, trust, agency relationship etc. (3) to maintain order and fair market competitions. For example, laws should be enacted to make monopolistic and unjust or inequitable competitions illegal. Only when these three objectives are given full legal force and the relevant regulations adhered to and implemented to the letter, will a healthy and sound real estate market be possible.

A complete legal system has three levels — basic laws, individual laws and departmental and regional regulations. Although the Law of Land Administration and the Law of Urban Property Administration already exist in China, they are not competent to be the 'basic law' for real estate given the 'chaotic' relations between them. There is much repetition as between the two Laws: some parallel laws run in both but some of their provisions contradict each other. In 'individual' laws, some empty and unpractical codes exist while other significant laws like Housing Act and Property Transfer Act await formulation. As for departmental and regional regulations, repetitive legislation is common — no thanks to the selfish desires for power of different administrative departments who care more for their own benefits than real estate management. To overemphasize their uniqueness, some local governments even have rules and regulations that are fundamentally contradictory to departmental regulations or laws.

Lack of good and efficient system in real estate legislation necessitates fine-tuning specific measures for implementation or judicial interpretations of relevant provisions, often bringing numerous troubles, hassles and obstructions to law enforcement, not to mention compromising the effects of justice and legislation. In some real estate disputes, the same case could have different or opposite rulings. This is because many civil liabilities are recognized by departmental and regional regulations, but they serve only as references in the People's Court.

It is therefore suggested that the NPC Standing Committee make a 'cleaning up' of the laws and regulations on real estate, formulate basic law for real estate in the spirit of property law, amend relevant clauses, supplement significant individual provisions, and rectify those contradictions between departmental and regional regulation and the current laws.

9.6.2. *Intensifying and Improving Macro-Control over Commercial Housing*

Since speculative ventures in real estate have some 'blindness' in themselves, excessive speculation will cause market upheavals, hamper the development of national economy, do harm to the interests of the people and go against social justice. Hence, China should intensify the real estate management through macro-control so as to facilitate the healthy development of real estate market.

In the absence of sound real estate laws, somehow certain policies have the regulating effects of laws in our country. During the reforms of our housing system, local governments have introduced a good number of policies that effectively promote the standardization of real estate market; yet there were also some 'ineffectual' policies in need of amendments. Here are some instances:

The 'Interim Measures for Submission of Income from the Sale of State-owned Housing to Finance Ministry' issued on Nov 23rd, 1994 by Ministry of Finance, Leading Group of State Council for Housing System Reform and Ministry of Construction ruled that 'administrative departments of real estate as well as institutions that practice overall budget management should turn over 85% of their income from the sale of state-owned housing"; institutions that practice budget management "by remainder" turn over 60%; institutions practicing self-supporting budget management turn over 30%; and corporations turn over 10%. For another instance, the 'Notification of Managing Collection of Income from the Sale of State-owned Housing' issued on June 14th, 1995 by Ministry of Finance and People's Bank of China emphasized collection of the income should be in time and in full amount. One consequence of these documents is lukewarm 'enthusiasm' in housing sales by property holders, which lead to stagnant sales of state-owned housing for over one year. The problem of overstock remained until the 'Meeting to Exchange Experience of National Housing Reforms' held in Shanghai on December 1995, which pointed out clearly that income from state-owned housing sales were special funds for housing construction and housing system reform, and therefore should belong totally to property holders instead of turning over certain percentages to the state. In direct consequence, the initiative of housing sales by property owners was rekindled by the new income distribution policy, pushing sales to soar.

Of course, there is no such thing as a 'perfect' policy, neither is there an immutable policy. Policy making is the result of weighing the pros and cons–as long as there are more advantages than disadvantages, the policy should be implemented. In addition, policies should follow the times and circumstances: today's good policies may become obstacles a few years later if they remain unchanged throughout. Thus macro-control policies should be legalized; they should be reasonable, opportune and expedient, and effective in playing their roles — leading people to make changes to their decision criteria. The view that policies must serve to prompt or lead people towards certain course of action is consistent with dialectics, which holds that internal causes (or factors) are the bases for change whereas external causes the conditions thereof, and that external causes become operative through internal causes. In our case, policies are the external causes that are leading market players such as housing buyers and developers. Hence, only when policies are well accepted by market players can they accomplish intended effects.

Housing price had gone up faster since 2006, and government departments made a series of policies including controlling land supply, increasing the supply for small households, levying more tax, intensifying tax monitoring and supervision, tightening credit, increasing down payment, limiting residents from buying second suites/apartments, strengthening the management over housing developed by foreign organizations and individuals etc, to lower the price and to facilitate healthy market development. But these policies did not work out so well due to rising costs and market demands. It wasn't until October 2007, when the global economic meltdown began, that the house price began to fall. Under the influence of public opinion and the prevalent expectation that price would continue to fall, the market slumped. There were even cases like intentional mortgage defaults and return purchases in some big cities. Market slump resulted in declining demands for steel, cement etc, and higher unemployment rate (since most peasant workers in cities worked on construction sites), making it even harder for realizing the results of implementing the policy of expanding domestic demand to counter the economic meltdown.

"Rescue packages" were introduced by local governments of some large and medium-sized cities. The General Office of the State

Council also issued 'Opinions on Facilitating the Healthy Development of Real Estate' on Sept 21, 2008 on www.gov.cn, the official website of the Chinese central Government, calling for more efforts on construction of government-subsidized houses and further improvement of people's living conditions in efforts to facilitate healthy development of real estate. Subsequent policies reaffirmed real estate's role as a 'pillar industry' of the national economy. These policies placed great emphasis on the importance of increasing 'ultimate' consumption like housing consumption. They also stressed on quickening the construction pace of government-subsidized houses; reducing transaction tax for some housing schemes; lowering the minimum real estate investment standard; intensifying credit support; encouraging financial innovations; and expanding financing channels for real estate etc.

It should be clear that the government's macro-control should observe the fundamental laws of the market economy, which include the law of value, the law of supply and demand and the law of competition. To manage the timing and enforcement of each policy, governments should keep in balance the interests of each party by careful analysis of the behavior traits and attitudes of buyers, developers, intermediate agencies and banks etc.

At present, our policy making on commercial housing should concern particularly about the houseless middle class. It is suggested that down payments should be lowered to 10% for those who purchase commercial houses with area below 60 m^2 and who pay less than 50% of their monthly income for monthly loan payments.

9.6.3. *Insist on Providing Proper, On-Going Guidance for the Directions of Public Opinion*

In recent years because of the rapid rise in house prices there are many readers who voice a 'big' variety of opinions on the Internet. Some scholars and media reports are inclined to amplify the gravity of the situation with some even demonizing real estate. It is imperative to identify and analyze these viewpoints on the Net and provide proper ongoing guidance so that public opinions will steer towards the right direction in boosting the housing system reform and guarantee the healthy development of commercial housing. I append below six points to keep in mind when dealing with the problems:

First, our secure housing support system should be appropriate, fair and effective, commensurate with the fact that China is currently still in the primary stage of socialism. With limited financial resources, it is already difficult to guarantee sufficient housing support for all low income households within the next three or five years, not to mention supporting those in the middle class.

Second, the price of commercial housing depends mainly on supply and demand of the market, meaning it is impossible for governments to intervene directly in the price but they can use macro-control methods to lead the market though. Governments should be aware of the actual problems of houseless middle class and provide appropriate support for them. As for those who intend to improve their living conditions or buy a second house, it is the individual buyer's decision to purchase or not according to the market situation.

Third, it is absolutely important to combat corruption in commercial housing. It has been mentioned earlier that a big part of the net income of some developers are "gray costs", or frankly the bribery cost.[21] To foster a 'clean' and corruption-free environment for real estate, government officials who seek bribes should be severely punished. Yet from the analysis of the cost of housing price, we could discern that anti-corruption measures are limited in dragging the price down, at the most 5–10% approximately. It is therefore unrealistic to lower the price of houses by a large percentage by merely combating corruption. We should be wary of the misleading theory that corruption is the principal cause of escalating housing price.

Fourth, governments should publicize and promote moderate consumption. With such a huge population and limited land resources, we also have serious problems with our environment, our outdated urban development as well as poor public services etc. Therefore moderate consumption on housing is of great necessity if not urgency. It may be true that people always harbor 'permanent' desires for improved housing, they should be aware of the realities of our country. From an analysis of foreign housing information, we could estimate that in developed countries the proportion of per-capita living space (m^2) and per-capita GDP (USD 10,000) is between 10 and 20. In 2008, China had USD 3267 in per-capita GDP and 26.7 m^2 in per-capita housing construction area (that was 18.7 m^2 for residential housing area). The proportion comes to nearly 30, even computing in terms of purchasing power parity, which is quite reasonable given our relatively low housing price and the fast growing market. It also proves that the per-capita housing level is generally consistent with our current development. Housing area of middle class homes in China's big cities such as Beijing, Shanghai, Shenzhen, Guangzhou etc is close to those of ordinary white collar households in New York, Tokyo, Singapore, Hong Kong, Taipei and like cities. Hence, the housing consumer should make their purchase decisions about area and location through careful consideration of their own purchasing power and opportunities. Renting (taking up a lease/tenancy) is not a bad choice if there are limited offers the purchasers desire in the meantime. In addition, governments should warn people about the consequences of over-consuming without strong financial capacities.

Fifth, governments should pay attention to the investment function of commercial housing. Today, public opinions on real estate speculators are so contrasting to their counterparts in the stock market that the former are constantly criticized while the latter receive much 'acclaim' and envy. The truth is, speculation in real estate and stock market are the same in nature — both are means for people to increase their income. Moreover, it should be made aware to people that capital in these two markets are interlinked: during the downturn of stock market, people turn to real estate, and vice versa.

Sixth, governments should strengthen people's legal awareness. To me, to label someone who pays monthly loan repayments as 'house slave' is incorrect and un-becoming. In the olden days, people could not buy their own house before they had enough savings. But thanks to bank mortgages they can realize their housing dream now. Hence, bank mortgage is an advantage and advancement for society — and paying monthly mortgage is the borrower's obligations under Contract Law so nobody should blame the government or the banks.

9.6.4. *Nurturing and Developing Second-Hand Housing Market*

Second-hand housing (also known as secondary commercial housing) is an integral part of commercial housing, and the two fuel and supplement each other. In many developed counties, secondary housing actually dictates the whole market for the main commercial housing. For example, in 2006, transactions of second-hand housing took up 86% of the commercial housing market in the US.[22] Developing secondary housing not only helps to re-vitalize commercial houses in stock, but also relieve some pressure off the primary market, which is beneficial to the overall commercial housing market development. China's secondary housing market has developed rapidly in recent years, with volume of transactions expanding with the years. Take Beijing as an example, in the first half of 2009, transactions of second-hand housing had exceeded that of new housing.[23] But problems exist in the development of second-hand housing — problems which deserve our intensive analysis and study. We need to seek solutions to these problems for the sake of fostering healthy market for secondary housing.

Firstly, information systems regarding the secondary housing market should be established to reduce problems arising from wrong or misinformation. Recently there are some intermediary agencies who use their housing resources and client information they collect through illegal means in collusion with speculators to drive housing price higher and higher, artificially 'heating up' the housing market. Pilot projects in large and medium-sized cities jointly sponsored by relevant departments such as information department, construction department, housing bureau, and industrial and commercial bureau etc are strongly recommended in order to serve people who wish to buy or rent second-hand housing.

Secondly, transaction tax on second-hand housing is too exorbitant. Compared with primary housing market, transactions of second-hand housing tend to invoke more tax in terms of amount and items, such as appraisal fees, intermediary fee, sales tax, personal income tax, contract tax, stamp duty, transfer fee, and housing maintenance fund etc, all of which can take up to 14.1% of the housing price. In the case of houses in the primary housing market, there are contract tax, stamp duty and housing maintenance fund, which account for only 3.505% of the housing price.[22] That is to say in a 1,000,000 RMB commercial housing deal, people have to pay 100,000 RMB more for second-hand housing than primary housing.

Thirdly, supervision over intermediary agencies should be strengthened. Owing to the lack of relevant information on secondary housing market, nearly 80% of the second-hand houses transact via real estate agencies that are quite often plagued by problems like unethical staff, overcharging, tax evasion, unfair competition etc. It is therefore important to strengthen supervision over real estate intermediary agencies.

9.6.5. *Promoting Financial Innovation in Real Estate*

Real estate goes hand in hand with financial systems. China's real estate financing comes mainly from commercial banks, from which house-buyers apply mortgage and developers loans. In this way, banks face capital flow problems for being long–term creditors of mortgage and loans. In addition, they have to bear default risks from both parties. Neither is it easy for developers as they are under pressing debt pressure and high financing cost, since they usually have to pay off the loans before the development cycle comes to an end. As for investors, most of them have difficulties increasing their proprietary income through real estate because they can get shut out easily for lack of sufficient capital for real estate investment. We should learn from developed countries on the development of real estate financing and encourage financial innovations for real estate.

Among financial innovations, financial derivatives represent the main vehicles: they aim to improve financing efficiency and hedging by diversifying risks. But they can also be used by speculators. Therefore China should encourage financial innovations actively but prudently so as to enhance our financial efficiency as well as financial competitiveness in international markets. Excessive speculation and potential risks should be avoided as far as possible, though it is impossible to stop investing just because of the risks. There is a saying in Institutional Economics: transactions always precede before institutional systems emerge, which implies that it is impossible for transactions to 'wait' until relevant institutional systems are ready and completed; rather, institutions evolve and 'perfect' themselves by overcoming the problems of transactions.

Pilot projects like REITs (Real Estate Investment Trusts) and MBS (Mortgage-Based Securities) are recommended as they could be suitable in China's current situation.

REITs, originated from the US in 1960, are a kind of securitized industrial investment funds that raise capital by issuing beneficiary certificates to investors. The funds will be kept in the custody of some special fund custodian organizations and entrusted to exclusive investment institutions for real estate investment. Investors will get their proportionate income from leasing and the like without assuming many risks.

The proposal for "carrying out REITs pilot projects and enlarging financing channels for real estate corporations" by State Council General Office's 'Opinions on Current Financing's Effects on Economic Development' launched on Dec 8, 2008 had received enthusiastic responses from banks, stock exchanges, governments and real estate corporations etc, who have henceforth actively prepared for the pilot projects. It is high time we formulate relevant policies, regulations and administrative procedures in regards to REITs in addition to getting and training of REIT professionals. By gathering and studying the preliminary experiences from various pilot projects, we should be able to define the mode and position of our Real Estate Investment Trusts.

A mortgage-based security (MBS) is an asset-backed security or securitized debt issued on a fixed monthly interest rate and represents a legal obligation to repay the principal from mortgage loans when due — most commonly applied to mortgaged residential properties.

In America, commercial banks repackage the loans and sell them to facilitate enhanced cash flows, but the banks themselves bear no responsibility to recall loan principals and interests. Issued by relevant entities, MBS realize securitization of mortgaged assets and constitute a secondary mortgage market — 'spreading' the banks' original risks to numerous MBS investors. Moreover banks need not hold the mortgage until due, and thus their liquidity increases. Therefore with China's strict mortgage quality control over our uprising real estate market, MBS is a suitable investment tool for people, given its characteristics of relatively low risk and high returns. What's more, MBS and REITs, which focus on commercial housing and leasing, can supplement each other. We should really give MBS a try.

Though the housing system reform in China is a tough and complex issue, we do learn from lots of precious experiences — even from our mistakes. We should follow the guidance of Deng Xiaoping's Theory, implement conscientiously in a people-oriented, overall, coordinated manner and utilize sustainable scientific concept of development, reflect calmly, establish clear target models, balance various interests, get the hang of the timing and exercise of policy making and be practical and diligent — this way, we should be able to advance and move forward in the urban housing system reform and help create favorable conditions for the 2011 housing system that suit, China's needs and circumstances.

References

[1] Cheng, S.W. (1999). The Reforms of China's Urban Housing Institutions — Target Models and Problems of Implementation, in Cheng, S.W. (ed.), Pandect, *A Systematic Analysis on the Reforms of China's Urban Housing Institutions*, Beijing: Democracy and Construction Press, pp. 1–51 (in Chinese).

[2] Beijing Information Office of United Nations Human Settlements Programme: Brief Introduction of United Nations Human Settlements Programme, http://www.cin.gov.cn/Habitat/cn/default.htm.

[3] Xinhua News Agency (2007). Per Capita Housing Area in China is 27 m^2 with 10 Million Familes Having Housing Difficulties. Accessed on September 18, China.com.cn (in Chinese).

[4] Cheng, S.W. (2007). The Reforms of China's Housing Institutions and Social-Economic Development, *Economic Affairs*, 4–10 (in Chinese).

[5] Fan, X.P. (2009). Preliminary Studies on the Existing Problems and Counter measures in Implementation of the Affordable Housing Policy, *Journal of Hebei University of Engineering* (Social Science Edition), 26 (1), 28–29 (in Chinese).

[6] Xu, D.Q. (2005). Stop Affordable Housing Program, *China Society Periodical*, 19, 11 (in Chinese).

[7] Xinhua News Agency (2007). Seven Departments Confirm that the Owner of Affordable Housing Owns Limited Property Rights, 20:12 November 30, 2007, Xinhua.net (in Chinese).

[8] Chen, B.G. (2009). Major Initiatives on Standard Management of Affordable Housing, Shanghai Construction, *Science & Technology*, 2, 34–35 (in Chinese).

[9] Cheng, S.W. (2006). *On Financial Reforms, Virtual Economy and Financial System Innovations*, Beijing: China Renmin University Press, pp. 59–66 (in Chinese).

[10] Xinhua News Agency (2009). Officials who colluded with businessmen in deals related to the 'Six Consecutive Numbers' Incident of Wuhan's Affordable Housing Are Punished, *Legal Daily*, June 29 (in Chinese).

[11] Huang, S.S. and Chen, H.M. (2009). *The Mystery and Puzzle of the Price of House in China*, Beijing: Social Sciences Academic Press (in Chinese).

[12] Cheng, S.W. (2009). Lessons for China from the Wall Street Financial Storm, *Financial Times*, June 15 (in Chinese).

[13] Li, A.H., Cheng, S.W. and Li, Z.R. (2006). Study on Housing Purchasing Power of Urban Residents, *Journal of Management Sciences in China*, 5, 8–17 (in Chinese).

[14] Yan,Y. and Cheng, S.W. (2008). Research on the Reference Cost of Chinese Commercial Residential Building, *China Soft Science*, 6, 115–123 (in Chinese).

[15] Land Cost Leads to High Housing Price; Need to Reduce the Pressure on Housing Developers/Enterprises in order to Cut Down the Price of Housing, *Legal Daily*, March 12 (in Chinese).

[16] Ministry/Department of Land Administration: No basis for the allegation 'Presence of 1.8 Billion Red Lines will affect Housing Price;

Land Cost Occupies 23% of the Housing Price. People.com.cn-People's Daily, June 24 (in Chinese).

[17] Cheng, S.W. (2003). Diagnosis and Treatment: Revealing the Stock Market of China, in Cheng, S.W. (ed.), Pandect, *Systematic Analysis and Adjustment Proposals on China's Stock Market*, Beijing: Economic Science Press, 1–47 (in Chinese).

[18] Sinhua News Agency (2009). The 4.06 Billion Yuan New Record has made the No. 15 Land of Guangqu Road "Double King of Real Estate" People.com.cn- Beijing Times, July 1, (in Chinese).

[19] Yan, Y., Cheng, S.W., Huang, H.T. and Wang, S.Y. (2006). Land Bubble Early-Warnings Models and Practical Analysis, *Systems Engineering, Theory & Practice*, 6, 1–7 and 40 (in Chinese).

[20] Li, M.F. (2007). The Problems Existing in our Current Real Estate Legislation and Measures to Deal with Them, *Coastal Enterprises and Science & Technology*, 11, 66–67 and 65 (in Chinese).

[21] Cheng, S.W. (2008). Part of the Housing Costs is Used for Bribery, *Beijing News*, December 29 (in Chinese).

[22] Lu, W. (2009). Suggestions on Improving Beijing's Second Hand Housing Market, *Housing Industry*, 5, 80–84 (in Chinese).

[23] Sales of Commercial Housing in the Second Hand/Secondary Housing Market have reached 100,000, Second Hand Housing Becomes the Mainstream, www.house.focus.cn, July 1, 2009 (in Chinese).

Chapter 10

Global Financial Crisis and the Strategy for China

The subprime mortgage crisis which originated from the USA during the spring of 2007 had spread successively along the industry chain, i.e., borrowers—commercial banks—real estate bond issuing institutions—investment banks—insurance companies, and along the product chain, i.e., mortgage loans—MBS—CDO—CDS, and then generated the financial turmoil in Wall Street. The storm finally spread from US to the entire world, and from the fictitious economy to the real economy as well. It resulted in the quick decline of the global economy, and many countries fell into recession. This crisis is regarded as the most serious financial crisis with the most extensive influence since the second half of the 20th century.

Marx once pointed out in Das Kapital that securities and other financial products based on loan capital and bank credit systems are a kind of fictitious capital. In countries whose fictitious economy is highly developed, fictitious capital can inflate greatly through financial engineering. Financial system operates at high risks with high leverage. Over-speculation in the financial derivatives markets becomes rampant. Although related financial institutions achieved very high profits during the period from 2002 to 2006 when real estate market boomed, they suffered liquidity crisis later from debt crisis and then credit crisis while the housing prices plunged later. Credit crisis is essentially the crisis of confidence and trust. Many people lost confidence on the recovery from the crisis and lost trust in financial institutions, financial system and even the government. At that time injecting liquidity into the market is only a temporary respite. The permanent cure should be restoring the public confidence and trust in financial institutions, financial system and the government.

We could draw some lessons from Wall Street's financial turmoil. First, the government's intervention in housing markets should be cautious and moderate. Second, excessive debt is the main cause bringing about deteriorating stability of financial system. Third, we must pay attention to prevent over-speculation in the financial derivative markets. Fourth, the central bank shouldn't take controlling inflation as the only objective of monetary policy. Finally, we should watch over the moral conduct of financial institutions and their employees to prevent untoward/corrupt behaviors.

Under the effects of global financial crisis and the economic cycle, China's economy began to decline seriously from the third quarter of 2008, and it was indeed a grave situation. On November 11th 2008, the government announced the adoption of an aggressive fiscal policy and a moderately lax monetary policy. The government arranged about 4 trillion RMB in the next two years to expand domestic demands and boost steady economic growth. This amount of investment would create more employment, increase more demand for production materials, improve the social security system, help energy saving, help reduce emission and pollution, boost consumption through wages, and prevent deflation. However, we should pay particular attention to social investment, support SMEs (small and medium-sized enterprises), insist on scientific and democratic decisions, and prevent corruption in the process of project budgeting and implementation.

In the first quarter of this year the decline of our economy slowed down somewhat, and some encouraging changes emerged. But, it was not the time to rejoice and be too optimistic. Since the economic growth of this first quarter was triggered by consumption, and the four trillion RMB investment would take some time to take effect. The serious situation of foreign trade couldn't be alleviated in a short time. Overall, our economy will gradually warm up by the middle of this year, with the second half better than the first half, and that the next year will be better than this year. It's very possible to realize the target of eight percent economic growth this year. But we should also follow conscientiously the scientific concept of development, pay more attention to energy conservation and environmental protection, avoid low-level redundant projects and surplus of production capacity. Our government and firms should be pro-active in seeking opportunities even in dangerous situations: we must re-adjust our domestic industrial structures and strengthen external cooperation.

The main reason we were impacted relatively moderately during this financial crisis is that our financial institutions are backed by the government and people have confidence in our government. Our financial system is not highly developed and there are hardly any investment banks, rating agencies or financial derivative products. Our banks are not short of liquidity and our financial supervisory and regulatory departments are always very cautious and prudent. However, we should also admit that there is a long way to go in our road to financial reforms. The international competitiveness of our whole financial sector is not high enough, and our voice in the international financial market is not loud enough. Moreover, the financial supervision and regulation as well as financial innovations in our country need to be strengthened further. In short, we should promote financial reforms actively and carefully along the lines of internationalization, marketization, and systematization. We also need to continue improving the financial service so as to increase efficiency and our international competitiveness.

10.1 Introduction

The subprime mortgage crisis which originated from the USA during the spring of 2007 had evolved into liquidity crisis and then credit crisis from debt crisis. It was a financial turmoil featured by bankruptcy of the subprime mortgage institutions, closing of investment banks and funds, and the severe shock of the stock market upheavals. The storm spread rapidly from US to the whole world, inducing shock and panic in the international financial markets. It also spread from financial sector to real economies, leading to the quick decline of the global economy. Many countries were drawn into economic recession. The huge scale, wide scope and fast spreading speed of the crisis was beyond people's expectation. This crisis is regarded as the most serious one and having most extensive influence since the second half of the 20th century.

As has been addressed by Marx in *Das Kapital*, securities and other financial products based on loan capital and bank credit system constitute a kind of fictitious capital.[1] In the recent decade, under the advocacy and operation of investment banks and rating agencies, fictitious capital consisting mainly of mortgage-backed securities (MBS), collateralized debt obligations (CDO) and credit default swaps (CDS) have been overly inflated in value. The leverage rate of US investment banks once reached more than 25 times, and generally they lacked effective supervision and regulation. In hind-sight, it is no wonder that this severe financial crisis broke out.

Our economy experienced a steady and healthy development in the past 30 years since the reform and opening-up, and our robust economy has made greater and greater contributions towards maintaining and promoting the prosperity of the world economy and its sustainable development. As our total economic output is huge enough and growing quickly, and we have the largest foreign exchange reserves in the world, the world has high hopes for China to take up a major role in helping to deal with the financial crisis. However, the fact is China is still a developing country; its GDP only accounts for six percent of the world, and its GDP per capita is even ranked lower than 100th in the world. So, China can only undertake obligations corresponding to its state power and developmental level.[2] President Hu Jingtao has already stated clearly that, in order to cope with the financial crisis effectively, countries in the world should enhance confidence, increase coordination and strengthen cooperation. Ever willing to continue being a responsible nation, China takes an active role in international cooperation to help maintain international financial stability and promote world economic growth. The steady and relatively fast growth of China is in itself an important contribution to international financial stability and world economic growth.[3] It is therefore imperative that we place paramount importance on dealing with our domestic problems and affairs.

The author has been concerned with the development of sub-prime mortgage crisis since 2007, and has provided his own opinions and comments about the formation and development of the crisis as well as the policies and strategies deployed to face it — in various speeches both inside and outside the country. This chapter integrates the studies made and viewpoints held on this topic. It uses the theory of fictitious capital to analyze the cause of the financial crisis and the lessons we can learn from it. It also explores some possible strategies for China and the potential directions of the financial reform in the future.

10.2. From Sub-prime Mortgage Crisis to Financial Crisis at Wall Street

Subprime mortgage crisis was the financial crisis caused by drastically rising defaults and credit contraction in US subprime mortgage sector. Subprime lending is the loan provided to borrowers with lower income and lower credit rankings by credit institutions such as banks. Encouraged by American government and the Congress, American commercial banks relaxed the standard requirements of housing credit, and in this way greatly promoted the development of subprime mortgage market. The down payment for these kinds of credit was very low. The median of the down payment by the first-time home-buyer was only two percent in 2005, with zero down payment accounting for 43%.[4] The usual payment method is to combine fixed interest rate with variable interest rate i.e, home buyers repay the loans with favorable fixed interest rate in the beginning years after purchasing the house (they didn't even need to pay the principal during these years), and then they repay the loans according to floating interest rate. But usually the interest rate of subprime credit is higher than the normal credit, and usually floating interest rate may rise drastically with time.

After releasing the mortgage loans, commercial banks didn't undertake the responsibilities to redeem the principals and interests. Instead, they would sell the whole package (with its rights and obligations) to third parties to obtain liquidity. The mortgage-based securities (MBS) are issued by some related institutions to realize asset securitization of the mortgage loans, thus generating the secondary market for mortgages.

In the years between 2002 and 2006, American housing market enjoyed a continuous boom. As the interest rate was low and the financial risk small, the subprime mortgage market developed rapidly. From 2001 to 2006, the average rate of increase of new subprime loan reached 38 percent. Due to the credit institutions' overly optimistic prediction of the real estate market — that when debtors default, the credit institutions would not lose after withdrawing the loans and auction them upon foreclosure proceedings. Thus they were willing to offer loans. At the same time the debtors expected the value of their houses to appreciate. They not only utilized mortgage to buy houses, but could also make profits by reselling their houses when they found it difficult to repay the loan. During the burgeoning period of American real estate's price surge, because of very low default rate, financial derivatives such as MBS, Collateralized Debt Obligations (CDO), and Credit Default Swap (CDS) could bring considerable profits at low risks. Credit rating agencies gave AA and above rankings to these derivatives and the related financial institutions. Many investors were following the crowd and 'chased' after the same things — and a lot of investment banks, funds, and insurance companies also purchased a great amount of financial derivatives as investment to make profits.

However, good things don't last long (or 'all good things must come to an end'). From the second half of 2006, with the slowing down of American housing market, home buyers find it increasingly difficult to resell their houses or obtain refinancing through collateralizing. At the same time, interest rate rose rapidly (from June 7, 2004, the Federal Reserve (FED) adjusted the interest rate 17 times, and the federal funds rate rose from 1 percent to 5.5 percent on June, 29, 2006). The repayment interest rate of subprime mortgage loan increased accordingly. Many debtors with poor financial conditions were facing serious repayment pressures, and fell into arrears and default. At about the same time, increasing oil price caused the slowdown of economic development, and many debtors couldn't repay the loans because of layoffs. The default rate of house credit rose rapidly, and the banks found it hard to recall their loans, with some banks suffering huge loss or even going bankrupt. The subprime crisis was triggered.

It is generally believed the subprime crisis began on February 22, 2007. On that day, HSBC disclosed its loss report related mainly to subprime mortgage and it wrote off 10.5 billion dollar MBS related to subprime mortgages.[5] After the occurrence of subprime crisis, lots of subprime mortgage institutions suffered heavy losses or even had to file for bankruptcy. On April 2, 2007, the second largest subprime mortgage cooperation-New Century Financial Corp. (NCFC) declared that it was filing bankruptcy petition and dismissed 54percentofitsemployees.Thereafter,thetenthlargestmortgageinstitutions-American Housing Mortgage Investment Corp., filed in the bankruptcy court for official protection on August 6, becoming yet another large mortgage institution seeking bankruptcy protection after NCFC. In 2007, there were at least 100 mortgage institutions that closed or were sold off.[6]

With the decline in house price and the slowing down of American economy, a lot of normal house mortgage credit began to experience default; this made the crisis spread further. In addition, some credit rating agencies added fuel to the fire by down-grading the rating of some financial institutions and financial products. A few hedge funds seized the opportunity to sell short, thus making the stock prices of many financial institutions such as credit institutions, investment banks and funds, insurance companies fall dramatically. The moves led to heavy losses and forced financial institutions to file for bankruptcy protection. Besides, many investment funds suffered heavily because they held products derived from subprime mortgage.

On July 16, 2007, two subprime debt hedge funds, High-Grade Structured Credit Fund (HGSCF) and High-Grade Structured Credit Enhanced Leveraged Fund (HGSCEL), belonging to the fifth largest investment bank in America, went bust. On October 30 and November 5, 2007, the CEO of Merrill Lynch, Stan O'Neal, and the president and CEO of Citibank, Charles Prince, resigned one after another because of the heavy losses on CDO. From December 2007 to January 2008, big financial institutions like Morgan Stanley, Citibank Group, JP. Morgan Chase, Merrill Lynch., and UBS announced their heavy losses caused by subprime mortgages successively.

Affected by the panics of investors, American bonds market constricted significantly, and dropped 28.27 percent points in the first quarter of 2008 compared with the same period in 2007; in the same period CDO dropped 93.73 percent, and asset-backed securities dropped 82.58 percent. At the same time, American stock market declined dramatically, falling 45 percent. Some commercial banks not only suffered heavily from the rising default rate of house mortgages, but also losses because of rising default rate of credit card payments.

After painful struggling, the fifth largest investment bank in Wall Street, Bear Stearns, finally succumbed: it couldn't overcome its liquidity debacle and declared a 30 billion dollar funding from JP Morgan at 9 a.m. on March 14, 2008.[7] It also obtained the support of American Government. On May 30, JP. Morgan completed the deal with a bidding price of 10 dollars per share. Meanwhile, financial institutions that issued CDOs and CDSs closely related to MBS also encountered liquidity problem, and had to dump their financial assets or seek for mergers.

After the eruption of the subprime crisis, America and Europe took multiple measures, mainly to try to provide liquidity. On August 10, 2007, global central banks injected funds to financial system jointly: the FED provided 38 billion dollars again over and above the basic amount of 24 billion-dollars given earlier. The European Central Bank too injected 248 billion Euros into the financial system. On February 13, 2008, American president Bush signed an economic stimulation plan amounting to 158 billion USD. On March 11, the FED declared a USD 200 billion project that permitted financial institutions, including major investment banks, to use their high risk bonds to exchange treasury bills with secured returns. On April 29, House Financial Services Committee legislated to provide 300 billion dollars to help home owners in financial distress and provide finance to those who were on the brink of losing their houses. From September 18, 2007 to April 30, 2008, the FED lowered the interest rate seven times. Federal fund rate was cut down from 5.25% to 2.0%. On July 16, American Securities and Exchange Committee (SEC) set an emergency restriction on the short selling of major financial companies, including Fannie Mae and Freddie Mac. On July 18, 2008, SEC set a 30-day restriction on short selling of 19 financial stocks, including Fannie Mae, Freddie Mac and Lehman Brothers Holding, Inc. On July 30, American president Bush signed a housing market assistance bill amounting to 200 billion dollars, aimed at bailing out Fannie Mae and Freddie Mac from the crisis and providing help to home buyers.

Since the economical growth rate reached 2.9 percent in the second quarter, an obvious increase compared with the rate of 0.9 percent in the first quarter, a lot of economists including Paulson, minister of the Treasury Department, believed that the main risk of subprime crisis had been 'released' and American economy had begun to recover. Unfortunately, things went contrary to people's wishes. The situation became even worse than before, and it finally shaped the Wall Street financial debacle.

The two largest house mortgage enterprises were Fannie Mae and Freddie Mac. MBS issued by these two companies were based on normal house mortgage credit and have definite credit standard which prescribes quite strictly the types of mortgages that can be offered. But under the encouragement of American government, as well as the impact of hedging funds (which entail high risks), the pension funds and the other funds, the strict standard requirements were relaxed. In 2007, these two companies held 394.8 billion MBS related to subprime mortgage and borrowed a great deal of money from the banks and other companies. Their debts reached 5.2 trillion dollars, 62.5 times than its core capitals (83.2 billion US dollars). With the continuous fall of real estate price, there appeared problems of repaying ability of normal mortgage borrowers, causing the rating of MBS issued by the two companies to decline rapidly, and their stock prices dropped. Liquidity problem arose. Their market values fell from 38.9 and 22 billion dollars in the end of 2007 to 76 and 33 billion respectively by the end of August in 2008. They were facing collapse and seemed not able to survive up to the election in November.[8] The institution bonds issued by the two companies took up 92 percent of the whole institution bonds. On one hand, decline of institution bonds would make the overall bonds market contract, and the capital would flow to equity market or overseas markets. On the other hand, as the institution bonds are the major products of global central banks' deposit, they might be dumped by the central banks of other countries. American government took over the two companies on September 7 by acquiring their preference stocks to provided funds. This resolved the crisis of bonds payment. The two companies issued one billion preference stocks to the Treasury Department, and the latter provided 100 billion dollars to the two companies respectively, maintaining their net book capital. The purpose was to tell the people that the two companies would not go bankrupt, and that the safety of their bonds would be assured. The government's moves also helped to recover the market confidence, stabilize the credit rating and the price, and at the same time bring down the mortgage interest rate in order to stimulate the depressing real estate market. In addition, the Fed joined hands with 10 big US banks to establish a 70 billion dollar stabilization fund to provide funds to the financial institutions facing risks of bankruptcy, and to ensure the liquidity of the market.

However, all the efforts couldn't stop the spreading of the crisis. During the short 24 hours between the night of September 14 to the night of September 15 (American Eastern time) in 2008, three surprising news items exploded in Wall Street, the international financial center, attracting world attention. The first was that on the night of September 14 the Bank of America announced a nearly 44 billion-dollar acquisition of Merrill Lynch, the second largest investment bank with a 94-year history.[9] The second was that the fourth largest investment bank, Lehman Brothers (with 639 billion dollars of assets) was forced to file for bankruptcy on September 15 because of 613 billion-dollar debts as the federal government and private capital refused to bail it out via acquisition.[10] The third was that the credit rating of the biggest insurance company, American International Group (AIG) was downgraded because it held too many default contracts. As loan providers couldn't be found to make it avoid bankruptcy, AIG applied to the Fed for short–term emergency credit in order to avoid bankruptcy during the 48 hours because of the downgraded credit rating, the high funds-raising cost and the pressures concerning its collaterals. At the request of AIG, on the night of September 16, the Fed announced without precedent in its history that it had permitted its subordinate New York Federal Deposit Bank to provide 85 billion-dollars inter-bank credit facility on condition that it would hold 79.9 percent equity capital of AIG, and it would have the right to suspend the distribution of bonus and dividends and of the common stocks and preference stocks issued before, in order to save AIG from the brink of bankruptcy.[11,12]

These serious 'accidents' that happened during the period from September 7 to 16 in 2008 greatly eroded people's confidence, caused the crisis to evolve into a credit crisis, forming the Wall Street Storm, or Wall Street financial tsunami as some people called it. Credit crisis is essentially the crisis of confidence and trust. Many people lost confidence in the future, lost trust in financial institutions, financial system, and even the government. Though the storm originated in US, many other countries had similar problems, and a global financial crisis erupted.

To cope with the financial crisis, many countries took measures using huge capitals to try to save the market. On September 15, 2008, European Central Bank and Bank of England provided 70 billion Euros and 20 billion pounds respectively to the financial market. On October 8, 2008, the central banks of major economic powers, including the Fed, European Central Bank, Canadian Central Bank, Bank of Sweden and National Bank of Switzerland reduced the interest rate jointly — in order to prevent the financial crisis from turning into economic crisis. But in fact, the sharp decline of economy was hard to stop. The estimated growth rate of global economy was below one percent, the lowest in 26 years. The economy of many developed countries experienced negative growth rate.

On November 15, 2008, G-20 summit meeting was held in Washington. G-20 leaders in their joint declaration expressed great concern about the financial market and global economy, and vowed to strengthen corporation, try to re-vitalize the global economic growth, realize the necessary reforms of world financial system so as to better face any serious challenges in the world economy and global financial markets.[13] On November 23, 2008, during the 16th APEC leaders' informal meeting held in Lima, the capital of Peru, it was stated in the informal declaration that the global financial crisis would 'abate' in 18 months.[14]

Thereafter, though many governments kept implementing policies to save the market, including the 'economic stimulus' plan of 787 billion USD passed by the US House of Representatives and Senate on February 13, 2009, the crisis was still developing, and even spread to the East European and developing countries. Many uncertain factors still exist, and the future is still hard to predict.

On April 2, 2009, the second summit of G-20 leaders was held in London. The participating leaders agreed on multiple issues such as macroeconomic policy coordination, financial market stabilization, financial regulation, international financial system reform and so on. There were some positive achievements.[15] After the meeting G-20 leaders signed a joint declaration and confirmed that the third summit meeting would be held in New York in September, 2009. However, the outcomes and decisions of the meeting are still waiting to be implemented, especially those pertaining to jointly maintaining the fair and open international trade environment and the measures taken against protectionism.

10.3. Financial Crisis: A View of Fictitious Economy

On the causes for the occurrence of the financial crisis, there are various and mixed opinions, including lax regulations, 'over-innovation', improper mixing of business in the industry, over-capacity of financial sector, or even a conspiracy theory involving the US government. The author suggests that we should not only 'look at the surface' or find out external factors contributing to the crisis; nor should we hold any subjective perceptions: we should attempt to find out the real, intrinsic reasons. Upon clear and in-depth analysis, I would conclude that an important reason for the outbreak of global financial crisis was the state of 'over-inflation' of fictitious capital attributable to excessive indebtedness and speculation.

10.3.1. *The Concept of Fictitious Capital*

Marx defined the so-called "fictitious capital" in Chapter 25, Volume 3 of *Das Kapital* where he refers to 'all financial products or securities based on loan capital and bank credit system' as fictitious capital. If investors buy stocks and bonds, that means they transfer the right of use of their capital to others, though they still keep the ownership of the capital, evidenced by a certificate, such as bonds, stocks, etc.

Investors could thus claim interests and principals from the bond issuer and require stock issuers to pay dividends and protect stockholders' interests. However, as the value of the certificate is supported by the issuer's promise ('credit ability') for making good the payment of interest and principal, or dividends, as the case may be, when the 'credit ability' evaporates, the certificate is just a piece of paper with no value. Marx thus calls it fictitious capital.

10.3.2. *Feature of Fictitious Capital: Inflation or Expansion*

One key feature of fictitious capital is that it can inflate on the basis of the banking credit system. Marx provides a simple illustration in his work: merchant A in London ordered some goods from producer C in Manchester through intermediary B intending to sell them to costumer D in East India. A, B, C and D all can discount the commercial bills offered by each other to the bank and get a short-term loan, and thus causing the 'inflation' of fictitious capital.

The author would like to extrapolate Marx's illustration thus: suppose the deal involves one million USD, and the valid transaction period is six months. After B and C, A and D, and A and B have signed the relevant contracts, they can ask for discounting from the bank using the contracts as commercial bills/paper, or borrow from the bank using the contracts as the collateral. In this way, producer C can get funding to buy resources, employ workers, and organize the production process. Intermediary B, buyer A, and customer D can also obtain loans individually from the bank. Therefore, one million USD could turn into four million USD which can be used in the six month period. Of course, the above example is a simplified one. In fact, banks will discount the payment when providing the loan, while the producer (C) will not start the production if it does not obtain a down payment.

Suppose in the 6 months, A, B, and D use the borrowed money to do other business in order to make profit, and if they have earnings, then B can pay one million dollars to C and take the goods, then transfer the goods to A and get one million payment to pay back its bank loan. A ships the goods to D and gets payments from D, and he returns the money to the bank. D sells the goods in India, and returns one million loan to the bank. If anyone gets into trouble and defaults, the whole chain will be broken. Although the defaulting party will be penalized according to the law, the bank will beget a new non-performing loan (NPL).

That was the case in Marx's era. Now, the inflation of fictitious capital is much more dramatic than in the past. Due to technological development and financial innovations, there is now a great variety of financial derivatives, seemingly endless and dazzling. The main objective of creating new derivatives is to fulfill different investors' different preferences or choices in terms of security, returns and liquidity. The other purpose is to hedge the risks. However, derivatives are also speculative tools and that's the reason for the inflation of fictitious capital.

Generally, the 'inflation' of fictitious capital can be categorized as follows:[16]

10.3.2.1. *Over-valuation*

When investors overvalue a security, this will cause the inflation of fictitious capital. For instance, in the stock market, if investors are too optimistic for a company's profitability, they would be willing to pay a higher price for the stock. Particularly in a bull market, many investors would chase after a stock owing to the 'herd mentality' or due to the psychology of 'fool's competition — hoping someone else will buy from you at even higher prices'. Bubbles are thus created and when they burst, investors will certainly suffer loss.

10.3.2.2. *Over-indebtedness*

When borrowers believe that their returns will be higher than the borrowing rate, they might borrow greater amounts to make more profit. Sometimes, their debts can be tens of times or even hundred times greater than their equities. When investors withdraw their loans owing to pessimism about the future prospects, or when they refuse to provide new loans, the borrowers could face the possibility of bankruptcy.

10.3.2.3. *Margin: (Using little money to 'guarantee' a larger amount)*

Less capital is used to 'guarantee' much larger transaction. For example, in futures market, a futures contract only need 5% margin to purchase.

10.3.2.4. *Multiplier effect*

We all know that because of monetary multiplier effect, the supply of currency by the central bank could be multiplied many times to become a considerable volume of currency in society. The same is true of the fictitious capital. For example, a bondholder may collateralize the bonds to the bank and borrow cash. He may then use the money as margins to buy futures contracts or other derivatives. Thus, the initial capital used to buying the bond can be utilized in buying into outstanding bonds, open-interest futures contracts (possibly 20 times the margins) or other derivatives. So, the capital is amplified tens of times. However, the bondholders' risk is also amplified from the low risk of bond to high risk of derivatives. He may earn higher return, or he might lose everything.

The reason for this financial crisis is over-inflated fictitious capital due to over-indebtedness caused by excessive speculation, which we call 'overly high leverage rate'. Leverage rate is defined as how many dollars worth of business can be done or generated by one dollar of capital. In the case of US, the leverage of commercial banks is about 8 to 12, and 25 to 40 for investment banks. With the support of federal government, leverage of Fannie Mae and Freddie Mac once reached 62.5, i.e, issuing 5.2 trillion bonds with 83.2 billion capital. For some AAA bonds, leverage could even reach 100.

Higher leverage rate helps produce higher efficiency of capital operations. Suppose leverage rate is 40. When returns rate is 1% higher than loans rate, actual returns may reach 40%, but risk will certainly increase. 25 thousand USD could do for you a business of USD one million; but if there be any trouble, the capital is definitely not enough and you have to borrow more or sell your equities.

10.3.3. *Expanding Risks of Fictitious Capital*

By the end of February 2007, the balance of sub-prime mortgage was about 1.3 trillion USD. [17] How could such a relatively small amount of sub-prime mortgage debt cause such a huge global crisis? Nobody can explain it clearly so far — because of the complexity of the process — and it warrants further intensive and detailed studies. Here, the author tries to provide a preliminary analysis, as follows:

Recent financial innovations help form an industrial chain: borrower—mortgage institutions including commercial banks—mortgage-backed bond issuing institutions—investment banks—insurance companies; a product chain: mortgage loans—MBS—CDO—CDS. Fictitious capital gets inflated continuously along these two chains, and the risk amplifies correspondingly. A debt crisis develops into a liquidity crisis, and finally evolves into credit crisis/credit crunch.

10.3.3.1. *Debt crisis*

When a borrower obtains mortgage loan from commercial banks and buys real properties, he is obligated to pay interests periodically according to the contract. If the borrower defers the payment, he has to pay punitive interests; if he defers beyond the deadline, the creditor may take possession of the ownership of the real estate according to relevant terms of the contract ('foreclosure proceedings'), and sell it in the auction market. So in primary mortgage market, the main risk is default risk. Mortgage institutions are the major risk undertakers. When real properties price plunge and the interest rate goes up, default begins from the sub-prime mortgage loans, since sub-prime mortgage borrowers are most vulnerable to risks among all. In October 2007, the default rate of sub-prime mortgage was about 16%.[18] In January, 2008, the figure shot to 21%.[19] In May 2008, the figure reached 25%.[20]

When real estate price decline seven further, some borrowers who, during normal circumstances could repay the loans, also lost their ability to pay back interests. Others defaulted intentionally since house price went much lower than its original purchase price. Default rate rose quickly, while legally auctioned house also increase greatly. 1.286 million real properties lost their rights of redemption in 2007, increasing 79% compared with 2006.[21] In 2008, the figure went up to 2.335 million, increasing 81% over 2007.[22] The total value of non-performing mortgage loans was 9.9 trillion USD at the end of 2006, and reached 10.6 trillion USD in the middle of 2008.[23] As the price of legally auctioned-off houses declines further, sales became even more difficult. The loan institutions suffered huge loss; their stock price went down sharply and some of them went bankrupt. Thus the debt crisis was born.

In addition, the debt crisis expanded form mortgage loans to car loans and other term installment loans, even credit card payments. Commercial banks were dealt heavy blows in the process.

10.3.3.2. *Liquidity crisis*

Mortgage-Backed Securities (MBS)

As the primary market of mortgage loans grew rapidly, secondary market for selling and transferring relevant securities emerged gradually alongside. In the securitization process, MBS was created. MBSs are bonds collateralized by mortgage loans issued with fixed monthly rates and payment of principal upon maturity. When house prices rose, interest rates on loan were kept low, and people's income was sufficient to pay interests and principals. MBSs were attractive because their rates were much higher than deposit interest rates.

At the beginning, the issue of MBS was supported by some government sponsored enterprise (GSE).The biggest two among them were Freddie and Fannie. Their main business was to buy mortgage loans from the secondary market, and then issue bonds or MBSs to investors. All these MBSs were implicitly assured or 'guaranteed' by the government, and thus had high credit. From 1989 on, MBS rates issued by Freddie Mac and Fannie Mae were 137 base points higher than 10-year government bonds on average, attracting investment from many institutions.

Along with the development of secondary market, private institutions could also conduct MBS issuing. Commercial banks are allowed to re-package mortgage loans and sell them to a Special Purpose Vehicle (SPV) to isolate bankruptcy risk. SPVs then issue MBSs. So-called 'risk isolation' means that creditors cannot claim repayment for the asset which have actually been sold to SPVs already — if the issuer goes bankrupt.

SPVs are actually "shell companies" registered in Caiman Islands or other places with tax incentives. They are usually set up by institutions unassociated with commercial banks, generally hiring no employee and no physical office, and they out source all business to other institutions. SPVs buy mortgage assets from commercial banks and issue MBSs to finance the move. They then pay the cost of buying mortgage assets using the proceeds. SPVs take interest and principals from mortgage borrowers through certain agencies, and appoint banks to pay interests and principals to MBS holders. Their assets and liabilities are generally equal.

The development of secondary market changed the mode in which commercial banks undertake solely the mortgage risk. Instead, risk can now be 'diversified' to MBS investors. Moreover, commercial banks need not hold the mortgage loans until maturity. Further, MBS allows institutions and investors all over the world to invest in US real estate markets, and 'spreads' the risk to the world. The value of MBS depends on mortgage payment rate and house price. When house price grew rapidly, MBS interest rates were higher than borrowing rates, the 'spread' (the price differential) had reached 2–3%. Many institutions were eager to borrow money by issuing bonds so as to invest in mortgage securities. By the end of Mar 2007, balance of MBS assets was 6.3 trillion USD, including sub-prime MBS of 900 billion. From 2001 to 2006, securitization rate of sub-prime mortgage increased from 54% to 75%.

In order to contain and prevent risk and protect investor confidence, the US government has set the following regulation for MBS issuing: First, to prevent reduction of principals due to borrowers' early payment, surplus assets are needed in issuing, i.e, credit assets supporting MBS should exceed the amount for issuing bond. Second, if borrowers could not pay interest in time in the early period for repayment, investors could force the issuer to redeem the security. Third, before any credit rating is made, SPVs should ask rating agencies to audit the MBS. If it does not get the expected rating, SPVs need to enhance its credit rating by asking for excess/additional collaterals from financial collateralization companies. This is called credit enhancement.

However, even the above regulations also cannot deal with the problems following real estate price decline. When debt crisis happened, MBS issuing institutions could not receive regular payments, and therefore had not enough cash to pay interests to investors and principals to those who request redemption causing liquidity problems. In this case, issuing institutions usually borrow from other institutions, or sell its own assets (stocks, or bonds), so as to obtain liquidity. However, since people did not hold hopes of an improved real estate market, credit rating of issuing institutions had been lowered greatly. So, other institutions were not willing to provide loan. At this time, investors' principals had already depreciated greatly, and increasing default rate further pressed MBS price downward. Besides, since MBS is a fixed-income security, when interest rate rises, the price will fall down, causing the stock price of issuing institutions to come down. Thus, issuing institutions could not obtain new funding by borrowing or selling assets. If the liquidity problems cannot be resolved or mitigated, related financial institutions would go bankrupt.

Collateralized Debt Obligations (CDO)

Through financial innovation, MBSs can be securitized further. Using the approaches of financial engineering, such as evaluation, reconstitution, and re-packaging, financial institutions have introduced and promoted great varieties of derivative products to the market, attracting buyers by their high rates of returns. Among the new products, the most famous one is probably collateralized debt obligations (CDO). CDO is a kind of structural asset-backed securities (ABS). Usually the CDO issuer forms a pool of all collateralized loans including mortgage loan, student loan and commercial loans, and then split it into different tranches according to the risks and the returns, then sell them to different investors according to their different risk 'appetites'. Typical CDOs are generally classified into senior, mezzanine (or medium), and equity tranches. Among them, equity tranche has the largest risk exposure, and suffers the loss first when default happens in the pool. Correspondingly, equity tranche provides higher returns than the others. Senior tranche (usually with AAA rating) has the priority to get payments for interests and principal over mezzanine and equity tranche, and has lower risk exposure than them. Hence, its returns are also lower. Risk and returns of mezzanine is between them, and the credit rating is also between AA and BB.

The issuing of CDO is similar to MBS. The issuers (usually investment banks) package their diversified collateralized assets to form the pool (underlying asset), then sell them 'truly' to SPV as a risk isolating approach. So, CDO holders could not claim repayment if collaterals did not achieve their required returns. SPV is the nominal issuer of CDOs, which are backed by the underlying asset. The proceeds from issuing CDO are used to pay the cost of buying underlying assets.

The managers of CDO (usually investment banks) hold the equity tranche, and attract investors by the (good) record of its past performance. Managers earn commission from the issuing procedure, and management fee for the duration of the contract. Rating agencies evaluate and audit the risk of the underlying assets, determine the proportion and scale of each tranche, ensure the quality of them, and renew the rating periodically.

Buyers of CDO are usually insurance companies, banks, pension funds, investment companies, investment banks, and hedge funds. The objective of most institutions is to earn higher returns (normally, CDO returns are 2–3% higher than corporate bonds with the same rating). More active investors use CDO for arbitrage. Hedge funds use CDO as collaterals to obtain loans from commercial banks with leverage of 5–15 times.

Besides, introduction of CDOs collateralized by other CDOs (CDOs of CDOs), CDO-squared, and CDO-cubed has made the securitization of debts and mortgages more and more complicated — in fact, so complicated that even financial specialists don't know how to explain them clearly. By the end of 2007, CDO value in US was about 19.8 trillion, and about 2.5 trillion accumulated CDOs issued in the world.

SPV is basically an off-balance sheet entity. Since regulators and stockholders do not know its existence, it's a 'regulatory lacuna'. Securitization provides the chance for institutions to transfer their mortgage assets to off-balance sheet SPVs, so as to avoid capital adequacy requirement, and to increase profit. However, risks also increase proportionately.[24]

When house price dropped and debt crisis emerged, defaults occurred widely to various collateralized loans. Repayment pressure forced financial institutions to sell their CDOs and this pushed the CDO prices down. According to the new Mark-to-Market (MTM) rule, financial institutions are required to value their assets according to the market price, which can be much lower than their normal value. Further, since bidding price was much lower than asking price at that time, institutions had to lower their asking price to complete the transaction. All these greatly reduced their profit margins, and further aggravated investors' panic, and caused more dumping. Price of nominally one dollar CDO even came down to as low as 7–11 cents. So the issuing institutions could still go bankrupt because of liquidity problems, caused by the fact that the income from selling off their assets couldn't pay off their debts.

To reduce risk, investors could get credit protection by buying insurance. MBS and CDO are usually insured by Monoline Insurance Institutions, which usually possess credit rating of AAA. However, when the credit rating of insured MBS goes down, insurance payments increase speedily, causing the credit rating of the insurance company to come down as well. Other products like municipal bonds are involved also. With the resultant liquidity problem, some insurance companies also had gone bust.

Credit Default Swap (CDS)

CDS is another innovation based on CDO, providing a tool against credit risk of MBS and CDO investors. CDS is basically an insurance product. Its buyer is the creditors who is concerned with the possible default by the debtor. The vendor/seller of CDO promises that if certain 'credit events'(for instance, the debtor defaults, goes bankrupt) occur, the buyer could use the collateral to exchange for the payment of debt. This kind of contracts usually mature in five years, and can be traded or transferred over-the-counter anonymously. All the trading records need not go public, making it difficult to regulate.

Like all the other derivatives, CDS can be used to hedge risk, protect creditors from the loss of default — and be used as speculative tools. CDS price is determined mainly by the solvency of debtors, including default probability, default time, value of collaterals, and financing cost. If real estate price goes up, and mortgage default rate is low, CDS price is relatively low. In such a situation, not only many investors will buy CDSs to obtain cheap credit protection, but also some speculators will hold cheap CDSs in order to make profits in case the price goes up, and could obtain high payment when credit events really occur. On the other hand, companies and other institutions may have the opportunity to sell a great amount of CDSs and earn more income at the time of low risk. Some investors can also sell (short) CDSs to make profit, even though they do not have any loans business. For the above reason, CDS market 'inflates' very quickly in the financial markets of developed countries, reaching 33-62 trillion USD in total 'open interest' value at the end of 2007.

As a speculative tool, CDS also affects the stock markets. If investors feel that that a particular company may fall into insolvency, they will buy lots of CDSs of this company. They will short sell the stock of the company, forcing the CDS price to rise so as to realize the profit on CDS market. However, it will be difficult for the company to get further loans due to its high CDS price, and so it may fall into financial distress. So we could see that CDS is actually a gambling tool for both the buyer and seller of CDSs.

When the subprime credit crisis erupted, 'credit events' occurred frequently. From 1998 to 2008, bad loans of CDS increased 100 times. Since the vendors of CDS would have to pay huge amounts for defaulting events and collaterals could not be liquidated easily, liquidity becomes a major problem for related institutions. For example, AIG once had USD 440 billion CDSs, and the US government had to provide bailout solutions to prevent its bankruptcy.

In summary, as real estate price dropped drastically, all derivatives in secondary market of mortgage loans, including MBS, CDO, and CDS, caused great liquidity problem to US financial institutions, and the debt crisis evolved into liquidity crisis.

10.3.3.3. *Credit crisis*

Following the evolvement of liquidity crisis, in the middle and late Sept 2008, many events occurred successively in US — the bankruptcy of Lehman Brothers, the takeover of Freddie and Fannie by the government, the acquisition of Merrill Lynch, and the urgent bailout of AIG — all these triggered serious credit crisis, generated the financial debacle in Wall Street, and caused the outburst of global financial crisis.

Credit system is the foundation stone of modern market economy, as well as the basis of fictitious economy. With the rapid 'inflation' and expansion of fictitious capital buttressed upon the credit system, fictitious economy developed rapidly in US and other developed countries. That's how these countries 'plundered' tremendous wealth from the world.

As aforementioned, when lots of borrowers/debtors lose their personal credit, it would cause a debt crisis, and when many financial institutions lose their credit, that will cause liquidity crisis. If individuals, institutions, companies, and even the government all lose their credit, then there will be a general credit crisis. When the credit system breaks down, the owners of capital will find it difficult to regain their ownership rights, which may be extinguished. Concerned with the lack of credit of the other party, investors fear for the security of their investments and this 'psychology of fear and worry' could spread rapidly. They have to dump their financial assets, and even withdraw their deposits from banks. The purpose of holding cash is to be able to carry out their financial obligations, avoid bankruptcy, and deal with possible difficulties in the future. At the same time, banks might fall into crisis or even go bankrupt if more and more borrowers default, and lots of deposits were withdrawn. Other related institutions might also dump their MBSs and CDOs, pushing their price down and hurting the debt market badly. Stock market also plunged because of dumping and price crash of financial institutions.

When the crisis broke out, 150 billion USD were withdrawn from the money market funds within two days. In the subsequent days, the outflow was five billion per two days. On September 16, the net value per unit of Reserve Primary Fund fell under one dollar because it had held bonds of Lehman Brothers — and investors rushed for redemption.[25] Before money market opened on the morning of September 18, total orders to sell reached 500 billion dollars, while the total value of the market was only four trillion dollars. It was fortunate that Federal Reserve injected 105 billion USD funding into the market on time. This saved the market from crashing.[26]

On September 21, the only surviving investment banks, Goldman Sachs and Morgan Stanley, applied to become' bank holding companies', signaling that the American investment banking industry had fallen apart. In the night of September 25, Washington Mutual, the largest deposits and loans bank, was takeover by Federal Deposit Insurance Company (FDIC). Most of its assets were transferred to J.P. Morgan Chase at a price of 1.9 billion USD.[27] On September 29, the Dow Jones Industrial Index lost 778 points in one day, the largest fall in history.[28] On the next day, the overnight LIBOR rate rose from 4.75 to 6.88%.[29]

In the face of serious credit crisis, US and European countries launched various bailout policies to inject liquidity into the banking system. However, these policies could not prevent the crisis from expanding to the real economy. The author suggests that credit crisis is indeed a crisis of confidence and trust. Injection of liquidity could only 'heal the superficial'. To 'heal the fundamentals', steps must be taken to restore public confidence and trust in the financial institutions, financial system and the government.

10.3.4. *Spreading of Financial Crisis to the Real Economy*

We could observe the following phenomena after the occurrence of the credit crisis:

First, banks cut down their loans. Facing increasing credit risk, banks had to tighten terms for loans, making it more difficult to obtain loans. Even inter-bank offering rates are going up sharply, resulting in firms and individuals finding it much more difficult to borrow money.

Second, investors are cutting on their investments. Because people could not trust other people or parties' credit, and are worried of losing their money in investments, the best way for them is to keep the money in their own pockets. When US stock market fell, some stock prices were even lower than their net asset value per share, or even lower than their net cash value per share. By simple logic, it would appear that these would be good buys. However, few people wanted to buy them. The reason was that they were in deep fear of misinformation or were afraid of getting misled or 'hood-winked' into buying them.

Third, consumers were cutting down their consumption. The losses in the stock markets had forced house prices to depreciate sharply and people had less money to spare. Consumers' general economic perspective turned to negative. They had to cut down expenditure and consumption, so as to prevent their financial situation from getting worse in the future.

Finance is the core of modern economy, while capital is its blood. Real economic growth relies on bank loans, investment and consumption. If banks cut their loans, investors cut their investment, and consumers cut their consumption, the real economy will be seriously impacted. True enough, global real economy declined drastically in the second half of 2008. In 2008, world economy only grew 2.5%. It's forecasted that growth rate will be negative for US, EU and Japan in 2009, and about 4–5% for developing countries. The average global growth rate will only be 1% in this year.

10.4. Financial Crisis: Implications to China

After the eruption of subprime mortgage crisis, domestic and foreign experts, scholars and economists have expressed a wide variety of views, trying to sum up relevant experiences and lessons. There are some insightful comments, but also some distorted views and misreading. The author studied in detail the developmental process and the causes of Wall Street's Finance Storm. Based on rigorous studies and in-depth analysis and considering China's actual situation, I have come out with the following preliminary revelations and suggestions:

10.4.1. *Government Intervention in the Real Estate Market should be Cautious and Moderate*

Housing is not only a expensive living necessity, but also an investment tool against inflation. The real estate industry is a 'pillar industry' of national economy. Its development could catalyze the demands for production materials, consumer goods and services. The development of real estate industry is closely related to the financial system. The purchaser of houses must depend on the bank mortgages, and the developer must depend on the bank loans: therefore the house price and the loan interest rate become the main factors affecting the market. According to economic principles, when the price of houses goes up, the supply of houses from the developer increases but the demand for housing demand decreases, and vice versa. Both supply and the demand will increase with the drop of the interest rate, whereas they will drop with the increase of the interest rate. At a certain price and interest rate, the supply and the demand of the market will reach an equilibrium. It is the market — the invisible hand — that plays the fundamental role in allocating resources in the real estate market.

According to principles of dialectics, everything remains in a state of flux and changes constantly. Balance or equilibrium is always relative, while imbalance is absolute. According to the tenets of emerging complex science, although every house-buyer decides independently when to buy and what kind of house to buy, the decision will certainly be affected by other people's decision and the external environment. The mutual influence of buyers, developers, banks and the government will generate a self-organizing effect and drive the market to develop towards a certain direction. Thus, although the market appears to be disordered from a microcosmic angle in the short–term, it has certain direction from a macrocosmic angle in the long–term. The market could advance in a wave-like manner and grow spirally, and that is the reason that the housing market fluctuates and rises periodically.

Because housing market involves the interests of millions of households, it is necessary for the government to exercise macro-control on the market in order to fulfill their responsibility to ensure justice and social fairness. However, government intervention in the market should be cautious and moderate; otherwise the consequences will be negative or even adverse. The subprime mortgage crisis occurred because both Clinton and Bush administrations made homeownership the major objective of their policies in their bids to win over the support of the low-income groups (mainly blacks and Hispanic residents). In trying to promote economic development, the policies of US government have always encouraged the real estate industries — including mortgage industries (Fannie Mae and Freddie Mac were two government-sponsored enterprises); they wished for the relaxation of lending requirements for borrowers.[30] Some senators of the US advocated: "Let all the blue-collar families own their own houses". So the Department of Housing and Urban Development (HUD) of US made relevant mortgage loan policies which encouraged the development of the subprime mortgage. These policies required that Fannie Mae and Freddie Mac should purchase more mortgages loans so as to enable low-income families and minority families to obtain affordable housing. Fannie and Freddie should regard their billions of investment in the subprime loan as 'public goods' to help develop housing for low-income families.[31] In 1996, HUD instructed that Fannie Mae and Freddie Mac should issue 42% of their mortgage loans to borrowers whose family income was below the median income in their community. The target was to rise to 50% in 2000 and 52% in 2005.[32]

With the prosperity and boom of the US housing market, banks began to offer more and more loans to high-risk borrowers, even illegal immigrants, driven by Fannie Mae and Freddie Mac, and tried to obtain high earnings from the high-risk loans. In general there were three types of high-risk loans. The first was the usual subprime loans issued to borrowers with no income, no job and no assets, sometimes known as NINJA loans. The second was adjustable or floating rate mortgages (ARM) which required the borrowers to pay interest only in the early years ('grace period'), but the pressure of servicing the debt would increase greatly when interest rates rise after the 'grace period'. Yet another one is self-chosen loans, whereby borrowers could choose monthly repayments, but any unpaid interest would be counted as principals. Of the aforementioned three types of sub-prime, ARM occupied about 80%. Meanwhile, the average interest margin between the subprime mortgage loans and the normal loans fell to 280 basis points in 2001, compared with 130 basis points in 2007. Besides, mortgage underwriting auditing was relaxed gradually. In 2007, 40% subprime loans were issued automatically, without appropriate auditing ad record.[33] This boosted the whole subprime mortgage market and made the issuance ratio of the subprime mortgage increase tenfold from 1994 to 2003, with its annual growth rate reaching as high as 25%.[34] The total amount of subprime mortgage loan increased from 35 billion dollars (5% of the gross loan) in 1994 to 160 billion dollars (13%) in 1999, and reached as high as 600 billion dollars (20%) in 2006.

When house price rises, the reduced housing demand will restrain the price rise to a certain degree. However, government policies had promoted the development of subprime mortgage, and the low interest rate policy of the US Federal Reserve supported the 'great prosperity' in the housing market from 2002. A lot of low-income families could get loans to purchase houses they could not afford before. These policies also encouraged housing investment and speculation. In 2005, 28% of houses purchased were for investment, while 12% for vacation use. The market risk increased greatly because speculators used high leverage in transactions involving these houses.

After the occurrence of the subprime mortgage crisis in early 2007, many low-income families couldn't afford the high interests by refinancing loans in the concession or 'grace' period and lost their houses in foreclosure. In September 2008, the US house price dropped more than 20% on average compared with the peak in mid-2006. This made many houses' net value to drop to zero or negative. It was estimated that 8.8 million borrowers' (accounting for 10.8% of all owners) housing assets had become negative assets in March 2008, and the figure reached 12 million in November 2008. Many borrowers chose to default intentionally, and cases of fraud in mortgage loans occurred commonly. In 2007 the sales of new American house sales fell by 26.4%, which was the maximum drop from 1980 (23.1%).[35] At the end of 2007, there were four million available houses for sale,[36] of which nearly 2.9 million were unoccupied.

The increasing mortgage default rate reduced the value of the securities such as MBS, CDO and so on, so the banks' net assets were reduced and financial situation weakened. Fannie Mae and Freddie Mac were also taken over by the US government for insolvency (their net asset values were 114 billion dollars on June 30, 2008, but their mortgage loans were up to 5.1 trillion dollars in which nearly half were outstanding accounts).

The global financial crisis triggered by the subprime mortgage crisis caused tremendous damage to the world. One lesson to be learned is that the government should respect the fundamental laws of the market economy, analyze carefully the attitudes and behavioral characteristics of buyers, developers, intermediary institutions, banks and others. The government should learn to handle properly issues relating to the balance of interests and benefits of all sides, and come out with appropriate policies and effective measures to address the problems in a timely manner.[37]

10.4.2. *Excessive Debt is Responsible for Destroying the Financial System Stability*

Fictitious economy is a metastable system with dissipative structure relying on fund exchange with the outside to maintain its relative stability. This kind of system can achieve stability by self-organization, but its stability can be damaged easily by small external perturbations. When its system stability is broken, it can swing within a certain range, between stability and 'motility'. On a macro level, the system can be considered as stable, which can be called local stability. But sometimes the system may change dramatically or even collapse, if it becomes instable. The system may restore to the metastable state by intrinsic restructuring after the system collapses, or it may die away. In general, the greater the inertia of the system, the smaller will be the probability of its collapse.[38]

There are many factors which cause the metastability, but the most fundamental factor is the intrinsic instability of fictitious capital. The 'inflation' and expansion of the fictitious capital — buttressed by the credit system — could bring danger to the credit system itself and eventually could even destroy it. The instability of fictitious capital also comes from the 'positive feedback effect' which exists in the fictitious economic system. For example, when a particular type of assets is dumped, more people will be induced to dump them. The interaction between people is the positive feedback effect which will result in amplification effect and cause the 'price' of the fictitious capital to rise or fall sharply.

The United States had abandoned the more conservative traditions of its forebears after World War II and had become a country which advocates conspicuous consumption. The consumerist culture emphasizes gratifying immediate demands. There is a widely accepted principle of "Buy now, pay later".[39] Prompted by this culture, the proportion of US household debt to annual disposable income increased from 60% in 1974 to 77% in 1990, and reached 127% in 2007 and 134% in mid-2008. The 'wealth effect' generated by the rise of house price prompted higher consumption and reduced savings. According to statistics from the US Bureau of

Economic Analysis, more than 99.5% of personal disposable incomes in US household were used to consume or service interests. Deducting items involving houses occupied by owners for own living, American family saving turned to negative from 1999, i.e., expenses had exceeded personal disposable income. In 2008, an American family had 13 credit cards on average. 40% of the families still had unpaid accounts in their credit cards; the number was only 6% in 1970.[40]

In the pre-crisis years, low interest rate and the inflow of massive overseas funds brought about a relaxation of credit conditions, and this boosted the housing market, and promoted debt-financed consumption. The pre-requisite for an indebted borrowers maintaining this metastable state is the capacity to repay principal and interests which requires that the rate of returns of the borrower's asset should exceed the interest rate of the loan. The increment can come from their income, or appreciation of their real properties or other fixed assets, or their investment. Once the aforementioned increment is not realized, the metastable state will be difficult to maintain, and the borrower might go on default in breach of the contract and go bankrupt.

Financial institutions are not only the creditors of the borrowers but also the debtors of their investors. When the borrowers break the contracts or go into bankruptcy, the capital inflow to the financial institutions will fall. Financial institutions will be hard-pressed trying to pay the agreed payments to their creditors; their metastable state will be broken, and they could even have to file for bankruptcy. So, excessive liability or indebtedness can destroy the stability of financial system, causing financial crisis.

Consumption accounted for more than 70% of the U.S. economy. Therefore the excessive financial liabilities of the US household consumption would inevitably lead to a large amount of US national liabilities or debts. From 1996 to 2004, the current account deficit of the United States increased 650 billion dollars, and its percentage in GDP increased from 1.5% to 5.8%.In order to compensate the current account deficit, the United States government encouraged and attracted foreign capital inflow by issuing treasury bonds, resulting in the capital account surplus. On the other hand, the United States government took advantage of the international currency status of US dollar and enlarged the dollar supply. When the financial crisis occurred, the United States government had to inject funds into the financial system by using US national financial resources to maintain its stability. However this left behind potential problems for the future US fiscal system.

10.4.3. *It is Necessary to Prevent Over Speculation in the Financial Derivatives Market*

As a kind of financial innovation, financial derivatives can improve financial efficiency and hedge or diversify risk. However, they can also be used as speculative tools. An important reason why the subprime mortgage crisis could trigger a global financial crisis was that the US government failed to prevent the over speculation in the financial derivatives market as it did not exercise sufficient financial supervision.

At the beginning of 1990's, in the name of innovations, large financial institutions of Wall Street entered the loan securitization market. Their objective was not to diversify risk but to chase after profits. They created a huge market by designing a great variety of financial derivatives for a variety of investors and canvassed these products aggressively. The securitization of mortgage loans meant that risks assumed by banks and other loan institutions could be transferred and could bring higher returns to the investors. However the existence and development of the subprime mortgage loan lowered the quality of bonds backing MBS and asset pool supporting CDO, and turned them into 'Toxic Assets' which were sold around the world. There were several factors contributing to the birth of these 'Toxic Assets'. First were the government's misguided policies (encouraging the development of the subprime mortgage, for instance). Then there was the lax supervision on the part of the regulatory authorities (relaxing the loan requirements and review procedures, and acquiescing in the existence of off-balance entities). The rating agencies also misjudged and misled investors in giving high ratings to these financial derivatives (rating 3.2 trillion dollars MBS and CDO as class AAA securities). In 2004, the decision of the U.S. Securities and Exchange Commission relaxed the restriction that the investment banks' leverage ratio should be 10–15 and enabled them to issue more bonds than before. But the revenue from issuing bonds was mainly used to purchase MBS and CDO. From 2004 to 2007, the leverage ratio of the top five US investment banks went up remarkably, and correspondingly their debts grew to more than 4.1 trillion dollars, accounting for about 30% of US GDP in the 2007 fiscal year. This meant that they could become insolvent when MBS devalue. Some financial institutions issued and purchased CDO with high leverage operations for high profits. Over speculation turned CDS (which was originally an insurance tool into a speculative tool fit for 'gambling'.

Over speculation resulted in the continuous accumulation of a large number of financial market bubbles. The metastable states of the financial market under the high price relied mainly on the support of the continuous inflow of funds. Once the credit system crashed, the bubbles would burst quickly because of the significant erosion of the investors' confidence, which would result in serious financial crisis. Due to the psychology from misunderstanding of derivative risks and "fool competition"(thinking that 'someone must be even more foolish than me, so I can escape by selling at the top price'), most investors did not quit until the crisis broke out, and hence they suffered huge losses. From January 1 to October 11 in 2008, the total value of the US stock market dropped from 20 trillion dollars to 12 trillion dollars, and the average depreciation of the other countries' stock market was about 40%.[41]

10.4.4. *The Central Bank should not Take Inflation as the Only Objective of Monetary Policy*

The original meaning of 'inflation' is that it is a monetary phenomenon. "Currency" is widely recognized as the medium of exchange, including banknotes and coins in modern society. So inflation represents the continuous rise of the general price level and the continuous depreciation of the currency due to the fact that the growth of money supply surpasses the growth of goods and service.

The central bank, which is authorized to manage the monetary policy of the government, regulates the money supply to control the inflation rate at a certain range by means of reserves rate, discount rate, open market operations and other monetary policy tools. The Fed, under Greenspan's leadership and the guidance of the general economic theory, usually focused on inflation control and paid less attention to addressing the asset price bubbles, such as the real estate bubble and the Internet dot com bubbles. And the Fed usually chose to respond only after the bubbles burst in its bid to minimize the collateral damage done to the economy, instead of trying to prevent the generation and the expansion of the bubbles.

In my opinion, when the scale of the fictitious economy increases continuously, the increase of the money supply may not necessarily lead to inflation if it can be absorbed by the housing market and the stock market. On the contrary, when the prices of houses and stocks fall, funds will be released into the real economy, and this could lead to inflation. For example, the US house prices rose rapidly from 2002, but the inflation rate was not high. The Fed believed mistakenly that the interest rate could be safely lowered. The federal funds rate was less than 2% in 2002–2004, the lowest record in the past 40 years. It was even less than 1% in the year from July, 2003 to July, 2004. Such low interest rates further accelerated the growth of the housing bubbles.

In addition, it should be noted that the general price level in any country today is more affected by the price of oil, grain and other commodities in the light of greater economic globalization. It means that 'imported inflation' is difficult to control by monetary policies. It will be counterproductive to deal with imported inflation by tightened monetary policy.

10.4.5. *The 'Moral Hazard' of Financial Institutions and their Employees should be Carefully Regulated*

Financial institutions, "the factory" in the fictitious economy, produce a wide range of financial products by financial innovations and sell to all kinds of investors both inside and outside the financial market. But in many financial institutions, especially investment banks, the income and bonus of their employees are closely linked to the short–term performance of these institutions. So they care more about year-end bonus, instead of the long–term healthy development of the company. In the financial system, all the people, from the mortgage brokers to the risk management managers of Wall Street, are more inclined to chasing after short–term profits and neglect long–term obligations. What is more, most senior administrators of the banks only cared about the returns rate of the investment and didn't really understand how CDS and other financial instruments worked.[42] In their pursuit of high profits, some financial institutions and their employees went against professional ethics and tempted the investors to purchase various financial derivatives by exaggerating their earnings or earning powers, concealing the risks using deceptive means.

The bonus of the investment bankers depend on the amounts they charge on the financial derivatives they have designed and not on the performance of these products and the profits which could be created in the future. Their bonuses were paid in cash and not by giving them equities stock, and couldn't be taken back when the financial derivatives performed badly. The earnings of the senior managers would not be affected by high-risks or improper operations either.[43] In fact, they earned high income from the high leverage rate adventure. The total amount of the bonuses paid to Wall Street senior managers in 2006 reached as high as 23.9 billion dollars. The yearly earning of Richard Fuld Jr., who was CEO of Lehman Brothers, reached as high as 34.4 million dollars in 2007.

The senior managers of Wall Street were even emboldened to ignore the risks because they believed that the government would rescue them for sure and would not let financial institutions close down because of bad debts. One good example was that New York Federal Reserve Bank rescued Long–Term Capital Management in 1998. It was amply and clearly shown that in this financial crisis, senior managers made huge earnings despite the loss incurred by their managed funds. They 'pushed' or passed the loss caused by high-risks to the government to bear but finally their losses were borne by the whole of society.

10.5. Maintaining the Sustainable and Healthy Growth of China's Economy

Under the impact of global financial crisis, China also encountered the problem of a slow-down in economic growth. The nation's GDP maintained a double-digit growth from 2004 to 2007. The growth rate was 10.0% in 2003, 10.1% in 2004, 10.4% in 2005, 11.6% in 2006 and 13% in 2007 — reaching the peak of this economic cycle. Under the dual impact of the global financial crisis and the country's economic cycle, the economic growth rate of our country dropped sharply to 9% in 2008, down four percentage points. Quarterly, the growth rate in the fourth quarter of 2007 was 11%. In 2008, quarterly growth rates were 10.6%, 9% and 6.8% respectively. Apparently, China's economic growth slowed from the third quarter of 2008, representing a serious situation. We should take positive measures quickly to ensure the continuous and healthy growth of our economy.

10.5.1. *The Economic Stimulus Plan of our Government*

The Government had announced on November 9, 2008 its wish to implement positive fiscal and appropriately relaxed monetary policies. It had arranged 4 trillion RMB funds to help stimulate strong domestic demands in promoting the steady growth of economy in the next two years. At the same time 10 measures to further boost domestic demands and promote the economic growth were identified. Chief among them were — providing support for infrastructure construction on railway, road, airport, and in the rural infrastructure construction; energy conservation and reduction of carbon emission projects, culture and education, innovation, reconstruction after Sichuan earthquake, etc. The revitalization plans of top ten industries have also been launched covering steel, automobile, shipbuilding, petrochemical, textile and light industries, non-ferrous metals, equipment manufacturing, electronic information and logistics.

It is expected that the 4 trillion RMB investment can play its part in the following aspects:

10.5.1.1. *It can provide more job opportunities*

Employment has always been an important economic and social issue. In the past few years, the number of employed people increased gradually with the rapid growth of economy. The teething problem of the employment of 12 million people was solved in 2007. But the employment pressure is still great. In our country there are 9 to 10 million people who graduate from various institutions and need jobs every year. Now there are about six million laid-off workers and this figure increases every year. In addition there are about nine million rural labor workers that need to transfer to the city every year. According to the study made by the Chinese Academy of Social Sciences, the registered unemployment rate in cities and towns was 4.0% at the end of 2007 while the actual unemployment rate was as high as 9.6%.[44] According to preliminary estimates, for every one percent drop in GDP there will be one million jobs lost. The National Bureau of Statistics and Ministry of Agriculture estimate that there were about 20 million laid-off, ex-farm workers who returned home — in consequence of the financial crisis — just before the 2009 Spring Festival in China.[45] Because many people could no longer adapt to rural life and the rural labor was in surplus, these unemployed 'migrant' workers would most likely stay back in the cities, causing social problems. The employment pressure will be alleviated by the investment on infrastructure and housing construction which could provide a large number of jobs.

10.5.1.2. *The investment can push up the demand for steel, cement and other production materials*

In recent years, the production of steel and cement has developed rapidly in our country and the output has been the biggest in the world. Affected by the financial crisis, the output and the price of steel and cement had dropped sharply. Their renewed demand can be promoted by the expansion of infrastructure investment.

10.5.1.3. *It can save the country's energy resources and protect the environment*

In previous years, fast economic growth was achieved at the expense of energy and environment in our country. It was estimated that the total cost for depletion of resources, ecological degradation and environmental pollution was 2.75 trillion RMB in 2005, accounting for 13.9% of that year's GDP.[46] A part of this 4 trillion RMB investment will be used for energy saving and carbon emission reduction in order to maintain the sustainable development of Chinese economy.

10.5.1.4. *It can help to improve further the secured housing system*

About 900 billion yuan will be used to construct low-rent housing and affordable housing, providing housing for people with low income or who are homeless. It can also stimulate their consumption.

10.5.1.5. *It can increase the momentum of consumption*

About 20% of this 4 trillion yuan worth of investment will convert to purchasing power through wages, which can help shore up their consumption.

10.5.1.6. *It can prevent deflation*

Affected by the financial crisis, Chinese CPI and PPI have begun to decline rapidly from the third quarter of 2008. By the end of January, 2009, the CPI increment had shown decline for the past nine months and PPI had a negative growth for the past two months. The danger of deflation does exist. This 4 trillion investment should bring CPI and PPI to a reasonable levels so as to prevent deflation.

In order to make the RMB 4 trillion investment work well, the following four issues should be carefully noted and addressed:

The first issue is how to utilize the 1.18 trillion yuan fiscal investment to drive social investment. According to a rough estimate, one RMB fiscal investment can drive or generate 5–8 RMB social investment in our country under normal circumstances. As it is now investors are more cautious, thanks to financial crisis, and are rightly concerned especially for those infrastructure projects with low returns and long payback period. So policies to encourage social investment are needed, such as increasing the issue of treasury bonds, relaxing the conditions for market access, simplifying the approval procedures of the investment projects, providing financial facilitation or incentives and so on.

The second problem is how to support the survival and development of small and medium enterprises (most of them are non-public or non state-owned enterprises). Small and medium enterprises are not only important driving forces in promoting economic development, but also important job providers. However banks are usually reluctant to provide loans to them because of their high management risks and transaction costs. So a sizeable number of small and medium enterprises closed down because their chain of capital breaks down. The government should therefore encourage the banks to support the survival and development of small and medium enterprises with friendly and favorable policies and economic means. For example, the government could allow banks to lend money to small and medium enterprises with a higher interest rate and provide fiscal subsidies for interest differential, or allow small and medium enterprises to obtain loans from banks, to be collateralized by their accounts receivable.

The third problem is how to minimize mistakes in policy decisions: we should insist on making decisions scientifically and democratically, and prevent the hasty launches of projects without serious and detailed feasibility studies.

The fourth issue or problem is how to prevent corruption that could transpire in the initial and implementation process of the projects.

10.5.2. *Economic Data Analysis of the First Quarter of 2009*

According to the data released by National Bureau of Statistics,[47] Chinese economic growth rate was 6.1% in the first quarter of 2009; the decline rate slowed down and some positive changes appeared. But I think we shouldn't be overly optimistic, because our economic growth was powered by a "troika" — which includes investment, consumption and exports. In 2007, their contribution was 39%, 38% and 23% respectively. In the growth rate of first quarter in 2009, consumption accounted for 4.3%, investment for 2.0%, and net export accounts for –0.2%, illustrating that economic growth was mainly driven by consumption. There were two groups of data which could be used as supplementary evidences. One was that the growth rates of primary, secondary and tertiary industry were 3.5%, 5.3% and 7.4%, respectively and the growth rate of tertiary industry was the highest. The other was that the total retail sales of social consumer goods obtained year-by-year rise of 15.0%. The real increase was 15.9% excluding CPI effects, up 3.6 percentage points. Except for the massive consumption (transport, shopping, dining and so on) during Spring Festival, government subsidies for encouraging rural electronic and electrical appliances consumption, consumption coupons, traveling coupons etc. boosted consumption in the first quarter. But this kind of 'boost' could not last long. It is still necessary to stimulate the economy by driving up investment and increasing net exports.

In the first quarter in 2009, our fixed asset investment was 2.8129 trillion yuan (RMB). It rose 28.8%, increasing 4.2 percentage points compared to the same period last year. Due to the time lapse between input and output, the stimulating effect of the first quarter's investment was still relatively small. It was noteworthy that the increase of the loans provided by financial institutions increased 4.58 trillion yuan in the first quarter, which exceeded 90% of the planned amount of loans for the whole year. This may be the consequence of too lax requirements. Moreover, the increase of medium and long–term loans was 1.85 trillion, accounting for only 40%. This shows that a lot of loans entered the stock market and the housing market, resulting in the 'concussive' upward trend of the stock market and the partial revival of the housing market. But this momentum cannot be sustained without follow-up funds.

The situation in foreign trade was very grave and it was difficult to improve in the short–term. The imports and exports totaled 428.7 billion dollars in the first quarter, year-on-year foreign trades dropped 24.9%, and the trade surplus was US62.3 billion dollars. The actually used FDI was 21.8 billion dollars, year-on-year it had dropped 21%. Our export enterprises were facing more difficulties owing to the lack of commercial credit and sharp rise of the default rates and breaches of contracts.

The author expects that China's economy will get better in the middle of 2009. The second half of 2009 will be better than the first half, and next year will be better than this year. The planned goals of economic growth rate for all regions this year are more than 8%, and our government has the capacity to pull out of the new economic stimulus plan if necessary. So it is entirely possible to achieve the objective of 8% economic growth rate. But in the process of economic development we should pay attention to carrying out 'the spirit and the letter' of the scientific concept of development, pay more attention to saving energy and protecting the environment, avoid low-level duplicate constructions and prevent increase in over-production capacity.

10.5.3. *Seeking Opportunities in Adversities*

In Chinese language, 'crisis'(危机) may be interpreted consisting of danger (危险) and opportunity (机遇). Chinese enterprises should strengthen management and modify the product structure in the financial crisis, improve the quality of employees by training, and seeking actively the opportunities of merger and acquisition.

The country should strive to change the mode of economic growth, from export-oriented economy to domestic demands oriented economy, from extensive growth relying on productive capacity expansion to intensive growth relying on innovations and technical progress. At the same time, the country should speed up economic restructuring, strive to conserve energy, protect the environment, and improve the social security system and the public services.

The financial crisis will strengthen financial cooperation among countries, especially with regards to cooperation in international financial supervision to prevent the 'accumulation' and spread of financial risks. In my opinion, economic globalization and regional integration are two parallel and mutually reinforcing processes, and financial crisis is also helpful to speeding up regional integration. The "10+1" free trade zone of Sino-ASEAN will be realized in 2010, and the cooperation between our central bank and the central banks of Japan, Korea and other countries are getting stronger. The SDR advocated by the Asian Development Bank is also under discussion.

Financial crisis will help to promote the reforms of the international financial system and to speed up the establishment of new international financial order. Nations of the world should make concerted efforts to build a stable, balanced, and fair international monetary system. This will not only be helpful in preventing the occurrence of financial crisis, but could also be helpful to establishing a multipolar world.

10.6. Advancing Resolutely the Financial Reform in China

Our country's financial reform has made remarkable achievements in the recent 30 years since the 'reform and opening-up'. In my view, the main reasons we only suffered a relatively minor shock during this financial crisis are that our financial institutions are backed by the government and people have confidence in our government. Our financial system is not advanced enough and there are hardly investment banks, rating agencies or financial derivative products. Our banks are not short of liquidity, and our financial supervision and regulatory authorities are very strict, prudent and cautious. However, we should also admit that there is still a long way to go for our financial reforms. The international competitiveness of our finance sector is not good enough. As the third biggest trading country in the world and a big buyer and seller, our voice in the international financial market is not loud enough. In addition, the financial supervision and regulation as well as financial innovations in our country need to be strengthened.

After the Wall Street's turmoil broke out, there were all kinds of public opinions, one of which is actually cast doubts on the direction and measures taken regarding our financial reforms. President Hu Jingtao once pointed, "As in a new and great revolution…the direction and way of the reforms and opening-up are totally correct, and there is no doubt about its effects and achievements. There will be no future if we stop or retrograde."[48] We must, on the premise of keeping economic and financial stability, try to handle properly and skillfully the relationships between financial innovation and regulation, the fictitious economy and real economy, and saving and consumption according to the wishes of Premier Wen Jiabao.[49] We should insist on promoting financial reforms actively and cautiously, and keep improving financial service to enhance effectiveness and our international competitiveness.

In my opinion, financial reforms should follow the following three main directions.[50]

10.6.1. *Internationalization*

The globalization of economy is a *fait accompli and* represents an inevitable historical trend. In this process, financial globalization is also on the schedule. From the trend of financial development, the characteristics of financial globalization can generally be summarized as follows:

The first characteristic is the increase in the fictitiousness of money: the exchange rate has become the tool of the policy game among countries. Since currency deviated from the gold standard and the gold exchange standard, there is no more objective standard to measure its value. In other words, money is to some extent virtualized; we can only use purchasing power to measure its value. The author proposes that there are two kinds of purchasing power. One is the domestic which can be measured by PPP, the other one is the international purchasing power which can be measured by exchange rates. In this case, the exchange rate regime of each country becomes a 'game' tool of policies. If a country doesn't have any import trade at all, variation of exchange rate will have no influence on its domestic purchase power. On the contrary, if a country depends all on imports, its domestic purchasing power will be determined by its exchange rate. But almost every country in the world lies in between these two extremes, so exchange rate cannot be determined by primary mortgage market alone. If every country were to take into consideration 'global' benefits, it's possible to reach "Pareto Optimality", and that benefits all. Unfortunately, no single country would consider the global benefits as first priority instead of benefits to itself all the time. So, to a certain extent, the exchange rate regimes of countries become a tool in economic 'games of battle'.

As everyone knows, the Plaza Accord and Louvre Accord led to Japan's economic recession for more than 10 years. At the time of East Asian financial crisis, there was a big pressure on the RMB for its devaluation. This time around, the pressure for the appreciation of RMB is also big. All these go to prove that the exchange rate regimes of countries have already become a tool or even a weapon in 'trade wars'. We therefore still need to hold on to the principle of 'our national interests and sovereignty come first'. Of course, we should take into account various factors, but on the issue of the exchange rate, we surely cannot follow the opinions or instruction of others.

The second characteristic is that the scale and speed of capital flow are both increasing. Thanks to the development of science and technology, all we need is to press a button to transfer trillions of funds to destinations tens of thousands of kilometers away within a short moment.

The third feature is that the integration of global financial markets is advancing day by day. That is to say, the relationship between the financial markets of all countries becomes closer and closer, even reaching the situation "Pull one hair and you move the whole body" of the "Butterfly Effect". The East Asian financial crisis began with a liquidity crisis in Thailand, but affected all the world finally. The recent American subprime mortgage crisis also affected Europe and other regions, resulting in the global financial crisis.

The final characteristic is that the financial innovation is developing rapidly and continuously. Financial innovation began with the Eurodollar after WWII. The past decades witnessed the birth of many new types of financial derivative products. This phenomenon resulted in the total value of financial derivative products reaching about 8 to 10 times the world's total GDP. Too many financial derivative products made people's heads spin and confused them. In the light of this situation, it has become an important and notable issue as to how to prevent over speculation in financial derivatives market in order to avoid financial risks.

In the face of the integration of the international finance, we must increase our international financial competitiveness and adapt through reform. First of all, we should learn from the experiences of others. In the area of financial innovation, we lack both knowledge and experience, not to mention their practical operation. So we are probably at a disadvantage in the competition among the international financial markets. For example, just in futures, we suffered setbacks in the China Aviation Oil, the China National Cotton Reserves Corporation, and the China National Cuprum Reserves Corporation affairs, causing great losses to us. We need to learn and understand the international financial products and their rules. We should cultivate talents with international vision and the ability for operating and managing international finance as well. We should use both strategies of attracting outside talents as well as developing and nurturing our domestic talents.

10.6.2. *Marketization*

To promote marketization, the author regards the marketization of interest rates as first priority. Interest rate is the cost of capital, and it actually depends on the risks and the transaction cost. So interest rates should be marketized. Both lending rates and borrowing rates should have a certain floating range according to the differences in risk and transaction cost.

The second matter is the marketization of exchange rates. Exchange rate itself reflects the international purchasing power, which keeps changing all the time. Our exchange rate regime should improve continuously with the demands and requirements of marketization. We should also promote the marketization of exchange rates to reflect the change of purchasing power and the relation between supply and demand.

RMB has appreciated nearly 20 percent since China implemented the managed floating exchange rate according to a 'basket of reference' in practice since July 2005, but this floating still doesn't follow completely the rules of the market. I would suggest we allow the exchange rate to float in a managed, targeted range. Only when it runs out of the range will the central bank need to adopt appropriate measures. Of course, there is no doubt that, finally, RMB will have to go for 'free' exchange rates. China opened its current accounts in 1996, but its capital accounts are still not opened. Among the 47 sub-accounts stated in IMF, we have opened about 20, so we still need to advance the process gradually. Much depends on our management ability, and we can liberate or set free the exchange rates only when we can regulate the system. On the choice of timing, we need to pay attention to the international environment and the relative strength of USD, Euro and Japanese Yen. It is just a problem of time for the completely free exchange of RMB. Although there is no timetable, it is not too far away. When the RMB becomes one of the commonly circulated currencies we could then say our exchange rate has been fully marketized.

Thirdly, we need to continue increasing the variety of participants in our market. Now among the banks, securities companies and insurance companies, the majority are still state-owned enterprises. There is very little foreign capital and not much private capital too. As has been expressed specifically in "the 36 terms of Non-Public Sectors Of the Economy (NPSOE)", we should encourage private capital to enter the small and medium-sized financial institutions. The more market participants there are, the better we can improve or 'perfect' our financial system. Of course there should be some specific rules regarding the participation — taking into consideration our national security. For example, we are stipulating that the share of a single foreign capital in a bank should not exceed 20% and the share of all the foreign capital should not exceed 25%.

10.6.3. *Systematization*

First, finance and economy are inter-connected and they cannot be separated or severed. We cannot consider finance alone. Finance is included in fictitious economy, while production, circulation and exchange belong to the scope of the real economy. Problems emerging in the fictitious economy will become contagious and spread to the real economy, and vice versa. The reason now the American government utilizes so much resource to save the financial market is to prevent the financial crisis evolving into economic crisis. We therefore must maintain the balance between the financial sector and the real economy, following the direction pointed out in the report of the Sixteenth National Party Congress.

Second, finance is a complete system, not a series of 'isolated islands' or components. The currency market, stock market, bonds market, insurance, futures and so on, are all connected in the system. We should consider questions systematically, and cannot "take stop-gap measures" or do what the Chinese say 'treat the head for headache and treat the foot for foot-ache'. From a long–term perspective, we should still promote mixed operation and integrated supervision and regulation progressively and steadily. Only through consolidated or integrated supervision and regulation can we prevent risk comprehensively and in an integrated way. Otherwise, it could lead to the situation where each supervisory and regulator department only cares and does its own work without any reference to other department — the so-called "each of the policemen only performs his duties at a particular stretch of the railway". If China Securities Regulatory Commission (CSRC) only assures the proper running of stock market, any risks would be driven to the insurance market or the currency market. If these two markets fall into trouble, it would affect the stock market as well.

Third, we should construct multiple financial markets. China's securities market has already reached a certain scale, but its bonds market is not developed enough. The bonds market has its own features in that although the profitability of bonds is lower than stocks, they are safer than stocks. The reason American government spent so much money and resources to save Fannie Mae and Freddie Mac this time is to prevent their possible insolvency. Once these problems occur, they would not only lead to many social problems but also result in international problems. Hence American government offered actual support to the MBS bonds issued by Fannie Mae and Freddie Mac. That is why we should not only develop the stock market, but also the bonds market, currency market, futures market and so on. Financial futures can begin with the stock index futures, and we should certainly pay great attention to avoid over-speculation and the possible risks in the process of development. There is a saying in institutional economics: "transactions precede institutions" — a transaction cannot be made until a perfect mechanism has been set up. The truth is that when there is a primary mechanism, we can find out the problems in the transaction and then solve them gradually.

The fourth is the systemization of supervision and regulation. The present system of one central bank and three commissions should give way to a coordinating institution. The systemization of supervision and regulation should go along the following steps: First of all, we should realize that the purpose of the supervision and regulation is to ensure the fundamental interests of the overwhelming majority of the people are safeguarded — in line with the motto "human beings first". Regrettably, when problems do arise, some supervisors often care more about the interests of the institutions' benefits. It is understandable that our banks, insurance companies and securities companies are all state-owned and their loss is also the country's loss. On the other hand, the wealth of the country and of the people should always complement each other. As the old saying goes: "A small river will be full of water if there is water in large rivers, and it will dry up if there is no water in large rivers." That seems to mean only when the country becomes rich will its people be rich. Similarly, if there is no water in small rivers, the large river will dry up as well. So enrich the people and the country will be strong; enrich the country and the people will be strong. They are complementary to each other. It's important for us to understand that protecting the benefits of the people is also protecting the benefits of the country. Supervision and regulation must begin with information disclosure, and must be transparent. Information disclosure is to allow financial consumers including investors, depositors and policy-holders, etc., the right to know. Only when information disclosure is done well, can it be convenient to analyze, find, announce and deal with events and problems. The supervision and regulation authorities may not be responsible for the ups and downs of the markets, but they must be responsible for the authenticity, completeness and timeliness of the information they release or disclose.

The final point is the systemization of the financial service. Financial institutions, including insurance companies, securities companies and banks, etc., should all be mindful of the concept of service. The financial industry itself is a service industry, so it naturally should adopt a good attitude of service and should learn to improve the quality of service at all times. At this point our financial institutions are in many aspects much worse than the foreign ones. I once heard a story from a Chinese student studying in Japan who once worked in a Japanese noodle house. The story was that the student once witnessed an employee of a Japanese bank came to the shop in the evening to help the boss put his cash earnings for the day into the bank. What surprised him most was that the bank employee brought a lot of small changes to the boss next morning to make it convenient for him to operate his business. I dare say that the service provided by Chinese banks is far from this level.

Rethinking this financial crisis, we should note the dual effects of fictitious economy on real economy. On one hand, fictitious economy can promote the growth of the real economy. On the other hand, the overexpansion of the fictitious economy and capital would harm the real economy as well. Moreover, the risks that have emerged in the fictitious economy will be transferred to the real economy; the financial crisis would evolve into economic crisis. In this case, we should think, analyze and summarize the lessons from this crisis more critically and rigorously. We should strengthen our confidence, and — under the leadership of the central government — work together to overcome the difficulties.

I gave a speech in Guangzhou on Nov 22, 2008 in which I pointed out that according to my personal analysis, Chinese economy and the world economy will be able to recover in 2011. On Nov 23, 2008, the summit conference of APEC announced that the financial crisis would end in 18 months. Whatever it is — 18 months or 24 months — the crisis will be gone sooner or later. Just as Shelly, the famous English poet, wrote in one of his poems, "If winter comes, can Spring be far behind?" As long as we work together closely, we will embrace another spring of our economy and of the capital market.

Reference

[1] Mark, K. (1975). *Das Kapital*, Translated by Bureau of Interpretation, Beijing: Renmin Press (in Chinese).

[2] Cheng, S. W. (2008). Opening Remarks on International Financial Forum, Beijing (in Chinese).

[3] Hu, J. T. (2008). Let Us Join Hands and Tide over Difficulties Together, Remarks on the Second G20 Financial Summit, November 15 (in Chinese).

[4] Knox, N. (2006). 43% of first-time home buyers put no money as down payment. *USA Today*, January 17.

[5] Timeline: Sub-prime losses, *BBC News Business*, May 19, 2008.

[6] Onaran Yalman (2008). Wall Street Firms Cut 34,000 Jobs, Most Since 2001 Dot-Com Bust, *Bloomberg*, March 24.

[7] Bear Stearns gets emergency funds, *BBC News Business*, March 14, 2008.

[8] Poirier, J. and Rucker, P. (2008). Timeline: U.S. plan for Fannie, Freddie to hit shareholders. *Reuters*, September 6, 2008.

[9] Landers, K. (2008). Lehman tumbles, Merrill Lynch totters on Meltdown Monday, *ABCNews* (Australia), September 16.

[10] Saporito, B. (2008). Getting Suckered by Wall Street — Again, *TIME*, September 16.
[11] Byrnes, N. (2008). The Fed Bails Out AIG, *Business Week*, September 16, 2008.
[12] Fox, J. (2008). Why the Government Wouldn't Let AIG Fail, *TIME*, September 16.
[13] Liu Y. and Ge X. W. (2008). G20 Financial Summit Announced the Declaration, *Renmin Daily*, November 16 (in Chinese).
[14] Bu X. M. (2008). APEC Set the Timetable to Deal with Financial Crisis: 18 Months, *Xinhua Net*, November 25 (in Chinese).
[15] Wu Y. M. (2009). President Hu Jingtao Attended the Second G20 Financial Summit and Obtained Relevant Achievements, *Renmin Daily*, April 4 (in Chinese).
[16] Cheng, S. W. (2009). The Fundamentals of Fictitious Economy and the Research Approaches, *Management Review*, 21, 3–18 (in Chinese).
[17] Will subprime mess ripple through economy? *msnbc.com*, 2007-03-13.
[18] Bernanke, B. S. (2007). The Recent Financial Turmoil and its Economic and Policy Consequences, Speech At the Economic Club of New York, New York, October 15.
[19] Bernanke, B. S. (2008). Financial Markets, the Economic Outlook, and Monetary Policy, Speech at the Women in Housing and Finance and Exchequer Club Joint Luncheon, Washington, D.C., January 10.
[20] Bernanke, B. S. (2008). Mortgage Delinquencies and Foreclosures, Speech at the Columbia Business School's 32nd Annual Dinner, New York, May 5.
[21] RealtyTrac Staff (2008). U.S. Foreclosure activity increases 75 percent in 2007, *RealtyTrac Inc*, accessed January 29.
[22] RealtyTrac Staff (2009). Foreclosure activity increases 75 percent in 2008, 2008 U.S. Foreclosure Market Report, *RealtyTrac Inc.*, Accessed January 15, http://www.realtytrac.com/home/.
[23] The End of the Affair, *The Economist*, November 20, 2008.
[24] Katz, A. and Katz, I. (2008). Greenspan Slept as Off-Books Debt Escaped Scrutiny, *Bloomberg*, October 30.
[25] Bernard , T. S. (2008). Money Market Funds Enter a World of Risk, *The New York Times*, September 17.
[26] Gray, M. (2008). Almost Armageddon: Markets Were 500 Trades from a Meltdown, *New York Post*, September 21.

[27] Dash, E. and Sorkin, A. R. (2008). Government Seizes WaMu and Sells Some Assets, *The New York Times*, September 25.

[28] Twin, A. (2008). Stocks crushed, accessed September 29, http://money.cnn.com/.

[29] Guha, K., Harvey, M., James, P. and Davies, P. J. (2008). Banking's crisis of confidence deepens, *The Financial Times*, September 30.

[30] Duhigg, C. (2008). Pressured to Take More Risk, Fannie Reached Tipping Point, *The New York Times*, October 4.

[31] Leonnig, C. D. (2008). How HUD Mortgage Policy Fed The Crisis, *The Washington Post*, June 10.

[32] Roberts, R. (2008). How Government Stoked the Mania, *The Wall Street Journal*, October 3.

[33] Trehan, V. (2007). The Mortgage Market: What Happened?" *National Public Radio* (NPR) Article, August 26.

[34] Angell, C. and Williams, N. (2005). U.S. Home Prices: Does Bust Always Follow Boom?" Federal Deposit Insurance Corporation, Accessed February 10 (Revised April 8, 2005), http://www.fdic.gov/.

[35] "New home sales fell by record amount in 2007, *MSNBC*, Accessed January 28, http.www.nbcnews.com/.

[36] Coy, P. (2008). Housing Meltdown, *Business Week*, January 31.

[37] Cheng, S. W. (2001). *Studies on Economic Reforms and Development in China*, Oxford: Oxford University Press, pp. 205–244.

[38] Cheng, S. W. (1999). Fictitious Economy and the Financial Crisis, *Journal of Management Science*, 2, 1–6 (in Chinese).

[39] Lasch, C. (2008). The Culture of Consumerism, Consumerism. Smithsonian Center for Education and Museum Studies 1, Accessed on September 15. http://smithsonianeducation.org/idealabs/ap/essays/consume.htm.

[40] Zakaria, F. (2008). There Is a Silver Lining, *Newsweek*, October 20.

[41] Zweig, J. (2008). What History Tells us about the Market, The Wall Street Journal, October 11.

[42] Steverman, B. and Bogoslaw, D. (2008). The Financial Crisis Blame Game, *Business Week*, October 18.

[43] Nocera, J. (2009). First, Let's Fix the Bonuses, *The New York Times*, February 21, p. B1.

[44] Li, Y. and Han, S. (2009). Unemployment Statistics Investigated by the Academy of Social Science is Much Higher than That Announced by the Ministry of Human Resources and Social Security, *Chinese Youth Daily*, January 2 (in Chinese).

[45] Xinhua News Agency (2009). Nearly 20 Million Farmer Workers Lost Their Jobs and Returned to Their Hometown in 2008, *China Net.*, accessed on February 2, http://www.chinanet.com. (in Chinese).
[46] Wang, X. (2008). Report Shows Real Price of Growth, *China Daily*, September 2012.
[47] Xinhua News Agency (2009). National Statistics Bureau Introduced Fundamental Information of National Economy in the First Quarter of This Year, *Renmin Net.*, accessed on April 16 (in Chinese).
[48] Hu, J. T. (2008). Remarks on the 30 Years' of Reform, Opening Ceremony, *Renmin Net*, December 18 (in Chinese).
[49] Wen, J. B. (2008). Each Country Should Deal with the Relationship Between Real and Fictitious Economy, *Chinese News Net.*, accessed on October 25 (in Chinese).
[50] Cheng, S. W. (2008). Three Directions of Financial Reform, *Beijing Daily*, October 6 (in Chinese).

Chapter 11

The Reform of RMB Exchange Rate System

In recent years, with rapid development of China and rise of our international position and status, the issue of RMB exchange rate has received a lot of attention. The RMB exchange rate, involving the nation's economy and people's livelihood, is an important issue that needs to be studied seriously and dealt with prudently. Since 2003, the appreciation pressure on RMB from United States, Japan and other western countries keeps increasing. Since this pressure won't disappear in the near future, it's of great importance for us to study the situation carefully: we need to move forward and advance the reforms of RMB exchange rate actively and prudently.

RMB exchange rate system includes two aspects: institution and regime. We have to study not only the choice of exchange rate regime and the determination of exchange rate level, the evolution of exchange rate system and its motivation, but also how to promote the evolution towards the desired objectives through policy guidance and strengthened regulation. In this chapter, I intend to apply the theory of fictitious economy, complex science and international finance to carry out some exploration and discussion on the RMB exchange rate system, including its arrangement, level, related policies and regulation; I would also propose some recommendations accordingly and attempt to specify some direction for further studies.

Currency is a special commodity that functions as a yardstick for value, exchange medium, payment tool, means of storage and world currency etc. It plays an important role both in the real economy and fictitious economy. According to the theory of fictitious economy, we can address the RMB exchange rate issue from the following aspects: 1) currency has been virtualized to a certain extent; 2) the difference between two types of purchasing power of currency; 3) the scale and speed of cross-border capital flows is growing rapidly; 4) the scale of fictitious economy is expanding; 5) exchange rates have become policy 'game tools'; 6) the dilemma in choosing exchange rate regime — whether to maintain the stability of exchange rate or to maintain the independence of monetary policy.

Exchange rate arrangement is the relationship between domestic currency and foreign currency. After currency was separated from the gold standard about 30 years ago, there are at present ten kinds of exchange rate regimes around the world according to their flexibility. They are: 1) free-float; 2) managed float; 3) target zone; 4) crawling zone; 5) basket peg; 6) crawling peg; 7) adjustable peg; 8) "truly fixed" exchange rate; 9) currency board; 10) currency union. In practice it has been proved that no country's exchange rate regime is immutable but the exchange rate is always adjustable with the changing domestic and international circumstances.

On July 21, 2005, China switched to a managed floating system which is based on market supply and demand and adjustable with reference to a basket of currencies. This reform increased the flexibility of RMB exchange rate and promoted the appreciation of RMB. However, as it is, there are still some shortcomings in this arrangement. Further reforms should be carried out to create positive condition for the ultimate objective, the full convertibility of RMB.

According to China's current internal and external environment and based on comprehensive comparison of various kinds of exchange rate regime, the author suggests that the "flexible target zone exchange rate regime" (double-layer, extendable and movable exchange rate target zone) is a better choice for China at the present stage. Since China's capital account is not fully open, in comparison with reference to a basket of currencies, it's better to implement the target zone exchange rate regime as this makes it possible for China to 'take the initiative and be proactive' on currency issues. Under this system, not only the stability of the exchange rate could be achieved, but also the exchange rate mechanism could function efficiently: we may have the advantages of both fixed and floating exchange rate systems.

The process of marketization of China's exchange rate would involve three stages: gradually extend both the hard and soft exchange rate target zones and finally culminating in the free convertibility of RMB. 1) Initial stage: the width of hard and soft target zone are ±1% and ±3% of the central exchange rate respectively; 2) Adjustment stage: the width of hard and soft target zone could gradually extend to ±5% and ±15% respectively; 3) Integrating stage: forming unified exchange rate target zone whose width is ±30% of the central exchange rate and then progressively move to the full convertibility of RMB. In establishing the RMB exchange rate target zone, a basket of currencies is to be preferred. But at the early stage, it's not appropriate to take the equilibrium exchange rate strictly as the central exchange rate. During the adjustment stage, the central exchange rate could slowly move towards the equilibrium exchange rate and at the integrating stage, the central exchange rate should move closer to the equilibrium exchange rate.

The target of the exchange rate policy could be attained in accordance with the requirements of the scientific development concept and should maintain the following 'balances' or equilibrium: 1) balance of reserves and usage; 2) balance of domestic and external demands; 3) balance of regulation and innovation; 4) balance of business interests and public interests. While implementing the "flexible target zone exchange rate system", we should try to improve the management of our exchange rate focusing on 1) preventing large inflows and outflows of hot money; 2) preventing speculative attack to our foreign exchange market; 3) maintain the government's credibility in respect of the commitment towards establishing the target zone.

Economic globalization is a irresistible 'historical tide'. In order to enhance China's international competitiveness and influence, the internationalization of RMB is inevitable. As there are many uncertainties and difficulties in the internationalization of RMB, it becomes more important for our scholars to study in depth the issues involved in the RMB exchange rate system We should find ways to improve the "flexible target zone exchange rate system" and provide support for policy decisions to realize the eventual free convertibility of RMB.

11.1. Introduction

In recent years, with rapid development of China and rising of our international position, the issue of RMB exchange rate has been highlighted. First of all, with our reforms and opening-up, China's export-oriented economy is developing rapidly and the dependence on foreign trade (the ratio of import and export volume of the GDP) rose from 9.7% in 1978 to 58.2% in 2008. Any change in the exchange rates will significantly affect the price of China's import and export commodities and thereby affect the performance and structure of foreign trade and even the development of our economy. Secondly, because of our rich human resources and lower prices, China's foreign trade surplus keeps growing from –1.14 billion dollars in 1978 to 295.5 billion dollars in 2008. This long-term imbalance in import and export leads to increased trade friction with foreign countries as well as mounting pressure on RMB for its appreciation. Thirdly, because China has many advantages such as rapid economic growth, great market potential, low-cost and high-quality human resources, good infrastructure and an improving investment environment, it has become more attractive to foreign investors these years. The amount of foreign capital investment every year increased from 1.956 billion dollars in 1985 to 92.4 billion dollars in 2008. Many world-famous multinational corporations have entered China. Obviously the RMB exchange rate will affect their investment decision. Fourthly, trade surplus plus net inflow of foreign capital has resulted in continuous surplus in China's capital and current accounts which brought foreign exchange reverses from 167 million dollars by the end of 1978 to 1946 billion dollars by the end of 2008. While the huge foreign exchange reverses can enhance our economic strength, it could also increase the risk we have to undertake when exchange rate fluctuates. Finally, as the incomes of urban and rural residents keep rising, the purchase of imported goods is increasing, and so is traveling abroad. Variation of the exchange rate will affect the real purchasing power of RMB and thereby affect people's consumption behavior and consumption structure. In addition, it should also be noted that the exchange rate may affect our fictitious economy, including factors relating to nation's economic stability and security such as the cross-border short-term capitals the price changes of financial assets, inflation or deflation and so on. The RMB exchange rate is an important issue involving the nation's economy and people's livelihood, and it needs to be studied seriously and dealt with prudently.

Since 2003, there has been increasing pressure on RMB for its appreciation from developed nations like America and Japan. In the G-7 summit held in the spring of 2003, the Japanese government had complained that RMB was grossly undervalued, and China was dumping cheap products to international market, leading to 'international deflation'. Later some U.S. congressmen also accused that China had exported a lot of cheap goods to America, took away job opportunities and brought about the huge trade deficit and economic depression in United States. Some congressmen threatened that if the value of RMB didn't appreciate 30% to 40%, they would propose legislation to impose 27.5% tariffs on goods imported from China. The international media added fuel to the flames by instigating the international community with the result that the expected RMB exchange rate was affected and this added to the pressure on our balance of payments.

On July 21, 2005, China implemented the reforms on the exchange rate system with the objective of enhancing the flexibility of RMB exchange rate and allowing the market mechanism to play a greater role in regulating foreign exchange's demand and supply. After that, the RMB appreciated continuously against U.S. dollar. By July 20, 2008, RMB had appreciated 20% cumulatively against the dollar. Although later the exchange rate of RMB against dollar fell slightly, the expectation for appreciation still remained strong. In addition, since the second season of 2008, RMB has started appreciating against the Euro and Japanese yen (on September 2, 2008, the exchange rate of RMB against Euro had risen to lower than 10 Yuan against 1 Euro). It could be expected that the appreciation pressure from Euro and Japanese yen will increase as well. China's economy will continue to develop rapidly and the dual surplus of China's BOP will sustain for a long time to come. China's dependence on foreign trade and the export-oriented economic structure shaped by large-scale foreign direct investment won't change in the near future: we will have to face the appreciation pressure on RMB exchange rate for a long time. Although the exchange rate issue concerns Chinese national monetary sovereignty and the international society has no right to require any changes in the exchange rate level, its system and related policies, the externalities of exchange rate still could become an excuse for western countries to mount pressure on China. Since this pressure won't disappear in the near future, it's of great importance for us to study the situation carefully in our efforts to advance the reforms of the exchange rate of RMB actively and prudently.

I had applied the methodologies of complex science to analyze the issue and believed that it should be viewed from two aspects, namely 'institution' and 'regime'. Institution refers to the status and structure of our exchange rate system at a certain point in time while regime means the processes and dynamics of evolution of the system. Institution and regime are also interdependent. Institution is the staring point and results of evolution while regime is the trajectory. The exchange rate system of RMB should contain these two aspects: we have to study not only the choice of exchange rate regime and the determination of exchange rate, the evolution of exchange rate system and its motivation, but also study how to promote the evolution towards the desired objectives through policy guidance and strengthened regulation.

I started to study the RMB exchange rate issue since 1997[1] and had presented views on exchange rate at home and abroad many times. While serving as the director of the Management Science Department of the National Natural Science Foundation between 1996 and 2004, I also conducted some research projects on the RMB exchange rate issue. This chapter aims to apply the theory of fictitious economy, complex science and international finance to explore and discuss on the RMB exchange rate regime with respect to its arrangement, level, related policy and regulation, and to propose recommendations accordingly and, it is hoped, to point out the directions for further studies.

11.2. The Issues of Exchange Rate from the Perspective of Fictitious Economy

Fictitious economy is a kind of economic mode corresponding to Real or Entity economy; it involves circulatory movements of fictitious capital relying mostly on the financial platform. It also involves the integration of the inter-relationships between related entities. Currency is a special form of 'commodity' serving as a general 'equivalent entity' with the following functions: value scale, exchange medium, payment tool, means of storage and world currency. Currency plays an important role both in the real economy and fictitious economy. According to the theory of fictitious economy, we could view the RMB exchange rate issue from the following aspects.[2]

11.2.1. *Currency has been Virtualized to Certain Extent*

Historically, since England first adopted the Gold Standard, gold had become the guarantee for paper money that had been issued widely at that time. The Gold Standard gradually became popular in Europe and became the foundation stone of the world currency system from 1870. After World War □, Gold Standard 'degenerated' into Gold Exchange Standard. After World War □, United States set the lowest dollar price for foreign central banks to buy or sell gold, and major European countries prescribed that currency could be freely convertible into gold or dollars in international payments. However, in 1971, the USA gave up converting dollars into gold freely at the fixed price (35 dollars per ounce). Since then, the international monetary system has been based on dollar and other currencies, and the official role of gold exchange in the world exchange rate ended. Currencies became completely 'un-pegged' from gold and couldn't be converted into gold at a fixed price freely. From then on, a country's currency is issued totally based on its total credit and not freely convertible and the currency is called 'fiat money'.

As a general 'equivalent entity', currency itself is a special commodity functioning as a yardstick for valuation. It can measure other commodities' values quantitatively, exchange with other commodities and transform the value of a commodity into price'. Currency changes the direct barter between commodities into an exchange with currency as medium. Most importantly currency can be circulated freely.

When currency was linked with gold, it reflected directly the value of labor contained in gold. Once currency became 'delinked' from gold, currency itself had been virtualized to some extent. That is to say, the currency itself is just a piece of paper and it has value only when issued based upon the country's credit. This means that people no longer use some 'reference material' with fixed value to define the currency's value; instead they use the currency's purchasing power to measure its value indirectly. As there is no mechanism for the currency to freely 'leave' the market under the constraints of the Gold Standard, the currency's purchasing power is determined by the relationship between the quantity of currency and the total production in real economy (including commodity and service mainly).[3]

A country's purchasing power can be expressed as follows:

$$Pi = (Ci + Si)/Mi$$

where, Pi is the purchasing power of country i
Ci is the amount of commodities in country i
Si is the amount of services in country i
Mi is the amount of currency of country i

Since the currency and gold have parted, the money supply of countries is no longer restrained by their gold reserves or gold equivalent reserves, but depends on the state's decision. Moreover, there is no common basal standard to measure the value of currency of various countries. Consequently the exchange rate is not fixed but uncertain, representing the virtualization of currency.

11.2.2. *Difference between Two Types of Purchasing Power of Currency*

As fictitious currencies no longer have a definite value, the value measured by purchasing power will vary from time to time and place to place. In recent years, many foreign scholars have advocated appreciating RMB according to PPP theory, and some domestic scholars also agreed with them. On June 15, 2004, I suggested that we distinguish between two types of purchasing power — the international purchasing power and domestic purchasing power, instead of simply taking purchasing power parity to determine the RMB exchange rate when discussing RMB issues with Fred Bregsten and others at the Institute for International Economics, Washington.

The theory of purchasing power parity had its inception in mid-16th century in Spain. It was developed by the Swedish economist Gustav Cassel (in 1916) who coined the term "purchasing power parity". Simply put, purchasing power parity theory postulates that the currency exchange rate between two countries depends primarily on the purchasing power of the two currencies.[4] That is to say, the demand of the domestic and foreign currencies is due to the demand of domestic and foreign goods and services, so exchange of national currency and foreign currency is equivalent to the exchange between the two countries of purchasing power of domestic and foreign currency. As the exchange rate is the domestic currency price of foreign currencies, so it depends on the ratio of the purchasing power of the two currencies, which is determined by the ratio of price levels between the two countries. This is the concept of absolute purchasing power parity. Considering that the price level data is difficult to obtain, we have introduced the concept of relative purchasing power parity, which equals the ratio between the inflation rates of the two countries multiplied by the base period inflation rate. Some researchers propounded theories that further relaxed the conditions, requiring neither proportional co-movements of relative price and exchange rate at home and abroad, nor the symmetry of domestic and foreign price indices.

With the purchasing power parity theory, people have long believed that it is a good way to predict long-term exchange rate movements. However, after currency and gold completely separated from each other, empirical studies showed that purchasing power parity did not apply for most currencies. So economists continued to improve and develop this theory, trying to make it applicable to new situations. Unit root test, co-integration techniques (including the

Engle-Granger two-step method, Johansen's maximum likelihood estimation method, etc.), variance ratio test, the fractional co-integration tests — all these advanced statistical tools have been widely used in the testing of purchasing power parity theory. There is also a growing number of economists who began to pay attention to the application of purchasing power parity in developing countries. Some economists pointed out that we need to find a long-term equilibrium exchange rate theory which can both interpret the RMB exchange rate fluctuations validly and guide exchange rate adjustment policies to reduce effectively the economic costs. Such theories include the theory of fundamental factors of the equilibrium exchange rate (FEER) theory, behavioral equilibrium exchange rate (BEER) theory and the equilibrium real exchange rate (ERER) theory.[5]

I believe that the purchasing power parity theory does not apply to the current RMB exchange rate because it is not freely convertible. There are differences between the international purchasing power and domestic purchasing power. As the exchange rate is determined by the government, and to some extent it represents the relationship between supply and demand, it only represents RMB's international purchasing power of purchasing foreign products and services at the relevant time. However, the purchasing power parity is based on the currency's domestic purchasing power. Since China and Western countries are different in market-oriented price index composition, foreign trade structure, labor productivity and so on and coupled with the impact of non-economic factors, the exchange rate calculated by purchasing power parity does not and cannot fully represent the value of Western currency after it was converted into RMB to purchase Chinese goods and services.

In addition, the correlation between a country's exchange rate and its domestic purchasing power is also related to the degree of foreign trade dependence and its foreign trade structure. In general, the exchange rate is positively correlated with foreign trade dependence. If the country's foreign trade dependence is zero, then the exchange rate has nothing to do with the purchasing power of the local currency. It can be further inferred that the exchange rate is positively correlated with the proportion of consumer goods in the foreign trade structure. Although China is a big trading country now, the proportion of consumer goods in foreign trade structure is low. Therefore the exchange rate and domestic purchasing power are of less relevance, which is one of the reasons why purchasing power parity theory does not apply to the RMB exchange rate.

Besides, exchange rates also depend on the interaction between people, as well as the impact of environment on people's behavior, and people's confidence in local currency. For example, expectation of RMB appreciation will promote the RMB's actual appreciation and the appreciation of the RMB would have a 'positive feedback', which further strengthens appreciation expectations.

It should also be noted that the purchasing power belongs to the scope or purview of commodity exchange in real economy while exchange rate calculation method is a static and equilibrium method based on purchasing power parity — involving consideration of national income, price levels, interest rates and so on. Even taking into account people's behavioral factors (mainly on exchange rate expectations), this method is only applicable in predicting the long-term exchange rate movements. In addition, the shortcoming of this approach lies in not considering comprehensively the impact of actual cross-border real capital and fictitious capital flow on the exchange rate.

All in all, I am not completely denying the role of purchasing power parity in predicting long-term trends of exchange rates. But I believe that we should consider fully various political and economic factors and make some amendments to the theory in order to set the RMB exchange rate at a reasonable level.

11.2.3. *The Scale and Speed of Cross-Border Capital Flows is Growing Rapidly*

According to the definition of IMF,[6] International Capital Flows can be divided into three types as follows: the first type is Foreign Direct Investment (FDI), consisting of equity capital, reinvested earnings and other capital. The second is Foreign Portfolio Investment (FPI), which includes stocks, bonds and financial derivative products. And the last is Foreign Other Investment (FOI), comprising long and short trade credits, loans, currency, deposit, non-tradable equities and bonds, insurance and pension reserves. In addition, International Capital Flows also can be divided according to time span: Foreign Long-term Investment (above one year) and Foreign Short-term Investment (one year and within one year).

With the development of the financial markets all over the world, the relaxed control of the capital flows, and the progress of information technology, financial transactions can go on round the clock and enormous amount of money or capital can be transferred to thousands of kilometers away within a second. These factors have contributed to the growing scale and volume of cross-border capital flows, and enhanced the trend that capital flows are mainly short-term. During the period 1986 to 2003, the average annual growth rate of world economy (real GDP) was about 3.5%, and international trade about 6.1%. The flow of international capital grew more rapidly.

Capital flows grew relatively slowly in the early 90s. In contrast, from 1998 to 2000, the capital flows grew 20%. In 2001, the global economy fell, and this is reflected in the reversal of capital flow. The capital flow returned to positive growth in 2002 and continued to grow rapidly in 2003 and 2004. In 2004, capital flow had grown 29.4% compared to the last year, totaling 960 billion dollars. In 2006, the scale of global capital flows was 1.3562 billion dollars, and it was estimated by IMF that it would grow to 1.448 billion dollars in 2007.

Since the 1990s foreign direct investments have grown at a furious rate, and the proportion of cross-border mergers and acquisitions (M & A) got larger and larger. In 2007, the global foreign direct investment volume grew to 1.83 billion dollars, and the total amount of M & A was 1.64 billion dollars, constituting 89.6% of the total flows.[7]

Cross-border Merger and Acquisition subsumes Cross-border Merger and Cross-border Acquisition. It is an activity whereby a company or investment fund in one country buys all assets or parts of the equities of a foreign company by certain payment methods (including paying in cash, exchange stocks or exchanging stock for assets). Companies merge in order to dominate the markets or to expand business, while the purpose of investment funds is to make profits by selling acquired companies after their values appreciate.

The impact of cross-border M & As on the exchange rate is very complex. In theory, lots of foreign capital flowing into the merging country (host country) will lead to the appreciation of the country's currency, which will raise the cost (of the M & A) and then reduce the foreign capital inflow. In practice however, if the impact of rising cost of M & A attributable to local currency appreciation on attracting foreign investment is not significant, foreign capital inflow will not decline.

Greenfield Investment belongs to the scope of real economy, and when the company merges with others by investing funds to expand business, its action also comes under the purview of real economy. Other companies merge by replacing or exchanging stock or replacing stock for assets — that action falls under the category of fictitious economy. The activity of investment funds to merge others often belongs to the category of fictitious economy, and the investing parties often make use of their expertise in administration and financing to increase the value of fictitious capital.

In terms of structure of global capital flow, the proportion of short-term capital is getting bigger and bigger. Foreign securities investment companies and other foreign investment form the majority of these short-term capital flows. All these investments are classified as "fictitious economic activities".

11.2.4. *The Scale of Fictitious Economy is Expanding*

With the growth of international economy, the rapid advances in information technology and financial innovation, the scale of financial market of all countries (especially developed countries) is expanding rapidly. In particular, driven by the rapid expansion of US dot com (Internet) economy bubbles during 1997 and 2000, the scale of fictitious economy based on fictitious capital transaction such as stock, bonds and financial derivatives expanded tremendously. The total value of over-the-counter transactions including the world's stock markets, bonds and financial derivative products went up to 50 billion USD — 10 times the GDP of all countries combined. In the global currency exchange market, the average transaction amount reached more than two trillion USD everyday, approximately 50 times the daily trade volume of the world. That is to say, only 2% of capital flow was actually utilized in international trade every day.

The current transnational financial activities, representing processes of choosing investors and financial supporters in the world, fall under the same "rules of the game" with the same financial tools. Among financial markets of different regions there are bridges connecting the two parties — allowing the capital to flow not only among the same kind of markets but also among different kinds of markets. All these have blurred the distinctions between long-time capital and short-time capital, between external finance and internal finance. The association and relation between financial markets of different countries are getting closer and this also means the speed in which risks can be transferred or passed on increases, as aptly described by the Chinese saying "move one hair and the whole body is affected".

After the 1970s, with the development of financial innovations, financial derivative markets emerged in some countries such as UK and US. These markets can be divided into two categories. One was the market of financial products — issued by banks — also called 'over-the-counter transactions.' The majority of trading was done by phone. These financial derivatives also changed the *modus operandi* of the banking industry and forced all the transnational banks to develop into "all-power" banks with rapid growth of off-balance-sheet business. The other was the 'tangible' market sponsored by financial futures exchanges. The currency derivative products traded in derivatives markets include forwarding contract, currency and interest rate swaps, perpetual interest rate agreement, financial futures, options and so on. According to the statistics of Bank of International Settlement (BIS), by the end of 2007, the total amount of derivatives reached 29.1 billion USD, in which swap and future contracts accounted half by half. The function of these financial derivatives is to hedge risk, but they also turn out to be tools for speculation with high risks. The recent global financial crises caused by the US sub-prime crisis were rooted in the over-expansion of financial derivatives related to mortgages.

11.2.5. *Exchange Rates have become Policy 'Game Tools'*

The exchange rate can only reflect the international purchase power: so with the ups and downs of the economic powers of countries, exchange rates may fluctuate most of the time. Meanwhile, governments can use the exchange rate as a policy tool. This can help governments gain more benefits from the current accounts or the capital accounts, and the adjustment of exchange rates turns out to be a 'gaming' behavior among governments. Theoretically, if the government of the country concerned set their eyes on the benefit for the whole, the adjustment of the exchange rate would possibly produce the 'Pareto effect' and result in win-win situations for all concerned. It is a pity that most governments consider their countries' own benefits first: it is no wonder that the exchange rate adjustments do not bring about the desired effects. This is evident in the adjustment process of international exchange rates in the 1980s.[8,9]

From 1981 to 1985, spurred by the devaluation of Japanese Yen and appreciation of US dollar, exports of Japanese products increased greatly, with exports to the USA increasing by 74%. This led to huge trade surplus of Japan-US trade. Against this background, and initiated by the USA, a summit meeting of the finance or treasury ministers and heads of central banks from the USA, Japan, Germany, France and UK was held at the Plaza Hotel in New York on September 22, 1985. The aim of this summit was to confer with each other on the exchange rate policies of the five countries, so as to reflect more appropriately and accurately the real development of their economies and to correct the imbalances of current accounts. The result of the consensus from the Summit meeting was the Plaza Agreement, which clearly stated that unified actions must be taken to devalue the US dollar against several main currencies — but in a gradual and progressive manner.

The Plaza Agreement is a precedent for the unified adjustment of exchange rate worldwide, and it helped achieve good results in a very short time. Central banks began to sell US dollars and buy Japanese Yen and Deutsche Mark and within one week after the summit, the US dollar devalued 8% against Japanese Yuan, and 6% against

Deutsche Mark. By the end of December 1986, the US dollar devalued nearly 20% against the two currencies. By then, some related countries argued that if the US dollar was allowed to continue devaluing freely, the economic development of all countries would be adversely affected. For this reason, the G7 summit held in Louvre Palace in France on 21st and 22nd February 1987 (including US, Japan, Germany, France, UK, Canada and Italy) discussed actions and policies to maintain the stability of exchange rates. Upon Italy's withdrawal, the six countries reached agreement and signed the Louvre Accord, in which the six countries agreed to control the fluctuation of exchange rates within a reasonable range; they would interfere if the exchange rates fluctuate outside the range. However, the US didn't stick strictly to the Accord to reduce its fiscal deficit. In particular, after October 19, 1987, with the sharp slump of the stock market, the US government focused all attention on their domestic economic problems and let the US dollars devalue freely. This had reduced the Louvre Accord to a piece of useless and defunct paper. Meanwhile, the continuous appreciation of Japanese Yen became one of the main factors contributing to economic bubbles of Japan which broke out in 1991. Subsequently Japan fell into recession for a very long time.

History tells us that we could never regard the exchange rate as just an issue of finance or economy, but also an issue of politics. For example, after the outbreak of the financial crisis of East Asia in 1997, China argued that the issue of exchange rate involved the sovereignty of China and vowed not to give in to pressure exerted by the West for RMB devaluation. This helped to maintain the stability of RMB exchange rate and benefitted the countries of East Asia in overcoming the difficulties and China gained praises from many East Asian countries. After 2003, we again confronted the pressure to appreciate RMB from the western countries. All the trials and tribulations we experienced had taught us to discern and 'read' the circumstance clearly, weigh and balance the pros and cons, as well as the possible risks to reach a correct and reasonable decision while maintaining our sovereignty in issues of exchange rate.

The experience of exchange rate 'gaming' also makes us realize that it is very difficult to reach a rational or reasonable outcome in a situation in which there are so many countries involved and there is a big gap between the USA and China in terms of national strengths. It's better to get a regional agreement with a few countries and form a grouping that can counter-balance US power. It will also help stabilize regional finance. This consideration was also the main incentive for the birth of the Euro. We can predict that, with the development of regional integration, financial integration will be the trend. The Development Bank of Asia was considering promoting the idea of Asian Current Unit (ACU), which is also a very new, persuasive example.[10]

11.2.6. *The Dilemma in Choosing Exchange Rate Regime*

There is an intimate link between the fictitious and the real economic systems. The fictitious economic system is generated from the real economic system, and is 'attached' to the real economic system. As the two economic systems are closely connected, risks arising from real economic system will transfer to fictitious economic system and cause its instability. The risks to the real economy are those in regards to products, decline in foreign trade, corporate bankruptcy and so on. Risks in fictitious economic system would also seriously affect the real economy, bringing about stock indexes fluctuation, real estate prices plunge, soaring bad loans in banks, currency devaluation and so on. Nowadays finance has become the core of the economy, and real economy can hardly function without fictitious economy. Consequently, if real economy is regarded as the hardware of economy, fictitious economy may be regarded as the software.[11]

As early as the 1950s, when the U.S. dollar-dominated gold exchange standard prevailed, there had been debates about whether fixed or floating exchange rate is the better system. A group of scholars led by Indieberger,[12] strongly recommended the fixed exchange rate regime, the reason being that floating exchange rate would cause exchange rate instability. Another group of scholars headed by Friedman[13] advocated the floating exchange rate regime. In their views, "The floating exchange rate isn't necessarily unstable; if it is unstable, it is mainly due to the instability of the economic base in spearheading international trade. Although nominally the fixed exchange rate is stable, its adoption may cause any instability of other economic factors to become protracted and severe.

The substance of the debate involves the aims of exchange rate regime. In an open economy, if maintaining exchange rate stability is the primary aim, then the fixed exchange rate system should be adopted — compromising monetary independence. If reducing the impact on the real economy caused by exchange rate fluctuation is the main aim, then the floating exchange rate should be adopted — thus compromising stability of exchange rates. Some economists have tried to search for an 'intermediate' regime (that has the best of both worlds) for exchange rates, but Mundell and others showed that it was difficult to achieve.

In 1960s, Mundell[14] and Fleming[15] developed the Mundell-Fleming model (M-F Model) of exchange rate. They applied the analysis of short-term demands on the circumstances of an open economy, and introduced factors describing foreign trade and capital flows; they analyzed different roles of fiscal and monetary policies under fixed or float exchange rate. The model assumes that: (1) Finance is completely open, that is, both the current and capital accounts are open; (2) Capital flows freely, that is, for all domestic and foreign currencies and securities, assets are freely inter-substitutable; (3) Output is determined by demand, and production supply is perfectly elastic; (4) The scale of domestic economy is small, which has no effect on foreign interest rates and the price level; (5) Interest rates remain constant in the relevant period; (6) Depreciation of domestic currency improves current account balance. Under these assumptions the monetary policy is ineffectual to economic stability if a fixed exchange rate regime is chosen (that is, it has no influence on income and employment), while fiscal policy is ineffectual on economic stability if a floating exchange rate is chosen. Thus, M-F model contains a "trilemma", meaning that among the three policy goals — free capital movement (open financial market), fixed exchange rate and independence of monetary policy (the money supply can be adjusted to achieve required interest rate level), only two of them can be changed.

The M-F model is the foundation of western currency exchange rate theories. Since then a large number of research had focused on relaxation or modification of assumptions of this model, as well as extension of this model.[16] Krugman[17] and Frankel[18] formalized the M-F model into "impossible triangle" model, and proposed a combination of "semi-independent and semi-stable". Yi and Tang[19] extended the "impossible triangle" model, and proposed an 'extended triangle hypothesis' addressing the influences of intermediate regimes. Shen and Shi[20] introduced international loan capacity variable of domestic currency into "impossible triangle" model, tried to expand "impossible triangle" model into a "tetrahedral hypothesis" and suggested that "impossible triangle" model is an example of "tetrahedral hypothesis". They think that the choice of exchange rate regimes is a dynamic conversion process. Depending on the difference and variation of factors in the country, the choice of exchange rate regime may take the form of a multiplicity of regimes co-existing and interconvertible among themselves.

11.3. The Choice of RMB Foreign Exchange Rate Arrangement

The exchange rate regime refers to the principles and methods that a country's monetary authority uses to regulate and manage the exchange rate level, and a series of arrangements and rules made thereof. In order to avoid vagueness in the meaning and generalization of the word "regime", we will adopt here "exchange rate arrangement" and define it as the relationship between domestic currency and foreign currency. Thus, exchange rate arrangement falls under the scope of institutions (structure) and it is relatively stable in a certain period, but gradually evolves in the long run.

11.3.1. *Evolution of Exchange Rate Arrangement*

Throughout the history of international finance studies, from 1880 to 1914 the fixed exchange rate regime under the gold standard system was adopted by the world and exchange rates between countries depended on their respective ratio of gold content–gold parity. After the outbreak of World War I, the gold standard system gradually disintegrated and exchange rate arrangements of all countries ran into chaos. In July 1944, 45 allied countries reached the Bretton Woods agreement, and established the gold exchange standard system based on USD (that is, the United States committed that 35 U.S. dollars was equivalent to 1 ounce of gold, U.S. Dollar reserves of other countries would be equivalent to gold reserves). This was the fixed exchange rate regime under the Bretton Woods agreement, and the exchange rate of other countries vis-à-vis U.S. Dollar could just float within the limits of 1% based on the U.S. dollar parity. In August 1971, the United States announced the depreciation of the U.S. Dollar stopped exchange with gold. The Bretton Woods agreement began to collapse, whereupon the exchange rate arrangements of countries of the world were in chaos again. In January 1976, members of the International Monetary Fund reached an agreement in Jamaica, acknowledging that fixed and floating exchange rates might co-exist at the same time, and all members could choose exchange rate arrangements freely. Henceforth all countries have their own exchange rate regimes and a unified regime could not be established — even until now.

After evolution of more than 30 years, there are mainly ten exchange rate arrangements in the world at present, which can be summarized according to the descending order of their flexibilities:

1) Free Float. Under this arrangement, the exchange rate depends on supply and demand; the central bank doesn't intervene in foreign currency markets at all and also doesn't have to make timely responses to the nominal exchange rates resulting from external or internal 'shocks', so large exchange reserves aren't needed. The shortcoming of this regime is that exchange rate fluctuations may lead to distortions in resource allocation and inflation can't be solved easily. In practice all governments do take into consideration the aims of exchange rate arrangement (exchange rate targets) when formulating and implementing monetary policies, so no country has adopted a completely free floating exchange rate.

2) **Managed Float.** In this arrangement the central bank intervenes in the foreign exchange market according to the exchange rate target, but doesn't have any pre-determined exchange rate parity. The central bank can intervene by means of hedging or other tools, leading to changes in foreign exchange reserves. Besides, it can intervene indirectly in the market by changing interest rates, liquidity and other financial instruments, which will not cause the change of reserves. The advantage of managed float is avoiding exchange rate fluctuations, but the main disadvantage is its lack of transparency on the part of the central bank, resulting in a number of uncertainties. Moreover, the central bank's intervention could only bring about short–term results but could sometimes bring about negative effects.

3) Target Zone. In this arrangement, the government determines the fundamental equilibrium exchange rate of domestic currency (central parity) and allows the nominal exchange rate to fluctuate freely around the central parity within a certain range, and fundamental equilibrium exchange rate can be pegged to a currency or to a basket of currencies. Monetary authorities would control fluctuation margins of the spot exchange rate around the central parity within the upper and lower limits of the target zone. However, in practice, there is no absolute obligation for the monetary authorities to intervene immediately when the spot exchange rate gets outside the target zone boundaries. For example, the European exchange rate mechanism founded in 1979 set the exchange rate fluctuation range of its members within 2.25%. The advantage of this exchange rate arrangement is that exchange rate fluctuation range and the central point can be made public, which will increase transparency of exchange rates and help guide the public's expectations, and thus monetary authorities don't have to intervene frequently in the foreign exchange market.

4) Crawling Zone. This exchange rate arrangement means that the exchange rate can fluctuate in a certain range, but central parity is not fixed and can change over time. The crawling of central parity can be a retrospective one — that is, adjusting central exchange rate according to past inflation. It can also be a forward-looking one — that is, adjusting central exchange rate according to the expected or target inflation. This exchange rate arrangement enables high-inflation countries to adjust central exchange rate but not the exchange rate range according to inflation. The disadvantage is that a retrospective crawling may introduce inflation inertia, while a forward-looking one may produce 'over-valued' exchange rates, and could lead to currency speculation.

5) Basket Peg. In this exchange rate arrangement, one country's currency doesn't peg to a certain country's currency but to weighted currencies of its major trading partners. The weight depends primarily on its own foreign trade structure, namely, the weight of one country's currency in the basket is usually the trade volume of the home country and the other country divided by the home country's total foreign trade volume. However, if the currency of the third country is adopted in bilateral trade, the currency weight of the third country should be increased correspondingly. Sometimes, the currency structures of external debts and foreign investment should be considered.

6) Crawling Peg. This exchange rate arrangement is comparatively suitable for high-inflation countries, i.e. the domestic currency pegging to the exchange rate is depreciated slowly according to inflation so as to maintain stability of real exchange rates. Sometimes, the crawling rate can also be deliberately set lower than the expected rate of inflation in an attempt to slow down inflation. The disadvantage of this arrangement is that stability of real exchange rate can't be maintained without the support of fiscal and income policies, and adjusting exchange rates according to inflation may cause inflation inertia, thus negating or nullifying the function of the exchange rate as a nominal anchor.

7) Adjustable Peg. Although monetary authorities promise to adopt a fixed exchange rate, and nominal exchange rate is fixed for a certain period, monetary authorities may adjust the exchange rate parity based on the operation of the real economy. After the collapse of the Bretton Woods system, most developing countries adopt this exchange rate arrangement. In such a regime or arrangement, the adjustment of the exchange rate is often announced 'suddenly', making exchange rates uncertain and causing inflationary pressures.

8) "Truly Fixed" Exchange Rate. In this case, a country's monetary authorities commit to one country or some countries that the exchange rate is fixed. However, as the promise or the commitment lacks any solid or legal foundation, it can hardly be kept when frustrated by special difficulties.

9) Currency Board. Under this arrangement, the monetary authorities issue local currency at a fixed parity according to reserves of foreign currency pegged to a particular foreign currency, and require enough pegged currencies to support the cash parts of the local currency to ensure that they can exchange in a fixed exchange rate at any time. Besides, the monetary authorities could maintain exchange rate stability by buying or selling local currency in the foreign exchange market. As there is great confidence that monetary authorities can maintain the fixed exchange rate, the regime or arrangement could help to maintain stability of exchange rates, but doesn't help in the adjustment of exchange rates. External shocks can only be absorbed through domestic economic activities, and the central bank lost its function as the lender of last resort.

10) Currency Union. In this case, more than one sovereign states use the same currency. The gist of this arrangement is that the common currency is issued by the central bank of currency union established by these countries. For example, European Monetary Union issues the Euro which is the unified currency of member countries of the European Union, issued by the European Central Bank. Another alternative way is adopting a ready currency which is usually the US Dollar. For example, Panama and a number of Eastern Caribbean States adopt the US Dollar-based monetary regime, that is, US Dollar is used as domestic currency, which makes these countries to relinquish their income due to 'minting tax' and lose their sovereignty over monetary policy. This is an extreme way of the fixed exchange rate arrangement.

In recent years, with the expansion of economic globalization, the increase of international capital flows and the integration of international financial markets, the impact of exchange rates on the macroeconomy is being felt and the influences thereof marked. The financial systems of Mexico, Thailand, Indonesia, Korea, Russia, Brazil, Turkey and Argentina, whose exchange rate arrangements are between the fixed and the floating exchange rate (intermediate exchange rate arrangement) suffered hits of different degrees, which even led to financial crises , forcing these countries to adopt the floating rate or the fixed exchange rate finally.[21] Obstfeld and Rogoff[22] suggested that something was amiss with various intermediate exchange rate regimes — between the floating exchange rate and the monetary union. Sommers[23] also opined that for those countries adopting intermediate exchange rate regime arrangements, there would be little 'space' to maneuver in their choice in regards to free movement of capital, and it would be getting more difficult to maintain exchange rates stability. However, Frankel argued that since most countries in the world still adopt intermediate exchange rate regime arrangements, governments 'more or less' need to intervene in foreign exchange markets.

Wolf[24] divided the exchange rate arrangements into six categories, and studied frequencies and duration of various types of exchange rates. He found that the traditional single-currency pegged out 147 times and pegged in only 39 times, while the number of peg-outs (exits) of other exchange rate regime arrangements was smaller than that of entry. The total number of strict peg in is 30 times without a single exit. The duration of strict peg regime is the longest and its average is 14.9 years; the average duration of the single currency peg and the currency basket peg regimes is 9.5 to 9.9 years, while the floating exchange rate regime lasts relatively shorter and its average duration is 4.5 to 6.2 years. This shows that the exchange rate regime arrangements of any country will not be static, but would be appropriately 'adjusted' or modified with the change of conditions at home and abroad.

11.3.2. *The Evolution of Exchange Rate Arrangements in China*

After the foundation of China, RMB was used as the legal currency and the floating exchange rate regime was adopted in accordance with the principles of "promoting exports, accumulating of exchange reserve resources, ensuring imports, encouraging remittances from overseas Chinese". However, as the fixed exchange rate regime under the Bretton Woods monetary regime was adopted by many countries all over the world, and the exchange rates had remained relatively stable, RMB exchange rate was basically stable and actually pegged to USD informally.

Due to the depreciation of the pound in 1967 which caused China's loss in exports, China began to turn to RMB-denominated settlements in the spring of 1968. With the collapse of the Bretton Woods monetary regime in 1971, China switched to basket-peg exchange rate arrangements, evolving from the fixed exchange rate regime into the managed floating one.

In 1979, China began to try different pricing methods in trade and non-trade foreign exchange receipts and implemented foreign exchange retention regime, allowing foreign companies to reserve a small part of export income themselves, with the rest turned in to the country according to an official exchange rate quotation, and thus a dual exchange rate regime arrangement was instituted. The official exchange rate was the managed floating of basket peg, while foreign exchange prices between enterprises float was based on supply and demand of markets. In April, 1980, the Bank of China started to issue foreign exchange certificates. Foreign exchanges owned by foreigners and domestic residents must be exchanged into foreign exchange certificates equivalent to RMB and before they could be used in specified areas within China.

In 1994, China abolished dual exchange rate regime and ceased foreign exchange retention rules. Foreign exchange certificates were no longer issued and instead a single, managed floating exchange rate regime was adopted based on market supply and demand. On July 1, 1996, China realized full convertibility of RMB under the current accounts. However, because of China's low level of exchange rate marketization, the exchange rate of RMB against US Dollar could only float within the range of 0.3% of the base rate. So the exchange rate regime arrangement of RMB was essentially a fixed one pegged to US dollar.

On July 21, 2005, China began to carry out managed floating exchange rate regime based on market supply and demand and regulated according to a basket of currencies. The People's Bank of China (PBC) would adjust floating range of the exchange rate at appropriate times according to market conditions and economic and financial situations, manage and adjust RMB exchange rate, keep RMB exchange rate basically stable at a reasonable and balanced level, promote balance of international payments, and maintain stability of macro-economy and financial market.

The reforms of the exchange rate regime arrangement enhanced the flexibility of RMB exchange rate and allowed appreciation of RMB. But currently there are still some shortcomings in the arrangement.

Firstly, transparency of exchange rate regime arrangements based on a basket of currencies is low. What kinds of currencies the basket contains and their weights are unclear. The central bank has much room for maneuvering in structuring discretion before making decisions. Thus, RMB exchange rate is not really based on market supply and demand. Such methods, depending on subjective decisions of the central bank, could easily lead to imbalance of exchange rates and are harmful to economic development whether overvaluation or undervaluation. If the exchange rate is undervalued for a long term, this will result in overdependence of enterprises on price competitiveness. Structural adjustment, industry upgrading and improvement of international competitiveness will all be affected.

Secondly, at present, RMB exchange rate is regulated largely depending on foreign exchange trading of the central bank in the market and is adjusted entirely based on the change in reserve assets, so the state possesses a large number of foreign exchange resources, but such a situation is extremely unfavorable to diversification and 'spread' of risks.

The primary aim of China's exchange rate policy should not be positioned on currency stability, but on the maintenance of the balance of international payments and promotion of economic development. If structural changes are occurring in an economic entity, the equilibrium exchange rate level must change continuously with factors such as labor productivity, economic development level, trade and capital flows and so on. Arrangements for RMB exchange rate should not only help mitigate foreign trade imbalance, improve trade conditions, optimize resource allocation, expand domestic demand and enhance international competitiveness of enterprises, help to optimize the structure of foreign capital and improve efficiency of capital utilization, but also help to enhance independence of monetary policies and improve the ability to take positive initiatives (to be proactive) and effectiveness of financial control, and help make full use of "two kinds of resources" and "two markets" to improve the level of openness. Moreover, the reforms of RMB exchange rate regime aim to satisfy the internal demand of establishing and perfecting the socialist market economic system and allowing the market to play a fundamental role in allocating resources. The reforms are also parts of the strategies for deepening the reform of economic and financial system and improving the macro-control system. These reforms are fully commensurate with the requests of the Central Committee and the State Council on establishing managed floating exchange rate regime based on markets, improving RMB exchange rate formation mechanism and keeping basic stability of RMB exchange rate at a rational and balanced level. They are also consistent with China's fundamental and long-term interests and contribute to scientific development and of vital significance to promoting the comprehensive, coordinated and sustainable development of economy and society.

Overall I would say the present time offers a better opportunity for China to reform the exchange rate regime. While the world economy has slowed sharply due to financial crisis, China still has a better macro-economic environment and international balance of payments, continuous external driving force for development and foreign direct investments to maintain our growth potential. Most importantly, our country has good economic fundamentals, as well as stable and good expectation of fast economic growth. Therefore, our government should seize this golden opportunity, further reform the existing RMB exchange rate regime arrangement, and create conducive conditions to achieve the ultimate goal of full convertibility of RMB.

11.3.3. *The Direction of Reform of RMB Exchange Rate Arrangement*

Since McKinnon propounded the phenomenon of "financial repression" in 1973 as a major obstacle to the economic development of developing countries,[25] more attention has been paid to the research of exchange rate regime arrangements in developing countries, with different theories proposed.

Black[26] proposed the concept of trade-weighted effective exchange rate to examine the choice of exchange rate regimes in developing countries and verified that costs and benefits of exchange rate regimes must be weighed regardless of any regime. Since the theory of exchange rate regimes in developing countries is relatively complex, and theories do affect to some extent decisions of exchange rate regime arrangements made by monetary authorities of developing countries, there is a need for systematic analysis before making any conclusions.

The American economist Heller H.R.[27] believes that the choice of a country's exchange rate regime depends on various economic factors. For countries in which the economy is very open, domestic financial markets are relatively underdeveloped, capital controls are more strict and economy scale is small, or in which the categories and countries of import and export commodities are highly concentrated, a fixed or a pegged exchange rate is suitable; otherwise, it would be appropriate to adopt a floating exchange rate.

Some economists in developing countries[28] believe that the economies of developing countries are generally backward and advanced technology and capital need to be imported from other countries. These countries are very dependent on foreign countries and don't have the necessary conditions to adopt floating exchange rate, so only pegged exchange rate can be adopted. As for which currency is to be adopted as anchor currency, much depends on the degree of openness and exposure of the country's economy to foreign trade as well as the political relation with foreign countries. Premised upon these reasons, Bird G.[29] proposed ten factors covering different aspects for references for developing countries to consider whether to adopt the floating exchange rate. These are, according to Bird: a country's economic fluctuations come mainly from overseas; economy is not open enough; commodities are too diversified; foreign trades are widely distributed geographically; high degree of integration of capital-markets both at home and abroad; inflation rate differentials are relatively large; the price elasticity of import and export commodities is high; international reserves are low; the society is more inclined to income growth; having a good long-term foreign exchange market etc. A country with a majority of the aforementioned factors would be well advised to choose floating exchange rate; otherwise, fixed exchange rate would be appropriate.

Yoshitomi and Shirai[30] believed that, if the source interference causing economic shocks comes from monetary factors — such as changes in money demand — fixed exchange rate is suitable. If the source comes from substantive factors, such as changes of preferences or prices, floating exchange rate is appropriate. If the source of interference comes from external shocks, then the floating exchange rate is suitable for isolating the domestic economy and reducing impacts of external shocks. Otherwise, if the source of interference is domestic, such as unstable fiscal and monetary policies, then it is appropriate to adopt a fixed exchange rate arrangement.

Since the 1990s, owing to frequent international currency crises, the choice of exchange rate arrangements in developing countries has become hot topics for research and debates. Some scholars[31] believe that it is not suitable for developing countries to adopt intermediate exchange rate regime. Other scholars[32] believe developing countries' lagging behind in financial systems is an "original sin", which will result in currency or maturity mismatch, so these countries should adopt regimes pegged to US dollar or regimes similar to that adopted by the Euro. Some other scholars[33] believe that developing countries "fear floating", and tend to maintain their exchange rates in a narrow range against a certain currency (usually US dollar).

Factors affecting the choice of exchange rate regime arrangements are complicated and great differences exist in these factors themselves. It comes as no surprise that exchange rate regimes are determined by a variety of diverse factors and hence there will be correspondingly diverse regimes or exchange rate arrangements. This will cause paradoxes in the research findings of different economists as they have chosen different factors in determining the exchange rate arrangements. Most economists study the choice of exchange rate arrangements from the perspective of a static, partial equilibrium, and the conclusions which they have reached based on limited factors may appear reasonable. However, as there are many factors influencing the choice of exchange rates, and these factors themselves change with the development of politics, economy and finance, their conclusions are biased and partial because of the dynamics of differences and changes of the factors. Thus, the choice of exchange rate regimes is not a 'one-off' or 'once and for all' matter, and every country would either voluntarily or be forced to change its exchange rate regime arrangements. Specific arrangements for the exchange rate regime may only be suitable for specific countries in a specific period.

As mentioned above, with the rapid development of China's export-oriented economy and the improvement of financial strength, our arrangement for exchange rate regimes (from US dollar pegged basically to references to a basket), has taken a big stride from the fixed exchange rate regime to a floating one. However, in the reform of RMB exchange rate regime, China still faces many difficulties and unfavorable conditions. For example, expectation of appreciation (of the RMB) would result in inflows of arbitrage capital; the capacity of domestic institutions to withstand exchange rate fluctuations is poor; lack of experience of risk management among our monetary institutions. In particular, the strong impact on the market brought about by adjustments of exchange rate policies under a high expectation of appreciation should be prevented. Moreover, China's market mechanism is not 'perfect' yet: there still exist restrictions in areas of trade and investment; marketization of interest rates has not been fully realized yet and prices obtained under such circumstances don't really reflect the true market supply and demand. Obviously, China still doesn't possess all the conditions for launching a completely free floating exchange rate arrangement. We should insist on the tenets of — being proactive, controllability and gradual advance — and try our best to achieve free convertibility of RMB.

Considering China's internal and external environment at present, I believe that adoption of "flexible target zone regime of RMB exchange rate" is a better choice under the present circumstances in China — basing on a comprehensive comparison of various arrangements for exchange rate. Exchange rate target zone is the 'zone' or scope for future exchange rate movements established by monetary authorities whereby monetary authorities undertake to maintain the exchange rate within the target zone through intervention in the market. Exchange rate target zone involves choice of the equilibrium exchange rate and width of target zone, transparency of target zone, modes and intensity in which monetary authorities intervene the exchange rate, relevant intervention policies and so on.

China's capital account has not yet been fully liberalized, hence it would be better — in the sense that we would be able (be proactive) to take the initiative in maintaining the stability of the RMB exchange rate regime — to adopt the target zone rather than adopting the exchange rate regime based on a basket of currencies. In this way, not only can we benefit from the basic stability of RMB exchange rate, but also the function of the exchange rate mechanism can be developed effectively, with advantages of both the floating and fixed exchange rate regime combined. In this way, any expectation of RMB appreciation will not vary in accordance with the remarks made by official monetary authorities; neither will it be determined by the amount of foreign currency assets the monetary authorities bought. It will be decided more by market supply and demand. The monetary authorities can set central rates of target zone in accordance with equilibrium rates of exchange measured using scientific methods. When market rates reach the boundary of target zone, the central bank immediately intervenes. The "honeymoon effect" that administrative mechanism of the target zone of the exchange rate produces (that is, the corresponding exchange rate which is lower or higher than the floating exchange rate due to expectation of depreciation or appreciation when it runs close to boundaries of target zone) will bring about small changes in exchange rates, and help advance the regulatory functions of markets, namely, discovering prices, guiding effective allocation of resources and stabilizing exchange rates. Meanwhile, speculation and pumps on currency baskets can be avoided. Chinese government has a more reasonable explanation to regulations of RMB exchange rate. Thus frictions with the external economy can be prevented or reduced effectively.

The "flexibility" the author advocates includes the following three aspects.

The first is dual target zone. Monetary authorities can divide the target zone into two kinds — soft and hard. The hard target zone refers to an open, transparent, and narrow zone that doesn't need to be frequently modified, and it is maintained through intervention of monetary authorities. The soft zone is not open and has a relatively wider range, to be determined and modified by monetary authorities based on international balance of payments and economic situations both at home and abroad.

The second aspect is extensibility (or expandability). The boundaries of the target zone aren't fixed, and can expand with the greater extent of financial reform and the degree of internationalization of RMB. Eventually, boundaries will be eliminated and full convertibility can be achieved.

The third is mobility. The central rate of target zone is fixed, but only relatively. When necessary or when expedient this can be adjusted according to the circumstances of international financial stability and domestic inflation etc.

11.3.4. *The Delineation and Expansion of Exchange Rate Target Zone*

Exchange rate target zone was first proposed by Fleming in 1974, and was used for the floating exchange rate rules of the IMF's executive board,[34] namely, exchange rate fluctuations should be limited to a "target zone". In 1976, Dutch Finance Minister Duisenberg[35] proposed a plan for establishing the target zone for European Union six-nation currency exchange rate. On March 13, 1979, the European exchange rate mechanism was formally established, adopting the regime of exchange rate target zone.[36]

In 1985 Williamson[37] proposed the "exchange rate target zone", which supported the opinion that the spot exchange rate should be floating around the fundamental equilibrium exchange rate (FEER) within a certain range, and monetary policy was used primarily to control the exchange rate to ensure it moves in a predetermined range. He also proposed that we should set the central rate and a certain fluctuation range among the three largest economies, the United States, Japan, West Germany (collectively known as "G3"). At the same time the three countries should adopt a coordinated monetary policy in order to stabilize international exchange rates. Frenkel and Goldstein[38] suggested that the exchange rate target zone has both the stability of a fixed exchange rate system, and also that of a floating exchange rate.

In 1991, Krugman P.[39] developed a rigorous theoretical model for the target zone. Krugman assumed that the exchange rate depends on the synthesis of money supply and other basic economic variables, as well as the expected value of future exchange rate. The key assumptions of this model are: 1) Exchange rate target zone is completely reliable and fixed; 2) There is inherently stable mechanism in the target zone and there is no need for the intervention of monetary authorities; 3) Other fundamental economic variables are random variables obeying the rules of Brownian motion. Flood *et al.*[40] proved that two of the assumptions may be problematical and they are: the assumption that the boundaries are completely reliable and that the target areas do not require the intervention of the monetary authorities. The target zone may be abandoned and thus transformed into free-floating exchange rate system, or may be reorganized into a new target zone. In addition, Obstfeld, M. and Rogoff, K.[41] suggested that, when the exchange rate reaches the boundaries, it would face the same problem with the fixed exchange rate system. It was also suggested that the Omstein-Uhlenbeck process with the characteristic of auto-regression should replace Brownian motion in Krugman's target zone model.

Miller and Weller[42] used the basic framework of D. Bush's model, and introduced a random variable in the process of price formation, then developed a 'sticky-price' target zone model. Sutherland[43] used the power series method to solve the exchange rate function of Miller and Weller's model, and proved that this model could explain the peak shape distribution (bell-shape distribution) of exchange rate statistics and the uncertainty of the relationship between exchange rate and interest rate.

Bartolini and Prati[44] suggested a soft target zone model. Its outstanding feature is that the reference standard for the exchange rate intervention has turned the exchange rate at each point in time into the behavior of exchange rate within a period of time. The fluctuation band of the soft target zone is different from the current fluctuation band of the exchange rate in the aforementioned model. It's a fluctuation band of the moving average of current exchange rates and past exchange rates. This feature means that monetary authorities can tolerate a short-term 'getting out' of the current band, but they need to undertake to maintain the exchange rate evenly at the required target zone in the long run. The soft target zone generally has a stronger ability to resist speculative attacks than the hard target zone.

In order to establish RMB exchange rate target zone, we must first identify the upper and lower limits or bounds. A narrower exchange rate target zone will be difficult in reflecting the flexibility of the exchange rate, while the broader exchange rate target zone will affect the stability of the import and export trade and capital flows. Yang and Wang[45] suggest that, in view of the ±2.25% zone widely used by the European Monetary System and ±6% used by some individual countries in specific cases, and taking into account that our country is still developing and there are more unknown variables in the financial system, we should relax the band of the target zone to ±5% or so, but the figure lacks empirical verification. According to the results of historical data analysis, Wang[46] proposes that, the upper and lower limits of the exchange rate target zone should be the sum of the equilibrium exchange rate with twice its variance. That is to say, the width of the target zone is four times the variance of the equilibrium exchange rate. However, no specific data has been provided. Guo[47] uses the method of least squares to analyze the data for our country from 1990–2005 and finds that the nominal exchange rate is always fluctuating around the equilibrium exchange rate within a range of 15%, thus setting this as the fluctuation range of the RMB exchange rate target zone.

The flexible RMB exchange rate target zone I proposed contains double target zones. In the hard-target zone, the exchange rate is determined by supply and demand in the market, and generally there is no intervention by the monetary authorities. Out of the hard-target zone, in the soft target zone, the monetary authorities could intervene when necessary. With China's exchange rate marketization, we could expand the two exchange rate target zones into three phases, and ultimately achieve the target of RMB free convertibility.

In the early phase, both target areas should be controlled within a narrow range. On the one hand, China's enterprises need a gradual process of adaptation, on the other hand, China's monetary authorities also need a change in management and a process of gaining experience. At this stage, the central bank should gradually 'lighten' or relinquish its function of directly intervening in the exchange rate in the market; more frequently the central bank should use tools of reserve rate, discount rate and open market operations to guide the behavior of participants in the foreign exchange market. Only when absolutely necessary would we directly deliver the foreign currency or the local currency to intervene in the exchange rate market. I propose, at this stage, that the width of the hard target zone should be ±1% of the central rate. Considering the fact that the standard deviations of the RMB exchange rate against the dollar, the euro and the yen are 0.50, 0.60 and 0.33 respectively[48] during China's exchange rate reforms from July 2005 to May 2009, it is still relatively prudent for us to relax the boundary to 1%. The soft target zone of the stage can be set at ±3% of the central exchange rate to control the larger, non-normal exchange rate fluctuations.

During the period of adjustment of the exchange rate target zone, with the gradual opening of China's capital accounts and continuous improvement of the market-oriented exchange rate, we could gradually (and in small increments) expand the hard target zone to within ±5% of the central exchange rate and expand the soft target zone to ±15% of the central exchange rate.

In the phase of the exchange rate target zone integration, more substantial expansion of hard and soft target zone is in order, and the former should expand faster than the latter. Ultimately, both the hard and soft target zones should be combined into a single one whose width is within ±30% of the central exchange rate. The final step is to gradually move the exchange rate towards complete convertibility.

11.4. The Determination of the RMB Central Exchange Rate

One of the most important issues in establishing RMB exchange rate target zone is the determination of the central exchange rate. We should first of all select a central currency, then determine the central rate of home currency against the central currency.

11.4.1. *The Options for the Central Currency*

The choice of central currency depend on the country's condition of foreign trade; this may be one or more (a basket of) foreign currencies. With the development of economic globalization, there will be an increasing number of countries which have opted for a basket of foreign currencies as the central currency. The foreign currency and their weight in the basket depend on many factors such as national import and export, foreign investment and foreign debt. Generally they include the U.S dollar, Euro and the Yen (G-3).

11.4.2. *Determination of the Central Exchange Rate*

It is generally believed that the equilibrium exchange rate is the real exchange rate when balance of international payments and full employment are achieved at the same time , that is , the internal and external equilibrium are realized at the same time. Swan[49] systematically discussed the relationship between the equilibrium real exchange rate and macro-economy, laying a theoretical foundation for the subsequent research of the equilibrium exchange rate. Based on Swan's research, Williamson J[50] not only presented the fundamental factors theory of the equilibrium real exchange rate that can be used for empirical analysis, but also measured the equilibrium real exchange rate of the US dollar, Japanese yen, Deutsche mark, British pound, French franc, Italian lire, Canadian dollar and other major currencies. The so-called fundamental equilibrium exchange rate is the real effective exchange rate that is consistent with macroeconomic equilibrium, describing an ideal status of macro-economy being at full employment and low inflation (internal balance) and sustainable current account reflecting the net capital flows (external balance). In 1994, Stein[51] proposed the theory of natural real exchange rate (NATREX) in response to the reasons of U.S. dollar exchange rate misalignment, as well as the U.S. current account deficit. He used this theory to estimate empirically the equilibrium real exchange rate of the dollar, Deutsche mark, French franc, Australian dollar and other currencies. This equilibrium exchange rate is defined as the mid-term real exchange rate, which enables international balance of payments — taking into account the main economic factors of main entities. In 1998, Clark and MacDonald[52] proposed the Behavioral Equilibrium Exchange Rate theory (BEER) and used it to analyze the exchange rate changes of dollar, Japanese yen and Deutsche mark. This is defined as the ultimate estimated exchange rate, which is computed by establishing a behavioral formula relating the real effective exchange rate and the related basic economic variables by econometric methods. The theory applies co-integration techniques developed in econometrics in recent years to find the statistical co-integration relationship between the real exchange rate and the determinants of various long-term exchange rates identified in the previous work and literature. Based on this theory, we could ascertain whether the equilibrium real exchange rate and the assessed exchange rate are imbalanced. In recent years, this theory has been widely used in the empirical study of measuring the equilibrium real exchange rate and solving the exchange rate imbalances.

Since the 1980s, some scholars have been studying the equilibrium exchange rates of developing countries. In 1989, Edwards[53] first proposed the equilibrium real exchange rate theory (ERER) of developing countries in which he fully considered the relevant macroeconomic characteristics of the developing countries, such as exchange controls, trade barriers, equilibrium exchange rate (usually black market exchange rates) and so on. Within this framework, he conducted an empirical study on the currency of Brazil, Colombia, India, Philippines, Malaysia, Thailand and other developing countries. Based on Edwards' research, Elbadawi[54] in 1994 proposed a more scientific theory of equilibrium real exchange rate for developing countries to achieve a better combination of theoretical analysis and empirical analysis. By integrating the theoretical literature on the equilibrium real exchange rate of the developing countries. Montiel[55] established a long term equilibrium real exchange rate model with micro-economic foundation that could be used to determine the actual exchange rate. He found that, as far as studying and researching on the problems of misalignment of exchange rates in developing countries are concerned, BEER had more advantages.

As for the detailed review on the equilibrium exchange rate theory, you can refer to Jiang and Li.[56]

11.4.3. *The Determination of the RMB Equilibrium Exchange Rate*

Foreign scholars have done some research on RMB Equilibrium Exchange Rate, and their main conclusions are that RMB is seriously undervalued. For example, Bosworth and Overholt have found that RMB equilibrium exchange rate is 1 dollar to 2 RMB if we take no consideration of the differences in income levels of relevant nations; but if differences in per capita income are taken into consideration, RMB is undervalued by 40%. Frankle has calculated that RMB is undervalued by 35% in 2000, and more than 35% in 2004 using the method of Revised Purchasing Power Parity.[57]

By referring to some western theories of equilibrium exchange rate, as well as by amending the model structure and parameters according to the actual situation of our country, domestic scholars have also studied the RMB Equilibrium Exchange Rate Theory. Their studies and findings may generally be classified into the following categories:

1. Based on the theory of PPP, such as Yu,[58] Li and Yu,[59] Wu and Zhou[60] etc, whose common conclusion is that the RMB is not undervalued or just undervalued slightly.
2. Based on the theory of ERER, such as Jin,[61,62] Ma,[63] Chu,[64] Zhang,[65] Lin,[66] Bu and Qin,[67] Zhang[68] etc.
3. Based on the theory of BEER, such as Zhang,[68] Liu,[69] Shi and Yu,[70] Qin *et al.*,[71] Zhang[72] etc.

Liu and Ren[73] also calculated the equilibrium effective exchange rate of RMB with the BEER model of Edward. They have constructed a theoretical model of the RMB equilibrium exchange rate by selecting the following — terms of trade, government spending on non-tradable goods, trade restrictions and the degree of transaction control, technological progress and debt-service ratio- as the fundamental elements affecting the real equilibrium exchange rate. At the same time, they have chosen the excessive supply of domestic credit and the ratio of fiscal deficit to the previous high-powered currency instead of the monetary and fiscal policy factors affecting the real exchange rate changes in constructing a theoretical model for RMB exchange rate. Through mathematical analysis, they concluded that RMB had experienced two obvious phases of underestimate (undervaluation) and overestimate (overvaluation) since the 1980s. RMB was underestimated both from 1986 to 1988 and from 1991 to 1995, but was overestimated from 1983 to 1985 as well as from 1989 to 1990.

Domestic Chinese scholars have done lots of research on the RMB equilibrium exchange rate and have achieved some success. However, the bases of their theories are not quite divorced from the scope of the aforementioned foreign theories and are not consistent, sometimes even contradictory because of different theories and models they have depended upon. Therefore, we need further research and innovation to strive for an early establishment of a theory and model of RMB equilibrium exchange rate suitable for China's current situation.

11.4.4. *The Determination of Centre Exchange Rate of the RMB Exchange Rate Target Zone*

I believe that we should use a basket of central currencies in constructing the RMB exchange rate target zone , in order to truly reflect our country's situation of foreign trade and balance of payments and fully reflect RMB's international purchasing power. We should take into account the structure of China's foreign trade, foreign investment and foreign debt in determining the foreign currency options and their weight.

In the early stage of exchange rate target zone, it's inappropriate to take the equilibrium exchange rate as the central rate strictly. There are two reasons for this. First, China doesn't possess the conditions required of a widely accepted RMB equilibrium exchange rate model. Secondly we should maintain the relative stability of RMB exchange rate to facilitate the smooth transition from the basket reference to the flexible exchange rate target zone.

At the stage of the adjustment of exchange rate target zone, the central exchange rate could move to the direction of the equilibrium exchange rate according to specific condition, and thereby facilitate the movement of entire target area in the expansion of the target zone.

At the stage of integration of exchange rate target zone, the central exchange rate would move increasingly closer to the equilibrium exchange rate. With the advances of China's reform, the expansion of opening up and the continuous improvement of the socialist market economy, the situation that the structure of China's foreign exchange market is 'single' or unitary and that the central bank monopolizes the market will definitely change gradually. Only upon the premise that enterprises and banks truly constitute the main body of the market could we determine the RMB exchange rate according to the laws of demand and supply. On this basis the equilibrium exchange rate can become the central exchange rate of RMB exchange rate target zone.

11.5. The Adjustment of the RMB Exchange Rate Policy

Policy has two aspects including policy objectives and policy implementation. The government guides the market system by policy measures to evolve to the policy objectives. I have emphasized repeatedly that there is no perfect policy, since every policy has its advantages and disadvantages. We should use a policy as long as it has more advantages than disadvantages. There is also no immutable policy because any policy could be appropriate at certain time and circumstances. It should be modified when the circumstances have changed. It should also be noted that the internal factors of system evolution are the self-organizing interaction between various components of the system and their environment. These lead the system towards a certain direction of evolution. When an external policy changes the behavior of market players, and thus the direction of the self-organized interactions, it can truly be said to be carrying out its function.

As a macro-economic policy involving internal as well as foreign affairs, exchange rate policy plays an important role in the country's economic development. Since July 2005, China's exchange rate policy goals are — to maintain the RMB exchange rate at a reasonable and balanced level, to promote the balance of international payments and ensure macroeconomic and financial market stability. Years of practice has shown that this goal is basically prudent and correct, and the policy measures implemented also achieved certain results.

However, it should be noted that because our nation is still in transition from the traditional planned economy to a socialist market economy, and the transformation of government functions has not been completed, it is still not easy for the market to play its fundamental role in resource allocation. In addition, owing to the adverse effects of international financial crisis, it is necessary and expedient to review and modify China's current exchange rate policy.

The author[74] once pointed out that under China's socialist market economic system, the goal of macro control should not only be limited to maintaining the traditional four aspects — including balance of international payments, promoting economic growth, increasing employment and stabilizing prices — but also ensuring that people's income and wealth grow, narrowing the gap between rich and poor, stimulating concurrent progress of economic, social, political and cultural development, and achieving sustainable development.

11.5.1. *Reserve and the Balance of its Use*[75]

Since the reform and opening-up, with China's rapid economic development, capacity of production for all kinds of products has increased continuously; the output of the real economy greatly exceeds domestic demand, leading to the rapid expansion of foreign trade. Foreign exchange reserves surged to 2.13 trillion U.S. dollars by the end of June,2009, ranked first in the world. Surge in foreign exchange reserves increased the difficulty of (the People's Bank of China) PBC's monetary policy operations and added operating costs, so that it has to pay a heavy price to maintain a stable exchange rate. The independence of monetary policy is seriously challenged by international economic factors. China's huge foreign exchange reserves constitute a great amount of the country's 'base money'. In the absence of appropriate hedging instruments, the influx of foreign exchange funds means that the central bank has to release great amounts of RMB to stabilize the exchange rate. According to the report of financial institutions' credit loan balance issued by PBC, China's foreign exchange reached RMB 17.79 billion Yuan by the end of June, 2009. Money supply exceeded demand, and there was a danger of inflation. In addition, huge foreign exchange reserves would help heighten expectation of RMB appreciation and this would exert greater pressure on RMB for it to appreciate.

The vast majority of China's foreign exchange reserves are U.S. dollar assets, especially large number of U.S. bonds. By the end of June 2009 we were holding more than 800 billion U.S. treasury bonds and that constituted great risks to our finance. Depreciation of U.S. dollar would bring high risks to China's foreign exchange reserves, and would definitely cause these assets to devalue. Possession of the 2.13 trillion USD foreign exchange reserves indicates that China has about 16 trillion RMB purchasing options. The idle status of these purchasing options implies that we are providing 2.13 trillion USD capital to countries in which we have trade surplus, and other countries as well — at a lower price to them.

According to calculations made by the author in 2006, a reasonable amount of foreign exchange reserves would be 650 billion U.S. dollars, in which strategic reserves, (including reserves for debt payment, reserves for temporary imports, foreign exchanges for foreign rescue usage and emergency usage) should be 450 billion U.S. dollars, tactical reserves (including funds for central bank intervention, foreign direct investment profit repayment, and residents' use of foreign exchange, etc.) occupy 200 billion U.S. dollars. Therefore, the use of foreign currency should be encouraged and strengthened — including payment for the import of necessary equipment, products and technology, the establishment of strategic resource reserves, increasing USD loan to well-performing companies supplemented with policy supports, the establishment of credit support mechanism for overseas investment, promote overseas investment for competitive domestic enterprises, manage multi-currency bond portfolios, conditionally open offshore financial services, and so on.

11.5.2. *The Balance of Domestic and External Demands*

Because China's domestic demand is insufficient, we have been encouraging exports to help drive domestic economic growth, and upon implementing this policy, consumption weights in GDP dropped from 67% from the 1990s to nearly 40%. In direct consequence of the global financial crisis, external demand dropped sharply and China's exports had declined greatly. In the first half of 2009, total imports and exports fell 24.5%; net exports contribution to China's economic growth was –2.9%. We therefore need to expand domestic demand, and try our best to gradually raise the proportion of consumption in GDP. This can be done by increasing wages and property incomes, improving the social security system and crediting system, adopting tax cuts and other methods to improve the people's purchasing power. We should increase people's income along with economic growth, narrow the gap between domestic regional economic developments, the income distribution gap, and promote domestic demands driven economic growth models. In order to do that, we must make changes to China's export-oriented exchange rate policy, strive to achieve balance of international payments, promote China's market-oriented economy and work towards sustainable economic growth.

11.5.3. *The Balance of Regulation and Innovation*

Over the years, China's foreign exchanges administration focused on preventing exchange rate risks and maintaining exchange rate stability, and generally do not encourage financial innovations. Low risk also means low efficiency, but exchange rate fluctuations present both risks and opportunities. When the exchange rate fluctuates with the market supply and demand, it provides advantages to allow the market to play its role in resource allocation, optimize resource allocation, and promote the internal and external balance. We should actively and prudently develop exchange rate-related financial derivatives, including swaps (exchange rate swaps), futures, options, and forwarding contracts. At the same time, our regulation should be legitimate, reasonable, appropriate and effective.

11.5.4. *The Balance of Corporate Interests and Public Interest*

China's foreign exchange policy objectives emphasize too much on stability. An important reason is the worry that companies' (especially large state-owned enterprises) interests may be harmed by exchange rate fluctuations. It's been taken for granted that our enterprises should be protected by the government, and when they incur losses from exchange rate fluctuations, they often ask for price increase or compensation: they seldom consider ways to improve competitiveness when they are in distress. We should let enterprises raise their quality in an international environment, reduce costs, enhance international competitiveness, and thus bring more benefits to the public.

In order to realize China's exchange rate policy objectives, we should first improve China's mechanism for the formation of exchange rate; from the current "with reference to a basket of currencies" to "flexible exchange rate target zone". We should also take actions to promote balance of international payments, prevent hot money inflows and outflows, and further advance reform and opening up of China's financial system along the directions of internationalization, marketization, and systematization.

11.6. Improvement of the RMB Exchange Rate Management

When adopting the system of "flexible exchange rate target zone", we should follow the principles of "independence, controllability and gradualness", manage the relevant relationships in the foreign exchange market, improve exchange rate mechanism, and improve RMB exchange rate regulation in respect of the following points:

11.6.1. *Prevent Large Amount of Inflow and Outflow of Hot Money*

After China's ascension to the World Trade Organization, along with the rapid development of foreign trade and the continuous large inflows of foreign capital, speculative capitals without clear background of actual trading (usually known as "hot money") will also pour in. According to the author's analysis of China's foreign exchange income and expenditure in 2004, foreign exchange reserves exceeded much more than the sum of China's trade surplus, foreign direct investment and foreign investment income, indicating that there were indeed "hot money" inflows. Because the differences resulting from different statistical calculations in foreign trade and foreign investment were too great and the error and omissions were numerous, it's difficult to compute accurately the amount of "hot money" inflows. The rough estimate was about 40–80 billion US dollar.[75] Although there might have been a small amount of "hot money" outflows due to the financial crisis in 2008, China's long-term economic outlook appears positive and therefore the net inflows of "hot money" is likely to continue in the future.

The net inflow of "hot money" will fuel the expectation of RMB appreciation, increase the pressure on RMB appreciation and erode the independence of our monetary policies, thereby affecting the effectiveness of macro-control, and increasing the risks arising from asset price and exchange rate variation. We must therefore monitor the cross-border flow of "hot money", in order to prevent it impacting on China's economy and finance. We should be wary of the fact that there are domestic and foreign parent companies and their subsidiaries that carry out related transactions, fake contracts or increase the amount of the pre-collected payments of remitted funds to china, or situations whereby large amounts of foreign exchange funds are found remitted in the name of individuals (since the statistics of individuals don't differentiate between residents and non-residents, investment or trade, it is easy to mask speculative capital), or some abnormal, fraudulent cases where fake projects are posing as real ones, over-borrowing, real estate speculation and the market penetration of collections — all under the name of foreign direct investment. It is necessary to suppress the underground 'banks' or money houses acting as the conduits of hot money flows and prohibit domestic enterprises trading foreign exchange through the black market.

11.6.2. *Prevent Speculative Attacks on China's Foreign Exchange Market by Hot Money*

When the nominal exchange rate deviates from equilibrium exchange rate for a long time, it will lead to the expectation of currency appreciation or depreciation. The expectation will be further strengthened by the difference between domestic interest rate and other country's interest rate as well as higher capital premium. Such a situation will likely induce speculative attacks from hot money, which could lead to sharp fluctuations in the exchange rates, and force the monetary authorities to release foreign currency or local currency to maintain a stable exchange rate. Today, when the speculative capital is capable of controlling multi-trillion dollar "hot money', such an attack would probably lead to the depletion of foreign exchange reserves or hyperinflation, and could force the government to abandon its exchange rate target zone and instead adopt a floating exchange rate system. In order to pre-empt such a scenario, the hard target zone committed by the government should be kept within a narrow range from the very beginning. When the exchange rate runs into the soft target zone, we should be very cautious and take appropriate actions expeditiously.

11.6.3. *Protect the Government's Commitment and Credibility to the Target Zone*

The credibility of exchange rate policy is that the public believes that the government will not abandon the exchange rate policy to pursuit short-term interest and deviate from the exchange rate target.[76] Good reputation of exchange rate policy is important to attaining the goal of policy stabilization for government, especially when adopting exchange rate target zone system. Only when the public has full confidence in the government's commitment will the hard target zone be successful. Therefore, the government should be very careful and prudent when determining and announcing its commitment to a hard target zone. The government should convince the public that the monetary authorities will not take any action to intervene in exchange rate in the hard target zone; this will help maintain the stability of the target zone by "honeymoon effect" formed by market forces.

Economic globalization is an irresistible historical trend and in line with our efforts to enhance China's international competitiveness and influence, internationalization of RMB is also a general trend. On the road towards RMB internationalization, there are still many difficulties and uncertainties, requiring in-depth studies of China's scholar's on the reform of RMB exchange rate system, so as to provide rationale for any decisions regarding the ultimate free convertibility of the RMB. I would propose further studying the "flexible RMB exchange rate target zone system" from the following aspects: first, summary and theoretical review of research, both domestic and foreign; second, historical variations and problems of the reform of RMB exchange rate formation mechanism; third, the empirical analysis of RMB exchange rate and the impact of exchange rate misalignment on China's economy; fourth, objectives and basic principles of the reform of the RMB exchange rate formation mechanism; fifth, regulatory mechanism of the RMB exchange rate target zone and the computation of RMB equilibrium exchange rate; sixth, RMB exchange rate target zone regulation policy and relevant supporting measures; seventh, other supplementary policies and recommendations on the reform of RMB exchange rate formation mechanism; eighth, further research directions. On the basis of our rigorous research and studies, we should be able to move our exchange rate arrangement from reference to a basket of currencies to a flexible target zone.

References

[1] Cheng, S. W. (1999). Analysis of the Asian Financial Crisis and Its Implications, in Cheng S. W. (ed.), *The overall analysis and perspective of the East Asian financial crisis*, Beijing: Democracy and Construction Publishing, pp. 1–50 (in Chinese).

[2] Cheng, S. W. (2007). *On Financial Reform*, Beijing: China Renmin University Press (in Chinese)

[3] Cheng, S. W. (2003). *Essays on Fictitious Economy*, Beijing: Democracy and Construction Publishing (in Chinese)

[4] Cassel, G. (1922). *Money and Foreign Exchange after 1914*, New York: The Macmillan Company.

[5] Zhang, X. P. (2000). The latest evolution of purchasing power parity theory and its application in RMB exchange rate, *The World Economy*, 9, 10–18 (in Chinese).

[6] IMF (1993). *Balance of Payments Manual*, 5th Ed.

[7] The United Nations Conference on Trade and Development (2008). World Investment Report, pp. 1–7 (in Chinese).

[8] Hashimoto, T., Hasegawa, M., and Hideaki, M. (1997). *On Japan's Economy System in 20th Century and Japan's Economy*, translated by Dai, X. F, Shanghai: Shanghai University of Finance and Economics Press.

[9] Song, G. X. and Sheng Y. F. (2003). The implications of international exchange rates coordination in 1980s, *Economic Herald*, 10, 54–56 (in Chinese).

[10] Asian Development Bank (2005). *Monetary and Financial Integration in East Asia*, translated by International Department, Ministry of Treasury, Beijing: Economic Science Press.

[11] Cheng, S. W. (1999). Fictitious economy and financial crisis, *Journal of Management Science in China*, 2, 1–6 (in Chinese).

[12] Kindleberger, P. (1972). The benefits of international money, *Journal of International Economics*, 2, pp. 425–442.

[13] Friedman, M. (1983). The Case for Flexible Exchange Rates, in Friedman, M. (ed.), *Essays in Positive Economics*, Chicago: University of Chicago Press, pp. 157–203.

[14] Mundell, R.A. (1963). Capital mobility and stabilization policy under fixed and flexible exchange rate, *Canadian Journal of Economics and Political Science*, 29, 475–485.

[15] Fleming, J.M. (1962). Domestic Financial Policies under Fixed and under Floating Exchange Rates, IMF Staff Papers 12, pp. 369–380.

[16] Cui, M. X. (2002). Studies of Modern Western Exchange Rate Theory, Beijing: China Financial Publishing House (in Chinese)
[17] Krugman, P. (1979). A model of balance of payments crises, *Journal of Money, Credit and Banking*, 11, 311–325.
[18] Frankel, J. A. (1999). No single currency regime is right for all countries or at all times, NBER Working Paper No. 7338.
[19] Yi, G. and Tang, X. (2001). A theoretical basis for the corner solution hypothesis of exchange rate regime, *Journal of Financial Research*, 8, 5–17 (in Chinese).
[20] Shen, G. B. and Shi, J. C. (2002). The choice of exchange rate regime: impossible triangle and its extensions, *World Economy*, 10, 3–9 (in Chinese).
[21] Song, H. (2003). *The Choice of Exchange Rate Regime Under Financial Globalization*, Beijing: China Financial Publishing House (in Chinese).
[22] Obstfeld, M. and Rogoff, K. (1995). The mirage of fixed exchange rate, NBER Working Paper No. 5191.
[23] Summers, L. (1999). Testimony before the Senate Foreign Relations Subcommittee on International economic policy and export, Trade Promotion, January 27.
[24] Wolf, H. (2001). Exchange rate regime choice and consequences, NBER Working Paper. No. 8112.
[25] McKinnon, R. I. (1973). *Money and Capital in Economic Development*, Washington DC: The Brookings Institution.
[26] Black, S. (1976). Exchange policies for less developed countries in a world of floating rates, Princeton Studies in International Finance, No. 119.
[27] Heller, H. R. (1978). Determinants of exchange rate practice, *Journal of Money, Credit and Banking*, 10, 308–321.
[28] Tang, S. Y. and Long, H. M. (2004). Examining changes in the RMB exchange rate regime from the evolution of exchange rate regimes in developing countries, *Hainan Finance*, 4, 10–14 (in Chinese).
[29] Bird, G. (2004). *International Finance and the Developing Economies*, New York: MacMillan Publishers, pp. 272.
[30] Yoshitomi, M. and Shirrai, S. (2000). Policy recommendations for preventing another capital account crisis, Technical Background Paper, Asian Development Bank.
[31] Eichengreen, B. (1994). International Monetary Arrangements for the 2lst Century, Washington DC: Brookings Institution.
[32] Eichengreen, B. and Hausmann, R. (1999). Exchange rates and financial fragility, NBER Working Paper. No. 7418.

[33] Calvo, G. and Reinhart, C. (2000). Fear of floating, NBER Working Paper No. 7993.

[34] International Monetary Fund. 1974 IMF Survey, Washington, DC.

[35] Wellink, N.(2008). Wim Duisenberg's legacy as President of the Netherlands Bank, Speech by Dr Nout Wellink, President of the Netherlands Bank and Chairman of the Basel Committee on Banking Supervision, at the inaugural event for the Willem F Duisenberg Fellowship, Amsterdam, 28 February.

[36] Chen, J. L. and Liang, Z. C. (2005). International experience on the target zone of exchange rate and its feasibility in China, *Academic Research*, 2, 33–38 (in Chinese).

[37] Williamson, J. (1985). The Exchange Rate System Policy Analyses in International Economics, Washington DC: Washington Institute for International Economics.

[38] Frenkel, A. and Goldstein, M. (1986). A guide to target zones, IMF Staff Papers, Vol. 3, No. 3, pp. 633–673.

[39] Krugman P. (1991). Target zones and exchange rate dynamics, *Quarterly Journal of Economics*, 106, 669–682.

[40] Flood, R. and Garber, P. (1984). Collapsing exchange rate regimes: some linear examples, *Journal of International Economics*, 17, 678–707.

[41] Obstfeld, M. and Rogoff, K. (1995). The mirage of fixed exchange rates, *Journal of Economic Perspectives*, 9, 73–94.

[42] Miller, M. and Weller, P. (1994). Exchange rate bands with price inertia, *Economic Journal*, 10, 1380–1399.

[43] Sutherland, A. (1994). Target zone models with price inertia: solutions and testable implications, *The Economic Journal*, 10, 96–112.

[44] Bartolini, L. and Prati, A. (1998). Soft exchange rate bands and speculative attacks theory and evidence from the ERM since August 1993, IMF Working Paper, pp. 98–156.

[45] Yang, M. and Wang, S. (2008). The path analysis of constructing RMB exchange rate target zone, *Economic Forum*, 12, 40–44 (in Chinese).

[46] Wang, Q. H. (2007). Empirical research of constructing RMB exchange rate target zone, *Finance and Economy*, 4, 17–20 (in Chinese).

[47] Guo, J. (2007). The Study of the RMB Exchange Rate Target Zone Based on Sticky-Price Target Zone Model, A Master's Degree Thesis, Hunan University. (in Chinese)

[48] Ding, Z. J., Ding, J. P., Wang, H., and Li, D. P. (2009). The four-year road reform of RMB exchange rate: trials and tribulations, *China's Foreign Exchange*, 7, 10–14 (in Chinese)

[49] Swan T. W. (1963). Longer-Run Problems of the balance of payments. Paper presented to section G of the Congress of the Australian and New Zealand Association for the Advancement of Science, Melbourne.
[50] Williamson, J. (1983). The Exchange Rate System, Policy Analyses in International Economics, Washington DC: Institute for International Economics.
[51] Stein, J. L. (1994). The Natural Real Exchange Rate of the US Dollar and Determinants of Capital Flows, in Williamson, J. (ed.), *Estimating Equilibrium Exchange Rates*, Washington DC: Institute for International Economics, pp. 133–175.
[52] Clark, P. B. and Macdonald, R. (1998). Exchange rates and economic fundamentals: a methodological comparison of BEERs and FEERs, IMF working paper.
[53] Edwards, S. (1998). Real Exchange rate in the developing countries: concept and measurement. NBER Working Paper, No. 2950.
[54] Elbadawi, I. (1994). Estimating Long-run Equilibrium Real Exchange Rates, in Williamson, J. (ed.), *Estimating Equilibrium Exchange Rates*, Washington DC: Institute for International Economics, pp. 97–131.
[55] Montiel, P. J. (1999). The Long-Run Equilibrium Real Exchange Rate: Conceptual Issues and Empirical Research, In Hinkle, L. E. and Montiel, P. J. (eds), *Exchange Rate Misalignment: Concepts and Measurement for Developing Countries*, New York: Oxford University Press, pp. 219–263..
[56] Jiang, B. K. and Li, H. D. (2006). Review of equilibrium exchange rate theory, *Contemporary Finance & Economics*, 2, 44–50 (in Chinese).
[57] Xu, Q. (2008). Review on RMB equilibrium exchange rate, *Commercial Research*, 4, 83–87 (in Chinese).
[58] Yu, Q. (1998). Asian financial crisis and China's exchange rate policy, *Economic Research Journal*, 10, 42–50 (in Chinese).
[59] Li, Y. X. and Yu, M. (2002). Calculation and applied research of RMB real effective exchange rate, *Studies of International Finance*, 10, 62–67 (in Chinese).
[60] Wu, J. and Zhou, Y. W. (2005). Some discussion on equilibrium exchange rate of RMB, *Forecasting*, 2, 52–54 (in Chinese).
[61] Jin, Z. X. (1995). On China's real exchange rate management reform, *Economic Research Journal*, 3, 27–33 (in Chinese).
[62] Jin, Z. X. (1996). On the equilibrium exchange rate formation mechanism during the transition period, *Economic Research Journal*, 3, 63–71 (in Chinese).

[63] Ma, G. (2000). China's real equilibrium exchange rate, NERI Working Papers, No. 5 (in Chinese).
[64] Chu, Y. Y. (2004). The empirical research of the equilibrium exchange rate of RMB, *Studies of International Finance*, May 2004 (in Chinese).
[65] Zhang, B. (2003). Renminbi equilibrium exchange rate-simplified General Equilibrium Model of a single empirical equation, *Journal of World Economy*, 11, 3–12 (in Chinese).
[66] Lin, B. Q. (2003). RMB Equilibrium Exchange Rate Estimates and Calculation of the Real Exchange Rate Misalignment, *Economic Research Journal*, 12, 60–69 (in Chinese).
[67] Po, Y. X. and Qin, W. H. (2002). Tariffs, monetary policy and the real equilibrium exchange rate in China, *Economic Research Journal*, 13–21 (in Chinese).
[68] Zhang, X. P. (2001). *Study of Equilibrium Exchange Rate of RMB.* Beijing: China Financial Publishing House (in Chinese)
[69] Liu, Y. (2004). Renminbi equilibrium exchange rate and exchange rate dynamics, *Economic Science*, 1, 83–92 (in Chinese).
[70] Shi, J. H. and Yu, H. F. (2005). Renminbi equilibrium exchange rate and China's exchange rate misalignment: 1991–2004, *Economic Research Journal*, 4, 34–45 (in Chinese).
[71] Qin, W. S., Jin, Y. H. and Po, Y. X. (2004). The reasonableness of the RMB exchange rate — RMB real exchange rate and the equilibrium exchange rate deviation analysis, *The Journal of Quantitative & Technical Economics*, 7, 26–30 (in Chinese).
[72] Zhang, Z. C. (2001). Real exchange rate misalignment in China: an empirical investigation, *Journal of Comparative Economics*, 29, 80–94.
[73] Liu, L. Y., and Ren, R. E. (2002). The empirical research of the equilibrium exchange rate of RMB, *Statistical Research*, 5, 28–32 (in Chinese).
[74] Cheng, S. W. (2007). The scientific concept of development and developing well and fast, *Journal of China Pudong Executive Leadership Academy*, 1, 6–14 (in Chinese).
[75] Cheng, S. W. (2006). On Financial Reform, in Cheng, S. W. (ed.), *Some Analyses and Suggestions of China's Foreign Exchange Reserves Surge*, Beijing: China Renmin University Press, 593–599 (in Chinese).
[76] Peng, Y. L. (2004). Analysis of policy credibility and reputation of RMB exchange rate policy, *The Study of Finance and Economics*, 30, 51–61 (in Chinese).

Chapter 12

Conclusion: Three Directions for China's Financial Reforms

It has been universally recognized that China has achieved great success in economic development. Over the thirty years of reform and opening, economic development has kept at an average annual growth rate of 9%. In recent years, though China's GDP only accounted for 6% of the world's total, the contribution rate is above 20%. China becomes a hot topic and the situation and direction of China economy have gained world-wide attention.

Over the 30 years of reform and opening, China's financial reform has obtained remarkable achievements. However, we should also admit that the overall international competitiveness of China's finance is not strong enough, and financial reform still has a long way to go. As a prominent player in international trade, China is both a big seller and a big buyer. However, the voices of China in international financial markets are not strong enough and often go unheeded. Our financial system and innovation must be strengthened.

How to further promote the financial reform positively and cautiously has become a very important issue, especially at the current time. Since the US Wall street financial debacle — which has caused a world-wide financial crisis — there appear many varied opinions and views among domestic circles. Some of the opinions query the direction and pace of the financial reforms. I want to cite the words of Chairman Hu Jintao that 'reforms and opening up represent a great, new revolution, the path and direction of which are entirely correct, the merits and achievements undeniable. To stop or reverse reforms and opening-up would lead us to a blind alley.' Therefore, we cannot halt or renegade: we should persevere in our efforts to advance the financial reforms in China upon the premise of financial and economic stability.

Now the Chinese economy is faced with three 'hidden' or 'covert' worries. One of the worries is that investment is increasing too fast. According to the author's research, the economic cycle of China is about ten years.[1] The current cycle began in 2001. From 2003, the growth rate reached above 10%. The figures were 10.1% in 2003, 10.4% in 2004, 10.7% in 2005, 11.4% in 2006 and 13% in 2007. Some people regard the situations as reflecting an overheated economy. The author thinks that it is only a rapidly increasing economy but not an overheated one. There are examples in the development of countries in the world where the growth rate had maintained at about 11%. In the 1960s, Japan initiated a 'Doubling the national income project' with the objective that the national income be doubled in ten years. The planned average annual growth rate was 7.2%, but the actual figure was 10.9%.[2] Nevertheless, investment in China is indeed overheated. It is characterized by too rapid growth rate, too many new projects with consequences such as overcapacity, inventory build-up, lowered efficiency and serious pollution resurgence problems. The second worry is the relaxing of lending restrictions which could lead to the problem of excess liquidity. Although the central bank has been carrying out tight monetary policies since 2008, it is still difficult to solve the problem of excess liquidity merely by raising the required reserve ratio and interest rate because there is a huge amount of foreign exchange reserves and cash in residents' hand. Moreover, the tight monetary policy has its negative effects. Since 2008, China has adopted the relatively moderate monetary policy and expansionary fiscal policy under the impact of the global financial crisis. The problem of excess liquidity becomes more pronounced. The writer has pointed out on many occasions that there exists the risk of inflation since the money supply exceeds the demand of real economy.[3] Besides, since the bank loans were mainly for local governments and state-owned enterprises, their debts increased rapidly and this could probably cause an increase in non-performing loans or bad debts. The third worry is the escalating foreign exchange reserves. In 2004, the trade surplus of China was 32 billion dollars. The figure was 101.9 billion in 2005, 177.4 billion in 2006 and 262.2 billion in 2007. The foreign exchange reserves have also increased tremendously due to the increasing trade surplus and other reasons. From 2004 to 2006, the foreign exchange reserves increased by 200 billion dollars every year. In 2007, foreign reserves increased by nearly 500 billion dollars. In the recent two years, although the growth rate of trade surplus has slowed down, the foreign exchange reserves continue to increase. Now the foreign exchange reserves have exceeded 2.3 trillion dollars. The dramatic growth of the foreign exchange reserves brings about tremendous pressure to the monetary policy of China and the exchange rate of RMB. Higher and higher expectations of the appreciation of RMB bring bigger difficulties in the modulation of exchange rate.

The savings rate in current China is very high. This affects China's economy and finance to a certain extent. The first reason for the high savings rate is the special propensity to save among Chinese or Asian people. Unlike American and Europeans, they prefer to save today's money for tomorrow's expense rather than borrowing tomorrow's money for today's expense. The second reason is the poor social security system in China. People always need to save money as a means of self preservation and protection. The third reason is that people are always worried about the risk of investment especially direct investment. Although the interest rate is low, at least the banks ensure the safety of their deposits. In Chinese people's mind, banks are state-owned and they are too big to fail. Banks always guarantee interest payments. Therefore, the reduction of interest will not have any appreciable effect on consumption. At present, the consumption level in China is not high and people are thrifty as far as consumption is concerned.

The high savings rate causes the three above mentioned problems. Since the savings rate is high, people deposit a large amount of money in banks. Banks are looking for ways to give out loans, leading to the ease of credit. Because of the ease of credit, people are eager to use the borrowed money for investment activities. Hence investments become overheated. Because domestic consumption is insufficient, a large amount of products, goods etc are exported. Meanwhile some local governments don't pay enough attention on sustainable development; they are more interested in accelerating economic growth via heavy investments.

Finance is the core of modern economy. The reform of finance plays an important role in the developing China's economy. The author hopes that scholars could pay more attention to the interaction between economy and finance in their research. Finance could have either a positive or a negative effect on economy and economy is the important foundation of finance. Once the economic conditions change, the finance will definitely be affected. Of course, finance could have adverse effects on economy. In promoting the financial reforms of China, we should understand the relationship between economy and finance and promote a harmonious development between them. The author believes that in order to ensure the sustained, steady and rapid development of Chinese economy, we should adopt a people-oriented, all-round, coordinated and sustainable scientific outlook on development and carry out financial reforms in the following three main directions.

12.1. Internationalization

Economic globalization has been an unstoppable historical trend. Along with the development of economic globalization, the globalization of finance has also now been on the agenda. From the development trends of the world finance, we could generally discern the characteristics of financial globalization as follows:

The first characteristic is the increase in the degree of virtualization of money. The exchange rate has become the tool of the 'game' between countries. Since currency broke away from gold standard and the gold-based exchange system, there is no objective measurement for the value of currency. That is to say, currency has been virtualized to some extent. With this development, the value of currency can only be measured by its purchasing power. In my opinion, purchasing power can be divided in two categories: one is domestic purchasing power, the other is the international purchasing power. Domestic purchasing power can be measured by Purchasing Power Parity (PPP). International purchasing power is mainly measured by exchange rates. If a country never imports, the change of exchange rate has no effect on its domestic purchasing power. On the other hand, if a country relies completely on imports, its domestic purchasing power relies totally on the exchange rate. However, every country in the world is somewhere between these two extreme situations. If every country takes into consideration global interests, a "Pareto effect" may emerge and everyone will benefit from it. Unfortunately, no country would take the global interest as first priority. Most countries will probably consider their own interests first. Under the circumstances, the exchange rate system becomes the tool of 'policy games' to some extent.

From the historical perspective, the Plaza Accord and the Louve Accord have led to the ten-year recession in Japan. At the time of Southeast Asian financial crisis, the pressure of appreciation on Renminbi had been great, so is the case in recent years. It is telling that the exchange rate problem has become the gaming tool of governments around the world. Therefore, China should act by the principles of the independence and sovereignty of the nation. Of course, China should take various factors into account, promote steadily but steadfastly the reform of RMB exchange rate, and work towards achieving the final for full RMB convertibility.

The second characteristic is that the size and spread of capital flow is increasing. The capital flows happen not only in developped countries but also in developing countries. Moreover, the capital flows are very fast at present. The development of science and technology makes it possible for hundreds of millions of capital to be transfered to thousands of miles away with a click of the mouse, for instance.

The third characteristic is that financial markets are increasingly linked with each other. The Southeast Asian financial crisis began as a liquidity crisis in Thailand and the crisis spreaded to the whole world. Recently, the US Wall Street financial turmoil also affected European and other regions. This shows that financial markets in different countries and different parts of the world have growing association with each other.

The last characteristic is that the financial innovations are developing continuously. After World War II, financial innovations began with the Eurodollar. In the following decades, innovative financial products have emerged one after another; financial derivatives were introduced into the market one after another. This makes the total sum or value of open contracts exceed the world GDP, with the former about ten times the latter. So many financial derivatives dazzle the people. Under the circumstances, how to prevent financial risks and over-speculation in financial derivatives becomes a problem worthy of our close attention.

Under the circumstance of international financial integration, we should improve the competitiveness of China in international finance and we should adapt to the characteristics of financial globalization. First we should learn from foreign experience. We should admit that our knowledge in financial innovation and financial derivatives is far from enough and our hand-on experiences even more meager. In the circumstances, we might experience failures in the competition in international financial markets. Just on futures, there existed problems such as Zhuzhou Zinc smelter group, China Aviation Oil, China Reserve Cotton, China Reserve Copper and similar problems that have caused great financial losses. We should therefore first study the international financial products and their related regulations.

Secondly, we must cultivate talents having internationalized perspectives and international finance management capacity. We should bring in people who are familiar with the theory and practical application of financial derivative products and at the same time train and nurture domestic talents in financial innovation. I would suggest setting up MBA specializing in finance in some renowned schools of management and set up the accreditation and quality certification for senior financial professionals along the line of the CFA system in the US.

Thirdly, we should make proper use of various financial innovative tools. Recently with the US Wall Street financial turmoil, some people think that we should not promote financial innovation. The author doesn't agree with them. Financial innovation and financial regulations restrict and promote each other. The aim of financial innovation is to increase the financial efficiency and decreasing or dispersing risks by hedging. However, they can also act as tools for speculation. A very important reason why the US sub-prime crisis triggered the global financial crisis is that American government failed to prevent over-speculation in financial derivatives markets via regulation. However, we shouldn't deny financial innovation merely for this reason. If the residential mortgage loans aren't securitized, the default risks of mortgagors would concentrate on banks, the losses caused by subprime crisis would be large and the banking system in US would even collapse.

China is adapting to the environment of economic globalization and has joined WTO. However, this doesn't obstruct China's cooperation with neighboring countries. The author once pointed out at the 16th OECC held in Seoul that economic globalization and regional integration complement each other and the appearance of NAFTA and EU manifests that regional integration has its developmental fundamentals.[4] After 8 years of efforts and development, the free trade zone of China and ten countries of ASEAN officially began operations on January 1, 2010. The trade zone covers regions with the largest population in the world. It is both the third biggest free trade zone in the world and the biggest free trade zone composed of developing countries. It has 1.9 billion consumers, a GDP of nearly 6 billion dollars and a total volume of trade of 4.5 billion dollars.[5] The development of free trade zone of China, Korea and ASEAN (10 + 2) and the free trade zone of China, Korean, Japan and ASEAN (10 + 3) are in progress. If the 10 + 3 trade zone can be achieved, its economic aggregate will make up 20% of the world and it will become one of three great economic 'pillars' besides EU and North America. This will be more conducive to the peace and development of the world. However, regional integration doesn't rule out the situation that its member could sign free trade agreement with other countries. For example, China has signed free trade agreements with Chile and Peru.

When we talk about regional integration, it is unavoidable to mention the issue of monetary integration. Nowadays, some scholars have already taken up the research of the possibility of pushing forward the Asian dollar and even RMB to be the Asian currency. Regional monetary integration is truly beneficial to the development of regional economy. It reduces the trivial formalities and price differences in the process of currency exchange. It will favor the flow of capital, labor force, products and services. However, regional monetary integration comes with an important pre-condition that the economic levels of member countries should be close to each other. Since the birth of the Euro, there have been some problems because economic levels of different countries in Eurozone are different and the extent of benefits for each country is also different.

In the long run, Asian currencies will be integrated. But as a prudent optimist, I think it's going to take quite a long time. It takes ten years to bring about the Euro dollar since the idea was first proposed and it would take longer for Asian dollar. Now, since the economic level of China is not high enough and China has not yet achieved full and free convertibility of the RMB, it is hard for RMB to become the world currency or the main Asian currency. However, this doesn't obstruct the cooperation between Asian countries. For example, the SDR, credit default swap based on RMB between the world's central banks, cross-border trade in RMB, etc. — these are some of the concrete examples of cooperation.

12.2. Marketization

Since 1993 when China officially proposed to set up the socialist market economy, we have achieved much progress in marketization. After the explosion of the global financial crisis some people in our country query about the direction of market reforms: some market economies had adopted government-sponsored measures to stimulate the economy. They therefore think that we should enhance government regulations and even revert to a planned economy. To me, such an opinion is very harmful.

The core idea of marketization is using market as the main means of allocating resources and 'adjusting' the economy. It requires every enterprise to produce the products demanded by buyers in a most economical way. Enterprises are cells of the markets. They are both producers and purchasers. Thousands of free and autonomous companies operate in the market and promote the economic development by self-organization. Therefore, from the view of management science, we can say that there is no market economy without enterprise system. However, the freedom is relative but not absolute because every company makes decisions not entirely free from the constraints created by other enterprises and by the external environment.

The apparently unordered movements of thousands of enterprises at the micro level propel the economy to develope towards a more rational macro direction. This is the result of self-organization.

From the view of system engineering, in some situations we can accelerate or postpone the development and change of the system by changes in the external environment. This process is named as the 'hetero' organization of the system. The government's input function upon markets can be summarized as the hetero organization of the market system: to influence the development of the market system by changing the external environment. Since we need to overcome problems such as "market malfunctions" — meeting the minimum requirements of lower income group, preventing actions that can harm public interests, protecting the country's security and alleviating the effects of changes in international economic environment on the development of national economy — the government should take necessary measures to modify and control the national economy on a macro scale.

Paul A. Samuelson concluded the function of governments in economy as increasing efficiency, maintaining fairness and stability in his book "Economics". He also pointed out the importance of preventing "government failure or malfunction" — decreased efficiency due to inappropriate interventions of the government, making things worse.[6]

Thus, on the one hand, we must be cognizant of the important role of the market — the invisible hand — in guiding the management of enterprises and stimulating economic development. On the other hand, we should also admit that the government — the visible hand — plays an important role in macro control. Therefore, the problem is to maintain a balance between those two hands. The government and the market should integrate closely with each other but not 'struggle' or 'fight' against each other. In the author's opinion, the macro-control of the government should follow the following three basic principles, namely: respect the laws of values, the law of supply and demand, and the laws of competition in a market economy. The government could bestow the power and rights of micro decision-making to entrepreneurs and focus on promoting the market economic system.[7]

The author thinks that measures adopted by western market economies to intervene are emergency and *ad–hoc* measures to deal with special issues such as financial crisis. We cannot implement these 'make-shift' measures in the long run. Since the financial crisis has cooled down somewhat, government intervention will gradually fade away. Certainly, there will be adjustment and improvement of some systems made on the basis of lessons learned in the financial crisis.

The first step in promoting financial marketization is the marketization of interest rates. Interest rate is the cost of capital and it is dependent on the risks and transaction costs. The interest rate is not fixed or static; it varies with risks and transaction costs. For example, the transaction costs of small loans in rural financial institutions are relatively high, so the lending rate should be increased. Of course, loans with fiscal discounts would be another problem. For another example, loans for medium sized and small enterprises have higher risks and transaction costs because the management in those enterprises is unsound, especially the financial management. Some small enterprises can't even manage loan application. Thus, the transaction costs are high and that is why I propose that the interest rate should be marketized. There should be a floating zone, not only for loan rate but also for deposit rate.

In the reform of interest rate maketization, a very important problem is how to determine the benchmark rate. At present, China adopts the Shanghai Interbank Offered Rate (Shibor) as the benchmark rate by reference to LIBOR. It is the arithmetic mean of RMB interbank offered rate quoted by 16 banks with higher credit ratings. It is an *ungesichert* ('unsecured') and wholesale rate of simple interest. Now, the announced types of Shibor include overnight, one week, two weeks, one month, three months, six months, nine months and one year. The National Interbank Funding Center is authorized to quote, compute and announce any information regarding Shibor. On every trading day, the center eliminates the highest and lowest quotes and calculates the arithmetic mean of all the other quotes for each type of Shibor and announces the figures at 11:30.[8]

The author once suggested in 1999 that we should adopt the method of issuing short term rolling treasury bills. For the three month's treasury bills, we should let the banks bid and underwrite for these bills and the benchmark interest rate obtained in the repo market.[9] However, at that time, China implemented a gloss volume management on treasury bills. That means limited bills were issued in one year.If we issue the three months' short-term treasury bills, the allowed volume of treasury bills becomes less. For instance, if the total volume of permitted treasury bills is 100 billion yuan and we issue the three months' short term treasury bills, only 25 billion treasury bills are allowed every three months. The Standing Committee of the National People's congress has passed the resolution to practice a 'balance remaining management' on treasury bills. This would be advantagous for the management of treasury bills and the protection against financial risks. Let's hope that the next step would be the establishment of the short term treasury bills market. It would provide a base reference for the interest rate maketization of China by via its operation.

The second point is the maketization of exchange rates. The exchange rate reflects the international purchasing power which is changing all the time. If we regard the total amount of goods and services as the numerator and the monetary aggregates as the denominator, the result would be the purchasing power of the currency. Since the money supply and the amount of goods and services are changing, the purchasing power is also changing. However, if the exchange rates are fixed, that would in practice violate the rules of the market. Under the circumstance, the exchange rate system of China should be improved and modified continuously in line with the requirements of maketization. We should promote the exchange rate marketization according to changes of purchasing power and the relationship between supply and demand.

The author once suggested a three-step strategy for the maketization of exchange rate.[9] The first step is the managed floating exchange rate which is basically fixed against US dollars. It is beneficial to us when the US dollar is 'hard' or a strong currency. The second step is changing from fixing against the dollar to fixing against weighting values of a basket of currencies — such as the basket exchange rate which is the weighting average of Euro, Japanese yen and dollar. The third step is to achieve full and free convertibility of the RMB.

Since July 21, 2006, China started a managed floating exchange rate system based on the market supply and demand adjusted by a basket of currencies and moved a great step forward from fixed exchange rate system towards floating exchange rate system. RMB has appreciated by nearly 20% since July, 2005. However, from the view of implementation, the system is not transparent enough. Therefore, the exchange rate of RMB is not truly based on the market supply and demand and this would lead to the maladjustment no matter whether the exchange rate is 'over-rated' or 'under-rated'. It is harmful to the economic development. In order to accelerate the transformation of the mode of economic development, it is necessary to reform the current RMB to alleviate the imbalance of external trade, improve the terms of trade, optimize allocation of resources, increase domestic demand and the international competitiveness, optimize the utilization of foreign capital structure to strengthen the independence of monetary policy, improve the effectiveness and initiative of financial regulation, fully utilize both domestic and international resources and markets, and push forward towards the goal of achieving the full convertibility of RMB under the principles of initiative, controllability and gradualness.

Upon comparing various exchange rate regimes and through personal research, I would suggest adopting a flexible RMB exchange rate — the 'double level' target zone system. In China, as the capital items are not fully opened, the suggested system would make us more capable of taking the initiative and be more proactive when compared with the system by reference to a basket of currencies. It not only has the advantage of keeping the basic stability of RMB exchange rates, but could facilitate the effective functioning of the exchange rate system. It has the advantages of both the fixed exchange rate system and of floating exchange rate system. The expectation of appreciation of RMB no longer changes with the words of monetary authorities and the exchange rate of RMB will not be determined by the volume of total foreign assets brought by monetary authorities but be decided by market supply and demand. The monetary authorities can set the central exchange rate in the target zone according to the equilibrium exchange rate calculated by scientific methods. When the market exchange rate reaches boundaries of the target zones, the central bank could then conduct interventionist operations. The 'honeymoon effect' of the exchange rate target zone management mechanism (when the exchange rate approaches the upper boundary or the lower boundary, there exists the expectation of depreciation or appreciation, as the case may be, which leads to the difference between the actual exchange rate and the corresponding data under the floating exchange rate system) will reduce changes in exchange rate and will perform the function of price discovery, efficient allocation of resources and stabilizing exchange rate. Meanwhile, it can also prevent the 'guessing' and probing of the reference currencies in the basket. The Chinese government would be able to give a reasonable interpretation of the controls on RMB exchange rate, thus effectively preventing or reducing conflicts with the external economies.

It is suggested we adopt a basket of center currencies when setting the RMB exchange rate target zones. Along with the progress of exchange rate marketization, we could develop the two exchange rate target zones step by step in three stages before finally attaining the goal of full convertibility of RMB.

In the early stages of constructing the exchange rate target zone, the width of hard target zone is within ±1% of central rate (the standard deviation of RMB to Dollar, the Euro and Japanese yen is 0.5, 0.60 and 0.33 respectively since the exchange rate reforms in July, 2005). The soft target zone in this stage can be set as within ±3% of the central rate to control the bigger, irregular fluctuations of exchange rate. At this stage, it is inadvisable to adopt strictly the equilibrium exchange rate as the central rate.

In the adjustment stage of exchange rate target zone, we could expand slightly the hard target zone to within ±5% of the central rate and expand the soft target zone to within ±15% of the central rate by a large margin with the gradually opening up of the capital account in China and the continous improvement of the marketization. At the same time, the central rate can be slowly moved to the equilibrium exchange rate according to specific circumstances, driving the whole target zone to move consequently.

In the syncretic stage of exchange rate target zones, we could gradually expand the hard target zone and the soft target zone by a large margin: make the former expand faster than the latter and finally combine the two zones into one to become a single exchange rate target zone of a width of ±30% of central rate. At this time, the central exchange rate should approach nearer and nearer the equilibrium exchange rate. We could gradually achieve the transition to full and free convertibility of RMB.

The ultimate goal of exchange rate system reform in China is very explicit, that is to achieve the convertibility of RMB and make RMB become an international currency. China had already opened its current account in 1996, though the capital account hasn't been opened yet. In the 43 separate accounts regulated by IMF, 20 accounts have basically been opened up. Further opening is still needed. I once exchanged views with Robert Mundell on this issue. Mr Mundell thought it would be a great occasion to put the convertibility of RMB into effect in 2008 since many foreigners would come to China for the Olympic Games. However, the author thought that conditions would not be ripe then. First of all, in order to achieve this goal, much depends on the management capability of the Chinese government. The convertibility of RMB can only be achieved under effective management. Second, the best occasion should be chosen according to the changing weights of the dollar, Euro and Yen. In the author's opinion, it is just a matter of time before China achieves the complete convertibility of RMB. Although there hasn't a time table yet, it won't be too far away. When RMB becomes one of the global currencies, we could say that the marketization of exchange rate system in China has been fully accomplished.

The third point of marketization is increasing the number of market participants. Now, in the banks, securities companies, insurance companies of China, state-owned equities still take the majority while foreign capital and private capital is less. For example, national banks are mainly state-owned commmercial banks. Some banks do bring in foreign strategic investors. However, there is a large amount of funds among the Chinese folks. Those funds can also participate in the operation of banks. The "36 rules for Non-public Economy" has explicitly specified that we should encourage funds of the common people to enter small and medium financial institutions. The financial system can be better improved with more participants in the market. Of course, the participants need to satisfy some requirement for sake of state's financial security. For example, it is regulated in China that the percentage of foreign investors' stockholding in banks cannot exceed 20% singly and 25% overall. Still, we need to bring more participants into the financial system of China.

The author once suggested establishing 'community' banks. In America, the number of community banks is very large. The advantage of community banks is their better understanding of the community and the conditions of the borrowers since these banks offer services mainly for the community. The community bank system is flexible for it doesn't have any 'historical burden' or no suspicious past. It is convenient to implement the floating interest rate and deposit insurance under this system. Besides, the cost of losing credit in the community is very high. People who default in a community cannot maintain a foothold in the community — they will 'lose face' and lose credibility. It is quite 'natural' for community banks to exist in the community and community banks should not rely on the government completely. We hope to use the community bank as a break-through in expanding participation of people's capital in financial industry. Neither will it meet the increasing demands for financial services nor will it accord with the direction of the marketization reform if the main bodies or institutions of the market are all state-owned banks.

The fourth point is offering more financial products and better financial services. Generally, the variety of financial products in China is limited and we can say that there is hardly any financial derivative product. Financial derivatives are developed to offer hedging tools and to mitigate or disperse risks by hedging. However, they can also be tools for speculation, undertaking high risks when there is over speculation.

In the past 20 years, financial derivatives have been increasing rapidly with an annual growth rate of more than 25%. At present, the amount of financial derivatives has reached a very large scale. According to preliminary statistics of BIS, the balance of over the counter open contracts came to 604.6 billion dollars by the end of June 2009. Among these open contracts, interest rate derivatives took up 72.3%, exchange rate derivatives took 1.1%, equity derivatives 0.6%, CDS 6% and others 12%. The financial futures and options account for more than 90% in international futures market. The author suggests that China should promote steadily the development of financial derivatives market.[10] On September 8, 2006, the Chinese Financial Futures Exchange Ltd. was established in Shanghai. It marked the beginning of financial futures in China. It would start from the stock index futures based on Shanghai-Shenzhen 300 Index. However, owing to a variety of reasons, the State Council did not agree to introduce the stock index futures until January 8, 2010.[11] In future, more new financial derivatives will be introduced with even greater and more intensified financial reforms.

The Insurance industry in China has also been developing rapidly. The total assets of national insurance industry reached 4.06 billion yuan at the end of 2008. The premium income in one year reached 1.11 billion yuan. However, the variety of insurance products is limited. The personal insurance premium income takes a percentage of 74% and the property insurance takes about 26%. Other insurances are rare. In addition, the scale of re-insurance is also too small and this is unfavorable in preventing risks. According to international experiences, the premium income of reinsurance should generally take up 20% of total income. However, In China, the figure is only about 5% which is far lower than the international standard. More efforts are needed to promote the development of re-insurance.

12.3. Systematization

The last direction is systematization.[12]

We should recognize the following points about systematization. Firstly, finance and economy are inseparable and we can't just discuss finance by itself. Finance belongs to the category of virtual economy. The real economy includes activities such as production, circulation and exchange. The problem that appears in virtual economy will spread to the real economy and problems in real economy will also spread to virtual economy. From the historical view of point, financial crisis always leads to the economic crisis. Therefore, we should handle correctly and prudently the relationship between the virtual economy and the real economy — to coordinate the development of both.

Secondly, finance is a 'total' system, not comprising 'solitary islands' or components that are unrelated to each other. The exchange market, stock market, bonds market, insurance and futures correlate with each other as a whole. Therefore, we should consider those problems systematically and in an integrated way. In the author's opinion, we should promote a mixed operation as well as integrated supervision in the long run since only by integrated supervision can we hope to prevent risks. Otherwise, different supervisory departments will each act in its own way. If the Securities Regulatory Commission only regulates the security market, risks will be diverted to insurance market or exchange market. When problems appear in those markets, security market will also be affected.

Thirdly, we should establish a multilevel financial market. We can say that the security market in China has already reached a certain scale. However, the bonds market is less developed. In fact, the bonds market also has its own characteristics — it is safer than stock. Not only do we need to develop the stock market but we also need to develop the bonds market, the foreign exchange market, the futures market and so on. Financial futures can begin to develop with the stock index futures. Of course, we should prevent the possible huge risks produced by over speculation and improve the supervision in the process. The supervisory institutions are not omnipotent. The supervision process is actually the mutual 'gaming' between regulators and the regulated. There is a well known saying in institutional economics that 'transaction precedes system or institution'. It is impossible for any transaction to stop proceeding and wait for the system to become 'perfectly completed' or 'fully constituted'. We can only discover the problems by letting the transactions proceed and try to 'perfect' or 'complete' the whole system after establishing the basic system.

The last point for systematization is the systematization of supervision. The systematization of supervision should accomplish the following objectives. Firstly, we should understand that the supervision aims to defend the most numerous people and put into practice the principle of "people come first". There are different protected groups in different markets. For example, banks should protect the legal rights and interests of the depositors. The securities industry should protect the interests of investors. The insurance industry should protect insurants. China didn't pay enough attention to this issue before and the reasons are as follows: one is the lack of supervisory experience; another reason is the specific conditions in China. Since banks, securities companies and insurance companies are all state-owned, the losses of these enterprises are also the losses of the nation. Thus, supervisors always consider more about the interests of institutions. In fact, the national interests and people's interests are the same. Therefore, we should achieve a people-oriented society and protect the legal rights of depositors, investors and insurants. We should realize that protecting people's interest is to protect the country's interests to a certain extent.

Protecting rights and interests should include three aspects. First, we should avoid losses caused by illegal actions: for example, the loss caused by the wrongful behavior and actions of corrupt people including officials and people. Second, the depositors, investors and insurants should have the right to be informed just as the consumers hold rights as consumers. The financial institutions should be transparent and be supervised. Third, investors should get their reasonable investment returns.

Secondly, we should enhance the 'sense of service' in financial institutions. Finance belongs to the service industry. People in the financial industry are supposed to establish a good service attitude and improve continuously the quality of services. On this issue, the financial institutions in China are far behind those foreign ones. The author once heard from a Chinese student who once studied in Japan and worked in a small noodle shop that the service staff in the bank of Japan helped the boss to deposit the cash income into the bank and sent a bucket of change to the boss the next morning. Banks in China probably cannot offer such good and meticulous services at present.

The last point is that supervision must begin from information disclosure to ensure the efficiency. Supervisory departments should be clear on the point that they can't violate the basic rules of market economy in the supervision process and they should guide the market forces to participate in supervision and not play against the market. That is to say, it is important to start from information disclosure and increase the transparency of supervision and transactions. As long as the information disclosure is authentic and complete, without delay and expedient, it becomes possible for people to make investment decision by analyzing the information. If the information disclosed is not authentic, incomplete and delayed, it is impossible to supervise or regulate well even when the supervision is greatly enhanced. Information disclosure is to afford consumers in China (investor, depositor, insurant, etc.) with the right to be informed. Only when the information disclosure is done well can we discover the problems through analysis, make announcement, and then take appropriate punitive actions if necessary .The supervisory and regulatory departments should not be responsible for the fluctuations of the market. However, they must be resonsible for the information disclosure and ensure its authenticity, completeness and timeliness.

References

[1] Cheng, Siwei (2008). *China Soft Science*, 11, 1–11 (in Chinese).

[2] Japan Economic Planning Agency (1980). National Income Doubling Programme (1962–1970), Beijing: The Commercial Press, p. 104 (in Chinese).

[3] Cheng, Siwei (2009). People's Daily Overseas, July 29.

[4] Cheng, Siwei (2005). China and Pacific Countries under the Framework of Economic Globalization and Regional Integration in *The Cooperation between China and the Pacific Economies*, Beijing: World Affairs Press, pp. 2–10 (in Chinese).

[5] China-ASEAN free trade zone was officially launched: *People's Daily online*, January 2, 2010.
[6] Samuelson, P.A, Nordhaus, W. (1998). *Economics*, 16th ed., New York: McGraw Hill Companies, Inc.
[7] Cheng S. W. (1998). How should the Government Manages Enterprises, in Cheng, S. W. (ed.), *The theory and practice of enterprise management by governments*, Beijing: Democracy and Construction Press, pp. 1–48.
[8] The introduction of Shanghai Interbank Offered Rate: www.shibor.org.
[9] Cheng, S. W. (1999). Analysis and Lessons from the East Asian Financial Crisis, in Cheng, S. W. (ed.), Pandect, *Fictitious Economy and the East Asian Financial Crisis*, Beijing: Democracy and Construction Publishing House, pp. 1–50 (in Chinese).
[10] Cheng, Siwei (2006). *On Fnancial Reformation*, Beijing: China Renmin University Press, pp. 622–628.
[11] The State Council consent to the margin trading pilot project and the introduction of stock index futures, *Xinhua.net.*, January 8th, 2010.
[12] Cheng, Siwei (2006). *On Financial Reform*, Beijing: China Renmin University Press, pp. 3–11.

Index